Early Modern Europe, 1450–1789

Covering European history from the invention of the printing press to the French Revolution, this accessible and engaging textbook offers an innovative account of the variety of people's lives in the early modern period and the global context of European developments. Six central topics – individuals in society, politics and power, cultural and intellectual life, religion, economics and technology, and Europe in the world – are explored in two chronological sections, 1450–1600 and 1600–1789. The text takes in Europe in its entirety, eastward to the Ottoman Empire, northward to Sweden, and southward to Portugal, as well as the European colonies overseas, and integrates religious, ethnic, gender, class, and regional differences. Students are encouraged to think about continuities as well as changes across this formative period, and throughout the text maps, illustrations, timelines, and textboxes of original sources and featured topics illuminate the narrative. Online resources include primary source material, art and music examples, and regularly updated bibliographies.

MERRY E. WIESNER-HANKS is Professor of History at the University of Wisconsin-Milwaukee and an experienced textbook author. Her recent books include *Discovering the Global Past* (2003), *Gender in History* (2001), and the second edition of *Women and Gender in Early Modern Europe* (2000).

The Cambridge History of Europe

The Cambridge History of Europe is an innovative new textbook series covering the whole of European history from c. 600 to the present day. The series is aimed at first-year undergraduates and above and volumes in the series will serve both as indispensable works of synthesis and as original interpretations of the European past. Each volume will integrate political, economic, religious, social, cultural, intellectual and gender history in order to shed new light on the themes and developments that have been central to the formation of Europe. Volume I covers the period from the end of antiquity to the flourishing of the Renaissance. Volume II charts the transition from the development of printing in the 1450s to the French Revolution. Volume III surveys the forging of modern Europe from 1789 to the First World War and finally Volume IV examines the period from 1914 to the present. The four volumes will combine chronological and thematic approaches to the past and will survey Europe in its entirety, from the Atlantic to Russia's Urals, and will situate European developments within a global context. Each volume will also feature boxes, illustrations, maps, timelines, and guides to further reading as well as a companion website with further primary source and illustrative materials.

Volumes in the series:

I: Medieval Europe
Matthew Innes

II: Early Modern Europe
Merry Wiesner-Hanks

III: The Making of Modern Europe, 1789–1919
Simon Dixon

IV: Twentieth-Century Europe
Geoff Eley

CAMBRIDGE HISTORY OF EUROPE

Early Modern Europe 1450–1789

MERRY E. WIESNER-HANKS

CAMBRIDGE
UNIVERSITY PRESS

CAMBRIDGE UNIVERSITY PRESS
Cambridge, New York, Melbourne, Madrid, Cape Town, Singapore, São Paulo,
Delhi, Dubai, Tokyo

Cambridge University Press
The Edinburgh Building, Cambridge CB2 8RU, UK

Published in the United States of America by Cambridge University Press, New York

www.cambridge.org
Information on this title: www.cambridge.org/9780521005210

First published 2006
Fifth printing 2010

Printed in the United Kingdom at the University Press, Cambridge

A catalogue record for this publication is available from the British Library

ISBN 978-0-521-80894-1 hardback
ISBN 978-0-521-00521-0 paperback

Contents

List of illustrations   *page vi*
List of maps   *ix*
List of boxes   *x*
Acknowledgments   *xiii*

Introduction   *xiv*

1 Europe in the world of 1450   *14*

2 Individuals in society, 1450–1600   *44*

3 Politics and power, 1450–1600   *78*

4 Cultural and intellectual life, 1450–1600   *116*

5 Religious reform and consolidation, 1450–1600   *148*

6 Economics and technology, 1450–1600   *184*

7 Europe in the world, 1450–1600   *216*

8 Individuals in society, 1600–1789   *252*

9 Politics and power, 1600–1789   *284*

10 Cultural and intellectual life, 1600–1789   *326*

11 Religious consolidation and renewal, 1600–1789   *364*

12 Economics and technology, 1600–1789   *402*

13 Europe in the world, 1600–1789   *438*

Index   *484*

Illustrations

1 Broadsheet, by the Protestant artist Matthias Gerung, 1546. *page 9*
© Abaris Books

2 Fifteenth-century engraving of Prague, anonymous. 28
© Snark / Art Resource, NY

3 Pilgrims ask for healing at the tomb of Saint Sebastian, oil painting
by Josse Lieferinxe. 36
© Nimatallah / Art Resource, NY

4 Painting of a family group by Lavinia Fontana. 54
© Scala / Art Resource, NY

5 Amorous scene of an older woman and a younger man. 66
© Abaris Books

6 The Battle of Lepanto, oil painting by Giorgio Vasari. 88
© Scala / Art Resource, NY

7 Dynastic alliances in sixteenth-century western Europe. 90

8 Rulers of western Europe, 1450–1600. 97

9 Rulers of northern, eastern, and central Europe, 1450–1600. 106

10 A sign advertising the services offered by a schoolmaster in Basel,
painted by Ambrosius Holbein. 121
© SEF / Art Resource, NY

11 Woodcut by the German artist Hans Burgkmair the Elder showing
the Emperor Maximilian. 138
© Foto Marburg / Art Resource, NY

12 Andrea Mantegna's *Dead Christ*. 140
© Erich Lessing / Art Resource, NY

13 Oil painting of the Madonna and Child with a young John the
Baptist by Raphael. 142
© Erich Lessing / Art Resource, NY

14 A sketch of Calvin made during a lecture by one of his students. 171
© Snark / Art Resource, NY

15 Armed procession of the Catholic League through a French city,
1590, in an oil painting by François Bunel. 179
© Erich Lessing / Art Resource, NY

16 Peasants sowing grain in October, from the Playfair Book of Hours,
from late fifteenth-century Rouen, in France. 192
© Victoria & Albert Museum, London / Art Resource, NY

17 Detail from Hendrik met de Bles's (1480–1550) painting of a copper mine. 200
© Erich Lessing / Art Resource, NY

18 Martin Waldseemüller's 1507 map of the world. 228
© Bildarchiv Preussischer Kulturbesitz / Art Resource, NY

19 Pietro Longhi's (1702–1785) painting of a luxurious urban household.   *263*
    ⓒ Réunion des Musées Nationaux / Art Resource, NY
20 Seventeenth-century French engraving of the skeleton and nerves.   *269*
    ⓒ Snark / Art Resource, NY
21 Rulers of western Europe, 1600–1789.   *303*
22 Jan Vermeer (1632–75), oil painting *The Glass of Wine*.   *311*
    ⓒ Bildarchiv Preussischer Kulturbesitz / Art Resource, NY
23 Rulers of northern, eastern, and central Europe, 1600–1789.   *315*
24 Statues created by Gian Lorenzo Bernini (1598–1680) enclosing the
    courtyard outside St. Peter's Basilica in Rome.   *353*
    ⓒ Scala / Art Resource, NY
25 Artemisia Gentileschi's *Judith Beheading Holofernes* (c. 1620).   *355*
    ⓒ Scala / Art Resource, NY
26 Rembrandt, self-portrait in oriental costume (1631).   *356*
    ⓒ Réunion des Musées Nationaux / Art Resource, NY
27 Witch flying off to a sabbath on a winged goat, from F. -M. Guazzo,
    Compendium Maleficarum, 1610.   *389*
    ⓒ Snark / Art Resource, NY
28 An engraving from about 1720 by the French artist Gérard
    Jean-Baptiste Scotin, titled *Dervishes in their temple after the dance*.   *398*
    ⓒ HIP / Art Resource, NY
29 Domenico Gargiulo's dramatic painting of the Revolt of Naples in 1647.   *411*
    ⓒ Scala / Art Resource, NY
30 Graph showing the growth of the European population.   *413*
31 The demographic transition model.   *417*
32 Isaac Claesz van Swanenburgh's painting of workers spinning and
    weaving wool in the Netherlands, *c.* 1600.   *426*
    ⓒ Erich Lessing / Art Resource, NY
33 An Indian miniature from about 1785 showing the wife of an East
    India Company officer surrounded by many servants.   *452*
    ⓒ Werner Forman / Art Resource, NY

Frontispiece illustrations

Introduction: A page of drawings by the German artist Albrecht Dürer.   *xiv*
ⓒ Erich Lessing / Art Resource, NY

Chapter 1: Fresco by Pinturicchio depicting a marriage ceremony.   *14*
ⓒ Erich Lessing / Art Resource, NY

Chapter 2: *The Great Staircase of the World*, or the *Ages of Life*, engraving by
Jasparde Isaac (d. 1654).   *44*
ⓒ Snark / Art Resource, NY

Chapter 3: Colored woodcut from the epic poem *Theuerdank* by the
German Emperor Maximilian I.   *78*
ⓒ Erich Lessing / Art Resource, NY

Chapter 4: Michelangelo's statue of the young king David as he prepares
to fight the giant Goliath.   *116*
ⓒ Alinari / Art Resource, NY

Chapter 5: Title page of Martin Luther's pamphlet, *Letter to the Christian Nobility of the German Nation Concerning the Reform of the Christian Estate* (1520).   148
© Foto Marburg / Art Resource, NY

Chapter 6: Woodcut illustration of grain measuring, from the *Royal Orders Concerning the Jurisdiction of the Company of Merchants and Shrievalty in the City of Paris*, 1528.   184
© Image Select / Art Resource, NY

Chapter 7: Columbus in the title-page woodcut from the 1494 Basel edition of his first letter describing his voyage.   216
© Snark / Art Resource, NY

Chapter 8: The title page of Thomas Hobbes's *Leviathan* (1651) with an engraving by the French artist Abraham Bosse.   252
© HIP / Art Resource, NY

Chapter 9: King Louis XIV of France standing before a map of Holland in 1672, by Charles le Brun.   284
© Giraudon / Art Resource, NY

Chapter 10: The title page and frontispiece illustration of an English translation of Isaac Newton's *Principia*, published in 1729.   326
© HIP / Art Resource, NY

Chapter 11: William Hogarth, *Hudibras and Ralpho in the Stocks* (1726).   364
© Image Select / Art Resource, NY

Chapter 12: A coffee vendor in about 1730, from a collection of engravings of artisans and artists published by Martin Engelbrecht.   402
© Bildarchiv Preussischer Kulturbesitz / Art Resource, NY

Chapter 13: William Blake's engraving of *Europe Supported by Africa and America*.   438

Maps

1 Geographic map of Europe   *page* 3
2 Atlantic islands settled by Europeans in the late fifteenth century   18
3 Political regions in Europe in 1450   23
4 Territories held by Charles V in 1526   103
5 Europe in 1559   108
6 Religious divisions in Europe in the later sixteenth century   168
7 Principal trade routes in the Indian Ocean   221
8 Columbus's voyages   226
9 Major European voyages, 1480–1525   231
10 Europe after the Peace of Westphalia, 1648   293
11 Europe in 1763   296
12 British industrial development in 1800   430
13 Major European voyages, 1600–1789   444
14 Colonial possessions of European states in 1648   448
15 Colonial possessions of European states in 1783   465

Boxes

1 Pius II calls for a crusade against the Turks   *page* 20
2 Village bylaws in England   25
3 University life in Ferrara   31
4 Elizabethan sumptuary laws   51
5 Lawsuit regarding a pregnancy out of wedlock   59
6 An Austrian marriage law regulates spousal relations   62
7 The Cambridge Group for the History of Population and Social Structure   72
8 Comments on the new weaponry   83
9 Edmund Spenser, *View of the Present State of Ireland* (1596)   93
10 The Inquisition at the local level   101
11 Habsburg–Valois wars   111
12 Royal proclamation about students' evening activities   123
13 Was Machiavelli Machiavellian?   125
14 Erasmus, *The Praise of Folly* (1511)   131
15 Cross-dressing and gender-blending on the Elizabethan stage   136
16 Artistic genius, powerful patron: Mimar Sinan and Süleyman   143
17 Martin Luther, *The Freedom of a Christian* (1520)   155
18 Debates about the Eucharist   157
19 Anabaptist hymns   162
20 Luise de Carvajal's mission to England   175
21 The Weber thesis   187
22 Petition requesting the prohibition of grain exports   195
23 The Fuggers of Augsburg   205
24 Journeymen's guilds   209
25 The kingdom of Prester John   223
26 Matteo Ricci on differences between the Europeans and the Chinese   234
27 Afonso I of Kongo writes to John III of Portugal   239
28 Theodor de Bry's images of America   246
29 Pepys's diary   257
30 Lovesickness or green-sickness?   266
31 Inoculation against smallpox   272
32 Onanism   278
33 The "crisis of the seventeenth century"   289
34 Warfare at sea   294
35 The Fronde   299
36 Gerrard Winstanley and the True Levellers   306
37 The memoirs of Jan Pasek   319
38 Alchemy and the history of science   334

39 Letters Between Kepler and Galileo, 1597   337
40 The *Encyclopédie*   345
41 Castrati   360
42 Quietism   373
43 Methodist hymns   379
44 Peter the Great's marital policies and the Russian Orthodox Church   385
45 Jewish Messianism   395
46 The draining of the English fens   409
47 Apprenticeship contract for an eleven-year-old boy, Paris 1610   422
48 Application for a patent, Venice 1568   431
49 Stock bubbles and government debt   434
50 The legacy of Captain Cook   445
51 The Code Noir   456
52 The transportation of children   460

Acknowledgments

The easiest debts to acknowledge are financial. I would like to thank the Regents of the University of Wisconsin System, who provided me with time off from teaching for three years over the last twenty, which gave me the opportunity to write several earlier books whose ideas emerge in these pages, as well as finish this one. A fellowship from the John Simon Guggenheim Foundation allowed me to write my first book that ventured beyond Europe, a venture that dramatically shaped the way I chose to discuss European history here.

My intellectual debts are much more difficult to acknowledge adequately. I cannot begin to thank all of the people with whom over the years I've discussed ideas and topics that emerge in this book, for this would include hundreds of friends, teachers, colleagues, students, acquaintances, and family members, spread out in many countries around the world. I am especially grateful to a group of fellow early-modernists, some of whom I've now known more than half my life: Darlene Abreu-Ferreira, Barbara Andaya, Natalie Zemon Davis, Grethe Jacobsen, Deirdre Keenan, Gwynne Kennedy, Susan Karant-Nunn, Diana Robin, Lyndal Roper, Ulrike Strasser, Hilda Smith, Gerhild Scholz Williams, and Heide Wunder. For this book, I also owe particular debts to colleagues and friends who helped me with especially tricky issues, or read over chapters and sections: Patrick Bellegarde-Smith, Scott Hendrix, Alan Karras, Aims McGinniss, Sue Peabody, Jeffrey Watt, and David Whitford. As always, none of this work would have been possible without the support of my husband Neil and my sons Kai and Tyr; my sons have never known me not to be writing, which may perhaps have influenced them to become the readers they are, and certainly contributed to their steadily expanding culinary skills.

Finally, I would particularly like to thank two people, one who helped me finish this project, and one who got it started. My colleague and friend Jeffrey Merrick read every word of the second half of the book (sometimes twice!) providing innumerable suggestions for improvement. I will never share your boundless enthusiasm for the eighteenth century, but with your help I've been able to approach it with respect. My mentor and friend Philip Kintner started me off on this journey with his course on the Renaissance at Grinnell College. I have certainly not written *the* book on the subject (though I have tried to) but I have written *a* book, a task you helped me to imagine doing. This book is dedicated to you.

Introduction

A page of drawings by the German artist Albrecht Dürer (1471–1528) that captures
many themes important to Renaissance culture. On the left, Dürer illustrates a
dramatic point in the Greek myth of the rape of Europa, though he sets it in a
landscape with sixteenth-century towns. On the right, he sketches a classically dressed
archer, a sage contemplating a skull, and three views of a lion. Thus on this one page
he brings together the importance of the classical past, the wisdom of the ancients,
the fleeting nature of human life, the wonders of the natural world, and the lure of
the exotic.

THE TITLE OF THIS BOOK, and perhaps also of the course for which you are reading it, is *Early Modern Europe*. The dates in the title inform you about the chronological span covered (1450–1789), but they do not explain the designation "early modern." That term was developed by historians seeking to refine an intellectual model first devised during this very period, which saw European history as divided into three parts: ancient (to the end of the Roman Empire in the west in the fifth century), medieval (from the fifth century to the fifteenth), and modern (from the fifteenth century to their own time). In this model, the break between the Middle Ages and the modern era was marked by the first voyage of Columbus (1492) and the beginning of the Protestant Reformation (1517), though some scholars, especially those who focused on Italy, set the break somewhat earlier with the Italian Renaissance. As the modern era grew longer and longer, historians began to divide it into "early modern" – from the Renaissance or Columbus to the French Revolution in 1789 – and what we might call "truly modern" – from the French Revolution to whenever they happened to be writing.

As with any intellectual model, the longer this tripartite division was used, the more problematic it seemed. The voyages of Columbus may have marked the beginning of European exploration and colonization, but there was plenty of earlier contact between Europeans and other cultures, and Columbus himself was motivated more by religious zeal – generally regarded as "medieval" – than by a "modern" desire to explore the unknown. The Protestant Reformation did bring a major break in western Christianity, but Martin Luther was seeking to reform the church, not split it, just like medieval reformers, of which there were many. Other developments traditionally regarded as marks of modernity, such as the expansion of capitalism, the growth of the nation-state, or increasing interest in science and technology, were also brought into question as scholars found both earlier precedents and evidence that these changes were slow in coming. (Similar points were also made by scholars rethinking the ancient/medieval break, who argued that the end of the Roman Empire was not as momentous as it had earlier seemed.) More philosophical issues also emerged: What exactly do we mean by "modernity"? Will it ever end? Has it ended? What comes afterward? The thinkers who first thought of themselves as "modern" saw modernity as positive – and "medieval" as negative – but is modernity necessarily a good thing?

If "early modern" is not as clear as it seems, what about the other part of the title, "Europe"? What is "Europe"? The answer most of us learned in school – one of the world's seven continents – can easily be rejected simply by looking at a globe. If a continent is a "large land mass surrounded by water" (which we also learned in school), then surely the correct designation for what is conventionally called "Europe" is the western part of the continent of Eurasia. If we look very closely at the globe, in fact, Europe is a small northwestern part of the huge continent of Afroeurasia, a term increasingly used by geographers and world historians for what is the world's largest land mass.

The idea of "Europe" derived more from culture than geography. The word "Europe" was first used by Greek writers in the seventh century BCE to designate their side of the Mediterranean (the sea whose name means "middle of the world," which it was to the ancient Greeks) from the other side, "Asia," which to the Greeks originally included Africa. They derived the word from the myth of Europa, the daughter of Agenor, a Phoenician king. In the myth, Europa was awakened by a dream in which two continents which had taken the shape of women argued over who should possess her: Asia said she had given birth to her and so owned her, but the other as yet unnamed continent asserted that Zeus would give Europa to her. Right on cue, Zeus fell in love with the beautiful Europa as she gathered flowers with her friends, and carried her away after changing into a bull. He took her to Crete, where she bore him a number of sons, including two who later became judges of the dead, and gave her name to the continent. In a tamer version of the myth, told by the ancient Greek historian Herodotus and repeated by later Christian writers, merchants from Crete carried Europa away in a ship shaped like a bull to marry their king. Herodotus notes that the (Asian) Trojans later abducted Helen, wife of the Greek king Menelaus – an event that led to the Trojan War – in part to avenge Europa. Like all mythology, either version of this story raises questions of interpretation: Crete is actually located between Asia and Europe; does this represent Greek ambivalence about Europe's separation from Asia? Is Zeus' abduction (some scholars use the word "rape") of Europa a demonstration and justification of men's rights over women and mothers' lack of rights to their own children, both of which were law in ancient Athens? Why were Zeus' children from this affair given such powers, rather than his children by his wife, Hera? And where was Hera during all this, anyway? If Europa was snatched away by merchants rather than Zeus, why didn't her father come after her?

Whatever we may think of this myth, it is clear that the idea of "Europe" came from Greeks asserting their distinction from people who lived on the other side of the Aegean or Mediterranean. In this it is much like the notion of "modern," that is, a term used consciously by people to differentiate themselves from others, to create a boundary between "us" and "them." Europe's geographical indistinctness has allowed its boundaries to be disputed and changed over time. The western border seems relatively easy to define because it is marked by the Atlantic Ocean – but is it? Are the British Isles part of Europe? (This may seem self-evident, but then there is the commonly used phrase "Britain and

Map 1. Geographic map of Europe.

Europe.") Is Iceland? Does Iceland become part of Europe once the Vikings get
there? Does Greenland? The eastern boundaries are even more vague; various
rivers were proposed as the dividing line, but none of them stretch the entire
way from the Arctic to the Aegean Sea. In the eighteenth century Swedish
and Russian officials suggested that the Ural Mountains and the Ural River,
which flows into the Caspian Sea, were the best boundary, in part because the
Russians wanted to assert that the main cities of Russia were clearly European.
This boundary is the one most commonly given today when discussing Europe
geographically, but for historical discussions it often seems too far east. Is the
story of Russia always part of European history? Is the story of the Ukraine?
During the period covered in this book – and until World War I – much of
eastern Europe, including almost all of the area known to the ancient Greeks,
was part of the Ottoman Empire, whose leaders were Muslim and Turkish, a
people originating in central Asia. Thus geographically the Ottoman Empire
was clearly part of Europe, but is its history "European" or not?

This questioning of terminology may seem both paralyzing and pedantic – don't we all basically know what "modern" and "Europe" mean? In fact, even historians who emphasize that these terms are problematic continue to use them because they are convenient and meaningful. Thus this book is still titled *Early Modern Europe*, though its chronology and geography are somewhat flexible. Concern with terminology is key to new ways in which history is being studied, researched, and presented, however. As they have for thousands of years, historians continue to ask "What can we learn about the past?" but they put greater emphasis on *why* we know what we do, and on the way that people in the past understood and recorded their own situation. Why did certain things get written down and preserved, so that they became the historical sources on which our understanding of the past is based? Who did the writing, and what was their point of view? How and why did people shape their own memories and create their own history? What was left out, or intentionally or unintentionally distorted? How were both the lived experience and stories about that experience different for different types of people – men and women, poor and wealthy, common and elite, rural and urban? How does our understanding of the past change if we include information from non-written sources, such as art, material objects, or oral traditions?

As they paid greater attention to the perspective of their sources, so historians also paid greater attention to the ways in which their own point of view shaped the story they were telling. It was no accident that the history of peasants and working people received greater attention after World War II, when the students attending colleges and universities – some of whom majored in history and eventually became historians – came more often from working-class families than they had earlier. It is not surprising that interest in women's history surged during the 1970s, when more women began to attend college and the feminist movement encouraged them to analyze their own situation. It is similarly not surprising that an interest in cultural diversity, historical encounters between different groups, and world history developed in the 1990s, along with new patterns of migration and an increasingly international intellectual community. In reference to the issues discussed at the beginning of this chapter, it is not surprising that doubts about "modern" and "Europe" emerged at a point when people were discussing the negative consequences of modern processes such as industrialism and globalization, and debating the adoption of the euro as a currency, the proper role of Europe in a post-colonial world, and the merits of various countries' membership of NATO and the European Union.

Every historian, like every person, approaches the past from his or her own perspective, which shapes the subjects one finds interesting, the methods one uses to find information, and the language one uses to describe one's findings. A point of view is sometimes described as "bias," but that word carries a very negative charge, and implies there can be history that is "unbiased," that is, simply a recounting of the facts of the past. Because the gathering of those facts is done by human beings, however, and the sources that reveal those facts were also made largely by human beings, every story is only partial.

This recognition of the limitations of history has occurred at the very same time that our knowledge of the past has widened dramatically, as peasants, workers, women, and various types of minority groups have been added to the picture of every region and era. Thus historians, particularly those wishing to examine a broad geographic era over a long time frame, are faced with two challenges: capturing the diversity of people's experiences while still outlining key developments, and paying attention to individual perspectives – their subjects' and their own – while still telling a story of the past that makes sense.

Structure of the book

This book is designed to cover more than three hundred years of European history, viewing Europe as both larger and more connected to the rest of the world than it often has been. Thus it definitely faces the challenges just noted, which emerge first as decisions about how best to structure the story. Any arrangement is an intellectual scheme imposed by an author on a group of events, developments, individuals, and groups. Some books arrange material over a fairly long period topically, which allows readers to see continuities and long-term changes, and better understand aspects of life that change fairly slowly, such as social structures, economic systems, family forms, or ideas about gender. Some books arrange material more or less chronologically, which works better for things that involve dramatic change, such as epidemics, wars, and revolutions.

This book splits the difference. It is arranged in two general sections, one covering roughly 1450–1600 and the other roughly 1600–1780. Within each section there are five topical chapters: "Individuals in society"; "Politics and power"; "Cultural and intellectual life"; "Religious developments"; "Economics and technology." Before, between, and after these two sections there are three chapters titled "Europe in the World" that each look at the relationships between Europe and the rest of the world in 1450, 1600, and 1789 in terms of travel, trade, exploration, colonization, and other types of contacts. Chapter 1 also provides an overview of European society in 1450 in each of the five topical areas, setting the stage for the rest of the book, while chapters 7 and 13 briefly summarize the major developments from all realms of life.

The book covers the basic events long identified with this period – the Renaissance, the Reformation, the rise of capitalism, the voyages of discovery, the growth of the nation-state, the scientific revolution, the Enlightenment – but also highlights ways in which historians see these as problematic, in the same way that they have interrogated "early modern" and "Europe." Each chapter discusses a historiographical debate or two, that is, disagreements among scholars about the ways in which material should be interpreted, processes analyzed, or causation ascribed. Such debates are not new in history, and the discussions here include both long-standing debates in historiography, such as those about the origins of capitalism, and very recent disputes, such as those about the origins of sexual identity.

Questions about the concept "early modern" have made it clear that any beginning date is relatively arbitrary; some of the processes understood as modern began in the Middle Ages, if not in antiquity. But developments in the field of history over the last several decades have made 1450 seem a better starting point than the more common 1500. Why? The focus on the ways in which the past gets recorded has led to greater interest in the mechanisms of recording as both cultural and technological phenomena. Around 1450, printing with movable metal type was invented in Germany by artisans – Johann Gutenberg and others – who adapted existing techniques from metallurgy, woodblock printing, wine pressing, fabric stamping, and paper-making. (Artisans in Korea developed a similar technology somewhat earlier, but there is no evidence that this spread from Korea to Germany.) Though the number of people who could read and write, and who were thus immediately influenced by this new technology, was quite small, its ultimate impact as a vehicle of social change was enormous. Gutenberg was recently ranked, in fact, as the "most influential person of the millennium" by a cable-television network.

In addition to printing, by the 1450s Portuguese ships were sailing regularly back and forth to Cape Verde in West Africa, bringing back gold and slaves through contacts with the Mali Empire and laying the groundwork for Portugal's later colonial empire. In 1453, the Ottoman Turks under Mehmed II conquered Constantinople, and began to establish themselves firmly as a European power. Both of these developments are significant in a European history that pays more attention to Europe's place in the world, and together they dramatically influenced Columbus, who was trying to find an alternative route to the East to challenge both the Portuguese and the Muslim Turks.

The year 1453 also marked the end of the Hundred Years War between England and France, a war whose last battles, like the siege of Constantinople, involved the use of artillery, which some military historians view as the beginning of modern warfare. It is hard to imagine any development that has had more impact on the lives of all types of people – not simply soldiers and their generals – than modern warfare. If we choose to see births as significant, the 1450s was an influential decade. Both Columbus and his patron Queen Isabella of Spain were born in 1451, and the man who gave his name to the New World, Amerigo Vespucci, was born in 1454; Leonardo da Vinci was born in 1452, and Henry VII, the first Tudor monarch, in 1457. Thus we can continue to debate the problematic notion of "modernity," but still find some (imperfect) markers in the 1450s.

The same is true for the point at which "early modern" became "modern." The beginning of the French Revolution in 1789 is the conventional breaking point, though historians have long recognized that using this date privileges the political history of western Europe. The late eighteenth century did bring significant developments in other areas and realms of life, however. During the 1780s, Edmund Cartwright invented the steam-powered loom, opening a spinning and weaving factory that used his new machines and represented a new type of workplace. In 1787, the first fleet of convicts set sail from Britain to Australia, carrying about a thousand people to a new colony on what was not yet designated a continent (that would come about a hundred years later). In 1792, Mary Wollstonecraft published *The Vindication of the Rights of Women*, the first explicit call for political rights to be extended to the female half of the population. In the early 1790s, Prussia, Austria, and Russia completed their carving-up of Poland, which disappeared from the map until the end of World War I. (The dates of the subsequent volume in this series – from 1789 to 1919 – thus make sense in women's and Polish history as well as general European political history; the end of World War I brought voting rights to women in many European countries along with the reestablishment of Poland as a country.) The years around 1789 therefore saw changes in economic structures, the process of colonization, political theory, and international relations, though the French Revolution has not lost its role as a major turning point.

Sources for early modern history

Everything we can learn about the past is ultimately based on original sources, that is, on documents and objects from the period we are investigating. Paying greater attention to the perspective of our sources and to our own perspective in evaluating them has not changed this. But what sources exist for early modern Europe? The easiest to access are printed materials, which became steadily more numerous as the technology of the printing press spread out from Germany after 1450. By 1500 over 200 cities and towns in Europe had presses, and scholars estimate that there were somewhere between eight and twenty million *incunables*. (Books printed in the first fifty years after the printing press was invented are called *incunables* or *incunabula*, from the Latin words meaning "in the cradle," because they come from the infancy of printing.) This vastly exceeds the number of books produced in all of western history up to that point, and the amounts were so fantastic that some people saw printing as an invention of the devil. This opinion did not halt the spread of printing, however, and by 1600, about 200,000 different books or editions had been printed, in press runs that averaged about 1,000 copies each. The book was thus the first modern mass-produced commodity.

Printers were not in the business for charity, and they printed anything that would sell: books for lawyers, such as classical legal codes like that of the Roman Emperor Justinian, collections of customary laws, and legal commentaries, all bound in fancy leather bindings in matching sets; books for doctors, surgeons, pharmacists, and midwives, such as herbals, books of instruction, and classical medical treatises; books for students, such as manuals of language instruction, grammars, dictionaries, cheap editions of the classics, often bound in paper in smaller formats so that students could easily carry them to class; books and other printed materials for members of the clergy, such as hymnals, Latin missals, breviaries, and psalters. All of these survive in far greater numbers than manuscript examples of the same types of texts.

Printed materials for what we might term the "general reader" are still more common, though it is important to recognize that even by 1789 most people in Europe could not read. Those who could were overwhelmingly urban, middle- or upper-class, and male. Their tastes in reading thus shaped the printed sources that are available to historians. What did literate people want to read? Until about 1700, they wanted to read religious materials; the best-selling authors, particularly after the Reformation in the 1520s but even before, were religious. This was *both* because people were very interested in religion in general and in their own salvation, and also because religious works were cheap, lively, illustrated, and gory. There were plenty of extremely expensive whole Bibles, but things like Luther's sermons or those of popular Catholic preachers such as Bernard of Siena were published in very small paperback editions of one, two, or three sermons, putting them well within the reach of most literate buyers. In terms of their tone, they were much more like a modern political debate – the sort of thing that occurs now on television, not in the press – than a complicated theological treatise. Particularly after the Reformation, religious opponents were often harsh in their invective, with lots of name-calling and scandal-mongering. Here, for example, is Luther: "Next one should take the pope, cardinals, and whatever servants there are of his idolatry and papal holiness, and rip out their tongues at the roots as blasphemers of God and nail them on the gallows, although all this is insignificant punishment in relation to their blasphemy and idolatry."[1] The illustrations in religious pamphlets were often just as dramatic, with woodcuts or engravings of Luther as the Anti-Christ or the pope as the Whore of Babylon. The pamphlet from which the quotation above comes has a woodcut illustration by Lucas Cranach showing four cardinals hanging on a scaffold with their tongues tacked up beside them. Books of saints' lives described not only their good deeds and acts worthy of emulation, but also their violent and tragic deaths. The Reformation produced religious martyrs on all sides, and books describing their deaths were very popular; the best-selling book in English for many years was John Foxe's *Book of Martyrs*, which describes in great detail the deaths of many Protestants during the reign of Mary Tudor. It is clear that people not only got religious inspiration, but what we might also call religious titillation from these best-sellers.

People did not spend all their time reading religious materials, however, and printers recognized very early that there was a market for other types of books and pamphlets. They printed historical romances, such as those of King Arthur and Tristan and Isolde, and by the seventeenth century novels that told of the triumphs and tragedies of contemporary fictional characters. They printed biographies of historical and contemporary figures, the more scandalous the better, and chronicles of city or regional history. "How-to" manuals were very popular, such as herbals and books of home remedies for everything from headaches to the plague. There were guides on how to manage your money,

Fig. 1. This single-sheet broadsheet, by the Protestant artist Matthias Gerung, shows Christ at the top deciding who will get into heaven and two linked devils at the bottom, one wearing the triple-crowned papal tiara and one a Turkish rolled turban. Graphic images like this were produced and printed by all sides in the religious controversies of the Reformation.

how to run a household, how to write love letters and business letters. There was pornography, graphically illustrated, and cookbooks, also often illustrated. There were guides for travelers with handy phrases, discussions of the weather, and descriptions of the strange customs of foreign lands.

After the voyages of discovery, printers discovered that people liked to read about the experiences of more adventurous travelers, and Columbus's letters and notebooks were reprinted frequently along with those of other travelers. Enterprising publishers frequently gathered together the most bizarre and exciting stories in one volume – "Tales from Foreign Lands" or something similar – often neglecting to mention these were gathered from many sources and often contained totally fictitious accounts mixed in with real ones. Among this kind of travel book, those that concentrated on strange animals and creatures, called "bestiaries," were especially popular. They described normal animals such as hedgehogs and porcupines (although giving wild stories about their habits and abilities), real ones someone had heard about such as giraffes or rhinoceroses, and fictitious ones such as centaurs, mermaids, and cyclopses. All of these animals were listed in alphabetical order, with no distinction made between those that were real and those that were not.

Books were generally bound in cloth or leather and were often passed around or handed down from one generation to the next. They are mentioned in wills and inventories (which continued to be hand-written, not printed), which are one of our best sources about what people were actually *reading*, or at least what they had in their possession, indicating that someone thought they *should* be reading it. Wills of quite ordinary people begin to mention printed books in the late fifteenth century, so that we know these early books were not simply in some monastery or noble library. Most of the books produced in the early modern period have long since disintegrated, of course, but many survive, and those judged important were reprinted in later centuries; modern editions of many types of works are thus widely available, either in print copies or increasingly on the web. Within the last twenty years those modern editions have included more works by women and men who were not members of the elite, thus making their ideas and words accessible to a much larger number of students and scholars. Each chapter in this book includes selections from works that were printed in the early modern period, some by well-known authors and some by less-familiar individuals.

In addition to books, printers also produced much smaller, cheaper booklets, with eight, sixteen, or twenty-four pages, often called "chap-books." They were written in very simple language with a small vocabulary, and were often illustrated, so that those who were illiterate or barely literate could also get something from them. Chap-books were sold by wandering peddlers who often sold other things as well, such as pins, needles, marbles, and (printed) playing-cards. It is difficult to tell how many of these chap-books were produced or exactly what they contained, as they had paper covers and most of them have long since disappeared. From those that have survived and from discussions of them in other sources, we can tell that many of them were about recent battles and heroes, new inventions, tools, techniques for farming and building, famous people and what was happening to them, or freakish events and strange occurrences. Similar subjects were also the subjects of single-sheet broadsides, usually illustrated and then sold on street corners. By the late sixteenth century printers began to combine these subjects together in almanacs, adding witty sayings, moral maxims, humor, horoscopes and other astrological predictions, long-term weather forecasts, and agricultural advice. By the early seventeenth century, printers in some European cities began to publish weekly newssheets, and by the early eighteenth literary and scientific pamphlets at regular intervals.

For many historical questions, then, printed materials provide a steadily increasing number of sources. For other questions, however, manuscript – which literally means hand-written – sources are the only way to find information. Governments slowly began to print their law codes and some official decisions or proclamations after the development of the printing press, but records of the meetings and proceedings of government bodies – city coun-cils, courts, representative assemblies – survive largely as manuscripts. Many records of the course of life – marriages, baptisms, births, deaths – were kept by church officials, who also recorded cases heard by church courts. Some of these records, especially for England, have been published, but most of them remain as manuscripts. The records of business – contracts, correspondence, lawsuits, expense records, ledgers, accounts – were kept by employees or by notaries; notaries also handled business matters for individuals, such as marriage con-tracts, adoption and apprenticeship agreements, petitions, wills, deeds, sup-plications, inventories. Notarial records survive for many European cities, but have seen only very selective publication. Individuals who could write pro-duced their own records – letters, memoirs, diaries, family chronicles – some of which have been published, but many not. Reading manuscript sources requires specialized training in paleography, for not only does the language of documents vary over time and from place to place, but the style of handwriting does as well. Many of the chapters in this book include some original sources taken directly from hand-written materials, translated by historians who have learned how to read old handwriting and understand languages that may be significantly different from modern European languages.

Manuscript sources significantly broaden the range of information available, for they can include information on individuals who would not otherwise make it into the historical record. Working people with few assets might still draw up a marriage or apprenticeship contract, an orphan might petition a city coun-cil or a nobleman for support, and anyone might show up in court records accused of a crime or serving as a witness. Manuscripts are not fully represen-tative, however, for they include more information about unusual situations than about normal everyday life, and more about people at the top of the social and economic heap than the bottom. In the situations given above, for example, though working people *might* draw up a marriage contract, middle- and upper-class people did so more regularly; most orphans were cared for by their relatives with no record of their situation; by their nature, cases that end up in court are those in which someone broke the law or deviated from community norms. Conflict-free families, friendly neighbors, and law-abiding individuals rarely show up in the historical record, so historians must always be careful not to regard what they do find as the norm.

Scholars must also be aware of the ways in which information is filtered; court records, for example, sometimes include direct testimony, and it is tempt-ing to read these as the authentic voice of the speaker, especially because they are one of the few places prior to the rise of mass literacy where the voices of people who could not read or write emerge. Such records were written by liter-ate, typically male individuals, however, whose perspective shaped what they heard and wrote down. The fact that many written records from this period – and other eras as well – are actually prescriptive sources such as law codes, sermons, and advice manuals, telling people how they should behave and what they should do, rather than descriptive sources, presents another problem of interpretation. They can provide a great deal of information about how their authors hoped or wished people would behave, but do not provide an accurate picture of people's actual, lived experiences.

Along with written sources, historians also use visual materials – paintings, sculpture, woodcuts, engravings, furniture, coins, buildings, kitchen implements, tombstones, needlework, jewelry, clothing, toys, tools – in short, any object produced or used during the period. Visual sources often support written texts; for example, almost all of the art that has survived from the Middle Ages is religious, reinforcing the impression gained from written works about the importance of religion in people's lives during this period. At times, however, the visual sources contradict the written record. For example, written descriptions and laws about mining during the fifteenth and sixteenth centuries generally mention only male miners, but paintings of mining show women engaged in various tasks such as washing and hauling ore; the illustrations in the most famous early modern reference work, the French *Encyclopédie* edited by Denis Diderot and Jean d'Alembert between 1751 and 1772, show women working at various occupations, but the text refers to male workers only. Historians are thus confronted with the issue of whether to believe the written or the pictorial record. Like written works, visual evidence can appear to be descriptive when it is actually prescriptive or idealized, showing things the way the artist wished they would be rather than the way they actually were. Images are an important means of communicating cultural values and teaching people how to behave, especially in a period when the majority of the population is illiterate, so they cannot be read as a mirror of real life.

Heightened attention to the limitations and perspectives of their sources, combined with interest in a wider range of individuals and issues, has meant that historians continually find new ways of gaining information. They apply modern technology to the physical remains of the past, using aerial photography, satellite imagery, DNA testing, forensic medicine, and soil composition analysis, among other methods. Though there is no way to capture oral history directly, they study folktales, popular songs, children's rhymes, and language itself to get some idea about oral traditions. Thus they often use materials and methods of analysis drawn from archeology, geology, anthropology, linguistics, and literary criticism, as well as history and art history. They comb libraries, archives, museums, private collections, attics, drawers, and people's memories for new sources, and also read and look at materials that have been known for centuries in new ways, demonstrating how fresh perspectives can reveal information that was always present but simply never noticed previously.

New types of sources, new theories about their meaning, and new methods of interpretation combine to form a picture of early modern Europe that is different than that of fifty or even twenty years ago. This book will present that new picture. It will also ask you to think about ways in which understandings of the past have been and continue to be created. Together these features may enable you to develop your own opinion about the significance of early modern Europe for our twenty-first-century world.

Further reading

Particularly in its first section "Formations of modernities," Stuart Hall, et al., eds., *Modernity: An Introduction to Modern Societies* (London: Blackwell, 1996), provides excellent summaries of ideas about the origins and development of "modernity" in many realms of life – intellectual, political, economic, social, and cultural. For a look at the way "modernity" was traditionally defined, see Louis T. Milic, ed., *The Modernity of the Eighteenth Century* (Cleveland: The Press of Case Western Reserve University, 1971). Many recent analyses, primarily by sociologists and social theorists, tend to be critical. See, for example, Anthony Giddens, *The Consequences of Modernity* (Stanford: Stanford University Press, 1991), and Arjun Appadurai, *Modernity at Large: Cultural Dimensions of Globalization* (Minneapolis: University of Minnesota Press, 1996).

On the issue of "Europe" as a concept, see Peter Burke, "Did Europe Exist before 1700?" *History of European Ideas* 1 (1980): 21–9, and Anthony Pagden, *The Idea of Europe: From Antiquity to the European Union* (Cambridge: Cambridge University Press, 2002). Denys Hay, *Europe: The Emergence of an Idea* (Edinburgh: Edinburgh University Press, 1957), and Robert Bartlett, *The Making of Europe* (Princeton: Princeton University Press, 1994), present thorough discussions of medieval notions of Europe. Martin W. Lewis and Kären E. Wigen, *The Myth of Continents: A Critique of Metageography* (Berkeley: University of California Press, 1997), offers an innovative analysis of the way in which culture shapes all types of geographic concepts.

The most important study of the impact of printing remains Elizabeth Eisenstein, *The Printing Press as an Agent of Change: Communications and Cultural Transformations in Early Modern Europe* (Cambridge: Cambridge University Press, 1980), which also appeared in an abridged, illustrated edition, *The Printing Revolution in Early Modern Europe* (Cambridge: Cambridge University Press, 1983). John Man, *Gutenberg: How One Man Remade the World with Words*, also published as *Gutenberg Revolution: The Story of a Genius and an Invention that Changed the World* (New York: Wiley, 2002), presents a rather idealized view of Gutenberg, but has good discussions of his milieu and excellent illustrations. The work of several French historians is insightful, and has been translated: Lucien Febvre and Henri-Jean Martin, *The Coming of the Book: The Impact of Printing 1450–1800*, trans. David Gerard, ed. Geoffrey Nowell-Smith and David Wootton (London: Verso, 1976); Roger Chartier, *The Cultural Uses of Print in Early Modern France*, trans. Lydia G. Cochrane (Princeton: Princeton University Press, 1987). More specialized studies include Arthur F. Marotti and Michael D. Bristol, eds., *Print, Manuscript, and Performance: The Changing Relations of the Media in Early Modern England* (Columbus: Ohio State University Press, 2000), and Brendan Dooley and Sabrina Baron, eds., *The Politics of Information in Early Modern Europe* (London: Routledge, 2001).

 For more suggestions and links see the companion website www.cambridge.org/wiesnerhanks.

Note

1 Martin Luther, *Against the Papacy at Rome, Founded by the Devil* (March 1545), translated and quoted in Mark Edwards, *Luther's Last Battles: Politics and Polemics, 1531–1546* (Ithaca, NY, and London: Cornell University Press, 1983), p. 163.

1 Europe in the world of 1450

Marriages for most Europeans in 1450 were arranged by their parents and family, and celebrated by a religious ceremony. This fresco by Pinturicchio (1454–1513), from a series in the Piccolomini Library in the cathedral of Siena, Italy, depicts a romanticized view of just such a ceremony at the highest social level, in which the future Pope Pius II brings together Princess Eleonore of Portugal and the Holy Roman Emperor Frederick III.

Timeline

1450s	Development of the printing press with movable metal type
1450s	War pitting Venice against Milan, Florence, and Naples
1450s	First contact between Portuguese and Mali Empire in West Africa
1450s	Lorenzo Valla uses his humanist skills to detect forged documents
1453	Ottoman Turks capture Constantinople
1453	End of the Hundred Years War
1458	Pius II becomes pope

IN the 1440s, the well-educated Italian nobleman Aeneas Sylvius Piccolomini (1405–64), who had served as a diplomat for several high church officials to Switzerland, Scotland, and England, moved to the court of the Holy Roman Emperor Frederick III (ruled 1440–93) in Vienna. Here he was crowned poet laureate, and engaged in high-level diplomacy for the emperor. He arranged Frederick's marriage to Eleonore of Naples, whose huge dowry solved the emperor's cash problem, and patched up relations between the emperor and the pope. Piccolomini was an indefatigable writer of letters, reports, and histories, all of which provide a vivid picture of Europe in the middle of the fifteenth century. Describing Vienna, he wrote:

> There are thick and lofty walls, with numerous towers and defenses prepared for war. The houses of the citizens are roomy and richly adorned, yet solid and strong in construction. Windows of glass let in the light from all sides, and the gates of the houses are mostly made of iron. On these many birds sing. In the houses there is a great deal of elegant furniture. The stables are full of horses . . . The churches are beautifully adorned and richly furnished. The priests abound in worldly wealth . . . It is really incredible how much produce is brought into the city day after day. Many wagons come in loaded with eggs and crayfish. Flour, bread, meat, fish, and poultry are brought in tremendous masses; nevertheless by evening nothing is left to be bought. It is unbelievable how much wine is brought in, which is either drunk in Vienna or sent to those outside by way of the Danube . . . Few people live in the city whose ancestors lived in the vicinity; old families are rare, and practically all the inhabitants are immigrants or foreigners.[1]

Aeneas was well rewarded for his talents. On returning to Italy, he was named a bishop and a cardinal, and in 1458 he was elected pope, taking the name Pius II.

The cosmopolitan Pius II was hardly typical, however. Most people living in Europe in the middle of the fifteenth century never traveled very far from their home village. They might go to a near-by market town to sell their products, but they could walk there and back in the same day. Some traveled slightly further to larger towns in search of work, or to pilgrimage sites close by in search of help from the Virgin Mary or the saints. In this stability, they were like agricultural producers throughout the world, who stayed near their fields and animals, both of which required regular tending. Their mental worlds were similarly local: family, weather, crops, village politics, neighborhood saints, community relationships. The world came to them in the form of peddlers bringing products and news, soldiers bringing damage and destruction, germs bringing illness and death. Thus the world beyond their village was as often a source of calamity as it was a source of wonder, or even concern.

Some people did not stay home, however, and the small minority that traveled the roads, paths, and – more often – seas in and around Europe created a web of networks that brought goods, ideas, and eventually change into even the most isolated villages, to say nothing of booming cities like Vienna. These travelers went for different reasons, and their contacts with the world beyond Europe were also varied, ranging from hostile encounters in a military campaign, to contracts for trade, to sexual relationships inside or outside marriage.

Merchants and missionaries

The opportunity to grow rich was a powerful motive for a few travelers, especially men who lived in seaports or cities located on important land trade routes. For centuries after his trip, literate urban dwellers avidly read the tales of the Venetian merchant Marco Polo (c. 1253–1324) who spent seventeen years at the court of Kublai Khan in China. Polo dictated the account of his travels to a writer of romance stories while they were imprisoned together as war captives after Polo came back from China; they were recopied and translated many times even before the development of the printing press. Polo's stories of the distances he traveled and the wonders that he found were exaggerated, but they inspired many men, including Christopher Columbus, who had a printed copy of Polo's stories in his sea chest when he sailed.

Urban merchants, in Italy, Germany, and the Low Countries (what is now Belgium, Luxembourg and the Netherlands) developed new business techniques, including various forms of contracts, some of them temporary partnerships and some more permanent arrangements called in Italian *compagnie*. (*Compagnie* literally means "bread together," i.e. sharing bread, and is the root of the English word "company.") These trading companies sponsored land and sea expeditions in search of better routes, sources of supply, and markets. Merchants from Florence, Venice, Genoa and other northern Italian cities established merchant colonies, or at the very least set up permanent agents in faraway locations. During the fourteenth century, merchants from Venice, Genoa, Barcelona, and other southern European cities developed permanent trading centers in most of the ports of the Middle East and many in North Africa. Genoese merchants dominated in the Aegean and the Black Sea, meeting caravans carrying goods from India, central Asia, and China. These caravans also brought the bubonic plague, which came into Europe from Asia in 1347. Venetian merchants paid more attention to Asian spices, traded up the Red Sea to Cairo, which in the mid-fifteenth century was the capital of the Mameluke Empire.

In these Near Eastern cities, European merchants often lived in enclaves separate from the rest of the population, with special privileges granted them by the local rulers. The same was true in northern Europe, where cities from Holland to Poland joined together in a mercantile association called the Hanseatic League (or Hansa for short) in which the German cities of Lübeck and Hamburg were the most powerful players. From the thirteenth to the sixteenth century, the Hansa controlled the fur trade with Russia, the fish trade with Norway and Sweden, and the wool trade with Flanders. Hansa merchants gained special concessions in cities such as Bruges, Bergen, and London, and often lived in special trading centers called "factories." In 1370, the Danish king tried to break the league's power, but a Hansa fleet seized Copenhagen and imposed severe peace terms on Denmark.

While Italian ships sailed the Mediterranean, the Aegean and the Black Sea, and German ships the North Sea and the Baltic, Portuguese ships inched further and further down the African coast, searching for better and more direct supplies of gold and slaves. Prevailing winds in the Atlantic meant that though ships could stick close to land when sailing south, they had to cut far to the west when sailing home to Portugal. Such travel patterns led to the Portuguese discovery in the late 1300s of the uninhabited Azores, the Cape Verde Islands, Madeira, and later São Tomé. Portuguese, Genoese, and Spanish ships landed on the inhabited Canary Islands, carrying off livestock and people. The inhabitants of the Canaries, called Guanches, were probably the descendants of North African Berbers and had been in the islands since at least the time of the Roman Emperor Augustus in the first century CE. They lived primarily herding sheep and goats. The Guanches, who may have numbered about 100,000 when Europeans first came to the Canaries, were eventually defeated by Spanish armies in 1496, although more by European disease than military action.

In the 1450s, a Genoese merchant sponsored by Portugal made direct contact with the Mali Empire of West Africa; trade in gold and slaves expanded dramatically. Portugal also encouraged colonization and farming in the Atlantic islands, which were soon exporting wheat and sugar. Hoping to see a population increase, the Portuguese crown brought in female slaves from Africa and later orphan girls from Portugal for the male settlers of São Tomé. Royal

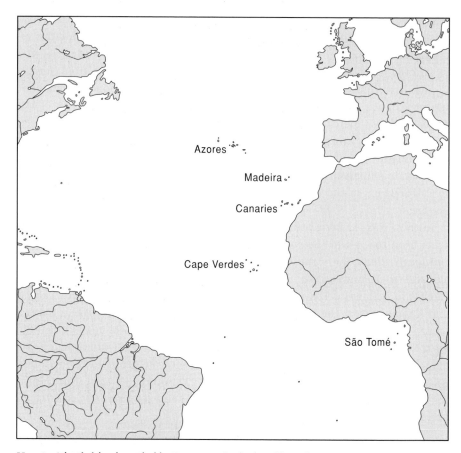

Map 2. Atlantic islands settled by Europeans in the late fifteenth century.

officials did not require marriage and did not even object very much when households included numerous women.

Though explicit royal support of population mixing on São Tomé was unusual, in many of the port cities of Italy and the Iberian peninsula, sailors, ship captains, pilots, peddlers, laundresses, slaves, ex-slaves, and drifters from a wide variety of backgrounds mixed very regularly. They shared practical knowledge as well as trading merchandise, which early explorers like Columbus – who spent his youth and young manhood in such cities – absorbed eagerly. They also shared beds; official prohibitions of sexual relationships across religious and sometimes social boundaries were enforced only sporadically among this mobile and marginal population. All of these encounters did not necessarily lead to toleration, however. Columbus learned Muslim geography, but still regarded his name (Christo-fero or "Christ-carrier") as a sign he was destined to oppose Islam. People may have socialized with others from all over the world, but they also accepted national stereotypes: Germans were drunkards, Moors and Italians were homosexual sodomites, Frenchmen engaged in sex with animals.

While economic motives inspired merchants to travel, and escaping creditors or legal authorities spurred sailors and peddlers, religious motives drew
others to the roads and sea routes. From ancient times, many of the world's
religions encouraged pilgrimages to holy sites. Chinese Buddhists went to India
seeking texts and relics, and Japanese Buddhists later went to China seeking
the same things. Christian pilgrims traveled to Canterbury in England, Maria
Wörth in Austria, or Czestochowa in Poland, and some ventured to the international pilgrimage sites of Jerusalem, Rome, Constantinople, or Santiago de
Compostela in northern Spain. Because making a pilgrimage to Mecca is one of
the duties of the believer in Islam, by 1200 there was a steady pilgrimage traf-
fic in the western India Ocean. Local shrines to holy people also drew Muslim
believers.

Inns, hostels, and shops were established along major routes, supplying pilgrims with shelter, food, and souvenirs like badges and relics. Women as well
as men made pilgrimages; certain sites promising safe childbirth and healthy
children became popular with Christian women, and Muslim women mixed
freely and unveiled with Muslim men while in Mecca. In theory, at least, peasants bound to the land were supposed to be allowed to go on a pilgrimage by
their lords if they had a specific request. Reports from real pilgrims mention
few who were very poor, but pilgrims were still a more varied group of travelers than merchants. By the middle of the fifteenth century there were steadily
more places they could visit, or sometimes the holy objects came to them in
the form of traveling collections of saints' bones and other relics.

The longer pilgrimage routes often crossed the territories of a number of
different rulers, and during times of war and conflict pilgrims were easy prey.
Attacks on pilgrims could sometimes have major consequences. Political turmoil in Palestine during the tenth century, and the conquest of Jerusalem by
the Seljuk Turks in the eleventh century, for example, led to attacks on Christian pilgrims to Jerusalem. These provided Pope Urban II with a justification –
some historians would say pretext – for advocating a military campaign against
the Turks, with the ultimate goal of conquering Jerusalem. Urban first issued
his call at a council of French bishops at Clermont in 1095, and for roughly two
hundred years after this western Christians engaged in a series of campaigns
against Muslims (and occasionally against eastern Christians) in Palestine and
the eastern Mediterranean. The Crusades – a title given to these campaigns
long after they were over – sometimes involved mass movements of troops
and the men and women who supplied them, and shaped Muslim–Christian
relations from that time forward.

Though the Crusades to the Holy Land are the best-known example of
religious conflict in the Middle Ages, other conflicts both within Christianity and between Christians and Muslims led people to travel far from home.
Beginning in the tenth century, Christian forces fought Muslims in Spain and
many islands of the Mediterranean, with Pope Gregory VII (pontificate 1073–85)
asserting that any land conquered from Muslims belonged to the papacy (an
assertion largely ignored by the conquerors). In the thirteenth century, Pope

Innocent III (pontificate 1198–1216) called for a military campaign to wipe out what he viewed as heresy in southern France, and northern French nobles and their supporters streamed southward. In the early fifteenth century, forces of the pope and the German emperor carried out military campaigns in Bohemia against the followers of Jan Hus, a religious reformer burned at the stake at the Council of Constance in 1415. By 1450, the heretics in southern France had been wiped out, most of the followers of Hus had been pacified (largely by letting them worship as they pleased), and Muslim territory in Spain had been reduced to the kingdom of Granada in the south. The largest theatre of Christian/Muslim conflict had shifted to the east, where the Ottoman Turks conquered much of Greece and the Balkans even before they captured Constantinople in 1453. For combatants on both sides, whether Christian knights or Muslim *ghazi* (warriors), opportunities for fighting in the name of God continued.

1 Pius II calls for a crusade against the Turks

Along with his letters, histories, and poetry, Pius II wrote autobiographical commentaries that were later combined into an extensive memoir. Throughout his pontificate (1458–64), he called for a campaign against the Ottoman Turks, though the response from European monarchs was tepid; he finally decided to lead one himself, and died in Ancona on the Adriatic Sea where he was assembling troops. His memoirs include a speech laying out his plans, in which he offers a rousing call to arms and summarizes some of the criticism of the church leveled by his contemporaries. Historians' views of Pius's sincerity in regard to the campaign against the Turks are mixed; some see him as motivated primarily by sincere worries about the future of Christendom, others by a desire to build up papal power and prestige. These two motivations were probably not separate in Pius's mind.

We [the pope is speaking of himself in the plural] shall imitate our Lord and Master Jesus Christ, the holy and pure shepherd who hesitated not to lay down His life for His sheep. We too will lay down our life for our flock since in no other way can we save the Christian religion from being trampled by the forces of the Turk. We will equip a fleet as large as the resources of the Church will permit. We will embark, old as we are and racked with sickness. We will set our sails and voyage to Greece and Asia . . .

We hear you whispering. You say, "If you believe war to be so difficult, how can you go on without securing adequate strength?" We are coming to that point. An unavoidable war with the Turks threatens us. Unless we take arms and go to meet the enemy we think all is over with religion. We shall be among

the Turks in the position in which we see the despised race of Jews among Christians. It is either war or infamy for us. "But," you say, "war cannot be waged without money." It occurs to us to ask where we are to look for money . . . All ways have been tried. No one has answered our prayers. We sent envoys to the provinces. They were scorned and derided. On every single thing we do the people put the worst interpretation. People say we live in luxury, amass wealth, are slaves to ambition, ride on the fattest mules and the most spirited horses, wear trailing fringes on our robes and walk the streets with puffed-out cheeks under red hats and full hoods, breed hunting dogs, lavish much on actors and parasites and nothing on the defense of the Faith. And they are not entirely wrong. There are many among the cardinals and the other members of the Curia who do these things . . .

What do you think we ought to do in such circumstances? Must we not seek a way to recover our lost credit? We must change to paths long disused . . . Abstinence, purity, innocence, zeal for the Faith, religious fervor, scorn of death, have set the Church of Rome over the whole world . . . By martyrs and confessors alike our Church was made great. It cannot be preserved unless we imitate our predecessors . . . there is no longer room for choice. We must go.

(From Leona C. Gabel, ed., and Florence A. Gragg, trans., *Memoirs of a Renaissance Pope: The Commentaries of Pius II: An Abridgement* [New York: Capricorn Books, 1959], pp. 356–9.)

 For additional chapter resources see the companion website www.cambridge.org/wiesnerhanks.

Military campaigns are one way for religions to gain or retain adherents, and individual or group efforts at conversion are another. Christian missionaries traveled in all directions from the Mediterranean, reaching Ethiopia by at least the third century, southwest India and Ireland by the fifth, Russia by the sixth, China by the eighth, and Iceland by the tenth. Traditions in many places hold that these churches are even older; the Christian community in southwest India, for example, regarded itself as having been established by the apostle Thomas in the first century, so they are often called the St. Thomas Christians. Stories tell of missionaries traveling further, as well; Saint Brendan of Clonfert (486?–577), an Irish monk, is supposed to have made it to North America in his small skin boat, for which he gained the title "the Navigator."

Christian communities in Asia and Africa were separated from European Christianity by the spread of Islam, which first motivated and accompanied Arab conquests in the Middle East, North Africa, and the Iberian peninsula, and then continued to expand in sub-Saharan Africa and South and Southeast Asia. Muslim legal scholars, Sufi mystics, and other types of religious leaders helped to spread and solidify Muslim teachings both within and beyond territories in which the rulers were Muslim. Effective missionaries in both Christianity and Islam often absorbed and modified indigenous traditions and customs, so that places sacred to specific gods became identified with saints or apostles in Christianity and local gods became manifestations of Allah in Islam. By 1450 there were thus wide variations in rituals, practices, institutions, and even doctrines in both religions, some of these sanctioned by the authorities and others not. Travelers from one part of Christendom or one part of the *dar al-Islam* (land of Islam) to another frequently commented on how strange – and often unacceptable – they found the practices of their co-religionists elsewhere.

Though merchants and missionaries were generally different men, they might very well have traveled together. Religious and economic motives were often similarly mixed in European contacts with the rest of the world. Italian merchants often wrote "in the name of God and profit" on the first page of their account books. According to the Byzantine historian Procopius, knowledge of silk-making and silkworm eggs were stolen from China – despite the emperor's threat of death to whoever did so – by eastern Christian monks, who brought the eggs back to Constantinople in their long walking staffs. The Byzantine emperors attempted to regulate and guard silk production just as the Chinese emperors had, to prevent a monopoly from developing and preserve Byzantium's status as the main supplier of silk to the Mediterranean. They were equally unsuccessful, and silk industries developed in Italian cities such as Lucca, though whether monks were again involved in the spread of silk technology is not clear.

Such ventures for God and profit occasionally merged into diplomacy. In 1287, Arghun, a nephew of Kublai Khan who was the ilkhan in Persia – the ruler of the westernmost regional Mongol Empire – sent Rabban Sauma, a Nestorian Christian priest of Turkic origin, as an envoy to the pope and the kings of France and England, hoping to create a coalition against the Muslims. (Nestorians were a splinter group within Christianity that disagreed with the rest of the church about the relationship between the divine and human natures of Jesus Christ; they split off in the fifth century and carried out missions in India and China.) A few years later, the pope sent John of Monte Corvino (1247–1328), a Franciscan friar, to Khanbalik, on a similar mission. Both the pope and the ilkhan envisioned themselves as the head of this alliance, however, and neither mission was successful. The journal of Rabban Sauma and the letters of John of Monte Corvino were not copied and printed to the extent that Marco Polo's writings were, but the events they described became well known in Europe.

In 1450, then, though most Europeans never traveled very far from their home towns and villages, some went great distances. They took land routes into Asia, following the roads on which silk had long traveled from China; they took sea routes to Asia, sailing down the Red Sea to Aden; they took sea routes down the African coast to the Mali Empire, then back by way of the Azores. The widening of geographic horizons was not a one-way process, however, for routes that once existed could also disappear or become more dangerous. By 1450 the Viking colony on Greenland had all died of starvation or been killed by Inuit, and the settlements in Iceland had been devastated by the Black Death, which reached the island in the early fifteenth century. Voyages in the North Atlantic were thus much fewer than they had been earlier, and memories of Viking trips to North America were turned into myths, their reality confirmed only in the late twentieth century through archeological excavations in Newfoundland. The Mongol Empire in China had broken apart, with the Ming dynasty that succeeded it dominated by scholar-bureaucrats who became increasingly suspicious of contacts with outsiders. Foreign merchants could stay in the carefully watched ports of Quanzhou and Guangzhou (Canton), but not travel around. Government support of naval expeditions and ship-building in China – which had led to seven huge naval expeditions into the Indian Ocean and the Persian Gulf led by Admiral Zheng He in the early fifteenth century – ended, and the navigational knowledge they had gained was lost. Though we recognize that 1450 marks the beginning of much greater European interaction with the rest of the world, it is doubtful whether many people living in that year would have noticed this trend.

Politics and power

Like all maps, those that portray political units involve judgments on the part of map-makers, and any map of Europe in 1450 is full of such judgments (see map 3). Beginning at the western edge of continental Europe: England and France were in the last stages of the Hundred Years War, with English holdings in France being slowly reduced to the town of Calais. Maps often mark shifting boundary lines between "English" and "French" holdings throughout the war, but these mask other changes that may ultimately be more important.

Map 3. Political regions in Europe in 1450.

Any map showing what is now France at the beginning of the war in 1337 would probably show solid lines between the great noble holdings – the duchies of Normandy, Burgundy, and Aquitaine, the counties of Anjou and Provence. Though their rulers were generally vassals of the king of France, they felt perfectly comfortable shifting their allegiance to England, or to no one, and opposing the centralizing moves of the French kings. By the end of the war in 1453, those lines are often shown as dotted or they have disappeared altogether. Local allegiances and traditions still made great differences, but regional units such as "Aquitaine" were increasingly understood as part of France, and not its neighbor.

In England, internal political divisions may have seemed less marked than those in France in the fourteenth century, but weak kings combined with warfare in the early fifteenth century to increase the power of feudal nobles. Their holdings were not as independent as those of the strongest French nobles, but particularly those with holdings along the borders of Wales and Scotland were quite independent, simultaneously feared and relied on for border defense by the English monarchy. English nobles in Ireland – some of whose families had been there for nearly three centuries – were even more autonomous; though the English attempted to draw a sharp line between Anglo-Irish and Gaelic territory and to prevent the mixing of the two populations, in reality the border was more nebulous and cultural assimilation was quite common.

In the middle of Europe, there were "Germany" and "Italy," off-hand designations used by contemporaries (and by us) for large areas politically subdivided into hundreds of different types of governmental units: kingdoms, counties, duchies, free cities, religious states ruled by bishops, abbots, abbesses, or the pope, and tiny territories ruled by lesser nobles. Even large-scale maps cannot capture the diversity of these units, for jurisdictions were often interwoven and overlapping, so that areas or individuals might be under the authority of – and pay taxes to – several political units simultaneously. In the northern part of central Europe, these units were loosely joined together under the title of Holy Roman Empire, with an emperor elected by a small group of secular and religious leaders. They had chosen a series of generally weak emperors from various noble houses through the fourteenth and early fifteenth centuries, but in 1438 settled on Albert II of the Habsburg family, whose family holdings included much of Austria and various territories in southern Germany. Habsburgs were chosen as emperor almost uninterruptedly from that date to 1806, though in 1450 their hold on the imperial office was certainly not assured, and the lines between the various states of the Holy Roman Empire continued to be more solid than those separating the various parts of France.

The Italian peninsula was even more divided than Germany. The Holy Roman Emperor had loosely controlled northern Italy in earlier times, but by the fifteenth century even this vaguely unifying force was gone. Northern Italy was made up of large and small city-states, each ruled by a merchant aristocracy or a single individual; in these often very wealthy states, one man or several hundred held actual power, though a few, such as Florence, still retained the façade of broader republican governments that existed briefly in the thirteenth century. The Papal States stretched across central Italy, and in the mid-fifteenth century the popes were busy establishing family dynasties and strengthening their military and political hold over this area. Southern Italy (and often Sicily) comprised the kingdom of Naples, whose crown was contested by France and Aragon. All of these states were jealous of each other's power, so they established alliances that shifted whenever one was perceived to be gaining strength, and invented modern diplomacy with permanent representatives at each capital.

Like Germany and Italy, Spain in the mid-fifteenth century was also a geographic concept masking political disunity. The kingdoms of Aragon and Castile were the largest units, but Aragon itself was made up of a group of separate principalities, and Navarre, Portugal, and the Muslim state of Granada were completely independent. Each kingdom had its own laws, courts, coinage, bureaucracy, and political institutions; even the *reconquista*, the centuries-long push to conquer Muslim holdings, did not create cultural or political unity. In northern Europe, the Union of Kalmar, created in 1397 under the rule of Queen Margrete of Denmark, brought together the kingdoms of Denmark, Norway, and Sweden under one monarch. As in Spain, each country retained its own laws, customs, and administrative council. The Union helped provide mutual defense against German power in the Baltic, though by the mid-fifteenth century powerful Swedish nobles were already rebelling against monarchs they perceived as pro-Danish.

On the eastern and southern shores of the Baltic, powerful nobles were also the most important group politically and economically. Rulers in this area, such as the dukes of Prussia, the grand dukes of Lithuania, the kings of Poland, and the princes of Muscovy, relied on nobles for support during disputes over borders and royal successions. Local lords were the ultimate legal authority in their own territories with little interference from royal officials, and they used this power to restrict the rights of peasants and townspeople. By contrast, the Ottoman sultans in the 1400s were

2 Village bylaws in England

Several times a year in most English villages, the villagers, or at least some of them, gathered for court proceedings during which the legal and financial affairs of both the lord and the village were handled. The courts often went beyond what we would recognize as judicial activities and issued new ordinances – which historians now term *bylaws* – in the name of the lord and the village to regulate activities in the village or its fields or forests. The following are a few of the many bylaws issued by the village of Great Horwood in central England.

1433
It is ordered by all the tenants that no one shall have his beasts on the green of the town by night until the end of autumn next to come under pain each one of 4d. [d. = denarius, or penny]. And there were chosen as wardens John Hayes and Robert Baynard.
And that every tenant be at Nether ford next Monday about Vespers with tools to clean the watercourse under pain of 1d. for default.

1465
It is ordered by the consent of all the tenants there that no one henceforth shall willfully allow his foals openly to go into the fields of grain after they are three weeks old unless tethered to their mothers under pain of each one doing the contrary paying 12d. namely for each foal every time.

1480
The township of Great Horwood is ordered to make anew part of the butts [mounds of earth on which targets for practicing archery are set] before the Feast of the Nativity of St. John the Baptist [June 24] under pain for each one in default of 8d., 4d. of which is to go to the parish church.
And if any one shoots his arrows at the metes [boundaries] and does not close the bars [of the gate] after him he shall forfeit to the lord as often as he does it 4d.

1503
It is ordered by common consent and assent that all tenants having hedges on the eastern part of the town aforesaid shall cause them well and sufficiently to be repaired, under pain for each of them falling into default of 12d.

1534
It is ordered that no one shall harbour or entertain any woman or women of ill fame more than one night under pain for each delinquent of 6s. 8d. [s. = shilling, worth 12d.]

(From Warren O. Ault, *Open-field Farming in Medieval England: A Study of Village By-Laws* [London: George Allen and Unwin, 1972], pp. 125, 132, 134, 141.)

developing centralized imperial institutions to rule their ever-expanding territory. They created a trained army and corps of administrative and tax officials, often co-opting existing local and religious authorities rather than displacing them. Thus within the Ottoman Empire regional territories such as Bulgaria, Serbia, Kosovo, and Albania still existed, though they were increasingly dependent on the sultan's government.

Throughout all of Europe, then, the mid-fifteenth century was a period in which political boundaries were shifting, as was the importance of different types of boundaries. Many lines on the map might more accurately be depicted as broad or blurry stripes, for frontier areas often had cultures and traditions distinct from those of the territories on either side.

There is another problem with viewing map 3 as a representation of political units in mid-fifteenth-century Europe: its scale. Other than in times of warfare, the political units that had the most impact on people's lives, and in which they were most likely to have some voice, were local. During the Middle Ages, in many parts of Europe villages developed political structures of their own that regulated what went on in the village and conducted relations with authorities beyond the village. Villages became what are often called "communes," with institutions of self-governance. These institutions were generally composed of the adult male heads of household, or a subset of these, who decided which crops the village would plant, supervised the harvest, watched over the village mill, and carried out similar functions. In some places village councils and courts had the authority to issue ordinances and make legal decisions, either in conjunction with the local lord or on their own.

Institutions of governance were even stronger in towns and cities, which won their independence from local lords in the twelfth and thirteenth centuries. Towns drew up charters that established administrative and supervisory offices, such as mayors, quartermasters, gate-keepers, tax collectors, and market overseers; they set procedures for tax collection and the maintenance of city walls and streets; they established citizens' militias, orphanages, various types of courts, municipal brothels and bathhouses, and funds to provide relief for the poor. On a day-to-day basis these village and city authorities had more control over many aspects of life than any territorial ruler.

Individuals in society

It is easy to see the limitations of making generalizations about any large group of people, yet we do it all the time. Fifteenth-century Europeans were no different. They arranged their society into three groups, according to a model made popular by church officials in the tenth and eleventh centuries: those who fought (nobles), those who prayed (members of the clergy), and those who worked (peasants). Like all models, this tripartite division oversimplifies the situation, particularly the situation by the fifteenth century. Yes, if we take Europe as a whole, the most powerful group in society was the nobility, but nobles themselves varied from wealthy monarchs who were the ultimate political authority in vast areas to impoverished knights who hired themselves out as mercenaries and controlled only a tiny piece of land or none at all. Clergy in Europe were similarly differentiated; bishops of large dioceses and abbots or abbesses of major monasteries often came from noble families and lived in splendor like their secular relatives, while village priests and nuns in small convents had barely enough to eat and engaged in manual as well as spiritual labor. Peasants ranged from wealthy landowners who were free of all labor obligations and employed others to assist them, to landless migrants who hired themselves out by the day or week.

The traditional tripartite division had been developed to describe western Christian Europe, so not surprisingly it left out Jews and Muslims. In the middle of the fifteenth century, there were large Jewish communities in many cities in Italy and Spain and in some cities of central and eastern Europe. Jews were prohibited from owning land in some parts of Europe, which meant they generally made their living in cities, congregating in neighborhoods that later became legally defined ghettos. In a wave of anti-Jewish sentiment, they had been expelled from some parts of Europe in the thirteenth and fourteenth centuries, including England and (temporarily) France. Expulsions would start up again in the later fifteenth century, including Bavaria in the 1480s and Castile and Aragon in 1492. The Ottoman Turks controlled most of Greece and the Balkans in 1450, ruling a population that was mixed in terms of religion, language, and ethnicity. Less than half the population of the Ottoman Empire was Muslim, and Jews and Christians were largely free to practice their own religion, educate their children, and control such matters as marriage. Non-Muslims paid substantial extra taxes to the government, so there were advantages in converting, though the Ottoman government, with an eye towards its treasury, did not actively encourage such conversions.

The traditional conceptualization of society also overlooked people who lived in towns and cities, who by 1450 numbered perhaps one-quarter of the population in the Low Countries, one-fifth of the population of Italy, and one-sixth of the population of Spain and Portugal. (Historians vigorously dispute how to define a "town"; some use functional characteristics such as commerce, production, and regional administration, while others use strictly demographic measures.) Towns began to grow in Europe during the eleventh century around a variety of cores – military camps, crossroads of trade, cathedrals, seaports – and gradually won some legal and political rights, often codified in a town charter. They developed institutions of self-government, regulated trade and production, and attracted migrants from the countryside. They were often hard hit by the first and subsequent outbreaks of the bubonic plague, though a few, such as Nuremberg in Germany, developed strict rules of quarantine that kept the plague outside the city walls.

Like nobles, clergy, and peasants, urban dwellers ranged across a broad socio-economic spectrum, from wealthy merchants who oversaw vast trading empires and lived in splendor that rivaled the richest noble to impoverished

Fig. 2. Engravings of city-scapes were very popular as book illustrations throughout the early modern period. This anonymous fifteenth-century engraving of Prague shows churches, houses, and other buildings packed in densely, several sets of walls, and an outlying suburb across the river from the main part of the city.

widows and orphans who depended on private, church, and – by 1450 in some towns – municipal charity to survive. The middle of this spectrum included artisans, shop-keepers, lawyers and other professionals, government officers, journeymen, and providers of the services that drew people to towns, such as tavern-owners, barber-surgeons, and money-changers.

Though the medieval tripartite model was thus quite out of date by the mid-fifteenth century, it still serves to highlight one significant way in which society was divided: by social rank, or what came to be called "estate" or "order." This division was based to a large degree on family of birth and function in society, though government service, talent, astute marriages, and occasionally money could help individuals – and sometimes their descendants – rise in rank. The concept of "estate" or "order" was also used to talk about other divisions of society: women were divided into virginal, married, and widowed "estates," and spouses of both sexes were described as part of the marital "order." The hierarchy of orders overlapped the hierarchy of wealth, but they were not exactly the same; those in the first estate were far more likely to be wealthy than those in the third, but even if they were poorer, they had a higher status. If this had not been the case, wealthy Italian merchants would not have bothered to buy noble titles and country villas as they began doing in the fifteenth century, and wealthy English merchants would not have been eager to marry their daughters and sons into – often impoverished – gentry families. Status was also tied in with considerations of honor. Among the nobility, for example, certain weapons and battle tactics were favored because they were viewed as more honorable, while among urban dwellers certain occupations, such as city executioner or manager of the municipal brothel, might actually be quite well paid, but were understood to be "dishonorable" and so of low status.

While estate, wealth, and honor established hierarchies that to some degree overlapped, gender created a different hierarchy. Europeans uniformly under-stood men to be superior to women in the fifteenth century, but disagreed about the degree to which rank could or should outweigh gender. Could a woman's being born into a royal family, for example, allow her to overcome the normal limitations of her sex? At a less exalted level, should the wife of a master craftsman have complete control of what went on in a shop and household in his absence, or should some of the decisions be left to the eldest journeyman?

Social, economic, and gender hierarchies thus intersected in complex ways in society as a whole in the fifteenth century, and their impact on any single individual was similarly complex. For example, poverty lessened the differences between men and women in terms of opportunities and life experiences, cre-ating an "equality of misery" for the poorest rural or urban dwellers. Poor women probably did not view this equality as a positive thing, however. Many women did recognize the liberation that came when they were widowed, and chose to remain unmarried; in making a decision about remarriage, women of middling ranks could be more independent than those of higher rank, whose marriages were a matter of family politics. Social and gender hierarchies did not operate in the abstract on individuals, but through many intermediate groups – families, guilds, neighborhoods, friendship networks, communities, villages – which will be explored in more depth in chapter 2.

Cultural and intellectual life

For most people in Europe, cultural and intellectual life in 1450 was still very closely linked to religion, though this was slowly beginning to change. Monasteries, convents, and cathedral schools had been the main avenues to basic literacy since the tenth century for all but the elite who could afford to hire private tutors; by the twelfth century, wealthy businessmen in a few cities had established small schools to teach reading and arithmetic, but even these used religious texts as their basic reading matter. Beginning in the twelfth century, some of these cathedral or municipal schools developed into universities, teaching law, medicine, theology, and philosophy to older male students, along with a more general curriculum – the "liberal arts" – to somewhat younger boys and men. Students at these universities, even those not studying theology or planning on a church career, were considered to be clergy in terms of legal jurisdiction and tax issues – the technical term is that they were in "minor orders" – though their regular participation in riots, drunken brawls, and similar disturbances often made this status a headache for city governments.

Universities shaped the culture and economic life of the cities in which they were located, such as Bologna, Oxford, Paris, or Salamanca, with rooming houses, dormitories (often called "colleges"), taverns, brothels, specialized stores, and other establishments catering to their needs. The number of universities increased slowly from the twelfth century onward; in 1300, there were fifteen to twenty universities in Europe, and by 1500, there were over fifty.

University education and the preparatory study that led to it were all conducted in Latin, which meant that scholars from Coimbra in Portugal to Kraków in Poland could communicate with one another, and that students could travel from one university to another, which they frequently did. Learning Latin served as a sort of male puberty rite for urban boys with an eye to careers that required university study, bonding them together and setting them off from the rest of the population, who spoke a variety of local dialects. Scholars corresponded and published in Latin until the eighteenth century, and university classes in many subjects continued to be held in Latin until the nineteenth century.

Though Latin dominated scholarly discourse, beginning in the fourteenth century writers in some parts of Europe began to use their local dialects rather than Latin for poems and stories, and these local dialects slowly developed into the vernacular literary languages of Italian, French, English, and others. This new type of literature was the result of – and spur to – increasing levels

3 University life in Ferrara

Rulers and city councils recognized that universities were a way to showcase their own piety and intellectual interests, and also support the economy. The following comes from a 1735 history of the university of Ferrara in Italy. In the first part, the author quotes from a petition brought by a group of citizens to the duke of Este, a wealthy nobleman, in 1442, asking for support to establish a university. The university was established, and two years later students had already developed extra-curricular traditions that were not part of the original plan, as the second part of the source makes clear.

The Wise Men [a board of advisors] and citizens were all of one mind: that a university be established in their city, which step would be of the greatest utility, praise and honor.

For, to begin with its utility, strangers will flock hither from various remote regions, and many scholars will stay here, live upon our bread and wine, and purchase of us clothing and other necessities for human existence, will leave their money in the city and not depart hence without great gain to all of us. Moreover, our citizens who go elsewhere to acquire an education and take their money there, will have an academy at home where they can learn without expense, and our money will not fly away. Besides, there are many excellent wits in this town of ours which remain undeveloped and lost, whether from the carelessness of their fathers or their own negligence or lack of money. These will be aroused by the presence of a university and the conveniences for study, and will be enabled to pursue their education without great expense. What praise, what honor there will be for our city, when the report shall spread through the whole world that we have our own seat of good disciplines and arts ...

On January 9, 1444, on the occasion of the assumption of his cap by the new rector, the students in arts in the house of Niccolò Pasetti which was located in the street of Santa Maria Novella held a noble banquet and public dances. Nay more, having set up in the same street a wooden image of a man, which we call in the vernacular Bamboccio, they tilted against it with spears and gave a prize to the victor with applause from all the banqueters and spectators ... Students each year divert[ed] themselves sometimes from the daily round of studies to cheerful and boyish pursuits. They turned to games and gala-making, especially either at the recurrence of the Bacchanalia [revived ancient Roman festivities in honor of Bacchus, the god of wine] or when the rectors of the university assumed the cap which was the insignia of their dignity. For then the nations of students, from the contribution which they demanded annually for the lecturers for that purpose, were wont to celebrate either by dances or jousting, fighting for a prize, or banquets, or some such rejoicing.

(From Borsetti, *Historia almi Ferrariae gymnasii*, I [1735], pp. 48–9, 52–3, translated and reprinted in Lynn Thorndike, *University Records and Life in the Middle Ages* [New York: Columbia University Press, 1944], pp. 334, 338. Reprinted by permission.)

---

of vernacular literacy in the cities of Europe; alongside schools teaching boys Latin, small schools, often little more than a room or corner of someone's house, had begun to teach boys – and a few girls – basic reading, writing, and figuring.

Vernacular languages slowly replaced Latin in official and business records, providing employment as notaries, secretaries, and clerks for men who had not gone to the university. This process served to broaden the circle of literate individuals – and of habitual readers – within one area, but it also separated those in one area more sharply from those elsewhere. In the twelfth century, everyone in Europe spoke a local dialect (their "mother tongue"), and a very few also spoke, read, and wrote Latin. By the mid-fifteenth century this was still true, but in addition some people spoke, read, and wrote dialects that were coming to be regarded as "French" or "Italian." Those whose mother tongue was a dialect that did *not* become a literary language, say people in Sicily, or Brittany, or Bavaria, or Wales, had to learn a language that varied from somewhat to extremely different if they wanted to become literate. Thus the development of vernacular literatures enhanced boundaries between what were becoming countries in Europe, and also enhanced a hierarchy of dialects within one country.

At the same time that literacy in the vernacular was expanding in many cities of Europe, some individuals in Italian cities began to call for a new type of education in Latin. They admired the works of ancient Greeks and Romans for both their content and style, and thought that the first-century Roman orator Cicero had set the highest standard. They established schools and academies in Italian courts and cities that focused on classical literature and history, calling their new curriculum the "studia humanitatis" or humanism. Humanists viewed education in the classics as the best preparation for a career in business or politics, for it taught one how to argue persuasively, write effectively, and speak eloquently. Conversely, they taught that a life active in the world should be the aim of all educated individuals, and that education was not simply for private or religious purposes, but benefited the public good. By the middle of the fifteenth century, humanist schools had opened in French and German as well as Italian cities, and gradually humanist education became the basis for intermediate and advanced education for a large share of the male middle- and upper-class population. Because of their emphasis on eloquence, action, and the public role of educated individuals, humanists were ambivalent about education for women, and never established schools for girls, though a few women of very high social status did gain a humanist education from private tutors. Convents remained the most important avenue for female literacy, and even the humanists strongly advocated Christian authors rather than the pagan classics for teaching girls and women.

Humanism is one aspect of the Renaissance, the self-conscious cultural movement begun by Italian intellectuals, artists, and writers that emphasized a break with the immediate past. Though they did not reject Christian teachings or separate from the church, Renaissance thinkers and artists put greater emphasis on the secular and material world. A new attitude toward artists, writers, composers, and other creators of culture began to develop, which emphasized their creative genius; certain types of art – particularly painting, sculpture, and architecture – began to be viewed as the product of an individual rather than a workshop, as "art" rather than "craft."

Humanist education and Renaissance art are extremely important looked at in hindsight, as they marked the beginning of major cultural shifts. It is important to remember, however, that they had absolutely no impact on the lives of the vast majority of fifteenth-century Europeans. Their cultural world remained one transmitted orally and visually – through stories told around the hearth, sermons preached by wandering friars, windows and objects in village churches. These oral and visual images continued to teach them to look forward to a paradise in heaven rather than seek fame in this world, a paradise where food would be plentiful and tasty, work would be short and easy, illness would be rare or unknown.

Religious institutions, ideas, and practices

Just as political structures ranged from supra-regional to local, so too did religious institutions. The Christian church in central and western Europe in 1450 was a hierarchy headed by the pope, who claimed spiritual authority over all Christians, as well as political authority over the inhabitants of the Papal States. Papal authority rested in theory on statements in the New Testament that were understood to give special powers to the apostle Peter, who was regarded as the first pope, along with decisions of church councils since biblical times which enhanced that power. In practice papal authority also rested on a strong centralized bureaucracy that had developed particularly after the end of the Roman Empire in the west in the fifth century. Key to this bureaucracy was a system of uniform church (or canon) law and church courts, which by the fifteenth century had jurisdiction over many aspects of life, including marriage and morality. Papal authority came into conflict with the power of secular rulers at various points in the Middle Ages, and problems in the church – including a schism from 1378 to 1415 in which there were two and later three popes – led some thinkers in the late Middle Ages to favor a form of governance in which the pope shared his power with a general council. This conciliar movement was supported by some rulers such as the kings of France, but was largely defeated after the schism when the popes tempered their more dramatic statements about universal power and concentrated on Italian issues.

The Byzantine Empire continued for a thousand years after the Roman Empire ended in the west, and the emperor often presided over church councils and had the final say in who became the head, or patriarch, of the eastern Christian church. The Christian churches in western and eastern Europe moved slowly apart in terms of structure, practices, and certain points of doctrine in the early Middle Ages. In 1054, the patriarch and the pope each excommunicated each other, and the schism was final, though there were occasional later attempts at reconciliation. The eastern church gradually became known as the Orthodox Church, the Greek word for following the correct and established faith. Church councils, composed of all Orthodox bishops who were willing and able to attend, set dogma and general policy, and the heads of the Orthodox churches in Bulgaria, Serbia, and later Russia operated quite independently of the patriarch in Constantinople in their decision-making. The lack of a unified code of canon law, a single administrative structure, and even a single language of operation (Greek, Syriac, Slavonic, and Russian were all in use) allowed for considerable local autonomy and diversity in Orthodox practices.

In both western and eastern Europe, significant power was held by bishops, whose territories – known as *sees* or *dioceses* with cathedrals as their headquarters – varied greatly in size. In the Holy Roman Empire, some bishops were secular political authorities as well as religious leaders, and in most parts of Europe bishops came from wealthy families and lived well. They were chosen in various ways, and were assisted in their administrative and spiritual duties by staffs of lawyers, priests, and officials. Each diocese was divided into parishes, which were staffed by parish priests who were supposed to have received enough education to say mass in Latin and carry out religious services such as baptisms, weddings, and funerals. By the fifteenth century, however, the offices (and income) of both bishop and priest were sometimes held by individuals who actually lived far away. Officials at the papal court frequently held several dioceses simultaneously, leaving the duties of the bishop to an assistant, while students at universities were supported with the income from a parish, with priestly functions left to a vicar, a lesser official who was paid a salary for his work. In the western church, councils held in the twelfth century had forbidden priests to marry, while in the eastern church married men could become priests, though not bishops. Priests and bishops were termed *secular* (from *saeculum,* meaning worldly in medieval Latin) clergy, as they lived and worked in the world.

Along with being a bishop or priest, there were other religious positions and affiliations open to men. They could join a monastery as a monk, living relatively cut off from the world under the leadership of an abbot. They could become Dominican, Franciscan or Augustinian friars, traveling from town to town preaching, ministering to the poor, or teaching at a university. Both monks and friars were termed *regular* clergy because they lived according to one of the monastic rules (*regulus* in Latin) established throughout the Middle Ages.

Women were never officially considered members of the clergy, but there were religious orders open to them. They could become nuns at a convent under the leadership of an abbess, technically cloistered, or cut off from the world, but in reality varying in the strictness of their enclosure. Convents generally required a dowry that could be used to support the nun during her lifetime, but poorer women could often join them as lay sisters, responsible for the physical needs of the residents while the nuns concentrated on spiritual matters. In some parts of Europe, women who wanted to emulate the friars' vows of poverty and obedience and work among the poor could become what were termed "third-order Franciscans," and in other areas similar groups attached to other religious orders developed. Most of these women wore distinctive dress and took some sort of vows, but only those who took final vows and lived in a convent are properly called "nuns"; "women religious" is the somewhat awkward, but correct, term for all of them.

Across Europe, individuals judged to be holy were of widely differing types. In addition to the various approved groups, there were also individual men and women who designed their own plans for a more intensive spiritual life; such persons were open to charges of heresy, or false belief, by the institutional church, but they often gained a reputation for holiness that far outweighed that of priests, monks, or nuns. There were also groups that hovered between acceptance and denunciation. The Beguines, for example, were women who lived communally in many cities in the Netherlands and Germany, devoting themselves to prayer and service to the poor; members took no vows, and

supported themselves by manual labor and teaching children. They were alternately blisteringly condemned and tepidly permitted by the papacy, but ultimately survived; several thousand Beguines live in Belgium and a few other
countries today.

Religion is not simply a matter of institutions, however, but also of beliefs,
rituals, and practices. It is very difficult to gain direct access to the beliefs of
ordinary Christians, for their religious ideas made it into the historical record
only when they came into conflict with those of the institutional church, such
as trials for heresy. Beliefs were expressed through rituals and actions, however,
and there is much historical evidence regarding these. People participated in
processions dedicated to the Virgin Mary or a specific saint to ask for a good
harvest or prosperity in their city. They asked for the assistance of saints to
get through childbirth (St. Anne, the mother of the Virgin Mary, was a favorite
for this), heal disease, or protect them while traveling. They paid church taxes
or made donations for the building and maintenance of churches and cathedrals, where they viewed religious relics regarded as holy; if they were wealthy,
they bought relics to have in their own homes or private collections. Parents
attempted to protect their children from the dangers of childhood with prayers
to the saints, religious images or objects, or pilgrimages to holy places. At least
once a year, and sometimes much more regularly, people confessed their sins
to the village priest, who then set certain actions, such as praying or fasting, as
penance for those sins. They bequeathed money for religious purposes in their
wills, including repairing church buildings and paying priests to say memorial
masses.

By the fifteenth century, every major life transition was marked by religious rituals for Christians. Very shortly after birth, children were baptized,
preferably by a priest but in emergency situations also by a midwife; unbaptized babies could not enter heaven, so baptism was sometimes carried out
on dead children, even though this was theologically unacceptable. Though
a church wedding was not required, most weddings in Europe were conducted by a priest, who often blessed the marital bed (sometimes with the
couple in it) later that day. Women who had given birth went through the
ritual of churching sixty days after the childbirth, in which they thanked
God for their safe delivery, and were welcomed back into the congregation.
There were rituals for the dying, in which the dying individual, family and
friends, and religious personnel could participate; after death there were
funerary rituals, and memorial prayers and masses designed to speed the soul
to paradise.

Not only were individual life events marked by religious ceremonies, but
the calendar was also set according to religious periods and days. The life of
Christ was reenacted in an annual cycle of special holy days (or holidays), with
days also dedicated to the Virgin Mary and various saints – Advent, Christmas,
Pentecost, Lent, St. John's Day, St. Michael's Day, the birth of Mary, All Saints'
Day, and so on. This intersected with the agricultural cycle of planting and
harvest. By 1450, as many as fifty days were marked off as special holidays

Fig. 3. Pilgrims ask for healing at the tomb of Saint Sebastian in this oil painting by Josse Lieferinxe (fl. 1497–1508). Certain churches, chapels, and shrines gained reputations for offering solutions to specific problems and became specialized pilgrimage sites; the most popular were surrounded by inns, hostels, food vendors, and souvenir stands selling pilgrim's medals and other trinkets.

in addition to Sundays, with restrictions on work, sex, and other activities. How seriously people took restrictions on work or sex during these days and seasons varied, as did their attendance at regular services. Weekly attendance at services was not always the norm, and though the church enjoined people to confess their sins to a priest at least once a year, many did not.

There is debate among historians as to the depth of people's understanding of Christianity, with some arguing that Christian beliefs were a thin veneer over long-standing traditional practices; ceremonies in which village priests and all the villagers walked around the boundaries of village land sprinkling holy water, or priests baptized magnets so that they could be used to find lost objects, are cited as examples of this. These very same rituals are also used by historians arguing how deeply Christianity permeated people's daily existence, however. Despite these varying opinions, it is clear from such rituals that there was little separation between aspects of life regarded as sacred and those viewed as secular for most people.

Jews and Muslims in Europe also celebrated a regular round of religious rituals. Both Jewish and Muslim boys were circumcised shortly after birth, and weddings and funerals for both groups involved the presence of a religious leader along with family members and friends. Religious life for Jewish men centered on schools where they learned Hebrew and studied religious literature, rabbinical courts where they studied and practiced Jewish law, and temples where they worshipped. Women did not learn Hebrew or study law (though they were not excluded from the temple) so their religious life centered on the home, where they cooked food, lit candles, and abstained from sexual relations in ways that followed religious prescriptions. For Muslim men, religious observances were also marked publicly, with prayer at a mosque or study at a Qur'anic school (*madrasa*). For Muslim women, religious observance was more domestic: observing the fast of Ramadan, saying prayers at home, wearing amulets with verses from the Qur'an. Neither Judaism nor Islam was hierarchical in the way that Christianity was, so there was no one individual with the authority of the pope, or even the authority of the patriarch of Constantinople. Both religions had developed codes of law that offered guidance on many issues (*halakhah* in Judaism, the *sharia* in Islam), but these were often interpreted and applied slightly differently by legal scholars and judges (called *kadi* in the Ottoman Empire) depending on the local situation.

Economics and technology

The cultural creations of the Renaissance were ordered and purchased by Italian merchants and bankers, the same sort of people who were sending ships throughout the Mediterranean. Merchant families in Florence became tax collectors for the papacy in the late thirteenth century, and subsequently opened banks in many European cities, making profits from investments, loans, and exchanges of money. Back in Florence, they invested in wool production, importing high-quality raw wool from England and Spain, hiring families to carry out the various stages of production, and promoting new techniques. Florentine cloth became the best in Europe, and was exported throughout the Mediterranean. In the fourteenth century, towns in the Low Countries, such as Bruges, Ypres and Ghent, became major cloth producers, and in the fifteenth century towns in England did as well. The English crown encouraged cloth production by setting a high tariff on the export of raw wool and a low tariff on the export of finished cloth; by the middle of the fifteenth century England was exporting more wool that had been made into cloth than raw wool.

Making cloth was one of the first types of production to be organized along capitalist lines in Europe, in which the raw materials, finished product, and sometimes the tools needed for production were owned by someone other than the person doing the actual work. Cloth merchants, called drapers, purchased raw wool, hired workers for all stages of production, and then sold the finished cloth. Some stages of production might be carried out in the drapers' homes or in buildings they owned, but more often production was carried out in the houses of those that they hired, who were paid by the piece rather than by the hour or day. Drapers in many towns, sometimes in combination with the merchants of other types of products, joined together to form a merchants' guild that prohibited non-members from trading in the town.

Mining was also a capitalist enterprise; silver mines in Germany and Bohemia, lead and tin mines in western England, copper mines in Spain and Sweden, iron mines in England, Poland, and eastern France, salt mines in the Alps, all provided opportunities for investment and for wage employment for workers. This investment paid for deeper tunnels, more use of machinery, and more complex smelting processes, which increased the volume and quality of metals of all types. These metals were essential to new techniques of warfare, which required much larger quantities of metals for armor, cannonballs, and shot.

Most goods were not produced by wage workers hired by investors, however, but through craft guilds. Craft guilds had first developed in the twelfth and thirteenth centuries; they organized the production and sale of a particular product, regulating the hours that could be worked, the number of workers in a shop, the amount of raw materials any shop could obtain, the quality standards required in finished products, and so on. They set down written ordinances stipulating their rules, and establishing means of governance and enforcement. Guilds were led by master craftsmen, adult male heads of household who had become members through producing a product judged acceptable – a "masterpiece" – and often paying a fee. Each craftsman led his own shop, which was located within his household unless his type of work required that he be at a specific location, such as a building site. He hired an apprentice or two (the number was set by guild regulations), boys of around ten, whose parents might sign an apprenticeship contract. These boys learned the trade while they worked; once their apprenticeship was finished (the duration was also set by regulations), they became journeymen, and either continued to work in the same shop or traveled around working for various masters. Some years later, they might have the opportunity to settle down, make a masterpiece, get married, and open their own shop. Though women, especially the wife, daughters, and servants of guild masters, worked in guild shops, they generally did not go through this formal training program and had no voice in the running of the guild; guilds recognized that wives were essential to keeping the household/workshop fed and clothed, however, and frequently required that all masters be married. The widow of a master might continue to operate the shop for a period of time after her husband's death, making her an attractive marriage partner for journeymen in the trade.

Larger cities in Europe could have hundreds of different guilds, each of which developed a strong sense of work identity and cohesion through ceremonies, celebrations, processions, and sometimes distinctive clothing. Guilds also had non-economic functions: they might have a special altar dedicated to a patron saint, establish a fund for orphans of masters, or arrange for carrying the casket in a funeral.

Though merchants' and craft guilds dominated the economic life of cities, most of the people who lived in cities were members of neither. They made their living producing goods and performing services not regulated by guilds: carrying goods from place to place, gathering and selling firewood, working as servants, washing clothes, selling used clothing, repairing houses, brewing beer, caring for the sick, making simple food items. If these failed, they might steal or beg, sleeping in whatever cellar or attic they could find. This less prosperous and more fluid segment of the population might be married, but, at least in northern Europe, they might also remain unmarried; demographers estimate that between 10 to 15 percent of the northern European population in this era did not marry, with most of these living in cities.

During times of famine or unrest urban populations generally grew as people flocked in from the countryside; cities tried to prevent this by restricting the distribution of food to home-town poor that they regarded as "worthy," that is, poor through no fault of their own. Such measures did not stop the flow of immigrants, however, which in the long run was fortunate as cities depended on immigration to maintain their population levels. Not until the nineteenth century did urban birth rates outpace urban death rates, for the tightly packed city population, crowded inside or just outside the walls, was an ideal breeding ground for every type of disease.

The growth of cities in western Europe was made possible by economic and political developments in the countryside. Labor obligations had begun to be replaced by cash rents in many parts of western Europe in the thirteenth century; attempts by landlords to reverse this trend after the Black Death had depopulated the countryside, provoked peasant rebellions, and were largely unsuccessful. Though some labor services, such as fixing roads or transporting goods to market, remained, peasants in many areas raised crops for themselves and for the market, not directly for their lord. A similar process had occurred somewhat earlier in eastern Europe; greater personal freedom and better economic conditions for peasants had contributed to growing towns and trade. This trend was reversed in the fourteenth and fifteenth centuries, however, and landlords used their political power to reintroduce serfdom. Urban populations stagnated and then declined, a development welcomed by landlords, who recognized that cities could provide a haven for runaway serfs.

Like the urban households of guild masters, peasant households were organized around a marital couple; agricultural tasks were highly, though not completely, gender-specific, so that the proper functioning of a rural household required at least one adult male and one adult female. Remarriage after the death of a spouse was faster in the countryside than the cities, and the number of people who remained unmarried was much smaller. Grain-growing was the most important part of agricultural production in most of Europe, for grain – eaten as bread or mush or drunk as beer – was the center of the European diet. Of all the requests in the Lord's Prayer, the most important prayer in Christian Europe, "give us this day our daily bread" was the only one that referred to material goods. To this grain was added whatever was locally available: berries, fruits, nuts, butter, a little meat, herbs, vegetables, cheese.

By the fifteenth century specialized agricultural production had also developed in certain areas, some of which became dependent on imported grain for basic survival. Southern Spain, Sicily, and Greece produced olives, southern France and central Italy wine, northern Italy silk, northern France and Germany flax for linen. The residents of coastal areas from Lithuania to Norway and from Portugal to Crete caught fish, which they dried or salted for long-distance transport. The trade in foodstuffs gradually became an increasingly important segment of long-distance trade, particularly when western European merchants hooked up with eastern European noble landlords to export grain their serfs had produced to the growing cities of the west.

Increasing shipments of foodstuffs and the growth of specialized regional economies were dependent on sea transport, which was in turn dependent on relatively reliable ships and at least rudimentary navigational instruments. The Vikings had learned how to build ships that were both shallow in draft so that they could maneuver up rivers and capable (or at least sometimes capable) of withstanding fierce storms in the North Sea and the North Atlantic. To this, European sailors in the twelfth century added a sternpost rudder – originally a Chinese invention – and a greater variety of sails: square sails for speed when the wind was from the rear, and triangular, or lateen, sails, for use when there was a crosswind. At about the same time, they began using simple magnetic compasses – either a magnetized needle floating on a wood chip or a pivoting needle on compass card – another Chinese invention that Europeans had probably learned about in the Indian Ocean. They also adapted Arabic astrolabes for figuring latitude by measuring the angle of the sun or the pole star above the horizon, and devised various ways for measuring speed, such as watching wood chips float by or using a log line, though these were very imprecise as there was no accurate way to tell time.

Ocean trading thus slowly became both faster and more reliable, though enterprising merchants realized that there were limits to this reliability, and devised ways to compensate for this, such as marine insurance for lost boats and cargoes, and joint-stock trading companies that spread the risk among many investors. The increase in seaworthiness was not accompanied by an increase in comfort for those on board. There were no sleeping quarters except for officers, so that the sailors slept right on the deck. (The hammock that would make sleeping on ships much more pleasant was a Native American invention.) Food on board was a monotonous diet of salt beef and pork, beans, chickpeas, and hard ship's biscuit, all shared with rats and roaches. This was washed down with large quantities of wine – perhaps a liter and a half a day – with barrels of water and wine the principal ballast keeping the ship upright.

Along with cargo, by the middle of the fifteenth century ships also increasingly carried cannons. Sea fighting in earlier centuries had primarily involved ramming and boarding, so that ships carried wooden structures called "castles" manned by soldiers, along with sailors. When cannons were first added, they were simply put on top of the deck of existing ships, but ship designs and naval tactics were gradually altered to make more effective use of the new weaponry.

Land warfare was also beginning to be changed by the use of gunpowder. Gunpowder, often called black powder, became known in Europe in the thirteenth century; it had been developed in China at some time between the tenth and twelfth centuries and was first used for land and sea mines and then to shoot rocks out of bamboo tubes. The Mongols spread this technology westward, and by the end of the fourteenth century cannons and black powder were being manufactured and used throughout Europe. Cannons were initially made of bronze – a mixture of copper and tin – using techniques first perfected for church bells of forming two halves, then banding them together. By the middle of the fifteenth century cannons had become effective against the walls of feudal castles, but they were heavy and difficult to move, so were used primarily as siege weapons rather than in the field.

These changes in military technology created more demand for metals, and also, of course, for gunpowder itself. Black powder is a mixture of charcoal (made from wood), sulfur (mined or dug up from the ground) and potassium nitrate (also known as saltpeter), which forms naturally by the decay of nitrogen-rich substances such as animal and human wastes. As black powder became more important, a guild of saltpeter collectors developed with rights to enter barns, sheds, outhouses, vacant buildings, and anywhere else waste or animal remains might have been deposited, which in wartime might even include cemetery grounds. Eventually saltpeter "plantations" were established, with the raw material furnished by pigeons and doves. The use of portable firearms such as pistols and muskets, which will be discussed in greater detail in chapter 3, further increased the demand for both metal and powder, and eventually transformed warfare even more than cannons did.

As you have read in the introduction, the most important technological development of the mid-fifteenth century – arguably even more important than gunpowder – was the invention of the printing press with movable metal type. In contrast to technology, what we would understand as purely scientific developments were not as evident in 1450. Both educated and uneducated Europeans shared a view of the body and the universe that derived from Aristotle, Galen, and the Bible. There were four basic elements – earth, air, fire, and water – that corresponded to four qualities – hot, cold, wet, and dry – and four humors (or fluids) in the body – blood, phlegm, black bile, and yellow bile. The qualities and the humors determined personality and caused illness, and they, along with God, created differences between men and women. Men were hotter and drier, with heat viewed as a positive force that made one energetic and creative; women were colder and wetter, with their bodies producing all sorts of strange fluids but their minds unable to be truly creative. Humans were set by God and by Nature on a motionless earth, about which the planets, sun, and moon moved; beyond this was the realm of the fixed stars and heaven, as changeless and motionless as earth.

Presenting a snapshot of all of Europe in 1450 in one chapter is very difficult, particularly a "Europe" that is geographically and socially broad and diverse. This diversity means, in fact, that a counter-example could be found somewhere in Europe for nearly every sentence in this chapter. Each of the following chapters will allow that diversity to be explored more fully, tracing social, political, intellectual, religious, economic, and technological changes and continuities. It may be harder to keep continuities in mind than to investigate changes, as continuities seem to require less explanation and are generally not as exciting or noticeable, particular when studying a period understood as "the birth of modernity." Many people living in this era, however, would not have been startled by what they saw around them had they been suddenly transported from 1450 to 1789; the final chapter of this book will help you assess what was really different, and for whom.

Further reading

For good overviews of the later Middle Ages, see David Herlihy, *The Black Death and the Transformation of the West* (Cambridge, MA: Harvard University Press, 1997); Maurice Keen, *English Society in the Later Middle Ages, 1348–1500* (New York: Penguin Books, 1990); John Aberth, *From the Brink of the Apocalypse: Confronting Famine, War, Plague, and Death in the Later Middle Ages* (London: Routledge, 2001). Two important collections with chapters on many topics are Thomas A. Brady, Jr., Heiko A. Oberman, and James Tracy, eds., *Handbook of European History in the Later Middle Ages, Renaissance and Reformation, 1400–1600*, 2 vols. (Leiden: E. J. Brill, 1994 and 1996) and Christopher Allmand, ed., *New Cambridge Medieval History*, vol. VII: *C. 1415–c. 1500* (Cambridge: Cambridge University Press, 1998).

Books that focus on European encounters with others before Columbus include Felipe Fernández-Armesto, *Before Columbus: Exploration and Colonization from the Mediterranean to the Atlantic, 1229–1492* (London: Macmillan Education, 1987); Janet

Abu-Lughod, *Before European Hegemony: The World System, A.D. 1250–1350* (New York: Oxford University Press, 1989); Jerry Bentley, *Old World Encounters: Cross-Cultural Contacts and Exchanges in Pre-Modern Times* (New York: Oxford University Press, 1993).

For political developments, see Denys Hay, *Italy in the Age of the Renaissance, 1380–1530* (New York: Longman, 1989); C. A. J. Armstrong, *England, France and Burgundy in the Fifteenth Century* (London: Hambledon, 2003); James Muldoon, *Empire and Order: The Concept of Empire, 800–1800* (London: Palgrave-Macmillan, 1999).

For late medieval urban life, see Charles Phythian-Adams, *Desolation of a City: Coventry and the Urban Crisis of the Late Middle Ages* (Cambridge: Cambridge University Press, 2002); David Nicholas, *Urban Europe 1100–1700* (London: Palgrave-Macmillan, 2003); Katherine A. Lynch, *Individuals, Families, and Communities in Europe, 1200–1800: The Urban Foundations of Western Society* (Cambridge: Cambridge University Press, 2003).

For religion, see Eamon Duffy, *The Stripping of the Altars: Traditional Religion in England, 1400–1580* (New Haven: Yale University Press, 1992); Robert N. Swanson, *Religion and Devotion in Europe, c.1215 –c.1515* (Cambridge: Cambridge University Press, 1995); Norman Housley, *Religious Warfare in Europe, 1400–1536* (Oxford: Oxford University Press, 2002); Andrew D. Brown, *Church and Society in England, 1000–1500* (London: Palgrave-Macmillan, 2003).

For economic and social changes, see Christopher Dyer, *Standards of Living in the Later Middle Ages: Social Change in England c. 1200–1520* (Cambridge: Cambridge University Press, 1989); Ruth Mazo Karras, *From Boys to Men: Formations of Masculinity in Late Medieval Europe* (Philadelphia: University of Pennsylvania Press, 2002); Tim Parks, *Medici Money: Banking, Metaphysics, and Art in Fifteenth-Century Florence* (New York: W. W. Norton, 2005).

 For more suggestions and links see the companion website
www.cambridge.org/wiesnerhanks.

Note

1 From Aeneas Sylvius Piccolomini, *Historia Frederici III imperatoris,* translated and reprinted in James Bruce Ross and Mary Martin McLaughlin, *The Portable Renaissance Reader* (New York: Penguin/Viking, 1953), pp. 208, 209, 211, 212.

2 Individuals in society, 1450–1600

The Great Staircase of the World, or the *Ages of Life*. In this engraving, Jasparde Isaac (d. 1654) depicts a man and a woman ascending from swaddled infancy to respectable middle age, and then descending to a shared deathbed.

All the world's a stage,
And all the men and women merely players;
They have their exits and their entrances;
And one man in his time plays many parts,
His acts being seven ages. At first the infant,
Mewling and puking in the nurse's arms;
Then the whining school-boy, with his satchel
And shining morning face, creeping like snail
Unwillingly to school. And then the lover,
Sighing like furnace, with a woeful ballad
Made to his mistress' eyebrow. Then a soldier,
Full of strange oaths, sudden and quick in quarrel,
Seeking the bubble reputation
Even in the cannon's mouth. And then the justice,
In fair round belly with good capon lin'd,
With eyes severe and beard of formal cut,
Full of wise saws and modern instances;
And so he plays his part. The sixth age shifts
Into the lean and slipper'd pantaloon,
With spectacles on nose and pouch on side,
His youthful hose, well sav'd a world too wide
For his shrunk shank; and his big manly voice,
Turning again toward childish treble, pipes
And whistles in his sound. Last scene of all,
That ends this strange eventful history,
Is second childishness and mere oblivion;
Sans teeth, sans eyes, sans taste, sans everything.
    (Jacques, in William Shakespeare's *As You Like It*
                    (1599), Act 2, scene 7)

Since the time of the ancient Greeks, western scholars had debated about how many stages made up a man's life. Some argued for four, corresponding to the four seasons, some twelve, corresponding to the months and the signs of the zodiac, and some three, five, six, eight, or ten. The most common number was seven, corresponding to the seven known planets (the planets out to Saturn plus the moon), and identified by St. Ambrose in the fourth century as infancy, boyhood, adolescence, young manhood, mature manhood, older manhood, and old age. The "ages of man" show up textually in philosophical discussions, essays, and poetry, verbally in songs, plays, and sermons, and visually in manuscript illuminations, stained-glass windows, wall paintings, and cathedral floors, so that everyone was familiar with them.

The ages of man began with stages of physical and emotional maturing, and then were differentiated by increasing and decreasing involvement in the world of work and public affairs. As Jacques says, a man moved from schoolboy to lover to soldier to official, roughly the same progression shown in the engraving by Isaac, with the clean-shaven lover in a fancy plumed hat, the mustached soldier carrying a long pike, and the bearded official in the elegant cape. As men moved from one stage to another, they were often shown with different objects symbolizing changing occupations or responsibilities. For men, only in adolescence was sexuality a factor, and marriage or fatherhood was almost never viewed as a significant turning point. When people described the stages of a woman's life, it was her sexual status and relationship to a man that mattered most: a woman was a virgin, wife, or widow, or alternately a daughter, wife, or mother.

The ages-of-man motif shows people as individuals – or occasionally as couples – and one of the marks traditionally associated with "modernity" is the increasing importance of persons as individuals rather than members of social groups. The nineteenth-century Swiss historian Jacob Burckhardt, who really created the modern idea of what the Renaissance was, saw "individuality" as one of its defining features: "In the Middle Ages . . . man was conscious of himself only as a member of a race, people, party, family, or corporation – only through some general category. In Italy [of the Renaissance] . . . man became a spiritual *individual*."[1]

In the century and a half since Burckhardt wrote, his notion of the individualism of the Renaissance has been rejected, rethought, and revised along several lines. Medieval historians have asserted that the individual was important in learned philosophy, theology, and political theory, as well as popular songs, poems, and stories, since at least the tenth century, or perhaps far earlier. Conversely, scholars of the Renaissance and early modern periods have emphasized that groups of all sorts – families, clans, neighborhoods, guilds – remained extremely important into the eighteenth century, or even into the twenty-first century for many people. This was particularly true for the nobility and for the broad mass of common people, but even among the subjects of Burckhardt's study – upper-class Italian men living in cities – corporate groups remained central to their understanding of themselves and their place in the world.

Along with these doubts about the "individualism" of the Renaissance, however, has come new interest in aspects of people's lives as individuals that were not part of what concerned Burckhardt. He focused on intellectual and cultural factors, but more recently historians have investigated people's physical bodies, identities as men and women, sexuality, and experiences with aging, thus returning to many of the same topics that for so long were part of discussions of the "ages of man." This newer scholarship on the individual simultaneously broadens and problematizes earlier studies. We now know a great deal more about all kinds of individuals than we did even twenty years ago, but we also recognize how much those individuals are enmeshed in various social relationships and networks of power, and how much they perceived of themselves as members of various groups. The brief discussion of the individual in society in the previous chapter worked inward from conceptualizations of the entire social order; this chapter will work outward from the individual to the ever-widening social circles that surrounded him or her.

The body

The body might seem to be a part of the natural world, not a cultural creation. We all experience our own bodies from the inside, feeling pain and pleasure, health and disease. Though evolutionary change has shaped the human body, it operates very slowly; there have certainly been no major changes in the physical structure of the body in the last five hundred years. All of these statements seem common sense, and yet they are disputed by historians of the body, who point out that understandings of the body are culturally specific and change over time. Some would even argue that because people in the past perceived and described their bodies differently, those bodies really *were* different, or at least they are unrecoverable as historical subjects in themselves, because all we can know about them are the words and visual images – the discourse – referring to them. This emphasis on the unrecoverability of actual experiences and the centrality of discourse is often loosely referred to as "deconstruction," "poststructualism," or the "linguistic turn" in history. It became very popular in the 1980s and 1990s when many historians were influenced by literary and linguistic theory, but was also hotly debated. Proponents of this point of view argued that historians should not be preoccupied with searching for "reality," because to do so demonstrates a naïve "positivism," a school of thought whose proponents regarded the chief aim of knowledge as the description of phenomena. Opponents argued that this went against the basic purpose of history, and that an emphasis on unchangeable linguistic structures denied people's ability to shape their own world – what is usually termed historical "agency." All historians recognize that their sources have limitations, they asserted, but historians also understand that sources refer to something beyond the sources themselves – a person who lived and died, an event that occurred or was blocked.

The linguistic turn affected many areas of historical study, not simply that focusing on the body, but study of the body throws the dispute – which is still going on, though with less vitriol on both sides – into high relief. On the one hand, bodies seem clearly to be tangible, physical objects, but on the other, various cultures have described their structure and functioning so differently that it is hard to imagine they are all talking about the same thing.

Understandings of the body in the centuries around 1500 were very different from the modern western body, though they had changed little in over a thousand years. For scientists, physicians, and other learned individuals, the Greek philosopher Aristotle (384–322 BCE), and the Greek physicians Hippocrates (c. 460–375 BCE) and Galen (129–199 CE) had explained human anatomy and physiology in a satisfactory way, and there was little reason to reject this. In fact, Galenic and Hippocratic precepts actually became more widely known in the sixteenth century than they had been earlier, when translations from Greek medical works were published in astounding numbers: nearly 600 editions of Galen's writings were printed between 1500 and 1600.

The Galenic body contained four humors – blood, phlegm, black bile and yellow bile – that influenced bodily health. Each individual was thought to have a characteristic temperament or "complexion," determined by the balance of the four humors, in the same way that we might describe a person today as having a "positive outlook" or a "Type A" personality. The organs were viewed primarily as channels for the humors, rather than as having only one specific function. Blood, for example, originated in the liver from the assimilation of food, then ebbed and flowed as a thick fluid in the veins, nourishing the body. Some of it seeped through the walls of the heart, where it mixed with air coming from the lungs, and then ebbed and flowed as a thin, almost spirit-like fluid in the arteries, energizing the body with its "life force." In Galenic theory there were thus two kinds of blood, one moving in the liver and the veins, and the other in the heart, lungs, and arteries; blood of both types was the dominant humor, carrying the other humors through the body.

Illness was caused by an imbalance in these humors, which was why the most common form of medical treatment was drawing blood, the only one of the humors for which the amount could be adjusted easily. (Black bile and yellow bile were never clearly identified, and the amount of phlegm the body produces is limited.) Diet, exercise, sleep, sexual activity, and relations with family and friends could also affect the balance of the humors, promoting good health or encouraging disease. Too much drink or worry, smoky rooms, bad companions, or too many arguments could make one "unbalanced" mentally as well as physically, with individuals dominated by black bile, also called *melancholy*, especially likely to become depressed or even insane.

Though the humors were distinct, under certain conditions they could also transform themselves into a different humor, or into any other fluid that the body produced, such as milk or semen. Thus during pregnancy women's menstrual blood nourished the fetus, and during lactation it turned into milk and continued to nourish the baby. During intercourse, blood turned into semen in men, and perhaps also in women, though learned individuals disagreed about whether women produced "seed" or were simply the vessels in which generation (what we would term "reproduction") occurred. The transformation of blood into semen led many physicians to recommend that men limit the number of their ejaculations, and poets sometimes described sexual relations as little deaths – "oh, I die, I die" was a standard poetic conceit for orgasm.

Heat was the primary agent in most of these transformations, and heat was also related to gender. Men were hotter and drier than women, which is why they went bald (their internal heat burned up their hair) and had bigger brains and broader shoulders (the heat expanded these). Heat also pushed the male sexual organs outside of the body, whereas women's lack of heat led to theirs remaining inside. Women's lack of heat was the reason they menstruated, for men burned up unneeded blood internally. The incorrect amount of heat created gender confusions: "virile" women who had more bodily heat than normal were seen as capable of producing semen, and effeminate men who lacked normal masculine heat were thought to lactate. Even menstruation was not completely gender-specific, for it was not clearly separated from other types of bleeding in people's minds, and was often compared to male nosebleeds or hemorrhoids or other examples of spontaneous bleeding.

The centrality of bodily fluids in medical theory led physicians to regard looking at a person's urine or taking their pulse as the best diagnostic tools for all kinds of illness; physicians were trained through a long university education and had a high social status, so that they regarded close physical examinations of patients as both socially beneath them and medically unnecessary. Medical training in the sixteenth century began to include more dissections, and anatomists such as the Flemish physician Andreas Vesalius (1514–64) critiqued Galen's claims about the structure of the body and the way it operated. Based on dissections he performed himself while lecturing at the University of Padua, Vesalius wrote his major work, *De humani corporis fabricia* (1543; *On the Structure of the Human Body*), which included detailed drawings. This and other medical discoveries caused some physicians to begin to doubt the humoral theory, but not until the late eighteenth century would the idea of the psychological effects of the humors die out among learned Europeans, and not until the nineteenth did bloodletting completely lose favor as a medical procedure.

Most people probably did not understand all the intricacies of the humoral theory, but they experienced bloodletting on a regular basis, performed by barber-surgeons, who also carried out other medical procedures on injured or ailing bodies, such as setting bones or lancing boils. People also used purgatives to rid their bodies of superfluous humors or of "poisons," and sought out other treatments to maintain health or treat illness that were not based strictly on the humoral theory. Practical experimentation over many centuries had provided a range of medicines made from herbs, salts, minerals, and other ingredients that were thought to be effective against specific illnesses or as general tonics to promote health. These could be purchased at apothecaries' shops if one lived in a city, or from men or women with a reputation as healers, or the ingredients could be gathered and mixed oneself, for early printed books included medical guides for making home remedies and cookbooks included medicines along with other recipes. Some of these ingredients were understood to work – and, indeed, *did* work, for they continue to be used in medical treatment today – through physical or chemical processes. Others were thought to be effective through their "sympathetic" qualities, that is, they resembled the affliction and could thus drive it away; spotted plants of various sorts, for example, were prescribed for diseases such as measles. Such sympathetic action shaded into the magical, for healers often recommended reciting certain sayings while taking the medicine, or prescribed rituals alone. Sometimes these rituals were regarded as outside of or in opposition to Christianity and their practitioners were suspect, though priests also engaged in healing rituals with saints' relics or holy water. Most people confronting illness probably tried a range of options sequentially or simultaneously: blood-letting, therapeutic mixtures, rituals, prayer.

Food was more important than medicine in keeping the body healthy and functioning. Bread was the center of the European diet, though its quality was highly variable depending on social status. Wealthy urban people ate fresh bread made from wheat flour that had been sifted until it was white, while poorer urban and rural people ate darker bread made from a mix of grains and baked or bought only sporadically, or mush made from grains or beans. To this were added vegetables in season, which in southern Europe meant leafy or root vegetables most of the year and in northern Europe meant primarily root vegetables in summer and fall and nothing in winter and spring. This scarcity of vegetables could cause scurvy, a disease caused by the lack of vitamin C; sauerkraut – cabbage pickled in salt and vinegar – was a useful antidote, developed in central Europe, and by the sixteenth century made and sold by female vendors in many cities.

Poor people in cities actually got much of their food already prepared from vendors. Bread or vegetables or even porridge require cooking facilities, to which the very poor, living in a basement or attic room, had no access. Meat was a luxury, eaten in the fall by rural families as they slaughtered the animals that would not make it through the winter, eaten more regularly by the wealthy, sometimes so much that they suffered from gout, a very painful inflammation of the tissues around the joints caused by too much uric acid and made worse by eating too much protein. Meat was judged more important for men than for women; according to German ordinances, male agricultural workers were to be fed meat and other foods twice a day, and women only vegetables, soup and bread. In these statutes only men were to be provided with wine, though it is clear from other sources that women drank wine and beer nearly as readily as men did.

The differences in dietary components – and the problems they caused – between poor and wealthy, men and women, were primarily a matter of economics, but they were also related to ideas about natural and social hierarchies. Birds were seen as more noble than pigs, as the former lived in the sky (and thus close to God) and the latter rooted around in the earth; thus birds were the proper food for high nobles, and pork was a food for peasants. Such foods not only symbolized the class of their eaters, but also transmitted qualities to them. Just as a child could absorb moral and spiritual qualities along with nutrition from the milk of a wet-nurse, so nobles could gain sensitivity and intelligence from eating delicate birds. Religious teachings also led to differences in dietary practices. Jews and Muslims did not eat pork, Catholic and Orthodox Christians did not eat meat on certain days, Muslims did not eat during the daylight hours at certain times of the year, Jews did not eat shellfish. Thus a test for how fully individuals who claimed to have converted from one religion to another had done so was requiring them to eat what their old religion judged taboo.

Covering the body had meaning as well, for clothing marked an individual's gender, class status, and religious allegiance. Sometimes this was officially regulated, as city councils and other governmental bodies passed sumptuary laws requiring groups of people to dress in specific ways. Jews were obliged to wear symbols on their clothes or hats of a specific color (often yellow), so that they would be easily recognizable. Prostitutes might also be ordered to sew stripes of yellow or red on their clothing, wear a specific type or color of cloak, or keep their hair uncovered. Anyone who was not a member of the nobility was prohibited from wearing gold, fur, certain fabrics, or specific colors, and anyone not a member of the urban elite was prohibited from wearing garments worth more

4 Elizabethan sumptuary laws

Sumptuary laws were passed during the reigns of Henry VIII and Mary, but were routinely ignored and were almost impossible to enforce. Several times during her reign Elizabeth issued admonitions to obey the existing laws, and also set out their stipulations in greater detail. This is an extract from a statute issued in 1574, which provides both a justification for the law and intricate details about prohibited clothing.

The excess of apparel and the superfluity of unnecessary foreign wares thereto belonging now of late years is grown by sufferance to such an extremity that the manifest decay of the whole realm generally is like to follow (by bringing into the realm such superfluities of silks, cloths of gold, silver, and other most vain devices of so great cost for the quantity thereof as of necessity the moneys and treasure of the realm is and must be yearly conveyed out of the same to answer the said excess) but also particularly the wasting and undoing of a great number of young gentlemen, otherwise serviceable, and others seeking by show of apparel to be esteemed as gentlemen, who, allured by the vain show of those things, do not only consume themselves, their goods, and lands which their parents left unto them, but also run into such debts and shifts as they cannot live out of danger of laws without attempting unlawful acts, whereby they are not any ways serviceable to their country as otherwise they might be ...

Wherefore her majesty willeth and straightly commandeth all manner of persons in all places

within 12 days after the publication of this present proclamation to reform their apparel ...

None shall wear in his apparel:

Any silk of the color of purple, cloth of gold tissued, nor fur of sables, but only the King, Queen, King's mother, children, brethren, and sisters, uncles and aunts; and except dukes, marquises, and earls, who may wear the same in doublets, jerkins, linings of cloaks, gowns, and hose; and those of the Garter, purple in mantles only ...

Velvet in gowns, coats, or other uttermost garments; fur of leopards; embroidery with any silk: except men of the degrees above mentioned, barons' sons, knights and gentlemen in ordinary office attendant upon her majesty's person, and such as have been employed in embassages to foreign princes ...

Hat, bonnet, girdle, scabbards of swords, daggers, etc.; shoes and slippers of velvet: except the degrees and persons above named and the son and heir apparent of a knight ...

Note that her majesty's meaning is not, by this order, to forbid in any person the wearing of silk buttons, the facing of coats, cloaks, hats and caps, for comeliness only, with taffeta, velvet, or other silk, as is commonly used.

(From Enforcing Statutes of Apparel, Greenwich, June 15, 1574, 16 Elizabeth I.)

 For additional chapter resources see the companion website www.cambridge.org/wiesnerhanks.

than a specified amount. These laws also regulated spending on celebrations such as weddings or baptisms according to social class, and were justified as a way to limit frivolous spending on luxuries, promote local production (many laws restricted the purchase of imported clothing or foodstuffs), and assure social order. It is clear from court records and from sermons and pamphlets decrying those who ignored them that sumptuary laws were not always followed, but governments – and in the case of Jews and prostitutes, church officials – continued to issue them well into the eighteenth century.

What one put in or on the body was clearly a moral as well as a material issue, and the body itself had moral and religious meaning. The bodies of Muslim and Jewish men were marked by circumcision, a procedure celebrated by prayer and festivities for most boys and by elaborate multi-day festivals with parades and banquets for the sons of the Ottoman sultan. Christianity taught that the resurrection of the body was one of the rewards for adherents, and that on this earth the actions of the body were significant – in Catholicism and Orthodoxy they helped to merit salvation, and in most varieties of Protestantism good works were marks of saving faith. As chapter 5 will discuss in more detail, though Protestants and Catholics in western Europe differed in certain points of theology, they were united in their efforts to impose order and discipline on both the individual physical bodies and the corporate social bodies of their adherents.

The life cycle: childhood and youth

Interest in the body as a historical subject is quite a new development, though as one delves into the sources of early modern history it is hard to see how it could have been avoided for so long, for early modern Europeans were clearly very concerned about the body, and left countless medical, legal, religious, and intellectual texts and images about it. The same is true of the life cycle; historians became interested in childhood only about thirty years ago, and in the aging process and old age only within the last decade, despite the many written and visual sources about the "ages of man."

The earliest studies of early modern childhood, such as those of Philippe Ariès, painted a grim picture for both boys and girls. Childhood, they argued, was not recognized as a distinct stage in life until at least the late eighteenth century, and children were raised harshly or regarded with indifference. These views were derived largely from child-raising manuals that advocated strict discipline and warned against coddling or showing too much affection and portraits of children that showed them dressed as little adults. This bleak view has been relieved somewhat in the last several decades by scholars using archival sources about the way children were actually treated; they have discovered that many parents showed great affection for their children and were very disturbed when they died young. Parents tried to protect their children with religious amulets and pilgrimages to special shrines, made toys for them, and sang them lullabies. Even practices which to us may seem cruel, such as tight swaddling, were motivated by a concern for the child's safety and health at a time when most households had open fires, domestic animals wandered freely, and mothers and older siblings engaged in productive work which prevented them from continually watching an infant or a toddler.

Children began their training for adult life at the age of four or five. Girls of all classes throughout Europe were taught skills that they would use in running a household – spinning, sewing, cooking, care of domestic animals. Peasant girls were also taught some types of agricultural tasks, and urban girls tasks that would help their father in his occupation. Boys were taught tasks appropriate to their station in life, and were more likely than girls to be taught to read or to receive at least a little formal schooling; the depictions of the ages of man that show both sexes often portray the female in the second age spinning, and the male reading.

Just as they disputed whether the early modern period had a clear concept of childhood, historians have also disagreed about whether there was a notion of adolescence. Once again, the trend has been to find more and more evidence that there was, although this varied across space and time. Some authors divided *adolescentia* from *juventus* (youth), seeing the former – for boys – as a time of raging lusts and wild behavior and the latter as a subsequent stage, when young men learned to control their actions and carried out their final preparations for adult responsibilities, including marriage. Physical maturing occurred in stages for men, as did maturing in legal and political terms; boys who were fourteen could generally marry, make contracts of apprenticeship for themselves, or enter universities, though they could not inherit land, unless they were a territorial ruler.

A number of different rituals served to mark these passages into adulthood. Urban boys who had been apprentices and journeymen in a craft guild might get permission to make a masterpiece and become a master, with a ceremony marking their entrance into the guild. New students at universities (*beani* in Latin) went through initiation rituals and periods of hazing, in which they wore distinctive hats and were required to serve older students. Noble boys might participate in tournaments and chivalric rituals marking their entrance into knighthood; gunpowder and more effective bows were lessening the importance of mounted knights in actual combat, but tournaments continued to be important avenues for young men to gain prestige and maintain their family's honor and status. At a certain age, rural or urban boys would be asked the join the gangs of young men (termed *abbeyes de jeunesse* in French) that carried out rituals of shaming, taunting, and harassing those whose actions they disapproved of, such as men who married older women or husbands whose wives were suspected of having extramarital affairs. Gangs of young men frequently roamed the streets of many towns in the evening, fighting with one another, threatening young women, and drinking until they passed out; in university towns these groups might be made up of students. Such activities were

Fig. 4. Paintings such as this family group by Lavinia Fontana (1552–1614) provide evidence for both sides in the debate about early modern childhood. Those who see childhood as bleak point to the elaborate adult-type dress of the boys and the formal posture of the older man; those who see it as pleasant note that the boys are shown with a pet and in physical contact with their father (or perhaps grandfather).

largely tolerated and viewed as a normal part of achieving manhood, though occasionally city authorities intervened if they became too wild.

For girls, physical maturity was marked by the onset of menstruation, termed menarche in modern English and "the flowers" or similar terms in the sixteenth century. Because of poorer nutrition levels, menarche probably occurred on average somewhat later than it does today. Menstruation carried a great many religious and popular taboos, for though all bodily fluids were seen as related, menstrual blood was still generally viewed as somehow different and dangerous. Hebrew Scripture held that menstruation made a woman ritually impure, so that everything she touched was unclean and her presence was to be avoided by all. By the early modern period in Jewish communities, this taboo was limited to sexual relations and a few other contacts between wife and husband for the seven days of her period and seven days afterwards. At the end of this time, a woman was expected to take a ritual bath (*mikvah*) before beginning sexual relations again. Among the Orthodox Slavs in eastern Europe, menstruating women could not enter churches or take communion. Western Christian churches were a bit milder, but canon lawyers and other Catholic and Protestant commentators advised against sexual relations during menstruation. This was originally based strictly on the religious notion that women were unclean during this period, though during the sixteenth century the idea spread that sex during menstruation was medically unwise as it would result in deformed or leprous children. Menstruation was used to symbolize religious practices with which one did not agree, with English Protestants, for example, calling the soul of the pope a "menstruous rag." According to popular beliefs, menstruating women could by their touch, glance or mere presence rust iron, turn wine sour, spoil meat, or dull knives, though how effective these ideas were at shaping the actual work in any household is difficult to say.

The life cycle: sexuality

Like the body and childhood, sexuality has become an increasingly common topic for historical investigation. The assertion of the women's movement that the "personal is political," combined with the growth of social history, led historians first to the sexual lives of women in the past, and then to those of men. Historical investigations have been an important part of gay and lesbian studies – which grew out of the gay liberation movement – as scholars have detailed changes in the ways in which same-sex relationships have been understood and practiced. Just as studies of women's sexuality led to studies of men's, studies of same-sex relationships led a few scholars to frame changes in male/female relationships as part of a history of heterosexuality, not simply the history of marriage or the family.

All of this scholarship has made clear that sexual categories and meanings change dramatically over time and across cultures. For example, though there were homosexual subcultures in a few cities and courts in earlier centuries, the idea that *everyone* has a "sexual identity" as a heterosexual or homosexual first developed in the nineteenth century. Ancient Greek and medieval Latin did not even have words for "sex" or "sexual," and the word "sexuality" only appeared in English and most other western languages about 1800. Because of this, some historians choose to avoid the word "sexuality" when discussing any era before the modern, but others point out that using modern categories to explore the past is not an unacceptable practice, because investigations of the past are always informed by present understandings and concerns; they note that earlier cultures were clearly concerned by the issues we view as part of sexuality, but contextualized them differently.

Medical and scientific texts provided one framework for sexual issues in early modern Europe. In medical terms, male sexuality was the baseline for any perception of human sexuality, and the female sex organs were viewed as the male turned inside out or simply not pushed out. Vesalius depicted the uterus looking exactly like an inverted penis, and his student Baldasar Heseler commented: "The organs of procreation are the same in the male and the female . . . For if you turn the scrotum, the testicles and the penis inside out you will have all the genital organs of the female."[2] This view of the correspondence between male and female sexual organs survived the Renaissance discovery of the clitoris, with scientists simply deciding that women had two structures that were like a penis. This idea meant that there was no precise nomenclature for many female anatomical parts until the eighteenth century because they were always thought to be congruent with some male part, and so were simply called by the same name. The parallels between the two could lead to unusual sex changes, for many medical doctors throughout Europe, including Ambrose Paré, solemnly reported cases of young women whose sex organs suddenly emerged during vigorous physical activity, transforming them into men; there are no reports of the opposite, however.

Because female sex organs were hidden, they seemed more mysterious than male organs to early modern physicians and anatomists, and anatomical guidebooks use illustrations of autopsies on women's lower bodies as symbols of modern science uncovering the unknown. Early modern sex manuals spread this idea to a wider public. The best-seller among these was the anonymous *Aristotle's Masterpiece*, first published in 1684 and reprinted in many different versions, often with a subtitle such as "The Secrets of Generation Displayed." Attributing the work to Aristotle gave it a claim to respectability, authority, and ancient pedigree; the real Aristotle, though he had nothing to do with it, would probably have agreed with many of its assumptions. One of these was the notion that both men and women needed to experience orgasm for procreation; only through orgasm would the female "seed" be released, an idea that was yet another example of female experience being simply extrapolated from male. This supposed connection between female orgasm and procreation allowed the manuals to go into great detail about ways to heighten sexual pleasure, while still claiming moralistically to be guides for happy marital life.

Sexuality was also a key issue in religious texts. Those written by Orthodox Slavic writers in eastern Europe saw all sexuality as an evil inclination originating with the devil and not part of God's original creation. Even marital sex was regarded as a sin, with the best marriage an unconsummated one; this led to a large number of miraculous virgin births among Russian saints, and to the popular idea that Jesus was born out of Mary's ear, not polluting himself with passage through the birth canal.

Western Catholic opinion did not go this far, but displayed an ambivalent attitude toward sexuality. Sex was seen as polluting and defiling, with virginity regarded as the most desirable state; members of the clergy and religious orders were expected to remain chaste, a policy that was enforced much more rigorously as part of the Catholic Reformation, as we will see in chapter 5. Their chastity and celibacy made them different from, and superior to, lay Christians who married. On the other hand, the body and its sexual urges could not be completely evil, because they were created by God; to claim otherwise was heresy. Writers vacillated between these two opinions or held both at once, and the laws that were developed in the Middle Ages regulating sexual behavior were based on both of them. In general, early modern Catholic doctrine held that sexual relations were acceptable as long as they were within marriage, not done on Sundays or other church holidays, done in a way which would allow procreation, and did not upset the proper sexual order, which meant the man had to be on top (what has since been termed the "missionary position"). Spouses were held to enjoy a mutual right to sexual intercourse (the "marital debt"), which would even excuse intercourse when procreation was not possible. It was better, for example, for a pregnant or menstruating woman to allow her husband to have intercourse with her if refusing this would cause him to turn to a prostitute. Sixteenth- and seventeenth-century Catholic authors adopted a more positive view of marital sex than their medieval predecessors, regarding sexual pleasure, even fantasies and variant positions, as acceptable as a prelude to procreative intercourse.

The Protestant reformers broke clearly with Catholicism in their view that marriage was a spiritually preferable state to celibacy, and saw the most important function of marital sex not as procreation, but as increasing spousal affection. Based on his own experience, Martin Luther stressed the power of sexual feelings for both men and women, and thought women in particular needed intercourse in order to stay healthy.

Western Christian authors and officials thus generally agreed that sexual relations were permissable as long as they were marital and "natural," though interpretations of the latter varied. Jewish authorities agreed, seeing procreation as a commandment of God, though marital sex still made one ritually impure. Islam regarded sex within marriage or other approved relationships as a positive good. Sexual relations did not have to be justified by reproduction, so that contraception was acceptable, though having children, and particularly having sons, was also seen as essential to a good life for Muslims.

Sexuality was also an important theme in popular literature. Many historians have viewed traditional popular culture in Europe as unrestrained, celebrating male sexuality with bawdy stories, obscene songs, and, after the development of the printing press, a range of pornographic literature. These songs and stories express a fear of rampant female sexuality, and often advocate beating as the proper way to treat women who showed too much independence: "Now will I sing so gaily, Hit thy wife on the head, With cudgels smear her daily" went the first of many verses of a sixteenth-century German song titled "Song of how one should beat bad women."

Medical, religious, and popular texts all discuss sexuality in theory, as do law codes and ordinances issued by religious and secular officials that regulated a range of sexual issues: premarital intercourse, adultery, rape, incest, sodomy. Court records providing information about actual cases also survive for many parts of Europe beginning in the fourteenth century; these can give us an idea about what types of sexual activities communities felt it most important to control in reality.

While a certain amount of wild behavior was tolerated in young men, it was not in young women, and punishments for sexual misconduct by unmarried women, particularly premarital intercourse and pregnancy out of wedlock, could be quite sharp. It was often very difficult for unmarried women to avoid sexual contacts. Many of them worked as domestic servants, where their employers or employers' sons or male relatives could easily coerce them, or in close proximity to men. Female servants were sent on errands alone or with men, or worked by themselves in fields far from other people; notions of female honor kept upper-class women secluded in their homes, particularly in southern and eastern Europe, but there was little attempt anywhere to keep female servants or day laborers from the risk of seduction or rape. Rape was a capital crime in many parts of Europe, but the actual sentences handed out were more likely to be fines and brief imprisonments, with the severity of sentence dependent on the social status of the victim and perpetrator. The victim had to prove that she had cried out and made attempts to repel the attacker, and had to bring the charge within a short period of time after the attack had happened. Women bringing rape charges were often more interested in getting their own honorable reputations back than in punishing the perpetrator, and for this reason sometimes requested that the judge force their rapists to marry them.

The consequences of unwed motherhood varied throughout Europe, with rural areas that needed many workers being the most tolerant. Once an unmarried woman suspected she was pregnant, she had several options. In some parts of Europe, if she was a minor her father could go to court and sue the man involved for "trespass and damages" to his property. The woman herself could go to her local court and attempt to prove there had been a promise of marriage in order to coerce the man to marry her. Marriage was the favored official solution, and was agreed upon in a surprising number of cases, indicating that perhaps there had been an informal agreement, or at least that the man was now willing to take responsibility for his actions. Marriage was impossible in many cases, however, and young women often attempted to deny the pregnancy as long as possible, hoping for a miscarriage.

If no other avenues were open to her, a pregnant woman might try to induce an abortion, either by physical means such as tying her waist very tight or carrying heavy objects, or by herbal concoctions that she brewed herself or purchased from a local person reputed to know how to "bring on the monthlies," that is, to start a woman's period again. Penalties for attempting or performing an abortion grew increasingly harsh during the early modern period, but it was hard to detect. (Contraception was even harder to detect, and though religious and secular authorities all opposed it, there were almost no cases in which it was an issue.) Abortion was legally defined as killing a child in the womb, who had gained a soul, which most authorities thought happened at the point in pregnancy termed "quickening," when the mother feels movement, usually about the fourth or fifth month. (The word "quick" is an old word for alive, as in the phrase "the quick and the dead.") A woman taking medicine to start her period before quickening was generally not regarded as attempting an abortion. Abortifacients of all types were never very effective, however, so women gave birth in outhouses, cowstalls, hay mounds, and dung heaps, hoping that they would be able to avoid public notice, and took the infant to one of the new foundling homes that had opened during the fifteenth or sixteenth centuries in many cities. A few did kill their children, a crime that carried the death penalty, often specified as death by drowning.

5 Lawsuit regarding a pregnancy out of wedlock

Despite the best efforts of political and religious authorities, women did get pregnant out of wedlock, and formal legal arrangements were sometimes made to support the child. These arrangements were recorded by notaries. In this document from Paris in 1547, a single woman and a man go on record to settle a lawsuit in progress regarding the woman's pregnancy and the subsequent birth of a child by the man. The woman's economic circumstances and means of earning a living are not specified. The man, as a legal practitioner given the title "master," was probably comfortably well off, though not rich. He promises to support the child for only two years; similar contracts often include a much longer period of support, but rarely beyond age seven or eight, at which point it was expected the child would be earning his or her own keep as a servant or day laborer.

Were present in person master Jherosme Honys, legal practitioner at the Palais in Paris, on the one hand, and Mathurine de Marville, living in Paris, rue Alexandre Langloiz, on the other hand, who have made and now make the agreements, compromises, and arrangements which follow.

That is to say that the said de Marville has promised and here promises to raise and support, well and duly, from this point on, a young girl named Claude, to whom she previously gave birth, child of the said Honys; in return for which the said Honys will be obliged and obliges himself to give and pay her, each month for the next two full years, one *écu soleil*, the first term of payment falling due the last day of February coming up.

And in addition to this, [Honys] has given four *écus d'or* in cash, and has promised and promises to pay her six *écus soleil* by the day and feast of Easter coming up, for maintenance and clothing of the said child; without Honys being in any way obliged to give anything else for the support of the said child, from this point on, if not of his own goodwill.

In consideration of the things above, the said Marville has released and here releases the said Honys of all things whatsoever, equally for what she is able or might be able to ask in original amount as for expenses in the legal process pending before whatever judges there might be, and of all other things whatsoever for which she could make demands and take legal action in whatever cause or way that might be, from the past up to now.

Thus etc., promising, etc., obligating, etc., each in his own right, etc., renouncing, etc. Done and passed in duplicate in the year 1547, Wednesday, the 25th day of January.

(Paris, Archives Nationales, Minutier central, Etude XI/27, Jan. 25, 1547. Trans. Carol Loats in Monica Chojnacka and Merry Wiesner-Hanks, eds., *Ages of Woman, Ages of Man: European Social History, 1400–1750* [London: Longman 2002], p. 56. Reprinted by permission.)

Along with extramarital pregnancy, other sexual activities were also regulated and punished during this period. During the Middle Ages, most European cities had allowed prostitution in licensed city brothels; the city leaders justified this by saying that it protected honorable women and girls from attacks by young men. In a few cities, such as Florence, authorities also noted that brothels might keep young men from homosexual relations, another far worse alternative in their eyes. During the fifteenth century, many cities began to feel increasingly uneasy about permitting the selling of sex for money, and, as noted above, began to require the women to wear distinctive clothing or not appear in public at all. After the Protestant and Catholic Reformations, moralizing authorities intent on social control and discipline called for the suppression of prostitution. Cities and states in central and northern Europe began to close their brothels and made soliciting a crime; southern European cities, especially those in Italy, licensed prostitutes and restricted their movements.

Church and state authorities also attempted to suppress same-sex sexual activity. After about 1250 they increasingly defined such actions as "crimes against nature," seeing them as particularly reprehensible because they thought they did not occur anywhere else in creation. Same-sex relations, usually termed "sodomy," became a capital crime in most of Europe, with adult offenders threatened with execution by fire. The Italian cities of Venice, Florence, and Lucca created special courts to deal with sodomy, which saw thousands of investigations, as did various courts in the Iberian peninsula, including the Inquisition. Almost all of the cases involved an adult man and an adolescent boy, and ranged from sex exchanged for money to long-term affectionate relationships. Actual executions were rare in Italy, and more common in the Iberian peninsula, where those charged with sodomy were sometimes tortured to reveal other names, so that sodomy accusations often occurred in waves. Many of those executed were from all-male environments such as monasteries or the military, or they were Italians or Muslim slaves, both groups that Spaniards regarded as particularly likely to be sodomites. Executions were generally carried out at public *autos da fé*, where bigamists, heretics, and relapsed Jewish or Muslim converts were also either executed or displayed for public ridicule. Executions for sodomy slowly tapered off in Spain in the early seventeenth century, at the same time that attempts to suppress both prostitution and same-sex relations increased in northern Europe, which we will trace in more detail in chapter 8.

Young people did not have to actually engage in illicit sexual behavior to be viewed with suspicion, for political and religious authorities often regarded unmarried young people as sources of disorder, and passed laws requiring them to live with older adults or otherwise restricting their behavior. (Such laws were also passed, and enforced, in colonial New England.) In Malmø, for example, the second largest city of the kingdom of Denmark, a city council ordinance issued in 1549 required all unmarried young men and servants to register annually at the city hall, and all unmarried young women to go into domestic service rather than living on their own. In Strasbourg, young women were even prohibited from living with their own widowed mothers, for this allowed them "to have more freedom to walk around, to saunter back and forth whenever they want to . . . [which] causes nothing but shame, immodesty, wantonnness and immorality."[3]

The life cycle: marriage

The most obvious solution for the problems of extramarital pregnancy or unmarried young adults sauntering around or starting drunken brawls was marriage, but marriage was not to be entered into lightly. The choice of a spouse often determined one's social and financial situation, as well as one's personal well-being and happiness, so that this decision was far too important to leave up to the young people themselves. Family, friends, and neighbors played a role in finding an appropriate spouse and bringing the marriage to realization. Particularly among the upper classes, there were often complicated marriage strategies to cement family alliances and expand family holdings. On the other end of the economic spectrum, communities and cities in some parts of Europe refused to give marriage permits to people who were poor. They worried that poor households would need public support, and saw marriage as a privilege open only to those who could afford it. This local restriction of marriage permits became state law in the early nineteenth century in many parts of central Europe, and lasted until after World War I.

Marriage was the clearest mark of social adulthood for both women and men. Craft guilds often required that masters be married, and participation in the governing body of villages or cities was limited to married men. Thus poor men who were refused marriage permits were also excluded from guild mastership and village decision-making. Marriage gave many women authority over dependent members of the household, including not only children but servants, slaves, and in craft households even apprentices and journeymen. Despite an emphasis on the individual among some thinkers, most fifteenth- and sixteenth-century theorists still conceptualized society as a collection of households, with a marital pair at the core of each household.

There are numerous examples of children and parents who fought bitterly over the choice of a spouse, but in the vast majority of marriages, the aims of the people involved and their parents, kin, and community were largely the same: the best husband was the one who could provide security, honor, and status, and the best wife one who was capable of running a household and assisting her husband in his work. Therefore even people who were the most free to choose their own spouses, such as widows and widowers or people whose parents had died, were motivated more by what we would regard as pragmatic concerns than romantic love. This is not to say that their choice was unemotional, but that the need for economic security, the desire for social

6 An Austrian marriage law regulates spousal relations

In addition to marriage contracts, local, territorial, and national law codes all regulated aspects of married life, including financial matters and spousal relations. This is a section from the Law Code of the territory of Salzburg, Austria from 1526.

It is to be accepted that both spouses have married themselves together from the time of the consummation of their marriage, body to body and goods to goods …

The husband shall not spend away the dowry or other goods of his wife unnecessarily with gambling or other useless frivolous pastimes, wasting and squandering it. Whoever does this is guilty of sending his wife into poverty. His wife, in order to secure her legacy and other goods she has brought to the marriage, may get an order requiring him to pledge and hold in trust for her some of his property. In the same way he is to act in a suitable manner in other things that pertain to their living together and act appropriately toward her. If there is no cause or she is not guilty of anything, he is not to hit her too hard, push her, throw her or carry out any other abuse. For her part, the wife should obey her husband in modesty and honorable fear, and be true and obedient to him. She should not provoke him with word or deed to disagreement or displeasure, through which he might be moved to strike her or punish her in unseemly ways. Also, without his knowledge and agreement she is not to do business [with any household goods] except those which she has brought to the marriage; if she does it will not be legally binding …

The first and foremost heirs are the children who inherit from their parents. If a father and mother leave behind legitimate children out of their bodies, one or more sons or daughters, then these children inherit all paternal and maternal goods, landed property and movables, equally with each other …

Women who do not have husbands, whether they are young or old, shall have a guardian and advisor in all matters of consequence and property, such as the selling of or other legal matters regarding landed property. Otherwise these transactions are not binding. In matters which do not involve court actions and in other matters of little account they are not to be burdened with guardians against their will.

(From Franz V. Spechtler and Rudolf Uminsky, eds., *Die Salzburger Landesordnung von 1526*, Göppinger Arbeiten zur Germanistik, Nr. 305 [Göppingen: Kümmerle, 1981], pp. 119, 154, 197. Trans. Merry Wiesner-Hanks.)

prestige, and the hope for children were as important emotions as sexual passion. The love and attraction a person felt for a possible spouse could be based on any combination of these, with intense romantic desire often viewed as more likely to be disruptive than supportive of a marriage. Marriage manuals, which became a common genre in the sixteenth century, reinforced these ideas; Catholic, Protestant and Jewish authors agreed that the ideal wife was obedient, chaste, cheerful, thrifty, pious, and largely silent, while the ideal husband was responsible, firm, and honorable.

Spouses did not live up to the ideals set for them all the time, of course, and people regarded it as important to stipulate many legal and financial arrangements with a marriage contract. Marriage contracts were not limited to the wealthy, but by the sixteenth century in some parts of Europe quite ordinary people, including servants and artisans, had marriage contracts drawn up before they wed. Contracts were especially important in second and third marriages, as they had to stipulate how any inheritance might be divided among all of the children. Only after all parties had signed the contract (often including the parents of both spouses, if they were still living) could the actual marriage ceremony proceed. Weddings varied throughout Europe, but they generally involved some sort of religious ritual, followed by as expensive a feast as the family could afford.

Just as marriage ceremonies varied according to region, so did marriage patterns. The most dramatic difference was between the area of northern and western Europe, including the British Isles, Scandinavia, France, Germany, and much of Italy and Spain, and eastern and southern Europe. In most of northwestern Europe, historians have identified a marriage pattern unique in the world, with couples waiting until their mid- or late twenties to marry, long beyond the age of sexual maturity, and then immediately setting up an independent household. (Demographers term this a *nuclear, ne-olocal* household structure.) Husbands were likely to be only two or three years older than their wives at first marriage, and though households often contained servants, they rarely contained more than one family member who was not part of the nuclear family. In most of the rest of the world, including southern Europe, most of eastern Europe, and a few parts of northwestern Europe, such as Ireland, marriage was between teenagers who lived with one set of parents for a long time, or between a man in his late twenties or thirties and a much younger woman, with households again containing several generations. (Demographers term this a *complex* family household, and make further distinctions between *extended* family households with one conjugal unit plus one or more other kin, and *multiple* family households with two or more kin-related family units.) There were regional and class variations from these patterns – in southern Italy and southern Spain nuclear families were more common than complex, which was also true among agricultural wage laborers in Hungary and Romania – but in the forty years since the demographer John Hajnal first identified these two family patterns, most research has supported his division.[4]

Historians are not sure exactly why this pattern developed, and its consequences are easier to trace than its causes: fewer total pregnancies per woman, though not necessarily fewer surviving children; a greater level of economic independence for newlyweds, who had often spent long periods as servants or workers in other households saving money and learning skills; more people who never married at all. In southern and eastern Europe most of the unmarried population lived in convents or monasteries, but in northwestern Europe this group was far too large for that, even before the Protestant Reformation led to the closing of most monastic institutions. Demographers estimate that from 10 to 15 percent of the northwestern European population never married in the early modern period, and that in some places in some eras this figure may have been as high as 25 percent. This may be one reason that most laws restricting unmarried people come from northern Europe, and the continuity in this pattern indicates that these laws were never very effective.

One of the key ideas of the Protestant Reformation was the denial of the value of celibacy and championing of married life as a spiritually preferable state. One might thus expect religion to have had a major effect on marriage patterns, but this is very difficult to document, in large part because all the areas of Europe that became Protestant lie within northwestern Europe. There were a number of theoretical differences. Protestant marriage regulations stressed the importance of parental consent more than Catholic ones, and allowed the possibility of divorce with remarriage for adultery or impotence, and in some areas also for refusal to have sexual relations, very serious physical abuse, abandonment, or incurable diseases such as leprosy. Orthodox law in eastern Europe allowed divorce for adultery or the taking of religious vows. The numbers of people of any Christian denomination who actually used the courts to escape an unpleasant marriage were very small, however, and apparently everywhere smaller than the number of couples who informally divorced by simply moving apart from one another. In parts of Europe where this has been studied, women more often used the courts to attempt to form a marriage, i.e. in breach of promise cases, or to renew a marriage in which their spouse had deserted them, than to end one. The impossibility of divorce in Catholic areas was mitigated somewhat by the possibility of annulment and by institutions which took in abused or deserted wives; similar institutions were not found in Protestant areas.

Jewish law allowed divorce (termed *get*) for a number of reasons, including incompatibility; in theory the agreement of both spouses was needed, and the economic division of the assets was to be based on each spouse's behavior. Muslim law allowed a man to divorce his wife at any time, though he was required to continue supporting her; wives seeking divorce – and this emerges more in actual court records than in theoretical law codes – gave up their right to this support. Muslim law also allowed a man to have up to four wives, but polygamy was relatively uncommon in the Ottoman Empire.

Place of residence and social class had a larger impact than religion on marital patterns. Throughout Europe, rural residents married earlier than urban ones, and were more likely to live in complex households of several generations or married brothers and their families living together. They also remarried faster and more often. Women from the upper classes married earlier than those from the lower, and the age difference between spouses was greater for upper-class women. Women who had migrated in search of employment married later than those who had remained at home, and married someone closer to their own age.

Along with significant differences, there were also similarities in marriage patterns throughout Europe. Women of all classes and religions were expected to bring a dowry to their marriage, which might consist of some clothing and household items (usually including the marriage bed and bedding) for poor women, or vast amounts of cash, goods, or property for wealthy ones; in eastern Europe the dowry might even include serfs or slaves. The size of the dowry varied by geographic area and across time as well as by social class. In fifteenth- and sixteenth-century Florence, for example, dowries required for a middle- or upper-class woman to marry grew staggeringly large, and families placed many of their daughters in convents instead of trying to find husbands for them, because convent entrance cost much less than a dowry. The dowry substituted in most parts of Europe for a daughter's share of the family inheritance, and increasingly did not include any land, which kept land within the patrilineal lineage. Laws regarding a woman's control of her dowry varied throughout Europe, but in general a husband had the use, but not the ownership, of it during his wife's lifetime, though of course if he invested it unwisely this distinction did not make much difference. During the late medieval period, women appear to have been able freely to bequeath their dowries to whomever they chose, but in many parts of Europe this right was restricted during the sixteenth century to prevent them from deeding property to persons other than the male heirs.

The life cycle: widowhood and old age

The loss of a spouse was another common feature of married life throughout Europe; people became widowed at all ages, and might easily be widowed several times during their lives. The death of a spouse brought a more dramatic change in status for women than it did for men. Women's link to the world of work often depended on their husband's professional identity, so that his death affected his widow's opportunities for making a living, while the death of a wife did not. We can see this distinction in the fact that the word for "widower" in most European languages derives from the word for "widow," whereas the more common pattern is for the female designation to derive from the male – princess from prince, actress from actor. The word "widower," in fact, does not enter common usage until the eighteenth century, when people began to think about the loss of a spouse more as an emotional than an economic issue; sources from before that time indicate clearly when women are widows, but only rarely that men have lost their wives.

Images of widows in this period are generally negative, with widows portrayed as ugly old crones or as greedy and sexually rapacious women looking for their next husbands (or sometimes as both). The reality was more complex. The death of a husband often brought financial hardship, and widows were more likely to be dependent on public or religious charity than married women. The poorest households in towns and villages were those headed by elderly widows; because the death of his wife did not mean a man had to change occupation, widowers did not become significantly poorer. On the other hand, widowhood provided social and financial opportunities for some women. Widows who had inherited money or property from their husbands or who had received their dowry back at his death were often relatively free to invest it or dispose of it as they wished. Aristocratic widows were often very active in managing their families' business affairs, and identified the rights and privileges attached to their position as *theirs*, and not simply belonging to them in trust for their sons. Widowhood could also place a woman in a position of great power over her children, deciding the amount of dowry for her daughters and assisting her sons in gaining positions of political influence.

This social and economic independence was disturbing to many commentators, who thought the best solution might be remarriage. Remarriage was also troubling, however, for this lessened a woman's allegiance to the family of her first husband, could have serious economic consequences for the children of her first marriage, and, if she was wealthy, might also give her what was seen as an inappropriate amount of power over her spouse. Thus both advice books and laws regarding widows reflect an ambivalence, though in actual practice whether a widow remarried or not was more determined by her economic and personal situation than by laws or theoretical concerns. Younger widows remarried much more readily than older ones, and widows with fewer children more readily than those with many. The opposite is true in the case of widowers; those with many children were most likely to remarry, and to

Wie ein altes Weyb bulet vmb eins Jünglings Leyb.

Fig. 5. Paintings and woodcuts, such as this one published in Nuremberg in 1570, often showed amorous scenes of older women and younger men, with the woman's money-pouch clearly depicted as the source of her attractiveness. Sixteenth century viewers would have understood the money-pouch also as a reference to female genitalia.

remarry quickly. In general, widowers were far more likely to remarry than widows; French statistics indicate that 50 percent of widowers in the sixteenth and seventeenth centuries remarried, while only 20 percent of widows did so. In general somewhere around one-fifth of all marriages were remarriages for at least one of the partners.

Widowhood was a clear legal status, but "old age" in the early modern period is harder to define. For women, the best marker might be menopause, which usually occurred somewhere in a woman's forties; the mean age at which women in northwestern Europe bore their last child was forty. For men there was no clear biological marker. Because life expectancy was less than it is today, however, even if people stopped having children before forty they still had children in their households for most of their later years of life. In eastern and southern Europe, older people often lived in three-generation multiple family households, or moved from the household of one married child to another. In northern and western Europe, older men and women whose children had all left home generally continued to live on their own as long as possible. Evidence from England indicates that middle-class children were more likely to assist their elderly parents by providing them with servants so that they could stay in their own households rather than taking them in; the elderly lived with their married children only among the poor.

Though we often romanticize earlier periods as a time when the elderly were cherished for their wisdom and experience, this was not necessarily so.

In many parts of Europe, parents made formal contracts with their children to assure themselves of a certain level of material support – e.g. "twelve bushels of rye and a place by the fire" – and public welfare rolls included many elderly whose children were still in the area but were not supporting them. In her advice book for women written in 1407, the French author Christine de Pizan reminds young women that "you owe honor to the elderly, so it follows that at all costs you must avoid mocking them and doing or saying injurious, derisive, or outrageous things, or bad things of whatever kind. Do not displease or find fault with them, as some wicked young people do who are very much to be reproached for it, who call them 'old boys' or 'old biddies.'"[5]

Older women were generally more in need of public support than older men, in part because their spouses were less likely or able to care for them than the wives of older men, who were generally younger or had no way to leave an ailing spouse. Younger relatives were also more willing to take in elderly men than women; older women often formed joint households with other older female relatives or simply acquaintances to pool their resources and expenses, a practice almost unknown among men. The higher percentage of elderly female welfare recipients may also have been partly due to the fact that there were simply more older women than men around. Despite the dangers of childbirth, female life expectancy seems to have been gradually growing longer than male throughout this period; by the eighteenth century in France, female life expectancy at birth was about thirty-four and male about thirty-one.

Aging brought physical as well as economic changes, and there is evidence that already in the fifteenth century these were viewed as more of a problem for women than men. Post-menopausal women were widely believed to experience increased sex drive, which might even lead them to seek demonic lovers in order to satisfy themselves. They were held to emit vapors from their mouths that could cause nursing women's milk to dry up or animals and children to sicken. They were thought to be especially concerned with the lessening of their physical attractiveness, for a Spanish physician's remedies to combat wrinkles were all directed at women. At the end of life, both men and women were viewed as physically and mentally infirm. Many illustrations of the ages of man show the people in the last stages as bent over and supported by a cane, and in *As You Like It* Jacques describes this stage as "second childishness and mere oblivion."

The life cycle: death

The very last stage of life was, of course, dying. The engraving by Isaac at the beginning of this chapter ends with a deathbed, and Death, shown as a skeleton in the foreground, presides over the right half of the staircase as individuals decline from the prime of life. Death was much less associated with old age in the early modern period than it is today, however. About one-quarter of children died before they were one, and another quarter before they were ten.

Thus people who survived to adulthood had already lived through the most deadly stage of life.

The frequency of death at an early age did not make people inured to grief, but did make having a "good death" a matter for all ages. Religious texts taught the "art of dying" (*ars moriendi*), instructing readers in how to make amends for their sins, avoid the Devil's snares, and prepare to meet God. Often illustrated with woodcuts of the "dance of death" in which Death leads people from all social ranks, they recommended making a will to dispose of earthly property, and also to make bequests for prayers or memorial services. Mothers were expected to instruct their children in how to have a good death, and to provide an example and spiritual model in their own deaths. Stories of good deaths were the subject of funeral sermons, which were gathered in collections and published as edifying reading. A particularly good death might merit a whole book by itself. For example, Phillip Stubbes, an English Puritan, details the short life and early death of his young wife in *A Crystal Glass for Christian Women* (1591), which went through twenty-four editions in the decades after it was first published.

For Christians before the Protestant Reformation, having a good death meant going through a series of religious rituals. The individual or the family called for a priest when they thought the hour of death was near, and he brought with him a number of objects and substances regarded as having power over death and the sin related to it: holy water to be sprinkled on and around the dying person, holy oil for anointing him or her; a censer with incense to be waved around; the priest's stole for the dying person to touch; a crucifix with an image of the dying Christ to remind him or her of Christ's own agony and death; lighted candles to drive back the darkness both figuratively and literally, often placed in the person's hand as he or she was just about to take a last breath (or "give up the ghost" as the phrase still goes); the communion host consecrated by the priest during the final ritual of Extreme Unction and then consumed by the dying person.

Once the person had died, the body was washed – usually by female family members or women who made their living this way – put in special clothing or a sack of plain cloth, and buried within a day or two. Family and friends joined in a funeral procession, again with candles, holy water, incense, and a crucifix, and marked by the ringing of church bells; sometimes extra women were hired so that the mourning and wailing were especially loud. The procession carried the body into the church, where there were psalms, prayers, and a funeral mass, and then to a consecrated space for burial, the wealthy sometimes inside the church – in the walls, under the floor, or under the building itself in a crypt – but most often in the churchyard or a cemetery close by. As cities grew, cemeteries were set up outside the city walls to provide more space. Individual graves did not have permanent markers, and as churchyards were used over hundreds of years, they became full of skeletal remains. As gravediggers dug a hole for the newest body, they often moved the bones they encountered to a special small building, called a charnel house or an ossuary, where they were available for public view. Standing at the graveside, the priest asked for God's grace on the soul of the deceased, and also asked that soul to "rest in peace."

This final request was made not only for the benefit of the dead, but also for that of the living. The souls of the dead were widely believed to return to earth. Mothers who had died in childbed might come back seeking to take their children with them. Executed criminals might seek to gain revenge on those who had brought them to justice; for this reason they were buried under the gallows, or at a crossroads, which put them permanently under the sign of the cross. Suicides, who were truly "unquiet souls" and the ultimate "bad death," were also buried at a crossroads, sometimes with a stake through the body to make sure it did not wander.

The souls of everyday people might also seek help from surviving family members in achieving their final salvation. If the individual had not provided for this in his or her will, family members hired priests to say memorial masses on anniversaries of the death, especially one week, one month, and one year afterward; large churches had a number of side altars, so that many masses could be going on at one time. Learned theologians sometimes denied that souls actually returned, and beginning in the twelfth century they increasingly emphasized the idea of purgatory, a place where souls on their way to heaven went after death to make amends for their earthly sins. (Those on their way to hell went straight there.) Purgatory is distinct from limbo, a place where the souls of unbaptized infants and noble pagans went after death, where they would remain permanently in a state of what the church termed "natural happiness" though excluded from the "beatific vision" of heaven.

Souls safely in purgatory did not wander the earth, but they could still benefit from earthly activities, for memorial masses, prayers, and donations made in their name might shorten their time in purgatory and hasten their way to heaven. When it was first discussed, purgatory was a rather neutral place, unpleasant largely because one was separated from God, but by the fifteenth century it had acquired the fire and brimstone of hell. The pain of souls in purgatory could be eased by prayers and masses, and also by purchasing or earning indulgences, documents that reduced the need for earthly penance or lessened time in purgatory in exchange for service or a donation to the church. Thus whether on the earth or in purgatory, the dead required things from the living, for death did not sever family obligations and connections.

Protestants denounced the selling of indulgences, rejected both purgatory and limbo as unbiblical, and denied that the living could do anything to assist the souls of the dead, whose destination was determined by God. Requiem masses were abolished and deathbed rituals were shortened and simplified, though family members were encouraged to remain with the dying so that they would not face death alone. Protestants were still concerned with having a "good death," however, and commemorated the deceased through lengthy funeral sermons and epitaphs, elaborate monuments, and generous donations to the poor.

The living also had obligations to the dead among Muslims and Jews. In both groups, deceased people were to be buried quickly, with special prayers said by mourners and family members. Muslim funeral practices involved washing the body, covering it completely with a cloth, and then carrying it to the burial ground by foot in a funeral procession; all Muslim men who saw a procession were to join it. Muslims said prayers and fasted on behalf of the dead, and maintained a brief period of official mourning. The Qur'an promises an eternal paradise with flowing rivers to "those who believe and do good deeds" (Qur'an, 4:57), and a hell of eternal torment to those who do not. Jewish funerals also involved prayers and readings from Scripture, with the body covered and treated respectfully. After a death, family members observed specified periods of mourning, with the normal activities of daily life curtailed. Every day for eleven months after a death and every year after that on the anniversary of the death, a son of the deceased was to recite Kaddish, a special prayer of praise and glorification of God. Judaism emphasized this life more than an afterlife, so that beliefs about what happens to the soul after death were more varied; the very righteous might go directly to a place of spiritual reward, but most souls went first to a place of punishment and purification generally referred to as Gehinnom. After a period that does not exceed twelve months, the soul ascends to the world to come; those who were completely wicked during their lifetime might simply go out of existence, or continue in an eternal state of remorse.

Family, kin, and community networks

Funerary practices made the links between individuals and their families visible, while marriage brought a husband and wife not only into a relationship with one another and their eventual children, but also into a broader web of family and kin relations. In the 1970s, several historians, including Lawrence Stone, posited a dramatic change in the early modern era from a "traditional" complex family in which broader kinship networks were important to a "modern" family in which the nuclear family was central and kin neither interfered nor helped very much. In contrast to Hajnal's geographic division of European family structures, this chronological division has not stood up very well in subsequent research.

One line of criticism has come from demographers and economic historians investigating family and household structure and composition, using sources such as marriage and death registers, birth or baptism records, poll tax surveys, land transfer records, and other types of legal documents. Historians working in some parts of Europe have discovered that nuclear families predominated as a living arrangement as early as the thirteenth century, while kin networks remained important in many matters, such as land transfers and property ownership, far into the nineteenth century, even if kin did not reside in the same household. Historians working in other areas have discovered that the proportion of people who lived in complex households actually increased rather than decreased during the period. In Russia, this increase was the result of the spread and sharpening of serfdom, which might be seen as a mark of this area's economic and social "backwardness," thus making the expansion of the more "traditional" family form not very surprising. In parts of western Europe, however, larger households resulted from the spread of industrial work such as textile production into rural areas, a development known as proto-industrialization and regarded by economic historians as a sign of economic development. (Proto-industrialization is explored in more detail in chapters 6 and 12.) Proto-industrialization had the opposite effect in England and Switzerland, however, where it led to earlier marriage, smaller and more nuclear households, and more unmarried women and widows living on their own. Demographic and legal records have thus led most historians to empha- size variability in household structures and in the importance of kin rather than any uniform pattern of change for all of Europe, or even for all of western Europe.

Inheritance laws, traditions, and patterns were also variable across Europe, and do not seem to have correlated with family structure very well. In general, inheritance was either partible, in which the total estate was divided among all the children or among all the sons, or impartible, in which one child, usually the eldest son, inherited all land and, in the case of aristocrats, the noble title. (Inheritance by the eldest son is termed primogeniture.) In areas with impartible inheritance, younger sons and daughters received a settlement in cash or goods, but this was almost never equal to the value of the eldest son's patrimony. Impartible inheritance meant that the family property stayed intact from generation to generation, but also that the lives and prospects of eldest sons were very different from those of their younger brothers and sisters. Partible inheritance could lead to impoverishment as family holdings became smaller and smaller, and gradually throughout the early modern period many areas with partible inheritance practices changed their laws to adopt impart- ible systems.

This change was not smooth or uncontested, however, and any change in inheritance laws provoked conflicts among legal authorities as well as individ- ual cases challenging the change. Certain aspects of inheritance, such as the rights of individuals to make donations, were governed by church law, so that ecclesiastical as well as secular officials frequently weighed in with opinions and objections. Inheritance provoked bitter conflicts even in areas with one clear system, for laws rarely covered every possible combination of multiple spouses, stepchildren, half-siblings, and cousins, or clearly set out the limits to which an individual could get around local traditions and choose heirs as he or she wished. The vicious hostilities among family members that emerge in the often voluminous legal records of such cases provides evidence for historians arguing that early modern families were cold and unpleasant, but arguments about money that have ended up in court are not likely to show families in any era in their best light.

7 The Cambridge Group for the History of Population and Social Structure

The Cambridge Group for the History of Population and Social Structure was founded in 1964 at Cambridge University by the late Peter Laslett, a historian, and (now Sir) Anthony Wrigley, a geographer, to study demographic change and family patterns. Records of individual life events such as birth, marriage, and death are generally available for England before they become common for the continent, and the Cambridge Group has made intensive use of them. Scholars associated with the Cambridge Group have studied the structure of households over long periods of time, using a technique known as family reconstitution, which involves linking all records for a relatively small group of people, say one village or one extended family.

Through family reconstitution, historical demographers can produce detailed statistics about such issues as nuptiality (rates of marriage), age at marriage, remarriage, fertility, infant and child mortality, and longevity. They can construct longitudinal analyses of change over time on all these issues. The work of the Cambridge Group, and similar study groups in other European countries, has been made much easier by the advent of computer-assisted data analysis, which allows the linking of information gleaned from much larger sets of records. Currently scholars from the Cambridge Group are using early modern demographic data to look at very specific questions, including the ways in which "shocks" experienced in the uterus, such as maternal famine, might have affected longevity, and the way position in the family – as oldest, middle, or youngest child – might have affected infant mortality.

This chart, based on Cambridge Group family reconstitution data for the period from 1580 to 1837, shows seasonality in infant and child mortality. The most deadly time of the year for both infants and toddlers was the late spring, when supplies of food were at their lowest. Another dangerous time for toddlers was late fall; children had usually been weaned by age two, so they were eating food that might be contaminated by diseases carried by insects, which were active at this time of year. The children had also lost the protective benefit brought by breast milk.

(From E. A. Wrigley et al., *English Population History from Family Reconstitution, 1580–1837* [Cambridge: Cambridge University Press, 1997], p. 345.)

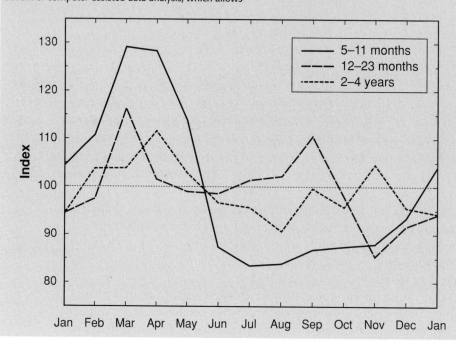

A second line of criticism of the model of a "traditional" extended family evolving into a "modern" nuclear one has come from scholars more interested in changes in ideas about the family and the meaning of family life than in its structure. They take issue not only with the Stone thesis of set points of change, but also with the methods and conclusions of the demographers.

Just because early modern records were structured according to households, they ask, how do we know that co-residence had the same meaning for family members in the sixteenth century it does today? One indication that it did not is the fact that co-resident relatives – cousins, nieces, nephews, or even sisters and brothers – were often referred to as "servants" by the household head and the census taker, though they might still have called the whole group a "family." How do we know which genealogical ties were significant, or whether other sorts of networks might have mattered more? And might this significance be different for women – who were often understood to be part of two families – than for men, or for eldest sons than for younger ones? Scholars interested in such questions have made extensive use of private family records, prescriptive literature such as sermons and advice manuals, letters, and wills to investigate the way that people thought as well as acted regarding their families.

A key finding of these studies is that the word "family" was actually used very rarely in the sixteenth century, perhaps because it had so many different meanings. Shakespeare, for example, only used it nine times in all of his writings, and never once in *Romeo and Juliet*; the feuding Montagus and Capulets were described as "houses," not families. Similar feuds – and the group loyalty that made them possible – can be found in many areas of Europe, centering on groups usually termed "clans" in English. Clans – *consortia* in Italy, *plemie* in Poland, *slachte* in northern Germany, *fis* in Albania, *cenel* in Ireland – thought of themselves as having a common ancestor, but did not worry about how they were actually related to one another and generally had methods of incorporating non-kin for political or economic reasons. Clans offered their members military support, political patronage, and economic advantages, and usually had ceremonies and symbols denoting clan membership. Both Burckhardt's idea of the rise of the individual and the Stone thesis about the rise of the nuclear family suggest that such clans were unimportant by the sixteenth century, but this was true for only a few parts of Europe. Until the eighteenth century, *fis* in parts of the Balkans functioned as fighting units and *slachte* in northern Germany provided fire and accident insurance; in 1745–6 Scottish clans rebelled (unsuccessfully) against George II, the Hanoverian king of Britain, seeking to put Charles Edward Stuart (1720–88), also known as Bonnie Prince Charlie, on the British throne. Thus broad kinship ties retained their power for many people, even if they were not exactly sure how they were connected genealogically with the group.

Until very late in the early modern period, and perhaps not even then, a person's name would not have provided a clear indication of kin connections or family membership. The modern western naming system of an individual first name and a hereditary surname seems to have developed among wealthy families in Italian towns in the twelfth and thirteenth centuries, but it spread only very slowly. By the sixteenth century the nobility of most of Europe had surnames, often taken from the place where they owned land, or, in Scandinavia, from the designs on their heraldic shields; the most powerful seventeenth-century Swedish Chancellor, for example, was named Axel Oxenstierna ("Ox

Forehead"). Slowly common people, especially those attempting to improve their status, adopted surnames from their occupations, physical characteristics, father's name, place of residence, or some other distinguishing feature. These slowly become heritable rather than changing with each generation, a process speeded up by church and state authorities who saw that such a system would make record-keeping and tax collection easier. In 1539 King Francis I of France ordered all families to adopt a permanent surname in the territory he ruled, though similar ordinances were not passed in Denmark until 1771 and in Austria until 1776. Peasants were generally the last to adopt permanent surnames, and in Iceland and a few parts of Scandinavia surnames never became heritable. Women in most of Europe kept their own surnames on marriage until the eighteenth or nineteenth century, though Christian women would often be identified in legal documents also as "wife of so and so," while Jewish women were identified as "daughter of so and so." Jewish men also generally used the name of their father as an identifier, as did Muslim men; prominent men might add the name of their grandfather and sometimes a long string of male ancestors to their given name in certain situations.

Clans were not the only type of group in which genealogical connections blended with non-kin ties. With the gradual adoption of infant baptism in late antiquity, Christians introduced the practice of godparentage, in which adults other than the parents sponsor a child at baptism. This creates a spiritual bond between the godparents and the child, and between the parents and godparents. In canon law, relatives by blood or marriage are prohibited from marrying; by the fifteenth century, this prohibition had been extended to seven degrees of kinship, which meant that individuals who shared a great-grandparent were officially prohibited from marrying one another. This prohibition extended to spiritual kin as well, so that marriage between godparent and godchild was forbidden, as was that between a godparent and a natural parent, and even between two unrelated godparents of the same child. This last prohibition was often ignored, especially as the number of godparents, especially in wealthy families, multiplied in the fifteenth century. In some parts of Europe, blood relatives were usually chosen as godparents, with children sometimes serving as godparent to younger kin. Peasants in England, France, and Germany more often chose a local notable, hoping that he or she might provide patronage or protection for the child later in life. Protestants limited the prohibited degrees of kinship in terms of marriage for blood relatives and in-laws, and rejected the idea that spiritual kinship should create any sort of barrier to marriage. Most Protestants retained the practice of godparentage, but limited the number of godparents and emphasized their spiritual, rather than practical, importance. The bonds between whole families created by godparentage (*compaternitas, compadrazgo*) became more significant in southern, Catholic Europe than in the north.

Along with godparentage, Christians were often linked through confraternities, voluntary lay groups organized by occupation, devotional preference, neighborhood, or charitable activity. Confraternities expanded rapidly in larger cities and many villages with the growth of the mendicant orders such as the Franciscans and Dominicans in the thirteenth century. Some confraternities specialized in praying for souls in purgatory, either for specific individuals or the anonymous mass of all souls. In England they were generally associated with a parish, so are called parish guilds, parish fraternities, or lights; by the late Middle Ages, they held dances, festivals, and collections to raise money to clean and repair church buildings and to supply the church with candles, altarcloths, and other liturgical objects.

Membership in a confraternity gave individuals spiritual, social, and charitable benefits, and in the case of male confraternities limited to members of the elite, political ones as well. Before the Reformation in the English town of Coventry, for example, only men who were members of the Trinity Guild could hold an office in the city government. In sixteenth-century Portugal, nobles and other wealthy men were often members of the Misericordia confraternities that monopolized most charitable activities and gained the support of the monarchy. Most men in confraternities were not members of the elite, of course, but the groups still gave them regular opportunities to reinforce their devotional life, express their faith outwardly, assist others, and get together with their peers. Across Europe, women had fewer opportunities to establish, join, or lead confraternities than did men. They appear more often as beneficiaries of the confraternities' welfare measures than as members, for some confraternities provided dowries that would allow poor girls to marry or enter a convent, opened institutions for repentant prostitutes (convertite), or established asylums for women who were felt to be at risk of turning to prostitution or losing their honor, such as orphans, poor unmarried women and widows, or battered wives.

Occupational groups such as craft guilds and journeymen's guilds provided additional opportunities for men – and in a few cases, women – to associate with their "brothers," so that by the sixteenth century a good share of the urban population would have been part of one fraternal organization or another, or perhaps several different groups at the same time. These groups took over some functions that kin groups had earlier performed, such as arranging funerals or providing for orphans. Both religious and occupational groups carried out tasks together, but they also offered opportunities during festivals and holidays to socialize and break up the daily routine of work.

For some people, religious or occupational groups augmented strong kin ties, while for others they may have offered an alternative to reliance on blood relations. Neighbors and friends provided still more possibilities for association, assistance, and economic exchange, though these have left fewer traces in the sources than family connections or formal associations. In fact, relations with neighbors generally made it into the records only when they broke down, when legal authorities were called in to reconcile disputes.

All of these groups created webs of obligation, reciprocity, emotion, and dependence, and helped individuals understand and negotiate the wider world through every stage of life. Men and women progressed up and down the "great staircase of the world" as individuals, but on each step most of them also saw themselves and were viewed by others as part of various groups. Even death did not change this, for the living were obliged to memorialize the dead with whom they had connections. Along with this sense of membership, families, guilds, and religious organizations also provided people with their most intimate experiences of relationships of power, for even the more egalitarian of these, such as religious communities of monks or nuns, had hierarchical structures of authority and leadership. All of these local groups formed the basis for broader hierarchies of power such as cities, territories, states, and nations, the subject of the next chapter.

Further reading

Along with Burckhardt, the classic discussion of individualism is Alan Macfarlane, *The Origins of English Individualism: The Family, Property, and Social Transition* (Cambridge: Cambridge University Press, 1979). Thomas C. Heller, ed., *Reconstructing Individualism: Autonomy, Individuality, and the Self in Western Thought* (Stanford, CA: Stanford University Press, 1986), provides essays that challenge or nuance Macfarlane.

Two studies that explore the cultural construction of the body are Thomas Laqueur, *Making Sex: Body and Gender from the Greeks to Freud* (Cambridge, MA: Harvard University Press, 1990), and Barbara Duden, *The Woman Beneath the Skin: A Doctor's Patients in Eighteenth-Century Germany* (Cambridge, MA: Harvard University Press, 1991). Food and drink have been examined in Barbara Ketchum Wheaton, *Savoring the Past: The French Kitchen and Table from 1300 to 1789* (New York: Touchstone, 1989), and A. Lynn Martin, *Alcohol, Sex, and Gender in Late Medieval and Early Modern Europe* (New York: Palgrave-Macmillan, 2001), while clothing and consumer goods are surveyed in Lisa Jardine, *Worldly Goods: A New History of the Renaissance* (New York: Norton, 1996), and Ann Rosalind Jones and Peter Stallybrass, *Renaissance Clothing and the Materials of Memory* (Cambridge: Cambridge University Press, 2000).

Scholarship on sexuality has exploded in recent years. For collections see Jacqueline Murray and Konrad Eisenbichler, eds., *Desire and Discipline: Sex and Sexuality in the Premodern West* (Toronto: University of Toronto Press, 1996); Louise Fradenburg and Carla Freccero, eds., *Premodern Sexualities* (New York: Routledge, 1996). For specific parts of Europe, see Eve Levin, *Sex and Society in the World of the Orthodox Slavs, 900–1700* (Ithaca, NY: Cornell University Press, 1989); Guido Ruggiero, *Boundaries of Eros: Sex Crime and Sexuality in Renaissance Venice* (Oxford: Oxford University Press, 1985); Michael Rocke, *Friendly Affections, Nefarious Vices: Homosexuality, Male Culture and the Policing of Sex in Renaissance Florence* (Oxford: Oxford University Press, 1995).

The two studies that first set out a rather bleak view of family life, and against which most later scholarship has reacted, are Philippe Ariès, *Centuries of Childhood: A Social History of Family Life*, trans. Robert Baldick (New York: Vintage, 1962), and Lawrence Stone, *Family, Sex, and Marriage in England 1500–1800* (Harmondsworth: Penguin, 1977). Christiane Klapisch-Zuber, *Women, Family, and Ritual in Renaissance Italy* (Chicago: University of Chicago, 1985), sees family life as especially difficult for women, while Alan Macfarlane, *Marriage and Love in England, Modes of Reproduction 1300–1840* (Oxford: Basil Blackwell, 1986), and Linda Pollock, *Forgotten Children: Parent–Child Relations from 1500 to 1900* (Cambridge: Cambridge University Press, 1983), present a more positive picture. André Burguière et al., eds., *A History of the Family*, 2 vols. (Cambridge, MA: Harvard University Press, 1996), and David I. Kertzer and Marzio Barbagli, eds., *The History of the European Family*, vol. I: *Family Life in Early Modern Times,*

1500–1789 (New Haven: Yale University Press, 2001), present a range of essays, while Trevor Dean and K. J. P. Lowe, eds., *Marriage in Italy, 1300–1650* (Cambridge: Cambridge University Press, 1998), and Martha C. Howell, *The Marriage Exchange: Property, Social Place, and Gender in the Cities of the Low Countries, 1300–1500* (Chicago: University of Chicago Press, 1998), explore specific parts of Europe. For a good overview of the various ways historians have investigated the family, see Michael Anderson, *Approaches to the History of the Western Family, 1500–1914,* 2nd edn (New York: Cambridge University Press, 1995). A recent demographic study of family structures and patterns is E. A. Wrigley, *English Population History from Family Reconstitution 1580–1837* (Cambridge: Cambridge University Press, 1997).

Rituals and ideas involving death and dying are explored in Ralph Houlbrooke, *Death, Religion, and the Family in England, 1480–1750* (Oxford: Oxford University Press, 1998), Bruce Gordon and Peter Marshall, eds., *The Place of the Dead: Death and Remembrance in Late Medieval and Early Modern Europe* (Cambridge: Cambridge University Press, 2000), and Craig Koslofsky, *The Reformation of the Dead: Death and Ritual in Early Modern Germany* (New York: Palgrave-Macmillan, 2000).

 For more suggestions and links see the companion website www.cambridge.org/wiesnerhanks.

Notes

1 Jacob Burckhardt, *Civilization of the Renaissance in Italy* (New York: Harper and Row, 1958), p. 143. First published in German in 1860.

2 Baldasar Heseler, *Andreas Vesalius' First Public Anatomy at Bologna 1540: An Eyewitness Report*, ed. Ruben Eriksson (Uppsala: Almqvist and Wiksells, 1959), p. 181.

3 Strasbourg Archives Municipales, Statuten, vol. XXXIII, no. 61 (1665). My translation.

4 John Hajnal, "European Marriage Patterns in Perspective," in D. V. Glass and D. E. C. Eversley, eds., *Population in History* (London: Edward Arnold, 1965), 101–43.

5 Christine de Pizan, *The Treasure of the City of Ladies: Or, the Book of Three Virtues* (Harmondsworth: Penguin, 1985), p. 157.

3 Politics and power, 1450–1600

In this colored woodcut from the epic poem *Theuerdank* by the German Emperor Maximilian I (1449–1519), groups of soldiers armed with arquebuses and swords do battle. The poem tells the story of Maximilian's courtship of Mary of Burgundy, casting him as a chivalric hero, which was important in the emperor's creation of his persona as "the last great knight."

Timeline

1453	End of Hundred Years War
1453	Ottoman capture of Constantinople
1469	Marriage between Isabella of Castile and Ferdinand of Aragon
1477	Marriage between Maximilian of Habsburg and Mary of Burgundy
1492	Conquest of Granada and expulsion of the Jews from Spain
1519	Charles V elected Holy Roman Emperor
1526	Battle of Mohacs between Hungarians and Ottoman Turks
1559	Peace of Cateau-Cambrésis
1571	Battle of Lepanto between Ottomans, Italians, and Spanish
1590s	Tyrone's rebellion in Ireland

OUSTED from his official position in the early sixteenth century, when a rival faction came to power, the Florentine diplomat Niccolò Machiavelli (1469–1527) had time to contemplate the politics in which he had been so thoroughly enmeshed. "A prince [by which he meant any ruler], should therefore have no other aim or thought, nor take up any other thing for his study, but war and its organization and discipline," he wrote. "When princes think more of luxury than of arms, they lose their state."[1] Several decades later, the English scholar and historian Polydore Vergil (1470?–1555) agreed with Machiavelli that too great a concern with wealth was destructive for rulers. In his *Anglia historia*, written about 1540, Vergil described King Henry VII (ruled 1485–1509), the father of the current monarch, in largely glowing terms, as "distinguished, wise and prudent ... brave and resolute." He ended on a sour note, however: "All these virtues were obscured by avarice ... [which] is surely a bad enough vice in a private individual, whom it forever torments; in a monarch indeed it may be considered the worst vice, since it is harmful to everyone, and distorts those qualities of trustfulness, justice, and integrity by which the state must be governed."[2]

Machiavelli and Vergil were both extremely perceptive observers of the politics of their era. Political power is always related to the ability to command resources from society, and in the fifteenth century the increasing cost of warfare favored rulers of large territories who could extract resources effectively and efficiently. Building on taxation systems and bureaucracies that had been gradually developing over several centuries, astute monarchs in Britain, France, and Spain further consolidated their power, developing tax policies that would support large armies when necessary instead of relying on nobles to supply them. They and their officials increased the size and scope of central institutions and government activities, and issued many more statutes and ordinances than monarchs had earlier. Through shrewd marital strategies, they created alliances with noble houses within their own territories and with ruling houses in other countries, which also strengthened their power. They backed explorers and pirates in their quest for riches from beyond the sea, and made use of new theories of rulership, which subsequent monarchs would extend even further. In the sixteenth century, monarchs restricted the independent power of the church, either by removing their territory from allegiance to the pope in the cases of England and Scotland, or asserting royal power over the church in the cases of France and Spain. These western European monarchs thus created what have since been called "nation-states," setting a pattern that was later followed by northern and eastern European monarchs as they created nation-states such as Denmark/Norway, Sweden, and Russia.

The growth of the nation-state, first in western Europe and then elsewhere, has long been viewed as the key political development of this era. In his study of the Renaissance, the nineteenth-century historian Jacob Burckhardt celebrated rulers and their officials who viewed the state as "a work of art ... the outcome of reflection and calculation," something to be created, shaped, and expanded, not simply inherited and governed.[3] Like Machiavelli and Vergil, Burckhardt viewed the actions and ideas of rulers as the most important factors in the creation of nation-states, and paid particular attention to the way they handled warfare, finances, and alliances.

Burckhardt was writing in 1860, the point at which Germany and Italy were being transformed – again by rulers, officials, and generals – from divided political entities into nations. It seemed to him, and to many others, that nations were an inevitable final stage in political development. Events of the twentieth century appear to reinforce this idea. Revolts against European colonization in the period after World War II resulted in the establishment of new nations in Asia and Africa. The breakup of the Soviet Union and Yugoslavia in the late twentieth century resulted in the creation of smaller units, such as Ukraine, Azerbaijan, and Croatia, but these are also understood to be nations. They all send representatives to the United Nations, a body whose title reinforces this conceptualization of world politics. Various ethnic groups around the world today are carrying out bitter military campaigns against their national governments, but their aim is also to establish new independent nations.

These historical and contemporary movements have made a world consisting of discrete nations seem almost natural, but they have also led scholars as well as activists and revolutionaries to consider the concept of a "nation" more closely – just what makes a "nation"? What makes it something that people are willing to die (or kill) for, when they would not be willing to die for their city or their favorite sports team or their family business, though they may have strong loyalties to all of these?

One of the most influential theoreticians on this question has been Benedict Anderson, who defines the nation as "an imagined political community."[4] By "imagined," Anderson does not mean fake or artificial, but intellectually and culturally created or brought into being. His definition thus fits very well with Burckhardt's description of the state as a "work of art ... the outcome of reflection and calculation," and both scholars see the creation of such political entities as beginning in the period covered in this chapter. They focus on very different processes and actors, however. While Burckhardt – and many political historians since – focus on rulers, Anderson investigates the ways that writers and bureaucrats used the new medium of print to transform certain vernacular languages into print languages, as we discussed in chapter 1. These print languages became a medium both of "national" unification and of drawing distinctions from others, used first in some parts of Europe, then by revolutionaries in the Americas, and then around the world. Printed essays, poetry, music, newspapers, and other works inspired loyalty to nations or to *ideas* of nations that were not yet political realities, and dying for one's country came to assume what Anderson terms "moral grandeur."

Though historians have sometimes focused only on one or the other, the creation of nation-states by rulers through warfare and taxes and by writers through songs and symbols was actually closely linked. Effective rulers used both warfare and the new medium of print to build up their power and to begin to transform what had been a dynastic realm into a "nation." They quickly adopted the new print technology and the newly developing national languages to make sure their new laws and decrees were circulated and understood throughout their territories. They supported writers and artists who linked royal power with national strength and prosperity. They absorbed – through war or marriage or a combination of these – smaller dynastic realms on the edges of their holdings, gradually creating more distinct "national" boundaries, which were reinforced by differences in print languages on either side of these borders.

This process was not always successful, however, and did not happen everywhere, as the story of Hungary makes clear. In the middle of the fifteenth century, under the leadership of John Hunyadi (1387–1456), a Hungarian nobleman of Romanian descent, the Hungarians defeated the Ottoman Turks. Hunyadi's son Matthias Corvinus (1443–90) became king of Hungary in 1458. Like the monarchs in western Europe, Matthias Corvinus strengthened royal power, patronized the arts, and developed sound tax policies. Major works were translated into or written in Hungarian, which is in a completely different language family than most European languages. A period of disorder followed Corvinus's death in 1490, however, and the nobles reasserted their power, which in turn led to a peasants' revolt. Using a huge army and siege cannon, the Ottoman Empire defeated the Hungarians at the Battle of Mohacs in 1526, and Hungary was divided into the small principality of Transylvania in the east, dependent on the Ottomans, and western and northern territories ruled by the Austrian Habsburgs.

Hungary thus did not become a nation, or even a unified political unit. It was instead divided between two of the strongest powers in Europe – the Ottoman Empire and the Habsburgs – both of which were dynastic realms that never developed into nation-states, but still lasted as political entities until the early twentieth century. Various linguistic and ethnic groups within them – including the Hungarians – dreamed of creating nations, but these remained literally "imagined communities" until the nineteenth or twentieth century. Thus the growth of nation-states is an important development during this period, but it is important to remember that most Europeans did not live in what we would understand as nations in 1600. In addition, though more Europeans could read and write in 1600 than in 1450, the vast majority could not, so they had little access to the developing national print languages; their sense of belonging to something beyond their village was provided by religion, not language or politics.

Military technology and organization

Though the history of Hungary is not one of the rise of a nation-state, it does provide an excellent example of Machiavelli's assertion of the key role of war and its financing in gaining and maintaining power. By the time of the Battle of Mohacs, changes in military technology and in the way that troops were recruited and provisioned had increased the cost of warfare dramatically. The Ottoman Empire was large and unified enough to absorb these costs; Hungary was not.

The most deadly and also most prestigious type of fighter in the fifteenth century was the cavalryman, wearing full plate armor and carrying a lance and sword; he rode a large warhorse which also wore plate armor. Such men-at-arms were almost always members of the nobility, and their primary function in battle was as frontline troops. They charged in formation at a steady canter with lances drawn against the enemy's front line, hoping to shock it into disarray, and then discarded their lances and fought with swords or maces in individual combat.

Heavy cavalry were regarded as the most important arm of the military in the fifteenth century, but their invulnerability was increasingly challenged. During the latter stages of the Hundred Years War, which ended in 1453, English footsoldiers armed with longbows were very effective against heavily armored French knights, and in other fifteenth-century wars soldiers used steel crossbows drawn by a windlass. Pikes were even more deadly than bows; footsoldiers armed with ten- to fifteen-foot long pikes, standing very close to one another with their pikes all facing outward – an arrangement termed the Swiss phalanx – were able to defend against a cavalry charge, as long as they held their position. Horses would not charge into a wall of pikes no matter how hard they were spurred, and with the cavalry line disrupted horses and their riders could be wounded or killed.

Gradually the pikemen were reinforced by footsoldiers carrying firearms. The first reasonably portable firearm was the harquebus (or arquebus), a short metal tube attached to a wooden handle, loaded down the muzzle with powder and a round bullet. (The woodcut that opens this chapter shows a soldier firing a harquebus.) The powder was initially lit by a slow-burning wick called a match-cord through a touchhole in the barrel – a firing mechanism termed a matchlock. Around 1500, wheel-lock firing mechanisms, in which iron pyrite creates sparks by being scraped along a metal wheel, were developed, producing the first self-igniting firearm. The wheel-lock was safer to the gunner than the matchlock as it did not require an open flame, but the harquebus was heavy and took so long to reload that two pikemen stood on either side of a harquebusier to defend him against a cavalry charge.

8 Comments on the new weaponry

Condemnation of gunpowder began in Europe almost as soon as the first artillery piece was fired. In 1366, the Italian humanist Petrarch wrote in *De remediis utriusque fortunae* that guns were invented by the devil, an idea that many later writers restated. "Would to God that this unhappy weapon had never been devised," wrote Blaise de Montluc, a French noble taken prisoner at the Battle of Pavia in 1525, "and that so many brave and valiant men had never died by the hands of those…who would not dare to look in the face of those which they had laid dead with their wretched bullets. They are tools invented by the devil to make it easier to kill each other." In his epic poem *Orlando furioso*, the Italian humanist Ludovico Ariosto agreed: "O wretched and foul invention, how did you ever find a place in a human heart? Through you the soldier's glory is destroyed, through you the business of arms is without honor, through you valor and courage are brought low, for often the bad men seem better than the good; through you valor no more, daring no more can come to a test in the field" (canto ix, verse 91). The Spanish author Miguel de Cervantes has his chivalric knight Don Quixote voice a similar complaint: "those diabolical engines, the artillery [are] an invention which allows a base and cowardly hand to take the life of a brave knight."

Some authors were more horrified by the physical than the social effects of gunpowder. In his treatise on wounds made by gunshot written in 1545, the French surgeon Ambroise Paré, who had treated soldiers on many battlefields in Italy, commented: "Verily when I consider with myself all the sorts of warlike engines which the Ancients used … they seem to me certain childish sports and games … for these modern inventions are such as easily exceed all the best appointed and cruel engines which can be mentioned or thought upon in the shape, cruelty, and appearance of their operations."

None of this criticism slowed the spread of gunpowder weapons. Rulers and nobles were quick to adopt them, and training in the use of artillery and portable firearms became a standard part of the upbringing of aristocratic boys. As François de la Noue, a French general who had lost his arm in battle, wrote in 1587: "All these instruments are devilish, invented in some mischievous shop to turn whole realms and kingdoms into desolation and replenish the ground with dead carcasses. Howbeit, men's malice had made them so necessary that they cannot be spared." De la Noue then provided in-depth guidance about how best to "profit by … the forms and effects of diverse sorts of weapons."

(Quotations from John Hale, "War and Public Opinion in the 15th and 16th Centuries," *Past and Present* 22 [July 1962]: 29, 30.)

 For additional chapter resources see the companion website www.cambridge.org/wiesnerhanks.

The musket, developed in the 1520s, was much lighter and easier to reload than the harquebus. Muskets also originally used matchlocks or wheel-locks to fire, but in the early seventeenth century a French courtier invented the flintlock firing mechanism, in which flint strikes a piece of steel to make sparks, which ignite powder in an attached flash-pan and this in turn (if things work correctly) ignites the main charge in the barrel. Flintlock weapons quickly replaced other types, and remained the most common portable firearm in Europe and European colonies until the middle of the nineteenth century. (They also provided several common English expressions, including "flash in the pan" for something that makes a lot of noise but has no lasting effect.) Musket balls could easily pierce armor, and though plate armor got thicker, this thickness resulted in increased weight, making horses so slow they were even more vulnerable; a nobleman had to figure he would lose his horse every time he went into battle. Military commanders generally arranged their troops with one pikeman to every two musketeers, though the later invention and adoption of the bayonet – a dagger attached to the end of the gun – made the same soldier both musketeer and pikeman. Infantry – that is, troops on foot – became the heart of early modern armies.

Footsoldiers had traditionally been commoners, not nobles, and the development of gunpowder made the traditional medieval tripartite division of society discussed in chapter 1 even more anachronistic. The loss of their unique status as fighters was not lost on nobles. Pistols, short-barrelled firearms first using wheel-locks and flintlocks, appeared to offer them a way out of their dilemma, a way to both use gunpowder and yet stay above the infantry – both figuratively and in actual combat.

Pistols were invented around 1510, and during several battles of the Habsburg–Valois wars in the 1550s, German mounted pistoliers, termed *Reiters*, humiliated heavily armored French cavalry armed with lances. *Reiters* were generally members of the lesser nobility – they had to be able to afford a horse – and their weapons were slowly adopted by nobles elsewhere, who abandoned lances and instead had three or four pistols along with their sword. (Pistols took a long time to reload, so pistoliers charged with several already loaded.) Cavalry firing pistols were used by military commanders against other cavalry or to break up large masses of footsoldiers.

Pistoliers still favored tactics that would allow them to display their individual prowess, however, which were not always the most effective militarily. Pistols fired at close range could easily pierce existing armor, so that pistoliers gave up full body armor for a thick breast plate and helmet that would at least protect their vital parts. This left their limbs and their increasingly unarmored horses more vulnerable, and both other pistoliers and footsoldiers aimed their weapons accordingly. Wounds caused by heavy pistol shot were much worse than those created by arrows, and contemporaries regarded the pistol as an especially deadly weapon. They certainly were for horses, and a significant part of the increased cost of warfare consisted of horses to replace those killed or injured by all types of weapons.

While hand-held weapons transformed actual battles, large artillery weapons altered military tactics. Early cannons fired rocks, which were not uniform in size and tended to shatter on impact. By the middle of the fifteenth century armies were using balls made of cast iron and cannons that could be disassembled for easier movement, which were much more expensive but much more effective. Cannonballs blasted holes in high castle or city walls, and defensive fortifications changed accordingly, becoming low, thick earthen ramparts that stood up to artillery quite easily. In the sixteenth century cities increasingly built more complex fortifications with outlying bastions in which they placed cannons, making it very difficult to take a city by force. Sieges grew longer, with starvation the most important tactic as armies cut off cities' lines of supply. (Direct campaigns against cities reemerged with the development of bomb-laden aircraft in World War II.)

Standing armies and navies

The new military technology required longer training and larger armies, which meant that those fielding military forces felt it necessary to maintain at least the core of a standing army from one conflict to the next. Standing armies were a key factor in the growth of nation-states, though the first European rulers to build a standing army were actually the Ottoman sultans. The nucleus of the Ottoman army was the Janissary Corps – from the Turkish *yeni cheri* ("new troops") – a group of professional soldiers recruited originally from non-Muslim war captives from newly conquered areas, and later primarily from the sultan's Christian subjects in Greece and the Balkans. Boys who became Janissaries were taken away from their families at a young age, raised in Turkish foster homes, and sent to schools for military and other training. They were legally slaves of the sultan, but they could gain power and prestige through their service; the most capable became senior officials and ambassadors as well as admirals and generals. The highest Janissary often held the office of grand vizier, second only to the sultan. In times of war, the Janissaries were supplemented by paid troops recruited from throughout the empire; at the time of the Battle of Mohacs, the Ottoman Sultan Süleyman the Magnificent (ruled 1521–66) regularly fielded an army of 150,000 troops every year, equipped with huge siege cannons.

By 1500, western European nations also had permanent armies, usually called the royal army or king's army, but these were much smaller than those of the sultan; French and Spanish armies fighting each other at about the time of the Battle of Mohacs each had only about 25,000 men. Armies grew in size throughout the sixteenth century, however, so that by the end of the century, Spain also had about 200,000 soldiers under arms. The combination of new weaponry, new tactics, and much larger armies has led some historians to see a "military revolution" in early modern Europe, but others note that such changes took centuries to implement: not exactly a revolutionary pace of change.

Though sultans and emperors could field an army of such size as easily as kings, this was beyond the financial reach of most nobles. Extremely wealthy nobles in some areas did maintain private armies with firearms and cannon – Robert Dudley, the earl of Leicester, in England and the duke of Grandía in Spain could both outfit hundreds of cavalry and footsoldiers in the middle of the sixteenth century – but even they could not support armies that numbered in the thousands. Monarchs attempting to build up their own power and monopolize legitimized violence passed regulations forbidding such private forces or ordering their disbanding, but the sheer expense was ultimately more effective than royal pressure. Those nobles who maintained private armies increasingly used them for local feuds or banditry, or they hired them out to fight for monarchs, gradually becoming company commanders in royal armies. Positions as officers of infantry companies were also often reserved for nobles, and the more astute of these learned the new techniques and tactics. The officer corps of many early modern armies was dominated by traditional elites, and military service was expected of nobles in many areas of Europe. Thus older forms of military organization adapted to the new realities of warfare.

Monarchs also hired professional military contractors of less exalted backgrounds, however. By 1450, almost all of those fighting, except the highest-ranking nobles, expected to be paid, either directly by a ruler or by their company's commander, who in turn was supposed to receive his company's pay from the monarch. Footsoldiers were recruited primarily from among the poorer groups in society with the promise of pay and bonuses, though military pay was often unreliable and soldiers sometimes went years without pay. When this happened, soldiers deserted, mutinied, or simply took what they needed from the surrounding countryside. Looting had long been a standard part of military life, for taking or destroying the property of one's enemies was recognized as an effective means of lessening their ability to continue fighting.

Soldiers often brought their wives, girlfriends, or other family members along on campaigns to cook for them and do their laundry, for armies did not provide such services; such individuals might well outnumber the actual troops, and spent much of their time searching the countryside for food and other provisions. Warfare was thus often accompanied by famine, and by diseases carried by the armies; such diseases, including typhus, dysentery, and pneumonia, were more deadly in malnourished populations. It is not surprising that a common subject for artists in the sixteenth century was the biblical image of the Four Horsemen of the Apocalypse, riding together: pestilence, war, famine, and death.

Military campaigns had traditionally been fought from March to October when food was available for men and animals, and the soldiers were simply sent home for winter. This was no longer advisable with a standing army – going home meant a high likelihood of desertion – but governments could not afford to build barracks for the troops. They were thus housed with civilian families, with the family expected to provide a place for a certain number of soldiers to sleep and keep warm. In theory the soldiers were supposed to pay for their food, but as their pay itself often remained theoretical, they simply took what they needed by force. The relationship between civilians and soldiers was therefore often very hostile, and neither group had enough to eat. The Spanish army fighting in Flanders in the late sixteenth century was the first to contract directly with local people to feed and clothe the army; such improved provisioning lessened mutinies and desertions, and was later copied by other armies.

Technological and organizational changes altered warfare at sea as well as on land during this period. War at sea may have as one of its objects the taking or holding of port cities or other land bases, but it is primarily about lines of communication and transportation. Such lines are just as important to private traders as they are to governments, and in the thirteenth to the fifteenth centuries most fighting at sea was sponsored by merchants or cities intent on securing or maintaining favorable trade routes (along with pirates seeking plunder). In the Mediterranean captains used oared galleys and in the Atlantic sailing ships, but in both cases these vessels were primarily trading ships, carrying cargo as well as troops. During the fifteenth century both types of ships began to carry heavy guns, though these were so expensive that arsenals increased very slowly. Guns were generally mounted facing forward, where they could be used both as siege weapons for the bombardment of coastal cities and to attack and defend merchant fleets. In the Mediterranean and the Baltic, specialized gun-carrying galleys were the most important type of warship in the sixteenth century; at the Battle of Lepanto in 1571 between the Turkish fleet and a fleet of Spanish, Venetian, Genoese, and papal ships, there were more than 200 galleys on each side. Galleys were not very useful in the more stormy Atlantic, however, and here improvements in ship design, hull construction, and rigging gradually gave sailing vessels the speed, seaworthiness, and endurance they needed to make them effective tools of warfare.

As on land, technical and tactical developments in naval warfare were accompanied by changes in recruitment, training, and organization of both commanders and crew. In contrast to standing armies, for which there is little use between wars, experienced seamen have skills that are in great demand wherever there is commercial shipping. Captains – and crews accustomed to working under them – were to be found in every seaport in the fifteenth and sixteenth centuries, familiar with using violence in defense of trade as well as the many difficulties of sea travel. In some parts of Europe, especially the Mediterranean, ship captains included younger sons of noble or wealthy urban families, but elsewhere they were more likely to be commoners, as the more technical aspects of shiphandling and gunnery were seen as demeaning. This social prejudice began to change in the sixteenth century, and slowly a corps of permanent sea officers, including both nobles and commoners, began to develop in many parts of Europe, with the social positions needed to command crew and the maritime skills needed to win battles. Skilled crew – gunners, topmen (who climbed aloft to handle sails and rigging), carpenters,

Fig 6. The Battle of Lepanto was often depicted by Italian artists as a conflict between good and evil as well as a naval battle involving galleys. In this oil painting by Giorgio Vasari (1511–74), Christ, St. Peter and other heavenly forces help the Christian fleet, while demons try vainly to help the Turks; the woman holding the cross and cup at the front left is a symbol of the Catholic faith.

sailmakers – were generally hired from merchant ships during time of war and might command fairly high wages. Unskilled men might be paid mercenaries, as soldiers were, but they might also be conscripted or impressed into service; the Danish and English navies both required seaside communities to provide and pay for a certain number of seamen during times of war. In navies with large galley fleets, such as those of France, Spain, and the Ottoman Empire, convicts, prisoners of war, and slaves were increasingly used as oarsmen, chained to their oars.

Taxes, bureaucracies, and marital politics

Standing armies played a central role in the consolidation of royal power, and military expenditures generally made up the majority of state budgets. Supplying those armies depended on extracting resources from society effectively and efficiently, which in turn depended on securing the ability to claim those resources. This process began centuries before 1450, and everywhere involved the establishment of legal codes, courts of law, bureaucracies, and taxation systems; in some parts of Europe it also involved the development of representative institutions.

After 1450 the size and scope of central institutions and government activities increased dramatically in some parts of Europe. Rulers issued new laws more frequently, and kings and their officials claimed the right to hear ever more legal cases, either on appeal or as the court of first instance. In the sixteenth century, states in many parts of Europe gained power over churches and their personnel, taxes, and courts. This was most dramatic in Protestant and Muslim areas, but even in Catholic Spain the rulers established their own Inquisition free of papal control, and in Orthodox Russia the leader of the church, the patriarch, came under the direct control of the tsar.

Because almost all of Europe was ruled by hereditary dynasties – the Papal States and some cities being the exceptions – claiming and holding resources also involved shrewd marital strategies, for it was far cheaper to gain land by inheritance than by war. Thus, like armies and bureaucracies, royal and noble sons and daughters were important tools of state policy. The benefits of an advantageous marriage, particularly if the wife had no brothers and thus inherited territory, stretched across generations, a process that can be seen most dramatically with the Habsburgs. The Holy Roman Emperor Frederick III, a Habsburg who was the ruler of most of Austria, acquired only a small amount of territory – and a great deal of money – by his marriage to Princess Eleonore of Portugal. He arranged for his son Maximilian to marry Europe's most prominent heiress, Mary of Burgundy, who inherited the Netherlands, Luxembourg, and the county of Burgundy in what is now eastern France. In his romanticized autobiography *Theuerdank* – the source of the woodcut that opens this chapter – Maximilian described his journey to woo Mary as a series of chivalric exploits. In reality, the marriage was a foregone conclusion arranged by their fathers.

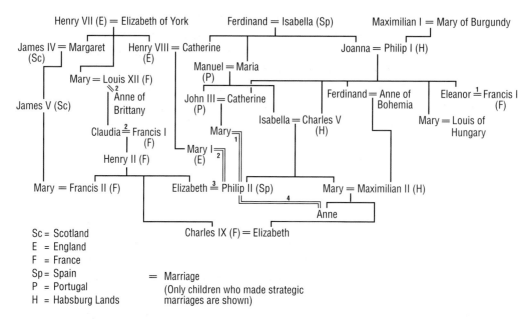

Fig. 7. Dynastic alliances in sixteenth-century western Europe.

Though he may not have wanted to admit it, Maximilian learned the lesson of marital politics well, marrying his son and daughter to the children of Ferdinand and Isabella, the rulers of Spain, much of southern Italy, and eventually the Spanish New World empire. His grandson Charles would eventually rule about half of Europe. Habsburg successes gave rise to the saying: "Let others wage wars; you, happy Austria, marry" (*Bella gerant alii, tu felix Austria nube*). The frequency with which the Habsburgs went to war, however, make this aphorism somewhat ironic.

Even popes and city leaders were often part of such marital strategies; papal nieces, nephews, and sometimes children were coveted marriage partners, as were the wealthy daughters of urban elites. Wealthy urban families, especially in Italy, also transformed themselves into hereditary dynasties through coups and alliances during this period, and cemented their position through marriages with more established ruling houses.

These processes of consolidation followed a similar pattern in many states, but everywhere there were local variations and different chronologies. Fifteenth- and sixteenth-century monarchs and their officials built on developments that stretched back centuries, so that some discussion of the medieval period is necessary to put their actions into perspective.

The British Isles

In England, centralization began under the Anglo-Saxon monarchs, who unified the kingdom and established a system of sheriffs, unpaid officials from well-off families responsible for collecting taxes, catching and trying criminals, and raising infantry. After the conquest of England in 1066 by Duke William of Normandy, the Norman kings assessed and collected taxes, required nobles to take oaths of allegiance, and used traveling circuit judges to work for uniform legal procedures throughout the country: what later became known as common law. (English common law is the basis of the legal system in the United Kingdom, the United States, Canada, Australia, and many other countries.)

Demands for taxes to fight the Crusades and war with France led the higher-level nobility to force the king to agree to a settlement limiting his power in 1215. This agreement, known as Magna Carta (Great Charter), has achieved almost mythical stature in history as the foundation of constitutional government, individual rights, and democracy. In reality it made almost no reference to the common people, but simply limited the king's powers vis-à-vis his barons, particularly his power to demand money. Later in the thirteenth century the king expanded his body of advisors from a group of upper nobility and high-level clergy to include relatively low-level knights and representatives from some towns; this group slowly evolved into a permanent representative body known as Parliament. This representative group gradually claimed the right to approve taxes and statutes, basing this on Magna Carta.

The easiest way for monarchs to avoid parliamentary approval of taxes was to stay out of foreign wars, for English monarchs could easily live off the income from their own personal holdings during peace time. That war increased the power of parliaments – and the nobles who dominated them – was a lesson well taught by the Hundred Years War, fought between England and France from 1337 to 1453. The war initially involved rival claims to the French throne and was widely supported on both sides; as it dragged on, the enormous costs of the war led to opposition, especially in England. Opposition occasionally took the form of peasants' revolts such as that led by Wat Tyler in 1381, but was more often expressed through parliamentary refusal to grant taxes unless the monarch granted something in return. Representatives met frequently during the war, with the group of knights and city residents (Commons) coming to meet separately from the higher nobles (Lords). Opposition to the war among these groups was one of the factors that contributed to the war's eventual end in 1453.

Immediately after the end of the Hundred Years War, the English nobility became embroiled in a civil war and succession controversy between two ducal houses, the Yorkists and the Lancastrians. This war, termed the War of the Roses because the symbol of the Yorkists was a white rose and that of the Lancastrians a red rose, saw first one side and then the other gain the throne. The desire for a reestablishment of order became stronger than either army, and in 1485 Henry Tudor, a Welsh nobleman with weak Lancastrian ties, defeated Yorkist forces and became King Henry VII. He initiated what would become his family's most important political strategy – astute marriages – marrying the daughter of the one and only popular Yorkist king, Edward IV (ruled 1461–70; 1471–83).

Henry VII was shrewd, cautious, and so unwilling to spend money that, as we have seen, courtiers such as Polydore Vergil accused him of being miserly and greedy. He called parliaments a few times early in his reign to confirm laws, but ruled primarily through his royal council, which included high nobles, high church officials, knights, lawyers, and professional civil servants. The council conducted diplomatic negotiations with foreign governments, and set up specialized bodies, such as the courts of Chancery, Requests, and Star Chamber, to handle cases more expeditiously than the common law courts did. Recognizing the importance of foreign trade and a healthy economy, Henry encouraged cloth production and built up the merchant marine to protect shipping; he secured a permanent right to customs duties on cloth exports, which would be an important part of royal revenues from that point forward.

Henry VII married his eldest daughter Margaret to King James IV of Scotland (ruled 1488–1513), and then arranged a marriage between his son Arthur and Catherine of Aragon, daughter of Ferdinand and Isabella, the rulers of Spain. Arthur died unexpectedly, and rather than lose this alliance and the dowry Catherine had brought with her, Henry wangled a papal dispensation to allow Catherine to marry his second son, Henry. Marriage to a brother's widow was technically not allowed in Christian canon law, but the pope in this case was persuaded to allow it with the argument that Arthur and Catherine had been children and thus had not consummated their marriage, along with strong royal pressure and donations to the papal coffers.

Henry built up the royal treasury largely by keeping England out of war, a lesson his son Henry VIII (ruled 1509–47) did not learn, though his granddaughter Elizabeth I (ruled 1558–1603) did. Henry VIII's need for cash to fight in Ireland and France was largely met by the confiscation and then sale of church lands following England's break with the papacy in Rome; had this not happened, the monarchy would have probably gone bankrupt. (For more on the break with Rome, see chapter 5.) In her early reign Elizabeth avoided becoming involved in the religious and dynastic wars of continental Europe, but by the 1580s this was no longer possible because of Spanish moves in the Netherlands. She needed both loans and taxes approved by Parliament to support troops on land as well as ships at sea. Parliament only met when it was called by the monarch – Elizabeth called it thirteen times in her forty-five-year reign – but once in session, it raised issues of policy beyond the approval of taxes and laws. Elizabeth did not agree with this expanded view of Parliament's role, and several times imprisoned members of the House of Commons for comments she regarded as seditious; she preferred to govern, as had her father and grandfather, through a small circle of advisors.

Though Elizabeth stayed out of continental wars as long as she could, this reluctance to take military measures did not apply to Ireland. Since the twelfth century, English kings had claimed authority over Ireland, backing this up by granting English nobles land in Ireland and by military intervention during times of unrest or rebellion. In the middle of the fifteenth century, attempts to keep all of Ireland under English control became too expensive. Ireland was unofficially divided into the area around Dublin ruled by the English deputy – known as the Pale – and the rest of Ireland controlled by Anglo-Irish and Gaelic lords. There were many revolts against royal overlordship, including one rebellion in the 1530s led by an Anglo-Irish nobleman, Thomas Fitzgerald, tenth earl of Kildare, several in the 1560s–1580s in the southern province of Munster, led by the earls of Desmond, and another in the 1590s led by Hugh O'Neill, third earl of Tyrone. These, combined with Anglo-Irish and Gaelic Irish armed opposition to the Protestant Reformation, led to increasing repression on the part of the English. Slowly English common law was imposed throughout Ireland, with Dublin emerging as the most Anglicized and most prosperous area.

9 Edmund Spenser, *View of the Present State of Ireland* (1596)

An extreme statement of English hostility to the Irish came from the poet and courtier Edmund Spenser (1552–99), who came to Ireland in the 1570s, hoping to gain land and wealth. He served with English forces during one of the many rebellions against English overlordship, and was awarded lands. During his stay in Ireland, he wrote a prose pamphlet, *View of the Present State of Ireland*, recommending the complete and violent suppression of the Gaelic language and Irish customs, using famine as a tactic. The pamphlet, written as a dialogue, was not published until long after Spenser was dead.

Eudoxus: But if that country of Ireland whence you lately came, be so goodly and commodious a soil as you report, I wonder that no course is taken for the turning therof to good uses, and reducing that savage nation to better government and civility. [He asks what has prevented this.]

Ireneus: I will then . . . begin to declare the evils which seem to be most hurtful to the commonweal of that land . . . they are also of 3 kinds; the first in the laws, the second in customs, the last in religion . . . [One of the customs was letting cattle graze freely, and living in isolated houses called bollies to be near them.] The people that live thus in these Bollies grow thereby more barbarous, and live more licentiously than they would in towns, using what means they list, and practicing what mischiefs and villainies they will, either against the government there . . . or against private men, whom they malign, by stealing their goods, or murdering [them]. For there they think themselves half exempted from law and obedience, and having once tasted freedom, do, like a steer that has been long out of his yoke, grudge and refuse ever after to come under rule again. [Eudoxus suggests changing the laws.]

Ireneus: And therefore where you think, that good and sound laws might amend and reform things amiss there, you think surely amiss. For it is vain to prescribe laws, where no man cares for keeping of them, nor fears the danger for breaking of them. [The Irish are] a people altogether stubborn and untamed and, if it were once tamed, yet now lately having quite shaken off their yoke and broken the bands of their obedience . . . [they can be tamed] only by the sword; for all those evils must first be cut away with a strong hand, before any good can be planted; like as the corrupt branches and unwholesome laws are first to bee pruned, and the fowl moss cleansed or scraped away, before the tree can bring forth any good fruit. [He then recommends destroying crops and animals.] The end I assure thee will be very short . . . for, although there should none of them fall by the sword, nor be slain by the soldier, yet thus being kept from maintenance, and their cattle from running abroad, by this hard restraint, they would quickly consume themselves, and devour one another. The proof whereof I saw sufficiently in those late wars in Munster [a province in Ireland]; for notwithstanding that the same was a most rich and plentiful country, full of corn and cattle, that you would have thought they could have been able to stand long, yet before one year and a half they were brought to such wretchedness, as that any stony heart would have rued the same. Out of every corner of the wood and glens they came creeping forth upon their hands, for their legs could not bear them; they looked [like] anatomies [of] death, they spoke like ghosts, crying out of their graves; they did eat of the carrions, happy where they could find them . . . yet sure in all that war, there perished not many by the sword, but all by the extremity of famine which they themselves had wrought [by their rebellion].

English officials in Ireland often recommended great brutality, particularly against the Gaelic Irish, whom they regarded as barbarous, pagan, "brutish," and "bestial." In the Desmond rebellions, English armies used scorched-earth tactics, destroying villages and crops; famine and disease killed perhaps one-third of the population of the province of Munster in the 1580s. Land was confiscated from Irish Catholics and given to Protestant English and Scottish landholders in what became known as the plantations of Ireland. Settlers were brought in from England, Wales, and Scotland, though there were never as many as the English crown wanted, nor were they as separate from the surrounding Irish as English policy dictated. After Tyrone's rebellion, the largest plantation was organized in the northern province of Ulster, the site of the most determined resistance to English rule; by 1640, it is estimated that there were about 40,000 "planters" in Ulster, most of them Protestant Scots. This English colonization sowed the seeds of mutual hatred and violence between Catholics and Protestants that has continued to the present day.

Scotland's political history during this period was in many ways similar to England's: succession controversies involving civil war and murder, struggles for power between the great nobles and the kings, the development of a parliament with control over the declaration of war and financial matters, and increasing levels of taxation. In the late fourteenth century, the Stuarts won a struggle among several claimants to the throne, establishing a dynasty that would rule for three centuries, though almost every monarch was a minor when he or she came to throne. The Stuarts generally maintained close ties with France, cemented by various marriages, and throughout the fifteenth century engaged in intermittent war with England. In 1503, James IV attempted to make peace with England by marrying Margaret Tudor. This amity did not last long, however, for James supported France in a war with England, and the English defeated and killed James at the Battle of Flodden in 1513. The marriage ultimately proved more important than the war, however, as it was through this marriage that the Stuarts later became the rulers of England.

War between Scotland and England broke out again in 1542, and the king of Scotland, James V (ruled 1513–42), died later that year, leaving a week-old daughter, Mary, who was immediately proclaimed queen, though the actual government was in the hands of a royal council. Mary spent most of her childhood in France, under the guidance of her mother Mary of Guise, and married the heir to the French throne. He died when they were both still teenagers, and Mary returned to Scotland in 1561. Scotland had become Protestant by this point, and Mary's marriage to her cousin Lord Darnley, a Scottish Catholic nobleman, combined with the perception that she favored Catholic France, led powerful Protestant lords to oppose her. A first rebellion was put down, but at the same time Mary grew to hate Darnley, though she had a son by him. She was implicated in a plot that killed him – in fact, she married the chief plotter – and in 1567 she was forced to abdicate in favor of her infant son James. She fled to England, where she was imprisoned by Elizabeth, for Mary was next in line to the English throne and Elizabeth worried – quite rightly – that she would become the center of Catholic plots to overthrow her. (Elizabeth's aunt Margaret was Mary's grandmother.) The one-year-old James was raised by Protestant advisors, and Mary – who never saw her son again – was eventually tried for treason and executed in 1587. With Elizabeth's death in 1603, James became the king of England and Ireland as well as Scotland.

France

In France, Philip Augustus (ruled 1180–1223) and his descendants enlarged the territory of the kingdom of France through military conquest, marriage, and inheritance; they ruled through a system of professional non-noble royal agents, called seneschals in the south and *baillis* in the north, who had judicial, financial, and military powers. Extended military actions sometimes required extraordinary taxes, and in the early fourteenth century the king decided that a national assembly was needed to approve taxes. These taxes included a levy on the clergy, which put him into direct conflict with the pope, who denied that kings had any legal or financial authority over members of the clergy. The national assembly was organized into three Estates, which were legally defined social classes – the First Estate (the clergy), the Second Estate (the nobility), and the Third Estate (residents of chartered towns called *bourgs*). This meeting of the national assembly, also called the Estates General, approved the king's taxes and royal policies vis-à-vis the pope, and during the Hundred Years War subsequent kings sometimes called the Estates General when they needed money.

Several of these Estates General granted the monarchy more permanent taxes than did the English parliaments, including the *taille* on land, the *aide* on sales, and the *gabelle* on salt. Some provinces of France had separate provincial Estates, which also imposed taxes that became more permanent. Because of these permanent taxes, the kings of France could more easily engage in warfare without needing to convene a representative body, as the kings of England had to do. The separate provincial Estates often opposed the calling of the Estates General, fearing it would lessen their independence and would itself cost too much, as delegates would need to travel great distances to meet. In both the national and provincial assemblies, each estate voted as a block, and gradually the First and Second Estates established the principle that they were exempt from taxes – the clergy supported the monarch through prayer, they argued, and the nobility through fighting. This meant that these two more powerful groups were less concerned about tax levels than their counterparts in England.

As in England, during the Hundred Years War the great nobles in France gained power, but Charles VII (ruled 1422–61), the king from the Valois line crowned at Reims through the actions of Joan of Arc, began to reassert the power of the monarchy. He created the first permanent royal army in western Europe, reorganized his royal council, and forced the pope to agree to the Pragmatic Sanction of Bourges, which gave the crown the right to name bishops and abbots and halted some papal taxes. His son Louis XI (ruled 1461–83) expanded the army, using funds gained through commercial treaties and the taxation of economic activities he supported such as silk weaving.

Louis sought to further expand the French kingdom, but in this he confronted the power of the duke of Burgundy, who was technically a vassal of the king of France but had allied himself with England in the later stages of the Hundred Years War. Through conquest, treaties, and marriage, by 1467 Duke Philip "the Good" (ruled 1419–67) held not only Burgundy but also Flanders, Brabant, Hainault (all in present-day Belgium and France) and Luxembourg; his son Charles the Bold (ruled 1467–77) sought to expand Burgundian holdings still further, and allied himself with the English by marrying the sister of Edward IV of England. His efforts might have led to a strong monarchy in the east of France, but Charles was killed in battle in 1477. Louis XI seized many of his vast lands, though some went to Charles's daughter Mary, who, as we have seen, married Maximilian of Habsburg, son of the emperor, the same year her father died. Marital politics expanded the French realm to the west as well as to the east; when the duke of Brittany died in 1489, his widow Anne married two kings of France in succession. She continued to rule an independent Brittany until her death, but eventually the duchy passed to the French crown.

During this period of territorial expansion and consolidation, the king's court developed larger and more permanent institutions. The most important of these was the *parlement* of Paris, the name given to the royal court acting on judicial business. The *parlement* of Paris was the supreme court of the territory under direct royal control, which was about one-third of present-day France in 1450, but grew steadily afterwards. Some regions of France also had their own *parlements*. The *parlements* could not legislate in the way the English parliaments could, though by tradition they had the right to examine royal edicts and forbid their registration if they did not conform to established law. Kings could compel a *parlement* to register an edict by personally appearing in the court (an event termed a *lit de justice*), however, so this power was limited.

In theory, a position as councillor in a *parlement* required legal training and skill, but the Valois kings Francis I (ruled 1515–47) and Henry II (ruled 1547–59) viewed these posts, along with most other positions in the royal bureaucracy and even the army, as open for sale. The sale of offices became an important means of raising revenue for French monarchs. Most offices were purchased by nobles, who then collected the income and other perquisites from the office and hired someone at a much lower salary to actually do the work required. Holding a royal office opened the possibility for receiving other forms of royal patronage, or for gaining a higher noble title; thus many purchasers were members of the lower nobility or eventually even wealthy non-nobles. Individuals who gained a noble title through office-holding were called *noblesse de robe*, nobles of the robe, a term derived from the robes worn by judges and officials, and set in opposition to the *noblesse d'épée*, nobles of the sword, the old nobility whose titles derived – at least in theory – from military service. High nobles viewed this avenue for social climbing with contempt, but it was a means for

England and Ireland	Scotland	France	Spain	Portugal
1422–61 Henry VI	1437–60 James II	1422–61 Charles VII	1454–74 Henry IV (Castile)	1438–81 Afonso V
1461–83 Edward IV	1460–88 James III	1461–83 Louis XI	1458–79 John II (Aragon)	1481–95 John II
1483–5 Richard III		1483–98 Charles VIII	1474–1504 Isabella (Castile)	
1485–1509 Henry VII	1488–1513 James IV	1498–1515 Louis XII	1479–1516 Ferdinand (Aragon)	1495–1521 Manuel I
1509–47 Henry VIII	1513–42 James V	1515–47 Francis I	1516–56 Charles I	1521–57 John III
1547–53 Edward VI	1542–67 Mary, Queen of Scots	1547–59 Henry II		1557–78 Sebastian I
1553–8 Mary I		1560–74 Charles IX	1556–98 Philip II	1578–80 Cardinal Henry
1558–1603 Elizabeth	1567–1625 James VI	1574–89 Henry III	1598–1621 Philip III	1580–98 Philip I (Philip II of Spain)
		1589–1610 Henry IV		1598–1621 Philip II (Philip III of Spain)

Fig. 8. Rulers of western Europe, 1450–1600.

the monarchy to cement allegiances with those slightly lower on the social scale, who were becoming an increasingly powerful and wealthy group.

The price of an office increased dramatically in the sixteenth century – a position as councillor on the Paris *parlement* went from 6,000 *livres* in 1522 to 60,000 in 1600 – and with royal expenses also rising, the sale of offices became an essential revenue stream for the monarchy. Because nobles escaped most taxes in France, however, the long-term fiscal implications of selling offices that carried with them noble titles were very harmful, particularly as many of these offices became hereditary.

Spain and Portugal

The political development of the Iberian peninsula was distinctive, yet in certain ways similar to that of England and France. At the same time as William was conquering England from Normandy, several Christian kingdoms in the northern part of the peninsula began to conquer the disunited Muslim states to their south. Castile, in the north-central part of the peninsula, became the strongest of the growing Christian kingdoms, with Aragon, in the northeast, the second most powerful. During the 1100s, the kings of Castile, Aragon, and several smaller states established representative assemblies (the *Cortes* in Castile, the *Corts* in Aragon), which, like the French Estates General, were structured with separate houses for the clergy, nobility, and urban dwellers. By the fifteenth century, the Castilian *Cortes* had relatively little power; so little, in fact, that representatives from the clergy and nobility simply stopped attending. The Aragonese *Corts*, by contrast, retained effective authority over the approval of taxes. During the twelfth century the region that is now northern Portugal gained its independence from Castile, and by the mid-thirteenth century, Portugal controlled all its present-day territory. Christian conquests continued, and by the late 1200s, Muslim territory in Spain had been reduced to the kingdom of Granada in the south. The Christian kingdoms of Aragon, Navarre, and Castile controlled the rest of what is now Spain.

Spain became unified first through marriage, and then through conquest. Both Castile and Aragon saw civil wars arising out of succession controversies in the 1460s, with France and Portugal supporting whichever heir seemed most likely to further their own interests. The monarchs of both countries had their eyes on Isabella, the heiress presumptive of Castile, but in 1469, she married Prince Ferdinand of Aragon, whose territory also included Naples, and the Mediterranean islands of Sicily, Sardinia, Mallorca, and Menorca. After they became monarchs their kingdoms remained separate, but under their heirs their lands became a more unified realm, though each state in Spain (and the territories beyond the peninsula) retained its own laws, courts, system of taxation, and representative body until about 1700. Following their own example, the royal couple made astute marriages for their children with every country that could assist them against their most powerful neighbor, France: their eldest daughter Isabella married King Afonso of Portugal; in a double wedding, their son John and their second daughter Joanna married the two children of Maximilian I and Mary of Burgundy, Margaret and Philip of Habsburg; their third daughter Catherine married Arthur, the eldest son of Henry VII of England. Death complicated this marital strategy, however. Afonso and John both died shortly after their weddings, Afonso actually in a fall from a horse while the wedding celebration was still going on. Isabella (the younger) was married again to Afonso's oldest brother Manuel, but she died shortly after giving birth to a son, who died as an infant. (Isabella and Ferdinand quickly recemented the Portuguese alliance with a marriage between Manuel and their fourth daughter, Maria, which eventually produced seven children, several of whom married their Habsburg cousins.) Arthur of England died less than a year after he married. All of this left Joanna as heiress apparent in Castile and Catherine a teenage widow. Joanna did eventually rule Castile, though her mental instability cut her reign short, and she became known as "Joanna the Mad." To the great outrage of her parents – who had hoped to use her in yet another alliance – Catherine and her dowry were held in England, and, after complicated negotiations she was married, as noted above, to Arthur's younger brother Henry. Catherine thus followed a pattern of marrying successive siblings set by her sister Isabella and her brother-in-law Manuel.

While marriages linked Isabella and Ferdinand with the rest of Europe, military victories enlarged their holdings. Immediately after their marriage they began military campaigns against Granada, the last remaining Muslim state on the peninsula, which were ultimately successful in 1492. After Isabella's death, Ferdinand conquered Navarre in 1512, and later Spanish troops also seized territory in what is now southern France, northern Africa, southern Italy, and the Canary Islands.

Isabella and Ferdinand also strengthened their position as monarchs through the systematic suppression of aristocratic power. They reorganized the main royal council, making it larger, stronger, and more professional, and filling it with lower-level nobility and educated non-nobles. Their successors established a huge number of additional councils, each responsible for one geographic area – Aragon, Naples, New Spain, and so on – or one aspect of government, with members and officials appointed by the monarch, not inherited by virtue of a noble title. To counter any rebellious nobles, Isabella and Ferdinand used the *hermandades*, brotherhoods of local vigilantes who acted as both police forces and judges; these were ordered to be disbanded in 1498 and replaced by a standing army.

The religious situation in the Iberian peninsula provided Isabella and Ferdinand with unique opportunities for further expansion of royal power. Around 1300, Jews had been expelled from England and France, and many of them had settled in the Muslim and Christian areas of the Iberian peninsula. Initially the rulers of both faiths welcomed them, but during the late fourteenth century attacks and riots against Jewish communities in Christian areas became more common, and many Jews converted (or were forced to convert), becoming *conversos* or "New Christians." Particularly in Castile, *conversos* were often well educated, serving as lawyers and physicians, local and royal officials, and even bishops and abbots. Their success enhanced popular resentment on the part of "Old Christians," and with the accession of Isabella, this sentiment gained a royal ear. Isabella was very devout, and she regarded *conversos* as a cancer within the Christian community; she and Ferdinand gained papal permission from Sixtus IV to establish an Inquisition to distinguish real from false converts. In contrast to earlier inquisitions, this was not under papal control but became a branch of royal government; it was established for Castile in 1480 and Aragon in 1481, making it the first institution common to both states. A separate Portuguese Inquisition on the Spanish model was established in 1526.

Investigations, trials, and executions of *conversos* began immediately, with officials of the Inquisition charged to search out the least sign of an incomplete conversion, such as not eating pork, or wearing clean clothes and not cooking on Saturday (the Jewish Sabbath). Some individuals and communities engaged in more clearly Jewish practices such as circumcision and Sabbath services, and maintained a kind of dual identity, blending Jewish and Christian beliefs and practices. Evidence of these practices has led some scholars to argue that most *conversos* were "crypto-Jews," while others view them as entirely assimilated until the Inquisition invented their devotion to Judaism. When brought before the Inquisition, most *conversos* argued that they were fully Christian and had been for generations. (We have no way of knowing exactly whether such an argument was a matter of expediency or the truth, of course, which is why there is such disagreement among scholars.) In countering this argument, Spanish officials developed what many historians see as a new type of anti-Semitism.

Christian hostility toward Jews had existed throughout the Middle Ages, but Jews were defined primarily as a religious group, unacceptable because they did not believe Jesus was the Messiah. To the officials of the Spanish Inquisition, however, Judaism was not simply a religious adherence that could be changed through conversion, but an essential (and unchangeable) aspect of a person's nature, housed in the blood and heritable. Thus it was more like noble status, which, despite the fact that in every part of Europe new families were frequently elevated to the nobility, was conceptualized as "having noble blood." These two hierarchies of blood – religious and social – converged in Spain during the sixteenth century, with the passage of laws requiring "purity of the blood" – having no Muslim or Jewish ancestors – for anyone claiming noble status. In some areas intermarriage between Old and New Christians had become common, so that families sought to hide their ancestors, as the revelation of "tainted" blood could mean disaster. (For discussion of the implications of these ideas in the Spanish colonies, see chapter 7.) The threat of an Inquisitorial investigation became a further tool in the hands of officials seeking to expand royal power against recalcitrant or politically suspect nobles, used particularly during the reign of Isabella and Ferdinand's great-grandson, Philip II (ruled 1556–98).

The Muslim areas of southern Iberia were home to significant numbers of Jews, including families who had lived there for centuries and others who had migrated there more recently. The conquest of Granada in January 1492 made this no longer a safe haven; later that year Isabella and Ferdinand ordered all Jews to leave Spain without taking any of their property with them. Historians estimate that about 200,000 Jews left Spain, about half to North Africa and the rest dispersed throughout Europe. Some went to Portugal, where, despite the presence of an Inquisition, the kings offered Jews and *conversos* twenty years' exemption from investigation. This did not necessarily mean they would be allowed to stay in Portugal, for in the same year the Portuguese crown sent 2,000 newly baptized Jews to its African island colonies, hoping they would intermarry with Portuguese Christians who were already there and increase the islands' population. Later in the sixteenth century Jews were officially expelled from Portugal as well as Spain, taking their talents, skills, and (despite the best efforts of the monarchs to prevent this) some of their wealth from both countries.

The conquest of Granada brought Muslims as well as Jews into Christian Spanish territory, of course. Initially Isabella and Ferdinand promised Muslims they could practice their faith, but this toleration was short-lived, and forced conversions began. Muslims in Granada rebelled in 1499, a revolt put down by force; at least 50,000 Muslims in Granada were baptized en masse, all Muslims in Castile were ordered to convert or leave, and Arabic-language writings relating to Islam were burned. Many Muslims, along with Jews, went to the Ottoman Empire, where they were welcomed by the sultan. Others converted, becoming Moriscos, another type of "New Christian" whose sincerity in conversion was often doubted by Christian authorities. The Inquisition had jurisdiction over those suspected of Muslim practices as well as Jewish. Men and women observed fasting during the Muslim holy month of Ramadan, performing daily prayers or washing themselves in a Muslim manner, wearing Muslim dress, carrying Arabic books or amulets, following Muslim funeral practices, or engaging in other suspicious activities were arrested, imprisoned, questioned, subjected to rituals of public humiliation, and occasionally executed at *autos da fé*. Officials recommended that children, especially boys, be taken from their parents and educated in Christian schools.

10 The Inquisition at the local level

The Inquisitions in the Iberian peninsula relied on unpaid lay agents, called *familiares*, to identify those suspected of beliefs or practices that deviated from Catholicism, and also encouraged people to inform on their neighbors or acquaintances. This created a climate of suspicion in some areas, as people reported on those whose ideas or behavior seemed odd, which they often attributed to being "New Christian" whether or not it had any relationship to Jewish or Muslim traditions. In this Portuguese Inquisitor's report, a woman describes two chance encounters, one involving an insult and another a discussion of burial practices.

And following this on the fifth day of the month of June of 1542 years, in Lisbon.

Isabel Fernandez, wife of Pero Reinel, who makes navigation charts, who lives in this city at the entrance way to the Misericordia at the rear of the terrace for old wheat, in the parish of See, was asked and testified under oath on the Bible if she knows of any person or persons who have said or done something against our holy Catholic faith. She said that she did not know anything else except that in this last Lent, she was going to the customs house and passing through the square of Pelourinho Velho, where items are sold at auction. They were selling some *tavoleiros* [special tins for baking cookies] and some women were buying the said *tavoleiros*. They placed a bid on them and a porter who was auctioning them, who is named Remedeo, carried the said *tavoleiros* to them to look at. They took them in their hands and were looking at them and were not pleased with them and left them. So then the said Remedeo told them, in a harsh voice: "These are the women who took the virginity from God!" Then she [the witness] left and afterwards encountered the said porter and reprimanded him for having spoken those words. He said that he was joking, and she [the witness] said that she does not know if the said Remedeo is a New

Christian or an Old, and yet that he appeared to be a New Christian. [She said] that there were many people present who she did not know nor did she know the women who took the said *tavoleiros* for it happened that she was passing by and heard the above mentioned and no more. Antonio Roiz [a secretary for the Inquisition] wrote it with the two marks that were made in truth and requested me the notary that I sign for her for [she] does not know how to write. She [the witness] said further that it was true that seven or eight months ago, more or less, a certain Isabel Fernandez, New Christian, a widowed woman who sold olive oil in the Feraria, came to her house one day. She started to talk, and she [the witness] asked her why when the New Christians when dead they were laid in [new] virgin graves, because the Old Christians rejoiced that the earth that ate their father and mother and grandparents would eat them. [In other words, that they were buried in the same ground with the rest of their family.] The said Isabel Fernandez retorted that she was astonished and did not know that, and that the reason the New Christians did that was because if they lay in graves where other dead had already been, all the sins of those who were buried there would be transmitted to them. She [the witness] replied to her by saying that this was the blindness in which they lived, and then said no more.

(Francisco Sousa Viterbo, ed., *Trabalhos nauticos dos portuguezes nos séculos XVI e XVII*, Part I [Lisbon: Typographia da Academia Real das Sciencias, 1898 (facsimile, Lisbon: Imprensa Nacional-Casa Moeda, 1988), p. 377 (341)]. Translated by Darlene Abreu-Ferreira in Monica Chojnacka and Merry Wiesner-Hanks, eds., *Ages of Woman, Ages of Man: Sources in European Social History, 1400–1750* [London: Longman, 2002], pp. 184–5. Reprinted by permission.)

Increased oppression led to another revolt in 1567. It took several years to subdue the rebels, after which King Philip II ordered all Moriscos in Granada to be dispersed throughout Castile, where they could be more easily watched by Christian authorities. Those who had taken direct part in the rebellion, including women and children, were subject to enslavement. This forced relocation created great hardships for Moriscos, and in many cases it increased, rather than decreased, their allegiance to their traditional cultural and religious practices.

In 1609, King Philip III began a series of decrees ordering Moriscos to leave all of Spain; those going to the "infidel lands" of the Ottoman Empire or North Africa were ordered to leave behind any children under the age of seven, turning them over to church officials or Old Christian families. More than 300,000 Moriscos left Spain during the period from 1609 to 1614, though slaves in Christian households, women who had married Christians, people who had taken monastic vows, and some tenants of Christian landowners were allowed to stay. It is impossible to know how many children were separated from their families, though strict rules set on their upbringing imply that there must have been a significant number. Morisco children were not supposed to be enslaved, but raised as good Christians by the families that took them in, and married to Old Christians whenever possible. Boys were not to be taught any trade in which they would need to read or use weapons, however, and children of both sexes had to repent their religious errors before the Inquisition. Royal and church policies thus simultaneously promoted the assimilation of the remaining Moriscos into Christian society and their continued distinctiveness as a group tainted by their heritage.

For their purging Spain of Jews and Muslims, and their military assistance in defending the Papal States, Pope Alexander VI gave Ferdinand and Isabella the title "Most Catholic Majesties." He also gave them, more importantly, the right to appoint bishops and retain much church revenue. Thus by being "most Catholic," Isabella and Ferdinand and their successors gained power over the church that other rulers would only gain by breaking with Rome.

Though in the short term Isabella and Ferdinand's marital politics were disrupted by death, in the long run at least one part of them was extremely successful. In 1516, with Ferdinand's death, the thrones to both Castile and Aragon were inherited by their grandson Charles, the son of their daughter Joanna and Philip of Habsburg, who became Charles I of Spain. With this, Charles gained a triple dynastic inheritance, as he already ruled the Low Countries and Habsburg holdings in central Europe. In 1519, at the age of nineteen, he was elected Holy Roman Emperor. (There had already been four emperors named Charles, so as emperor he was Charles V.) Charles married Isabella of Portugal, his cousin and sister-in-law, who served as his main representative in Spain when he was elsewhere in his realm, which was often.

Charles's vast holdings were split apart at his abdication in 1556, and his eldest son Philip II inherited the throne of Spain. Philip continued his great-grandparents' policies of expansion, invading and conquering the islands that became known as the Philippines in 1565 and, during a succession controversy

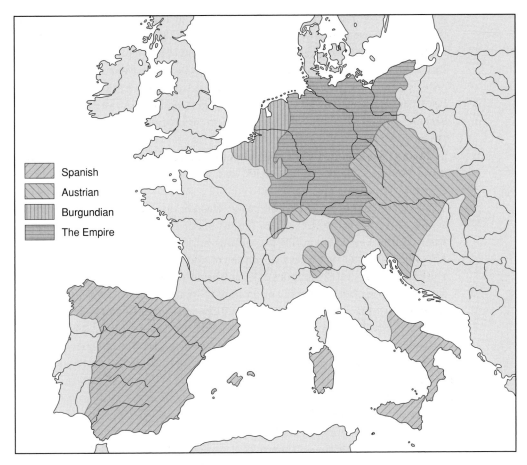

Map 4. Territories held by Charles V in 1526.

Spanish

Austrian

Burgundian

The Empire

in which he was one claimant to the throne, Portugal in 1580. He also inherited their zeal for religious uniformity, and the Inquisition tried and executed suspected Protestants as well as *conversos* and Moriscos. These policies led, as we have seen, to a revolt by Moriscos in Granada, and, as we will see in chapter 5, to a revolt in the Netherlands. Both Charles and Philip fought wars against France, the Ottoman Empire, and other European powers; Philip was at peace at most six months of his forty-two-year reign. Wars sucked the royal treasury nearly dry of all the gold and silver pouring in from the Americas. American precious metals, higher taxes, loans, and the sale of offices could not cover the costs of the army and the ever-expanding bureaucracy in Spain, and Philip was bankrupt by the time of his death in 1598.

Eastern and Northern Europe

Rulers in eastern and northern Europe sought to expand their power and holdings in many of the same ways as those in western Europe did. Viewed from the Christian perspective, the fourteenth and fifteenth centuries saw Christian forces in many places engaged in campaigns against non-Christians, just as they were in Spain. Christian Hungarians and Transylvanians fought Muslim Ottomans in southeastern Europe. Christian Poles, Livonians (modern-day Latvians), and members of the Teutonic Knights – the last remaining crusading order – fought pagan Lithuanians in northeastern Europe. Teutonic Knights, Poles, Swedes, and Muscovites all fought pagan Mongols in much of what later became Russia. The view from the Muslim side similarly presents many parallels with western European monarchies, for the Ottoman sultans were also fighting in the name of their religion, developing centralized institutions, creating more specialized bureaucracies, and, as noted above, expanding and modernizing their army and navy.

The Ottoman Turks created the most effective institutions in eastern Europe during this period, as well as the largest state. The word Ottoman was taken from Osman Bey, the chief of a group of Turks who settled in northwestern Anatolia (modern-day Turkey), a frontier region between the Byzantine Empire and the holdings of the Seljuk Turks, in the thirteenth century. They served as mercenaries for both groups, and gradually increased their own holdings. Ottoman forces entered Europe in 1345, and dramatically defeated a huge army of French, Burgundian, and Hungarian troops at Nicopolis in 1396. Their advance stopped briefly while they fought Mongol forces under Timur in the east, but began again in the fifteenth century and by the middle of the century they held the entire area south of the Danube. In 1453, they took Constantinople, which they renamed Istanbul and made the capital of the Ottoman Empire.

Janissaries recruited and trained for military positions provided the initial personnel in the Ottoman bureaucracy. Villages were organized into districts called *timars*, under the authority of a cavalry officer or government official, who collected taxes for the sultan and handled legal disputes. These districts were organized into a hierarchy of larger units, with each level under the authority of a trained official. As the Ottomans expanded, they sometimes gave local leaders the control of *timars*, requiring conquered peoples to pay taxes but allowing them to keep their own laws and traditions. These traditions included religion, for the Ottomans did not regard religious uniformity as important. They also charged non-Muslims higher taxes, so were not eager to have all their subjects convert. Their relations with Christian and Jewish communities (whom the Muslims viewed as related "Peoples of the Book" as they were based on the same biblical tradition as Islam) were formalized in the *millet* system, in which the head of each religious community served as an intermediary between the sultan's government and the people. Religious communities paid taxes just as villages did, but they could practice their religion openly, retain their own systems of religious law, and teach their children. Christian and Jewish leaders often held high government offices, and Ottoman authorities welcomed *conversos* and Jews as well as Moriscos and Muslims when they were expelled from Spain.

The Ottomans expanded southward around the Mediterranean as well as into Europe, first engaging in a series of naval wars with the Venetians and the Genoese, and then conquering Syria and Iraq from a rival Turkic group, the Safavids, with the same mixture of skilled infantry and heavy artillery they would later deploy against the Hungarians. In 1517, Sultan Selim "the Grim" (ruled 1512–20) invaded the Mameluke Empire, and within a few months had taken the entire eastern Mediterranean, Egypt, North Africa, and the Arabian peninsula. This included all the holy places of Islam, and to reinforce this religious authority they moved the caliph of Cairo, the head of Sunni Islam, to Istanbul.

Selim's successor Süleyman then turned his attention back northwards, conquering Bosnia, Croatia, Romania, the Ukraine, and, as we have seen, Hungary in the 1520s. This advance was stopped outside Vienna in Austria, but Turkish naval forces drove the Spanish out of their North African ports and planned an invasion of Italy that was halted by the combination of the loss of the naval Battle of Lepanto and the need to confront a reinvigorated Safavid Empire in the east. Though it would have been impossible to predict this at the time, the boundaries between the Ottoman Empire and the rest of Europe stabilized in the 1570s, leaving the Ottomans as rulers of about a third of Europe and half the shores of the Mediterranean for the next three hundred years.

North of the Ottoman Empire, several Christian dynasties also built up their power and worked toward creating stronger states. Like Aragon and Castile, the crowns of Poland and Lithuania were joined together by a marriage, though this one also involved a conversion – in 1386, Queen Jadwiga of Poland married Jagaila (Jagiello in Polish), the grand duke of Lithuania, who was baptized with the Christian name of Wladyslaw and promised to convert his subjects. Each country remained largely self-governing, and under the Jagiellonian dynasty Poland–Lithuania expanded its territory to cover a large part of central and eastern Europe, including what is now Belarus and Ukraine. In 1493, the first national parliament (the *sejm*, pronounced like "same" in English) was established in Poland, and in 1569 Poland and Lithuania were united under a single parliament. Nobles dominated this parliament, however, and when the last Jagiellonian monarch died in 1572, they asserted their right to be consulted on foreign policy matters and to elect the kings. They often chose foreigners without local bases of power rather than elevating a native noble family to the monarchy.

Poland–Lithuania defeated the Teutonic Knights and their allies the Livonian Brethren of the Sword, military religious orders who together controlled much of the Baltic region, several times during the fifteenth century. This halted the advance of Germans eastward, which had begun in the fourteenth century under the protection of the Teutonic Knights. In 1525, the Teutonic Knights themselves underwent a conversion, when their last Grand Master, Albert of Brandenburg, a member of the Hohenzollern family, became a Lutheran. Albert changed their territory from a religious state to the secular duchy of Prussia, under the overlordship of the king of Poland–Lithuania.

To the east of Poland–Lithuania, the decline in the power of the Mongols in the late fourteenth century allowed the grand dukes of Muscovy to

Denmark/ Norway	Sweden	Poland/ Lithuania	Russia	Ottoman Empire	Holy Roman Empire
1448–81 Christian I	1448–81 Christian I	1445–92 Casimir IV	1425–62 Basil II	1451–81 Mehmed II	1440–93 Frederick III
1481–1513 John	1481–1513 John	1492–1501 John Albert	1462–1505 Ivan III	1481–1512 Bayazid II	1493–1519 Maximilian I
1513–23 Christian II	1513–23 Christian II	1501–06 Alexander	1505–33 Basil IV	1512–20 Selim I	1519–56 Charles V
1523–33 Frederick I	1523–60 Gustavus I	1506–48 Sigismund I	1533–84 Ivan IV	1520–66 Süleyman I	1558–64 Ferdinand I
1534–58 Christian III	1560–8 Eric XIV	1548–72 Sigismund II		1566–74 Selim II	1564–76 Maximilian II
1558–88 Frederick II	1568–92 John III	1575–86 Stephen Batory	1584–98 Theodore	1574–95 Murad III	1576–1612 Rudolf II
1588–1648 Christian IV	1592–1604 Sigismund (of Poland)	1587–1632 Sigismund III	1598–1605 Boris Godunov	1595–1603 Mehmed III	

Fig. 9. Rulers of northern, eastern, and central Europe, 1450–1600.

expand their holdings. During the fifteenth century, the grand dukes Basil I (ruled 1389–1425) and Basil II (ruled 1425–62) firmed up their alliance with the eastern Christian church and rewarded high-ranking landowners (boyars) with positions as army officers and government officials. Ivan III (ruled 1462–1505) married the niece of the last Byzantine emperor, thus both symbolically and genealogically tying himself to the legacy of Rome. Church and court officials began to talk of Moscow as the "third Rome," and Ivan's grandson Ivan IV (called "the Terrible," ruled 1533–84) gave himself the title of Caesar (Tsar in Russian) in 1547 to further reinforce this link. Ivan IV was even more effective than French or Spanish monarchs at curbing the independent power of the great nobles. Using a special police force, he ordered the arrest and murder of hundreds of aristocrats and gave his victims' estates as payment to those landowners – usually members of the lesser nobility – serving in his army or government, often referred to as the "service nobility" and thus similar to the French *noblesse de robe*. Ivan III and Ivan IV expanded Muscovite territory both westward and eastward, annexing several cities, including Novgorod, whose inhabitants were massacred. They attacked Livonia, and seized Tatar states east of the Ural Mountains in order to control access to the Caspian Sea.

Northern Europe also saw a series of conflicts between rulers and the nobility in the thirteenth and fourteenth centuries, set against a backdrop of moves by German cities who had joined together to form the Hanseatic League to gain monopoly control of the fur and fish trade. In 1388, Swedish nobles turned to Queen Margrete of Denmark, the widow of King Haakon VI of Norway, for help in opposing the Germans. Their combined efforts were successful, and in 1397 a treaty set up the Union of Kalmar uniting Denmark, Norway, and

Sweden under Margrete. The treaty provided for a common foreign policy, but separate national councils and the continuation of existing laws in each country. Both Denmark–Norway and Sweden (which included what is now Finland) developed representative assemblies (*Riksdag*), with lawmaking and taxation powers. The Swedish Riksdag was unique, because along with the usual estates of clergy, nobility, and bourgeois, it had a fourth estate for peasants.

During the early sixteenth century, Swedish nobles became increasingly dissatisfied with the Union of Kalmar, and after several years of war, in 1523 the Swedes defeated the Danes and established their own monarchy under Gustav Vasa, a member of a prominent Swedish noble family. Like his contemporaries Francis I of France and Henry VIII of England, Gustav Vasa (ruled 1523–60) centralized his administration and increased royal power over the nobility and the church. He built an extremely efficient army and navy, both of them used frequently over the next century and a half. Hostilities and alliances among northern European powers shifted constantly, with the Danes and Swedes sometimes united – against the German city of Lübeck, and later against Emperor Charles V – and sometimes fighting against each other, as in the Northern War (1563–70), which involved major naval battles fought by specialized battleships and ultimately ended in Danish defeat. The Danish and Swedish royal houses were frequently linked by marriage to those of the rest of Europe – the Danish King Christian II married the sister of the Emperor Charles V, the brother of the king of Sweden married the daughter of the king of Poland–Lithuania – so that northern conflicts were often supported by money and troops coming from elsewhere.

Central Europe

As a successful and durable multiethnic political unit, the Ottoman Empire provides one type of counter-example to a narrative that highlights the rise of nation-states in this era. Central Europe provides another. Except for the northern tier of Scandinavian countries, the middle third of Europe did not develop into nations until the nineteenth century. This did not mean, however, that these areas were cut off from the changes in military technology, the growth of government institutions, or the marital politics that were so important for the rest of Europe; in fact, central Europe led the way in some of these developments. In 1152 Frederick Barbarossa (ruled 1152–90) was chosen as the emperor of the Holy Roman Empire, a confederation of principalities, duchies, cities, bishoprics, and other types of regional government stretching from Denmark to Rome and from Burgundy to Poland. Barbarossa himself was from the Hohenstaufen family, the hereditary rulers of the duchy of Swabia in what is now southern Germany. Like his contemporaries in England and France, Frederick Barbarossa appointed officials to oversee the empire, developed royal courts of justice, and required vassals to take oaths of allegiance.

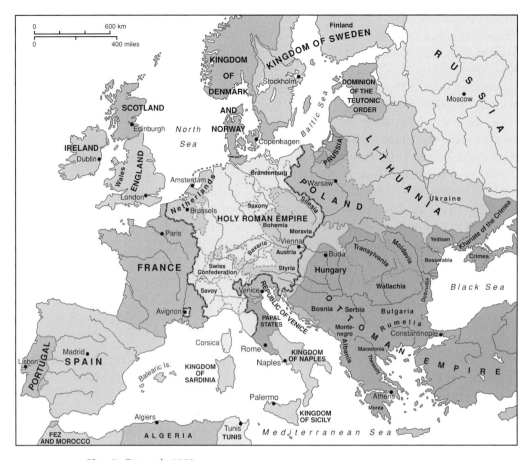

Map 5. Europe in 1559.

Two primary and related problems prevented subsequent emperors from transforming the empire into a centralized state. First, the various regional states, particularly the larger and more powerful among them, succeeded in keeping the emperorship an elected office. Until the middle of the fifteenth century, men from various powerful regional dynasties – the Luxembourgs, the Wittelsbachs, the Habsburgs – all vied for the office, as they made strategic marriages with women from each other's families and other ruling houses, through which they expanded and consolidated their family holdings. In 1438 the emperorship went to Albert II of Habsburg, and it would remain with the Habsburgs with only one short break until the Empire was dissolved in 1804. Despite this continuity, not until the mid-sixteenth century were Habsburgs relatively assured the office would be theirs; the election of Charles V in 1519 still cost enormous amounts of money and involved extensive political maneuvering. Thus even if they happened to be emperor, the rulers of central European regional territories put their main efforts into their inherited family lands, developing armies, appointing officials and often establishing representative institutions called diets (*Landtage*). The smaller territories, including more than fifty imperial cities and thousands of free imperial knights who might hold only a few square miles, worried about being swallowed up by their larger neighbors, but their support of stronger imperial power to counter this was sporadic and relatively weak.

Second, the battle for power between popes and secular rulers, which had taken place all over central and western Europe, was particularly strong in the Empire, as the popes claimed the right to crown emperors, and emperors claimed authority over papal lands. Gradually both of these claims disappeared. With the Golden Bull of 1356, a decree issued by the imperial Diet and Emperor Charles IV (ruled 1355–78), seven leading territorial rulers in Germany, three of them archbishops and four of them secular princes, became the electors, and a papal coronation was no longer required. Papal armies combined with those of northern Italian cities defeated those of the emperor at various points, and by the early fourteenth century the emperors had very little permanent power in Italy. For centuries after this, however, factional disputes within and between Italian cities, or between a city and the pope, often led one side to ally with the emperor, so that imperial troops and influence continued to be a factor in Italian politics. Popes were unwilling to cede power over taxation or the appointment of church officials to the emperors in the ways they did – or were forced to do – with western European monarchs.

This situation became particularly significant in the early sixteenth century, when papal tax collectors were desperately trying to cover the costs of the building of St. Peter's in Rome, and increased their activities in the Empire substantially. As we will see in chapter 5, papal tax collection was one of the sparks that set off the Protestant Reformation, and the emperor's weak hold over German territorial princes was an important factor in its spread. The resulting religious divisions in the Empire kept imperial institutions weak. Emperor Maximilian I did set up an imperial supreme court and established a general tax, but the separate institutions established by territorial princes had more real impact on people's lives. As in France, most taxes were paid by peasants, who had no representation in any of the regional diets; these diets had little legislative function, and rulers generally simply proclaimed ordinances without consulting them. In their own territories, which grew, as we have seen, through conquest and astute marriages to include Bohemia and part of Hungary, as well as Spain, the Low Countries, Naples and Sicily, and the Spanish colonial empire, the Habsburgs established separate institutions of government, including councils, law courts, offices and bureaucracies. These often worked to weaken the imperial institutions even further.

The territorial rulers are often seen as the most important players in the Empire, sort of mini-nation-states, a few of which, such as Austria and Brandenburg, would later follow an inevitable path to nationhood. This overemphasizes their power at the time, however, for both in Germany and even more so in central and northern Italy, cities were as important politically and perhaps more important culturally and economically than territories ruled by noble houses.

Beginning in the twelfth century, growing urban communities from Hamburg to Siena had fought for, bought, or maneuvered their independence from local nobles. In Italy many of these nobles moved into the cities, intermarrying with urban merchant families, while in Germany they were less likely to do this, gaining access to merchant wealth by highway robbery and small-scale wars rather than marriage. In both places merchants became the most powerful social and political group, establishing legal codes, institutions of government, and taxation policies that favored their interests. In most cities they were able to defeat revolts by those lower on the social scale in the thirteenth and fourteenth centuries, so that even cities such as Venice or Florence or Nuremberg, which had constitutions or charters of government, were in reality dominated by a few hundred (or even fewer) merchant families.

Conflicts among elite families for power within a city could be very fierce, and in the fourteenth and the fifteenth centuries many Italian cities were taken over by powerful individuals (*signori*) either subverting or ignoring the existing structure of government, and hiring mercenaries to enforce their aims. Many of these individuals, such as Giangaleazzo Visconti (ruled 1378–1402) in Milan, sought legitimacy from the pope or emperor, and transformed their takeover of government into a hereditary dynasty. Both German and Italian cities controlled some of the countryside outside the city walls (called the *contado* in Italian) and many of the Italian cities sought to expand their holdings, becoming city-states. This put them into conflict with one another, giving the *signori* further opportunities to gain power, particularly those who were themselves captains of mercenary companies. (Such individuals are called *condottieri*.) In the fifteenth century, the larger Italian city-states of Milan, Florence, and Venice sought to annex their smaller neighbors as they fought with each other, forming, breaking, and reforming alliances among themselves or with outside powers to achieve a balance of power whenever one city was perceived to be gaining too much strength. By the end of the fifteenth century, Italian cities also sought to use states outside the peninsula as part of this balance of power, a policy that proved disastrous as Italy became a battleground for the aspirations of many of the rulers of Europe.

The shifting system of alliances in Italy depended on obtaining accurate information about those who were alternately enemies and friends. The Italian city-states initially relied on merchants and bankers traveling or living in other cities to pass along information, but in the fifteenth century they began to send out permanent representatives whose functions were to send back a constant stream of foreign news and win the loyalty of important people. These representatives created modern diplomacy: they established permanent embassies, which gradually came to be understood as islands of foreign sovereignty; they kept extensive records; they made both open and secret alliances. The larger Italian city-states soon had ambassadors throughout Italy, and by the 1490s at the major courts in the rest of western Europe. Ferdinand of Aragon was the first monarch to set up Italian-style embassies – in Burgundy, England, and the papal court in Rome – and by the early sixteenth century other monarchs of western Europe had done the same, often employing Italians as diplomats. In official statements discussing ambassadors, their duties were often described as preserving peace, particularly among Christians, but in reality ambassadors served the interests of one particular government.

The city-states are often seen as holding Italy back, preventing the development of a nation, but they can also be seen as models for the future. By the nineteenth century a balance of power among a system of multiple states was a key political goal for leaders in all of Europe, with diplomats as well as soldiers responsible for both maintaining it and furthering the ends of their home country.

11 Habsburg–Valois wars

Lines of conflict in sixteenth-century Europe were complex and frequently shifting, but the primary rivalry pitted the house of Habsburg against the house of Valois, the kings of France. The prelude to this conflict was war in Italy. Aragon and France both claimed the kingdom of Naples and Sicily in southern Italy through different lines of descent, and the death of its ruler in 1494 provided an opportunity to enforce these claims. Naples was also involved in shifting alliances in Italy itself, and in 1494 entered into an agreement with Florence to take over Milanese territories; Milan asked France for support, and French armies invaded Italy, moving quickly all the way to Naples. Spanish armies took Naples back a decade later, and Spanish and German troops together pushed French troops out of Italy. Meanwhile other areas came into dispute, including the kingdom of Navarre, which lay between France and Spain, several areas between France and the Holy Roman Empire, and the city of Milan. The young Charles V became king of Spain as well as ruler of the Habsburg lands and Holy Roman Emperor, the ambitious Francis I became king of France, and the conflict escalated. The French invaded Navarre in 1521 and Italy again in 1522, and Charles responded by sending imperial forces, which eventually sacked the city of Rome in 1527. The wars in Italy involved shifting alliances on an international scale, and brought troops from all over Europe to the peninsula, wrecking the economy – and sometimes the physical structure – of many cities. Soldiers fighting in Italy took syphilis with them when they returned home, which the French labeled the "Italian disease" and most of the rest of Europe the "French pox." The system of diplomacy established by Italian city-states made the situation worse instead of better. Italian ambassadors at the French court and those of Spain at courts throughout Europe were instrumental in the French decision to invade, and continued to feature in the long series of wars that followed.

Four Habsburg–Valois wars (1521–5, 1526–9, 1535–8, 1542–4) were interrupted by brief periods of peace, during which time the emperor was often fighting Protestant troops in Germany or Ottoman troops in eastern Europe. The French allied with the Ottomans, Scotland, Sweden, Denmark, and various German princes, and fighting often took place on the Mediterranean as well as on land. Charles skillfully used promises of territory to placate many of France's allies, and this, combined with imperial troops advancing to within sight of Paris, forced Francis to agree to a peace treaty. Fighting began again in 1551, and was finally ended with the Treaty of Cateau-Cambrésis of 1559, in which France abandoned its claims in Italy. At this point France itself was being torn apart by religious wars. Conflict with France – and with the Ottomans – was one reason Charles was not able to respond immediately with great military force to the spread of Martin Luther's ideas, so the Habsburg–Valois wars were one reason for the success of the Protestant Reformation. Decisions by Italian city-states to ally with outside powers against one another increased hostilities among them, and Italy remained divided until 1870.

Power at the local level

The Italian city-states and the German imperial cities are the most visible example of politics at the level where it had the greatest impact on most people's day-to-day lives: the local. Their history reminds us that in all of Europe, underneath the highest layer of intermarrying hereditary dynasties, cities, villages, parishes, *timars*, and many other smaller governmental units all had authority over people and their families. Just as national or territorial rulers did, these lower levels of government demanded taxes, developed bureaucracies, and issued ordinances. They created and maintained courts that set punishments for those who did not pay their taxes, obey officials, or follow ordinances. Though most men could not hope to become an official for a national or territorial ruler, they might gain a position as village constable, gate-keeper, church sexton, or market overseer.

Some of these more local institutions of government were run by the church. Christians throughout Europe paid taxes to their local parish and were under the authority of church courts for matters involving marriage, morality, and a variety of other issues. Other of these institutions were secular. By 1450 villages in many parts of Europe had become what were called communes, with institutions of self-governance such as councils or courts that regulated planting and harvesting, and might represent the village as a whole to outside political authorities. In some places such groups could issue ordinances and make legal decisions, either in conjunction with the local lord or on their own.

The towns and cities that won their independence from local lords and gained charters had even stronger institutions of governance. In Germany and Italy, as we have seen, they might be under the jurisdiction of only the emperor or of no higher political authority at all, but even in areas in which national monarchies developed, cities collected taxes, passed and enforced ordinances, built and maintained walls and fortifications, and established courts, hospitals, orphanages, and often municipal brothels.

Larger cities were often dominated by a merchant oligarchy, and in smaller towns and villages the men from wealthier families were often the most powerful, but in many places all adult men swore an oath annually to defend and protect their town, so that they were at the very least symbolically part of a political community. They were citizens, a word that is linked etymologically and conceptually in many European languages to living in a city or community – in Latin the word *civitas* means both citizenship and community; in French a city is a *bourg* and its residents are *bourgeois*; in German *Burg* is a walled city or fortress and its residents are *Bürger*. Citizenship in a city or town did not bring direct voting rights in this period, but it did bring preferential legal treatment, often lower taxes than those paid by non-citizens, the right to live in the city and buy property there without seeking anyone's permission, the right to be free from the demands of anyone living outside the city, and the right to claim certain services if one fell ill or became incapacitated, such as staying in a city hospital or receiving public support. In short, it brought many of the same benefits we associate with citizenship today, particularly the right to live and work undisturbed in a particular location. Citizenship was thus a coveted commodity, and, like property or a monarchy, became heritable.

The importance and heritability of citizenship meant that – again as with property or a monarchy – distinctions were made on the basis of gender. Until about 1500 women were regularly listed as "citizeness" (*Bürgerin, bourgeoise*) in court records, though they do not seem to have been part of the annual oath-swearing. This label gradually became more rare, as cities sought various means to restrict the number of citizens, and as Roman law – which viewed women as mentally weak – spread in Europe. Women in towns and cities very occasionally held minor offices such as churchwardens, market inspectors, or gate-keepers, especially if they were the widow of a man who had held this office, and in more places held official positions as city midwives. In these positions, they swore oaths of office just as men did. They never held high positions in urban or village government, however. Women inherited and governed nations and regions, of course, but those female rulers did not grant or allow other women a more significant political role than male rulers did. They named no women as ministers or judges, or sold them the government offices that were so often for sale to men.

Whether one was a citizen of a town or a member of a village commune could shape relationships of power, legal standing, and access to wealth at the local level, so these were important issues. At all higher levels, however, such matters made little difference. In 1600, as in 1450, political power was in the hands of rulers, nobles, and the occasional commoner favored because of capability, attractiveness, or talent. The growth of the nation-state may appear to have lessened the power of hereditary aristocrats. It did end their ability to maintain their own armies and collect their own taxes, but traditional elites adapted to new circumstances very well, obtaining posts of command in the new standing military forces, offices in the expanded bureaucracies, and opportunities for wealth through the new systems of taxation. In some countries, nobles, clergy, and a few wealthy townspeople had a voice in political decisions through representative institutions, but their more important source of power was their inherited family status, maintained and enhanced by careful marital strategies.

Rulers in the fifteenth and sixteenth centuries did not limit their activities to what we would consider politics, but often attempted to shape the cultural and religious lives of their subjects as well, recognizing that these were integral to maintaining power. As both Jacob Burckhardt and Benedict Anderson have emphasized, nation-states were brought into being by writers and artists as well as soldiers and tax collectors. Painters, composers, poets, and essayists did not limit themselves to political matters, however, or work only or always for royal patrons. At the same time as some of Europe's creative minds were devising new weaponry and new laws, others were creating new artistic techniques, new forms of literature, and new musical instruments. As we will see in the following chapter, a few made both deadly weapons for powerful rulers and exquisite paintings.

Further reading

For general studies of political developments during this era, see Richard Bonney, *The European Dynastic States: 1494–1660* (Oxford: Oxford University Press, 1991); Thomas Ertman, *The Birth of Leviathan: Building States and Regimes in Medieval and Early Modern Europe* (Cambridge: Cambridge University Press, 1997).

For military developments, see John R. Hale, *War and Society in Renaissance Europe, 1450–1620* (Baltimore: Johns Hopkins University Press, 1985); Bert S. Hall, *Weapons and Warfare in Renaissance Europe: Gunpowder, Technology, and Tactics* (Baltimore: Johns Hopkins University Press, 1997); Jeremy Black, *European Warfare, 1494–1660* (London: Routledge, 2002); Jan Glete, *Warfare at Sea, 1500–1650: Maritime Conflicts and the Transformation of Europe* (London: Routledge, 2002). The original essay positing a "military revolution" in the early modern period was by Michael Roberts. It is included in Clifford J. Rogers, ed., *The Military Revolution Debate: Readings on the Military Transformation of Early Modern Europe* (Boulder, CO: Westview Press, 1995). See also Jeremy Black, *A Military Revolution? Military Change and European Society, 1550–1800* (Basingstoke, UK: Macmillan, 1991), and Geoffrey Parker, *The Military Revolution: Military Innovation and the Rise of the West, 1500–1800*, 2nd edn (Cambridge: Cambridge University Press, 1996).

For discussions about the relationships between centralizing states and the nobility, see Samuel Clark, *State and Status: The Rise of the State and Aristocratic Power in Western Europe* (Toronto: McGill-Queen's University Press, 1995); Jonathan Dewald, *The European Nobility, 1400–1800* (Cambridge: Cambridge University Press, 1996); John Adamson, ed., *The Princely Courts of Europe: Ritual, Politics and Culture under the Ancien Régime, 1500–1750* (London: Weidenfeld and Nicolson, 1999); Hillay Zmora, *Monarchy, Aristocracy and the State in Europe, 1300–1800* (London: Routledge, 2001).

There are many discussions of the political histories of specific western European countries during this period. For England, see John Guy, *Tudor England* (Oxford: Oxford University Press, 1988); Steven Gunn, *Early Tudor Government, 1485–1558* (Basingstoke, UK: Macmillan, 1995); Susan Doran, *England and Europe in the Sixteenth Century* (Basingstoke, UK: Macmillan, 1998); Susan Brigden, *New Words, Lost Worlds: The Rule of the Tudors, 1485–1603* (London: Allen Lane, 2000). For Ireland, see Steven G. Ellis, *Ireland in the Age of the Tudors, 1447–1603: English Expansion and the End of Gaelic Rule* (London: Longman, 1998). For France, see James B. Collins, *The State in Early Modern France* (Cambridge: Cambridge University Press, 1995); Mack P. Holt, ed., *Renaissance and Reformation France* (Oxford: Oxford University Press, 2002). For Spain, see John H. Elliott, *Imperial Spain, 1469–1716* (London: Edward Arnold, 1963); John Lynch, *Spain under the Habsburgs*, 2 vols. (Oxford: Oxford University Press, 1991, 1992).

Interactions between Christians, Jews, and Muslims in Spain have been surveyed in Mark D. Meyerson and Edward D. English, eds., *Christians, Muslims, and Jews in Medieval and Early Modern Spain: Interaction and Cultural Change* (Notre Dame, IN: Notre Dame University Press, 1999) and Mary Elizabeth Perry, *The Handless Maiden: Moriscos and the Politics of Religion in Early Modern Spain* (Princeton: Princeton University Press, 2005). The role of the Spanish Inquisition in these, and in shaping Spanish society, has been discussed in William Monter, *Frontiers of Heresy: The Spanish Inquisition from the Basque Lands to Sicily* (Cambridge: Cambridge University Press, 1990); Henry Kamen, *The Spanish Inquisition: A Historical Revision* (New Haven: Yale University Press, 1997).

For political developments in central Europe, and particularly the role of the Habsburgs in these, see Helmut G. Koenigsberger, *The Habsburgs and Europe, 1516–1660* (Ithaca, NY: Cornell University Press, 1971); Michael Hughes, *Early Modern Germany, 1477–1806* (Basingstoke, UK: Macmillan, 1992); Andrew Wheatcroft, *The Habsburgs: Embodying Empire* (London: Viking, 1995); Peter H. Wilson, *The Holy Roman Empire,*

1495–1806 (London: St. Martin's, 1999). A new study in English on Poland is Daniel Stone, *The Polish-Lithuanian State, 1386–1795* (Seattle: University of Washington Press, 2001). For the Ottoman Empire, see Peter F. Sugar, *Southeastern Europe under Ottoman Rule, 1354–1804* (Seattle: University of Washington Press, 1977); Daniel Goffman, *The Ottoman Empire and Early Modern Europe* (Cambridge: Cambridge University Press, 2002); Colin Imber, *The Ottoman Empire, 1300–1650: The Structure of Power* (Basingstoke, UK: Macmillan, 2002).

For the Italian city states, see Dennis Romano, *Patricians and Popolani: The Social Foundations of the Venetian Renaissance State* (Baltimore: Johns Hopkins University Press, 1987); Richard Mackenney, *The City State, 1500–1700: Republican Liberty in an Age of Princely Power* (Basingstoke, UK: Macmillan Education, 1989); Philip Jones, *The Italian City-State: From Commune to Signoria* (Oxford: Clarendon Press, 1997); Thomas James Dandelet, *Spanish Rome, 1500–1700* (New Haven: Yale University Press, 2001). The classic study of the beginnings of diplomacy remains Garrett Mattingly, *Renaissance Diplomacy* (Boston: Houghton-Mifflin, 1955).

 For more suggestions and links see the companion website www.cambridge.org/wiesnerhanks.

Notes

1 Niccolò Machiavelli, *The Prince and the Discourses*, trans. Luigi Ricci, revised by E. R. P. Vincent (New York: Random House, 1950), p. 53.

2 Denys Hay, ed. and trans., *The Anglia Historia of Polydore Vergil, AD 1485–1537*, book 74 (London: Camden Society, 1950), p. 147.

3 Jacob Burckhardt, *The Civilization of the Renaissance in Italy*: vol. I (New York: Harper and Row, 1958), p. 22.

4 Benedict Anderson, *Imagined Communities: Reflections on the Origins and Spread of Nationalism*, rev. ed. (London and New York: Verso, 1991), p. 6.

4 Cultural and intellectual life, 1450–1600

Michelangelo's statue of the young king David as he prepares to fight the giant Goliath, commissioned by the city of Florence to celebrate one of the times that a republican government ousted the Medici family from power. It stood outdoors on the main city square from 1504 to 1873, when it was moved indoors to protect it from the weather, and became an iconic symbol of Renaissance artistic brilliance.

Timeline

1350s	Petrarch begins to teach in Florence
1430s	Donatello produces bronze free-standing statue of David
1450s	Johan Gutenberg invents printing press
1462	Marsilio Ficino establishes Platonic Academy in Florence
1503	Leonardo paints the *Mona Lisa*
1508–12	Michelangelo paints frescoes in the Sistine Chapel
1514–17	Scholars working in Spain produce the Complutensian Polyglot
1513	Niccolò Machiavelli writes *The Prince*
1516	Thomas More writes *Utopia*
1532	François Rabelais publishes the first part of *Gargantua and Pantagruel*
1550	Giorgio Vasari publishes *Lives of the Most Eminent Painters, Sculptors, and Architects*
1576	Jean Bodin publishes *The Six Books of the Republic*
1596	Shakespeare's *Romeo and Juliet* probably first performed
1605	Miguel de Cervantes publishes first part of *Don Quixote*

"THE great Ruler of Heaven looked down," wrote the Italian artist, architect, and author Giorgio Vasari (1511–74), and seeing "the presumptuous opinion of man more removed from truth than light from darkness, resolved ... to send to earth a genius universal in each art ... so that the world should marvel at the singular eminence of his life and works and all his actions, seeming rather divine than earthy."[1] In his *Lives of the Most Eminent Painters, Sculptors, and Architects*, a series of biographies of artists published in 1550, Vasari coins a word to describe the new types of art made by this singular genius – Michelangelo Buonarotti (1475–1564) – and other painters, sculptors and architects only slightly less talented: Renaissance (*rinascita* or "rebirth" in Italian). Writers and thinkers of the fourteenth and early fifteenth centuries such as Petrarch (1304–74) and Lorenzo Valla (1405–47) had already seen themselves as reinvigorators of the classical past, but Vasari thought that this rebirth had gone beyond

the original. "Many works today," he wrote, "are more perfect and better finished than were those of the great masters of the past."[2] Their creators were,
in Vasari's eyes, not simply skilled and highly trained artisans, but "rare men
of genius," who should sign and take full credit for their work. This notion of
the artist as creative genius did not apply to all branches of art, but to those in
Vasari's title – painting, sculpture and architecture – which were subsequently
dubbed the "major" arts. Other types of art, such as needlework, porcelain manufacture, goldsmithing, and furniture-making, were "minor arts," "decorative
arts," or "crafts," and the names of those who made them were not important.

Along with inventing the term "Renaissance," Vasari also influenced how we
understand other aspects of art and culture. He is often regarded as the first
art historian, and his categories continue to shape the way that art history is
taught and museums are arranged. Vasari's term "Renaissance" came to be used
for a whole era and not simply its art. Because it derived from broad cultural
changes and not specific events, the Renaissance happened at different times
in different parts of Europe. "Renaissance" is used to describe fifteenth-century
Italian paintings, sixteenth-century English literature, and seventeenth-century
Scandinavian architecture. As we discussed in the Introduction to this book,
some scholars see the Renaissance as the beginning of the "modern" era, while
others see it as a sort of transition between medieval and modern. Others
choose to limit the term only to art, and object to its being used more generally
because it is not a discrete period. Like "Europe," however, "Renaissance" is a
term that is too widely used to avoid, even if there is disagreement about its
limits.

Vasari's distinction between "art" (made by "rare men of genius") and "craft"
(made by everyone else) has been extended to other cultural realms in early
modern Europe: certain forms of writing, such as poetry, history, and epics,
came to be defined as "literature," while other types of writing, such as letters and diaries, were excluded from this category; certain forms of music
became "classical," while everything else was "popular" or "folk"; instruction
that occurred in institutional settings was "education," while that going on in
the family or workshop was "training" or "tradition." Scholars traced a growing split between professional and amateur, and, to a lesser degree, between
learned and popular culture. High culture and advanced intellectual accomplishments were urban, supported by wealthy elites, and done by individuals –
predominantly men – who had been formally trained or educated.

Research into all aspects of cultural life over the last several decades, however, has pointed out that the divisions between art and craft, learned and
popular, high and low, are more pronounced in hindsight than they were at
the time. Vasari may have prized painting, sculpture, and architecture, but
patrons carefully ordered and paid enormous amounts for candlesticks, silver and gold tableware, enameled or jewel-encrusted dishes, embroidered altar
cloths, enormous tapestries, and portrait medallions, along with paintings and
statues. Embroiderers as well as painters experimented with perspective, paid
greater attention to proportion, shadowing, and naturalistic representation,

and took their subjects from antiquity. Writers paid as much, or even more, attention to literary conventions in their letters than in their poetry or drama. Folk tales told orally for centuries became part of literary works in many countries, and people telling stories increasingly included those that someone had read in a book. Highly learned individuals participated in festivities involving all kinds of people that poked fun at their own intellectual pretensions and satirized other hierarchies of power and status. Educated individuals did form a community among themselves with concerns different from the vast majority of the population, but they also shared many values and traditions with their less-educated neighbors.

Schools and education

Social position, gender, geographic location, religion, and other factors all influenced one's chances of ever joining the community of scholars or artists, beginning with the very first steps, learning to read and write. It is often difficult to find much information about basic education, as children were taught by their own parents or by neighbors who could read, a process that left no trace in any record. Older women in many villages and towns ran small "cranny schools" which combined child care with teaching young children their letters and the recitation of Bible verses or psalms. Parish records from parts of France and England refer to village schools that taught reading, writing, singing the liturgy, and some arithmetic; in Italian cities, men taught middle- and working-class boys reading, writing, bookkeeping, and accounting in *abbaco* schools. Church ordinances in parts of Spain from the late fifteenth century ordered priests and sacristans to teach reading and writing, and fathers to send at least one son for such studies, but there are few records about how well these aims were realized. Jewish children learned the Hebrew letters and texts of basic prayers at home, and then might attend a school organized by the synagogue to study the Torah and other books of Hebrew Scripture in Hebrew and the vernacular. In the towns of the Ottoman Empire, schools established by private individuals or religious organizations taught boys, and occasionally girls, to read, write, and recite the Qur'an.

In the sixteenth century, Protestant reformers called for the opening of schools to teach reading in the vernacular and inculcate proper religious values, but this process proceeded more slowly than they hoped. There were over 100 different ordinances regulating the curriculum, hours, and structure of schools in the cities and states of Germany by 1600, but ordinances were often issued well before many schools were opened. By 1580, in the province of Electoral Saxony in central Germany, only 50 percent of the parishes had licensed German-language schools for boys, and 10 percent for girls; licenses to teach from England at about the same time indicate that some dioceses had English-language elementary schools in about half of their parishes. By 1675 in Electoral Saxony the numbers had increased to 94 percent for boys and 40 percent for girls. Those numbers are quite large, but it is important to remember that children did not attend such schools for the whole day, or for very long; boys often went for half a day for three or four years, and girls for an hour or so a day for one to two years. The level of literacy achieved was thus not very high. Though reformers regarded separate schools for girls and boys as the best organization, this was generally not feasible in smaller towns, and children attended mixed-sex schools. In larger towns and cities, girls and boys were separated, with the girls taught by female schoolmistresses and the boys by schoolmasters, both paid through a combination of student fees and salary; in Antwerp in 1576 there were seventy licensed schoolmistresses and eighty-eight schoolmasters. Boys who had mastered reading in the vernacular might start basic Latin training, while girls were taught sewing and embroidery; all children received a very heavy dose of religious instruction, with readings from religious texts, hymn-singing, worship services, and prayer part of the daily curriculum.

Catholic reformers also called for instruction in basic Christian doctrine, and informal catechism schools that taught reading and writing along with memorization developed in Italy and Spain; those for boys were taught by men and those for girls by women. Many of these met for only two hours on Sundays and religious holidays, but they were able to get across the basics of literacy to at least some of their pupils; in 1550 in the Spanish dioceses of Toledo and Cuenca, about half the men brought up for questioning before the Inquisition could read in Spanish. Some of these "colleges of children of the doctrine," as they were called in Spain, were specifically established for orphaned or poor boys, who were thought to be especially at risk of never learning proper religious or moral values.

Though we now teach reading and writing at the same time, during the early modern period children were taught to read before they were taught to write. In part this was a financial matter, as learning to read required fewer resources than learning to write – one slate or hornbook for teaching basic letters and a few psalters or saints' lives or parts of the Bible for mastering whole words and sentences, as compared to many slates and then paper and ink and pens for writing. In part this was also a philosophical issue, for political and religious authorities regarded the most important function of education as teaching children the ideas of others, not having them express their own.

The fact that people learned to read without learning to write makes measuring exact levels of literacy very difficult, for the ability to sign one's name is often taken as the basic indication of literacy. In East Anglia, in eastern England, for example, 49 percent of male tradesmen and craftsmen and 6 percent of women in the decade of the 1580s could sign their names, proportions that had only risen to 56 percent and 16 percent in the 1680s. From other types of sources, however, such as wills and the inventories taken at death, we know that the proportion of people who could read was much higher, but there is no way of arriving at exact figures. The safest generalization is that literacy levels were highest among the urban upper classes of northwestern Europe,

Fig. 10. A sign advertising the services offered by a schoolmaster in Basel, painted by
Ambrosius Holbein (c. 1494–1519), whose father and brother, both named Hans, were
well-known portraitists. Small schools like this were very common in German and Swiss cities;
the text at the top promises that the master will teach "young men and women honestly for a
reasonable price."

and lowest among the rural peasantry of south and east Europe, and that they
slowly increased from 1450 to 1750. By 1750 almost all upper-class men and
women could read, but still only a small minority of male or female peasants
could. The greatest gap between male and female literacy was in the middle
of the social scale; by 1750 in many cities of Europe the majority of male
artisans could both read and write, but their wives and sisters could not. Parish
registers, marriage contracts, and wills throughout the early modern period
generally reveal that about twice as many men as women from similar social
classes could sign their names, and that the women's signatures are more
poorly written than the men's, so that their names might have been the only
thing these women ever wrote.

Once a Christian boy had learned to read and write in the vernacular, or
even before that if his parents were wealthy and the opportunity was available,
he might be sent to a Latin grammar school, or to a college or academy that
offered many years of education. As noted in chapter 1, during the Middle Ages

secondary and higher education was largely controlled by the church, but by 1450 rulers and city governments had begun to support secular schools and academies. This process continued in the sixteenth century, with cities hiring and licensing schoolmasters and determining the subjects taught. Along with Latin grammar, rhetoric, and dialectic, boys might be offered Greek, natural philosophy, modern foreign languages, and arithmetic; some schools used medieval texts, while others adopted a more humanist curriculum centered on classical Latin works such as those of Cicero, Quintilian, Terence, and Julius Caesar. Grammar schools and colleges produced the literate notaries, secretaries, and officials needed by expanding national and local governments; they were supported by powerful patrons, who expected them to train their sons in moral values and civic leadership as well as in the more practical skills of rhetoric and mathematics.

Protestant reformers supported these Latin schools, and they became the training ground for pastors and other church officials. In England, Latin grammar schools were established with private and royal funding; historians estimate that there may have been as many as 400 grammar schools in England by 1500, and another 400 opened in the century after that. In Protestant parts of France and Switzerland, schools modeled on the college established in 1559 by the reformer John Calvin in Geneva taught the Geneva catechism along with Latin grammar. In Catholic areas the church often objected to municipal schools, and sometimes accused teachers of heresy, but in the early sixteenth century cities paid little attention to such charges. By the later sixteenth century, members of the new religious orders that began as part of the Catholic Reformation decided that the best way to shape education was not to protest municipal schools, but instead to staff them. Grammar and secondary schools in France, Spain, Poland, and other Catholic areas were increasingly staffed by Jesuits or members of other religious orders, who also opened their own colleges. By 1556, the Jesuits were running thirty-three colleges in seven European countries, and by 1600 there was a Jesuit college in nearly every city and town in Spain, which offered free instruction in Latin grammar, philosophy, theology, geography, religious doctrine, and history for boys. These trained clergy as well as laymen, for an important aim of Catholic reformers was improved clerical education. Several female orders, particularly the Angelicals and the Ursulines, ran schools for girls, though these were generally within convents after the middle of the sixteenth century, when the Council of Trent reinforced the requirement that all female religious be cloistered. In Protestant areas, education for girls beyond basic literacy in the vernacular was available only through private tutors.

Latin grammar schools and colleges were generally open only to Christians, with even converted Jews forbidden to teach in Spain in 1573. Jews in some areas established separate secondary schools for boys, which taught Latin and arithmetic as well as Hebrew and doctrine. Boys seeking more intensive religious training could attend a yeshiva, where they studied the Talmud and other texts; yeshiva studies often lasted many years, and centered on formal discussions and disputations. In the Ottoman Empire, as elsewhere in the Muslim world, colleges (*madrasas*) attached to mosques trained legal scholars, *muftis* (jurists who gave authoritative opinions – *fatwas* – on legal questions), and judges in Islamic law and tradition. Arabic was the language of religious law and Persian the language of elevated literature throughout the Muslim world, so that, as in Christian Europe, highly educated people across a wide area shared a common language. The most prestigious colleges, where professors received the highest salaries, were those established in Istanbul by Sultans Mehmed II and Süleyman I, whose graduates hoped for careers in the sultan's household or as military judges.

Universities offered the highest level of education in Christian Europe, and by the early sixteenth century there were over fifty universities in Europe; more were established in the century that followed as Christian national and territorial rulers, like the Ottoman sultans, increasingly saw a need for educated officials and regarded founding universities as part of a ruler's job. Italian universities, such as those at Bologna and Padua, focused on law and medicine, drawing students from all over Europe. Paris had the most renowned theological faculty. Students at Italian universities were generally young men who had already mastered Latin in an academy or college. Students at northern European universities such as Paris and Oxford included teenage boys studying for a bachelor's degree; they often lived in residential colleges endowed by private donors under the supervision of teachers with master's degrees. Paris and Salamanca were the largest universities in Europe, with thousands of students; most universities were much smaller, with several hundred students coming largely from the surrounding area and thirty or forty professors.

Though older faculty often fought change, during the sixteenth century most universities gradually adopted humanist curricula that emphasized original Latin, Greek, and Hebrew texts rather than relying solely on medieval commentaries. Humanist teachers of medicine added anatomy and the study of medicinal plants to the reading of classical texts by Hippocrates and Galen, which slowly changed medical practice. Humanist teachers of law, most prominently Andrea Alciati (1492–1550),

12 Royal proclamation about students' evening activities

Kings and other rulers who had established universities often took a keen interest in both the scholarly and extra-curricular life of students. King John III of Portugal issued the following proclamation regarding the University of Coimbra in 1539, writing to the university's rector, who was also a bishop:

Reverend Bishop, Rector, Friend: I, the King, send you many greetings. I have been informed that some students of that university, not respecting what amounts to the service of God and me and the honor of their persons, go about at night with weapons making music and other acts not very honest through that city, which results in scandals for its citizens and residents and little authority and honor to the university. And since I get grief from such things occurring, I order that you inform yourselves of this and reprehend those who do this according to the quality of the person. Have the bailiff of the university called and tell him on my behalf that he keep a watch for this and comply with my ordinances. And thus the ordinances that I have made about this, for [if] not done in this manner I will attend to the situation [so] that it is well as it pleases me. You [are to] write to me about what is happening in this situation, documented well. [June 20, 1539]

(Mário Brandão, ed., *Documentos de D. João III* (Coimbra: Universidade de Coimbra, 1937), vol. I p. 153, 153, trans. Darlene Abreu-Ferreira), in Monica Chojnacka and Merry Wiesner-Hanks, eds., *Ages of Woman, Ages of Man: Sources in European Social History 1400–1750* [London, Longman, 2002], p. 48. Reprinted by permission.)

 For additional chapter resources see the companion website www.cambridge.org/wiesnerhanks.

based their interpretation of Roman law on the text of the *Corpus juris civilis*, the legal code of the sixth-century Roman Emperor Justinian, rather than on medieval legal commentary. A reinvigorated Roman law gradually became the basis of municipal and national law codes in France and Germany, favored by humanist lawyers over older Frankish and Germanic law because it was more systematic and comprehensive. The *Carolina constitutio criminalis*, for example, a standardized code of criminal procedure drawn up for the Emperor Charles V in 1527, was gradually adopted in most of the territories of the Holy Roman Empire. In Spain, appointment to high administrative offices was limited to those who had studied law for at least ten years, which increasingly meant that officials had been exposed to humanist learning.

The Protestant and Catholic Reformations had disruptive effects on many European universities. Religious wars led some universities to close completely for years at a time, and the secular authorities who had jurisdiction over universities began to demand oaths of religious orthodoxy from students and teachers. Pope Pius IV required all professors and students seeking degrees at universities in Catholic territories to swear allegiance to Catholicism in 1564, and in the 1580s Elizabeth I similarly required faculty and students in England to swear to the Elizabethan Articles of Religion. She dismissed teachers suspected of Catholic or Puritan leanings, and even executed several teachers at Oxford for refusing to give up their Catholic beliefs. Thus, by 1600, though university education was still in Latin so that in theory scholars all across Europe could communicate with each other, religious differences had made scholarly contact, mobility, and exchange more difficult.

Political theory and humanist thought

Religious differences shaped not only the structures of learning and scholarship, but also the content of thought in the sixteenth century, which was influenced as well by the social and political changes we have traced in the previous two chapters. This can be seen most clearly in political theory, which is often conceptualized in response to actual political developments. Thus in the fourteenth century, after a series of confrontations between the popes and various rulers, most political theory was concerned with the proper relationship between church and state, with the balance shifting slowly toward those who viewed secular government as having more legitimate authority. Rulers were sanctioned by God, and their primary function was just like God's: to judge and protect those under their authority. In the early fifteenth century, scholars in Italian cities, which were often divided by political factions, taken over by home-grown or regional despots, and attacked by foreign armies, looked to the stability of Rome as a model state. Some of them, especially those influenced by the writings of Cicero, a first-century BCE Roman orator and opponent of Julius Caesar, argued that republicanism was the best form of government. Others used the model of Plato's philosopher-king in the *Republic* to argue that rule by an enlightened single individual might be best. Both sides agreed that educated men should be active in the political affairs of their city, a position historians have since termed "civic humanism."

The most famous (or infamous) civic humanist, and ultimately the best-known political theorist of this era was Niccolò Machiavelli. He was the secretary to one of the governing bodies in the city of Florence, responsible for diplomatic missions and organizing a citizen army. Power struggles in Florence between rival factions brought the Medici family back to power, and Machiavelli was arrested, tortured, and imprisoned on suspicion of plotting against them. He was released, but had no government position, and spent the rest of his life writing – political theory, poetry, prose works, plays, and a multi-volume history of Florence. The first work he finished – though it was not the first to be published – is his most famous, *The Prince*, which uses the example of contemporary rulers, especially the papal general Cesare Borgia (1475?–1507), to argue that the function of a ruler is to preserve order and security. Weakness would only lead to disorder, which might end in civil war or conquest by an outsider, clearly situations that were not conducive to any people's well-being. To preserve the state a ruler should use whatever means he needs – brutality, subterfuge, manipulation – but should not do anything that would make the populace turn against him; stealing or cruel actions done for a ruler's own pleasure would only lead to resentment and destroy the popular support needed for a strong, stable realm. "It is much safer for the prince to be feared than loved," Machiavelli advised, "but he ought to avoid making himself hated."[3] Effective rulers exhibited *virtù*, which is not virtue in the sense of moral goodness, but the ability to shape the world around them according to their will.

Cesare Borgia, Machiavelli's primary example, was the son of Rodrigo Borgia, a Spanish nobleman who became Pope Alexander VI (pontificate 1492–1503). Cesare Borgia combined his father's power and his own ruthlessness to build up a state in

13 Was Machiavelli Machiavellian?

Within forty years of Machiavelli's death, the word "Machiavellian" was applied to individuals judged to be unscrupulous in their methods of achieving a goal, and it continues to be a term of criticism today. In psychology, "Machiavellian intelligence" is used to describe social skills that involve deception and the ability to use cunning to form coalitions. In the seventeenth century, even his first name became a synonym for the Devil, "Old Nick." Why has Machiavelli been viewed so harshly?

Medieval political philosophers debated the proper relationship between church and state, but regarded the standards by which all governments were to be judged as emanating from moral principles established by God. Machiavelli argued that governments should instead be judged by how well they provided security, order, and safety to their populace. A ruler's moral code in maintaining these was not the same as a private individual's, for a leader could – indeed, should – use any means necessary. This more pragmatic view of the purposes of government, and Machiavelli's discussion of the role of force and cruelty, was unacceptable to many.

The fact that Machiavelli was Italian also became mixed in with these judgments. By the sixteenth century, Italian merchants were often resented in the same way that Jews had been earlier, being regarded as unprincipled and avaricious. Diplomacy was a new Italian invention, viewed by many as centered on the clever use of flattery and deception. Italians served as diplomats and advisors to rulers all over Europe, but they were frequently accused of secret dealings and plots, which at times escalated into anti-Italian hysteria. The Italian advisor of Mary Queen of Scots, for example, was stabbed to death by Protestant nobles in 1566.

Not everyone agreed with this negative view. Francis Bacon, the English scientist and politician, praised Machiavelli for just what others found so distasteful. "We are much beholden to Machivel and others," he wrote in *The Advancement of Learning* (1605), "that they write what men do, and not what they ought to do" (bk II, xxi, 9). He quickly added, "All good moral philosophy is but the handmaid to religion" (bk II, xxii, 14), but this comment may have been motivated by "Machiavellian" expediency more than real sentiment.

central Italy. He made good use of new military equipment and tactics, hiring Leonardo da Vinci (1452–1519) as a military engineer, and murdered his political enemies, including one of the husbands of his sister, Lucrezia. Despite his efforts, his state fell apart after his father's death, which Machiavelli ascribed not to some weakness, but to the operations of fate (*fortuna* in Italian), whose power even the best-prepared and most merciless ruler, the one with *virtù*, could not fully escape, though he might try.

Fortuna was personified and portrayed as a goddess in ancient Rome and Renaissance Italy, and Machiavelli's last words about fortune are expressed in gendered terms: "It is better to be impetuous than cautious, for fortune is a woman, and if one wishes to keep her down, it is necessary to beat her and knock her down."[4] Fate presented a new – and, given Machiavelli's words, one might even say ironic – challenge to both ruling houses and political theorists in the sixteenth century. Though Machiavelli mentions only male rulers by name, and *virtù* is linked conceptually and linguistically with *vir* (man in Latin), dynastic accidents in many areas led to women serving as advisors to child kings or ruling in their own right – Isabella in Castile, Mary and Elizabeth Tudor in England, Anne in Brittany, Mary Stuart in Scotland, Mary of Guise, Catherine de' Medici and Anne of Austria in France. Theorists vigorously and at times viciously disputed whether this was appropriate: could a woman's being born into a royal family and educated to rule allow her to overcome the limitations of her sex and become a successful ruler? Should it? Or, stated another way: which was (or should be) the stronger determinant of character and social role, gender or rank?

The most extreme opponents of female rule were Protestants who went into exile on the continent during the reign of Mary Tudor, of which the Scottish reformer John Knox is the best known. In his *The First Blast of the Trumpet Against the Monstrous Regiment of Women* (1558), Knox compared Mary Tudor and Mary Stuart with Jezebel, arguing that female rule was unnatural, unlawful, monstrous, and contrary to Scripture; being female was a condition that could never be overcome, and subjects of female rulers needed no other justification for rebelling than their monarch's sex. Knox's work was published just as Elizabeth assumed the throne, however, and a number of courtiers, including Thomas Smith and John Aylmer, realized that defenses of female rule would be likely to help them win favor in Elizabeth's eyes, and they advanced arguments against viewing a woman's sex as an absolute block to rulership.

Jean Bodin (1530?–96), the French jurist and political theorist, returned to Scripture and natural law in his opposition to female rule in *The Six Books of the Republic* (1576), but also stressed what would become in the seventeenth century the most frequently cited reason against it: that the state was like a household, and just as in a household the husband/father has authority and power over all others, so in the state a male monarch should always rule. Robert Filmer carried this even further in *Patriarchia*, asserting that rulers derived all legal authority from the divinely sanctioned fatherly power of Adam, just as did all fathers. Male monarchs used husbandly and paternal imagery to justify their assertion of power over their subjects, as in James I's statements to Parliament: "I am the Husband, and the whole Isle is my lawfull Wife … By the law of nature the king becomes a natural father to all his lieges at his coronation … A King is trewly *Parens patriae*, the politique father of his people."[5]

Bodin's arguments in favor of male rule were shaped not only by the reality of female monarchs, but also by the religious wars in France during the 1560s and 1570s. (For more information about these, see chapter 5.) Catholics and Protestants (called Huguenots) engaged in military campaigns, plotted and carried out assassinations, and sometimes massacred adherents of the other confession; the most brutal of these was the St. Bartholomew's Day Massacre in 1572, in which royal troops and Catholic mobs killed thousands of Huguenots, first in Paris and then in other French cities, often mutilating the corpses afterwards. There is sharp debate among historians about exactly who planned these killings, but after they were over the king admitted that he ordered at least some of them, and those doing the killing clearly believed they were doing the king's will. In response, Protestant writers began to argue that the power of a monarch should be limited, and that when a ruler became a tyrant, the people – or at least those people who otherwise had some authority, such as office-holders or representative groups – had the right, or even the duty, to rebel. The most influential of these works was the anonymous *Defense of Liberty Against Tyrants* (1579), probably written by the Huguenot nobleman Philippe Duplessis de Mornay.

Bodin's *Six Books of the Republic* was an answer to this resistance theory. For Bodin, all political authority came from God, and kings were answerable to God alone; husband/fathers had absolute authority in their households, but this never gave them the right to resist, or even question, the actions of a divinely ordained monarch. To do so would lead to anarchy, which was worse than the worst tyranny. Bodin's opinions were not shared by all Catholics, however. Radical Catholics later wrote their own resistance propaganda, which actually authorized the regicide of a ruler judged to be ungodly. Resistance theory on both sides was often written in very inflammatory language and published in pamphlet form, so that it was widely read.

Along with influencing political theory, war shaped thinking and scholarship in other significant ways. Humanists in Florence at the end of the fourteenth century had become interested in Greek philosophy and literature along with Roman when Coluccio Salutati, the chancellor of the Florentine republic, convinced the city to hire Manuel Chrysoloras, the most eminent Byzantine scholar of classical Greek. The conquest of Constantinople by the Turks in 1453 brought other Greek-speaking scholars, such as Johannes Argyropoulos (1410–87) westward. Florentine intellectuals, most prominently Marsilio Ficino (1433–99) became increasingly interested in the ideas of Plato. Under the patronage of Cosimo de' Medici (1389–1464), the most powerful man in Florence, Ficino began to lecture to an informal group of Florence's cultural elite – this became known as the Platonic Academy, but it was not really a school – and translated Plato's dialogues into Latin. Angelo Poliziano (1454–1494), a tutor in the household of Lorenzo de' Medici (1449–92), Cosimo's grandson, translated Homer into Latin, and developed methods of textual criticism relying on comparisons of manuscripts and a search for the oldest among them that are still used today. Through these translations, Greek learning became available to a much wider western European audience.

Ficino, who would eventually become an ordained priest, regarded Plato as a divinely inspired precursor to Christ, and attempted to synthesize Christian and Platonic teachings. Plato's emphasis on the spiritual and eternal over the material and transient fitted well with Christian teachings about the immortality of the soul. Platonic ideas about love – that the highest form of love was spiritual desire for pure, perfect beauty uncorrupted by bodily desires – could easily be interpreted as Christian desire for the perfection of God. Ficino and his most brilliant student, Pico della Mirandola (1463–94), found such ideas not only in Christian and Platonic writers, but also in works they regarded as even more ancient, such as Hebrew mystical texts called the Cabala, metaphysical and astrological works attributed to the shadowy ancient writer Hermes Trismegistus (called Hermetic texts), and number mysticism from the pre-Platonic Greek philosopher Pythagoras. Ficino and Pico understood all these texts to be teaching the same truth: that the universe was a hierarchy of beings from God down through spiritual beings to material beings. For Ficino humanity was the crucial link right in the middle, for humanity was both material and spiritual, body and soul; humans themselves were also arranged in a hierarchy, from the rational and spiritual elite who can understand complex philosophy to the unlearned masses. For Pico, humanity was even more important; as he explains in the brief treatise, *Oration on the Dignity of Man* (1496), man is the one part of the created world that has no fixed place, but can freely choose whether to rise to the realm of the angels or descend to the realm of the animals. It is unclear in Pico's treatise exactly how this fits with Christian teachings about the importance of Christ in human salvation (and unclear exactly how women fit into his understanding of "man"), but for Ficino and the rest of the Florentine Platonists, this glorification of human nature had a clear scriptural base, for the Bible taught that fashioning humans was God's final act in creation, and implied that God regarded them as worth redeeming.

Ficino's Platonized Christianity emphasized spiritual contemplation and study more than active involvement in the world, which many historians see as a turning away from the ideals of civic humanism. This happened at roughly the same time as the French and Spanish campaigns in Italy, which began in 1494, a period in which courts revolving around powerful noblemen were also becoming the most important cultural centers. These military and political developments did not cause the new interest in Platonic thought, but Ficino's emphasis on the superiority of an elite fitted well with the new rulers' concepts of themselves, particularly in combination with Machiavelli's notion of *virtù*, though these were based on diametrically opposite views of human nature. Setting a pattern later emulated by rulers of nation-states, Italian noble rulers hired humanist scholars, along with poets, artists, and musicians, to glorify themselves and their families, making patronage of the arts and scholarship an expected part of governing a territory.

Italy had been a destination for religious pilgrims, merchants, and university students for centuries; the Florentine Academy, other humanist schools, and sophisticated noble courts drew young men to Italy from all over Europe, with the French and Spanish military campaigns bringing in still more foreigners. At the same time, Italians trained as humanists traveled beyond the Alps as teachers, diplomats, canon lawyers, merchants, and writers; Aeneas Sylvius Piccolomini, for example, traveled widely in central and eastern Europe as a papal ambassador before he became Pope Pius II (pontificate 1458–64). The historian Polydore Vergil, the scholar and theologian Peter Martyr Vermigli (1499–1562), and the artist and engineer Leonardo da Vinci lived for several years in northern Europe. These kinds of links, combined with the printing of humanist texts, carried humanist ideas and institutions of learning beyond Italy.

Humanist scholars gained influence as the headmasters of Latin grammar schools and professors of Latin grammar, rhetoric, and dialectic in many universities, but even more through a growing interest in their ideas and writings within the social elites in larger cities and at royal or noble courts. Johann Reuchlin (1455–1519), for example, who had studied in France, the Empire, Switzerland, and Italy, became a legal counselor and judge for several different German states. Conrad Celtis (1459–1508) was crowned the poet laureate by the German emperor and gained imperial patronage to open a humanist academy in Vienna; Celtis also organized humanist discussion groups – called "sodalities" – among young middle-class men in German cities such as Heidelberg and Ingolstadt, which became a network through which ideas and cultural patterns were spread. In France, Jacques Lefèvre d'Etaples (1460–1536) was the tutor to King Francis I's children, and at the end of his life lived with a group of his followers at the court of Marguerite d'Angoulême, Francis's sister. In England, Thomas Linacre (1460–1524) became the physician to King Henry VIII and the tutor to his children, and in 1518 he founded the Royal College of Physicians. In Spain, Antonio de Nebrija (1444–1522) became a historian to the royal crown and the head of a team at the new university of Alcalá producing a multi-language edition of the Bible (the Complutensian Polyglot) under the patronage of Cardinal Francisco Jiménez de Cisneros (1436–1517), the head of the church in Spain. All of these men had studied and traveled in Italy, sometimes as students at Italian universities and sometimes simply as guests of Italian scholars.

Scholars and thinkers from outside of Italy often shared the ideas of Ficino and Pico about the wisdom of ancient texts. Reuchlin mastered Hebrew through study with several Jewish scholars because of his interest in the Jewish Cabala, and late in his life he defended the reading and ownership of Hebrew books in a controversy that grew to involve both the emperor and the pope. Lefèvre turned his attention first to a better translation of Aristotle, and then to publication of the works of various medieval mystics, such as Ramon Lull and Hildegard of Bingen, and other writers whom he thought had lived in the first centuries of Christianity. Cisneros bought and borrowed the oldest texts he could find for the Complutensian Polyglot, which ultimately included a Hebrew grammar and dictionary along with the biblical texts.

By the early sixteenth century, humanism outside of Italy had developed to the point that a long period of Italian study and travel was no longer essential. The Dutch humanist Desiderius Erasmus (1467?–1536), the most famous scholar of his time in all of Europe, did not go to Italy until he was nearly forty. He then spent his time primarily at the print-shop of the Venetian printer / publisher Aldus Manutius (1449–1515), working alongside other scholars as he collected Greek and Latin sayings for his *Adages*. This work presented and explained over 3,000 classical sayings, serving as a guide to classical learning and a source of appropriate quotations for centuries. Sir (and later St.) Thomas More (1478–1535), the most famous English humanist, learned his Greek and Latin in England, and never even traveled to Italy. More was a lawyer who held a number of positions in the City of London and at court before his surprise elevation to the most senior legal position in the land – that of Lord Chancellor – in 1529. He was in touch with Europe's leading humanists and many of his Latin compositions and translations were read across the continent. He is most famous for his controversial dialogue *Utopia* (1516). *Utopia*, a word More invented from the Greek words for "no – where," describes a state somewhere beyond Europe in which problems that plagued More's fellow citizens, such as poverty and hunger, have been solved by a beneficent government, but in which dissent and disagreement are not tolerated. Whether this followed in the humanist tradition of satire or represented More's own views was unclear to his contemporaries, and has been a matter of scholarly debate ever since.

More and Erasmus typify another aspect of humanism in the early sixteenth century – its increasing concern with reforming the Christian church. Though Italian humanists such as Ficino had been interested in Christian texts and ideas, they were not interested in the church as an institution or in the beliefs of ordinary Christians. More, Erasmus, the French scholar Lefèvre d'Etaples, the Spanish theologian Juan de Valdés (1500–1541), the Spanish educator Juan Luis Vives (1492–1540), the German knight and satirist Ulrich von Hutten (1488–1523), and eventually many others were, for they regarded humanist learning as a way to bring about reform in the church and a deepening of people's spiritual lives, both of which they regarded as essential. They connected humanism with the movement for reform of the church that was already going on, using textual analysis of Scripture and the writings of the church fathers such as St. Ambrose, St. Jerome, and St. Augustine to criticize many practices of the contemporary church.

This movement of "Christian humanism," as it has since been termed, is most associated with Erasmus, who published a new Latin translation of the New Testament alongside the first printed Greek text in 1516, a six-volume edition of the works of St. Jerome, and many other scholarly works on biblical texts. Erasmus also wrote a number of works which became popular with the growing number of middle-class readers – the *Enchiridion* (1501), a guide to

Christian living that focuses on inner, spiritual experience; *The Praise of Folly* (1511), a witty satire poking fun at political, social, and especially religious institutions; and the *Colloquies* (1518), a series of dialogues that became the most popular textbook of Latin conversation in grammar schools. In his scholarly and popular writings, and in the hundreds of letters he sent to scholars, friends, rulers, and admirers around Europe, Erasmus accused the church of greed, corruption, and desire for power, and called for a renaissance of the ideals of the early church to accompany the renaissance of classical learning already going on. This renewal would be based on what Erasmus termed his "philosophy of Christ," which emphasized inner spirituality and personal morality rather than scholastic theology or outward observances of piety such as pilgrimages or venerating religious relics: objects associated with saints and other holy individuals, such as bones or clothing, thought to have special powers. On the latter issue, Erasmus is reported to have commented that it was unfortunate there were only twelve apostles, because fourteen of them were buried in Germany.

The movement of Christian humanism is one important root of the Protestant Reformation. A popular saying of the time was "Erasmus laid the egg that Luther hatched" though Erasmus himself denied this,

14 Erasmus, *The Praise of Folly* (1511)

Erasmus dedicated his satire to his close friend Thomas More, and its Latin title *Moriae Encomium* can also mean "In Praise of More." The main text is "an oration of feigned matter spoken by Folly in her own person." Folly is a demi-goddess – like Justice – who argues that everything in life comes from her; her speech includes both silly comments and biting criticism.

What is more sweet or more precious than life? And yet from whom can it more properly be said to have come than from me? . . . What man is it that would submit his neck to the noose of wedlock, if, as wise men should, he should first truly weigh the inconvenience of the thing? Or what woman is there would ever go to it did she seriously consider either the peril of child-bearing or the trouble of bringing them up? . . . Is not war the very root and matter of all famed enterprises? And yet what more foolish than to undertake it for I know not what trifle, especially when both parties are sure to lose more than they get in the bargain? . . . But to speak of the arts, what set men's wits on work to invent and transmit to posterity so many famous, as they conceive, pieces of learning but the thirst of glory? With so much loss of sleep, such pains and travail, have the most foolish of men thought to purchase themselves a kind of I know not what fame, than which nothing can be more vain . . . Next come those that commonly call themselves the religious and monks, most false in both titles, when a great part of them are farthest from religion . . . [And] as if the church had any deadlier enemies than wicked prelates [high officials such as bishops], who not only suffer Christ to run out of request for want of preaching him, but hinder his spreading by their multitudes of laws merely contrived for their own profit, corrupt him by their forced expositions, and murder him by the evil example of their pestilent life.

(Erasmus, *The Praise of Folly*, trans. John Wilson [1668] [Ann Arbor: University of Michigan Press, 1958], pp. 15, 16, 35, 41, 101–2, 119.)

despaired at the religious divisions the Reformation created, and first privately and then openly broke with Martin Luther. Many other Christian humanists also refused to become Protestants. The Reformation (which will be discussed in chapter 5) has traditionally been viewed as the end of humanism, as it initially made moderate reform programs coming from within the church hierarchy more difficult and restricted lines of communication among scholars. Some of the reform measures advocated by humanists were later taken up as part of the Catholic Reformation, however, so that Christian humanism can actually be seen as a root of both the Protestant and Catholic Reformations.

Other aspects of humanism also continued in the later sixteenth century. Whether Protestant or Catholic, schools from grammar schools to universities continued to emphasize classical languages, with Greek and Hebrew added to Latin as standard parts of advanced training. Government officials, courtiers, and noble gentlemen were expected to have at least a basic knowledge of Latin, and middle-class parents increasingly recognized that humanist training might open doors to advancement for their sons. Even those who did not have a classical education had increasing access to the most important Latin and Greek works through vernacular translations; by the end of the sixteenth century translations of Aristotle, Thucydides, Cicero, Livy, Ovid, and many others authors were available in Italian, French, Spanish, English, and German. Original works of vernacular literature drew on the stories and themes of the classical past as well, adapting and retelling them orally as songs and plays as well as in print. Humanists since Petrarch had, in fact, written all kinds of popular vernacular literature alongside their classical scholarship, which were often – sometimes to the dismay of their authors – much more popular than their scholarly works.

Vernacular literature and drama

Both the expansion of education and the religious controversies of the sixteenth century created a larger and more avid reading public for vernacular works, and enterprising authors and publishers responded. As discussed in the introduction, the best-selling works between the invention of the printing press and 1700 were religious; between 1518 and 1525, one-third of *all* books printed in German were by Luther. Printed religious works varied from expensive leather-bound Bibles to eight-page pamphlets or chapbooks with paper covers, or even single-sheet broadsides, usually illustrated and often scandalous, scurrilous, or gory. The same qualities could be found in other popular non-fiction printed works, such as travel literature, accounts of recent events, or biographies, though how-to manuals also sold very well. Baldassar Castiglione's *The Book of the Courtier* (1508–16), which sets out proper behavior for courtiers and court ladies (or those aspiring to such positions), sold very well in its original Italian, and was translated into Spanish, French, English, German, and Polish. The personal qualities Castiglione praises – reserve, discretion, good manners, solidity, and learning worn lightly for men, and purity, modesty, beauty, agreeableness, and affability for women – became ideals for people much further down the social scale than his original audience.

Both middle-class people and courtiers read poetry and prose fiction along with religious works and instruction manuals, and some of them tried their hand at writing these as well. A circle of poets grew up at the court of Lorenzo de' Medici in Florence, who patronized writing in Italian as well as humanist scholarship in Latin. Lorenzo himself wrote love lyrics, sonnets, pastorals, odes, and carnival songs, many of them meditations on nature or on the fleetingness of human life: "Fair is youth and void of sorrow;/But it hourly flies away./Youths and maids, enjoy today;/Nought ye know about tomorrow." His circle included the young artist Michelangelo and the humanist Poliziano, all of them influenced by Platonic concepts of beauty and love. Humanist sodalities or similar groups in other European cities offered people an opportunity to discuss and share works written in the vernacular as well as Latin; though most of these groups were made up only of men, because they were less formal than universities or academies, women sometimes participated. In Poitiers in France, for example, Madeleine and Catherine des Roches (1520–87 and 1542–87), a mother and daughter, shared their poetry with a humanist circle. Members of such groups read their works aloud or circulated them in manuscript, and often never published them. Thus even at this elite social and educational level, older forms of cultural transmission continued.

Italian was the first modern European language to be transformed into a literary language, a process that began with Dante Alighieri's (1265–1321) decision to write the Divine Comedy in his northern Italian Tuscan dialect instead of Latin. The sonnets of Petrarch and the prose fiction of Giovanni Boccaccio (1313–75) further solidified this language as "Italian," with authors from elsewhere in Italy, such as the Venetian poet and church official Pietro Bembo (1470–1547), adopting and defending it.

The epics, romances, and lyric poetry of medieval troubadours laid the foundations of modern French, and by the sixteenth century authors such as Marguerite d'Angoulême were combining chivalric themes with Platonic and Christian ideals; her *Heptameron*, a collection of seventy-three lively stories about people from all walks of life published shortly after her death, was extremely popular in France and was quickly translated into English. A circle of seven poets at the French court under the leadership of Pierre de Ronsard (1524?–85) defended the use of French as a literary medium, writing in what they saw as a new style that combined classical, Italian, and French forms. They dubbed themselves the *Pléiade*, taken from a Greek word for a group of seven, used to describe seven poets in ancient Alexandria, and the seven daughters of the mythical figure Atlas, who were said to have eventually become a constellation of seven stars.

Other authors whose works were widely read frequently drew on medieval romances and epics as well as classical traditions. Several writers in sixteenth-century Italy, for example, retold the story of the Frankish knight Roland (Orlando in Italian), though *Orlando furioso* (1515) by Ludovico Ariosto (1474–1533), a poet at the court of the Este family in Ferrara, may have been mocking epics more than emulating them. Orlando goes mad when the young woman he is pursuing falls in love with someone else, but his wits are restored to him by another knight who travels to the moon to retrieve them. In France, the former friar and physician François Rabelais (1483–1553), adapted bawdy stories about the giant Gargantua and his son Pantagruel that had been told orally for centuries and printed in cheap chapbooks. Rabelais' novels – which eventually grew to five volumes – show the two giants living life to its fullest, whether in terms of learning, drinking, eating, or sex; along with contemptuous satire and vulgar humor, they have serious discussions of politics, philosophy, religion, and education. This combination got Rabelais into trouble with theologians at the University of Paris, but he was shielded from serious consequences by the patronage of church officials and members of the royal family, including Marguerite d'Angoulême.

Many of the scenes in *Orlando furioso* or *Gargantua and Pantagruel* would have fitted very well into *Don Quixote* (1605; Part II, 1615), the major work of Miguel de Cervantes (1547–1616), and often regarded as the greatest masterpiece in Spanish literature. Cervantes studied in Italy, fought and was wounded in the Battle of Lepanto, was captured by pirates, was sold as a slave, and was eventually ransomed at a price that would ruin his family. He wrote romances, more than twenty plays, only two of which survive, and toward the end of his life *Don Quixote*, which tells the story of the country gentleman Don Quixote and his faithful squire Sancho Panza, whose encounters with every kind of person in Spanish society are shaped by Don Quixote's often misguided idealism. Cervantes wrote in Castilian, the language of central Spain, which became literary "Spanish." The era in which he wrote is often called the "Golden Age" by Spanish literary scholars, who base their judgment on the works of many other authors besides Cervantes, especially the prolific playwright Félix Lope de Vega (1562–1635), whose roughly, 1800 plays – 500 of them extant – include tragedies, historical drama, romances, comic love intrigues, and plays that blend all of these.

Lope de Vega's plays were staged for all types of audiences; court performances could be very elaborate, with expensive costumes and complex stage settings, while public performances were much simpler. The same was true for drama elsewhere in Europe, which provided the best way for people who could not read to experience and create vernacular literature. All sorts of plays were put on as part of church holidays or city festivals, by local groups or traveling companies of players. Mystery plays depicted biblical episodes, miracle plays told stories from the lives of the saints, and morality plays presented religious and moral allegories, with comic or satiric interludes often interspersed between the acts of these more serious plays. Towns or groups within towns – either craft guilds or specifically organized dramatic societies called "abbeys" or "chambers of rhetoric" – competed with one another to write and put on the best play. Itinerant performers used puppets, trained animals, and acrobatic tricks to attract viewers, and sometimes included tooth-pulling and selling medicines as part of their entertainment. In the Ottoman Empire, artisans' guilds and the sultan sponsored festivals that included acrobats, fireworks, mock battles, and the staging of scenes of workshops, fortresses, and mosques.

Humanist scholars rediscovered the works of Greek and Latin playwrights, and wrote tragedies in Latin and comedies in the vernacular based on these. One of the most popular of the latter was Machiavelli's *Mandragola* (1524), in which he wove the themes of fortune and nature into a story involving a young woman, her young lover, her old husband, her scheming mother, her wily priest, and a love potion made out of a mandrake root. Most imitations of classical drama were tediously boring, however, and people preferred instead to attend performances of traveling Commedia dell'Arte troupes, in which actors and actresses dressed up as certain stock characters – Harlequin, the trickster servant, Pulchinello, the lecherous old hunchback, Scaramouche, the swaggering soldier, Columbine, the witty and mischievous maid, and Pantalone, the miserly merchant. Dialogue in Commedia dell'Arte plays was improvised, gestures were exaggerated, and comedy was slapstick – a word that comes from the stick or bat carried by Harlequin – all of which made the plays easy to understand and fun to watch. Playwrights such as Lope de Vega incorporated characters based on Commedia dell'Arte types into their plays as side characters, where they provided commentary and subplots that enhanced the central story.

Plays of all types were also very popular in England, where writing in the vernacular had developed out of the dialect spoken in the city of London and the nearby royal court of Westminster. Before the Hundred Years War, English kings and nobles, many of them descendants of Normans, had spoken French, but the war made the use of English a matter of national pride. The writings of Geoffrey Chaucer (1343–1400), a diplomat and royal official, especially his *Canterbury Tales*, solidified this language while still incorporating classical models, just as Petrarch and Boccaccio had done in Italian. Later English poets such as Edmund Spenser (1552–99) and Sir Philip Sidney (1554–86) built on this base, composing in English but blending in classical structures, conventions, and philosophical concerns, and often using verse forms derived from Italian, such as the sonnet. Christopher Marlowe (1564–93) began to use blank (unrhymed) verse for his plays as well as his poems, often centering the plot around a figure whose life is destroyed by an aspect of his own character, such as passion or ambition. Marlowe's plays are filled with violence, bloodshed, and brutality, making them popular with London audiences, who regularly filled the increasing numbers of public theatres that staged plays.

Those theatres also staged the plays of William Shakespeare (1564–1616), who is often simply described as "the greatest playwright who ever lived"; Shakespeare dominates English literature in a way that no single writer dominates any other European literature, not even Dante or Lope de Vega with his 1,800 plays. Shakespeare came from a middle-class background in a medium-sized town, probably attended a Latin grammar school, but had no further formal education. He married and had three children, then went to London, where he became an actor and playwright for the Lord Chamberlain's Men, a company of professional actors. He later became the part owner of several London theatres, and spent most of the rest of his life in London, writing plays and apparently taking minor roles in them. Shakespeare's talent was so great that some people have doubted whether someone from such a middling background could actually have written the plays, but his use of classical and historical sources, and of both medieval and humanist forms of language, demonstrate how widely humanist education had spread.

Literary critics generally approach Shakespeare's plays as texts, but his contemporaries watched them as performances, so that their impact went far beyond London's literate minority. Assessing that impact – or that of any play

15 Cross-dressing and gender-blending on the Elizabethan stage

Many of the plays written for the early modern English stage include cross-dressed characters, including nine of Shakespeare's surviving thirty-eight plays. In many ways every professional production involved cross-dressing, however, because all the female characters on the English professional stage were played by male actors until 1660. Some of these were boys apprenticed to mature actors whose voices had not changed, while others were young men who specialized in women's roles, playing them into their thirties.

Why did the English professional theatre companies not hire women? The answer used to be "tradition," but women performed in guild and village plays, in traveling troupes of musicians and actors, and in masques, which were dramatic court entertainments with lavish costumes and special effects. Women were common in French and Italian companies, which occasionally performed in London with their female actors. Recent explanations have included the strong anti-theatrical prejudice in England, cultural taboos about women's public speech, the desire of the relatively new professional companies to distinguish themselves from amateur village productions, and the attempt to appeal to a range of sexual orientations in the audience by presenting attractive women who were actually boys.

Whatever the reasons – and Shakespeare scholars do not agree – playwrights added to the complexity by having female characters dress as men, and then comment on their layered and ambiguous gender identity. At the end of Shakespeare's *As You Like It*, Rosalind (who has been dressed as a boy for much of the play) comes out in women's clothing and says, "It is not the fashion to see the lady in the epilogue," but only a few lines later says to the audience, "If I were a woman I would kiss as many of you as had beards that pleased me."

Elizabethan audiences appear to have accepted this practice easily, and delighted in extended dialogues filled with double-entendres about beards, swords, and other aspects of manhood. They did not expect realism in theatre, where all performers were pretending to be what they were not, a "counterfeiting" that was one of the main reasons moralists objected to theatre. Lower-class actors dressed as lords were also cross-dressing, blurring distinctions of social status that were seen as even more natural than those of gender.

or literary work that might have been shared orally – is difficult, however, as there are very few sources that provide evidence about the cultural life of people who could not read and write. We know from a variety of sources that people often told stories to one another while they were working, or in the evenings sitting in a tavern or at home around a fire. They certainly talked about the day's events, people they knew, and other aspects of village life, but they also told stories, recited poems, and sang ballads about famous people, mythological creatures, and amazing heroes. Such "fairy tales" were first written down in the seventeenth century by the French poet Charles Perrault (1628–1703), and later by the Grimm brothers, but it is clear they circulated long before that.

Some oral traditions, such as stories about Christian or Muslim saints or the knights of King Arthur, were widely shared among many types of people, but others were specific to certain population groups and served as markers of membership in that subculture. Sailors, for example, developed rituals blessing ships or marking a man's first passage across a particular geographic point, and rhythmic shanties that made certain tasks, such as raising the anchor, easier. Miners built chapels dedicated to their own patron saints – such as St. Anne, the mother of the Virgin Mary, who, like the earth the miners dug, held a treasure inside her – put on plays on the days honoring those saints, and told stories about the spirits of the mines who might reveal hidden riches. Journeymen who traveled in search of work took songs and poems with them, and developed naming rituals for new members of their group similar to baptisms. Village women gathered together to spin and tell stories in *veillées* in France or *Spinnstuben* in Germany, and women in Serbia and Galicia – and elsewhere – had their own work songs. Beggars, thieves, and other criminals developed their own slang terms and initiation rites, creating a "counter-culture" that writers often included – in embellished and romanticized form – in their plays and stories.

Music and art

Oral culture involved music along with the spoken word. Plays included music, particularly as interludes called *intermedi* between scenes, while fairs, market places, and inns provided a place to both listen and perform. Shepherds made and then played bagpipes and flutes as they watched their flocks; street singers accompanied themselves on hurdy-gurdies, fiddles, guitars, or harps, and then sold copies of their ballads; court musicians provided music for banquets and dances; monks and nuns chanted eight services (called the Divine Office) daily. Village families sometimes sang as they worked or as they came together at night around the hearth-fire; wealthier urban and aristocratic families sang or played instruments together, and courtiers sang or played accompaniments on a lute. Writers sometimes worried about women using music to lure men into the dangers of love, but by the end of the sixteenth century singing and playing an instrument, especially the lute or the harpsichord, was seen as an "accomplishment" appropriate for a middle- or upper-class young lady. Although by the later sixteenth century amateur performers sometimes used printed music, including special tablecloths with the music for each vocal part or instrument printed separately around the edge, most of this music was transmitted orally, with players improvising on pieces they had learned.

Alongside this amateur music, nobles and church officials hired professional musicians and composers, both for special occasions such as weddings or processions and as permanent staff. Josquin des Prez (*c*. 1440–1521), generally seen as the most important composer of the early sixteenth century, began his career with a position at the chapel of the pope, and Giovanni Pierluigi da Palestrina (*c*. 1525–94) later became the pope's official composer. By the early sixteenth century, printers recognized the market for printed music, and by the late sixteenth century the works of major composers were printed very quickly and shipped throughout Europe, so that musicians from Poland to Portugal could play the same pieces. Composers such as Orlando di Lasso (1532–94), the choirmaster to the dukes of Bavaria in Munich, gained international reputations as their music was widely performed. Nobles and bishops maintained ensembles of singers, generally all male, with boys, castrati, or men singing falsetto taking the higher parts. Women did sing, play instruments, and compose in convents, however, and in the 1580s, the Este dukes at Ferrara established a separate group of singing women, the *concerto di donne*, which quickly became the fashion at other courts as well. During the sixteenth century the most important musicians and composers were trained north of the Alps, especially in the Low Countries, and the courts of the German emperor and many of the territorial rulers in Germany became centers of musical culture.

Vocal music was the center of musical composition, with the basic compositional technique the counterpoint, in which independent melodic lines – usually four – were combined in polyphonic (that is, multi-voiced) harmony. Secular vocal music was usually sung by small groups, but sacred vocal music was sung by increasingly large choirs. The four-part pattern of

(fol. 142 b)   Die geschicklheit in der musiken und was in seinen ingenien und durch
in erfunden und gepessert worden ist.
(Cod. 3o33.)

Fig. 11. This woodcut by the German artist Hans Burgkmair the Elder (*c.* 1473 – *c.* 1553) shows the Emperor Maximilian surrounded by musicians and musical instruments, including flutes, recorders, sackbuts (akin to trombones), viols, drums, a lute, a harp, and a small pipe organ. Both women and men play various instruments, which would have been common in private performances, though professional court musicians were almost always male.

soprano/alto/tenor/bass also extended to instruments, as families of different-sized versions of one particular instrument – recorders, viols, shawms (a type of oboe), sackbuts (trombones) – were also popular. Instruments that could play several notes at one time, such as keyboard instruments, harps, and especially lutes, accompanied soloists or groups of singers, while trumpets and drums were used for playing fanfares on battlefields and ceremonial occasions. Small village churches and large urban cathedrals had organs to accompany choir and congregational singing, and the position as organist at a major church was a coveted one.

Roman and Greek literature and art served as models for humanist writers and Renaissance artists, but there was no way for anyone to know how Roman and Greek music had sounded. Humanist writers adopted Plato's notion of a relationship between musical harmony and other harmonies in the universe, and they, along with musical theorists such as Gioseffo Zarlino (1517–90) and Vincenzo Galilei (1520–91), the father of the famous scientist, advocated music that expressed emotion and brought harmony to the soul. Composers of vocal music, including French motets and Italian and English madrigals, sought to translate the meaning and mood of texts into musical language using changes in tempo, pitch, rhythm, and key to illustrate words or phrases.

Precisely because it could affect the emotions, music became a matter of debate during the Reformation. Martin Luther saw it as an important tool for strengthening faith, and wrote hymns for the congregation itself to sing, sometimes setting them to popular secular tunes. Other Protestants regarded all music as inappropriate for use in worship, or limited sacred music to unison singing of psalms, with no instrumental accompaniment. (Organ music was so popular, however, that Sunday afternoon concerts were sometimes held in Protestant churches that had banned organ music during the service.) Catholic reformers also worried whether complex multi-part harmonies were suitable in church, and ruled that ecclesiastical music should be composed and sung so that "the words can be clearly understood by all." Hundreds of songs were written praising the heroism of martyrs on the author's side and satirizing the ideas and leaders of the other side in the religious controversies of the sixteenth century; they were often sold as printed broadsheets, with words and suggestions of popular tunes that would work as the melody.

Though the differences between professional and amateur in music grew during the sixteenth century, in terms of types of instruments and complexity of compositions played, people of all classes still sang and played instruments regularly, and regarded what they did as "music." They also used paint, wood, metal, cloth, and thread to decorate their surroundings and their persons, but it is less clear whether they would have used the word "art" to describe their products. As noted at the beginning of this chapter, Vasari clearly did not, and it is his definition of "art" – painting, sculpture, and architecture – that later became standard. More recent scholarship has broadened to include other genres and forms, but it has generally not rejected Vasari's notion that this art had a new and innovative style.

Vasari highlights the contributions of Italians, beginning with Giotto di Bondone (1266–1337), in painting and Donatello (1386–1466) in sculpture: spatial depth, dramatic scenes, classical themes and settings, expressions of weight and force, and (in painting) pure colors. During the fifteenth century, individuals who were both artists and artistic theorists, such as Piero della Francesca (c. 1412–92), Andrea Mantegna (1430/1–1506), and Leon Battista Alberti (1404–72), became intrigued with problems of perspective, developing systems of

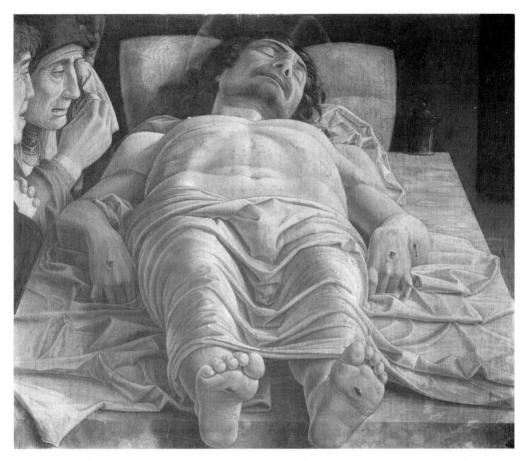

Fig. 12. Andrea Mantegna's *Dead Christ* shows the Virgin Mary, St. John the Evangelist, and an unknown pious woman mourning over the body of Christ. Mantegna, who was the court painter for the Gonzaga family of Mantua, painted sharp sculpture-like details and used the art of foreshortening to dramatic effect.

perspective with a single vanishing point and mastering foreshortening (the portrayal of three-dimensional figures on a two-dimensional surface in proportions that match those seen by the eye). Alberti was a humanist scholar and author as well as an artist and architect, writing prose and poetic works in Latin and Italian on literature, love, law, the family, the horse, geometry, cryptology, and fame at the same time as he was writing treatises on painting and architecture and designing palaces and churches.

Artists and their patrons viewed the purpose of art as the imitation of nature, which they recognized meant creating an illusion of reality rather than copying it. Sandro Botticelli (1444/5–1510), for example, worked on *contraposto* (the shape of the body when the weight is mostly on one foot) and the way that fabrics draped. Leonardo da Vinci both theorized about and, in his actual paintings, statues, and buildings, experimented with the effects of light on different sorts of surfaces, systems of proportion based on the human body, and compositional structures based on geometric forms (especially the triangle).

In architecture, Filippo Brunelleschi (1377–1446) designed a new hospital for foundlings, set up by the silk-workers' guild in Florence, in which all proportions – of the windows, height, floor plan, and covered walkway with a series of rounded arches – were carefully thought out to achieve a sense of balance and harmony. Brunelleschi later turned his talents to designing and constructing a dome for Florence Cathedral, based to some degree on Roman domes, but higher and more graceful.

In the fifteenth century, Florence was the center of the new art in Italy, but in the early sixteenth century this shifted to Rome, where wealthy cardinals and popes wanted visual expression of the church's and their own families' power and piety. Michelangelo, a Florentine who had spent his young adulthood at the court of Lorenzo de' Medici, went to Rome in about 1500, and began the series of statues, paintings, and architectural projects from which he gained an international reputation: the *Pietà, Moses*, the redesigning of the Capitoline Hill in central Rome, and, most famously, the ceiling and altar wall of the Sistine Chapel. Pope Julius II, who commissioned the Sistine Chapel, demanded that Michelangelo work as fast as he could and frequently visited the artist at his work with suggestions and criticisms. Michelangelo complained in person and by letter about the pope's meddling, but even his "singular eminence" did not match the power of the pope and he kept working. The statue of David, commissioned by the Florentine city council as a symbol of the city, and tombs for members of the Medici family, did take him back to Florence at various points, but in 1546 Pope Paul III appointed him as chief architect of the new St. Peter's basilica. This had originally been designed by another northern Italian architect, Donato Bramante (*c.* 1443/4–1514), and would eventually take more than 150 years to complete. Bramante's relative Raphael Sanzio (1483–1520) got the commission for frescoes in the papal apartments, and in his relatively short life painted hundreds of portraits and devotional images, becoming the most sought-after artist in Europe. Raphael also oversaw a large workshop with many collaborators and apprentices – who assisted on the less difficult sections of some paintings – and wrote treatises on his philosophy of art, in which he emphasized the importance of imitating nature and developing an orderly sequence of design and proportion, which he called *buona maniera* (good style).

Venice became another artistic center in the sixteenth century. Titian (1490–1576) produced portraits, religious subjects, and mythological scenes, developing techniques of painting in oil without doing elaborate drawings first, which speeded up the process and so pleased patrons eager to display their acquisition. Paolo Veronese (1528–88) and Jacopo Tintoretto (*c.* 1518–94) learned from Titian, as did Doménikos Theotokópoulos, a painter born on Crete who came to be known as El Greco (1541–1614). These and other sixteenth-century painters developed an artistic style, known in English as "mannerism" (from *maniera* or "style" in Italian), in which artists sometimes distorted figures, exaggerated musculature, and heightened color to express emotion and drama more intently. Until the twentieth century, "mannerism" was a negative term, as critics and art historians preferred the more naturalistic and elegant style of

Fig. 13. In this oil painting of the Madonna and Child with a young John the Baptist, Raphael places the intimate group in a peaceful countryside that looks much like the landscape of north-central Italy where he grew up. Raphael painted a whole series of Madonnas, in which Mary's tranquil loveliness brings together pagan ideas of beauty and Christian devotion.

16 Artistic genius, powerful patron: Mimar Sinan and Süleyman

© Vanni/Art Resource, NY

The battle between Pope Julius II and Michelangelo over the speed with which the artist was completing the Sistine Chapel paintings has become famous, the subject of novels, films, and even cartoons. Several decades later, another brilliant artist and his domineering patron were having a similar fight. In the 1550s, Süleyman the Magnificent hired Mimar ("architect" in Turkish) Sinan to design and build a vast religious complex in Istanbul, called the Süleymaniye. Work had been delayed, and rumors spread to the sultan that the architect was incompetent and that the main dome of the central mosque was ready to collapse. In a rage, Süleyman stormed to the building site and threatened Sinan with the same fate as the architect of an earlier sultan, his great-grandfather Mehmed, known as the Conqueror. That architect, also

named Sinan (though no relation), had disagreed with the sultan about whether they should use some antique columns in a new mosque he was building, and the sultan threw him in prison, where he died.

Mimar Sinan responded by promising that the mosque would be finished in two months, a promise that everyone at the sultan's court thought was insane. Sinan stuck to his promise, and two months later the mosque was finished, with a central dome that was enormous and perfectly sound. The Süleymaniye mosque impressed (and continues to impress) visitors from many countries, and Mimar Sinan went on to design and build many more mosques, schools, palaces, and other buildings. He outlived Sultan Süleyman by more than twenty years.

Botticelli or Raphael, but modern critics and artists have appreciated its sense of movement, vivid colors, and passionate expressions.

Italy was not the only part of Europe to see extensive and innovative artistic production. In Hungary, King Matthias Corvinus and some of his successors hired Italian artists to rebuild the royal palaces in a more classical style, and in France and Spain architects blended classical styles emanating from Italy with local traditions and building materials, designing buildings that were generally more vertical and ornamented than those in Florence or Rome. In the Ottoman Empire, Mimar Sinan, the chief architect for the sultans for over fifty years (1538–89), developed a new design for building mosques that was later widely adopted.

In the Netherlands, the dukes of Burgundy patronized goldsmiths, armor-makers, sculptors, manuscript illuminators, and especially tapestry-makers, and Netherlandish works were shipped throughout Europe to avid buyers. Painters such as Jan van Eyck (before 1395–1441), Rogier van der Weyden (c. 1399–1464), and Hans Memling (c. 1433–94) perfected techniques of painting in oil in ways that captured the textures of physical objects, as well as conveying deep emotions. Hieronymus Bosch (1450-1516) and Pieter Brueghel (the Elder, c. 1525–69) drew on popular sayings and biblical stories to depict scenes of everyday life that often serve as humorous or more biting moral allegories about human weakness.

In Germany, wealthy cities such as Cologne, Augsburg, and Nuremberg supported numerous painters and sculptors. In Nuremberg Albrecht Dürer (1471–1528) produced woodcuts, engravings, and etchings that rendered the human form and the natural world in amazing detail, and, like Raphael, wrote treatises on proportion and measurement. Matthias Grünewald (c. 1480–1528) concentrated on religious themes, using elongated forms, vivid colors, and expressive forms to provoke an intense emotional response. Lucas Cranach the Elder (1472–1553) painted a huge number of altarpieces, portraits, and mythological scenes; he was one of Martin Luther's closest friends, and created a style of art that reflected Protestant ideas and themes. Other German artists were not so fortunate; though Luther approved of art as a means of teaching, other reformers were more hostile to any kind of image in churches, and iconoclastic riots in many towns in the 1520s and 1530s destroyed paintings and statues. This hostile atmosphere led Hans Holbein (the Younger, 1497–1543) to leave Basel for England, where he became court painter to Henry VIII.

Whether in Italy or northern Europe, most Renaissance artists trained in the workshops of older artists; Botticelli, Raphael, Titian, and at times even Michelangelo were known for their large, well-run, and prolific workshops. Though they might be "men of genius," artists were still expected to be well-trained in proper artistic techniques and stylistic conventions, for the notion that artistic genius could show up in the work of an untrained or "primitive" artist did not emerge until the twentieth century. Beginning artists spent years copying drawings and paintings, learning how to prepare paint and other artistic materials, and, by the sixteenth century, reading books about design and composition. Younger artists gathered together in the evenings for further drawing practice, and by the later sixteenth century some of these informal groups had turned into more formal artistic "academies," the first of which was the Compagnia e Accademia del Disegno, begun in 1563 in Florence by Vasari under the patronage of the Medicis.

Artistic works, whether single portraits or huge buildings, were generally created for specific patrons – private individuals, groups such as guilds or religious confraternities, convents, city councils, and territorial rulers. The military leaders who ruled many Italian states by the fifteenth century, for example, ordered elaborate armor, inlaid and etched with natural objects and battle scenes, had their portraits painted or had equestrian statues erected of themselves in that armor, and had palaces or tombs designed to look like something out of Arthurian stories. Burckhardt's idea of the growing importance of the individual in the Renaissance, traced in chapter 2, was based in part on the large number of portraits ordered by wealthy nobles and merchants, though they also paid for religious scenes in which they and their family members were pious onlookers. Botticelli's painting *Adoration of the Magi* includes three members of the Medici family as the three wise men presenting gifts to the infant Jesus, and also shows other members of the Medici intellectual circle: Pico della Mirandola, Poliziano, and Botticelli himself. Patrons varied in their level of involvement as a work progressed; some simply ordered a specific subject or scene, while others oversaw the work of the artist or architect very closely, suggesting themes and styles, and demanding changes while the work was in progress. As we have seen, the relationships between Michelangelo and Pope Julius II during the painting of the Sistine Chapel, and between Sinan and Sultan Süleyman the Magnificent during the building of the Süleymaniye mosque, were extremely tempestuous. As certain artists became popular and well known, they could assert their own artistic style and pay less attention to the wishes of a patron, but even major artists such as Raphael or Titian generally worked according to a patron's specific guidelines.

The centrality of the patron/artist relationship diminishes somewhat if we look beyond Vasari's "major arts" to printed images and decorative objects. Simple woodcuts were very cheap, well within the range of artisans, and were readily available through booksellers in towns or peddlers in the countryside. Enterprising printers arranged for copies of popular engravings and woodcuts, giving artists such as Dürer an audience far larger than just the people who had seen one of his actual works. Carved wooden altarpieces mass-produced in the Netherlands were sold to churches from Portugal to Poland; they had standardized sizes and scenes rather than being made to order. Nobles and middle-class people adorned their homes with statuettes, small-scale paintings and reliefs, elaborate tableware, inlaid furniture, embroidered tablecloths, painted ceramic dishes, and a variety of other products that they bought ready-made; large workshops fabricating these items were set up in Italy, the Netherlands, and elsewhere, with the stages of production subdivided between workers.

All of the most famous and most prolific Renaissance artists were male; there are no female architects, and Properzia de' Rossi (1490–1530) is the only female sculptor whose name is known. Several women did become quite well known as painters. Stylistically their work is very different from each other, but their careers show many similarities. The majority of female painters were the daughters of painters; one of the earliest identifiable female painters, Caterina van Hemessen (1528–after 1587), even signed her work "Caterina, daughter of Jan van Hemessen," indicating she recognized the importance of this relationship.

Those who were not the daughters of painters were often the daughters of intel-lectuals or minor noblemen with ties to intellectual or artistic circles. Many were eldest daughters or came from families in which there were no sons, so their fathers took an unusual interest in their careers. A significant number came from aristocratic families, whereas most male painters had an artisanal background. Many women began their careers before they were twenty, and pro-duced far fewer paintings after they married, or stopped painting entirely. Of those who married, many married painters. Women artists were generally more successful when there were only a very few of them, for they could then be viewed as novelties. This was the case with Sofonisba Anguissola (1532/5–1625), the first Italian woman to gain international recognition for her art. Anguis-sola spent ten years as a court painter to Philip II of Spain, and was extremely popular as a portrait painter. The women who took her as a model, such as Lavinia Fontana (1552–1614) and Fede Galizia (1578–1630), never received the same level of praise, and were openly resented for their success at winning public commissions.

Women were not allowed to study the male nude, which was viewed as essential if one wanted to paint large history paintings with many figures, so they generally painted portraits, smaller paintings with only a few subjects, or, by the seventeenth century, still lifes and interior scenes. Neither did women learn the technique of fresco, in which colors are applied directly to wet plaster walls, because such works had to be done in public, which was judged inap-propriate for women. Concerns about propriety and morality thus limited the media they could use as well as their subject matter.

Worries about morality shaped far more than the works of female artists as the sixteenth century progressed. Though Catholic writers defended the veneration of religious images against Protestants who wanted to do away with them, they also called for decorum and decency in all portrayals of the human form. They were particularly scandalized by nudity, even that of the infant Jesus or saints being martyred, and debated painting over certain body parts in the naked figures of Michelangelo's *Last Supper*. Religious and secular authorities throughout Europe saw threats to public order and propriety everywhere, and thought that God would not look favorably on cities or communities where people did not live a moral or upright life.

Such moral concerns have often been seen as a product of the Protestant Ref-ormation, culminating in what is traditionally called "Puritan morality" or a "Puritan" attitude toward the world. In fact, worries about order and morality predated the Protestant Reformation, especially among urban dwellers, and would eventually be just as powerful among Catholics as among Protestants. As we will see in the next chapter, religious reformers in the sixteenth century had strong opinions on nearly every aspect of Renaissance culture – education, humanism, political theory, vernacular literature, art, and music. Those opin-ions shaped all of these, and much more, in a Europe increasingly divided over religious issues.

Further reading

Discussions of basic education include R. A. Houston, *Literacy in Early Modern England: Culture and Education 1500–1800* (London: Longman, 1988; 2nd edn, 2001); George Huppert, *Public Schools in Renaissance France* (Urbana: University of Illinois Press, 1984); Paul Grendler, *Schooling in Renaissance Italy: Literacy and Learning 1300–1600* (Baltimore: Johns Hopkins University Press, 1989). For more advanced education, see Anthony Grafton and Lisa Jardine, *From Humanism to the Humanities: Education and the Liberal Arts in Fifteenth and Sixteenth-Century Europe* (Cambridge, MA: Harvard University Press, 1986).

Charles G. Nauert, Jr., *Humanism and the Culture of Renaissance Europe* (Cambridge: Cambridge University Press, 1995), provides a thorough introduction, as do the many works of Paul Oskar Kristeller, such as *Renaissance Thought and its Sources* (New York: Columbia University Press, 1979). Charles Trinkaus, *"In Our Image and Likeness": Humanity and Divinity in Italian Humanist Thought* (South Bend, IN: University of Notre Dame Press, 1995), examines humanists' views on human nature. For single humanists, see Peter Ackroyd, *The Life of Thomas More* (New York and London: Nan A. Talese, 1998); James Tracy, *Erasmus of the Low Countries* (Berkeley: University of California Press, 1996). On political thought, see Quentin Skinner, *The Foundations of Modern Political Thought* (Cambridge: Cambridge University Press, 1978), and Gordon Schochet, *Patriarchalism in Political Thought* (New York: Basic Books, 1975).

Stephen Greenblatt, *Will in the World: How Shakespeare became Shakespeare* (New York: Norton, 2004), interweaves what we know about the life of the playwright with a broader analysis of Elizabethan culture, while Jean Howard, *The Stage and Social Struggle in Early Modern England* (London: Routledge, 1994), and Stephen Orgel, *Impersonations: The Performance of Gender in Shakespeare's England* (Cambridge: Cambridge University Press, 1996), also set English theatre in the context of broader social issues.

Richard A. Goldthwaite, *Wealth and the Demand for Art in Italy, 1300–1600* (London and Baltimore: Johns Hopkins University Press, 1993), analyzes the economic context of Renaissance art, while Peter Burke, *The Italian Renaissance: Culture and Society in Europe* (Princeton: Princeton University Press, 1986), discusses the social setting, and Lauro Martines, *Power and Imagination: City-States in Renaissance Italy* (New York: Vintage Books, 1980), examines the political background. Craig Harbison, *The Mirror of the Artist: Northern Renaissance Art in its Historical Context* (Upper Saddle River, NJ: Prentice-Hall, 1995), provides a good overview of northern European developments, while Suraiya Faroqhi, *Subjects of the Sultan: Culture and Everyday Life in the Ottoman Empire* (London: I. B. Tauris, 2000), examines art, literature, and popular culture. Allan W. Atlas, *Renaissance Music: Music in Western Europe, 1400–1600* (New York: Norton, 1998), provides an excellent introduction to the topic. Charles Nicholl, *Leonardo: Flights of the Mind* (New York: Viking, 2004), provides a broad rendering of Leonardo's life and times.

 For more suggestions and links see the companion website www.cambridge.org/wiesnerhanks.

Notes

1 Giorgio Vasari, *Lives of the Artists*, trans. George Bull (Harmondsworth: Penguin Books, 1965), p. 205.
2 Ibid., p. 253.
3 Niccolò Machiavelli, *The Prince*, trans. Leo Paul S. de Alvarez (Prospect Heights, IL: Waveland Press, 1980), p. 101.
4 Ibid., p. 149.
5 *The Political Works of James I*, ed. Charles Howard McIlwain (New York: Russell and Russell, 1965), pp. 272, 307.

5   Religious reform and consolidation, 1450–1600

Title page of Martin Luther's pamphlet, *Letter to the Christian Nobility of the German Nation Concerning the Reform of the Christian Estate* (1520), in which Luther calls on secular authorities to reform the church. Thousands of copies of the first edition sold in weeks, with readers attracted by the message and by Luther's forceful language.

Timeline

1415	Execution of Jan Hus at the Council of Constance
1492	Jews expelled from Spain
1521	Luther's address at the Diet of Worms
1525	German Peasants' War
1531	Zwingli's death at the Battle of Kappel
1533	Henry VIII breaks with the Church of Rome
1536	Calvin comes to Geneva
1540	Society of Jesus officially recognized by the pope
1545–63	Council of Trent
1555	Peace of Augsburg
1572	St. Bartholomew's Day Massacre
1579	Northern provinces of the Netherlands form a union against Spain
1598	Henry IV of France issues the Edict of Nantes

IN 1521, Martin Luther (1483–1546), a professor of theology at the German university of Wittenberg, stood before the Diet of Worms, an assembly of representatives from the nobility, church, and cities in the Holy Roman Empire. Speaking loudly to the group, which included the Emperor Charles V, Luther refused to give in to demands that he take back his ideas. "Unless I am convinced of error by the testimony of Scripture and plain reason," he said, "I cannot and I will not recant anything, for to go against conscience is neither right nor safe. Here I stand, I cannot do otherwise." By the nineteenth century, these words were viewed as the beginning of modern religious individualism and freedom of conscience, joining Renaissance art and the voyages of Columbus as the origins of the modern world. "Here I stand" was the title of what was for decades the most popular biography of Luther, published in 1950 by Roland Bainton, the leading Reformation scholar of his day. These words continue to be highlighted in the twenty-first century; they are on socks for sale in gift shops in Luther's hometown, and in both television documentaries and movies, one of which describes Luther as "rebel . . . genius . . . liberator."

149

While the popular view of Luther as heroic revolutionary remains strong, most scholars of religion today put less emphasis on Luther alone as the source of religious change. They point out that from the twelfth century onward a number of groups and individuals increasingly criticized many aspects of western Christianity, including doctrines they judged to have no biblical basis, institutions such as the papacy or church courts, the tax collection methods and fiscal policies of the church, the ways in which priests and higher officials were chosen, and the worldliness and morals of priests, monks, nuns, bishops, and the pope. Various measures were suggested to reform institutions, improve clerical education and behavior, and even alter basic doctrines. Occasionally these reform efforts succeeded in changing the Roman church, and in at least one area, Bohemia (the modern-day Czech Republic), they led to the formation of a church independent of Rome, a century before Luther.

In Luther's own day there were a number of other reformers, such as Ulrich Zwingli (1484–1531) at Zurich in Switzerland, who also rejected many basic doctrines of the medieval church, including the importance of good works, the authority of the papacy, and the binding force of tradition. They developed their ideas largely independently of, and sometimes in opposition to, Luther's influence. Luther called Zwingli a heretic because he developed a different interpretation of the presence of Christ in the Eucharist, the ceremony during which Christians consume bread and wine, understood as representing or as containing the glorified body and blood of Christ. He called peasants who extended ideas about spiritual equality to the earthly realm "venomous, pernicious, and Satanic." Luther's harsh reaction to those who disagreed with him indicates that there were clear limits to his ideas about the primacy of conscience and the possibility of individual interpretation. If these are the marks of "modern" religion, then Luther was very much a "medieval" thinker.

Even the famous words "Here I stand" have not stood up to scholarly scrutiny. Luther did appear at Worms and defend himself, and his words as written down by several in attendance were roughly similar to the speech given above; these eye-witness accounts do not include "Here I stand," however, which was added later as a – very effective – rhetorical flourish.

This de-emphasis on the centrality of Luther has not meant that historians have de-emphasized the importance of religion in the early modern period, however: quite the opposite. The reform movement of which Luther was a part lasted far longer than the few decades during which he was active, and had political, social, economic, and intellectual ramifications far beyond what is today usually understood as the "religious" realm of life. The ideas of Luther and other reformers were attractive to political leaders, who broke with the papacy and the Roman church and established their own local churches: churches that came to be labeled "Protestant" after a 1529 document issued by German princes protesting an imperial order that they give up their religious innovations. Their motivations were mixed and varied; spiritual aims blended with desires to end the economic and political power of the papacy in their territories, gain the income from church lands, and oppose neighboring states who remained Catholic. Once European states were divided into different Christian confessions, political and religious authorities acted together to teach their populations more about their particular variant of Christianity – a process historians have called "confessionalization." (Different groups within Christianity, now generally called *denominations* – such as Baptists, Methodists, Presbyterians, Catholics – were called *confessions* in the sixteenth century.) Rulers and clergy tried to improve clerical education, opened the schools for lay people traced in chapter 4, and encouraged or required attendance at sermons or other services. They also sought to make their states and their communities more moral and orderly, in a process historians term "social discipline." Catholic theologians believed that without good works individuals could not call upon God's saving power, while Protestant theologians saw them as the fruit of a saving faith given by God. Thus for both Catholics and Protestants, one's sexual, leisure, and workplace activities – and those of one's neighbors – continued to be important in God's eyes. Order, piety, and morality were marks of divine favor. Religious and political authorities passed laws against blasphemy and dancing, increased the punishment of those judged deviant, including witches, people who had sex outside marriage, converts from non-Christian religions, and practitioners of magic. In Catholic areas the power of bishops and church courts was strengthened and in Protestant areas special courts were established to handle marriage and morals cases; the motto of one of these courts was "discipline is the sinews of the church."[1] Officials began to keep registers of marriages, births, baptisms, and deaths, which allowed them better to monitor the behavior and status of individuals. This process of confessionalization and social discipline – what some scholars have dubbed the "long Reformation" – lasted well beyond the sixteenth century, as educating people and encouraging (or forcing) them to alter their behavior took far longer than either Protestant or Catholic reformers anticipated.

Throughout Europe the emphasis on political and social order led to the persecution of Christians whose understanding of Christianity differed from that of those in power. Catholic leaders imprisoned and executed Protestants, while Protestants imprisoned and executed Catholics and other types of Protestants. Individuals and groups that developed doctrines seen as "radical" – such as communal ownership of property, a rejection of infant baptism, or a questioning of the Trinity – were harassed and suppressed by all sides. Both Protestants and Catholics hunted, arrested, and executed people believed to be witches, viewing them as in league with the devil and thus opponents of proper religious and social order. (Witchcraft will be discussed in detail in chapter 11.)

This attempt to get rid of internal enemies was accompanied by religious wars in different parts of Europe from the mid-1520s onward; war plus religious persecution led to large numbers of refugees moving from place to place. In some places, especially France and the Netherlands, popular riots designed to rid the community of the symbols of other religions sometimes turned against people as well as property. The suppression of ideas judged religiously deviant, and the use of violence to wipe them out, had not been unknown in western Europe before the sixteenth century – both a crusade and a special papal inquisition had been sent against the Albigensians, a heretical group in southern France in the thirteenth century, for example – but the extent of both increased significantly.

Eastern Orthodoxy – divided into different national churches including Greek, Russian, and Serbian – did not see a dramatic split in the sixteenth century the way the western church did. Orthodoxy was affected by movements of moral reform, and secular rulers in some places increased their control over church life in the same way that Protestant rulers did. As we will see in more detail in chapter 11, the Russian patriarchate was moved from Kiev to Moscow, and in 1589 came under the direct control of the tsar. With the expansion of Turkish holdings in the Balkans, many Orthodox Christians lived under Muslim rule. The limits of Christian independence were set by the sultan, who also had both religious and political authority over his Muslim subjects.

Movements to enhance religious uniformity throughout Europe had negative effects on the Jews. In 1492 Jews were expelled from Spain, and in the sixteenth century first Venice and then other Italian cities ordered Jews to live together in areas separated from Christians, which the Venetian Senate and then other authorities called "ghettos," a word derived from the Italian word for foundry because Venetian Jews were relegated to an island where a foundry had been located. In his later works, Luther called Jews "disgusting vermin," and recommended that they be expelled from the Empire; his words provoked anti-Jewish riots in Braunschweig.

Thus the significant religious developments of this era range far beyond the theological disputes in the western church of the 1520s and 1530s, and far beyond the ideas of a single individual. Certain figures, however, including Martin Luther, Henry VIII of England, and Ignatius Loyola, are still extremely important, in both the ways their actions shaped religious change and the ways their personal histories typified the interweaving of religion with other developments of this era.

The early Reformation

Western Christianity in the middle of the fifteenth century was a powerful political, intellectual, and economic institution, and also a lived experience of rituals, practices, and beliefs. Dissatisfaction with the church and calls for reform involved both these aspects of the church. People complained that absentee bishops, or bishops who held more than one diocese, did not supervise priests very well; that monks and friars were greedy and immoral, wheedling money out of people, maintaining concubines, and living too well; that priests were barely able to read and write in any language, and just mumbled the

mass in Latin without understanding what the words meant. Educated reformers such as Erasmus and Lefèvre agreed with these anticlerical criticisms, and
also saw many popular religious practices as foolish or misguided. Instead of
spending their time on pilgrimages or their money on relics or indulgences,
people should help the needy or pray, they asserted.

In the late fourteenth century John Wyclif (c. 1330–84) in England and in
the early fifteenth century John Hus (c. 1372–1415) in Bohemia, both university
teachers of theology, added theological issues to these critiques of church structure and practice. Both of them denied papal authority, called for translations
of the Bible into the local language, and questioned the accepted interpretation of specific practices. Wyclif rejected the idea of transubstantiation – that
the bread and the wine are transformed into the body and blood of Christ
by the words of the priest during the Eucharist – and Hus called indulgences
useless. Wyclif's followers (called Lollards) were persecuted in the fifteenth century; some were executed, some recanted, and others met secretly in houses,
barns, and fields to read and discuss the Bible and other religious texts in
English. Historians differ on how widespread Lollard beliefs were by the time
that Protestant ideas came to England, for they were intentionally hidden and
thus are difficult to trace; the Lollard emphasis on biblical literacy certainly
created groups of individuals who were open to Protestant views and practices.
John Hus was tried, condemned, and executed as a heretic at the Council of
Constance in 1415 (despite being granted a safe-conduct to go there by the
emperor), but his followers were successful in defeating the combined armies
of the pope and the emperor many times. In the 1430s the emperor finally
agreed to recognize the Hussite church in Bohemia and Moravia.

Wyclif and Hus prefigure Luther in many ways: all three held positions
as university teachers, called for a return to the Bible, condemned the institutional church, popular practices, and theological doctrines, and gradually
grew more severe in these condemnations. All three of their movements drew
on "imagined political communities" (to use Benedict Anderson's phrase again)
created by language – English, Czech, German – to oppose the supra-national
power of the pope, and, in the case of Hus and Luther, to oppose the emperor
as well.

Luther was the son of a copper miner and mine owner from Saxony in central Germany, who enrolled at the University of Erfurt, intending to study law.
In 1505, caught in a thunderstorm, he vowed to St. Anne – by tradition, the
mother of the Virgin Mary – to become a monk if his life was spared. Much
to his father's great dismay, he took this vow seriously, joined a monastery of
Augustinian friars at Erfurt and switched his studies from law to theology. He
was a very scrupulous monk, and was troubled by fear of damnation, doubts
about his own worth, and his own sinfulness. These doubts led him to fast
frequently and wear a hair-shirt, but they did not keep him from obtaining
a doctorate in theology and accepting a position as professor at the new University of Wittenberg in 1512, where he spent the rest of his life. He followed

standard university procedures in lecturing, going verse by verse through a specific book of the Bible and giving commentary.

In working through the letters of Paul, Luther found the basis of an understanding of essential Christian doctrines different from the one he had been taught. His understanding is often codified as "faith alone, grace alone, Scripture alone" (*sola fide, sola gratia, sola Scriptura*). For Christians, salvation and justification come through faith, not good works, though true faith leads to love and to the active expression of faith in helping others. Faith is a free gift of God, not the result of human effort. God's word is revealed only in Scripture, not in the traditions of the church. Luther understood the sacraments as signs of God's promise of the forgiveness of sins, and regarded baptism and the Eucharist as the only true sacraments.

At the same time that Luther was engaged in scholarly reflections and professorial lecturing, Archbishop Albert of Mainz, who controlled the area in which Wittenberg was located, sought to become the bishop of several other territories as well, for which he needed special dispensation from Pope Leo X. To obtain this he needed money, which he borrowed from the Fuggers, a wealthy German banking family in Augsburg. Pope Leo, a member of the Medici family, was constructing family chapels and tombs (for which he hired Michelangelo) and continuing the building of St. Peter's basilica in Rome. He authorized a special St. Peter's indulgence, which promised the living and the dead the remission of church penalties for the payment of a fee, and allowed Albert to keep a portion of the revenue collected in the territories over which he was bishop to pay back the Fuggers. Albert hired a friar from the Dominican order, Johann Tetzel, to run the indulgence sale. Tetzel was a very effective salesman, hawking indulgences – printed on the newly developed printing press – in a way that promised full forgiveness for sins or the end of time in purgatory for one's dearly departed relatives; people traveled for miles to buy them.

Luther was disturbed by what seemed to him a combination of the worst of both institutional corruption and misguided popular beliefs. He wrote a letter to Archbishop Albert, laying out his ideas – in a style very typical of a university professor – as ninety-five theses, or scholarly points of argument, against indulgences. Later biographies of Luther reported that he also nailed these theses to the door of the Wittenberg castle church on October 31, 1517, the day before All Saints' Day, when church attendance would be high. Such an act would have been very strange – they were in Latin and written for those learned in theology, not normal church-goers – but it has become a standard part of Luther lore, much like "Here I stand." Whether the theses were posted or not, they were quickly printed, first in Latin and then in German translation. Luther was ordered to come to Rome, which he was able to avoid because of the political situation in the Empire, but he did engage in formal scholarly debate with a representative of the church, Johann Eck, at Leipzig in 1519. He refused to take back his statements, and continued to develop his reform ideas, publicizing these in a series of pamphlets in which he moved further and further away from Catholic theology. Luther clearly understood the power of the new medium of print, and so authorized the publication of his works. Printers also quickly realized that Luther would sell, so they printed additional unauthorized versions of his more popular works as fast as they could.

In his writings, sermons, and university lectures, Luther asserted that both popes and church councils could err, that secular leaders should reform the church if the pope and clerical hierarchy did not, that there was no distinction between clergy and lay people (an idea often described as "the priesthood of believers"), that requiring clergy to be celibate was a fruitless attempt to control a natural human drive, and that marriage brought spiritual advantages so was the ideal state for nearly all human beings. He gathered followers from among the faculty at Wittenberg, most prominently Philipp Melanchthon (1497–1560), a professor of Latin and Greek, and by the early 1520s from other parts of central Germany as well. His appearance at the Diet of Worms only created an even broader audience for reform ideas, and throughout central Europe other individuals began to preach and publish against the existing doctrines and practices of the church.

In Zurich, Ulrich Zwingli, the priest at Zurich's major church, agreed with Luther about the primacy of faith and Scripture; he preached against indulgences, the veneration of saints, religious images, clerical celibacy, and the worship of Mary, and began translating the Bible into Swiss German. He advocated a simpler service than Luther did, with no liturgy, church decorations, or music other than the singing of psalms. He and Luther disagreed vehemently about the meaning of the Eucharist, and despite attempts by reformers such as Martin Bucer (1491–1551) of Strasbourg to bring the two together, the reform movement split into two wings: those who followed Luther, often called *Evangelical*, and those who

17 Martin Luther, *The Freedom of a Christian* (1520)

In 1520, right after the Leipzig debates, Luther published three significant pamphlets that marked his clear break with the papacy: *Address to the Christian Nobility of the German Nation*, demanding that German rulers reform the church; *The Babylonian Captivity of the Church*, condemning the papacy for holding Christians in "captivity" for centuries by distorting the meaning of the sacraments; and *The Freedom of a Christian*, summarizing his own beliefs. In this brief pamphlet, written in Latin for the pope but translated immediately into German and widely published, Luther wrote that Christians were freed through Christ – not their own actions – from sin, death, and the devil, though the true Christian life was one of service to one's neighbor.

What can it profit the soul if the body is well, free, and active, and eats, drinks, and does what it pleases? For in these respects even the most godless slave of vice may prosper. On the other hand, how will poor health or imprisonment or hunger or thirst or any other external misfortune harm the soul? Even the most godly men, and those who are free because of clear consciences, are afflicted with these things. None of these things touches either the freedom or the servitude of the soul . . . One thing, and only one thing, is necessary for Christian life, righteousness, and freedom. That one thing is the most holy Word of God, the gospel of Christ . . . as the soul needs only the Word of God for its life and righteousness, so it is justified by faith alone and not any works . . . a Christian is free from all things and over all things so that he needs no works to make him righteous and save him, since faith alone abundantly confers all these things . . . in his spirit. But as long as he lives in the flesh . . . and remains in this mortal life on earth . . . a man cannot be idle, for his body drives him and he is compelled to do many good works to reduce it to subjection [that is, to make sure his desire for power, money, fame, food, or other earthly things does not take over his life]. Nevertheless the works themselves do not justify him before God, but he does works out of spontaneous love in obedience to God.

(From *Luther's Works,* ed. Harold Grimm [Philadelphia: Muhlenberg Press, 1957], vol. XXXI, pp. 345, 346, 348, 359 reprinted by permission.)

 For additional chapter resources see the companion website www.cambridge.org/wiesnerhanks.

followed Zwingli, called *Reformed*. In general, Zwinglian Reformed ideas spread more widely in Switzerland and south Germany, and Lutheran Evangelical ideas in northern Germany and Scandinavia.

Both Luther and Zwingli recognized that, if reforms were going to be permanent, political authorities as well as concerned individuals and religious leaders would have to accept them. Zwingli worked closely with the city council of Zurich; it was the city council that decided it would accept only the authority of Scripture in matters of religion, officially changed the structure of the church service, ordered that religious images be removed from the churches, and established a new court to adjudicate marriage and morals cases, which had previously been under the jurisdiction of the bishop's court. In other cities and towns of Switzerland and south Germany, city councils similarly took the lead, appointing pastors that they knew had accepted Protestant ideas, requiring them to swear an oath of loyalty to the council, and overseeing their preaching and teaching. Some historians have argued that cities were especially fertile grounds for reformed ideas in which the religious and political community were understood to be coterminous. Even before the Reformation, city authorities passed and enforced laws that sought to make their cities more moral and bring all activities under the control of the city council; reformed ideas thus provided theological justification for what they were doing already, which helps explain the speed at which many cities accepted them.

Luther lived in a territory ruled by a noble – the Elector of Saxony – not a city, but he also worked closely with political authorities, viewing them as fully justified in asserting control over the church in their territories. Indeed, in his 1520 *Address to the Christian Nobility of the German Nation* he demanded that German rulers reform the papacy and ecclesiastical institutions, and in *On Secular Government* he instructed all Christians to obey their secular rulers, whom he saw as divinely ordained to maintain order. In terms of the process of the Reformation, Luther's hopes were largely fulfilled. Individuals may have been convinced of the truth of Protestant teachings by hearing sermons, listening to hymns, or reading pamphlets, but territories became Protestant when their ruler, whether a noble or a city council, brought in a reformer or two to reeducate the territory's clergy, sponsored public sermons, confiscated church property, and closed convents and monasteries. This happened in many of the states of the Empire during the 1520s and in Denmark-Norway under Christian III (ruled 1534–59) in the 1530s. In Sweden, Gustavus Vasa (ruled 1523–60), who came to the throne during a civil war with Denmark, also took over control of church personnel and income, and Protestant ideas spread, though the Swedish church did not officially accept Lutheran theology until later in the century. In every area that became Protestant, there was a slightly different balance between popular religious ideas and the aims of the political authorities. In some areas certain groups, such as clergy or journeymen, pushed for reforms, while in others the ruler or city council forced religious change on a population that lacked interest or was hostile.

18 Debates about the Eucharist

The central ritual in Christianity, based on Jesus' words to his disciples as he gave them bread and wine at the Last Supper (Matthew 26: 26–8; Mark 14: 22–5; Luke 22: 17–19) is variously called "the Eucharist," "the Mass," "Holy Communion," "the Lord's Supper," "the Breaking of Bread," and "the Sacrament of the Altar." No issue was debated as sharply in the Reformation. The Catholic doctrine of transubstantiation, made dogma at the Fourth Lateran Council in 1215 and reaffirmed at the Council of Trent, taught that at the moment a priest repeated Christ's words "this is my body, this is my blood," – these are called the "words of institution" – the substance of the bread and wine are transformed into the body and blood of Christ. The outer form of consecrated bread and wine, termed the "accidents," did not change, but the inner substance, what we might call the essence, was really Christ. This ritual, in which the priest offered up Christ as a visible sacrifice, renewing Christ's sacrifice on the cross, could only be done by an ordained priest, giving him a power that no lay authority had. The priest's central role was emphasized in the ritual itself by the fact that he was the only one to drink the wine. The Eucharist was effective in itself (*ex opere operatum*), not dependent on the moral or spiritual state of the priest or the recipient.

Luther rejected the doctrine of transubstantiation, but he took the words of institution literally, believing that sin was being forgiven in the Eucharist and that Christ was really present in the consecrated bread and wine of the Eucharist. This "real presence" was the result of God's mystery, however, not the actions of a priest, and faith was absolutely necessary to make the sacrament effective; the Eucharist is a sign of the fellowship of believers with one another and with Christ, what Luther calls Christ's "testament." Some Lutherans, such as Philipp Melanchthon, preferred to emphasize the presence of Christ with the bread and wine during the ritual itself, and the Formula of Concord (1577), trying to accommodate all views, established the lasting Lutheran position: in the Lord's Supper Christ is "in, with, and under" the bread and wine. (This position was later termed "consubstantiation," but this word was not used in the sixteenth century.) Luther called for both the bread and the wine to be administered to all who wished to participate, and communion "in both kinds" became standard in Protestant services.

Ulrich Zwingli understood the Eucharist differently than Luther, as a memorial service in which Christ was present in spirit among the faithful, not in the bread and wine. The "is" in the phrase "this is my body," really means "signifies," and the sacrament is a sign of God's grace already given, not a means of giving that grace. Many thinkers in the radical Reformation adopted views along these lines, with some viewing communion as an important memorial of Christ's sacrifice and others denying its centrality as they emphasized the inner workings of the spirit more than visible rituals. Luther attacked both Zwingli and the radicals in several pamphlets of the mid-1520s, calling them "fanatics." Luther, Zwingli, and many other reformers met at Marburg in 1529 to see if they could reach agreement, but found that on the issue of the Eucharist they could not, though they did agree to tone down their rhetoric.

John Calvin followed the lead of south German and Swiss reformers such as Martin Bucer who tried to work out a doctrine of the sacraments that could be acceptable to all Protestants. He held, like Luther and Melanchthon, that Christ's body and blood were conveyed in the sacrament, but in a spiritual sense; the sacrament was a means of giving grace, a "sacred feast" and divine seal of God's promise of salvation through which believers become one flesh with Christ. Theologically Calvin was closer to Luther than to Zwingli, but Luther and his successors refused to come into formal agreement. Zwingli's followers and Calvin's did accept several joint statements of doctrine, which served as the basis for a Reformed understanding of the Eucharist.

In England, Thomas Cranmer articulated a position quite similar to Calvin's, that Christ remained corporally in heaven but was "verily and truly" in the sacrament. The various statements defining the doctrines of the Church of England issued during Elizabeth's reign also use language about the body of Christ "given, taken, and eaten [in a] heavenly and spiritual manner." Thus, though they could not agree on a uniform understanding, all Protestants rejected the idea that the Eucharist was a sacrifice. The Council of Trent responded by decisively reaffirming that Christ "now offering [himself] by the ministry of priests" is "the same who then offered himself on the cross."

The Reformation in England

The relationship between popular pressure and reform from above is sometimes a matter of dispute among historians, and in this the Reformation in England is the best example. Books and individuals brought Lutheran ideas into

England very early, especially in the universities and the city of London, though they were strenuously opposed by the king, Henry VIII and his lord chancellor Thomas Wolsey (1475?–1530), who was also a cardinal. Henry was married to Catherine of Aragon – the daughter of Ferdinand and Isabella, those marriage brokers extraordinaire – who had originally been married to his older brother Arthur, who had died as a youth. To marry Catherine, Henry had been required to obtain a special papal dispensation, as marriage to a brother's widow went against canon law. The marriage was about average for royal marriages – they neither especially hated nor loved one another – but it had only produced one living heir, a daughter, Mary. By 1527, Henry decided that God was showing his displeasure with the marriage by denying him a son, and appealed to the pope to have it annulled; he was also in love with a court lady-in-waiting, Anne Boleyn (1504–1536), and assumed she would give him the son that he wanted. Normally an annulment would not have been a problem, but the troops of Emperor Charles V were at that point in Rome, and Pope Clement VII was essentially their prisoner. Charles V was the nephew of Catherine of Aragon, and thus was vigorously opposed to an annulment, which would have declared his aunt a fornicator and his cousin Mary a bastard. (An annulment declares that there never was a marriage, making children of such a union illegitimate.)

The military situation in Rome, added to the fact that an annulment would have called into question the pope's right to grant a dispensation from something proscribed by the Bible, led the pope to stall, though Cardinal Wolsey put immense pressure on him. Wolsey was removed from office, arrested, and charged with treason, though he died before coming to trial. Working through Parliament and other officials, Henry gradually took over control of the English church. In 1533, he married Anne, and shortly afterward appointed Thomas Cranmer (1489–1556), a Cambridge scholar, as archbishop of Canterbury. Cranmer announced that Henry's marriage to Catherine was void and his marriage to Anne valid, allowing her to become queen. Henry had forced the pope to agree to Cranmer's appointment by threatening to withhold all taxes, but this move was too much, and the pope excommunicated Henry. Later that year, to Henry's great dismay, Anne gave birth to yet another daughter, Elizabeth.

Henry and his new principal minister, Thomas Cromwell (1485?–1540), ordered everyone holding office in England to agree that Henry was the "supreme head of the Church of England" and dissolved the monasteries, transferring their assets to the royal treasury, and later disbursing them to Henry's supporters. For the rest of his reign, Henry alternated between Protestant religious measures, such as supporting translations of the Bible, and Catholic ones, such as forbidding clergy – including monks and nuns whose convents he had closed – to marry. His own religious opinions were idiosyncratic, with the strongest held being his firm belief in the authority of the monarch over everything, temporal and spiritual.

There is no dispute about these events, nor about the fact that Henry's marriage and succession problems were the direct cause of the English Reformation. What is debated is how the king's moves intersected with popular theological conviction. Some historians see the fact that most clergy and officials accepted Henry's moves (Thomas More being one of the few who did not, for which he was executed), and that the return to Catholicism under his daughter Mary did not outlast her death, as evidence that English people were already deeply dissatisfied with the Catholic Church. Others argue that most people were quite content with the traditional Catholicism of communal celebrations and structured ceremonies, and that they resisted Henry's changes as much as they could. In 1536, for example, opposition to Henry's closing of the monasteries combined with discontent about rising taxes, and a revolt led by priests and nobles began in the north of England. Called the "Pilgrimage of Grace," it disbanded when promises were made to address its demands, though these promises were ignored and Henry later executed many of its leaders. More recent scholarship has pointed out that people rarely "converted" from Catholicism to Protestantism overnight, particularly in a situation like the one in England where changes were often piecemeal and where the religious policies of the crown itself varied. People responded to an action of the crown being played out in their own neighborhood – the closing of a monastery, the ending of masses said for the dead – with a combination of resistance, acceptance, cooperation, and collaboration.

This process of cultural accommodation and compromise continued under Elizabeth I. She required officials, clergy, and nobles to swear allegiance to her as the "supreme governor of the Church of England." She initially chose the word "governor" rather than "head" to provide a loophole for English Catholics to remain loyal to her without denying the primacy of the pope. She also realized that "head" might be viewed as inappropriate for a woman, for treatises about the family and proper gender relations always referred to men as the "head." Many of the leaders of the Church of England under Elizabeth were influenced by continental reformers that were closer to Zwingli than Luther in their ideas, so that the Elizabethan church is part of the Reformed wing of Protestantism. Later the term Anglican would be used to describe the Church of England, but this word was not used during Elizabeth's time.

Though Elizabeth said she "would not make windows into men's souls," that is, inquire too closely into what people believed, her subjects were required to be members of the Church of England and to attend church. By later in her reign, doubts about the loyalty of her subjects if there should be a joint Spanish-papal invasion led to increasing fines and imprisonment of "recusants," the term given to Catholics who refused to attend services. Every political authority in Christian Europe, whether Catholic, Evangelical, or Reformed, accepted this policy of religious uniformity and an official state church. (Because of their links to political authorities, who were called "magistrates" in the sixteenth century, Evangelical and Reformed thinkers and churches are often termed *magisterials*.)

The radical Reformation

Some individuals and groups rejected the idea that church and state needed to be united, and sought to create a voluntary community of believers as they understood it to have existed in New Testament times. In terms of theology and spiritual practices, these individuals and groups varied widely, though they are generally termed "radicals" for their insistence on a more extensive break with the past. Many of them repudiated infant baptism, for they wanted as members only those who had intentionally chosen to belong; some adopted the baptism of believers – for which they were given the title of "Anabaptists" or rebaptizers by their enemies – while others saw all outward sacraments or rituals as misguided and concentrated on inner spiritual transformation. Some groups attempted to follow Christ's commandments in the gospels literally, while others reinterpreted the nature of Christ. Radicals were often pacifists and refused to hold any office or swear oaths, which were required of nearly everyone with any position of authority, including city midwives and toll-collectors, as well as anyone involved in court proceedings. Some groups attempted communal ownership of property, living very simply and rejecting anything they thought un-biblical. Different groups blended these practices in different ways, and often reacted very harshly to members who deviated, banning them from the group, and requiring other group members – sometimes including spouses – to shun, or have no contact with, the offending member until he or she changed behavior and asked for forgiveness. Others, however, argued for complete religious toleration and individualism; that idea was especially common among those radicals who rejected the idea of the Trinity and viewed Christ as thoroughly human.

Individuals known for their more radical ideas include Andreas Bodenstein von Karlstadt (1486–1541), who taught with Luther at the University of Wittenberg and celebrated the first communion service in German there; Conrad Grebel (c. 1498–1526), an associate of Zwingli's in Zurich who conducted the first adult baptism in 1525; Kaspar von Schwenkfeld (1489–1561), a German nobleman who asserted that Christ worked directly in the human soul so that no external ceremonies were very important; Menno Simons (c. 1496–1561), a Dutch pastor who developed a very Christ-centered theology and opposed the use of violence; Jacob Hutter (1500?–36) an Austrian hatmaker turned preacher who set up a system of complete communal sharing of property among his followers; Fausto Sozzini (1539–1604), an Italian reformer who saw the importance of Christ in his resurrection, not his divine nature, and thought that true religion was consistent with reason. Highlighting the role of specific individuals when looking at the radical Reformation may be even more misleading than focusing only on Luther in the magisterial Reformation, however, for the majority of those who accepted radical beliefs were not highly learned. They were artisans and peasants who opposed hierarchies within the church, wanted the congregation to have a more active role in the church service, and expected the second coming of Christ – predicted in the Book of Revelation – to be imminent. Many of them were women, and a key issue facing many Anabaptist groups became that of "mixed marriages," that is, whether spouses who differed in matters of religion should be allowed – or even required – to divorce and remarry.

In some cases eschatological ideas about the end of the world were linked with political insurrection. Some radical reformers, including Thomas Müntzer (d. 1525), supported the peasants in the 1525 German Peasants' War (see below), for which he was eventually executed. In Münster, a city in northwestern Germany, several charismatic preachers gathered increasing numbers of followers when they predicted that the city would be the site of a New Jerusalem that would survive God's final judgment. In 1534 people streamed into Münster to be rebaptized, a city council sympathetic to these views was elected, and those who refused rebaptism were expelled. Material goods were redistributed, polygyny was introduced (justified because the immigrants included many unmarried women), and leaders in Münster proclaimed their city an independent kingdom. This attempt to transform society according to radical religious principles was absolutely unacceptable to both Catholic and Lutheran authorities, and combined armies successfully besieged the city and executed its leaders.

The insurrection at Münster and the radicals' unwillingness to accept a state church were both used as justification for intense persecution. The emperor made Anabaptism a crime punishable by death in 1529, and both Catholic and Protestant religious and political leaders complied. Over the next century thousands of radicals were tortured and executed in many parts of Europe, often in very gruesome ways; Jacob Hutter, for example, was burned at the stake, and many female Anabaptists were drowned. Records of their trials are one of the few sources we have for the religious ideas of people who were illiterate. From these records, we learn that many unlearned men and women had memorized large parts of the Bible by heart and could argue complicated theological concepts. Anabaptists themselves compiled accounts of trials and executions, along with letters and other records, into martyrologies, which were published and read widely.

Persecution also led radical leaders and their followers to migrate to parts of Europe that were more tolerant. Sympathetic nobles in the Empire sometimes allowed them to live in their territories, as did nobles in Moravia (in modern-day Slovakia and the Czech Republic), Silesia (in modern-day Poland) and other parts of eastern Europe. Eventually many of these groups were forced to move even further. In the seventeenth century Polish Socinians (the anti-trinitarian followers of Sozzini) went into exile in Transylvania (in modern-day Hungary) and Mennonites and Hutterites moved to southern Russia. In the eighteenth century Schwenkfelders went to Pennsylvania, and in the nineteenth century

19 Anabaptist hymns

Hymns were an important means of conveying religious ideas, and sometimes of memorializing heroic actions. The following is a hymn detailing and praising the martyrdom of a husband and wife, Jeroen Segersz and Lijsken Dircks, who were executed as Anabaptists in Antwerp. Segersz was burned at the stake in 1551, and Dircks was drowned in the River Scheldt several months later; her execution was delayed because she was pregnant at the time of her trial and the court waited until the child had been born to put her to death, a common practice for women who were executed. The hymn includes references to specific verses of the Bible; the Bible was extremely important to Anabaptists, and many of them had memorized large sections of it.

1   Most faithful is the Lord our God
    [2 Cor. 1: 4] Comforts his own from morn to
        night.
    When Jeroen, together with his Wife,
    From evil suffered sorrow great,
    So they [Josh. 1: 5, Heb. 13: 5] were not
        forsaken
    By God, in their sad, dark affliction,
    [Ps. 91: 15] Who in their need did come to aid
        them,
    Through his spirit most wondrously.

2   The Markgrave and his fellow Sophists,
    Put on a good show with their wares,
    But Jeroen spoke, with no dissembling,
    "And should the fool stand up right now,
    And say: 'The power to leave is in your hands,
    All you need say is: "I regret it"'':
    From my course I would not want to stray,
    For I possess the truth, I know."

3   Then Markgrave he spoke with fury wild:
    "I'll have you thrown into the fire
    Alive, if you won't hear!"
    Jeroen laughed at all the ranting,
    Spake bravely: [Acts 21: 13] I'll gladly suffer all
    Of what you might do unto me,
    For this my faith!" (For doing battle
    Well armed that Champion was).

4   Two Priests he once took on, together,
    Punished them so, with God's own word,
    That they ought well to've been ashamed;
     For that they were angry and enraged,
    They burned with fury at Jeroen,
    Smashing their fists upon the table,
    Insisting that Peter had begun
    The papacy, the first mass held by Andrew.

5   Well, these finally quit the field,
    But Jeroen to the rack was brought,
    Much he suffered pain and torment,
    Gileyn's helper racked him long,

And while he lay there, bound up tight,
With water Gileyn poured him full;
The cruel Wolves about him stood,
Expecting his need to make him speak.

6 When he had suffered all of this,
    And lay in strong walls imprisoned,
    He was indeed so much at peace,
    All his burden up and left him,
    For he could hardly get to sleep
    Through rejoicing and joy so great,
    Which he gleaned while in the Emperor's
        chair,
    Granted to him by the Lord.

7 Thus did the Sheep the Wolf escape;
    But then he turned his craft on Lijsken,
    Thinking he would make that woman recant;
    But her pillar was the word of God,
    And she endured, remained [Matt 24: 13,
        Mark 13: 13] fast standing
    Against the Anti-Christ's rough rabble,
    Who so harshly did pursue her,
    Even coming around to Scripture.

        . . .

11 The Sophists and the Hypocrites,
    So very much were angered,
    That they could not tear to bits
    God's children through their teachings false.
    And so the Council did decide
    That those dear lambs so sweet they would
    Cast out, away, to their deaths.
    That's how they quenched their cruel hearts!

12 Jeroen, going to the sacrifice,
    Was very well prepared to die;
    Big Hendrik, standing there as well,
    Patiently waited for death with him.
    They stepped together, the two of them,
    Thus to the stake, and had no fear,
    For their Father they did long,
    [Ps. 31: 6, Luke 23: 46, Acts 7: 59] To whom
        they did commend their Spirit.

13 Jeroen had to leave his love,
    That was for him a sorrow great;
    For she was fruitful with their child.
    And when she had borne that child,
    In torment, with great labour,
    They threw that small sheep in the Scheldt.
    Take this example to further spread
    God's praise to all tormented Brethren.

(Hermina Joldersma and Louis Grijp, ed. and trans., *'Elisabeth's manly courage': Testimonials and Songs of Martyred Anabaptist Women of the Low Countries* [Milwaukee: Marquette University Press, 2001].)

Hutterites moved to South Dakota, where they have survived to the present day. (The Hutterites in South Dakota migrated to Canada because they were persecuted for their pacifism during World War I; after the end of the war, they gradually returned to the United States, where they still live communally.) Many other religious groups, such as the Baptists, Unitarians, and Quakers, have their roots in the radical Reformation. The radicals' notions that religious allegiance should be voluntary, and that church and state should be separate, later became part of the United States Constitution, and are widely accepted in Europe today.

Social change and the Reformation

The radicals represent one way that the ideas of early reformers were pushed further; as we have seen, many of their ideas had social, economic, and political implications, which is in part why they were seen as so dangerous. Groups that linked Protestant ideas directly to various political and social programs were also threatening. In 1522–23, free imperial knights, who controlled small territories in the Empire and numbered in the thousands, revolted against larger territorial princes. Their grievances were primarily economic and military – knights were becoming less valued because of the military changes traced in chapter 3, and their small estates could not support them adequately because of inflation – but they used Lutheran ideas to justify their movement. Armies led by territorial princes quickly suppressed the revolt and burned a number of knights' castles; the Knights' Revolt thus succeeded only in making some princes more wary of the new religious ideas.

The German Peasants' War of 1524–26 had much more far-reaching consequences than the Knights' Revolt. Peasants in many parts of Germany objected to new laws limiting hunting and fishing rights, rising levels of taxation, and the imposition of labor obligations; in 1524 what began as a protest about fishing in a forbidden stream quickly became a widespread rebellion, the largest mass uprising in Europe before the French Revolution. Local groups of peasants formed regional revolutionary organizations and military alliances in southwestern and then central and southeastern Germany. In March 1525 a union of these groups issued the Twelve Articles of Memmingen, a manifesto that called for the abolition of serfdom, hunting and fishing rights, a reduction in taxes and labor services, and the right of the community to elect and dismiss pastors to ensure that the "pure gospel" would be preached. Most dramatically, the Twelve Articles stated that any practice not in accordance with the gospels should be rejected, thus linking the word of God, what was often termed "divine law," with issues of social justice. All of this was expressed in clear language, and the Articles were published as a small pamphlet that was quickly reprinted many times. The demands of the Twelve Articles were backed by military action, and peasant armies seized castles, noble houses, abbeys, and a few cities; in other cities townspeople themselves revolted, calling for civil rights and religious reform. Peasant and urban armies included former mercenaries, so that they were not completely inexperienced, but they had almost no cavalry or artillery and few firearms. Once experienced imperial mercenaries returned from fighting in Italy, and the forces of territorial rulers organized to fight the revolt, peasant armies were crushed with brutality and vengeance.

Though peasant grievances long predated the Reformation, the ideas of Luther and Zwingli about Christian freedom and the reshaping of Christian life certainly influenced the way peasant calls for change were expressed. The response by magisterial reformers was uniformly hostile, however; as noted above, in *Against the Robbing and Murdering Hordes of Peasants* (1525), Luther urged rulers "as God's sword on earth to knock down, strangle, and stab the insurgents as one would a mad dog." He and other reformers asserted that their message was not to be linked with economic, social, or political grievances, and that peasants and poor city people both owed their superiors obedience. Spiritual reasons never gave individuals the right to oppose political authority by force, an idea Zwingli also affirmed in *Whoever Causes Insurrection* (1526). Not surprisingly, the magisterial Reformation lost much of its popular appeal after 1525, though peasants and urban rebels sometimes found a place for their social and religious ideas within radical groups.

At the same time as they were reacting so harshly to radicals and peasants, Luther and Zwingli decided to marry, Luther to a former nun, Katharina von Bora (1499–1552), and Zwingli to a Zurich widow, Anna Reinhart (1491–1538); both women quickly had several children. Most other Protestant reformers also married, and their wives had to create a new and respectable role for themselves – that of pastor's wife – to overcome people viewing them as simply a new type of priest's concubine. They were living demonstrations of their husband's convictions about the superiority of marriage to celibacy, and were expected to be models of wifely obedience and Christian charity.

Though they denied its sacramental nature, many Protestant reformers praised marriage in formal treatises, commentaries on the Book of Genesis, household guides, and – most importantly – wedding sermons. They stressed that it had been ordained by God when he presented Eve to Adam, served as a "remedy" for the unavoidable sin of lust, provided a site for the pious rearing of the next generation of God-fearing Christians, and offered husbands and wives companionship and consolation. A proper marriage was one that reflected both the spiritual equality of men and women and the proper social hierarchy of husbandly authority and wifely obedience. Protestants did not break with medieval scholastic theologians in their idea that women were to be subject to men, a subjection rooted in their original nature and made more pronounced by Eve's primary responsibility for the Fall. Women were advised to be cheerful rather than grudging in their obedience, for in doing so they demonstrated their willingness to follow God's plan. Men were urged to treat their wives kindly and considerately, but also to enforce their authority, through physical coercion, if necessary; both continental and English marriage manuals use the metaphor of breaking a horse for teaching a wife obedience, though laws did set limits on the husband's power to do so. (In England the law held that the stick a husband could use had to be thinner than his thumb; this is the origin of the phrase "rule of thumb.") A few women took Luther's idea about the priesthood of all believers to heart and wrote religious pamphlets and hymns, but no sixteenth-century Protestants officially allowed women to hold positions of religious authority, though monarchs such as Elizabeth I and female terri-torial rulers of the states of the Holy Roman Empire did determine religious policies.

Because, in Protestant eyes, marriage was created by God as a remedy for human weakness, marriages in which spouses did not comfort or support one another physically, materially, or emotionally endangered their own souls and the surrounding community. The only solution might be divorce and remarriage, which most Protestants came to allow. Protestant marital courts in Germany, Switzerland, Scandinavia, and later Scotland and France allowed divorce for adultery and impotence, and sometimes for contracting a contagious disease, "malicious" desertion (meaning intentional desertion, as opposed to unintentional desertion such as extended army service), conviction for a capital crime, or deadly assault. Some of them allowed both parties to marry again, and some only the innocent.

This was a dramatic change in marital law, as Catholic canon law had allowed only separation from bed and board with no remarriage, but it had a less than dramatic impact. Because marriage was the cornerstone of society socially and economically, divorce was a desperate last resort, and in many Protestant jurisdictions the annual divorce rate hovered around 0.02 to 0.06 per thousand people. (By contrast, the 2000 US divorce rate was 4.1 per thou-sand people.) This was still higher than the divorce rate in England and Ireland, however, for the Anglican and Anglo-Irish churches rejected divorce and contin-ued to assert the indissolubility of marriage. This rejection led England later to adopt a totally secular divorce process. Beginning in 1670, divorces for adultery were granted by Act of Parliament, a procedure that remained the only avenue for divorce in England until 1857. These acts were very rare; there were only 325 in the entire period from 1670 to 1857, with only four of these filed by women.

Religious wars

Radicals and peasants were not the only ones to be met by violence, for the Reformation brought with it more than one hundred years of religious war in Europe. What we might term round 1 of these wars, from 1529 to 1555, involved Zwinglians, Lutherans, and Catholics in Switzerland and Germany; round 2, from 1560 to 1609, involved Catholics and Calvinists in France and the Netherlands; and round 3, the Thirty Years War from 1618 to 1648, involved nearly all of Europe. Thus one of the consequences of the Reformation was an increased chance of being killed for one's own religious beliefs, the beliefs of one's ruler, or simply by accident in a religious war. All of these wars involved political and dynastic issues as well as religious ones. Indeed, it is probably misleading to separate the two, for rulers and others who held political power clearly did not.

Switzerland in the early sixteenth century was officially a part of the Holy Roman Empire, though it was really a loose confederation of thirteen largely autonomous cantons. The cantons were often hostile to one another, and powers from outside the Swiss Confederation, particularly the papacy and France, could take advantage of these tensions. Popes, the kings of France, and emperors also used Switzerland as a source of mercenaries, paying large pensions to Swiss military captains to act as recruiting officers and commanders. Along with calling for religious reforms, Zwingli called for an end to the mercenary system, what he termed "trading blood for gold." This did not mean that he rejected military action to further his aims, however. As the leader of the Zurich city council, he made a number of treaties with other cantons that had accepted reform, and those that had not also formed an alliance. These Catholic cantons allied themselves with Ferdinand, the Habsburg ruler of Austria, which Zwingli countered by planning a grand anti-Habsburg alliance involving France, England, and many other states of Europe. This never materialized, but the two sides met militarily in 1531 at Kappel, just south of Zurich, a battle in which Zwingli was killed.

Both sides quickly decided that a treaty was preferable to further fighting; the treaty basically allowed each canton to determine its own religion, and ordered each side to give up its foreign alliances. This weakened the unity of the Swiss Confederation and did not stop mercenary recruitment, but it did establish a policy of neutrality that is still characteristic of modern Switzerland.

At the same time as Protestants and Catholics were forming military alliances in Switzerland, political authorities were doing the same in Germany. Hoping to end religious divisions, the Emperor Charles V (ruled 1519–56) called an Imperial Diet in 1530, to meet at Augsburg. Luther's associate Melanchthon developed a statement of faith, later called the Augsburg Confession (or *Confessio Augustana* in Latin), and the Protestant princes presented this to the emperor. He refused to accept it and ordered all Protestants to return to the Catholic church and give up any confiscated church property. This threat backfired, and Protestant territories in the Empire – mostly north German princes and south German cities – formed a military alliance called the Schmalkaldic League, with the Augsburg Confession as its statement of belief. The Augsburg Confession remained an authoritative statement of belief for many Lutheran churches, especially those outside of Germany, for centuries, while a subsequent statement of belief, the Formula of Concord, drawn up in 1577, was accepted by the majority of German Lutherans. (Several Lutheran colleges in the United States are named Augsburg, Augustana, and Concordia in honor of these statements.) Luther altered his ideas about the right of resistance somewhat; though private persons were never to oppose their rulers, those who had political authority, such as princes, could oppose those above them in a political hierarchy, such as the pope and emperor, when they were clearly in league with the anti-Christ.

The emperor could not respond militarily to the Schmalkaldic League, as he was in the midst of a series of wars with the French – the Habsburg–Valois wars, fought in Italy and along the eastern and southern borders of France – and the Turks under Süleyman the Magnificent had taken much of Hungary and besieged Vienna. The 1530s and early 1540s saw complicated political maneuvering among many of the powers of Europe. The emperor, the pope, France, England, Protestant and Catholic princes and cities in Germany, Scotland, Sweden, Denmark, and even the Turks made and broke alliances, and the Habsburg–Valois rivalry continued to be played out militarily. Various attempts were made to heal the religious split with a church council, but the intransigence on both sides made it increasingly clear that this would not be possible, and that war was inevitable. Charles V realized that he was not only fighting for religious unity, but also for a more unified state against territorial rulers who wanted to maintain their independence. He was thus defending both church and empire.

Fighting began in 1546, and initially the emperor was very successful, taking a number of Protestant leaders captive and forcing the south German cities to come to terms with him. This success alarmed the pope, however, who did not want Charles to become so powerful that he could limit papal authority in Germany. He withdrew papal troops, and Charles called an Imperial Diet in an attempt to end the war. The agreement drawn up at this diet created only a temporary lull in the fighting, and Protestant rulers regrouped, allying themselves with the French. The French were Catholic, but by this time territorial rulers were more concerned with limiting the power of the emperor than with religious ideology.

After a brief period of fighting, both sides agreed to a diet to draw up a more permanent settlement. Neither the emperor nor papal representatives were present at this diet, so the main actors were the territorial rulers, and the agreement they drew up, the Peace of Augsburg, reflected their concerns. According to the terms of the Peace of Augsburg, accepted in 1555, Lutheran princes, knights, and cities were guaranteed security, with both sides ordered to maintain "eternal, unconditional peace"; each territory was given the right to decide whether to be Lutheran or Catholic (a principle codified in the phrase *cuius regio, eius religio* – literally whose the region, his the religion); inhabitants who disagreed with their ruler were to be allowed to leave; all church lands taken by Lutheran rulers before 1552 were to be retained by them; individuals who were territorial rulers because of their position as officials in the Catholic

Map 6. Religious divisions in Europe in the later sixteenth century.

church were to give up their title and lands if they became Lutheran. The terms of the treaty were to be preserved not by the emperor, but by a deputation of princes.

The Peace of Augsburg accomplished what its makers hoped it would: it ended religious war in Germany for many decades, and put political, religious, and economic life clearly in the hands of the territorial rulers, who became increasingly authoritarian. They became the primary agents of confessionalization and social discipline, developing and expanding institutions of control such as church courts, reforming poor relief by regulating begging and reforming social welfare, supporting schools and universities that would impart correct doctrine to students and train pastors loyal to state churches. Limitations and problems in the Peace of Augsburg would become clear by the late sixteenth century, but it was immediately evident that this agreement ended Charles V's hope of creating a united empire with a single church. He abdicated in 1556 and moved to a monastery, transferring power over his holdings in Spain and the Netherlands to his son Philip, and his imperial power to his brother Ferdinand.

Calvinism

One of the limitations of the Peace of Augsburg was the fact that it recognized only Lutheran Protestantism and Catholicism as legitimate confessions, and by 1555 the most dynamic form of Protestantism was that inspired by John Calvin (1509–64). Calvin was born in France and originally studied law; in about 1533 he became a Protestant and fled to Geneva, where he quickly published the *Institutes of the Christian Religion*, a synthesis of Protestant thought arranged in a logical, systematic way. In the *Institutes*, Calvin sets out his key doctrines: God is infinite in power and sovereignty; humans are completely sinful and depraved, saved only through the atoning power of Jesus Christ; redemptive grace and the possibility of union with Christ are free gifts of God; there is no free will, for God determined who would be saved through the redemptive power of Christ and who would not. The latter idea, called *predestination*, had been asserted by Christian thinkers since St. Augustine in the fourth century and discussed even earlier, but Calvin made it absolute. God's decision occurred at the beginning of time, foreordaining some to eternal damnation and others to eternal salvation. Even Adam and Eve did not have free will, for God had determined what their actions in the Garden of Eden would be. This "terrible decree" – Calvin's own words – was based simply on God's will, which is the highest justice.

One's own actions could do nothing to change one's fate, but many Calvinists came to believe that hard work, thrift, and proper moral conduct could serve as signs that one was among the "elect" chosen for salvation. Any occupation or profession could be a God-given "calling," and should be done with diligence, thanksgiving, and dedication. Salvation had already been decided, so that human energies could be put to fulfilling God's will in the world. Calvinism appealed to a wide spectrum of people, but it proved especially popular with urban merchants, professionals, and artisans, who were attracted to its vigor and dynamism.

Calvin's writings attracted the attention of city leaders in Geneva, who had just thrown out their bishop and were setting up new city and church governance structures. They asked for Calvin's assistance in this, and he spent the rest of his life – with one short break – in Geneva, transforming the city into a community based on his religious principles. Calvin was firm in the notion that the leaders of the church should have ultimate authority, and that church and state should act together. The most powerful organization became the Consistory, a group of pastors and lay elders, or presbyters, charged with investigating and disciplining deviations from proper doctrine and conduct, and ensuring the welfare of the city. A well-disciplined city, like a well-disciplined individual, might be seen as evidence of God's election, and would certainly provide an appropriate setting for those on their way to heaven. Thus the Consistory sought out religious dissenters, but also those guilty of drunkenness, profanity, gambling, adultery, family fights, absence from church, dancing, and premarital sex. Its punishments ranged from scolding to corporal punishments such as whipping to excommunication, which brought civil death as well as separation from the church, as excommunicants could not make a will, plead in court, inherit property or otherwise act as a legal person. Those charged with serious crimes, such as adultery, murder, heresy, or witchcraft, were tried by a civil court that could enforce the death penalty. Most public amusements, such as theatre, dances, dice and card games, and even drinking, were prohibited or restricted, both because they could lead to more clearly immoral action and because they were a waste of time for the elect. Religious images were removed from churches. Deacons were appointed to oversee poor relief and the care of widows and orphans. Members of the Consistory regularly questioned people about what was going on in their neighborhoods, and encouraged children to report suspicious or improper activities of older family members.

Along with the Consistory, Calvin set up an academy for those who wished to become clergy, providing them with theological instruction and practical, on-the-job training as local chaplains or assistant pastors before sending them out on their own. Young men trained at the Genevan Academy spread Calvinist ideas into France, the Netherlands, Germany, England, Scotland, Hungary, and Poland, often working with local leaders who had visited or been religious refugees in Geneva and had been impressed by what they saw. In areas that were officially Catholic, such as France and the Netherlands, they organized churches secretly. In areas that were Protestant, such as England, they worked within the state church to move theology and discipline in a Calvinist direction, which came to be called "Puritanism." In areas where nobles were relatively free to make decisions about religion on their own lands, such as Germany and Poland, Calvinism became the state church, even though it was not officially recognized by the Peace of Augsburg. In Scotland, John Knox (1505?–72), who had studied with Calvin in Geneva, worked with the Scottish Parliament to set up a Calvinist state church, the "Kirk" of Scotland, with consistories called kirk sessions or presbyteries enforcing discipline. Scottish settlers took Calvinism to Ireland later in the century, where the state church was similar to the Church of England, but most people were still Catholic.

Fig. 14. A sketch of Calvin made during a lecture by one of his students, capturing the reserve that comes out in Calvin's letters as well.

Because they were working in areas larger than just one canton, Calvinists outside Geneva established regional representative institutions to make decisions about broader issues of church policy. All bodies from local consistories to regional institutions involved lay elders in setting church policy; thus, though Calvinism is sometimes called a "theocracy" because pastors had a great influence on all aspects of daily life, what was more novel in the sixteenth century was lay men having a strong voice in running the church. This enhanced the appeal of Calvinism for many groups, who also combined it with political grievances. Nobles in France who accepted Calvinism saw it as a way to combat the power of the monarchy as well as the papacy, while urban residents in the Netherlands saw it as a way to assert their independence from their Habsburg rulers, especially Charles V's son Philip II, who was intent on strengthening royal authority.

The Catholic Reformation

The successes of Calvinism spurred the Catholic Church into more vigorous responses to Protestant challenges, which had begun somewhat fitfully in the 1530s. Many historians see the developments within the Catholic Church after the Protestant Reformation as two interrelated movements, one a drive for internal reform linked to earlier reform efforts, and the other a Counter-Reformation that opposed Protestants intellectually, politically, militarily, and institutionally. In both of these movements, the papacy, new religious orders, and the Council of Trent that met from 1545 to 1563 were important agents.

Beginning with Pope Paul III (pontificate 1534–49), the papal court became the center of the reform movement rather than its chief opponent. Paul appointed reform-minded cardinals, abbots, and bishops who improved education for the clergy, tried to enforce moral standards among them, and worked on correcting the most glaring abuses. Reform measures that had been suggested since the late Middle Ages – such as doing away with the buying and selling of church offices (termed simony), requiring bishops to live in their dioceses, forbidding clergy to hold multiple offices (termed pluralism), ending worldliness and immorality at the papal court, changing the church's tax collection and legal procedures – were gradually adopted during the sixteenth century. Paul III and his successors supported the establishment of new religious orders that preached to the common people, the opening of seminaries for the training of priests, the end of simony, and stricter control of clerical life. Their own lives were models of decorum and piety, in contrast to the fifteenth- and early sixteenth-century popes such as Alexander VI (pontificate 1492–1503), Julius II (pontificate 1503–13), and Clement VII (pontificate 1523–34), who had concentrated on building and decorating churches and palaces and on enhancing the power of their own families. (Alexander was a member of the Spanish Borgia family, and accomplished his aims partly through the military actions of his son Cesare and the marriages of his daughter Lucrezia.) By 1600 the papacy had been reestablished as a spiritual force in Europe, with its political hold on central Italy suffering no decline in the process.

Reforming popes also supported measures designed to combat the spread of Protestant teaching. Paul III reorganized the Sacred Congregation of the Holy Office, giving it jurisdiction over the Roman Inquisition and putting its direction in the hands of a committee of cardinals in Rome. The Inquisition was given the power to investigate those suspected of holding heretical opinions or committing acts deemed theologically unacceptable, and was very effective at ending Protestantism, first in the Papal States and then elsewhere in Italy, though local authorities sometimes limited the scope of its investigations. Paul III's successors Paul IV (pontificate 1555–9) and Pius IV (pontificate 1559–65) promulgated an Index of Prohibited Books, which forbade the printing, distribution, and reading of books and authors judged heretical. (The Index was formally abolished in 1966, and the records of the Congregation of the Holy Office were opened to scholarly study in 1998. Many of its records had been carted off to Paris during the time of Napoleon, where they were sold as scrap paper.)

Reforms involved religious orders as well as the papacy. Older religious orders, such as the Benedictines, Augustinians, and Franciscans, carried out measures to restore discipline and get back to their original aims. New religious orders such as the Theatines, Barnabites, and Capuchins worked among the poor and sick, establishing hospitals and orphanages and preaching and administering the sacraments in poorer districts.

The most important of the new religious orders was the Society of Jesus, or the Jesuits, founded by Ignatius Loyola (1491?–1556). Loyola was a Spanish knight who became acquainted with the works of religious writers and mystics while his leg was mending after being broken in several places during a battle in the first Habsburg–Valois war. Like Luther, he went through a period of inner turmoil and crisis of conscience, but resolved this through a rigorous program of contemplation rather than a new theological approach. He later described his techniques – in Spanish, so that they could be read by those who did not know Latin – in the *Spiritual Exercises*, which sets out a training program of structured meditation, designed to develop spiritual discipline and allow one to meld one's will with that of God. The ultimate aim of Loyola's program was not a mystical losing of oneself in God, however, but action on behalf of God. Though Loyola had not studied as a humanist, his stress on the individual will and the possibility – with God's assistance – of self-control and holiness certainly fitted with the ideas of Ficino and Pico.

Loyola had, in fact, not studied formally at all, a deficit that he recognized. He enrolled first at a preparatory school to improve his Latin, and then studied briefly at several Spanish universities. In 1528, he went to Paris to study theology, and quickly gathered a group of like-minded young men around him, including Francis Xavier (1506–52), who later became a missionary in Asia. Most of the members of this group were not priests, but they took the standard monastic vows of poverty, chastity, and obedience, and also declared that they owed special obedience to the pope. After some initial misgivings, Pope Paul III responded in 1540 by recognizing the group as a new religious order, the Society of Jesus, whose main purposes were the entwined processes of education and conversion. The Jesuits founded schools, taught at universities, and preached popular sermons. They became confessors to influential people, and through this gained influence at many European courts. The order itself was highly centralized and arranged in a military-style hierarchy under a Superior General; Jesuits were not under the control of local bishops, an independence that the bishops often resented. Though Loyola's *Spiritual Exercises* offered a quick four-week program for those beginning the process of self-discipline, training for admission into the order took many years, during which time a young man went through military-like training designed to transform him into a spiritual soldier controlled from within. Only those who had passed rigid examinations were allowed to become professed fathers and take the special fourth vow of absolute obedience to the papacy.

Their training and discipline made Jesuits extremely effective. Under the leadership of Peter Canisius (1521–97), they established colleges in Vienna, Cologne, Munich, Mainz, and other cities in the southern part of the Holy Roman Empire, reconverting some areas that had become officially Protestant and strengthening the loyalty of areas that had been wavering. In 1565 Canisius sent ten members of the order to Poland-Lithuania, where many of the nobles were Protestants of various types – Lutheran, Calvinist, Socinian – and the official policy was one of religious toleration. Jesuits established several colleges for training noble boys, and became confessors to the Polish monarchs; loyalty to Catholicism grew, and in the early seventeenth century King Sigismund III Vasa (ruled 1587–1632) repudiated the policy of toleration with little resistance. Jesuit missionaries went to Brazil, the Spanish New World colonies, West Africa, India, the East Indies, Japan, and China, where they worked to convert indigenous people and minister to the European soldiers, traders, and settlers who were there. (Missionary activity outside Europe will be discussed in more detail in chapters 7 and 13.)

In 1580, Robert Parsons (1546–1610) and Edmund Campion (1540–81) began a Jesuit mission in Protestant England, providing spiritual guidance and religious services for English Catholics, and encouraging them to resist Elizabeth's policies of religious uniformity. Campion was arrested and executed as a traitor, and Parsons returned to the continent to organize or expand colleges for Englishmen who wished to become Catholic priests. Despite the threat of arrest and execution, Jesuits and other priests stayed in England, where they were often sheltered by women from prominent Catholic families. Married women, according to common law, controlled no property, and imprisoning a woman would disrupt family life. Thus though Elizabethan officials fined and imprisoned Catholic men for recusancy (refusing to attend church), they were generally unwilling to apply the law to women, and English Catholicism increasingly centered on households.

20 Luise de Carvajal's mission to England

Women's requests to serve as missionaries were almost always denied, but a few women were given permission to minister to Catholics in England. One of these was a Spanish noblewoman, Luise de Carvajal y Mendoza (1566–1614), who was jailed several times for attempting to convince English Protestants to convert to Catholicism. The following is a portion of a letter she wrote to Joseph Creswell, the director of the English Jesuits in Spain and Portugal, which gives a vivid account of street-corner religious debates.

I can tell Your Grace that I have walked between the cross and holy water, as they say there, because I have been in prison, and since it was in the public jail, it would be useless for me to keep silent about it. The reason was because, arriving one day at a store in Cheapside [a part of London], leaning on the door sill from outside, as is my custom, the occasion offered to ask one of the young attendants if he was Catholic presented itself, and he responded, "No, God forbid!" And I replied, "May God not permit that you not be, which is what matters for you." At this the mistress and master of the shop came over, and another youth and neighboring merchants, and a great chat about religion ensued. They asked a lot about the mass, about priests, about confession, but what we spent the most time on (over two hours) was whether the Roman religion was the only true one, and whether the Pope is the head of the Church, and whether St. Peter's keys have been left to them [the popes] forever in succession.

Some listened with pleasure, others with fury, and so much that I sensed some danger, at least of being arrested. But I thought nothing of it, in exchange for setting that light before their eyes in the best way I could. And in these simple matters of faith there are known methods [of convincing] which are very handy

for anyone, and with which one can wage war on error. And although they might not take it very well at first, in the end those truths remain in their memories, to be meditated upon and open to holy inspirations, and God's cause for their salvation or condemnation is greatly justified. And there are very many who never manage to find out even where the priests are, and among the lay Catholics, not many want to run that risk [of contact with priests] without a guaranteed benefit. And the merchants of Cheapside exceed the rest of the city in malice, error, and hatred for the Pope, as well as in the quantity of its residents and money. And some of this can be observed in the fact that, when I have spoken on several occasions with others about exactly the same things, they have always taken it affably.

The mistress of the shop tried to stir everyone to anger, as did another infernal young man who was there, younger in age but with greater malice. The woman said it was a shame that they were tolerating me and that, without a doubt, I was some Roman [Catholic] priest dressed like a woman so as to better persuade people of my religion. Our Lord saw fit that I speak the best English I've spoken since I've been in England, and they thought I was Scottish because of the way I spoke …

While in jail I spoke about religion much more than I had out of it, with all the jailers and officials and their families and friends whom, with my permission, they brought to speak with me. And they listened nicely. And I didn't want to let the chance slip by, remembering the Holy Apostle who says that the word of God is not tied down.

(From Elizabeth Rhodes, *This Tight Embrace: Luisa de Carvajal y Mendoza (1566–1614)* [Milwaukee: Marquette University Press, 2000], pp. 265–79. Reprinted by permission.)

The unusual situation of Catholics in England allowed recusant women to play a more prominent role in the maintenance of Catholicism than was possible for women elsewhere in Europe. The year after the Jesuits obtained papal recognition, Isabel Roser, who had been an associate of Loyola's in Barcelona, sought papal approval for an order of women with a similarly active mission of education, along with care of the sick and destitute. Loyola was horrified at the thought of religious women in regular contact with lay people, and Pope Paul III refused to grant approval. Despite this, Roser's group continued to grow in Rome and the Netherlands. Several years earlier, Angela Merici (1474–1540) had founded the Company of St. Ursula, a group of lay single women and widows also dedicated to the poor. This received papal authorization, and later in the century became a religious order focusing increasingly on girls' education. Once they became a religious order, however, the Ursulines came under increasing pressure to become cloistered nuns, that is, to cut themselves off from the world in enclosed convents. Many Ursuline houses fought this, though others accepted claustration willingly, having accepted church teaching that the life of a cloistered nun was the most worthy role for a woman in the eyes of God. Ursuline houses were generally allowed to continue teaching girls, though now within the walls of the convent, and especially in France, they became the most important providers of education for girls.

The exclusion of women from what were judged the most exciting and important parts of the Catholic Reformation – countering Protestants and winning converts – is reflected in the relative lack of women from the sixteenth century who were made saints. Only 18.1 percent of those individuals from the sixteenth century who were made saints were women, whereas 27.7 percent of those from the fifteenth century had been women. Sixteenth-century male saints tended to be missionaries, reforming bishops and popes, or opponents of Protestantism, while female saints were generally mystics or reformers of existing religious orders. The best known of these – indeed, the most famous religious woman of the sixteenth century – was Teresa of Avila (1515–82), a Carmelite nun who recorded her mystical visions in a spiritual autobiography, founded new convents, and reformed her Carmelite order. Though Teresa did not advocate institutionalized roles for women outside the convent, she did chafe at the restrictions placed on her because of her sex, and thought of the new religious houses she founded as answers to the Protestant takeover of Catholic churches elsewhere in Europe.

An affirmation of the necessity of cloistering for all women religious was just one of many decrees issued by the Council of Trent, an ecumenical council convened by Paul III in 1545, which met with several breaks over the next eighteen years to define Catholic dogma and reform abuses. In terms of dogma, Trent reasserted traditional Catholic beliefs in response to Protestant challenges: good works as well as faith are necessary for salvation; tradition along with Scripture contains essential Christian teachings; the mystery and power of the mass centers on transubstantiation, which can only be effected by an ordained priest; seven sacraments are efficacious and, except for emergency baptisms, can be administered only by a priest; the Virgin Mary and the saints are to be venerated; priests and monks are to be celibate, and to give up their concubines.

The Council of Trent also issued a large number of disciplinary decrees, though these were not accepted in all Catholic areas of Europe the way Tridentine dogmatic decrees were. (Regulations from the Council of Trent are termed "Tridentine" from the Latin name for the city of Trent, Tridentum.) These called for bishops to live in their dioceses, forbade the outright sale of indulgences (though not the pope's power to grant them), strengthened the jurisdiction of bishops, and required every diocese to establish a seminary.

Priests were to be trained to instruct and teach the laity, and were to keep records of how well their parishioners were fulfilling their spiritual obligations, especially the duty to confess and receive Communion during the Easter season.

In its final session, the Council passed the decree *Tametsi*, which laid out Catholic marriage doctrine. To be valid, a marriage would now have to be celebrated before witnesses, one of whom had to be the parish priest; priests were ordered to keep records of all marriages in their parishes. Divorce with remarriage was not allowable for any reason, though spouses who absolutely could not live together could ask for a separation from bed and board; annulment was still a possibility, but only for very extreme cases such as total impotence.

Tridentine decrees set out ideals that were realized only very slowly; their impact would not be felt until the seventeenth or even the eighteenth century in many parts of Catholic Europe. By the time the Council finally disbanded in 1564, however, the Catholic Church had clearly begun to change. The church had revived traditional doctrine, provided the means for the enforcement of theological uniformity through such measures as the Inquisition and the Papal Index, and begun to reform itself through the new religious orders with their emphasis on discipline and education.

This revitalization was not simply a matter of the church hierarchy, but also of devotional life at the local level. Confraternities of lay people were established or expanded in many urban parishes and even in villages. Venice had 120 confraternities in about 1500 and almost 400 by about 1700. They held processions and feasts, engaged in penitential flagellation, handed out charity to the poor, conducted funerary services for their members, purchased candles, furnishings, and art for churches, administered hospitals and orphanages, and supported local shrines and altars. Most confraternities were limited to men, though there were a few all-female confraternities, often dedicated to the rosary, the Virgin Mary, St. Anne (the mother of the Virgin), or another female saint. Jesuits relied on confraternities organized under their auspices, called Marian sodalities, for financial and political support in their charitable, educational, and missionary activities. Some of these, such as the French Congregation of the Holy Sacrament or the Portuguese Misericordia confraternity, were secret bodies of courtiers and officials who provided support for the monarchy as well as engaging in devotional and charitable activities. Such support was important when the leaders in this reinvigorated Catholic Church fielded armies against Protestants who were themselves more militant.

Later religious wars

The first theatre of conflict in the second round of religious wars was France. In 1559, France and Spain ended the long series of Habsburg–Valois wars by signing the Treaty of Cateau-Cambrésis, which affirmed Spanish dominance in Italy. These wars had been ruinously expensive for the French monarchy, which, as we saw in chapter 3, sold offices to raise revenue. Francis I (ruled 1515–47) also made a treaty with the papacy, the Concordat of Bologna, in which he agreed to recognize papal supremacy over any church council in return for the right to appoint all French bishops and abbots, thus dramatically expanding the number of offices the French monarchy could sell or give as rewards. The Concordat gave the French monarchy control over the personnel of the French church and a vested interest in maintaining Catholicism.

Religious reformers in France such as the Christian humanist Lefèvre d'Etaples debated Lutheran ideas as early as the 1520s, but the ideas of Calvin found far wider acceptance, particularly among urban residents and nobles. Calvin was himself French and wrote in French, and sent pastors trained at the Genevan Academy to French cities and noble households. Nobles in France saw accepting Calvinism as a way to combat the power of the monarchy, while urban artisans were attracted by the role it gave to the laity and its emphasis on work and order. French Protestants (called Huguenots) and their Catholic opponents used violent actions as well as preaching and teaching against each other, for each side regarded the other as a poison in the community that would provoke the wrath of God. Protestant teachings called the power of sacred images into question, and mobs in many cities took down and smashed statues, stained-glass windows, and paintings. They ridiculed and tested religious images, throwing them into latrines, using them as cooking fuel or building material, or giving them as toys or masks for children. Though it was often inspired by fiery Protestant sermons, this iconoclasm is an example of men and women carrying out the Reformation themselves, rethinking the church's system of meaning and the relationship between the unseen and the seen. Catholic mobs responded by defending images, and crowds on both sides killed their opponents, often in gruesome ways. Such murders led to open warfare during the 1560s, with the French monarchy generally backing the Catholics, but sometimes adopting a more conciliatory policy and arranging for truces.

In 1572, it appeared as if the French monarchy wanted to make the truce more permanent, as the royal government invited the leaders of both sides to Paris to celebrate the lavish royal wedding of a Protestant prince (Henry of Navarre) to the sister of the king. A few days later, on August 24 (St. Bartholomew's Day), most of the prominent Protestant wedding guests were assassinated on the order of the royal council, and thousands of other Protestants from all walks of life were slaughtered by mobs. The violence spread to other cities, where thousands more were killed, not through spontaneous mob action but on the direction of municipal authorities. This planned and orchestrated bloodshed, which became known as the St. Bartholomew's Day Massacre, drove some Protestants into exile but others to renewed warfare and, as we

Fig. 15. Armed procession of the Catholic League through a French city, 1590, in an oil painting by François Bunel (1522–1599). Public processions by both sides in the French religious wars heightened tensions and provoked riots.

saw in chapter 4, to developing political theories justifying rebellion against a tyrannical ruler.

The war dragged on for fifteen years, exhausting both sides and frequently provoking further riots and assassinations, including the fatal stabbing of King Henry III (ruled 1574–89). This murder left the Protestant Henry of Navarre – the unfortunate bridegroom of the St. Bartholomew's Day Massacre – as the king of France (he ruled as Henry IV, 1589–1610). Despite – or perhaps because of – his own experiences, Henry was more pragmatic than doctrinaire in matters of religion, a position that was termed "politique." Recognizing the fact that most French people were Catholic, Henry first declared Catholicism the official religion of France, and a few years later agreed to become Catholic himself. Radicals on both sides were aghast, and Catholic propaganda asserted that Henry's conversion was not genuine, claiming he had said "Paris is worth a mass." But mutual fatigue and an increasing fear of disorder – which would indeed erupt shortly in a massive peasant uprising in south-central France called the Croquants – led more moderate forces on both sides to accept Henry as king and stop fighting. Henry confirmed this truce in 1598 in the Edict of Nantes, which stated clearly that Catholicism was the state religion of France, but gave Huguenots the right to live and worship freely in certain defined areas and the right to maintain about 150 fortified towns. The toleration accorded by the Edict of Nantes was thus limited, and the Edict itself would be revoked in 1685 under Louis XIV (ruled 1643–1715), but it did provide many years of religious peace.

Iconoclastic riots and hostility to a monarch were also part of religious wars in the Netherlands. This country, which Charles V had inherited from his grandmother Mary of Burgundy, was made up of seventeen quite independent provinces, many of them centered on towns such as Bruges, Ghent, Amsterdam, and Antwerp that were wealthy centers of trade and production. Charles, who had grown up in the Netherlands, was able to limit the spread of Lutheran ideas, but his son Philip, who had grown up in Spain and inherited the Netherlands along with Spain and the Spanish possessions in Italy and the New World when Charles abdicated in 1556, was much less effective against Calvinism. Merchants and artisans in the thriving towns were attracted to it because of the sense of purpose it offered and its validation of labor. Philip was not willing to tolerate this, and nor was his half-sister Margaret of Parma (ruled 1559–67), whom Philip appointed as regent while he stayed in Spain. Margaret began to repress Calvinism, and at the same time she raised taxes; these two moves together sparked a wave of iconoclastic rioting in 1566. Philip responded by sending an army under the duke of Alva to stop the riots and punish those who were destroying religious images. Alva carried out his task ruthlessly, executing hundreds of men after trying them through a special court that became known as the "Council of Blood." These harsh moves were ineffective, and led instead to open rebellion and civil war against Spain.

Spanish armies were initially unsuccessful, but gradually they affirmed their hold on the southern ten provinces, which included Bruges, Ghent, and Antwerp. Calvinism was prohibited and the area (modern-day Belgium) remained Catholic and under the control of the Spanish Habsburgs. The seven northern provinces, including Holland and Utrecht, formed a union in 1579, which later became the United Provinces of the Netherlands. Philip did not accept this, and war continued, with the Dutch troops gaining victories under the leadership of a local nobleman, William of Nassau, prince of Orange (1533–84), known as William the Silent. William was shot by a French assassin loyal to Philip, and the leaders of the United Provinces looked beyond their borders to other Protestant areas for assistance against the Spanish. They particularly appealed to England, and when it looked as if Spain would continue its advance into the northern Netherlands, Elizabeth reluctantly sent money and troops. At just the same time, Mary, Queen of Scots, cousin and heir to the childless Elizabeth, became implicated in a plot against Elizabeth's life. This conspiracy had the backing of the Spanish monarchy, and Mary was beheaded as a traitor. Philip received papal sanction and the promise of a huge payment if he invaded England, a move that he was already contemplating as the only way to reassert religious uniformity in Europe.

Philip increasingly isolated himself in the newly built palace of the Escorial near Madrid, planning the invasion from afar. He authorized the assembly of a huge fleet of ships in Lisbon, designed to attack the English coast directly and transport Spanish troops from the Netherlands to England in a land invasion. The fleet of about 130 ships, which official documents called "la felícissima armada" (the most fortunate fleet), left Lisbon in 1588. This was a year later than originally planned because English pirates had burned ships, supplies and most of the storage barrels as they lay stacked on the docks and new barrels had to be built. It was a disaster.

The experienced general whom Philip was relying on died during the year's delay. The new barrels were made of wood that had not been seasoned, so that they leaked, spoiling the food and water inside. Plans had not been communicated clearly to the Spanish troops and they were not prepared to be picked up, although ultimately this did not matter as Spanish pilots and captains were not able to get near the shore in any case. The Spanish ships were less maneuverable than the English ones, and some sank under English fire or burned when hit by lighted "fire-ships." Shifting winds in the English Channel led many Spanish vessels to just sail right by into the North Sea, ultimately foundering in storms or off the Irish coast, where delighted (Catholic) people plundered the ships and killed any survivors.

As a single event, the Spanish Armada was not as significant as it is sometimes portrayed, for about half the ships made it back to Spanish ports and war in the Netherlands continued through the rest of Philip's reign. Spain was unable to send enough troops to reinforce its hold on the entire Netherlands, however, for the booming Dutch economy provided plenty of ships, weapons, and manpower. Dutch pirates preyed on Spanish shipping and attacked colonial ports, while Dutch merchants organized to expand foreign trade through more peaceful, though no less ruthless, means. In 1609 the Spanish King Philip III (ruled 1598–1621) finally agreed to a truce, effectively recognizing the independence of the United Provinces.

At the beginning of the seventeenth century, the religious map of much of Europe was the product of just such uneasy truces. Italy, Spain, and Portugal were firmly Catholic, Scandinavia, England, and Scotland firmly Protestant, and Russia firmly Orthodox, but the middle of Europe was religiously divided. These religious divisions meant that policies of confessionalization and social discipline continued, and, as we will see in chapter 9, they would combine with dynastic and political disputes to lead to the Thirty Years War (1618–48), a conflict that would involve almost every European power. Though the combatants did not acknowledge it openly, the Thirty Years War would also involve economic issues, particularly trade and the wealth trade created, which shaped European society in the early modern period as much as the religious changes of the Reformations, as we will see in the next chapter.

Further reading

John Bossy, *Christianity in the West, 1400–1700* (Oxford: Oxford University Press, 1985), provides a lively, brief overview of the major changes and continuities in this era. Solid surveys of the Reformation include Euan Cameron, *The European Reformation* (Oxford: Clarendon Press, 1991), which focuses only on Protestants, and Carter Lindbergh, *The European Reformations* (Oxford: Blackwell, 1996), which includes some discussion of Catholic issues. Harold J. Grimm, *The Reformation Era, 1500–1650*, 2nd edn (New York: Macmillan, 1973), remains a thorough treatment of the relationship between religious change and other issues. R. Po-chia Hsia, *A Companion to the Reformation World* (Oxford: Blackwell, 2004), includes essays on a range of topics, each with a long bibliography, as does Hsia's *Re-formation and Expansion, c. 1500–c. 1660*, vol. VI of the Cambridge History of Christianity (Cambridge: Cambridge University Press, 2006).

Heiko Oberman, *Luther: Man Between God and the Devil* (New Haven: Yale University Press, 1989), provides a thorough grounding in Luther's thought, while François Wendel, *Calvin: The Origins and Development of his Religious Thought* (New York: Harper and Row, 1963), does the same for Calvin. G. H. Williams, *The Radical Reformation*, 3rd edn (Kirksville, MO: Sixteenth Century Essays and Studies, 1992), remains an important broad analysis.

Good surveys of the Catholic Reformation include Michael A. Mullett, *The Catholic Reformation* (London: Routledge, 1999), and R. Po-chia Hsia, *The World of Catholic Renewal, 1540–1770* (Cambridge: Cambridge University Press, 1998), which includes extended coverage of colonial Catholicism. Louis Chatellier, *The Europe of the Devout: The Catholic Reformation and the Formation of a New Society* (Cambridge: Cambridge University Press, 1989), focuses especially on France, while Sarah Nalle, *God in La Mancha: Religious Reform and the People of Cuenca, 1500–1650* (Baltimore: Johns Hopkins University Press, 1992), offers a well-documented analysis of one particular town. John W. O'Malley, S.J., *The First Jesuits* (Cambridge, MA: Harvard University Press, 1993), looks at the beginnings of the Jesuit order, while Dauril Alden, *The Making of an Enterprise: The Society of Jesus in Portugal, its Empire and Beyond, 1540–1750* (Stanford: Stanford University Press, 1996), analyzes the worldwide mission.

Specialized studies of the Reformation in France include Barbara Diefendorf, *Beneath the Cross: Catholic and Huguenots in Sixteenth-Century Paris* (Oxford: Oxford University Press, 1991), and Mack P. Holt, *The French Wars of Religion, 1562–1629* (Cambridge: Cambridge University Press, 1998). For England, see Christopher Haigh, *English Reformations: Religion, Politics, and Society under the Tudors* (Oxford: Oxford University Press, 1993); Peter Marshall, ed., *The Impact of the English Reformation 1500–1640* (London: Edward Arnold, 1997); and Ethan Shagan, *Popular Politics and the English Reformation* (Cambridge: Cambridge University Press, 2003). For Germany, see Robert W. Scribner, *Popular Culture and Popular Movements in Reformation Germany* (London: Hambledon Press, 1988), and Susan C. Karant-Nunn, *The Reformation of Ritual: An Interpretation of Early Modern Germany* (London: Routledge, 1997). For the Low Countries, see Alastair Duke, ed., *Reformation and Revolt in the Low Countries* (London: Hambledon, 1990). For eastern Europe, see Karin Maag, ed., *The Reformation in Eastern and Central Europe* (New York: Scholar Press, 1997).

For analysis of the ways in which religious messages were conveyed, see Robert W. Scribner, *For the Sake of Simple Folk: Popular Propaganda for the German Reformation* (Cambridge: Cambridge University Press, 1981), and Mark U. Edwards, Jr., *Printing, Propaganda and Martin Luther* (Berkeley: University of California Press, 1994). For discussions of toleration and persecution, see J. Coffey, *Persecution and Toleration in*

Protestant England: 1558–1689 (London: Longman, 2000), and Brad Gregory, *Salvation at Stake: Christian Martyrdom in Early Modern Europe* (Cambridge, MA: Harvard University Press, 1999).

 For more suggestions and links see the companion website
www.cambridge.org/wiesnerhanks.

Note

1 This was the motto of the Calvinist consistory at Nîmes in France, translated and quoted in Raymond A. Mentzer, "*Disciplina nervus ecclesiae*: The Calvinist Reform of Morals at Nîmes," *Sixteenth Century Journal* 18 (1987): 89–115.

6 Economics and technology, 1450–1600

A woodcut illustration of grain measuring, from the *Royal Orders Concerning the Jurisdiction of the Company of Merchants and Shrievalty in the City of Paris*, 1528. Governments at many levels tried to regulate the price and distribution of grain and bread to keep it affordable, but steady inflation in the sixteenth century made this very difficult.

Timeline

1401	First publicly controlled bank founded in Barcelona
1450s	Enclosing common land for sheep becomes more common in central England
1460	First stock exchange set up in Antwerp
1500	European population returns to pre-Black Death level of 80 million
1556	Georgius Agricola publishes *De re metallica,* a major treatise on mining
1557	Spain declares bankruptcy for the first time
1560	Grain exports from Poland ten times what they had been a century earlier
1572	Parishes in England begin to levy a "poor tax" on residents
1580s	Dutch ship-builders invent the *fluyt*
1590s	Amsterdam opens a workhouse for the "able-bodied" poor
1600	Grain prices four to seven times what they had been a century earlier
1603	Serfs in Russia completely tied to the land

I N a famous scene from *Don Quixote*, the knight Don Quixote and his faithful squire Sancho Panza hear along a stream "strokes falling with a measured beat, and a certain rattling of iron and chains that, together with the furious din of the water, would have struck terror into any heart but Don Quixote's." The noise "is but an incentive and stimulant to my spirit," says Don Quixote, "making my heart burst in my bosom through eagerness to engage in this adventure, arduous as it promises to be." After secretly tying his horse's legs together, Sancho Panza convinces Don Quixote to wait until morning, and tells him a long story to pass the time. Once it was light, the two:

> began to move towards that quarter whence the sound of the water and of the strokes seemed to come ... they came upon a little meadow at the foot of some high rocks, down which a mighty rush of water flung itself. At the foot of the rocks were some rudely constructed houses looking more like ruins than houses, from among which came, they perceived, the din and clatter of blows, which still

185

continued without intermission. Rocinante [Don Quixote's horse] took fright at the noise of the water and of the blows, but quieting him Don Quixote advanced step by step towards the houses, commending himself with all his heart to his lady, imploring her support in that dread pass and enterprise, and on the way commending himself to God, too, not to forget him. Sancho, who never quitted his side, stretched his neck as far as he could and peered between the legs of Rocinante to see if he could now discover what it was that caused him such fear and apprehension. They went it might be a hundred paces farther, when on turning a corner the true cause, beyond the possibility of any mistake, of that dread-sounding and to them awe-inspiring noise that had kept them all the night in such fear and perplexity, appeared plain and obvious; and it was (if, reader, thou art not disgusted and disappointed) six fulling hammers which by their alternate strokes made all the din.

Sancho Panza immediately burst into laughter "so heartily that he had to hold his sides with both hands to keep himself from bursting," whereupon Don Quixote struck him with his lance and ordered him not to talk about the incident. "[How] am I," he asked Sancho Panza, "a gentleman ... to know and distinguish sounds and tell whether they come from fulling mills or not ... when perhaps I have never in my life seen any as you have, low boor as you are, that have been born and bred among them?"[1]

In this scene, Miguel Cervantes captures not only Don Quixote's often misguided sense of gallantry and heroism, but also some of the economic changes going on in sixteenth-century Europe. What the knight and his squire mistake for giant opponents is a water-powered fulling mill, in which mechanical stampers beat woven cloth with water and special clay called fuller's earth to make it thicker, bulkier, and more windproof. Fulling had long been done by hand – or actually by foot, for fullers stamped the cloth in special tubs – but in the sixteenth century wind and water power began to be used to power fulling mills, which dramatically reduced the number of workers needed. Mechanical fulling equipment was quite expensive, so that fulling mills were generally owned by investors, not by those who tended the machines. Lifting soggy cloth in and out of fulling mills, and spreading it out to dry, was still hard physical labor, not the sort of thing that a gentleman like Don Quixote would ever do. Don Quixote probably wore cloth that had gone through a mechanical fulling mill, but, as he says, only a lower-class person such as Sancho Panza would have been "born and bred among them," that is, near the noisy and unpleasant mills. Cloth was the most important commodity handled by merchants, and changes in cloth-making were at the heart of the expansion of the early modern European economy.

The transformation of the European economy through investment in new, larger-scale processes of trade and production – what is usually called the "rise of capitalism" – has, along with the Renaissance, the Reformation, and the growth of the nation-state, long been viewed as a central factor in the development of the modern world. That recognition began in the eighteenth century. In the same way that Vasari saw Italian artists of his own era as taking art to levels it had never before achieved, the Scottish economist Adam Smith

(1723–90), in *Inquiry into the Nature and Causes of the Wealth of Nations* (1776), saw recent developments as offering great possibilities for economic growth. For Smith, people had a natural tendency to trade with one another. This inclination led to the specialization of labor, as first individuals, then groups, then regions, and ultimately nations, concentrated on products and tasks that they could produce or carry out better than their neighbors. The highest level of development, production, and innovation, the greatest "wealth of nations," would best be achieved by allowing free trade and open competition in both products and labor, an economic system later called capitalism, though Smith himself did not use this word.

Economic theorists since Smith have also seen capitalism as a powerful system that became increasingly dominant in the European economy during the early modern period. The German philosopher Karl Marx (1818–83) agreed with Smith that capitalism promoted economic growth, though he saw the origins of that growth not in free exchange, but in an unequal relationship between workers (the "proletariat") and the entrepreneurs who employed them and who owned the raw materials and equipment (the "means of production"). In Marx's view, the wages paid to the workers are always less than the value of the goods they produce, and the difference between the two is the profit, which flows to the

21 The Weber thesis

Why would investors and entrepreneurs want to make more money than they needed to live well? Luther and other clerical commentators attributed this to greed, one of the seven deadly sins and thus part of basic human nature. The German sociologist Max Weber (1864–1920), noting that capitalist forms of production developed more quickly and vigorously in Protestant, especially Calvinist, areas, saw a causal link between the two. In *The Protestant Ethic and the Spirit of Capitalism*, first published in 1904–5, Weber argued that anxiety about predestination led Calvinists to search for signs that they were among the "elect" chosen for salvation; they came to believe that hard work in one's chosen vocation (a word that comes from the Latin word for "calling," and implies that God or nature has called one to this particular line of work), proper moral conduct, and a disciplined, ascetic lifestyle could serve as such signs. This "Protestant ethic" made business activities and the maximization of profit morally legitimate, and a way to honor God, particularly if they were accompanied by restricting one's consumption.

The "Weber thesis," as this line of argument has come to be called, has provoked a century of debate among historians, who point to fifteenth-century Italian Catholic merchants who began every ledger "in the name of God and of profit," and seventeenth-century Dutch Calvinists who spent money lavishly on paintings, books, and tulips. They note that if there is a correlation between Calvinism and business success, it might better be explained by greater opportunities for schooling often available in Protestant areas, or the fact that some Calvinists were refugees or religious minorities enmeshed in close networks that could serve as business connections. Some contemporary economists have pointed to the importance of what they term "cultural factors" in explaining economic growth, however. These include "the desire to achieve," respect for property rights, and effective law enforcement, all values that Calvinists, and their English and American successors, the Puritans, firmly supported.

 For additional chapter resources see the companion website www.cambridge.org/wiesnerhanks.

entrepreneurs who organize production and handle trade, not to the workers themselves. In an economy dominated by noble landlords, excess profit went largely into consumption: buying fancy houses, clothing, or other goods; in a capitalist economy, some or most of the profits were invested in productive enterprises designed to make still more profit.

The development of capitalism was slow, uneven, and complicated. It involved changes in the organization of production and the handling of money, and also an increase in the amount of goods manufactured, bought, and sold. This expansion of the European economy was driven in part by a growth in population. Population statistics before the advent of regular registrations of births, baptisms, marriages, and deaths are sketchy, but many demographers set the population of Europe at about 80 million in 1300. Famine, plague, and other diseases killed off at least a quarter of the population in the next century, but by about 1500 it had climbed again to pre-plague levels and over the next century it climbed gradually to about 100 million. Rulers and their officials regarded the growth in population as a good thing, for more people offered the possibility of greater economic and military power.

The rising population brought problems as well as opportunities, however. The demand for food increased, leading to a sharp rise in food prices, especially the price of grain, which increased between four- and sevenfold across Europe during the period from 1450 to 1620. Prices of firewood and charcoal also rose, as people chopped down trees for fuel or to increase the amount of land under the plow. Forests contracted sharply in size, and new land was created as coastal areas and marshes were diked and drained. The hardest hit by rising prices were those who had to buy all or most of their food, especially the urban and rural poor; this led to bread riots and other types of violence. In 1497, a crowd of poor people in Florence attacked the city's public granary, provoking a riot in which some of them were trampled or crushed to death. In 1585, the city council in Naples ordered that the standard loaf of bread would be smaller but cost the same, a common practice in cities during times of shortage. A mob seized one of the council members – who was also suspected of speculating on grain prices – killed him, mutilated his corpse, and sacked his house. Crowds did not regularly kill officials, but they often rioted, seizing grain, flour, or bread and then selling it at what they regarded as a "just" – that is, lower – price.

Governments, private groups such as guilds and trading companies, and even the church often attempted to shape economic growth by imposing tariffs and taxes, setting wage rates, establishing monopolies, and passing other sorts of regulations. National governments attempted to build up their own industries by setting high tariffs on imported manufactured goods and promoting exports, a policy later called "mercantilism." Mercantalists saw the amount of trade and production as fixed, so their policies were directed at grabbing a bigger piece of the pie, and then taxing it.

Government and personal responses to rising prices generally made things worse. Governments devalued coins, which meant they minted coins with less precious metal content – either by making smaller coins or mixing precious metals with other metal such as lead – but this only drove prices up faster as people demanded more of the devalued coins for any purchase. Merchants and millers hoarded grain and flour in hopes of greater profits to come, which drove prices up further, and cities and nations prohibited the export of food, which often kept food from where it was especially needed. Most famines in Europe were quite localized: one valley might have too little rain, while the next one was fine, or one village might experience especially devastating hailstorms right at harvest-time, which missed neighboring villages.

The increasing population meant there was no shortage of tenants, and landowners raised fees, fines, and rents; rents on land in England may have increased as much as ninefold between 1510 and 1640, while grain prices went up fourfold. Rural rebellions such as the German Peasants' War (1524–5) or Kett's Rebellion in England (1549) combined religious demands with those for a rollback to earlier levels of rent or fees, and iconoclastic riots in the cities of the Netherlands often occurred in years of sharp upturns in the price of grain. There was also no shortage of workers, especially those who had little specialized training, so that wages increased much more slowly than food or rent, and real wages declined. In eastern Europe, as we will see in more detail below, landlords increased rents and labor services, and eventually reintroduced serfdom, as they sought ways to take advantage of rising grain prices.

Wages increased more slowly than prices for manufactured goods, and enterprising investors saw the opportunity for enhanced profits in manufacturing. They developed new forms of capitalist organization for the production of goods, hiring families of workers while retaining ownership of the raw materials, tools, and finished products. The fulling mill that so threatened Don Quixote was one example of this. Some of these merchant-entrepreneurs were able to profit from the enormous amounts of gold and silver coming into Europe from the Americas. This influx of precious metals drove down the value of coinage, which was made from gold and silver, the same way that an increase in the supply of any commodity reduces its price. The long increase in prices, which economic historians label the "price revolution," enhanced the wealth and power of long-standing elites, such as eastern European noble landholders, and of relative newcomers, such as western European merchant-entrepreneurs.

Trade, production, and population growth are all important factors in explaining Europe's economic expansion. In the early modern period, however, that expansion did not change the fact that the vast majority of Europeans lived in rural villages, growing crops and raising animals for their own use, for the use of their landlords, and for sale. In 1450, about one out of every twenty Europeans lived in a town or city with more than 10,000 inhabitants; by 1800, that proportion had only climbed to about one out of every ten. There were places, such as the Netherlands, where by 1800 three out of every ten people lived in cities, but these were offset by Scandinavia, northern Spain, and eastern Europe, where there were almost no cities at all. Thus any discussion of the European economy must begin in the countryside.

Late medieval agriculture

As local historians have made clear, patterns of land ownership varied from one region of Europe to another, one village to another, and sometimes from one family to another within a village. Some land, termed "allodial," was owned by the peasants who farmed it, who might owe fees for certain services, but no other direct obligations. Most land was held by an absentee landlord, however, which might be an individual or an institution such as a monastery. The peasants who farmed it paid rents, taxes, and fees to the landowner, which had earlier been paid in labor or agricultural products, but which by the mid-fifteenth century in western Europe were increasingly paid in cash. This transformation to cash payments had been accompanied by a disappearance of serfdom, so that peasants were no longer legally tied to the land, but were tenants of the landowner. They still often owed fees based on earlier feudal rights, such as special fees to mill grain or press grapes, to buy, sell, or inherit land, or to take a case to court, and in some areas still had a few labor obligations (called the *corvée* in France), such as carting the landlord's produce to market or repairing roads and bridges. Peasants also generally paid taxes and fees to support the church, which were collected by the village priest and then shared with his superiors. The priest himself was often poor, and integrated into the economic life of the village, so that he farmed during the week alongside his parishioners.

Landlords generally appointed officials from outside the village to oversee the legal and business operations of their holdings, collect taxes and fees, and handle disputes. The lords or their officials also held courts at regular intervals, which handled legal matters such as fights, assaults or robberies, litigation between villagers, and infractions of laws or customs regarding the fields, roads, or public places. These courts relied more on the collective memory of village traditions and customs than on written laws, so that groups of responsible adult men, in England called *jurors*, were often asked to decide issues, such as who had the right to a certain piece of land, by simply talking among themselves or to others who might know. Because of this, jurors were chosen from among those most likely to know the facts of the case, the opposite of modern jury selection.

Landlords and government officials had direct power in the countryside, but by the fifteenth century villages in many parts of Europe had also developed institutions of self-government to handle issues such as crop rotation, and to choose additional officials such as constables, church wardens, and ale-testers without the lord's interference. How they were chosen or elected was more often a matter of oral tradition than written law, but both those who chose officials and the officials themselves were almost always adult men and generally heads of household. Women had no official voice in the running of the village, though they did buy, sell, and hold land independently. (There was a handful of cases of women chosen as churchwardens in England, a minor office charged with assisting in the physical upkeep of a parish church and oversight of parish affairs, but they do not seem to have been elected.) Especially as widows, women headed households and were required to pay all rents and taxes. In areas of Europe where men were gone for long periods of time foresting or fishing, such as Portugal or the Basque region of Spain, or where men left either seasonally or more permanently in search of work elsewhere, women made decisions about the way village affairs were to be run, though they did not set up formal institutions.

Gender formed one kind of hierarchy among peasants, and wealth formed another. In most villages, there was a small group of better-off farmers, called "yeoman" in England, a term that is now also used for other parts of Europe, who were able to hire additional laborers beyond family members to produce for the market. There was a larger middle-level group who held just about enough land to support a family, usually about 10 to 30 acres. Many families were landless or nearly landless, supporting themselves by wage labor. The epidemics and wars of the fourteenth and early fifteenth centuries had improved the economic situation for the peasants of all wealth levels who had survived; in 1450, wages and rents were relatively low compared to prices for agricultural products. Better-off peasants bought or leased land that had been abandoned, joining more substantial noble and bourgeois landlords in many parts of Europe to raise specialized commercial crops along with or even instead of grain, purchasing the grain they needed for bread and beer from local or long-distance merchants.

Most parts of Europe depended on grain-based agriculture – wheat in central and southern Europe, rye and oats in the north – with a gender division of labor typical of that in grain-growing societies. These gender divisions were partly the result of physical differences, with men and adolescent boys generally doing tasks that required a great deal of upper-body strength, such as cutting grain with a scythe or clearing new land. Women and girls, along with older people and children of both sexes, bound grain into sheaves, watched animals, and picked up fallen grain kernels, a process called "gleaning." Gender divisions also resulted from women's greater responsibility for child care, so that women carried out tasks closer to the house which could be more easily interrupted for nursing or tending children, and from cultural beliefs, so that women in parts of Norway, for example, sowed all the grain because people felt this would ensure a bigger crop. These divisions often broke down, however, especially during harvest, bad weather, or periods when the population was low because of epidemics. In much of Scandinavia, northwestern Europe (Ireland, Scotland, Wales, Brittany), and mountainous or upland areas throughout Europe, most of the land was devoted to grazing sheep, goats, and cattle. Along the coasts, people depended on fishing for much of their food, either eating fish or trading them for grain and other agricultural products with those living further inland; in fishing communities small family groups and small houses predominated, with wives and daughters drying and salting fish for later use or sale while husbands and sons went out in the boats.

In western and central Europe villages were generally made up of small houses for individual families, with one marital couple, their children (including step-children) and perhaps one or two other relatives – a grandmother, a

Fig. 16. Peasants sowing grain in October, from the Playfair Book of Hours, from late fifteenth-century Rouen, in France. In areas where the land was extremely fertile and the weather fairly mild, people often planted one grain crop in the fall, so that it could be harvested earlier in the summer, and another crop on the same field later in the summer.

cousin whose parents had died, an unmarried sister or brother to one of the spouses. The family group was thus largely nuclear, and some households contained only an unmarried person or a widow, or several unmarried people living together. Villages themselves were nucleated: that is, the houses were clumped together with the fields stretching beyond the group of houses. Each house might have a tiny yard for smaller animals such as chickens and ducks, and a vegetable garden. During the medieval period, the fields of many villages in western and northern Europe were farmed in what is termed open-field agriculture, in which the village as whole decided what would be planted in each field, rotating crops according to tradition and need. Some fields would be planted with crops such as wheat or rye for human consumption, some with oats or other crops for both animals and humans, and some would be left unworked or *fallow* to allow the soil to rejuvenate. The exact pattern of crop rotation varied from location to location, but in most areas with open-field agriculture the holdings farmed by any one family did not consist of a whole field but of strips or plots in many fields. Families might share plow animals and work their holdings together, especially in areas where heavy soil necessitated teams of six or eight oxen, though they held their small fields separately. Most families were also allowed to let their pigs, oxen, cows, and sheep graze in the woods or meadows beyond the fields, and to gather firewood, nuts, mushrooms, and other foods from these areas, called the *commons* because they were held in common by the whole village.

In southern and some parts of eastern Europe, though nuclear families and single-person households were not unknown, extended families were more likely to live in the same household or very near to one another than in northern Europe. Father and son, or two married brothers, might share a house with both of their families, forming what demographers call a stem or complex household. The milder climate in the Mediterranean area allowed for more frequent planting and a greater range of agricultural products; families here tended to farm individual square plots rather than long strips.

Commercial agriculture developed most intensively in more urbanized regions of Europe, where city populations provided a concentrated market for crops. In Flanders, peasant farmers worked their land more intensively by multiple hoeings, plowings, and weedings, and planted legume crops such as peas and beans or clover to rejuvenate the soil rather than letting the land lie fallow. They let their stock graze on specific fields rather than wander common land, and the resultant droppings fertilized the soil for the next year's grain crops. Human and animal refuse from near-by cities, known euphemistically as "night-soil" and gathered from streets and chamber-pots by specialized night-soil collectors, furnished more fertilizer, which further increased crop yields. In northern and southern Italy and southern Spain, noble and middle-class landlords put together large estates, often called *latifundia*, where tenant farmers intensively cultivated rice, grapes, olives, hemp (for rope), dyestuffs, and fruit, along with grain and cattle. In Spain, wool became the primary commercial crop, with herders driving the sheep hundreds of miles each year from the north in the summer to the south in the winter. This transhumant sheep-grazing took them across fields and croplands, and in the thirteenth century a special organization, the *Mesta*, had been established to deal with the inevitable conflicts that resulted.

Rural developments in western Europe

In both areas with specialized agriculture and places where traditional grain-growing predominated, the relative prosperity of most peasants in the fifteenth century generally gave way to the impoverishment of the majority by the late sixteenth. Landlords increased rents and fees faster than agricultural prices rose, and centralizing states, always in need of money, increased tax levies. Wealthier peasants were sometimes able to take advantage of the situation and purchase more land, but this came from middling and poor peasants, who were reduced to holding nothing but a cottage or no property at all. In

England, by 1620 around 40 percent of rural residents held only a cottage and a garden without fields, and in southern Spain, almost three-quarters of the rural population had no land at all.

This process of the increasing polarization of wealth in the countryside proceeded slightly differently in different parts of Europe. In Spain, government officials sold off communal lands known as *baldios* to wealthy aristocratic or ecclesiastical landlords, depriving peasants of places to let their stock graze or gather firewood. Those same noble landlords also purchased positions as tax collectors, thus assuring their exemption from paying taxes. They were not interested in agricultural improvements, but in extracting as much from their tenants as possible. Rents and taxes became so high that many peasant families could not pay them, and they lost their leases, swelling the ranks of the landless poor.

In Italy, wealthy urban residents increasingly bought land around major cities such as Florence, Pisa, and Venice. They rented it out to tenant farmers, often through share-cropping contracts termed *mezzadria* in which the owner supplied the seed, animals, and tools as well as the land. Landowners increased the interest rates in *mezzadria* contracts and other rents, and the city governments that controlled the countryside fixed prices artificially low to try to control inflation and assure urban residents of enough food. Tenants were caught in the middle, and the number who were well-off declined; village organizations of self-government could do little to halt this. Neither peasant tenants nor wealthy landlords saw any benefit in agricultural improvements, and landlords increasingly spent their excess income on fancy country houses, elaborate furnishings, art, and other types of conspicuous consumption.

The situation was no better in France, where the religious wars destroyed crops and villages, and government policies exempted land owned by nobles and often that owned by bourgeois urban residents from taxes. This made land attractive to upper- and middle-class buyers, but as they purchased more and more land, the tax burden was spread among fewer and fewer people. Only in the Netherlands, where taxes and rents on rural land remained moderate and leases long-term, did prosperity continue for a broad spectrum of the peasant population.

Agricultural developments in this era have been studied – and debated – most intensively for England, particularly the process of enclosure, in which fences or hedges were built around fields and common land, and marshes and fens were drained to yield new land; the resulting consolidated plot of land was used by one owner rather than the whole village. In the early sixteenth century, when wool prices were very high, land was enclosed primarily to transform croplands into pasture; as Thomas More put it, sheep were devouring men. Later in the century enclosed lands were also planted with new types of crops such as clover or turnips, or used for convertible husbandry, in which fields were rotated every few years between crops and pasture, thus enhancing crop yields through natural fertilizers. These changes increased existing divisions

22 Petition requesting the prohibition of grain exports

Growing populations meant an increase in the demand for food in many areas, with a resultant rise in prices. Merchants sought to make the highest profit, which sometimes led to shortages, even in areas where food was produced. In 1591 the town council of Velas, on the Portuguese Azorean island of S. Jorge, dealt with a petition from some concerned citizens about the impending departure of locally grown grains.

Year of the birth of our lord Jesus Christ of one thousand five hundred and ninety-one in this town of Velas of this island of São Jorge: Having gathered together in the town council the distinguished officials João Teixeira and Pero Gomez d'Avila, ordinary judges, and Amtonio Gonçalvez Tagalas and Francisco Breves, councillors, and the procurators Amtonio Gonçalvez, procurator of the council, and Mateus Lopez and Mellchior Garcia, shoemakers, and Amtonio Gonçalvez, weaver, procurators of the masters. By the said procurators of the council as well as the ones for the masters: it was said and requested to the said officials that it had come to their attention that in this region some provisions had arrived for some local individuals to freight wheat from the land that they rent out and the harvest that they have on this island. They requested, in the name of God and of the King our lord, that their Graces [that is, the town officials] as fathers of the people look after the necessity that so urgently exists in this region for the said wheat. All the laborers in wheat complained that there was a third less wheat than they had last year, and this from the best land that there was on this island. Last year, with much more [locally grown] wheat, ninety or one hundred *moios* [1 moio = 828 liters] of wheat from outside [still] entered this town and all was used.

Every year what this region has from the outside always comes to eighty or one hundred *moios* of wheat, and all is used due to the little cultivation that there is of it [here]. They were informed that on this island there was also a shortage in districts that were supplied every year, for which reason they were ready to collapse with great distress because of not having a source [of wheat]. For this they requested of their Graces that they have a hand on what is gotten from the land, even if it is only a little, and with much vigilance not allow it [to be] loaded nor taken to any [other] area, and that guards be placed on the ports and on land and that the ports be sealed. If their Graces do not do this they protested thus: that if any persons perish for lack of the said wheat, their Graces account for it with God our Lord. The said officials, seeing the plea from the procurators and the outcry from the people from the lack of the said wheat, had the ports sealed and ordered that it be announced that no boatman nor carter be so insolent as to freight out any wheat or barley or rye or any victuals without first showing the dispatch and judicial licence at the risk of a fine of fifty *cruzados* and the owners losing the wheat or barley or rye or victuals as already ordered another time. It was announced by Amtonio Mateos and Bras Afonso, town criers. Mateus Dias wrote it.

(António dos Santos Pereira, *A Ilha de S. Jorge, séculos XV–XVII* [Ponta Delgada: Universidade dos Açores, 1987], ff. 74–75v [326–7], trans. Darlene Abreu-Ferreira, in Monica Chojnacka and Merry Wiesner-Hanks, eds., *Ages of Woman, Ages of Man: Sources in European Social History, 1400–1750* [London: Longman, 2002], p. 152.)

between wealthy and poor peasants. Yeoman peasants along with urban and noble landholders expanded their share of land ownership and their income per unit of land, while poorer peasants were often forced to sell their tiny plots, especially once they lost access to common land. The process was slow and uneven – by 1650, only 10 percent of the farmable land in England was enclosed – but it affected the area around London, which provided a huge market for wool and food, particularly intensively.

Throughout much of southern and western Europe, then, inflation, high rents, and burgeoning taxes increased the number of poor families who owned only a house or nothing at all, and survived solely by the labor of their members. Husbands and wives sometimes hired themselves out as a team, he cutting grain with a scythe while she bound it; they were generally paid according to how many bundles of grain they produced, one of the earliest

examples of piece-work. From maximum wage regulations, enacted by governments in the sixteenth century in an attempt to slow inflation, we can see that
female agricultural laborers hired on their own were to be paid about half of
what men were, and were also to be given less and poorer-quality food, which
often formed the most important part of an agricultural worker's income. An
ordinance from south Germany in 1550, for example, notes that male laborers
were to be fed soup and wine for breakfast, beer, vegetables, and meat at midday, and vegetables and wine at night, while women were to receive only soup
and vegetables in the morning, milk and bread at midday, and nothing in the
evening; they thus received less food, decidedly less protein, and no alcohol.
The difference between male and female wages meant that in families with
just a small plot of land, women often did all of the agricultural work on the
family plot, while men worked for wages on other people's land or in extractive
industries such as fishing, forestry, or mining.

Men and women in the countryside with too little land to support themselves also served as a labor pool for expanding handicrafts. Peasant households had long made fabric, rope, baskets, barrels, household items, and farm
tools for their own use or to trade with neighbors; women made cheese and
butter from their own milk and whole families wove linen and wool from
their own flax and sheep. They sold these in nearby market towns, or sometimes to urban merchants. In some areas, these merchants increasingly supplied rural individuals or households with raw materials they had not grown
themselves – wool from Spanish sheep, silk from Italian silkworms, cotton from
Egypt – and sometimes supplied the households with tools such as spinning
wheels or handlooms as well as raw materials. These cottage or domestic industries (this is also sometimes called the "putting-out" system, as work was put
out to households by capitalist investors) expanded unevenly across Europe,
in some areas coming to employ a majority of the rural population. That happened more often after 1600 than before, so this process will be traced in more
detail in chapter 12.

No matter how many family members worked, however, their wages could
not keep pace with inflation. Real wages for agricultural laborers and rural
artisans in England were cut in half during the period 1500 to 1650, and those
around Paris by two-thirds. There was often too little work available at even depressed wage levels, and large numbers of landless agricultural workers drifted
continually in search of employment or better working conditions, in addition
to those who migrated seasonally following the harvests. It appeared to many
contemporaries that poverty was increasing at an alarming rate, and that more
of the poor were what they termed "sturdy beggars," that is, able-bodied men
and women who could work if they chose rather than those who were poor
through no fault of their own, such as orphans, infirm elderly people, or the
handicapped. Most cities in Europe began to pass laws forbidding healthy people to beg, ordering them to go back to their home area, or forcing them into
workhouses. These laws were motivated both by increases in the actual numbers of the poor, and by changes in attitudes toward them, as first Protestant

and then many Catholic authorities came to regard beggars not as opportunities to show one's Christian charity, but as dangerous vagrants to be expelled or locked up.

Neo-serfdom and slavery in eastern Europe

In eastern and east-central Europe, poor migrants were rarely a problem. This was not the result of better economic conditions, however, but of a reintroduction of serfdom that tied people to the land, forbidding them to move or even travel. In the medieval period, serfdom had declined faster in eastern Europe than in the west. By the middle of the fifteenth century, labor services (called *robot* in Czech, the origin of the word "robot" in English) had almost disappeared, rents were low and long-term, and communal village organizations were strong. This changed dramatically over the next century. Ruling houses in eastern Europe were weak and frequently changing, dependent on noble landowners (called *Junkers* in German) for money, troops, and political backing. Often acting through the parliaments they controlled, such as the *Sejm* in Poland or the Diets of Prussia and Hungary, these noble landowners introduced laws that raised rents, required ever more extensive labor services, and ultimately bound peasants legally to the land. They gave themselves tax exemptions and monopolies on trade, crippling older cities such as Danzig and limiting the development of new cities.

These measures were progressively sharpened. The 1497 Russian legal code, for example, restricted peasants' right to move to a two-week period, the 1603 code abolished this completely, and the 1649 code set no limit on the lords' authority over their peasants, and who could buy, sell, and trade them. On estate surveys, peasants were listed as private property, with legal contracts and later newspaper advertisements describing their sale. During the American Revolutionary War, nearly 30,000 young men from Germany were sold to the British as soldiers. There were a few limits to landlords' power; they could not kill their serfs outright, and in some areas village communal organizations remained strong enough to negotiate limits on labor services or rents. Peasants also engaged in work slowdowns, rituals in which a landowner or his manager was insulted or killed in effigy, and at times even armed rebellion or the murder of officials or landlords.

Because the nobles were the primary judicial and police officials on their lands, however, such actions were often counter-productive. In Hungary, for example, the Diet's restrictions of peasant freedom and expansion of labor obligations led to a peasants' revolt in 1514. Peasants under the leadership of György Dózsa (1470?–1514), a veteran of wars against the Turks, attacked estates, but the nobles united against them and Dózsa and other leaders were brutally executed. Later that year the Diet sharpened serfdom even further, while giving the nobles the power to elect the king and granting them freedom from taxation and military service (except in defensive wars). These laws, known as the Tripartitum, were the basis of the Hungarian legal code until the revolution of 1848.

Neo-serfdom was just as onerous in its labor obligations and limitations on freedom as earlier European serfdom, but it was very different economically in that it was designed for the market, not for subsistence. Landlords sold the grain produced on their estates and taken in as taxes and rents on peasant land both regionally and internationally; in Poland, for example, rye exports to the west were 6,000 tons in 1460, 70,000 tons in 1560, and 200,000 tons in 1618. Nobles sold grain locally to the increasing number of peasants who had become landless when they could no longer afford their rents, and to the armies regularly engaged in dynastic/religious wars or battles with the Turks. Some landlords specialized in other types of commercial crops, such as wine-grapes, hops, and flax, but grain remained their primary product. Increases in the price of grain during the sixteenth century encouraged landlords to raise rents, further expand labor obligations, buy more land, and put still more land into grain cultivation; all of these resulted in more short-term profits and were safer and easier than trying new crops or new agricultural techniques. In the long run, however, such practices lowered yields and productivity, and hindered economic growth of all types, not simply in agriculture.

The situation was so terrible for serfs that slavery sometimes seemed a better option. Slaves were quite common in Muscovy – perhaps 10 percent of the population – where they included the offspring of slaves, military captives, indentured servants, and people who had enslaved themselves or their whole family to pay off debts. Most slaves lived in rural areas and worked the land, but some were estate managers, household workers, or soldiers, although a series of slave rebellions in the early seventeenth century led the government to prohibit military training for slaves. In the mid-sixteenth century, a central office for recording and handling all types of slaves, the Slavery Chancellery, was established in Moscow. About half the slaves were limited-contract slaves, who after the 1590s were freed on the death of their owners. The fact that slave status was thus not heritable, and that slaves did not pay taxes, led peasants to sell themselves more frequently, especially after the legal changes in 1649 made serfdom even more onerous. Once the government realized what was happening, it converted all slaves back into serfs, which effectively ended slavery per se, although Russian serfdom by this point was not much different than slavery.

Russians, along with Ukrainians, Poles, and other eastern Europeans, were also captured by Crimean Tatars and sold as slaves into the Ottoman Empire; perhaps as many as 2.5 million slaves were handled through the Crimean town of Kaffa in the period 1500 to 1700. The Ottoman state used slaves for construction projects, galley service, and in the army, while private individuals used them for agricultural and especially domestic work. Islamic tenets encouraged slaveholders to free their slaves after a long period of service, and census records indicate that slaves were only about 5 percent of the population of the Ottoman Empire. The regular freeing of slaves meant that there was a steady demand for new ones, however, which by the sixteenth century included Africans imported through Egypt, Roma (Gypsies) brought in from India, and Slavs traded by Italian merchants, as well as Russians sold by the Tatars.

Most agricultural work in the Ottoman Empire was not done by slaves, however, but by peasants who farmed small family holdings, growing grain along with fruits, olives, and vegetables. They raised sheep and goats, which supplied milk, along with wool and hair to be spun into yarn and woven into cloth. Some agricultural goods were sold to provide money for taxes, though taxes were also paid in kind longer than they were in western Europe. Significant production for regional or international markets did not begin in the Ottoman Empire until the eighteenth century, when large amounts of new land were put under cultivation for the first time. Until then, stretches of empty land often separated quite small villages, a situation that provided little incentive or capital for agricultural innovations.

Shortly after the Ottomans conquered an area, officials surveyed all the taxable resources, measuring the land, assessing its fertility, and counting the households. The state then divided the land into *timars*, administrative units assessed at a certain value of tax revenue. Military officers and government officials were given the right to collect the taxes from one or more timars instead of being paid directly in cash. As we saw in chapter 3, timars were sometimes granted to lords or monasteries that had previously held the land – there were Christian timar holders, though their numbers decreased over time – but the taxes demanded were less than had been imposed before the Ottoman conquest.

Mining and metallurgy

Armies fighting over territory and religion throughout Europe were enormous consumers of grain and other foodstuffs, and they also had an insatiable appetite for metal, particularly after the development of gunpowder-based weapons. By one calculation, a siege of an average-size city at the end of the sixteenth century used more than 10,000 cannonballs *per day*, to say nothing of the metal required to make the artillery that shot those cannonballs. Warfare used huge quantities of copper, lead, tin, iron, and various mixtures of these, and the demand for metal in architecture, housing, and other crafts increased as well.

Metals require large amounts of fuel to be smelted, which in the Middle Ages had primarily meant wood or charcoal made from wood. Wood prices increased and many areas were deforested, leading to a search for alternative fuels. This problem began to be solved by mining coal, and coal production dramatically expanded in certain areas. Around the city of Liège in the Low Countries it nearly quadrupled in the first half of the sixteenth century, and in the English counties of Northumberland and Durham it grew tenfold from 1500 to 1650.

Fig. 17 Detail of a painting of a copper mine by Hendrik met de Bles (1480–1550), showing a furnace for smelting in the background with a water-wheel-powered bellows, and a sluice trough in the foreground. Workers include both men and women.

Coal and metals were often found in different places, however, and relatively inexpensive transportation networks needed to be devised to bring these two bulky, heavy commodities together. Water was the easiest way to do this, which explains why the Rhineland-Palatinate, an area of Germany where the rivers Rhine, Neckar, and Main join, produced as much iron as all of France; nearly one-quarter of the population of the Rhineland-Palatinate were involved in iron production. Coal did not burn cleanly enough to produce high-quality iron or steel, however. (Steel is an iron alloy that contains less than 2 percent carbon.) For that charcoal was still required, which is why Sweden, with copper and iron mines, but more importantly with virtually endless forests that could be turned into charcoal, became Europe's largest single supplier of copper and iron.

Mining and metal production in the Middle Ages were largely organized in the same way as other crafts were, with groups of artisans in guilds or associations who leased the land on which ore was to be found from landowners. As the demand for metals went up, however, complex machinery was needed to dig and maintain deeper tunnels and speed up production processes. This was too expensive for artisans, but as the price and possibility for profit were also going up, other players became interested. Rulers, including the popes and various members of the Habsburg family, opened or expanded mines; the popes had a monopoly on alum, a mineral used for fixing dye in cloth, and the Habsburgs held copper and silver mines. In eastern Europe, noble landowners opened new mines and iron foundries on their estates, using some of the profit they had earned from the grain trade to build blast furnaces, gravitational or hydraulic pumps to get water out of mine shafts, devices for ventilating shafts, and other types of machinery. As part of their increased labor obligations, serfs on these estates were required to cut wood or haul raw materials. Private individuals and family firms also expanded mining operations through large amounts of initial investment and the increasing use of machines.

Mining and the production of metals came to involve an elaborate division of labor, as well as significant investment of capital. Adult men did most of the work underground, and broke the ore into large pieces. Older men, adult women, and children sorted, washed, and further broke apart the ore, and also prepared charcoal briquets for use in smelting. Miners were often hired as families, though only the adult men were listed in records; for example, men might be paid per basket for ore, but it was expected that this ore would be broken into small pieces and washed, jobs done by their wives, sisters, and children. One of the best sources for understanding this division of labor, as well as other aspects of mining, is *De re metallica* (1556), a huge well-illustrated treatise on mining and metallurgy written by the German humanist Georgius Agricola (1494–1555). Agricola describes surveying techniques, machines, laboratories, and the organization of operations, and provides standardized language to describe mining operations. His text includes nearly 300 illustrations, and provides thorough grounding in both the practical aspects of mining and more theoretical issues about the relationships between humans and their natural environment.

Commerce and banking

Metal products formed a significant share of the goods handled by European merchants, who bought and sold many other types of merchandise as well. Their most important commodities were raw wool and finished cloth. Merchants from Venice and Genoa traded silk, velvets, and fine woolens produced in northern Italy eastward to Constantinople and westward and northward to wealthy nobles in Spain, France, and Germany. During the sixteenth century, they were joined, and sometimes supplanted, by Dutch, English, and French merchants handling what were called "new draperies": cheaper, lighter cloth made of wool, cotton, linen, or blends.

Responding to – and creating – changes in fashion, merchants added new types of textile products to the cloth they traded. Knitting had been introduced into Europe from the Islamic world through Spain in about the thirteenth century, and knitted hose and stockings, of both silk and wool gradually replaced bias-cut woven stockings among the upper classes. Knitted materials cling to the body and stretch more easily than woven ones, making them more practical and flattering. With the introduction of knitted stockings, men's jackets and doublets became shorter and shorter, showing off a greater expanse of often brightly colored leg. They grew so short that fashionable men began wearing elaborate "cod-pieces" to cover their private parts, often stuffed and decorated with bows and embroidery.

Stocking knitting became a common occupation for the poor in many parts of Europe, as it required almost no capital investment; knitters used yarn from their own sheep or yarn supplied by merchants, who then paid the knitters for their labor and sold the stockings both regionally and internationally. Knitting stockings was speeded up with the introduction of the knitting frame – in which double-pointed needles are arranged on a stand, and the knitter works around the needles – and in some towns guilds of stocking-knitters formed to control production, modeled on the craft guilds in other products. As in other guilds, master stocking-knitters were predominantly male, as were the merchants who organized stocking-knitting in rural areas where no guilds developed. Pressure from merchants, the relative availability of the raw materials, and the simplicity of the equipment prevented the establishment of strong guilds of stocking-knitters in most parts of Europe, however, and knitting remained a "free art," open to anyone in terms of both production and trade.

Lace-making also remained a "free art," and lace became a major commodity for merchants in the southern and northern Netherlands. Here urban craft guilds had lost much of their power in the religious wars of the 1560s–80s, when Antwerp and other cities and towns were besieged and sometimes destroyed; after the wars, city governments were dominated by merchant-entrepreneurs. These merchants hired urban residents as well as villagers to make ribbons, trimmings, and even cloth as well as lace, lowering their costs by subdividing and simplifying the steps of production so they could hire less-skilled workers at lower wages.

In the Ottoman Empire, Italy, and southern France, merchants expanded silk production, growing the mulberry trees that silkworms eat and hiring large numbers of young women to unwind cocoons, spin silk thread, and weave. Turkish and Italian silk was never quite as good as Chinese, but it was much cheaper, and wealthy people throughout Europe could afford luxurious fabrics made of silk such as velvets, brocades, and satins. Clothing styles in the sixteenth century often included many layers of fancy silk, with slashes cut in the top layers so that the bright colors of the layers underneath showed through. Silk was so profitable that investors even tried to develop silk production in England and Germany, but the winters were too harsh for silkworms.

Particularly in the northern Netherlands, which became the Dutch Republic, new technology enhanced organizational changes to increase production. The "Dutch" ribbon loom, for example, allowed a single worker to weave up to twenty-four ribbons at a time. Wind power was tapped to full cloth, and fulling mills similar to the one that startled Don Quixote were built in many parts of the Dutch countryside. Because the Netherlands is so flat, falling water was not a common power option, but the Dutch adapted technology developed for water-mills to wind power, using wind-mills to grind grain, crush seeds for oil, saw wood, and for many other uses. These technological innovations required large amounts of capital, much of which was provided by the partnerships and companies that had originally been established to share the risk in trading ventures.

The Dutch combined new technology, a simplification of production processes, and a sharper division of labor in ship-building and textile production. In the early sixteenth century, Dutch shipyards were producing many types of ships, from small fishing yawls to huge galleons, supplying a merchant fleet that at its height in the seventeenth century may have numbered over 15,000 ships. Toward the end of the century Dutch ship-builders invented the *fluyt*, or fly-boat, a long, flat-bottomed ship made of pine or fir, soft woods that could be cut by wind-driven sawmills. Because there was little piracy in the North and Baltic Seas where the Dutch primarily traded, *fluyts* carried no guns, but could be crammed with bulky cargos such as grain, fish, lumber, wine, and metals. *Fluyts* were mass-produced quickly and cheaply in the area just north of Amsterdam, a district called the Zaanstreek. Because they were rigged simply, they needed only half the crew of other ships for the same amount of cargo, making them much cheaper to operate as well as produce.

Dutch ships brought raw materials from all over Europe and later from around the world to the Netherlands, where merchants invested in "traffics" (*trafieken* in Dutch), firms that specialized in processing and refining products for reexport. Raw sugar was refined into white table sugar and raw diamonds cut into gems in Amsterdam, gin distilled in Schiedam, tobacco cut in Rotterdam, whale blubber boiled into whale oil in the Zaanstreek, clay made into ceramics at Delft, and paper, leathergoods, and glass produced in many Dutch towns. These products were shipped internationally, and also sold locally to prosperous farmers and city residents over the canals and rivers that crisscrossed the Dutch countryside.

New types of financial organization also played a role in this commercial expansion. In the fifteenth century, the most important European banks were run by Italian merchants in Florence, Venice, and Genoa. They loaned money to individuals and governments, issued maritime insurance on overseas voyages, speculated in foreign exchange, and accepted deposits of coins. Deposit banks with similar functions became common in major cities, but they often made speculative loans and frequently failed. These failures led to the creation of public banks, overseen by government officials, of which the first was the Taula de Canvi of Barcelona, founded in 1401. In the middle of the sixteenth century, Naples and Palermo founded public banks, and the northern Italian cities soon followed; those in Genoa were specifically designed to handle the gold and silver coming in from the Spanish New World. Public banks were opened in Amsterdam and other Dutch and north German cities in the early seventeenth century, and gradually took over more and more business from private merchant banks.

Though both private and public banks issued various forms of paper bills of exchange and statements of deposit, most business in the fifteenth and sixteenth centuries was carried out with coins – gold florins or ducats or écus or nobles for the large transactions of nobles and merchants, large silver gros tournois or groats or guldiner or taler for rents and major purchases, smaller silver deniers or copper pennies, or coins made of a mixture of metals (called billon) for everyday purchases. Mints that made coins were monitored and taxed by government authorities, but generally operated privately. When governments needed money, they ordered mints to make smaller coins or use less precious metal, thus increasing the amount of taxes flowing to the government for the same amount of metal. Debased gold coins grew smaller and their purity declined from 24 carats to 18 or even less, while "silver" coins turned black because of their high copper content, or grew so thin that they crumbled and bent. Merchants thus often weighed coins rather than counting them, and relied on networks of information about which coins were to be particularly avoided, though debasement still led to inflation.

Certain coins, especially Venetian gold ducats and gold florins minted first in Florence and then elsewhere, were widely recognized and became a standard in international exchange in the fifteenth century. In the sixteenth century, these were joined by the larger Spanish doubloon and the English sovereign, both made from New World gold. New sources of silver in central Europe and the New World also allowed for larger silver coins, such as the English crown, the French franc, and the Spanish piece of eight, so called because it was worth eight of the older Spanish silver coins. Thus when pirate rhymes talk of "gold

23 The Fuggers of Augsburg

Jacob Fugger (1459–1525), a merchant-banker from Augsburg, began his career as a typical merchant. His grandfather had been a successful weaver, eventually employing other weavers and prospering by selling cloth in Augsburg's growing textile trade. Jacob continued to sell cloth, both traditional heavy woolen cloth and newer, lighter varieties, including cotton and fustian, a blend of cotton and linen. He used business techniques that had first been developed in the cities of northern Italy, developing a network of branch offices in many parts of Europe and eventually overseas. His agents kept detailed financial records, using account books, ledgers, registers, and double-entry bookkeeping; they also spied on competitors, sending regular reports back to the central office in Augsburg. These reports were preserved and copied in manuscript by later members of the Fugger family, though they were never printed or circulated in the early modern period. (They were published in the 1920s, and the idea developed that they had formed the basis of "Fugger newsletters" and were part of early journalism, but this is incorrect.)

Jacob Fugger loaned money to nobles, church leaders, and rulers, accepting control of mining properties as security on the loans. He gradually established a monopoly of silver and copper mining in Tirol, Hungary and Slovakia, which provided him with 1.5 million florins profit. That profit was recirculated into further loans, and Fugger made an enormous fortune; his contemporaries called him "Jacob the Rich." He financed the imperial election of Charles V – a Habsburg – in 1519, for which he was given control of mercury and silver mines in Spain; one of these, the Almadén mercury mine, employed more than a thousand people by 1600. Fugger was a firm opponent of the Protestant Reformation, and even more opposed to peasant demands for change. He made sure that plenty of copper for casting cannons was delivered from his eastern European mines during the German Peasants' War. That copper was also put to the same use closer to its origin, when a miners' revolt broke out in mines run by a Fugger subsidiary in Slovakia in 1525. Miners discontented with their shrinking wages in an era of rising prices attacked company officials, and, like the peasants, mixed in some Lutheran ideas; they were defeated, and their leaders arrested and executed.

Though the Fuggers had plenty of metal because of their control of mining operations, they also used various types of non-metallic money: paper bills of exchange, bank notes, and personal promissory notes. The Fuggers were patrons of the arts, commissioning paintings, buying books, collecting ancient sculpture and coins, and supporting musicians and composers. Jacob also had philanthropic concerns, building a housing development called the *Fuggerei* for poor families in Augsburg, many of them less successful weavers. The *Fuggerei* charged very low rents, but required tenants to be Catholic and pray for Jacob's soul; the housing development continues in operation today, still charging only a token rent.

Jacob Fugger and his descendants became fabulously wealthy by loaning money to rulers and church officials, especially the Habsburg family, but this was also their downfall. Spain declared bankruptcy in 1557, 1575, and 1607, which meant that the Fuggers could not claim repayment on their loans. Loans to Spain and the Spanish-ruled Netherlands represented more than half the Fuggers' assets, and by the middle of the seventeenth century it was clear these would never be repaid; the company was dissolved in 1650.

doubloons and pieces of eight," they are referring to large Spanish gold and silver coins made from New World metal.

Most people – and no doubt many would-be pirates – never saw large gold or silver coins. They paid their taxes and rent and bought food and clothing with small silver or copper or mixed-metal coins. If they needed cash quickly, they went to a local moneylender, who often took an item of clothing or household goods as security on the loan, so acting as a pawnbroker as well. Stands with men and women selling used merchandise of all types, along with other small items not regulated by guilds such as soap or wooden dishes, filled the market place of any early modern city. They received their goods from people who needed money, or from the households of people who had died. Many cities required such individuals to register, pay a fee, and swear an oath not to take in stolen merchandise, not to make agreements with each other to fix prices, and not to take more than a certain rate of commission. During outbreaks of the plague, they were forbidden to sell clothing or bed linen from sick people, and during times of war, they were specifically prohibited from selling soldiers' booty. Such regulations were difficult to enforce. "Thieves' markets" sprang up from time to time, were closed down, opened in another place in town, and were closed down again. Sellers hid things when market officials were nearby, leading a frustrated city council in Nuremberg at one point to prohibit female pawnbrokers from sitting while selling, as they suspected the women were hiding illegal merchandise under their long skirts. The market for used merchandise was simply too good and the need for ready cash too great; even smaller towns and villages had a pawnbroker/moneylender or two who facilitated the movement of capital at the lowest level and sold small items. Men and women also loaned their neighbors and family members money through informal agreements, which allowed them to buy food or tools, or perhaps pay back gambling debts.

The activities of village pawnbrokers differed in scale, but little in kind from those of Europe's wealthiest and most successful merchants. Successful merchant-entrepreneurs also diversified their activities, buying and selling a range of products, making loans, exchanging currencies, and investing in trading ventures and extractive industries such as mining. The Fuggers of Augsburg were the most successful, but other merchant families made fortunes nearly equal to that of the Fuggers. The Mendes family of Portugal (later known as the Nasi family), who had been forcibly converted from Judaism, fled to the Netherlands, and established large-scale banking operations in Antwerp. Gracia Nasi (1510–68), the widow of the firm's founder, ran the family business from Antwerp, Venice, Ferrara, and eventually Constantinople, making an alliance with Süleyman the Magnificent for trading and financial privileges. She reconverted to Judaism, and established an "underground railroad" to get Jews out of Portugal and Spain, convincing Süleyman to grant her a long-term lease on property in Greece where these refugees could resettle. Like Jacob Fugger, Gracia Nasi patronized learning and the arts, especially the publication of Hebrew books, and a number of Jewish scholarly works from the sixteenth century were dedicated to her. Her nephew Joseph Nasi (1524–79) became a close adviser to Sultan Selim II (ruled 1566–74), and the governor of several territories. His power declined when the Turks reestablished their commercial ties with France, however, and his hopes for a commercial empire centered in Constantinople ended when the Turkish fleet was defeated at Lepanto in 1571.

In the first half of the sixteenth century, Antwerp was the largest center of financial activities in Europe and one of the world's richest cities. Shortly after Portuguese voyages to the East Indies began bringing in significant amounts of spices, Portugal made Antwerp the main outlet for spices in Europe, and the Habsburg emperors favored Antwerp bankers and merchants. The English Merchant Adventurers, a confederation of independent merchants, mostly from London, that controlled the export of English cloth, established their continental base in Antwerp. The first stock exchange or *Bourse* was set up there in 1460, and in 1531 this moved into an elaborate new building, the first building in the world designed to be a stock and trade exchange. Sir Thomas Gresham (1519–79), an English merchant and royal official in Antwerp, admired this building so much that he convinced Queen Elizabeth to build an exchange patterned after it in London; this Royal Exchange was built in 1566–7, and became the center of London's commercial and banking activities.

The most profitable business arena was loaning money to governments, for which interest rates could be extremely high, but this was also very risky. Along with the Fuggers, other banking houses in Genoa, Antwerp, Amsterdam, and London made huge loans to governments, who could not keep up with their financial needs in an era of inflation and frequent warfare, despite charging higher and higher taxes. Some of these were repaid and some were not, for there was no way that a private bank could collect when a government declared bankruptcy.

Antwerp reached the height of its prosperity about 1560, just before the revolt of the Netherlands. In 1576, Spanish troops housed in Antwerp, who had received no pay because of the bankruptcy of the Spanish crown, mutinied; they seized everything of value, burned many buildings, raped women, and slaughtered about six or seven thousand city residents. This "Spanish fury" was followed by another round of destruction, the "French fury" in 1583 when the duke of Anjou, the brother of the French king, attempted to take Antwerp from the Spanish. This was unsuccessful, but Dutch troops later blocked Antwerp's access to the sea, limiting its role in international trade. With this, Amsterdam became Europe's most important financial and commercial center, aided in its rise by the immigration of Protestant and Jewish merchants and artisans from all over Europe, including Antwerp.

Towns and cities

The wealth and commercial success of merchants were both a cause and consequence of their domination of urban politics. Though some merchants, like Cosimo de Medici and Jacob Fugger, chose to influence city government through informal means, in most cities merchant families enhanced their power by membership of the council or councils that governed the city. Council members generally served for life, and they often rotated in and out of the office of mayor. In some cities certain seats on the council were reserved for the elected representatives of specific groups, especially craft guilds, but more often the existing council members chose the replacements for members who had died. Many city councils tried to limit membership to an exclusive group of families in the sixteenth century, though men from newly rich families were generally still able to turn their financial success into membership of the city's political and social elite.

Some cities in Germany and Italy remained independent city-states through-out the early modern period, but elsewhere in Europe centralizing monarchs asserted their power over cities. Urban leaders often recognized that cooper-ating with monarchs could give them advantages, allowing them to shape national as well as local financial and trade policies, and influence other gov-ernment decisions. Men from wealthy merchant families – especially second and third sons, who often trained as lawyers – became royal officials, and gradually, in many parts of Europe, the urban elite and royal service merged into a single oligarchy of wealthy, educated men whose families intermarried. As we saw in chapter 3, service to a monarch might eventually bring a noble title, formalized in France as a position in the *noblesse de robe*. Originally mem-bers of the *noblesse de robe* could not transmit their titles to their heirs, but by the seventeenth century these ranks also became hereditary. They were, in fact, often simply purchased outright for the tax advantage conferred by noble status.

Even those cities located within centralizing monarchies, such as London and Paris, had a level of autonomy that rural areas did not. All cities could build walls to regulate the flow of people and goods, charge taxes, hold markets, and form a citizens' militia. Legally and juridically, a city was a corporate community, embodied in the adult male heads of household who were its citizens; women, and men who were not citizens, had to pay taxes and supply troops for the citizen militia, but they had no political voice.

Almost all European cities were enclosed by walls with gates and watch-towers; as immigration from the countryside swelled the urban population, spaces between houses were filled with new buildings and additional stories were built on existing houses. Once this was no longer possible, houses were built right outside the walls, and eventually these suburbs might be enclosed within a second or third ring of walls. With the development of effective siege cannons, city fortifications were often enhanced by thicker walls, massive bas-tions, and permanent defensive guns. Citizens paid special taxes to build and maintain these walls, and their construction provided work for the city's poor and recent immigrants.

The physical structure of most cities can serve as a metaphor for urban social, economic, and political structures. In contrast to today, the center of most cities was the most desirable neighborhood, with the large houses of mer-chants, lawyers, and other wealthy individuals close to the cathedral, church, or main market place that marked the hub of the city. Here the city built government buildings, including elaborate city halls, courts, and public gra-naries. Slightly out from the center were the homes of craft guild masters and professionals; goods were produced or services performed on the first floor or at the front of the house, while the family, along with servants, apprentices, and sometimes journeymen, lived at the back or in the upper stories.

The craft guilds described in chapter 1 continued to organize the production and distribution of most products well into the eighteenth century or even

24 Journeymen's guilds

Conflicts between masters were often accompanied by conflicts between masters and journeymen. During times of economic expansion, apprentices and journeymen looked forward to the day when they too could become masters, marry, and establish their own shop and household. During times of decline or uncertainty, guilds often restricted the number of new shops and limited membership to sons of masters or those who married a master's widow or daughter. Many journeymen continued to work for a master all their lives, becoming essentially wage laborers. They began to think of themselves as a group distinct from masters rather than as masters-in-training, and formed special journeymen's guilds, termed *compagnonnages* in French and *Gesellenverbände* in German. They held initiation rituals, when they were often given a new name and taught a secret oath, met regularly in taverns or private drinking rooms, and held memorial services for those who had died.

Journeymen had little opportunity to accumulate property or money, so they became particularly concerned with what has been called the "symbolic capital" of honor and skill, and acted harshly against those they saw as dishonoring the guild. Their idea of "honor" was very different from that developed by craft masters and merchants. For journeymen, frequent travel, physical bravery demonstrated in fights and contests, spending all one's money on drinks for friends, and camaraderie all gave one status, while for masters and merchants honor involved stability, honesty, reliability, and authority over one's family and

servants. Both masters and journeymen were groups of men, and the differing notions of honor became the core of two very different ideals of masculinity, ideals that later shaped working-class and middle-class notions of what made a true man.

Political authorities and guild masters feared journeymen's guilds would provoke social and political unrest, and often banned them. The Diet of the Holy Roman Empire banned separate journeymen's associations in 1530, 1548, 1551, 1566, 1570, and 1577, but the frequency with which this ruling was repeated is a good indication of its ineffectiveness. Journeymen enforced their demands by boycotting a master or sometimes an entire town, spreading the word as they traveled. In many parts of Europe, journeymen won the right to live on their own rather than with the master's family, and to determine who would be allowed to work in guild shops. They refused to work next to those they regarded as dishonorable, which often included married journeymen and women. State authorities trying to promote the free movement of labor in the eighteenth century ordered journeymen to accept their married colleagues, but opposition remained strong. In the minds of most journeymen, getting married meant one had clearly broken with an ideal of masculinity that prized connections among men and the ability to move around easily; a man who married was thus not a real man. Journeymen's associations survived well into the nineteenth century, when they continued to carry out strikes and supported many of the 1848 uprisings.

longer. In theory, all guild masters were equal, following the same rules about the size of their shops, hours of operation, and access to raw materials. In practice, richer masters often hired servants to undertake the less-skilled parts of production, or pushed for fewer restrictions on the number of journeymen allowed in each shop. Sometimes they even hired poorer masters and their workshops outright, effectively reducing those masters to wage laborers and transforming themselves into capitalist entrepreneurs. These moves were occasionally accompanied by formal changes in guild regulations, but more often by a lack of enforcement of existing rules, as guild officials charged with their enforcement were often the same wealthy masters who benefited when they were flouted. If guilds succeeded in preserving their traditional rights within the city, wealthier masters or merchants hired families in nearby villages to produce goods outside of guild rules.

The households of merchants and masters depended on the work of servants, who made up between 15 and 30 percent of the population of most cities. Larger commercial and manufacturing centers had a higher percentage of servants than the smaller cities, whose economies were more dependent on agriculture. Perhaps one out of every twelve people in early modern France were servants, two-thirds of them female. Children might begin service as young as seven or eight, traveling from their home village to a nearby town. They often depended on friends and relatives to find positions for them, gathered at certain spots in the city where employers knew to look for servants, or in some cities of Germany and France used the services of an employment agent. Some urban servants were in fact slaves, purchased from eastern Europe in Italian households or from northern and western Africa in Spanish and Portuguese ones. Most households with servants could afford only one, a woman whose tasks were highly varied; she assisted in all aspects of running the household, and generally ate and slept with the family, for there was rarely enough space for her to have separate quarters. Even in wealthier households with many rooms, servants were rarely separated from their employers the way they would be in the nineteenth century, but lived on quite intimate terms with them.

No matter what their age, servants were legally considered dependants of their employers, and could be punished or dismissed by them with little recourse. Male heads of household in particular were expected to oversee the conduct of their servants at all times. The city council of Frankfurt, for example, required employers whose maids became pregnant to pay the costs of the delivery and care for the maid and her infant for three months no matter who the father was. They reasoned that the pregnancy would not have happened had the master been keeping a proper eye on his servants. Though servants usually came from poor families, they identified in many ways with their employers, and tended to wear fancier clothing than poor people who worked for wages. This upset bourgeois notions of the proper social order, and many cities expanded their sumptuary laws to forbid servants to wear fine materials or jewels, even if they had been given these by their employer. Ordinances regulating the conduct of servants became stricter during the sixteenth century. Some laws even charged servants with causing the general inflation, as they were now demanding wages instead of being satisfied with room and board.

The control of servants and journeymen was important to urban elites, but they were more worried about the large numbers of people who neither lived nor worked in households of responsible, tax-paying citizens. Tax records from early modern cities indicate that half or even more households did not own enough to pay any taxes at all. These were people – married, single, or widowed – who lived in attics and cellars, in rooms they shared, or in flimsy housing just inside or just outside the city walls. They supported themselves any way they could. Men repaired houses and walls, dug ditches, and hauled goods from ships; women laundered clothing, spun wool, and cared for invalids; children carried messages or packages around the city or the surrounding countryside. The poor found work in city orphanages, infirmaries, and hospitals, where the poor made up most of the patients as well as being the care-givers. They made and sold small simple items that were unregulated by guilds, such as wooden dishes, pins, or soap. They gathered nuts or firewood outside city walls, carried them through the gates, and sold them for a few pennies. They bought eggs from villagers, cooked them in a small pot on a charcoal brazier, and sold them as a quick meal. They bought and sold used clothing and household articles, or worked in taverns and inns. Sometimes they engaged in criminal activities, stealing merchandise from houses or wagons and then fencing it, or cutting the strings of money-pouches or purses. Or they did all of these at once, taking advantage of whatever opportunities they could.

For women, and some men, selling sex for money – what later came to be called prostitution – could provide a living or augment other work. As discussed in chapter 2, in 1450 most major cities in Europe and many of the smaller ones had an official brothel or an area of the city in which selling sex was permitted, but over the following centuries such activities were restricted. Many cities set down strict rules for the women and their customers, and in the sixteenth century most Protestant and then Catholic cities in northern Europe closed their municipal brothels, arguing that the possible benefits they provided did not outweigh their moral detriments. Harsh punishments were set for prostitution, including public flogging and incarceration in prison or a syphilis hospital. Selling sex was couched in moral rather than economic terms, as simply one type of "whoredom," a term that also included pre-marital sex, adultery, and other unacceptable sexual activities. Religious reformers such as Luther described women who sold sex in very negative terms, and also regarded "whore" as the worst epithet they could hurl at their theological opponents.

Closing the official brothels did not end the exchange of sex for money, of course, but simply reshaped it. Smaller, illegal brothels were established, or women moved to areas right outside city walls, such as Southwark and Bankside outside London. Police and other authorities were influenced or bribed to overlook such activities. For Italian city authorities, this fluid situation was more worrisome, and they tended to favor regulation over suppression. They also viewed selling sex as a significant source of municipal income. From 1559 until the mid-eighteenth century in Florence, for example, all women registered as prostitutes were required to contribute an annual tax based on their income which went to support a convent for those women who wished to give up prostitution; payment of extra taxes would allow a woman to live where she wished in the city and wear whatever type of clothes she chose.

Hauling, day labor, peddling, stealing, selling sex, and other types of short-term work were often not enough to support an individual or a family, particularly when rising prices made bread and other foodstuffs increasingly expensive. By the late sixteenth century, three-quarters of a poor family's income went for food, about half of that for rye bread, wheat bread being far too expensive. The only options were begging and charity, but, as noted above, attitudes toward beggars and toward the poor grew harsher in the sixteenth century. Cities passed laws prohibiting begging, and many opened workhouses where the able-bodied poor were put to work at simple tasks, such as spinning wool or beating hemp; London's Bridewell opened in the 1550s, and Amsterdam's workhouse in the 1590s. To make sure they did not decline into the sin of idleness, orphaned boys were apprenticed to learn a trade and orphaned girls sent into domestic service.

Poor relief was handled by a combination of institutions: private philanthropic organizations, monasteries, voluntary charitable groups, city and village agencies, parish (and, in Catholic areas, episcopal) councils. Beginning in the 1520s, both Protestant and Catholic cities in western Europe tried to centralize and consolidate the dispensation of charity, control begging, and put everyone who could to work. They often established "common chests" or central collections of alms and gifts, and appointed men and women as overseers of the poor, to visit people in their homes and run almshouses. In Catholic areas, orders such as the Franciscans who survived by begging opposed the new poor laws, arguing that the poor had a right to beg and that begging allowed people to show their Christian charity. Most Catholic clergy and rulers did not have such misgivings, however; acts of mercy such as donating to the poor were certainly meritorious good deeds, but they were to be funneled through structures established and controlled by bishops. Franciscans and other mendicant orders were allowed to beg, but Catholic rulers preferred that they solicited contributions through personal appeals, not on the streets.

In both Catholic and Protestant areas, authorities hoped that voluntary contributions would provide enough money for poor relief, but they also recognized that compulsory contributions might be necessary, especially during times of famine or epidemic diseases. In 1572, parishes in England were given the right to levy a regular poor tax on parish residents, and over the next century most parishes began to do this. People could only collect support in their home parish, however, not in London or another city where they might have migrated to look for work. Poor laws in many places made sharp distinctions between the "worthy poor" – orphans, widows, the elderly, working families with many children, those whom illness or accidents had incapacitated, respectable people who had fallen on hard times – and the "unworthy poor" – vagrants and idlers who came from somewhere else. The worthy poor were to be taken care of in their own homes or in municipal hospitals, and the unworthy poor sent to workhouses, where they were often joined by debtors and people awaiting sentences.

Workhouses and jails could never hold all of the poor, and other sorts of punishments were used as well, particularly for those who combined begging and vagrancy with other criminalized activities. Flogging, branding, and bodily mutilation – such as slitting nostrils, slicing cheeks, amputating ears or noses – were common punishments imposed throughout Europe into the eighteenth century. Repeat offenses or more serious crimes might merit execution, most commonly by hanging, but also by more grisly means such as burial alive, boiling in oil, burning at the stake, or breaking at the wheel.

Executions were public ceremonies, in which the convicts were marched through city streets on busy market days to a permanent gallows, accompanied by armed guards and clergy. Particularly notorious or famous criminals would draw a huge crowd, and their penitent speeches from the gallows would be recorded, printed, and sold as cheap broadsheets. The executions of even everyday criminals offered the possibility of a good speech and a grisly spectacle, so were popular forms of entertainment. At the middle of these events was the public executioner, who also carried out floggings and other corporal punishments. He was often well paid (and strong-armed), but was considered socially dishonorable; executioners were often required to live outside city walls, and their children could not enter craft guilds or marry those from honorable occupations.

Banishment and penal servitude were other punishment options for vagrants and criminals. Beggars and thieves might be flogged, and then ordered to leave a city and its territory for a specified period of years. In the late fifteenth and sixteenth centuries, France, Spain, and the Italian city-states began to sentence men to galley service – rowing in the increasingly large military ships; by the seventeenth century galley labor was the most common punishment for male convicts in France. Galleys were particularly important in naval battles in the Mediterranean, though they were less significant in the Atlantic. Ship design and naval technology changed significantly in the eighteenth century, and galleys were no longer effective, leading France and Spain to abolish galley service in 1748. During its heyday, galley service provided a model for land-based penal servitude, when convicts were sentenced to work in mines and dockyards, or on plantations. Such sentences removed convicts not only from their home city, but from Europe itself, as colonial empires provided first Spain and then England with a new means of ridding themselves of those considered undesirable. The transportation of convicts also brought a profit to governments, as mine and plantation owners paid more for workers than it cost to transport them.

Economic transformations are sometimes called "revolutions" – the Commercial Revolution, the Price Revolution, the Industrial Revolution – and their effects can be as transformative as any political revolution. They are much slower processes, however, and often lack a clear beginning or end. The "rise of capitalism" is one of these long, slow transformations. Economic historians sometimes joke that no matter when or where you look, capitalism always seems to be rising – there were business-owners who hired workers in the Roman Empire, merchants who engaged in diversified, long-distance trade in the Indian Ocean in the twelfth century, entrepreneurs who invested in machinery in Ming China. Conversely, even in the twenty-first century, large parts of the economy continue to operate largely outside the market – parents "invest" time and money in their children, family members carry out unpaid labor in the home or a family business, friends and neighbors share and exchange goods and services.

Despite these continuities, however, by 1600 the economy of many parts of Europe was quite different from what it had been two centuries earlier. In northern Italy, the Netherlands, London, Paris, and a few other places, wealth came primarily from trade and production, not land. Investment in equipment and machinery to process certain types of products, such as metals and cloth, had increased significantly. Governments at all levels were reacting to economic changes, bestowing privileges such as tax exemption or licenses to trade, though they did not have well-thought-out economic policies. In western Europe labor was more mobile, while in eastern Europe serfs had become tied to the land. Rural areas in both western and eastern Europe were more specialized in what they produced, dependent on the import and export of commodities. Those trading networks did not stop at the borders of Europe, for by 1600 they extended around the world. As we will see in the following chapter, not only did mechanically fulled cloth from Europe clothe Don Quixote and Sancho Panza, but also sailors and nuns in the Philippines, and slaves and planters in the Caribbean.

Further reading

An excellent introduction to economic developments in this era is Robert S. Duplessis, *Transitions to Capitalism in Early Modern Europe* (Cambridge: Cambridge University Press, 1997). See also the classic studies by Ralph Davis, *The Rise of the Atlantic Economies* (Ithaca, NY: Cornell University Press, 1973), and Fernand Braudel, *Civilization and Capitalism, 15th–18th Century*, 3 vols. (London: Collins, 1982–4). Considerations of several areas are included in Maarten Prak, ed., *Early Modern Capitalism: Economic and Social Change in Europe* (New York: Routledge, 2001). A recent collection on the Weber thesis controversy is Hartmut Lehmann and Guenther Roth, eds., *Weber's Protestant Ethic: Origins, Evidence, Contexts* (Washington, DC: German Historical Institute, 1993). For government actions in shaping the economy over the long term, see Charles Tilly, *Coercion, Capital, and European States, A.D. 990–1990* (Oxford: Oxford University Press, 1990), and Charles Tilly and Wim P. Blockman, eds., *Cities and the Rise of States in Europe, A.D. 1000–1800* (Boulder: University of Colorado Press, 1994). For the effects of long-term inflation, see David Hackett Fischer, *The Great Wave: Price Revolutions and the Rhythm of History* (Oxford: Oxford University Press, 1996).

For the rural economy, see Jan de Vries, *The Dutch Rural Economy in the Golden Age, 1500–1700* (New Haven: Yale University Press, 1974); Margaret Spufford, *Contrasting Communities: English Villagers in the Sixteenth and Seventeenth Centuries* (Cambridge: Cambridge University Press, 1974); Peter Kriedte, *Peasants, Landlords and Merchant Capitalists* (Cambridge: Cambridge University Press, 1983); Philip T. Hoffman, *Growth in a Traditional Society: The French Countryside, 1450–1815* (Princeton: Princeton University Press, 1996). For eastern Europe, see Vera Zimányi, *Economy and Society in Sixteenth and Seventeenth Century Hungary (1526–1650)*, trans. Mátyás Esterházy (Budapest: Akadémiai Kiadó, 1987), and Antonie Maczak, Henryk Samsonowicz, and Peter Burke, eds., *East-Central Europe in Transition from the Fourteenth to the Seventeenth Century* (Cambridge: Cambridge University Press, 1985).

For banking, see the older, but still useful, Raymond de Roover, *Business, Banking, and Economic Thought in Late Medieval and Early Modern Europe* (Chicago: University of Chicago Press, 1974). For trade and production, see D. C. Coleman, *Industry in Tudor and Stuart England* (London: Macmillan, 1975), and John Munro, *Textiles, Towns and Trade: Essays in the Economic History of Late-Medieval England and the Low Countries* (Aldershot: Macmillan, 1994). For more detailed information on cloth and clothing, see N. B. Harte and Kenneth G. Ponting, eds., *Cloth and Clothing in Medieval Europe: Essays in Memory of*

Professor E. M. Carus-Wilson (London: Heinemann, 1983). For ship-building, see R. W. Unger, *Dutch Shipbuilding before 1800: Ships and Guilds* (Assen: Van Gorcum, 1978).

Studies of urban developments include Paul M. Hohenberg and Lynn Hollen Lees, *The Making of Urban Europe, 1000–1994* (Cambridge, MA: Harvard University Press, 1995); Peter Clark and Bernard Lepetit, *Capital Cities and their Hinterlands in Early Modern Europe* (Aldershot, UK: Macmillan, 1996); S. R. Epstein, ed., *Town and Country in Europe, 1300–1800* (Cambridge: Cambridge University Press, 2001). For guilds, see Richard Mackenney, *The World of the Guilds in Venice and Europe, c. 1250–1650* (Totowa, NJ: Barnes and Noble, 1987), and Steven Epstein, *Wage Labor and Guilds in Medieval Europe* (Chapel Hill, NC: University of North Carolina Press, 1991).

For issues regarding poverty, see Catharina Lis and Hugh Soly, *Poverty and Capitalism in Early Modern Europe* (Atlantic Highlands, NJ: Humanities Press, 1979); Maureen Flynn, *Sacred Charity: Confraternities and Social Welfare in Spain, 1400–1700* (Ithaca, NY: Cornell University Press, 1989); Brian Pullan, *Rich and Poor in Renaissance Venice: The Social Institutions of a Catholic State to 1620* (Cambridge, MA: Harvard University Press, 1971); Robert Jütte, *Poverty and Deviance in Early Modern Europe* (Cambridge: Cambridge University Press, 1994).

 For more suggestions and links see the companion website www.cambridge.org/wiesnerhanks.

Note

1 Miguel de Cervantes, *Don Quixote,* trans. John Ormsby (New York: W. W. Norton, 1981), ch. 20.

7   Europe in the world, 1450–1600

Columbus offers a goblet to a group of naked, hesitant island residents in the
title-page woodcut from the 1494 Basel edition of his first letter describing his voyage.
The galley in the foreground bears little resemblance to his actual ships, and the
entire woodcut was adapted from one the printer already had on hand. Such images
shaped European ideas about the New World for centuries, however.

Timeline

1405–21	Chinese voyages to the Indian Ocean under Zheng He
1492	Columbus lands in the Caribbean
1494	Treaty of Tordesillas divides the world
1497	Vasco da Gama reaches India
1497	John Cabot leads the first English expedition to New World
1515	First sugar mill is built in the western hemisphere
1521	Magellan is killed in the islands that become the Philippines
1521	Cortés and his allies defeat the Aztecs
1532	Pizarro conquers the Inca Empire
1540s	Japanese lords allow the Portuguese to trade in Japan
1557	Archbishopric established in Portuguese Goa
1560s	Spanish silver fleet begins regular sailings to the Philippines

O N the return voyage from his trip to what he thought were islands off the coast of Asia, Christopher Columbus wrote a letter to Lord Luis de Santángel, the secretary of the Aragonese royal treasury and one of his key supporters. A storm drove his ship into Lisbon in early March 1493, and Columbus sent the letter by land from there to Barcelona, where Isabella and Ferdinand were holding court, so that it would arrive before he got there.

I have decided upon writing this letter to acquaint you with all the events which have occurred in my voyage, and the discoveries which have resulted from it. Thirty-three days after my departure from Cadiz [on October 12, 1492], I reached the Indian sea, where I discovered many islands, thickly peopled. Of which I took possession without resistance in the name of our most illustrious Monarchs, by public proclamation and with unfurled banners. To the first of these islands, which is called by the Indians Guanahani, I gave the name of the blessed Savior [San Salvador], relying upon whose protection I had reached this as well as the other islands.

Describing the physical features of the land, Columbus wrote, "All these islands are very beautiful, and distinguished by a diversity of scenery; they are filled with a great variety of trees of immense height ... There are very extensive fields and meadows, a variety of birds, different kinds of honey, and many sorts of metals, but no iron." Turning to the people, he commented:

> They are naturally timid and fearful. As soon as they see they are safe, however, they are very simple and honest, and exceedingly liberal with all they have ... the women seem to work more than the men. I could not clearly understand whether the people possess any private property ... I did not find, as some of us had expected, any cannibals among them, but on the contrary men of great deference and kindness.[1]

Columbus's letter was immediately passed on to a printer in Barcelona, who published it in Spanish, the language in which he wrote it. By the time Columbus reached the Spanish court, a copy of the letter had already been sent to Rome, where it was translated into Latin and published in several editions. By the end of 1493, Latin editions had also been published in Basel, Paris, and Antwerp, some decorated with woodcut images of ships and voyages copied from earlier books such as the illustration opening this chapter, but with captions labeling them as Columbus landing in the "Indian Sea." The first Latin translation was subsequently translated into a rhymed Italian version, printed in Rome and Florence with a title-page woodcut of King Ferdinand looking out over Columbus landing on an island. (The printer's introductions in many editions, and the visual images that accompany the texts, omit any mention of Isabella.) By the end of the year, educated people all over Europe had access to Columbus's letter, and it formed the basis of their first impression of what would soon be understood as a "New World."

Columbus may have sailed off into waters that were unknown to European sailors, but he carried with him firm ideas of what he would find, as his letter indicates. He expected cannibals, but found none, though he reported that people told him there were cannibals on a nearby island. He expected to find Amazon-like women, and found none, but again heard that on another island there were women who "dwell alone ... and employ themselves in no labor suitable to their sex, but use bows and javelins." He expected to find gold, and found a little, though was told there was another larger island nearby "which abounds in gold more than any of the rest." He expected to be well received, and reported that at each new island the native men he had captured and brought on his ships cried out "with a loud voice to the other Indians, 'Come, come and look upon beings of a celestial race.'" Whether this is indeed what the men were saying we will never know. Columbus had captured native men "in order that they might learn our language and communicate to us," but does not report that he or his men learned the local language. Columbus's actual encounters thus did little to alter his preconceptions; if something he expected was missing, it must be on the next island.

Examining the ways in which Columbus's cultural assumptions shaped both his own and other Europeans' responses to the New World, the Mexican historian and philosopher Edmundo O'Gorman coined the phrase the "invention of America." The America that took shape in Europeans' minds – and which in turn influenced their subsequent relations with indigenous peoples – was a blend of expectations and actual encounters. Those expectations were based on notions of cultural difference that were the product of centuries of trade, warfare, missionary activity, and other encounters across much of the "Old World." In those encounters, people confronted others of different ethnicity, race, language, and religion, and they had to develop ways of understanding these differences. Some scholars describe this process as "creating the Other," "defining the Other," "constructing the Other," or sometimes even "Othering." In creating "the Other," groups also came to define themselves. The encounter between Europeans and indigenous peoples in the New World was thus a continuation of a long-established process, but also something radically new and shocking, for these were people and lands unknown to the ancient Greeks, the source of the greatest wisdom in Renaissance Europe.

European relations with the rest of the world used to be studied separately from Europe itself, as what was termed "overseas history" or "colonial history" that was affected by, but did not influence, developments in Europe. Studies of individual colonies and of Europe by itself have certainly continued, but it has become increasingly clear that the histories of Europe and its colonies – colonies and "metropole" are the common terms – are completely intertwined. Relations between Europeans and non-Europeans were not simply discoveries or conquests (though they were both of these), but cross-cultural encounters involving exchanges of people, material goods, and ideas, and they began in classical or even prehistoric times. This recognition of global interconnections has come in an era when most former European colonies have become independent states, so this more integrative approach is often termed "post-colonial."

The Italian political theorist Antonio Gramsci has been especially important in post-colonial studies, particularly in his notions of "hegemony" and "subaltern." Hegemony means the control or domination of one person or group or nation over another, but Gramsci emphasizes that this is often achieved by granting special powers and privileges to some individuals and groups from among the subordinated population, or by convincing them that the new system is beneficial or preferable. The notion of hegemony explains why small groups of people have been able to maintain control over much larger populations without constant rebellion and protest. "Subaltern" refers to people who have been subordinated by their race, class, culture, gender, or language. Colonies contain many different subaltern groups, but so do the colonizing countries, and insights drawn from subaltern studies are now being applied to the study of "subaltern" groups such as racial and ethnic minorities in Europe and the United States. At the same time, some scholars also argue that post-colonial theory has been overused; not all of the world was colonized by Europeans, they point out, and "subaltern" peoples shape their own history and are not simply victims of subjugation.

Post-colonial theory developed at the same time as history as a field was undergoing the "linguistic turn" we discussed at the beginning of chapter 2, with its heightened attention to the ways in which the perspective of sources shapes what can be learned about the past. Though "constructing the Other" was a many-sided process, in many parts of the world European responses to non-Europeans left far more sources, both written and visual, than the opposite. As we have seen with Columbus's letter, those sources can sometimes tell us as much about the Europeans who wrote them as the non-Europeans they were encountering. Some scholars would argue, in fact, that such sources are so shaped by preconceptions that they can reveal little or nothing about the people described, so that the only possible focus of scholarly study is the text itself. Others find this approach limiting and unsatisfying, and consider European observations, imperfect and biased as they are, as nonetheless valuable for analyzing other cultures. They, too, stress, however, that we must be extremely careful and not simply take the available sources at face value.

In the fifteenth century, the world began to become interconnected in a way it had not been before, a process one new survey of world history has termed the "great world convergence."[2] The pattern of that convergence was directly shaped by existing lines of contact, however, so that to view Columbus and the impact of his voyages in context, we must first understand his competition.

Indian Ocean connections

The most regular lines of cross-cultural encounter in the centuries before Columbus were the sea routes of the Mediterranean, the Indian Ocean, and the South China Sea, over which boats carried all types of cargo. Buyers, sellers, bankers, sailors, captains, navigators, and other people seeking their fortunes came together in bustling port cities from Venice in the west to Hangzhou in the east. More than fifty languages might be spoken on the streets of such cities, for trade offered the possibility of fabulous wealth for merchants and investors, and a steady job for many. Transport over land was difficult and expensive, and remained so throughout the early modern period, but travel by sea grew steadily cheaper and more secure with improvements in ship-building, navigational instruments, port facilities, and business procedures.

Ships carried all types of merchandise, but spices from the "Spice Islands" (now the Moluccas, part of Indonesia) and other parts of South and Southeast Asia were the most important luxury product. Spices – pepper, cloves, nutmeg, mace, cardamom, cinnamon, and ginger – served not only as flavoring for food, but also as ingredients in perfumes, love potions, pain killers, and funeral balms. In an era before refrigeration, spices also helped preserve meats and masked the taste of meat that was slightly spoiled. By the fifteenth century, ships carrying spices sailed directly across the Arabian Sea and the Bay of Bengal on the two sides of India, using compasses and astrolabes for navigation and a variety of sails for maneuverability. Many of these ships also carried Muslim pilgrims going to Mecca and other Muslim holy places. The spread of Islam in the Near East, East Africa, and South and Southeast Asia had encouraged trade in other ways as well, for merchants could count on the same laws applying wherever they bought and sold merchandise.

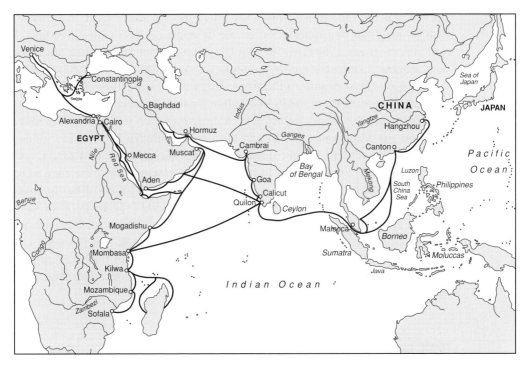

Map 7. Principal trade routes in the Indian Ocean.

Indian, Arab, Malay, Persian, and Turkish merchants, many of them Muslim, controlled the trade in spices and other luxuries in Asia and the Near East. Once goods got to Cairo or Constantinople they were often handled by Christian merchants, whose families had stayed in the Near East after the Crusades were over, or by Jewish merchants who had lived in these cities for centuries or recently migrated to them because of Christian persecutions in Europe. The Christian merchants came especially from northern Italian cities such as Venice, Genoa, Pisa, and Florence, and used new types of business procedures to spread risks among investors and keep better track of their ventures. Venetian merchants set up permanent offices in Cairo, where they dealt in spices traded up the Red Sea, while Genoese merchants went to Constantinople and the Black Sea, where they met caravans carrying goods over the silk roads. (A Genoese ship may have carried the first wave of the plague to Europe in 1347.) A few Italians went to the coastal cities of western India, which were becoming cosmopolitan mixtures of Hindus, Buddhists, Muslims, Jews, and Christians, all intent on expanding their profits.

Wherever they came from and wherever they went, merchants bought and sold slaves along with other merchandise. Italian merchants bought young women in Russia and North Africa to be household slaves in Venice, Genoa, and other Mediterranean cities. Spanish and Portuguese merchants bought North African men captured in war, and sold them to the military for use as galley slaves, when they rowed merchant vessels and warships. In the last sentence of his 1493 letter, Columbus offers help in this regard, "I promise, that with a little assistance afforded me by our most invincible sovereigns, I will procure them ... as many men for the service of the navy as their Majesties may require."[3] Turkish merchants bought Russians, Ukrainians, and Poles who had been captured in eastern Europe, selling them for use as household slaves, soldiers, textile workers, or in the sultan's palace. Arabic and African merchants crossed the Sahara Desert in both directions with slaves – West Africans going to the Mediterranean, eastern Europeans going to West Africa. Indian and Arabic merchants bought slaves in the coastal regions of East Africa, taking them to the west coast of India or further eastward. Because they were often taken far from home, slaves in many places were outsiders, differing from their owners in terms of religion, language, or physical appearance. They were defined as "Other," though this did not prevent sexual relations between male owners and their slaves. Laws usually forbade owners to kill their slaves, and religious teachings advised owners to treat them kindly, or (in Islam) to free them in their wills, but in no part of the world was slavery itself seen as wrong.

Chinese and Portuguese voyages

By the fifteenth century, people who had been on the fringes of the Indian Ocean/Mediterranean trading network became more active. From Ming dynasty China, the Ming Yongle emperor (ruled 1403–24) sent seven huge naval expeditions into the Indian Ocean and the Persian Gulf led by Admiral Zheng He (1371–1433), a Muslim from southwestern China. These were designed to gain control over foreign trade with China and convince people of Chinese power. These expeditions reached the Philippines, the east coast of Africa, and the Red Sea, but the voyages cost far more than the value of the goods brought back. After Zheng He and the Yongle emperor died, Chinese emperors and officials became more concerned about land attacks from the Mongols than about demonstrating Chinese power overseas, and sent no more expeditions.

At almost the same time that the Yongle emperor sent Zheng He on his voyages, the younger son of the king in a tiny country on the far western end of the Mediterranean also decided to increase his country's influence. Prince Henry of Portugal (1394–1460), later dubbed Prince Henry the Navigator, supported Portuguese explorations down the west African coast and military expeditions against Muslim forces in North Africa. When he was only twenty-one, he conquered the Muslim city of Ceuta in Morocco and became its governor. He learned about the land routes between Ceuta and central Africa, but thought that going by sea might provide better and more direct supplies of gold and slaves. Henry eventually planned and raised the money for over fifty voyages, and also supported map-makers, astronomers, and mathematicians, who made charts and calculations to assist ships' captains.

Portuguese colonies were established on many of the Atlantic islands, including the Azores, the Canaries, the Cape Verde Islands, Madeira, and São Tomé, where Portuguese and Italian investors obtained charters from the Portuguese king to grow and process sugar. Portuguese captains sailed further and further down the African coast, making contacts with rulers in Mali and the Kongo to provide gold and slaves. They used new types of ships, called caravels, which carried several different types of sails, and new instruments, including compasses, astrolabes, and log lines. These tools for navigation were not very accurate, but in experienced hands they allowed mariners to feel secure sailing far out of sight of land, which they had to do on their return voyage back to Portugal because of the wind patterns.

The most important motivation for Portuguese voyages was trade with Africa, but they were also trying to find a sea route to the Indian Ocean that would allow them to buy spices directly and avoid Arab, Ottoman, and Italian middlemen. In 1488, Bartolomeu Dias (1450?–1500) rounded the southern tip of Africa, but his tired sailors forced him to return to Portugal. In 1497, the Portuguese king Manuel I sponsored a fleet of four ships under the command of Vasco da Gama (1469?–1524), equipped with the best new technology and astronomical charts developed by Prince Henry's scholars. Da Gama's ships rounded Africa and sailed up its east coast until they reached towns where they

25 The kingdom of Prester John

Along with searching for gold and slaves, Portuguese captains were also hoping to connect with the Christian kingdom of "Prester John" reported to be somewhere in Africa. Prester (short for presbyter, or priest) John was a mythical Christian ruler first mentioned in European sources in the twelfth century, thought to be a descendant of one of the three kings from the East who presented gifts at the birth of Jesus. About 1165, a letter supposedly written by him to the Byzantine emperor began to circulate in Europe; hundreds of copies in different languages still exist, so many people certainly read it. In the letter, John describes himself as the fabulously wealthy and powerful ruler of a kingdom of Christians in central Asia, whose kingdom was filled with fantastic animals as well as "men with horns, one-eyed men, men with eyes before and behind, centaurs, fauns, satyrs, pygmies . . . [and] some people subject to us who feed on the flesh of men." European geographical knowledge of "the Indies" was vague, and the exact location of his kingdom was unclear; over the next several centuries it was thought to be in Mongolia, Persia, India, or Armenia. At the same time, other sources identified the king of Ethiopia (or Abyssinia) as Prester John. Abyssinia had become Christian by the fourth century, and many people there remained Christian after the spread of Islam in Africa, so that the ruler of Abyssinia was actually a better possibility as the heir to Prester John than any ruler in Asia. Portuguese explorers carried letters of introduction to Prester John with them on their voyages along the African coast, and thought they had reached his kingdom when they reached Ethiopia.

The story of Prester John is not based on historical evidence about Ethiopian or Asian rulers, however, but on wishful thinking. Though the location of this kingdom varied, its key quality was always a willingness to unite with Christian Europeans against Islam. The world map of 1507 that first used the word "America" put the kingdom of Prester John in the Himalayas, though another world map of 1516 placed it in Africa.

 For additional chapter resources see the companion website www.cambridge.org/wiesnerhanks.

could find mariners with experience in the Indian Ocean. Da Gama hired an Indian ship's pilot to navigate, and reached Calicut on the west coast of India by sailing directly across the Arabian Sea. Indian and Arabic merchants who were already there resisted da Gama, and he left for Portugal with fewer spices than he had hoped, though King Manuel I still rewarded him richly and gave him the title "Admiral of the Indian Ocean." Manuel sent da Gama back three years later to enforce Portuguese interests, this time with twenty warships; da Gama bombarded Calicut, defeated an Indian fleet, and conquered the city. Returning to Portugal with a huge amount of spices, gold, jewels, and other plunder, he was made a count. These riches, and the profits of Portuguese ventures on the west coast of Africa, meant that the Portuguese experience was the opposite of Zheng He's voyages, and Portuguese rulers had no doubts about whether they should keep sending more.

Columbus's background and voyages

Word of Portuguese voyages drew all sorts of people to Lisbon, including Columbus, whose story provides examples of all the themes important to post-colonial scholars and whose ideas were the beginning of the "invention of America." Columbus had grown up in the Italian port city of Genoa, where he had spent time as a boy listening to mariners and merchants and seeing the wealth that trade could bring in boxes and chests on the Genoese docks. He joined the crew of a merchant ship as a teenager, and while in his twenties settled in Lisbon with his brother, making maps to support himself. He married a woman whose father was one of Henry the Navigator's captains and a governor of the Portuguese colony of Madeira; the couple lived on Madeira for a while, and Columbus visited many other islands and the Portuguese trading posts on the west coast of Africa. Here he saw the possibilities for wealth and trade that overseas colonies could offer.

In Portugal, Columbus also got to know the group of geographers and astronomers that Henry the Navigator had brought together, but he apparently did not listen very well to what they were saying. Instead he paid more attention to what he was reading, which included works by ancient geographers and medieval travelers, both actual and armchair. He read *Natural History*, written by the first-century Roman official Pliny, which included quite accurate descriptions of the peoples, animals, and landscape of Africa and west Asia, combined with reports about cannibals, dog-faced boys, and people with feet so big they used them as umbrellas. He read the *Geography* of the second-century Greek scholar Ptolemy, which stated that the size of the earth was about one-quarter smaller than it actually is, and that Asia stretched out for half the circumference of the earth, when it is actually just a little more than one-third. He read the *Travels* of the thirteenth-century Venetian merchant Marco Polo detailing his trip to the court of Kublai Khan, which also retold the story of Prester John. He read the *Imago mundi*, written in 1420 by Pierre d'Ailly, the bishop of Cambrai and chancellor of the University of Paris, an encyclopedic account of the inhabitants of the world. From these books, Columbus developed his ideas of "the Indies": full of gold and beautiful landscapes, but also of men who might be cannibals or women who might be Amazons.

Figuring out what most literate early modern people might have read is purely conjectural, based on what they refer to in their own writings or what was likely to be in circulation in the places they lived. In Columbus's case, there is much less guessing involved, for the actual copies of many of the books he carried in his sea chest have survived, with annotations and marginal notes in his own hand. We know that his copy of Pliny was in Italian, printed in Venice in 1489, his copy of Ptolemy was printed in Rome in 1478, and his copies of Marco Polo and Pierre d'Ailly were also printed versions from the 1480s. We thus have a clearer understanding of what shaped his preconceptions than we do for almost any other early modern person. Some scholars of the Protestant Reformation have wondered whether Luther's message would have had much impact had the printing press not been available to spread it, and we can ask a similar question about Columbus – would he have left Lisbon had printing not given him access to all of these ideas?

He may very well have done so, because he was also influenced by direct contacts with at least a few contemporaries who thought as he did. The most important of these was Paolo dal Pozzo Toscanelli (1397–1482), a well-connected Florentine humanist, physician, astronomer, and mathematician. From his reading and his calculations, Toscanelli became convinced that the distance between Europe and Asia sailing westward was only about one-third of the globe. In this he was particularly influenced by Ptolemy, whose work was unknown in Europe before the fifteenth century, but, given the respect Renaissance scholars felt toward the ancient world, had quickly become a classic. Toscanelli shared his opinions, and a map based on them, with a cleric friend in Lisbon, who he hoped would take them to the king; Columbus heard about this, and asked for a copy, which Toscanelli sent shortly before he died. The map has disappeared, but part of the letter, in a copy in Columbus's own hand, has survived, and in it Toscanelli enthusiastically reports of the spices, gold, silver, and people with "great feelings of friendship for the Christians" that would greet a voyage westward.

Toscanelli's ideas had no impact at the Portuguese court; nor did Columbus's attempts to get backing for a voyage west based on them, for the king's council knew that almost all geographers thought the distances were much longer, so that a trip west would be far too costly. Columbus next tried the Spanish court, where for many years he got the same reaction, for the same reasons: his calculations were wrong, and it was too expensive. Their "Most Catholic Majesties" Isabella and Ferdinand grew more interested, however, once Columbus indicated he planned to use the wealth gained from his trip to recapture Jerusalem from the Muslims. He asserted that he was destined by God to spread Christianity, a destiny symbolized by his first name, Christo-fero, which means "Christ carrier" in Latin. (Columbus often signed his first name using the Greek symbols for Christ.) In 1492, Spanish armies conquered Granada, the last act in the centuries-long *reconquista*, and Spanish soldiers no longer had a mission on the Spanish mainland. Several weeks later, Columbus received the support of Queen Isabella, and later that year he left Spain with three ships and about ninety crew members. He carried Chinese silk in his sea chests along with his many books, and an Arabic-speaking Spaniard as a translator, figuring that someone at the Chinese court certainly spoke Arabic.

About five weeks after setting sail from the Canary Islands, Columbus's ships landed at an island in the Caribbean, which, as we have seen, he named San

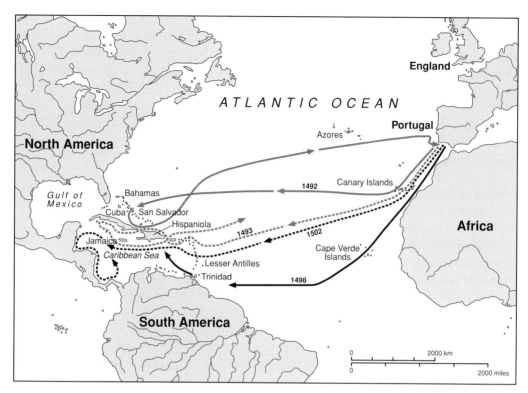

Map 8. Columbus's voyages.

Salvador, Spanish for Holy Savior. He was certain that he had reached an island off Asia, and called the inhabitants, who were members of the Taino people, "Indians." Looking for Japan or the Asian mainland, he explored numerous islands for several months, then set off again for Spain, taking several captured Tainos with him.

Columbus was greeted in triumph, but his subsequent expeditions were not uniformly successful. The second was huge, with over a thousand men, but most of these were treasure-seekers who went home disappointed after a few weeks. Columbus and his brothers governed different island colonies, never very successfully, and on his third voyage in 1498 he could find so few willing men that Ferdinand and Isabella had to release prisoners to serve as crew. On this voyage he explored what is now the coast of Venezuela, finding the mouth of the enormous Orinoco River, which made him realize this had to be a large land mass and not just an island. (Islands do not receive enough rainfall to allow large freshwater rivers to form.) He wrote in his journal that he had found a "very great continent . . . until today unknown," and that God had made him "the messenger of the new world." This was the first time that he used the words "new world" (*mondo novo*) for what he had found, though he still believed that Asia was just to the west, and the maps he and his brother sketched show the coasts of Central and South America – labeled *mondo novo* – vaguely attached to Asia. On his fourth and final voyage, he sailed along the coast of Central America looking for the passage to China, and was then marooned for more than a year on Jamaica while the governors of nearby Spanish colonies refused to help him. He died in 1506, just two years after returning to Spain for the final time, and two years after the death of his strongest supporter, Queen Isabella.

Early voyagers after Columbus

Columbus's reputation was not always glorious during his lifetime, but the news of his first voyage spread immediately throughout Europe and other mariners and adventurers found backers for their own expeditions. Another young man from Columbus's home town of Genoa, Giovanni Caboto (1450?–1498?) followed the same career path as Columbus, working on merchant ships in the Mediterranean, becoming a map-maker, and moving westward looking for support for longer voyages. He ended up in England, where he changed his name into English – John Cabot. Cabot thought that it would be faster to take a northern route to China, got the backing of King Henry VII of England and merchants in the port city of Bristol, and in 1497 made the first English voyage to North America, landing on the bleak and rocky shore of Canada somewhere near where the Viking colony on Newfoundland had been five hundred years earlier. Like Columbus, Cabot found no gold or treasure, but he did find the richest fishing area in the world, what was later called the Grand Banks. (These would remain an important source of the world's fish for centuries, until they had to be closed because of overfishing in the late twentieth century.) His voyage also gave England a claim to the mainland of North America and led to the founding of the English colonies in America, though Cabot himself disappeared on a second voyage.

Amerigo Vespucci (1454–1512) was born in Florence, worked for a banking firm run by the Medici family, moved to Spain, got involved in overseas trade, and served as a ship's captain on several Spanish and Portuguese voyages. He wrote vivid and extensive descriptions of his voyages, including a letter to his old employers the Medici detailing his trip along the coast of Venezuela that trumpeted the wonders of this "new world" and claimed that he had "found a continent." Just as Columbus's first letter had been, Vespucci's letter was published many times in many different languages, and along with "New World," the word "America" began to appear on maps and charts of what is now South America. The first to use this was the German map-maker Martin Waldseemüller (1470?–1522?), who justified his decision with the comment: "I see no reason why, and by what right, this land of America should not be named after that wise and ingenious man who discovered it, Amerigo, since both Europe and Asia had been allotted the names of women."[4] (Europe and her mother Asia were the Greek demi-goddesses discussed in the Introduction.) By just a few years later, map-makers – including Waldseemüller – and

Fig. 18. Martin Waldseemüller's 1507 map of the world, made from twelve separate woodblocks, the first to use the word "America." Waldseemüller includes the "thousands of islands" off the coast of Asia mentioned by Marco Polo, and frames the map with pictures of the four winds, Ptolemy, and Amerigo Vespucci. The only surviving copy of the map, which measures four feet by eight feet when assembled, was purchased by the US Library of Congress in 2003 for $10 million, and is on display there.

others knew they were wrong, and that Columbus had reached the same place before Vespucci; they wanted to omit "America" from future maps, but the name had already stuck. The Flemish cartographer, mathematician, and instrument maker Gerardus Mercator (1512–94), who invented the projection most commonly used to show the globe on a flat surface, used the word America for both land masses for the first time on his world map of 1538, and later the designations "North" and "South" were added.

While Spanish and English ships were exploring the coasts of the "new world," the Portuguese were as well. They sent fishing fleets to the Grand Banks, and built small settlements on the Canadian coast for salting and drying fish and processing whale blubber into oil. Some Portuguese scholars believe Portuguese ships were actually in the Grand Banks before Cabot and before Columbus, but so far no physical or textual evidence has been found to back up this assertion. In 1500, Bartolomeu Dias, the Portuguese explorer who had first rounded the southern tip of Africa, commanded ships in an expedition led by Pedro Alvares Cabral (1467?–1528?), another Portuguese adventurer. They were on their way down the African coast to India, but the fleet drifted off course, and landed in eastern South America. They found trees that were the color of glowing coals, and called both the trees and the country Brazil, after the word for this color in Portuguese, "brasa." Dias died during the voyage home when a storm sank his ship, but Portugal claimed Brazil.

Portugal's claim to eastern South America was supported by an international treaty drawn up several years before Cabral's voyage, before anyone in Europe knew that South America existed. Right after Columbus returned from his first voyage, the rulers of Portugal and Spain realized that their expeditions might lead to disputes over who had the rights to certain areas. They appealed to the only international authority available, Pope Alexander VI, who drew an imaginary line down what he thought was the middle of the Atlantic Ocean, giving Portugal everything to the east and Spain everything to the west. This line of demarcation was moved about 1,000 miles westward the next year in the Treaty of Tordesillas (1494), so that it ran right through South America, though no one knew it yet. Cabral's landing confirmed what the pope had already pronounced, and Portugal became the ruler of Brazil, even though a Spanish expedition was exploring the mouth of what would later be called the Amazon River in the same year.

In the eyes of Spain, Portugal, and the pope, the Tordesillas Line continued around the entire world, which meant the Philippine Islands off the coast of Asia were supposed to belong to Portugal. The first European expedition to land in the Philippines was a Spanish one, however, and in later treaties Portugal agreed to give up the Philippines to Spain in trade for a larger part of South America. This expedition was led by a sea captain who was actually Portuguese, Ferdinand Magellan (1480?–1521), who had spent many years sailing around the Indian Ocean, southeast Asia, and the Spice Islands. Magellan was unable to convince the king of Portugal to fund a voyage to reach the Spice Islands by sailing west, but in 1518 the teenaged king of Spain, Charles I (who was elected the Holy Roman Emperor Charles V the following year), agreed to support him. Magellan set off with five ships, first to Brazil, then down the coast of South America to the frigid waters near Antarctica, where one of his ships sank and the crew of another mutinied and turned around for home. He finally found a way around the southern tip of South America, through what is now known as the Straits of Magellan, and gave the ocean into which he sailed the name "Pacific," which means peaceful, because it seemed much calmer than the Atlantic.

Magellan's voyage was far from peaceful, however. The Pacific was so huge that food ran out, and the crew boiled their leather bags along with the ships' rats to eat. With no fruits or vegetables, they suffered from scurvy, a disease caused by lack of vitamin C, which made their joints grow sore, their gums bleed, and their teeth fall out. Once in the Philippines, Magellan and some of his crew took part in battles between local groups, and Magellan was killed. Only one of his ships, with eighteen survivors from the original crew of 240, and several men from the Spice Islands, made it back to Spain. Juan Sebastian del Cano, the captain of the ship that actually made it back, was first given credit for circling the globe. One of the survivors, an Italian named Antonio Pigafetta, had kept a detailed journal of the whole voyage, however, which praised Magellan's courage and skills; after it was published, the fame and credit shifted to Magellan. Thus it was printing, rather than the explorations themselves, that provided the key to fame for both Vespucci and Magellan.

With the Tordesillas Line, the pope may have divided the world in a way that satisfied Spain and Portugal, but other European nations were not included. Just a week before Magellan was killed in the Philippines, Martin Luther was standing in front of Charles V – the same ruler who had backed Magellan – declaring his independence in matters of religion. The Protestant Reformation ended the authority of the pope in half of Europe, and Protestant countries such as England and the Netherlands saw no reason to follow the pope's division of the world. They claimed territory for themselves based on their own voyages, and even Catholic countries such as France eventually simply ignored the Tordesillas Line. European claims to territory were based much more on actual voyages, military force, and the establishment of colonies than on imaginary lines drawn by popes.

European voyages of exploration in the century after Columbus are generally remembered by the names of their captains as individual heroic exploits, but for people in the busy port cities of Spain, Portugal, England, and France, these voyages must have seemed very similar to one another. A captain, often an Italian with experience in the Mediterranean, or later a Spanish or Portuguese mariner who had been to the Atlantic islands, or still later an English, French, or Dutch adventurer, recruited sailors and soldiers from among the men and boys hanging around the docks and taverns hoping to make their fortune. He also had to find merchants willing to risk the cash needed to pay for the voyage in the hopes of fabulous profits in return, and perhaps a noble

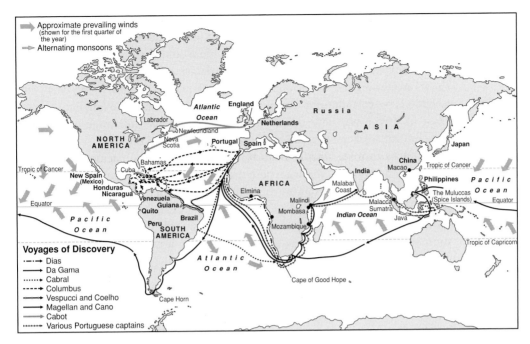

Map 9. Major European voyages, 1480–1525.

willing to provide additional money with the prospect of gaining wealth and a government position in the new territory or at home. Once he found them, he and his backers approached a ruler, hoping for formal approval and more financial assistance. Especially if they were Catholic, they also scouted around for a few missionaries, usually monks or friars who were accustomed to a harsh life and so could withstand the rigors of life on a ship. Sending only one ship was far too dangerous, so groups of ships, each with its own captain but with one man given supreme command, set out together. They sailed off, and some years later a few ships came back, bringing gold, pearls, spices, and slaves if they had gone east or stranger products, such as parrot feathers or cochineal insects for making red dye, if they had gone west. Many ships and men never returned.

For the men on these ships – and in the first decades they were all men – the voyages would have also seemed much the same. Sailors, soldiers, and whoever else was on board slept on the deck, ate a tasteless and dull diet, and alternated between boredom and terror. Alcohol was the only painkiller (though it was no help against sea-sickness), but it could make crews rowdy, so that effective captains had to be capable of disciplining rough and brutal men as well as being good navigators and skilled sailors. Shipwrecks, disease, accidents, malnutrition, and knife-fights all killed far more crew members than any battles with an enemy.

While they may have seemed similar viewed from the perspective of European port cities, the European voyages differed dramatically in terms of their effects on the rest of the world. In much of the Indian Ocean and eastern Asia, existing trading networks and structures of power just shifted a little to allow Europeans to collect some tribute and handle some trade. In parts of southwest India, eastern Africa, and island Southeast Asia, European weapons and the money brought by trade allowed some rulers to gain more power over their neighbors, which changed the political balance. This was also true on the west coast of Africa, but here those weapons, and the need for huge numbers of agricultural workers, also led to a steady expansion of the slave trade. African slaves came to make up the majority of the population in many parts of the Caribbean and South America. There they took the place of native peoples, who had died not so much from the guns Europeans carried on their shoulders, but from the germs they carried on their clothing, skin, and breath. In the New World, the impact of European voyages was initially disastrous and ultimately dramatic, creating completely new types of societies.

Europeans in Asia: merchants and missionaries

In the Indian Ocean, Portuguese mariners tried to dominate the centuries-old trade in gold, spices, silk, and other goods. They decided that the best way to do this was to build fortified trading posts along coasts that ships sailed near or narrow passageways between bodies of water. Under the leadership of Admiral Afonso de Albuquerque (1453–1515), Portuguese fleets captured the port of Goa on the west coast of India, Malacca in what is now Indonesia, and Hormuz, at the mouth of the Persian Gulf. They quickly built forts at all these places, and required all merchant ships to buy licenses or risk having their cargoes confiscated and their captains executed if they met a Portuguese warship.

Cannons and sturdy ships made this Portuguese protection racket possible. Indian, Turkish, and Arabic warships were usually long, light rowed galleys with a few cannon, built for quick actions close to shore. Portuguese ships were bulkier and better able to withstand storms at sea, with more heavy, long-range guns, able to bombard cities as well as blast holes in other vessels. They often attacked quickly, before galleys were able to travel from their home ports, and threw their opponents off guard with new types of tactics, like blockading harbors. The Portuguese were far from home, with no backup if they lost, so they were ruthless or even foolhardy against what were always larger local forces. They also used disputes among local groups to their advantage, gaining bases or ports from one ruler in return for helping him attack his neighbors.

Though Chinese emperors did not support long ocean voyages after those of Zheng He, large Chinese cargo ships sailed all over the South China Sea, trading silk and porcelain for pepper, spices, and cotton. They also brought silver mined in Japan to be made into coins in China, although trade with Japan was technically illegal because Chinese rulers saw the Japanese as uncivilized raiders and pirates. Chinese merchants settled in port cities in what is now Vietnam, Thailand, Indonesia, and the Philippines, where they often introduced local rulers to Chinese art and culture. This rich trade attracted Portuguese merchants, and from their fortified trading posts along the coasts of Africa, India, and Southeast Asia, Portuguese ships landed in China in the 1520s. The Chinese they first contacted found them even more uncivilized than the Japanese, so it took them decades to get permission to trade.

What changed the minds of Chinese officials was not an improvement in Portuguese manners, but the fact that in the 1540s the Portuguese landed by accident in Japan. They were given permission to trade by Japanese regional lords (*daimyo*), and European goods such as glassware, tobacco, clocks, and especially firearms were welcomed in Japan. The increasingly powerful *daimyo* Oda Nobunaga (1534–82), engaged in a military campaign to unify Japan, bought and then copied European artillery and hand-held weapons, and also collected western European art and artifacts. The Portuguese sent large well-armed ships to handle this new trade with Japan, and Chinese officials recognized these ships could also provide safe transport for Japanese silver to China. They relaxed their restrictions on Portuguese traders, who grew wealthy on shipping products all over east and southeast Asia, as well as to Europe and Africa. By the late sixteenth century, along with Japanese silver, Portuguese ships also brought American silver and new American crops such as sweet potatoes and maize, which came across the Pacific to the Philippines in Spanish ships.

Along with merchants, members of various religious orders, especially the Jesuits, were welcome at the courts of some of the *daimyos* in Japan and the court of the Chinese emperor. In China, they discussed religious issues, astronomy, and other subjects with Confucian scholars. Other missionaries gained converts among more ordinary people. The emperors generally tolerated Christianity because it did not require people to give up their allegiance to the emperor, and Christianity joined Confucianism, Taoism, Buddhism, and Islam as religions or philosophies practiced in China. Both missionaries and merchants operated within limits set by the government, however, and did not go far from major cities.

Missionaries were also sent to other areas with Portuguese trading posts. The conversion of local people was a slow process in the early sixteenth century, and the Portuguese clergy were often quite lax, living with local women just as soldiers and merchants did. With the arrival of clergy inspired by the Catholic Reformation in the 1540s, more rigorous standards were demanded of the clergy, and rules governing converts became stricter. Bishoprics were established in many colonies, and even an archbishopric and a separate Inquisition in Goa, which held the first *auto da fé* in Asia in 1563. Anyone who had converted and been baptized fell under its jurisdiction, which included former Hindus and animists as well as Portuguese "New Christians" whose ancestors had converted from Judaism or Islam decades earlier; *autos da fé* took place regularly until the late eighteenth century.

26 Matteo Ricci on differences between the Europeans and the Chinese

Matteo Ricci (1552–1610) was a highly educated Jesuit who joined the mission in China in 1583. He had studied astronomy and mathematics, and could build his own scientific equipment. He learned Chinese, translated and composed scientific, historical, and religious works, and in 1601 was given permission to join the emperor's court in Beijing, where he remained for the rest of his life. Ricci kept journals during his entire stay in China, which were edited and published by a fellow Jesuit after his death. Here he talks about differences between Chinese and European political systems; he is particularly impressed with the respect accorded scholars in China.

The Chinese place absolutely no trust in any foreign country, and thus they allow no one at all to enter and reside here unless they undertake never again to return home, as is the case with us. Their conception of the greatness of their country and of the insignificance of all other lands made them so proud that the whole world seemed to them savage and barbarous compared with themselves; it was scarcely to be expected that they, while entertaining this idea, would heed foreign masters …

Only such as have earned a doctor's degree or that of licentiate are admitted to take part in the government of the kingdom, and due to the interest of the magistrates and of the King himself, there is no lack of such candidates. Every public office is therefore fortified with and dependent upon the attested science, prudence, and diplomacy of the person assigned to it, whether he be taking office for the first time or is already experienced in the conduct of civil life …

Civil and military accounts and the expenses of all government departments are paid out of the national treasury, and the size of the national budget is far in excess of what Europeans might imagine. Public buildings, the palaces of the King and of his relations, the upkeep of city prisons and fortresses, and the renewal of all kinds of war supplies must be met by the national treasury, and in a kingdom of such vast dimensions the program of building and restoration is continuous …

Before closing the chapter on Chinese public administration, it would seem to be quite worthwhile recording a few more things in which this people differ from Europeans. To begin with, it seems to be quite remarkable when we stop to consider it, that in a kingdom of almost limitless expanse and innumerable population and abounding in copious supplies of every description, though they have a well-equipped army and navy that could easily conquer the neighboring nations, neither the King nor his people ever think of waging a war of aggression. They are quite content with what they have and are not ambitious of conquest. In this respect they are much different from the people of Europe, who are frequently discontent with their own governments and covetous of what others enjoy. While the nations of the West seem to be entirely consumed with the idea of supreme domination, they cannot even preserve what their ancestors have bequeathed them, as the Chinese have done through a period of some thousands of years …

Another remarkable fact and quite worthy of note as marking a difference from the West, is that the entire kingdom is administered by the Order of the Learned, commonly known as the Philosophers. The responsibility for orderly management of the entire realm is wholly and completely committed to their charge and care. The army, both officers and soldiers, hold them in high respect and show them the promptest obedience and deference, and not infrequently the military are disciplined by them as a schoolboy might be punished by his master. Policies of war are formulated and military questions are decided by the Philosophers only, and their advice and counsel has more weight with the king than that of the military leaders. In fact very few of these, and only on rare occasions, are admitted to war consultations. Hence it follows that those who aspire to be cultured frown upon war and would prefer the lowest rank in the philosophical order to the highest in the military, realizing that the Philosophers far excel military leaders in the good will and respect of the people and in opportunities of acquiring wealth.

(From *China in the Sixteenth Century: The Journals of Matteo Ricci,* trans. Louis J. Gallagher, S. J. [New York: Random House, 1942]. Reprinted with permission.)

Goa was just north of the province of Malabar, where there had been well-organized Christian churches since missionaries had come here from Syria in the fifth century, or even earlier; the Christians here regarded the New Testament apostle Thomas as the true founder of their church, and so are often called the St. Thomas Christians. Throughout their history, the St. Thomas

Christians had loose affiliations with eastern patriarchs, but they had no bishops. Each congregation was largely independent, led by married hereditary archdeacons rather than celibate priests. They were, of course, not under the authority of the pope, a situation that disturbed Portuguese officials. In 1599 the archbishop of Goa convinced some church leaders to swear allegiance to Rome, agree to the principle of a celibate clergy, and recognize the decrees of the Council of Trent. This was not acceptable to every congregation, however, and gradually two separate Christian communities developed in southwest India, one allied with the papacy and one not.

In the early years of Portuguese colonial ventures, there was an expectation that an indigenous clergy would develop, and a seminary was opened in Portuguese Goa, soon taken over by the Jesuits. Most seminarians were of high-caste groups or had European fathers, so this situation provides a good example of Antonio Gramsci's notion of hegemony: local elites participated in enforcing European authority. Non-Europeans were never accepted as full members of religious orders in any Portuguese colony, however; no amount of training could alter their subaltern ethnic status.

The Portuguese "empire" in Asia, then, altered trading patterns somewhat, but had little significant impact on powerful states such as China and Japan, except for the relatively small number of converts to Christianity. European ventures in Asia did not alter people's daily lives significantly, and most Asian people were probably not aware that Europeans had now been added to the international mixture of merchants and traders that had been active in coastal cities for more than a thousand years. If European traders stayed long enough, in fact, they often married local women, raised mixed-race children that spoke the local language, and sometimes converted to Islam, so that they blended even more easily into the multi-ethnic urban populations.

In Europe, Portuguese voyages provided wealth to merchants and a few mariners, and some taxes and fees to the rulers of Portugal, especially from the silver trade with China. This influx of money was not enough to allow Portugal to withstand a Spanish invasion and conquest in 1580, however, though the conquest did make the flow of silver and other goods in and out of Asia in European ships even smoother.

Europeans in Africa: slavers and sugar growers

At first, the impact of European voyages along the West coast of Africa was not much stronger than in Asia. Tropical diseases such as malaria, yellow fever, and sleeping sickness killed Europeans quickly, so that Portuguese traders often stayed only a short while, as close to the coast as possible. They set up permanent fortified trading posts, but relied on existing trading networks to buy and sell goods. The kings of Portugal made treaties with the rulers of West African states such as Benin, Oyo, and Kongo, supplying them with wool and silk cloth, tools, and weapons, in return for gold, cotton cloth, ivory, and slaves.

A few missionaries ventured further inland, first searching for the Christian kingdom of Prester John, and when they never found it, working to convert the people they did meet. They had the greatest success in the kingdom of the Kongo, a powerful state including parts of what is now the Republic of Congo, Zaire, and Angola. Jesuit and Capuchin missionaries gradually learned Kikongo, so that they could hear confessions and preach in the local vernacular; the first book printed in a Bantu language was a bilingual catechism in Portuguese and Kikongo, written in 1556 and printed in 1624.

Kongo was ruled by the *manikongo*, or king, who had both religious and political power and appointed governors for its six provinces. Converts to Christianity included the *manikongo* Nzinga Nkuwu (ruled to 1506), who took the Christian name João I, the same name as the king of Portugal. The next *manikongo*, Nzinga Mbemba, whose Christian name was Afonso I (ruled 1506–43), was raised as a Christian, and worked to convert his subjects to Christianity. Many of the ideas of Christianity – a heavenly realm, priests with special powers, an initiation ritual involving water and signifying rebirth, angels and demons – were similar to religious ideas already present in West Africa, which meant it was not difficult for people to accept Christian teachings. The rulers and Kongolese church leaders revised Christian ideas and practices according to their own values, just as Europeans had done when Christianity first spread north from the Mediterranean. Christianity became an important part of Kongolese culture, with so many churches in Mbanza, the capital of Kongo, that people called it "Kongo of the Bell."

At the same time as Christianity was spreading in the Kongo, another import was beginning to have disastrous effects – sugar. Sugar cane is native to the South Pacific, and was taken to India in ancient times, where farmers learned to turn cane juice into granules that could be stored and shipped easily. It then went to China and the Mediterranean, where islands such as Crete, Sicily, and Cyprus had the right kind of warm, wet climate for growing sugar. The Atlantic islands off the coast of Africa also had this kind of climate, and shortly after they were discovered by Europeans, sugar growing and processing began here. Producing sugar takes both expensive refining machinery and many workers to chop and transport heavy cane, burn fields, and tend vats of cooking cane juice. This means that it is difficult for small growers to produce sugar economically, and what developed instead were large plantations, owned by distant merchants or investors. The earliest sugar plantations in Europe and Africa were worked by both free and slave workers from many ethnic groups, but by the 1480s the workers in many sugar plantations, especially those on the Atlantic islands off the coast of Africa, were all black African slaves.

Columbus saw the possibilities of sugar first-hand when he lived on the island of Madeira, and he took sugar cane cuttings to the Caribbean on his second voyage. The first sugar mill in the western hemisphere was built in 1515 in what is now the Dominican Republic. Brazil also had the right kind of climate, and by the middle of the sixteenth century investors from all over

Europe were setting up sugar plantations there. By 1600 Brazil was Europe's largest source of sugar, and sugar had become a normal part of many people's diets. Per capita consumption in England was several pounds per person per year, still tiny compared to modern sugar consumption (the United States has the world's largest per capita sugar consumption, at about 150 pounds a year), but much more than it had been in the Middle Ages, when sugar was such a luxury that people thought of it more as a drug than a food. Sugar may not be physically addictive, but the human demand for sugar seems insatiable, as long as the price is low enough.

Slavery and shipping kept the price of sugar low. Sugar growers in the Caribbean and Brazil first tried to force native peoples to do the back-breaking labor that sugar demands. In the Caribbean, Spanish settlers (*encomenderos*) were given rights to compel native labor in the *encomienda* system, but the native peoples either died or ran away. Few Europeans were willing to wield machetes and haul cane in the hot sun for any amount of wages. The solution was the same one that had worked on the Atlantic islands – import enslaved Africans and set up huge plantations, where large numbers of workers supplied the sugar cane to keep complicated refining equipment running all the time. Slave-traders from West African coastal areas went further and further inland to capture, buy, or trade for more and more slaves. Some rulers tried to limit the slave trade in their areas, but others profited from it, and raiders paid little attention to regulations anyway. They encouraged warfare to provide captives, or just grabbed people from their houses and fields. The slave trade grew steadily, and first thousands and then tens of thousands of people a year, the majority of them men and boys, were taken from Africa to work on sugar plantations. For 350 years after Columbus's voyage, more Africans crossed the Atlantic than Europeans.

Slaves were marched from the interior of Africa to the coast, where they waited in locked pens to be loaded onto ships. On board, they were crowded into the filthy, stinking space below the decks, sometimes with not enough room to sit up. Food and water were limited for everyone on the ship, and even more so for slaves, who also suffered beatings and brutal treatment at the hands of the crew. On early slave trips as many as half the slaves died on the trip across the Atlantic – later called the "middle passage" – though later mortality declined as ship-owners realized they could make better profits if they kept the slaves alive. At every stage, slaves resisted their capture by refusing to work, sabotaging equipment, running away, or rebelling. In most islands of the Caribbean and on the South American mainland, communities of escaped slaves, known as "maroons," came together in forested or swampy areas, free from the control of plantation owners or government officials.

Slavery was a part of many societies around the world in 1500, but the plantation slavery of the New World was different from earlier slavery in two ways. One of these was the fact that almost all the slaves were black, and almost all the owners and managers were white, so that plantation slavery had a racial element that slavery in other parts of the world did not. Both European Christians and Arabic Muslims saw black Africans as inferior, barbaric, and primitive, attitudes that allowed them to buy and sell African slaves without any concern. By linking whiteness with freedom and blackness with slavery, the plantation system strengthened these racist ideas; slaves became the ultimate Other, only barely human. In fact, plantation owners came to think of their slaves more as machines than human beings; like machines, slaves would wear out and need replacing. Brazilian owners figured that most slaves would live about seven years, and they calculated the costs of buying new slaves into the price they hoped to get for their sugar. Some Christian missionaries objected to this treatment, especially for slaves that had converted to Christianity, but officially the Catholic and later Protestant churches accepted slavery. Sometimes church leaders even praised slavery, saying that though it might make people's lives on this earth worse, it gave them the opportunity of getting into heaven by becoming Christian, so in the long run they were better off.

The second new thing about plantation slavery was how much it depended on the international trading networks created as a result of European voyages. Plantations were centered on the monocultural production of one commodity, first mostly sugar, and later other crops such as coffee, indigo, and cotton, which meant that everything else needed on the plantation had to be imported. Ships that brought slaves to the Caribbean and Brazil – and later, in smaller numbers, to North America and the rest of South America – took raw sugar and molasses to Europe. Raw sugar was refined into white sugar in the Netherlands, and used to make sweet wine in Portugal and its Atlantic islands. One kind of sweet wine is still called Madeira, the name of the island where Columbus and his family had lived, and the site of the earliest European sugar plantations. Sugar and wine were shipped to England and other parts of Europe in exchange for cloth, manufactured goods, and machines. Ships took flour and lumber from North America to tropical plantations, and carried molasses on the way back, which was processed into rum. Rum and wine were on every European ship crossing any ocean, for they could be sold at a profit almost anywhere and were part of the crews' daily rations. West Africa, Europe, and the Caribbean formed three points in what is often called the "triangle trade" of the Atlantic, which will be discussed in greater detail in chapters 12 and 13; any leg of this triangle offered opportunities for wealth.

Slavery is often perceived as a very backward system, in contrast to modern industrial factories, but in many ways plantations *were* factories, mass-producing one specific thing to be sold as widely as possible. The slave trade by itself did not bring spectacular profits, but the plantation system was an essential part of a business network that provided steadily increasing wealth for European merchants and investors. During the sixteenth century, European governments expanded their navies to help control pirates and built more and better seaports, making trade a bit more secure. By a century after Columbus,

27 Afonso I of Kongo writes to John III of Portugal

In the 1520s, the Christian king of Kongo, Afonso I, wrote a series of letters to King John III of Portugal asking him to limit the importation of European goods and stop the enslavement of his people, and commenting on other matters. These are the first extant sources that discuss the effects of European actions from an African perspective. João did answer Afonso, but did nothing about the slave trade.

Sir, Your Highness should know how our Kingdom is being lost in so many ways that it is convenient to provide for the necessary remedy, since this is caused by the excessive freedom given by your agents and officials to the men and merchants who are allowed to come to this kingdom to set up shops with goods and many things which have been prohibited by us, and which they spread through our Kingdoms and Domains in such an abundance that many of our vassals, whom we had in obedience, do not comply because they have the things in greater abundance than we ourselves; and it was with these things that we had them content and subjected under our vassalage and jurisdiction, so it is doing a great harm not only to the service of God, but the security and peace of our Kingdoms and State as well.

And we cannot reckon how great the damage is, since the mentioned merchants are taking every day our natives, sons of the land and the sons of our noblemen and vassals and our relatives, because the thieves and men of bad conscience grab them wishing to have the things and wares of this Kingdom which they are ambitious of; they grab them, and get them to be sold. And so great, Sir, is the corruption and licentiousness that our country is being

completely depopulated, and your Highness should not agree with this nor accept it as in your service. And to avoid it we need from those your Kingdoms no more than some priests and a few people to teach in schools, and no other goods except wine and flour for the holy sacrament. That is why we beg of Your Highness to help and assist us in this matter, commanding your factors that they should not send here either merchants or wares, because it is *our will that in these Kingdoms there should not be any trade of slaves nor outlet for them* [emphasis in original] …

Many of our people, keenly desirous as they are of the wares and things of your Kingdoms, which are brought here by your people, and in order to satisfy their voracious appetite, seize many of our people, freed and exempt men, and very often it happens that they kidnap even noblemen and the sons of noblemen, and our relatives, and take them to be sold to the white men who are in our Kingdoms; and for this purpose they have concealed them; and others are brought during the night so that they might not be recognized.

And as soon as they are taken by the white men they are immediately ironed and branded with fire, and when they are carried to be embarked, if they are caught by our guards' men the whites allege that they have bought them but they cannot say from whom, so that it is our duty to do justice and to restore to the freemen their freedmen, but it cannot be done if your subjects feel offended, as they claim to be.

(Translated in Basil Davidson, ed., *The African Past* [Boston: Curties Brown, 1964], pp. 67–8. Reprinted by permission.)

captains, investors, and government officials knew they were still taking risks with ocean voyages, but the possibilities of profit usually outweighed those risks.

The slave trade had dramatic effects on West Africa, encouraging warfare and destroying families and kinship groups. In fact, one in five African-Americans may descend from people who were originally from the kingdom of Kongo. Eventually the slave trade weakened the authority of the *manikongo*, and Kongo broke apart into smaller states; this took more than a century, however, for the Kongo was actually at its largest and most powerful during the reign of Garcia II (ruled 1641–61).

Europeans in the New World: conquerors and miners

Spanish conquests in the Caribbean and in Central and South America were like the Portuguese conquests in the Indian Ocean area in many ways. They were quick and ruthless, depended on military technology, and took advantage of hostilities that already existed among different groups of native peoples. The Spanish, and later other groups of Europeans, had one weapon in the Americas that the Portuguese did not have in Africa and Asia, however – germs. Tropical diseases kept Europeans out of the interior of sub-Saharan Africa until the development of modern medicines to prevent and combat them, but the reverse was true in the Americas, where the impact of European voyages was devastating, even for people who never saw a ship or a soldier. Europeans brought with them diseases that were common in Eurasia, such as measles, mumps, bubonic plague, influenza, and smallpox, against which natives of the Americas had no resistance. These diseases spread through the Caribbean islands, and then in the more densely populated areas of Central and South America, killing more than 90 percent of the local population in some places.

Once Europeans reached the mainland of Central and South America in the late 1490s and early 1500s, diseases often spread ahead of actual groups of explorers or soldiers. For germs to be transmitted, only a few or even one native person had to come into contact with a Spanish landing party and then return to their village, spreading germs to other people as they did normal things like preparing food, carrying children, or talking about what they had seen. People became sick and died quickly, so that when European troops got to an area several weeks or months later, they found people who were already weak and fewer in number. This dramatic drop in population allowed the Spanish and Portuguese, and later the French, English, and Dutch, to set up land-based empires, not simply a string of trading posts. Soldiers and explorers were given positions as governors or royal officials, and settlers arrived soon afterwards.

Both guns and germs were important in the European conquest of the two largest New World empires, the Aztecs in central Mexico, and the Incas in the Andes. The way these empires had grown before the Spanish landed also helps explain why small European forces succeeded so easily. Both the Aztecs and the Incas built their empires through military conquest in the fifteenth and early sixteenth centuries; their neighbors resented their power and their demands for tribute, so they often helped the Spanish or became their allies.

The Aztec Empire was founded by the Mexica people, who migrated into central Mexico from the north around 1300, settling on the shores and islands in Lake Texcoco in the central valley of Mexico. Here they built their capital city of Tenochtitlán, which by 1500 was probably larger than any city in Europe except Istanbul. As they migrated, the Aztecs conquered many neighboring tribes, and war came to be seen as a religious duty. The Aztecs believed that the all-important sun god Huitzilopochtli demanded the sacrifice of captured warriors and other youthful victims to maintain his energy, so that crops would grow and life continue. Because of this, Aztec warriors took prisoners instead of killing defeated soldiers, and demanded that conquered tribes pay tribute and supply additional people for ritual sacrifice.

In the Andes, the Inca Empire first grew up around Lake Titicaca, and in the fifteenth century expanded its territory; by 1520 it stretched for 3,000 miles along the west coast of South America. Like the Aztecs, the Incas associated themselves with the sun god, whom they called Inti, though Inti did not require human sacrifice. They saw their emperor, also known as the Inca, as the link between people on earth and the sun in the sky. The Incas demanded tribute and taxes from the groups they conquered in the form of crops and forced labor (termed the *m'ita* system). One of the most important tasks throughout the Inca Empire was building and maintaining an extensive system of roads and bridges, along which were special huts for runners who carried oral messages to the runner in the next hut, a sort of pony express on foot. This system allowed news to travel about 150 miles a day, but it would also allow infectious diseases to be carried just as swiftly.

In the decades after Columbus's first voyage, Spanish settlements in the New World were limited to islands in the Caribbean, though explorers went back and forth to the American mainland several times. Spanish horses and Spanish soldiers gradually grew more accustomed to tropical climates, and in 1519 Hernando Cortés (1485–1547), led a group of 600 men and several hundred horses to the Mexican coast. He made allies among the Tlaxcalan and other native peoples who opposed the Aztecs, particularly after he used cannon to bombard the villages of those who did not side with him. By the time he reached Tenochtitlán, he had several thousand troops. The Aztec emperor Moctezuma let Cortés and his followers into the city, but, like the Portuguese in China, the Spanish behaved badly to their hosts, and they were thrown out in a bloody battle. They left behind an invisible enemy, however, in the form of smallpox germs, and many people sickened and died. Cortés gained more allies from among the Aztecs' enemies, and after a long battle took Tenochtitlán from the weakened Aztec forces. He and his allies then fought Aztec armies in other areas, and by 1521 he had taken permanent control of the whole empire. He shipped Aztec art back to Europe, where it was seen and appreciated by Renaissance artists, including Albrecht Dürer.

About ten years later, the Spanish explorer Francisco Pizarro (1478?–1541) conquered the Inca Empire. Pizarro had become rich after settling in Panama City, where he heard stories of a fabulous empire somewhere to the south. He organized several expeditions to search for this empire, and in 1532 captured one of the Inca leaders, Atahualpa (1500?–33), and killed thousands of Incas. Pizarro had even fewer men than Cortés, but the Spanish took the Incas by surprise in this attack. The Incas themselves were not united, as the powerful emperor Huayna Capac (ruled 1493–1525) had recently died in a plague – perhaps one that came to America with the Spanish – and not all Incas backed Atahualpa. Atahualpa paid a huge ransom for his release, but the Spanish killed him anyway. Pizarro founded the city of Lima as Peru's capital, and the Spanish used this as a base for the exploration and conquest of most of South America. King Charles I of Spain made Pizarro governor of Peru, but he was killed a few years later by another Spanish explorer who wanted to be governor.

King Charles I – the same King Charles who became the German Emperor, listened to Luther and sent Magellan – also made Cortés governor of Mexico, which was renamed New Spain. In both Peru and Mexico, the Spanish founded new towns, built Christian churches, and set up agricultural plantations like those in the Caribbean. Spanish conquerors and settlers were given large estates and rights to the labor of native people through an *encomienda* system modeled on that first established in the Caribbean. Along with ministering to immigrants, Spanish clergy began preaching to the local residents, first in Spanish, which few people understood, and then in the languages spoken in the Americas as the missionaries learned them. They set up missions away from the new Spanish towns and from existing Indian villages, trying to convert native people to Christianity and to teach them European ways; these missions took people away from their own culture, but also protected them from plantation owners who wanted to enslave them.

The discovery of silver mines in northern Mexico and in the Andes Mountains of Peru speeded up the pace of conquest. As we discussed in chapter 6, though merchants and bankers in Europe and Asia sometimes used paper forms of money for complex business transactions, most buying and selling was done in coins, and most of these were silver, which people also used to pay their taxes. More silver meant more coins available, and also more taxes for the government, which taxed both mining and trade. The Spanish government saw the silver mines as a great opportunity, and gave the rights to mine silver to private investors in exchange for 20 percent of the silver they mined. Mine owners brought in managers with experience mining in Europe, together with machinery and materials for smelting silver ore to make it pure, and imported goods so they could live like the elites of Europe; they organized the mines as capitalist enterprises, just as mines were organized in Europe. The government wanted to make sure this silver got back to Europe, so they built forts, encouraged the construction of sturdier ships and better weapons, and hired soldiers. In the Andes, they adapted and expanded the Inca system of forced labor, drafting Indians through the *encomienda* system to mine and transport silver from the unbelievably rich mines at Potosí. The Indians were also forced to mine mercury, which was needed to extract the silver from silver ore but is highly poisonous. Mission priests sometimes objected to these harsh demands, but the government replaced them with priests who were more willing to follow orders.

The Spanish government could do nothing about the spread of germs, however. Dangerous conditions in the mines and poisoning from the mercury used to smelt silver combined with disease to kill people even faster. Especially in the Andes, people fled to remote villages rather than work in mines, and there were never enough Spanish troops to force their return. The Spanish brought in African slaves from their Caribbean colonies, for they would not have local family connections and so would find it harder to run away, but they also died in great numbers. The mine owners responded to problems in finding and keeping workers by trying new types of more efficient machinery, and eventually by providing wages and improved working conditions. The forced labor of native people survived in some areas until the eighteenth century, however, and the enslavement of Africans even longer.

Spanish officials had originally imagined that their colonies in Central and South America would contain separate communities of Europeans and Indians, and a hundred years after conquest this was true to some degree. By about 1600 there were perhaps 200,000 people in the Spanish and Portuguese colonies who were, or pretended to be, of purely European ancestry. They lived in cities, wore clothing made of English wool or Chinese silk, ate from Dutch dishes, drank sweet Portuguese wine, and worshiped in churches designed by Italian architects. This European minority held the positions of power in the government, church, and private business. Away from the cities, there were millions of people of purely Indian ancestry living in villages, hunting or raising the same animals and growing the same crops they had for centuries. This was especially true in areas such as the Amazon River basin where there were no precious metals and there was no possibility of growing sugar. European diseases had killed people even in the remotest areas, but officials or soldiers rarely traveled in these areas, and even missionaries were very few.

The number of European women who migrated to the Spanish and Portuguese colonies was much smaller than the number of men, however, so this separation between Native Americans and Europeans was impossible to maintain. European men entered into relationships with indigenous women, and a mixed society developed, especially in and around mining towns and the new cities. African slaves and their children added to this mixture, so that increasing numbers of people in Central and South America were of mixed race, termed *castas* or *mestizos*. Spanish and Portuguese authorities, and the Catholic Church, were forced to develop policies and institutions to regulate a society very different from the one they had envisioned, a process we will discuss in more detail in chapter 13.

Global connections

Silver speeded up the development of a mestizo society in Latin America, and it also speeded up the development of global trading connections. Silver and gold from Mexico and Peru went to Spain in armed convoys, where they supplied the Spanish monarchy with one-fourth of its total income. Beginning in the 1560s several huge silver-ships also sailed every year from Acapulco in Mexico to Manila in the Spanish colony of the Philippines. There the silver was traded to Chinese merchants for silk, porcelain, spices, and other luxury goods, to be sold to European mine-owners and city-dwellers in Latin America or carried still further to wealthy nobles in Spain. Those Chinese merchants also bought Japanese silver, and took it all to China, where the economy was expanding and needed more and more silver to make coins. Silver taken to Spain paid for equipment and supplies for both mines and sugar plantations in the colonies, and also for guns and tools taken to West Africa, where they were traded for slaves. American silver and gold contributed to the inflationary "price revolution," and often ended up with German bankers who had loaned money to Charles V to finance his election as emperor or to later Spanish kings to finance their wars.

Global connections were not just a matter of metals and money, however, but also the intentional and unintentional sharing of many things, for European voyages linked parts of the world that had been cut off from each other for tens of thousands of years. These links were sometimes disastrous, as in the spread of infectious diseases to people in the Americas who had no immunity. But other links, what historians call the "Columbian exchange," were very beneficial. Food crops and animals traveled both ways across the Atlantic. Europeans brought horses, cattle, pigs, sheep, and chickens from Europe to the Americas, where they often escaped into the wild and thrived; a herd of a hundred cattle that the Spanish abandoned in the grasslands of the Rio de la Plata area in what is now Argentina grew within several decades to over 100,000. They also brought wheat, which grew well on the plains of both North and South America, along with wine-grapes and olives. From Africa they bought bananas, coffee, and coconuts. They took maize and potatoes back to Europe, growing them first as food for animals and gradually as food for humans as well. Tomatoes, peppers, sweet potatoes, peanuts, and manioc went from South America to Africa and Asia, as did pineapples and avocados. (About 30 percent of the foods eaten in the world today originated in the Americas.) This exchange of plants and animals improved nutrition around the world, and allowed a slow increase in the total global population, despite the tremendous loss of life because of epidemic disease.

The Columbian exchange involved products that brought pleasure as well as nutrition. We have already traced sugar's travels from Asia to the Americas; chocolate, which the Aztecs believed had been brought from paradise, went in the other direction. Both the Aztecs and the Mayas cultivated the cacao beans from which chocolate is made, and Cortés took them to Spain. Like the Aztecs, the Spanish developed the habit of drinking cups of chocolate, which they sweetened with imported sugar. (Aztecs and Mayas drank their chocolate, a word that comes from the Maya words for "sour water," unsweetened.) Drinking chocolate spread to France and England, where by the 1600s people were also drinking coffee imported from Arabia and Africa, and by the 1650s tea imported from India and China.

By the early 1600s global trade was providing another addictive substance along with the caffeine found in chocolate, tea, and coffee – nicotine. Native Americans grew and smoked tobacco long before Columbus, who took some tobacco seeds back to Spain with him, where farmers began to grow tobacco for use as a medicine that helped people relax. The French ambassador at Lisbon, Jean Nicot (1530–1600) – whose name is the origin of nicotine and of the botanical name for tobacco, *Nicotiana* – introduced the use of tobacco in France, originally in the form of snuff. English merchants brought tobacco to the Ottoman Empire, where coffeehouses filled with pipe smoke became popular places for men to gather. Ottoman religious leaders complained that coffeehouses kept people away from their religious duties, and Sultan Murad IV (ruled 1623–40) outlawed both coffee and tobacco, but his measures were ineffective.

Though products were exchanged in all directions, they were carried primarily in western European ships. Europeans were one group among many in the Indian Ocean and South China Sea, but elsewhere they came to dominate oceanic shipping. This provided great profits, and allowed them to dictate the terms of trade even in areas where they did not have colonial empires. This trade also stimulated the growth of many industries in Europe, from shipbuilding to textiles, as Europeans increasingly exported manufactured goods in exchange for unprocessed or partially processed raw materials, such as sugar, precious metals, and timber. International trade and the demand for European manufactured goods enhanced an economic expansion that was already underway for certain parts of Europe, a story we will take up in greater detail in chapters 12 and 13.

The first century of European colonization also had political effects, for the creation of the first global empires meant that arenas of conflict and sources of power were no longer confined to Europe itself. The conquest of the Americas initially glorified the Spanish (and to a lesser degree the Portuguese) monarchy and the Catholic Church; both acquired immense new lands to rule and people to govern. The wealth brought by Spain's overseas colonies made it the most powerful country in Europe around 1600, a connection that was widely recognized, as English and French actions to weaken Spain always involved cutting off trade with the Americas. Western European countries came to view overseas possessions as essential adjuncts to their military and economic power, which helped foster nationalism by encouraging a race for trade, treasure, and colonies. English pirates – often dignified by the term "privateer" – were motivated primarily by a desire for wealth in their attacks on the Spanish treasure fleet and South American ports, but they often obtained the approval of the English monarch, and were expected to provide a cut of their haul to the national treasury. Sir Francis Drake (1543?–96), for example, the most famous of these "sea dogs," got money, ships, and eventually a knighthood from Queen Elizabeth. He seized Spanish ships, commanded English warships against the Spanish Armada in 1588, and looted Spanish towns in the Caribbean and on the north coast of South America, termed the "Spanish Main." On his trip around the world in the late 1570s, he raided the west coast of South America, where the towns were completely unfortified. Drake began his career as a slave-trader, and ended it as a member of the House of Commons.

Hatred of Spain was enhanced in the sixteenth and early seventeenth centuries by stories that circulated orally and in print about Spanish atrocities in the New World. This "Black Legend" (in Spanish *Leyenda Negra*) was based especially on the writings of Bartolome de Las Casas (1474–1566), a Spanish

28 Theodor de Bry's images of America

© Bildarchiv Preussischer Kulturbesitz/Art Resource, NY

The most famous and widely reproduced images of the New World in the late sixteenth and early seventeenth centuries were those of the Flemish engraver Theodor de Bry (1527?–98), who brought out a series of multi-volume accounts based on many sources beginning in 1590, including an illustrated edition of Las Casas. De Bry was a Protestant who had fled his homeland during the Dutch Wars of Religion, and used his engravings to demonstrate the evils of Catholicism as well as the nobility and exoticism of the Indians. In this engraving, from the fifth volume of his *Americae* series, published in Frankfurt in 1595, Spanish soldiers violently suppress a revolt of African slaves. This volume is based on the published text and woodcuts of an Italian adventurer, Girolamo Benzoni, who traveled in the Caribbean in the 1540s and 1550s. Benzoni hated the Spanish, and his book provides countless stories of their mistreatment of natives and Africans, though other sources indicate that reactions to slave revolts were indeed brutal.

Dominican missionary who became bishop of Chiapas in Mexico in 1544. Las Casas took part in royal investigations into the treatment of Indians, and in response to assertions by various officials that enslaving them was justified because Indians were less than human, he published a series of essays in 1552–3 detailing, condemning, and probably exaggerating Spanish abuses. In Las Casas's writings, all Indians were childlike innocents and all the Spanish were violent, cruel, and greedy. His writings led to a royal prohibition of the enslavement of Indians, though this was widely ignored, and may have played a role in the increasing importation of African slaves, which Las Casas endorsed, though he later regretted this. Translated into other European languages, often with titles such as "The Tears of the Indians," they provided a justification for New World conquests by other European nations and became a staple of Protestant propaganda.

Las Casas's portrayal of the indigenous peoples of the Americas as peaceful and harmless was only one of several stereotypes developed and popularized by Europeans. Other writers, some of whom had actually been to the New World and some of whom had not, viewed Indians as savage, wild, and bestial, while others portrayed them as dignified, virtuous, and stately: "noble savages" similar to the "noble pagans" of ancient Greece and Rome. Both positive and negative accounts often describe or portray Indians as naked or only partially clothed, or as dressed only in feathers, clearly viewing them as exotic. The accounts of explorers or works based on these accounts were translated and reprinted many times – Vespucci's letters saw sixty editions – often with illustrations that reinforced these perceptions. Illustrations were copied and reproduced separately from textual accounts, so that people who were illiterate came to share these views.

The discoveries in the New World posed an intellectual problem for educated Europeans, because they had to fit the peoples of the Americas into a world view based on Christian teachings and classical models. If the Flood described in the Old Testament truly covered the whole world, then the Indians must be descendants of Noah. But when and how did they get there? How could the ancient Greeks and Romans so revered by humanists not have known about them? How were the differences between peoples to be explained? What was the true difference between civilized and barbarian? Las Casas tackled these questions in a massive ethnography and comparative history, *Apologética historia sumaria*, arguing that all peoples were equally rational and on the same road to civilization, and that New World cultures were actually superior to the Greeks and Romans. In contrast to his essays describing Spanish cruelty, this work was never published until the twentieth century, though other, shorter considerations of these issues were.

One of these was the *Historia natural y moral de las Indias* (Natural and Moral History of the East and West Indies), written by the Spanish Jesuit theologian José de Acosta (1540–1600), who had spent more than twenty years in Peru and Mexico. Acosta's work, which was published in several languages in the late sixteenth and early seventeenth centuries, arranges world cultures into a hierarchy, with Europeans, Chinese, and Japanese at the top, Aztecs and Incas in the middle, and Africans and other "savages" at the bottom. Acosta's arrangement both shaped and reflected Jesuit policy. Jesuits in China accepted Chinese men as members of the Jesuit order and even as priests more readily than darker-skinned Christians elsewhere, viewing them as members of highly developed cultures and thus better prepared for leadership positions. The first Chinese priest, Luo Wanzao (baptized Gregorio Lopez) was ordained in 1654, and was later named a bishop, though his appointment was fought by many in the church hierarchy.

Most Europeans were not as willing as Acosta to share the top of the cultural hierarchy with any other group, and even fewer accepted Las Casas's notions about the equal rational capacity of all peoples. The relative ease with which the Spanish conquered the Caribbean, Central America, and the Andes region created a strong sense that Europeans were destined to impose Christianity and civilization on these "new" peoples. This combined with assessments of African inferiority bolstered by the expansion of the African slave trade to create a greater sense of European cultural superiority than had been evident earlier. Overseas conquests gave Europe new territories and sources of wealth, and also new confidence in its technical and spiritual supremacy.

The first recorded celebration of Columbus Day on October 12 was in New York City in 1792, though more extensive festivities began among Italian-Americans in the late nineteenth century, and the day was made a U.S. federal holiday in 1937. The view of Columbus in these celebrations was as heroic and triumphant: Columbus was the first "modern man," who ventured into the unknown just to find out what was there and stuck to his dreams despite the ridicule and scorn of his contemporaries. In the early twentieth century, several countries in Latin America began celebrating October 12 as *Día de la Raza* ("day of the race"), commemorating the blending of European and indigenous cultures in the formation of *mestizo* society. Both holidays have been sharply contested in the last several decades. Edmundo O'Gorman, the Mexican historian who first coined the term "the invention of America," resigned as the director of the Mexican Academy of History in 1987 because he objected to celebrations of cultural blending that avoided the discussion of European domination. Events in 1992 marking the 500th anniversary of Columbus's first voyage ranged from celebratory television specials and recreations of the voyages to funerals for indigenous cultures and protests at statues of Columbus in Europe and the Americas. Some communities have renamed the day "Indigenous People's Day," and in Venezuela, in 2002, *Día de la Raza* was officially renamed *Día de la Resistencia Indígena* (Day of Indigenous Resistance). Even those who continue to sponsor parades now tend to recognize the mixed effects of Columbus's voyages, and the less attractive qualities of his character. Neither side in this controversy disputes the enormous consequences of the "great world convergence": the connections and encounters that became more global in their scope with the European voyages.

This global network was only one of many things that had changed dramatically in the 150 years since the invention of the printing press and the Portuguese voyages to the West African coast in the 1450s. The printing press was an important factor in an expansion of literacy, particularly among urban, middle-class men in western Europe, but by 1600 artisans in certain trades and middle-class women could often read as well. Both printing and literacy shaped, and were shaped by, the Protestant and Catholic Reformations, as printed materials aided the spread of religious ideas, and religious controversy provided an eager audience for books and pamphlets. The division of Christian Europe certainly competes with exploration and colonialism as the most important difference between 1450 and 1600. That division was accompanied by – and again played a role in – the establishment of firmer national boundaries, as smaller states combined or were absorbed by their larger neighbors. Thus by 1600 Aragon and Castile had become a unified Spain (and had conquered Granada) and Brittany and some of Burgundy had become parts of France. These political changes were the result of military campaigns in which large armies used new types of weapons combined with clever martial strategies on the part of astute rulers. They were bolstered by the development of expanded government bureaucracies and taxation systems, which also occurred in central and eastern Europe, though strong centralized nation-states had not developed there. Eastern and western Europe were more closely linked by trade in 1600 than they had been in 1450, with grain flowing west and manufactured goods flowing east, as well as to many other parts of the world. This expansion of trade and manufacturing went hand in hand with the growth of cities in certain areas, especially the Low Countries and the national capitals in western Europe, as Paris and London joined Istanbul as major metropolises.

Many other aspects of life had changed little since 1450, however. Most people continued to live in small villages and make their living by farming, with grain as their primary crop. While people and goods moved regularly around the world by water, land transport remained very difficult. Local and more widespread famines continued, contributing to infant and child mortality that remained high, with only half the people born making it to age ten. The precariousness of life was one reason for the continued importance of religion, as a matter of both personal observance and powerful institutions. Europe was religiously divided in 1600, but the decades of religious wars that had hardened those divisions had not lessened people's sense of the centrality of spiritual matters and the quest for salvation. Though Renaissance humanists praised the genius and contributions of certain individuals, the family remained people's primary source of identity and support. Expanding wealth allowed some individuals and some families to increase their social stature, but did not upset a hierarchy in which being born noble was the best assurance of power and prosperity. Hierarchies of wealth and inherited status continued to intersect with hierarchies of gender, for whether one was born male or female shaped every life experience and every stage of life.

Had Pope Pius II, whom we met in chapter 1 commenting on Vienna, suddenly been transported from 1450 to 1600, he would no doubt have immediately noticed that his authority as pope was geographically diminished in Europe, but now extended to lands he had never imagined existed. Other than this, it is difficult to know if he would have found the changes or the continuities more striking. As we begin to examine Europe after 1600, the second half of this "early modern" period, we will need to keep the balance between change and continuity in mind, between the "early" in that term, and the "modern."

Further reading

Edmundo O'Gorman's pioneering study of European ideas about the New World was first published in Spanish; an expanded and modified version appeared in English as *The Invention of America: An Inquiry into the Historical Nature of the New World and the Meaning of its History* (Bloomington: Indiana University Press, 1961). In the last several decades, it has been joined by numerous others: Tzvetan Todorov, *The Conquest of America: The Question of the Other*, trans. Richard Howard (New York: Harper and Row, 1984); Peter Hulme, *Colonial Encounters: Europe and the Native Caribbean, 1492–1797* (London: Methuen, 1986); Urs Bitterli, *Cultures in Conflict: Encounters Between European and Non-European Cultures, 1492–1800*, trans. Ritchie Robertson (New York: Polity Press, 1989); Peter Mason, *Deconstructing America: Representations of the Other* (London: Routledge, 1990); John F. Moffitt and Santiago Sebastián, *O Brave New People: The European Invention of the American Indian* (Albuquerque: University of New Mexico Press, 1996). For analyses of encounters in other parts of the world, see Stuart Schwarz, ed., *Implicit Understandings: Observing, Reporting and Reflecting on the Encounters between Europeans and Other Peoples in the Early Modern Era* (Cambridge: Cambridge University Press, 1994); O. R. Dathorne, *Imagining the World: Mythical Belief versus Reality in Global Encounters* (Westport, CT: Bergin and Garvey, 1994), and *Asian Voyages: Two Thousand Years of Constructing the Other* (Westport, CT: Bergin and Garvey, 1996). Encounters with and representations of Africans have been the focus of fewer studies; the best introduction to this issue from a European perspective is Kim F. Hall, *Things of Darkness: Economies of Race and Gender in Early Modern England* (Ithaca, NY: Cornell University Press, 1995).

A good introduction to Antonio Gramsci's notion of hegemony is Joseph V. Femia, *Gramsci's Political Thought: Hegemony, Consciousness and the Revolutionary Process* (Oxford: Clarendon Press, 1981), or Gramsci's own work, *Selections from the Prison Notebooks of Antonio Gramsci* (New York: International Publishers, 1971).

For the Indian Ocean, see K. N. Chaudhuri, *Trade and Civilization in the Indian Ocean: An Economic History from the Rise of Islam to 1750* (Cambridge: Cambridge University Press, 1989), and Sanjay Subrahmanyam, *The Portuguese Empire in Asia, 1500–1700: A Political and Economic History* (London: Longman, 1993). Subrahmanyam has also written a study of Vasco da Gama, *The Career and Legend of Vasco da Gama* (Cambridge: Cambridge University Press, 1998). Two older studies that are very valuable are J. H. Parry, *The Spanish Seaborne Empire* (New York: Knopf, 1966), and C. R. Boxer, *The Portuguese Seaborne Empire, 1415–1825* (New York: Knopf, 1969).

For European expansion before Columbus, see the classic works of J. H. Parry, *The Age of Reconnaissance* (Berkeley: University of California Press, 1963), and Carlo Cipolla, *Guns, Sails, and Empires: Technological Innovation and the Early Phases of European Expansion* (New York: Minerva Press, 1965), and the newer studies, Felipe Fernández-Armesto, *Before Columbus: Exploration and Colonization from the Mediterranean to the Atlantic, 1229–1492* (London: Macmillan Education, 1987) and J. R. S. Phillips, *The Medieval Expansion of Europe* (Oxford: Oxford University Press, 1998). Fernández-Armesto has also written an excellent biography of Columbus, *Columbus* (Oxford: Oxford University Press, 1992). For a broad survey of European colonization, see Geoffrey Vaughn Scammell, *The First Imperial Age: European Overseas Expansion, c. 1400–1715* (London: Unwin Hyman, 1989). For the role of Africans in European expansion, see Philip Curtin, ed., *The Rise and Fall of the Plantation Complex: Essays in Atlantic History* (Cambridge: Cambridge University Press, 1990), and John Thornton, *Africa and Africans in the Making of the Atlantic World, 1400–1680* (Cambridge: Cambridge University Press, 1992). A good brief survey of the slave trade is Herbert S. Klein, *The Atlantic Slave Trade* (Cambridge: Cambridge University Press, 1999).

For a discussion of the impact of New World voyages from the point of view of literary critics, see Stephen Greenblatt, *Marvelous Possessions: The Wonder of the New World* (Chicago: University of Chicago Press, 1991), and Anthony Pagden, *European Encounters with the New World: From Renaissance to Romanticism* (New Haven: Yale University Press, 1993). From the point of view of historians, see J. H. Elliott, *The Old World and the New, 1492–1650* (Cambridge: Cambridge University Press, 1972), and Roger Schlesinger, *In the Wake of Columbus: The Impact of the New World on Europe, 1492–1650* (Wheeling, IL: Harlan Davidson, 1996).

 For more suggestions and links see the companion website www.cambridge.org/wiesnerhanks.

Notes

1 R. H. Major, ed. and trans., *Select Letters of Christopher Columbus* (London: Hakluyt Society, 1847), pp. 1, 4.
2 Ross Dunn and Elizabeth Cobbs Hoffman, *Spinning Planet: A Short History of Humankind* (Boston: McGraw-Hill, 2007).
3 Major, *Select Letters*, p. 15.
4 Martin Waldseemüller, *Introduction to Cosmography* (1507), trans. in George Kish, *A Source Book in Geography* (Cambridge, MA: Harvard University Press, 1978), p. 319.

8 Individuals in society, 1600–1789

The title page of Thomas Hobbes's *Leviathan* (1651), with an engraving by the French artist Abraham Bosse. The top half shows a huge crowned king, with a sword in one hand and a bishop's staff in the other, rising above a countryside with villages, a walled city, and a church, while the bottom shows various symbols or elements of sacred and secular power.

THE title page of *Leviathan*, a political treatise arguing the need for an authoritarian, unchallengeable ruler, written by the English philosopher Thomas Hobbes (1588–1679), is one of the most famous images of society from the seventeenth century. Though the head of the king is that of a single individual, his body is made up of the tiny bodies of many men. In *Leviathan*, Hobbes argues that the true basis of government is not a divine right conferred by God, but the agreement – the word he uses is "contract" – of the residents of a state to form a society with an absolute ruler at its head who has both civil and ecclesiastical authority. Once they have done this – and it does not have to be in historical memory – they have no right to rebel; if they do not do this, they will live in a pre-political state of nature driven by fear and passion, a state that Hobbes describes as "solitary, poor, nasty, brutish, and short" (*Leviathan*, ch. 13). The title-page engraving illustrates this theory; the men, most of them dressed as gentlemen but a few as artisans, peasants, and clergy, seem to be in the process of fitting themselves into the body of the ruler, literally incorporating (a word that comes from the Latin word for body, *corpus*) themselves into his form.

Using the body as a metaphor for society or the state did not originate or end with Hobbes; many of the words we still regularly use to discuss groups that act as units, such as corporate or corporation or Marine Corps, have their origin in this imagery of a body. This metaphor was employed to support many different and sometimes contradictory ideas in the early modern period, however. In Bosse's engraving and Hobbes's treatise, it is *individuals* who incorporate themselves into the ruler, making a contract that creates "an Artificiall Man." Other writers and illustrators saw the body politic as created by God, rather than by a human contract, and as made up of different social groups rather than individuals. The ruler was always the head, but the eyes and ears were the king's advisors or the clergy, the hands knights, the thighs merchants, the feet peasants, the toes servants, and so on. The body was a hierarchy, but one in which each part was dependent on the others.

Political authors and playwrights illustrated this point by telling and retelling the "fable of the belly," a tale attributed to the Greek author Aesop, in which other parts of the body rebel against the stomach, which seems to be useless. They refuse to nourish it, and, of course, the entire body sickens. This story could be used to make quite different points, however, sometimes by two characters in the same work. In Shakespeare's *Coriolanus* (1608), the Roman patrician Menenius Agrippa uses the fable in the opening scene to denounce rebellion by plebian "mutinous members" against "the senators of Rome [who] are this good belly" (*Coriolanus*, I.i.152, 153). Later in the play, however, citizens and officers criticize Coriolanus because he "loves not the common people," calling them "curs," "slaves to buy and sell," or "boils and plague," instead of recognizing they are the feet and hands on which he depends.

Rebellion of the members or tyranny of the head were only two of the problems that could plague the social body. Bodies could have two heads, which made them monstrous; the English writer John Milton (1608–74) used this analogy in 1641 to argue against the power of bishops, which had become, in his thinking, a "swollen Tumor" growing so "huge and monstrous" out of the neck that it challenged the proper head, the king.[1] Writers discussing the appropriate relations between husband and wife noted that no household should have two heads, though some did give wives the somewhat lesser, though still important, position of "heart." The word "head" was linked closely enough to masculinity that Elizabeth I chose to have herself designated the supreme "governor" of the Church of England, rather than the "head" as her father had been. Her successor, James I, linked husbands and heads even more clearly, declaring in his first speech to Parliament in 1603; "I am the Husband, and the whole Isle is my lawful Wife; I am the Head, and it is my Body."[2]

Like the physical body, the social body could become ill, another analogy with a long history. Just as consumption (tuberculosis) made the body thin and weak, so war led to weakness and a loss of population; just as palsy made the body useless, so making or importing new fashions was a waste of money that could be put to better uses; just as an infected and swelling spleen made the body sick, remarked James I, so the growth of London threatened the realm. Any of these diseases could spread, as gangrene could spread in a diseased body, and the proper remedy might be the same as for gangrene – chop off the infected part. As one character says about Coriolanus, "he's a disease that must be cut away." The analogy between the body and society was thus not simply one of structure, but also one of function; both were healthy only when all parts functioned as they should, and both required treatment when one part became ill and could not, or would not, function.

In chapter 2, we looked at the individual life cycle and at some of the social structures in which early modern people were enmeshed. Those aspects of life did not change dramatically in the two hundred years after 1600: the seven ages of man continued to be used to describe the life cycle, sumptuary laws continued to regulate spending, rural households continued to be larger than urban ones, widows continued to have a rougher time than widowers, death continued to take many children, religious and occupational groups continued to augment kin ties. This chapter will focus more on the way individuals and groups functioned, or were thought to function, and what happened when illness or social conflict interfered. We will begin with a discussion of several influential theories relating to the social and physical body, and then explore various arenas in which individual and corporate bodies interacted.

Sources and theories about the body and the body politic

Treatises of political theory such as *Leviathan* provide one type of source for understanding ideas about the role of individuals in society. Personal documents, such as letters, journals, and diaries, provide another. Letters were sent through all sorts of channels – traveling acquaintances who passed them along to other travelers, merchants going to fairs, people on pilgrimages, and (for the wealthy and powerful) privately hired messengers. At the beginning of the sixteenth century, the Taxis (or Tassis) family, who had served as couriers for the pope and other Italian rulers, was commissioned to set up a communication system in all the lands under Habsburg rule. This territory stretched from Spain to Bohemia, and slowly regular postal routes were established, which were open to anyone who paid the fee, not simply to specific business or government clients. The postal service was a private enterprise, not a branch of the government, and the Taxis company made contracts with rulers beyond the Habsburgs as well. Postal systems and post offices were set up in France, England, and Scandinavia in the first half of the seventeenth century, with mail coaches instead of individual riders handling the increased volume. Postal maps existed for all of Europe by 1700, showing roads, bridges, and post offices.

The regular delivery of mail is such a normal part of daily life today that we notice only when it is interrupted, but it was a major innovation in early modern Europe. People who could write did not have to rely on private contacts or the whims of travelers to correspond directly with one another, and began to use the post for regular communication. Though most letters from any era have long since disintegrated, so that it is difficult to arrive at exact figures, the volume of written personal communications increased significantly with the regular postal service. Paper provided letter writers as well as printers with a cheap surface, and writing letters became a large part of many people's daily activities.

We know that people spent time each day writing letters not only from the letters themselves, but also from journals and diaries that describe this, along with their other activities. Personal journals have survived in numbers that steadily increase throughout the early modern period, mostly from people at the upper end of the social scale, but quite a few from middle-class individuals, such as the German merchant Mattheus Miller, and a few from the laboring classes, such as the English lace-maker's apprentice Mary Hurll. Explorers such as Columbus, Vespucci, and Pigafetta wrote open letters and kept journals describing their voyages. Men, and a few women, in various occupations kept daily records of their professional activities; the English scientist Robert Boyle (1627–91), for example, kept a diary of his experiments and observations, while the Dutch midwife Catharina van Schrader (1656–1746) kept notebooks of every one of the more than 3,000 births she attended over her long career. Such journals vary from terse and businesslike to rambling and thoughtful. Protestants, especially Calvinists and Quakers, were encouraged to engage in spiritual self-reflection on a regular basis, and in England and other places where literacy rates were relatively high, many people kept spiritual journals. Catholics were more likely to discuss spiritual matters orally with their priest, but in certain cases they, too, were encouraged to write them down. The confessors of several Spanish holy women (termed *beatas*) ordered them to dictate or write about their devotional practices and mystical visions. The most famous of these, Teresa of Avila, edited and refined her work over many years, turning it into a full spiritual autobiography.

Some writers combined business, religious, and family matters with introspection in ways that reveal a great deal about their personal qualities as well as the society in which they lived. Glickl bas Judah Leib, traditionally known as "Glückel of Hameln" (1646?–1724) was a Jewish woman born in Hamburg who assisted her husband in his growing trade in gold, pearls, jewels and money. When she was in her early forties, her husband died accidentally, and she continued his business, traveling widely. To help her get over her sorrow, she also began to write her memoirs, which contain much about her family and business life, but also stories drawn from history and tradition through which she sought to understand and explain the events of her life. "In my great grief and for my heart's ease," she wrote, "I begin this book ... upon the death of your good father, in the hope of distracting my soul from the burdens laid upon it." Her book would be a long endeavor written over many years, eventually describing the death of her second husband as well as her first. The text survived in two family copies to the nineteenth century, when it was published, first in the Yiddish in which it was written, and then in translation. Glickl's text provides a detailed look at the economic and social life of central European Jews as a group, as well as information about how one seventeenth-century woman responded to a son and a second husband who disappointed her and to a God who sometimes seemed distant; in recent translations, her memoirs have served as a source of inspiration as well as historical information.

Samuel Pepys (1633–1703) was an English civil servant who worked in several branches of government. He eventually became the top administrator of the navy, a member of the House of Commons, and president of the Royal Society. He kept an extensive diary covering the years 1660 to 1669, including a discussion of the dramatic political events of those years and of the many theatrical and musical performances he attended. He also recorded in great detail his rather fumbling sexual encounters with a number of women – one of which his wife walked in on – coding these in French, Italian, or Spanish words so that they were even more secret than the shorthand he used for the rest of the diary. This shorthand made transcription difficult, and the diary was not published until the nineteenth century, when a bowdlerized version omitting anything even vaguely sexual appeared; the full diary was not published until the 1970s, though it is now available in several versions on the web. The diary provides historians of music and drama with information about actors and audiences, and social historians with information about aspects of daily life, such as lice in wigs or excrement piling up in streets and cellars. Pepys also turned his talent for close observation inward, recording his strengths and weaknesses, thoughts and emotions, in what Claire Tomalin, a recent biographer, has termed his contemplation of the "unequalled self."

29 Pepys's diary

In recording his daily activities, Pepys blends comments about family life, routine government operations, major political events, and goings-on in his neighborhood and around London. Here are two diary entries for February 1660, when Parliament was debating restoring Charles II to the throne after his father had been deposed and executed in the English Civil War. At this point Pepys was a clerk in the Exchequer, or treasury department.

February 16

In the morning at my lute. Then came Shaw [Pepys's colleague at the Exchequer] and Hawly [another work colleague, who was also Pepys's neighbor], and I gave them their morning draft [of ale, a common morning food] at this time at my house. So to my office, where I wrote by the carrier to my Lord [the Earl of Sandwich, a distant cousin] and sealed my letter at Will's [a tavern] and gave it old East [probably a servant] to carry it to the carrier's, and to take up a box of china oranges and two little barrels of scallops at my house, which Captain Cuttance sent to me for my Lord. Here I met with Osborne and with Shaw and Spicer [two colleagues], and we went to the Sun Tavern in expectation of a dinner, where we had sent us only two trenchers [platters]-full of meat, at which we were very merry, while in came Mr. Wade and his friend Capt. Moyse (who told us of his hopes to get an estate merely for his name's sake), and here we staid till seven at night, I winning a quart of sack of Shaw that one trencherfull that was sent us was all lamb and he that it was veal. [In other words, they made a bet about what type of meat was on the platter.] I by having but 3d. in my pocket made shift to spend no more, whereas if I had had more I had spent more as the rest did, so that I see it is an advantage to a man to carry little in his pocket. Home, and after supper, and a little at my flute, I went to bed.

February 17

In the morning Tom that was my Lord's footboy came to see me and had 10s. [shillings] of me of the money which I have to keep of his. So that now I have but 35s. more of his. Then came Mr. Hills the instrument maker, and I consulted with him about the altering my lute and my viall [violin]. After that I went into my study and did up my accounts, and found that I am about 40l. [pounds] beforehand in the world, and that is all. So to my office and from thence brought Mr. Hawly home with me to dinner, and after dinner wrote a letter to Mr. Downing [Pepys's supervisor at the Exchequer] about his business and gave it Hawly, and so went to Mr. Gunning's [a prominent clergyman] to his weekly fast, and after the sermon . . . we went and walked in the park till it was dark. I played on my recorder at the Echo, and then drank a cup of ale at Jacob's. So to Westminster Hall, where I heard that some of the members of the House were gone to meet [about the restoration of King Charles] . . . Hence we went to White Hall, thinking to hear more news, where I met with Mr. Hunt [a neighbor], who told me . . . that some of the members of the House had this day laid in firing into their lodgings at White Hall for a good while, so that we are at a great stand to think what will become of things . . . Hence . . . to Harper's, and there drank a cup or two to the King, and to his fair sister Frances' good health, of whom we had much discourse of her not being much the worse for the small pox, which she had this last summer. So home and to bed. This day we are invited to my uncle Fenner's wedding feast, but went not, this being the 27th year [i.e. his 27th wedding anniversary].

(From *The Diary of Samuel Pepys*, ed. Henry B. Wheatley [London: G. Bell and Sons, 1924], vol. I, pp. 55–7.)

 For additional chapter resources see the companion website www.cambridge.org/wiesnerhanks.

Both Glickl's and Pepys's works are unusual in their personal insights, but they are also unusual in that they seem to have been written only for private or family reading. Today we draw a fairly sharp line between a private diary or letter and a published book of memoirs, but in the early modern period this line was not as clear. Members of the nobility and the educated elite sent letters to friends or colleagues knowing (and indeed, often hoping) that these would be copied, circulated in manuscript, and eventually published. The French noblewoman Marie de Rabutin-Chantal, marquise de Sévigné (1626–96), for example, wrote regularly to her friends and relatives, providing court news, Parisian gossip, and witty commentary; over 1,100 letters have survived. She quickly learned that her letters were being copied and read widely, and so crafted them with this in mind, though she still included her personal feelings. Daily journals, especially those of well-connected people, were often written in the same way, with an eye to their eventual publication. We have already traced the impact of the journals of Columbus, Vespucci, and Pigafetta, but even the journals of less adventurous sorts proved interesting for people to read. The English clergyman John Beadle's *The Journal or Diary of a Thankful Christian* (1656), for example, was a best-seller and a model for others.

This semi-public nature of many personal documents means that we cannot use them as direct windows into people's inner thoughts and emotions, for their writers often framed their journal with a wider audience in mind, and were careful to present a persona that would enhance their reputation or at least be acceptable. This is actually true of all personal documents. Letters and diaries, even those that the writer expects will remain private, are written within a specific cultural background in which certain emotions, ideals, and fantasies are regarded as appropriate for people of a specific age, gender, and social class. In the early modern period, for example, anger was generally seen as more appropriate for men and thus masculinized a woman who became extremely angry, whereas intense heterosexual passion was seen as feminizing a man. This did not mean that women never became angry and men never felt passion, but such expectations may have affected how men and women described their feelings, even to themselves. Thus we may think of personal documents as strictly *descriptive* sources, depictions of reality, when they are actually to some degree also *prescriptive* sources, reports of what their writers wished were true.

Sources that are unambiguously prescriptive, such as sermons, laws, and moral tracts, also provide information about individuals in society. A close study of one type of prescriptive source, books of manners and conduct, led the German sociologist Norbert Elias to assert in 1939 that the early modern period saw a "civilizing process" in western Europe. Manners books increasingly taught that basic bodily functions, such as blowing one's nose, eating, defecating, and sleeping, should be done in specific ways: nose-blowing should be done on a specially made item, the handkerchief, not on the tablecloth, one's bare hand, or a sleeve; eating should be done with a fork, not with one's hand or knife; urinating and defecating should be done in private, not on the street or while chatting with others; sleeping should be done in special clothing, not naked, and beds should not be shared with strangers.

In some cases, these changes in behavior were regulated by actual laws, and are related to the process of social discipline after the Reformations we discussed in chapter 5, as Protestant and Catholic authorities attempted to make people more moral, pious, and orderly. Elias, and many other scholars, have been more interested in less formal ways that codes of conduct are established and regulated, and especially in ways that people in Europe gradually internalized more controlled habits and social behavior. Feelings of shame, embarrassment, modesty, and delicacy made what was once perfectly acceptable seem rude; topics that appeared in early sixteenth-century conduct books, such as when and how to spit, fart, or burp, became too disgusting to mention, much less do. Open expression of strong emotions, especially negative ones such as anger or aggression, grew increasingly unacceptable. Children learned "proper" behavior from their parents long before they could read books of manners, so that by the time they were adults they regarded controlled behavior as "natural," as coming from their own inner selves rather than from externally imposed social convention.

This "reformation of manners" was, in Elias's opinion, related to political, social, and economic changes. As power was increasingly centralized, the state claimed a monopoly on the legitimate use of violence, and people had to settle conflicts in non-violent ways. Nobles demonstrated their superiority through "courtliness" or "courtesy" (common terms for good manners), rather than through military prowess. Middle-class urban residents sought to learn and imitate courtly manners as a demonstration of their improving economic status and increasing political influence, providing a wide market for conduct books such as Castiglione's *The Book of the Courtier*. Self-restraint became a marker of class status, with the "lower orders" those who still spat, fought, or drank in public.

Studies of the "civilizing process" since Elias have been based on many other types of sources along with books of conduct, including personal documents, public sources such as court records, and visual evidence. This research has generally supported Elias's contention that self-restraint, formality, and discipline were becoming widespread ideals, policed by external agents such as courts and clergy and by internalized feelings of shame and guilt. There is disagreement about how fully or quickly these ideals were becoming reality, however. Middle- and upper-class people did try to change the behavior of the lower classes through the political and religious institutions they controlled, in what historians have called a "reform of popular culture," but this was a very slow and incomplete process.

Notions about what was civilized and what uncivilized shaped European ideas about race as well as social class. As they created empires, Europeans came to view themselves as "civilized" and superior to the "savages" in areas being colonized, not only because of their religion, but also because of their "gentility" and more restrained deportment. The French philosopher Michel Foucault has highlighted other negative effects of the "civilizing process" within Europe itself. He points to the establishment of workhouses for the poor and vagrants, and mental institutions for those judged insane or deviant as examples of what he calls the "Great Confinement," in which those who upset notions of the proper social order were removed from public view. These institutions were never as widespread as some reformers and government officials wished, but they did serve as a threat about the consequences of behavior judged to deviate too greatly from accepted social norms.

The social body: orders and classes

Leviathan portrays the social body as a collection of individuals, but it was also thought of – and functioned – as a collection of groups. Medieval Europeans had conceptualized society in three basic groups: those who pray (the clergy), those who fight (the nobility), and those who work (everyone else). These groups were termed "orders" or "estates," and many medieval representative assemblies, including those of France and the Low Countries, were organized into three houses by estate. In England, the higher-level clergy joined the nobility in the House of Lords, with the House of Commons the rough equivalent of the third estate elsewhere. Both the House of Commons and assemblies of the third estate primarily represented the interests of towns, not the majority of the population who were peasants. Only in Sweden did the peasants have a special fourth house in the national assembly with their own representatives.

The society of orders was a system of social differentiation based on function – or at least theoretical function – in society. It worked fairly well in setting out socio-legal categories for membership in representative bodies, and highlighted the most important social distinction in both medieval and early modern Europe: that between noble and commoner. Status as a noble generally brought freedom from direct taxation and rights of jurisdiction over a piece of property and the people who lived on it. Even in the Middle Ages, however, and more strikingly by the seventeenth century, the more fixed and inherited hierarchy of orders was interwoven with a more changeable hierarchy based on wealth: what would later come to be termed social class.

Within each order there were vast differences in status, power, and wealth. The clergy included prince-bishops who lived in opulent palaces and poor parish priests who farmed their own fields, while the nobility ranged from wealthy counts with vast estates to poor gentlemen with a single run-down house or knights with no land at all. In England, distinctions were made between true nobles with heritable titles, represented in the House of Lords, and gentry, who paid taxes, had no clear set of privileges, and sent representatives to the House of Commons. Everywhere in Europe the third estate consisted of very diverse individuals, from affluent merchant-bankers and powerful judges to poverty-stricken artisans.

Wealth allowed some male commoners to buy or gain noble titles, and female commoners to marry into noble families, so that these categories were not static; in the English county of Lancashire between 1600 and 1642, for example, more than one-third of the gentry families died out, but their numbers were replaced by wealthy social-climbing commoners. Monarchs sometimes attempted to restrict entrance into the nobility to avoid erosion of the tax base, but the temptation to gain cash quickly by selling titles massively outweighed concerns about long-term revenue streams. The steady influx of newcomers with no military function meant that the old basis for noble status was increasingly anachronistic, but commoners' willingness to spend vast sums of money for a noble title also indicates the continuing privileges and social cachet of noble rank. The nobility maintained its status in most parts of Europe by taking in and integrating competing social elites; where wealthy commoners did not bother acquiring noble titles, such as the Dutch province of Holland, nobles lost their social and political role.

Wealth and ability also allowed lower-level nobles to climb higher, especially once monarchs recognized that selling inflated noble titles was an excellent way to make money. James I invented the title of "baronet" in 1611, while Spain had fifty-five titled nobles in 1520, and nearly ten times that number in 1700. In England, a noble title brought prestige and certain legal privileges, while in Spain and France it brought freedom from many taxes, so that the long-term financial implications of such sales for the royal treasury were significant.

The most common way to gain a noble title was to buy one, but the fastest way to climb in terms of title, status, and actual power was through gaining royal or princely favor at court. Courts were cultural, political, and economic centers in which rulers dispensed favors, offices, gifts, and rewards. At Louis XIV's court at Versailles, the palace built by the king outside Paris in 1660, nobles vied with each other to carry out tasks associated with the physical needs of the monarch – bringing in breakfast, handing napkins, emptying the royal chamber pot. Though we may view these activities as demeaning or disgusting, they offered great opportunities for personal access to the ruler, as did attendance at card-parties, festivities, and entertainments. French nobles hoping to gain positions moved to Versailles, where they lived in cramped rooms and ate high-priced cold food bought from vendors, rather than the more lavish fare they would have been served on their own estates. English and Austrian nobles were more fortunate, for their rulers continued to live much of the time in London and Vienna; though nobles had to move to be near them, London and Vienna offered far more in terms of food, housing, entertainment, and other amenities than Versailles.

Nobles themselves attended to the needs of the monarch, and they also sought positions at court for their adolescent children, especially if the young men or women were physically attractive, intelligent, and talented in music, conversation, or dance. Their function was largely to serve as decorative objects and high-status servants, and – as the name lady- or gentleman-in-waiting implies – wait for and wait on the ruler. Success at court for either an adult or adolescent called for deference, understanding of ceremony and protocol, discretion, charm, skill, and luck. As we have seen, for women – and for men with a few monarchs – sexual attraction could also be a powerful tool, with royal mistresses and male favorites gaining wealth, influence, and the power to dispense favors of their own.

Those who were legally noble generally made up about 1 or 2 percent of the population, although in Spain and Poland nearly one out of every ten people was technically noble. In western Europe, nobles owned about one-half to two-thirds of the land, and in eastern Europe almost all of it. Most nobles did not own very much, however, and some, such as the impoverished *hidalgos* of Spain, owned nothing at all, surviving by payments for mercenary service. Middle-level nobles owned enough land to live comfortably, and often served as royal judges, commanders in princely armies, or bishops of smaller bishoprics. At the top were aristocratic families whose vast tracts of land might provide them with an income of more than a hundred times that of a country gentleman. The Mendoza family in Spain controlled more than eight hundred villages, and the Radziwills in Lithuania more than ten thousand.

Inheritance systems shaped the fortunes of noble families over generations, and they varied throughout Europe. In areas with partible inheritance, which included parts of France, the Empire, and eastern Europe, land and other property was divided among sons (and occasionally among all children), diminishing the family fortune over time. In areas such as England with a tradition of primogeniture, in which the eldest son inherited all land and the noble title, family wealth remained more concentrated. The advantages of this system were increasingly clear to nobles throughout Europe, who pushed for the introduction of primogeniture or other forms of inheritance, termed strict settlement or entail, that prohibited the sale or division of family lands. Younger sons generally received stipends of cash, but were expected to augment this with income from a government office or position in the church or military. Daughters received dowries, the size of which determined the young woman's value in the marriage market; a larger dowry would attract higher-status suitors, though social-climbing lower nobles or wealthy urban merchants might be willing to accept a lower dowry in return for the prestige and access to power that marrying into a noble family could bring. Daughters who were sole heirs sometimes inherited the family lands and the right to a title (which they passed to their husbands) and sometimes not. Gaining this inheritance might involve a protracted legal battle with uncles or male cousins, however, who argued that gender should be more important than degree of familial relationship in determining access to land and position.

In the sixteenth century, nobles and gentry in most of Europe lived in the countryside, although in northern and central Italy, and southern France and Spain, they often lived in large households in town, where they might attend the court of the pope or a ruling duke or count. In the seventeenth and eighteenth centuries, nobles who could afford it built sumptuous houses in national and regional capitals, where they sought royal princely patronage and joined in the cultural activities of the court. They also maintained a steady

Fig. 19. In this painting, the Italian artist Pietro Longhi (1702–85) shows a luxurious urban household in which women, accompanied by their servants, introduce themselves. Formal personal visits, afternoon coffees, and dances were important parts of the social "season" for wealthy women and men.

round of their own social activities, especially during the "season," the winter months when life on country estates would have been uncomfortable and boring. By the eighteenth century, nobles in western Europe did not have the independent power or vast wealth that many of their counterparts in eastern Europe did, but they maintained their privileged position.

Though nobles were increasingly attracted to city life, cities were also where the hierarchy of orders met the hierarchy of wealth most dramatically. By 1500, and much earlier in cities in Italy and the Netherlands, a number of urban merchants and bankers were wealthier than all but the highest level of nobility.

Over the next centuries, some of these men climbed into the nobility through marriage, service to a monarch, or purchasing a title. More of them heightened social and political distinctions within cities themselves, often beginning this process by limiting membership in the city councils they controlled to a small circle of families. They might hope to marry into nobility, but, as in the German city of Nuremberg, they also prohibited men who married the daughters of city councilors from joining the council themselves.

The most significant distinction within cities was that between citizen and non-citizen, as we discussed in chapter 3. Urban citizenship, described in England as having the "freedom" of a city, made one a member of a corporate group with legal privileges and claims on public assistance; it also brought responsibilities, including serving in or providing troops for the city militia, and paying local taxes. Like noble titles, the status of citizen was heritable.

Cities also allowed people to purchase citizenship, especially after demographic catastrophes, and sometimes granted citizenship free of charge for special services to the city or if applicants for citizenship practiced an occupation deemed desirable, such as midwifery or surgery. Toward the end of the sixteenth century, though national capitals continued to expand and flourish economically, many smaller cities stagnated. They responded not by making it easier to immigrate, but by increasing the standard fees for citizenship to bring in more money, and granting citizenship free of charge less often. In 1599, for example, the entrance fees for citizenship in the Swiss city of Basel were raised from 10 gulden to 30, beyond the reach of all but the wealthiest immigrants. Cities often tolerated outsiders who performed needed manual labor, and sometimes developed an in-between category for permanent residents too poor to obtain citizenship, but the native-born still had distinct advantages.

In many cities, sumptuary laws attempted to create easily visible distinctions between social groups. Nobles were set off by their fine silk clothing, university-educated physicians and lawyers by their velvet- or fur-trimmed robes, servants by their rough dark clothes and aprons. Individuals tried to evade these laws by wearing the clothing restricted to the group above them, though there were fines prescribed for doing so. Wearing a disguise or attempting to pass oneself off as someone else was taken much more seriously, and could warrant the death penalty. Doing so successfully was difficult, for it meant not only acquiring different clothes, but also different speech patterns, gestures, eating habits, and mannerisms. With the reformation of manners these distinctions became increasingly elaborate. Using a fork and an individual plate for eating was initially a marker of status, but as common people came to use forks, elites developed complex table settings with specialized utensils and dishes that poorer folk could neither afford nor use properly. Refusal to honor distinctions of status was a sign of rebellion in early modern society, whether it was German peasants disobeying their landlords in 1525 or non-noble deputies in the French Estates-General keeping their hats on in the presence of the king in 1789.

A healthy state depended, in the eyes of most observers, on each group performing its allotted function without, in the words of the English writer Robert Burton, "discontents, common grievances, complaints . . . rebellions, seditions, mutinies, idleness, riot . . . That kingdom, that country" where such things did occur was "melancholy, hath a sick body, and needs to be reformed."[3] For many writers, maintaining the health of the body politic was best accomplished by measures similar to those physicians used to treat illness: execute rebellious subjects as one would amputate a gangrenous limb, or banish them as one would quarantine a family infected with the plague.

The inner body: emotions and passions

Robert Burton's words about a sick body politic were a small part of his enormous consideration of illness in the human body, *The Anatomy of Melancholy* (1621). Like most physicians and medical writers of the time, Burton viewed emotions and mental states as linked to imbalances in the four bodily humors: too much blood made one bold, courageous, and *sanguine* (from the Latin word for blood, *sanguis*); too much phlegm made one sluggish, apathetic and *phlegmatic*; too much yellow bile (choler) made one angry, irritated, and *choleric*; too much black bile made one sad, depressed, and *melancholy*.

Melancholy was the most worrisome of these states. A certain amount of melancholy could be a source of genius, inspiring music and poetry, but too much could lead to madness and both physical and mental illness. Physicians prescribed physical and spiritual treatments for their melancholic patients: a change in diet or sleeping patterns, vomits, bleeding, travel to a different climate, sex, music, astrology, wearing amulets, magic, prayer. In the early seventeenth century – the height of the witch hunts, as we will see in chapter 11 – a few medical thinkers speculated about the demonic sources of mental illness, but both learned and unlearned people generally differentiated between people who appeared to be possessed and those whose problems originated in their own bodies. Those judged mentally ill were usually cared for by their own families, though from the sixteenth century onward public hospitals and private asylums were also available in some places. Some patients were confined, though others worked in the surrounding town or countryside to support themselves if they were able. The postal service run by the Taxis family, for example, hired patients at asylums in central Germany to deliver letters and packages, regarding them as reliable messengers.

Melancholy was linked to love as well as mental illness. Of all the emotions, love has been the most hotly debated, both by early modern writers and by recent historians. Romantic love appears as a literary theme in European literature long before 1450, and found expression in the sixteenth century in poetry and drama. From the late seventeenth century, powerful romantic passion inspired much of the action in the new literary form of the novel, so much so that moralists recommended young women be prevented from reading novels so that they did not get too excited. In the eighteenth century, many of these novels were actually written in the form of exchanges of letters – what are termed "epistolary novels" – modeling themselves on the real exchanges of letters people were used to reading. Samuel Richardson's *Pamela; or, Virtue Rewarded* (1740), which tells the story of a virtuous servant girl's victorious struggle against her master's attempts to seduce her, was one of the most popular of these. Similar stories of virtue triumphing over vice, and of chaste love triumphing over sexual passion, were published by many authors in the eighteenth century. There were also counter-stories, such as Pierre Choderlos de Laclos's *Les Liaisons Dangereuses* (Dangerous Liaisons, 1782), another epistolary novel in which two amoral people successfully manipulate the passions of a young woman for their own amusement.

30 Lovesickness or green-sickness?

For early modern physicians, love caused a range of illnesses. Love that was too intense could lead to lovesickness, which in the Middle Ages was generally viewed as an ailment afflicting aristocratic men, but in the early modern era became more associated with young women. Love might lead women to hysteria – a word that comes from the Latin word for womb – in which passion took over their ability to control their bodies or their minds. Robert Burton criticized both infatuated love and religious passion, arguing that neither gave people any special insight, but made them ill. Repressing or refusing love was also dangerous, however, for this could lead to "green-sickness," an ailment in young unmarried women that caused the stoppage of menstruation and turned the skin pale or greenish. In *Romeo and Juliet*, Juliet's father shrieks, "out you green-sickness carrion," when she refuses to marry the man he has chosen for her. Doctors treated green-sickness with warming remedies that would heat the body and cause the thickened blood to flow again, of which the best was sexual intercourse (in marriage, of course). This would release both the young woman's blood and her pent-up sexual desire.

In the nineteenth century, the same set of symptoms were deemed "chlorosis" (a Latinized translation of "green-sickness"), and judged to be the result of iron-deficiency anemia, which could be tested by new tools such as the hemoglobinometer that measured the level of iron in the blood. The recommended treatment was still marriage, though now this was seen as a way to protect women's frail and weak condition from the harshness of industrialization, which was viewed as the cause of chlorosis. Iron-deficiency anemia still exists as a medical condition, though after the 1930s young unmarried women were no longer seen as especially susceptible to it. Historians of medicine point out that illness is to some degree culturally constructed; the changing understandings of green-sickness provide a good example of this.

Love, along with other passions, was a matter for philosophical speculation as well as literature. In his *Treatise on the Passions of the Soul* (1649), the French philosopher René Descartes (1596–1650) asserted that the passions subjected the soul to the desires of the body, though he argued that reason could always triumph over passion. Descartes did not discuss the role of gender differences in this, though later philosophers did, contending that men had a more powerful rational capacity, while women were dominated by their emotions. Thomas Hobbes and Adam Smith developed another line of thought about the passions, arguing that they were all reflections of human beings' selfishness and love of themselves. Self-interest could be a negative force, but it could also be channeled into socially useful activities, such as (for Hobbes) supporting effective governments or (for Smith) engaging in trade or manufacturing.

Early modern thinkers debated the merits of melancholy or the limits of passion primarily within the individual, and more recently historians have also been interested in the role of the emotions in family life. Some argue that the "modern" family, in which couples choose their own spouses based on romantic sentiments rather than parental or community preferences, and in which strong emotional bonds develop between parents and children, originated in the eighteenth century. Before then family interactions were cold, with mothers indifferent to their infants, siblings jealous of the power of the oldest brother, parents callous toward their children's wishes, and spouses formal and uncaring in their relations with one another. This notion has been countered by other scholars who have found mothers and fathers deeply saddened, sometimes to the point of madness or suicide, by the deaths of their children, and spouses at all social levels affectionate and supportive. There is plenty of evidence to support both sides of this argument, and it is not something that can be assessed quantitatively, for the sources are primarily the personal documents discussed above, which are limited in total number, skewed toward the upper classes, and may not reveal people's real feelings in any case.

The quantitative evidence relating to families that does exist is also open to widely varying interpretations. For example, age at first marriage for women in western European cities appears to have declined in the eighteenth century, especially among the poorer classes. Does this mean that young women who had left their villages for larger towns in search of employment were reveling in their ability to choose a husband based on love rather than having to go along with their parents' wishes? Or does it mean that they unemotionally assessed their opportunities for wages compared to those of men, and grabbed the first likely prospect for a husband, realizing they would never earn enough to support themselves on their own? Similarly, do high numbers of children left at orphanages or foundling homes mean that poor mothers were uncaring, or that they were willing to put the chances for the survival of their children ahead of their own feelings?

These debates have made most scholars careful about extrapolating from their own research to making generalizations that apply to all of Europe, or even to all social classes within one country, but by and large the scholarly consensus has swung in favor of more continuity than dramatic change in familial and parental love and affection. There does seem to have been an increase in the desire for privacy among middle- and upper-class families, both privacy *for* the family as a unit and privacy *from* other family members within the household. Thus, for households that could afford it, servants increasingly had separate quarters, and rooms within houses were more compartmentalized, with doors that could be closed.

Privacy did not extend to lower-class families in either theory or practice. Poor people in cities lived in very crowded quarters, often renting a tiny attic or cellar room for an entire family, and continuing to share beds and eating utensils. Local communities sometimes refused to allow poor people to marry, as they worried that poor families would require public support; emotional relationships were no excuse for burdening the community coffers. This control of marriage became state law in some of the territories within the Holy Roman Empire in the early nineteenth century, with political authorities describing marriage as a privilege available only to those who were economically solvent; such restrictions were not lifted until after World War I.

The analyzed body: anatomy and medical theory

Melancholics and young women suffering from green-sickness were not the only ones whose outer body revealed their inner state, for humoral theory explained physical health and illness as well as one's mental state. Newer ideas about anatomy that developed in the seventeenth century also connected the mind and the body.

Learned writers, first Andreas Vesalius and then many others, criticized the prevailing Galenic understanding of anatomy and physiology. In several works, the English anatomist and royal physician William Harvey (1578–1657) demonstrated that the veins and arteries are one system, with the same blood being pumped throughout the body by the heart. Based on dissections, experimental proof, and logical argument, Harvey explained the workings of the heart muscles, the function of the valves in the veins, and the path of blood through the heart. He saw blood as even more important than it had been in the Galenic system, however, identifying it as animate and linking it with the soul. Harvey also viewed semen as powerful, and suggested that an egg found inside a female could become fertilized at a distance without physical contact, in the same way that magnets exerted their energy across space.

Galileo Galilei (1564–1642) and Pierre Gassendi (1592–1655) studied the physical principles of bodily processes: how the pores secreted, how the mouth and stomach digested, how blood flowed through the blood vessels. They, and others, thought about the body in mechanical terms: as, in Galileo's terms, an assemblage of small machines. Just as machines need oil to prevent friction and pumps need a free flow of liquid to work properly, they reasoned, the body needed a free flow of various fluids to maintain good health. These were now observable fluids such as blood, digestive juices, and glandular secretions rather than the Galenic four humors, however, with illness described in terms of blockages, restrictions, and obstructions, rather than imbalance. Later medical writers studied respiration, with Joseph Priestley (1733–1804) and Antoine-Laurent Lavoisier (1743–94), identifying the "vital air" carried by the blood as oxygen, necessary for both life and combustion.

The work of anatomists and medical writers was made easier by improvements in the microscope undertaken by Dutch lens-makers, especially Anton von Leeuwenhoeck (1632–1723). Leeuwenhoeck's microscope allowed him to see single blood cells circulating through capillaries (an action that Harvey had not been able to explain) and spermatozoa (what he called "animalcules") in semen, demonstrating that something physical was clearly responsible for fertilization. The latter discovery led Leeuwenhoeck to argue that each sperm was the seed of an individual, and that sperm contained the full formative structure of the embryo, including its sex. This "spermatic" view of embryology was countered by "ovists" such as the Swiss physiologist Albrecht von Haller (1708–77), who thought that the embryo-in-miniature existed preformed in the female ovum. Ovists were often ridiculed by the male scientific community,

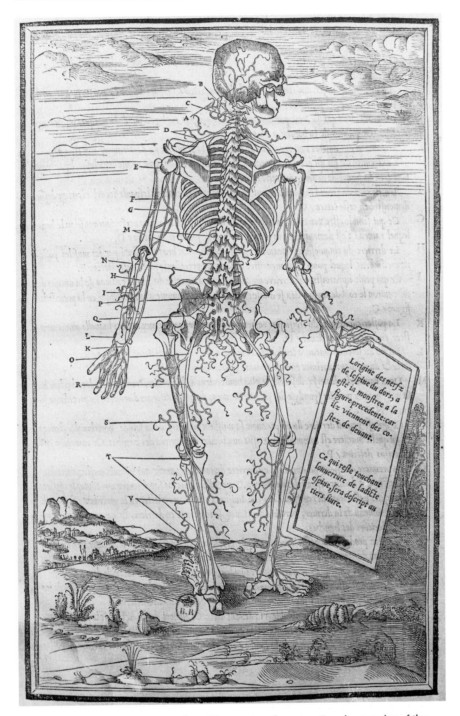

Fig. 20. Anatomical illustrations, such as this seventeenth-century French engraving of the skeleton and nerves, were important features in medical textbooks and training from the sixteenth century onward. Artists often placed the figures in naturalistic settings, posing them holding objects as if they were alive.

however, and were limited by the fact that the mammalian ovum had not yet been definitively identified. Both of these "preformationist" positions also had to explain how the embryo's future children could be contained within it, and then *that* embryo's within it ad infinitum, a puzzle that led back, in both serious and satirical works, to the ovaries of Eve. This conundrum contributed to a recognition that somehow both parents must be involved, but not until the identification of the ovum in 1827 – a remarkably late date given its size relative to that of spermatozoa – would the modern view of conception begin to emerge.

The mechanical view of the body as a system of hydraulic and pneumatic machines was opposed in the eighteenth century by "vitalists," some of whom asserted the importance of the soul as a "life-force" or "life-principle," and others of whom located this life-force in the body itself. The latter group often based their arguments on research on the nervous system and on the ability of plants and some animals (such as starfish) to regenerate body parts that had been severed. Good health, for these vitalists, was a matter of stimulating or "exciting" the nervous system and allowing muscles to freely contract and expand.

Some anatomical research was conducted by individuals with positions at university medical schools, but in general the critique of Galen did not translate immediately into a rejection of the notion of humors in the training or practice of physicians. The older humoral notion of the body's physiology could also be combined with newer ideas in eclectic ways, with anatomical theorists blending and balancing mechanism, vitalism, and other theories in their attempts to explain how the body operated.

The treated body: medicine and public health

Medicine as practiced was even more diverse than medical theory, both in terms of the approaches of medical practitioners and the range of practitioners available, though all practitioners regarded their work as important for individuals and for society at large. The highest-status – and highest-paid – medical practitioners were university-trained physicians, whose course work remained largely theoretical and all in Latin until the eighteenth century, when a few daring professors began to lecture in the vernacular. Physicians were in charge of the internal body, so their advice was sought for illnesses that appeared to come from within, such as fevers.

After the outbreak of the plague in 1348 or of other epidemic diseases, towns and cities, first in northern Italy and then elsewhere, appointed official city physicians or boards of medical commissioners. These individuals were charged with developing and enforcing measures that would limit the spread of disease – quarantining infected houses or streets, disposing of corpses and the belongings of the dead, prohibiting public gatherings, and setting out *cordons sanitaires*, "sanitary cordons" around uninfected areas. At first these commissions disbanded once the threat posed by an epidemic had passed, but by the sixteenth century northern Italian and German cities often made these positions permanent, and charged physicians with the routine supervision of public health. City physicians and commissions developed (and tried to enforce) sanitary regulations about the disposal of waste, supervised other medical practitioners, and investigated reports of new diseases. In the seventeenth century, some cities, territories, and states expanded the role of these boards – often called a *collegium medicum* – to include developing and offering a licensing examination for any physician who wanted to practice in the area. Officials in centralizing states slowly came to regard a large and healthy population as essential to the well-being of the state, and called for the keeping and study of better vital statistics, including birth, death, and morbidity rates, as a basis for health policies.

Hospitals were increasingly viewed as important institutions for maintaining public health. In the centuries before 1450, hospitals were primarily charitable institutions whose main function was caring for the spiritual and physical needs of the ill, infirm, mentally ill, or elderly poor; they gave such people beds, food, and a (relatively) clean place to die. Many cities also had leper- or pest-houses for those with contagious diseases; with the advent of syphilis in the 1490s, special "pox-houses" were set up in German and Italian cities for those who were infected with this new disease. Medieval hospitals and pest-houses were often small privately endowed institutions that were inefficiently run. City governments, first in Italy and then elsewhere, gradually consolidated these into large general hospitals over which they exerted stricter oversight and control. Like the poor in general, residents in these hospitals were often divided into "worthy" and "unworthy." Care for the latter group – which included vagrants and beggars who were sometimes rounded up off the streets against their will – involved enforced labor and strict moral discipline. Even the "deserving" poor, such as widows and orphans, might be expected to work as much as they could while in the hospital, however, for work was viewed as spiritually fulfilling, and thus as contributing to the healing process.

Treatment for illness was always a part of hospital care, and during the seventeenth century mercantalist ideas about the importance of a growing and productive population led to more attention to strictly medical issues within hospitals. Regular rounds in hospitals examining and treating patients gradually became a part of medical training, with physicians recording their clinical experiences in casebooks. Medical reformers emphasized the role that hospitals could play in research and the rehabilitation of workers and soldiers. In Britain, philanthropic "alliances against misery" began to open voluntary hospitals in the middle of the eighteenth century, describing their function as the maintenance of public health and vigor as well as the treatment of individual illness.

The impact of public health measures and improvements in hospitals was limited, however. London, Genoa, and other cities saw devastating outbreaks of the plague in the middle of the seventeenth century, with smaller outbreaks continuing in western Europe until the early eighteenth and in eastern Europe until the later eighteenth century. Even after the plague had disappeared – and the reasons for this are not entirely clear – infectious diseases such as cholera

31 Inoculation against smallpox

Innovations in medical treatment often came through individuals who learned through observation, not formal training. Local medical practitioners in several parts of the world, including the Ottoman Empire, West Africa, and probably China, recognized that survivors of smallpox did not contract the disease again. They thus took pus from the sores of a smallpox sufferer and intentionally scratched it into the skin of a healthy person, a process called variolation (from *variola*, the Latin term for smallpox), or inoculation. That person became infected with what was hoped was a mild case of the disease, and was thus protected, though it was difficult to determine the proper dosage, and some inoculated people died. The Royal Society of London heard about this practice in the early eighteenth century, but it got its best boost from Lady Mary Wortley Montagu (1689–1762), an aristocratic English woman whose husband was sent as the British ambassador to the Ottoman Empire in 1717. Lady Montagu had been scarred by smallpox as a young woman, and was intensely interested when she watched Turkish women inoculate their children. She had both of her children inoculated, and on returning to England wrote essays in popular journals and letters to powerful individuals urging the practice. Across the Atlantic, the prominent Boston minister Cotton Mather became aware of Ottoman reports, and also learned about inoculation from his slave Onesimus, who had been inoculated as a child in West Africa. When three of his children nearly died in a smallpox epidemic, Mather became an advocate of inoculation, working with Dr. Zabdieh Boylston, a Boston physician. They wrote up their experiments for the Royal Society in 1722, and this report, combined with Montagu's writings, convinced the Prince and Princess of Wales to have themselves and their children inoculated. Most religious and medical authorities opposed inoculation, however, and many of the general public were suspicious; Mather's house was set on fire. The practice still spread, largely as a sort of home remedy, though sometimes inoculated individuals introduced cases of smallpox into the general population as they were not quarantined in the way Ottoman practice taught. At the very end of the eighteenth century, Edward Jenner (1749–1823), an English surgeon (his medical degree was honorary, and was awarded to him when he was sixty-four), learned from local farmers that people who had had cowpox (*vaccinia*) were immune to smallpox. Jenner experimented with cowpox inoculations – he called them vaccinations – and these were largely successful, though the practice was not widely accepted until after Jenner's death.

still killed huge numbers of people, especially in crowded cities. Not until the early twentieth century would anyone who was not poor generally enter a hospital, for they remained places most people exited feet first.

University-trained physicians were expensive, and hospitals were dangerous, so people more regularly consulted with surgeons for various types of ailments. In theory, surgeons were to treat the outer body and physicians the inner, but in practice surgeons often treated illnesses such as syphilis or cancerous tumors as well as externally visible problems. Before 1700 surgeons were generally trained through a guild system rather than at universities, so they did not hold an MD degree and were not referred to as "doctor." They were trained to use knives and other instruments in their practice – something that university-trained physicians rarely did – and so were often grouped together in a guild with barbers, who might also do routine blood-letting along with cutting hair. Though the occasional dissection that university medical students observed as part of their training was usually done by a surgeon (with the professor lecturing as the surgeon did the actual cutting to reveal body parts), the training of surgeons did not involve regular dissections. The status of surgery improved in the eighteenth century, however, in keeping with ideas that practical experience and experimentation were effective teaching tools. Surgeons were given more training, sometimes in hospitals and sometimes in special surgical academies, and surgery was added as a course of study in some medical schools.

Along with physicians and surgeons, apothecaries regularly provided medical advice along with medications made of herbs, minerals, metals, salts, and many other ingredients. Apothecaries were trained through apprenticeship, and were supposed to dispense drugs only on the advice of a physician, but in practice they often acted on their own. Their medications included, and often mixed, ingredients understood to heal in different ways: some "sympathetically" mimicked the illness, such as the spotted plants prescribed to cure measles; others worked astrologically, by drawing on the power of an alignment of the stars and planets; others operated through alchemical processes, such as the mercury, sulfur solutions, or drinkable gold (*aurum potabile*) that contained the secret "elixir of life"; others worked only when certain phrases were repeated or prayers said as they were ingested. Most ingredients, especially those that poorer people could afford, were natural plant and mineral products whose effects had been discovered over centuries of trial and error.

Knowledge about such treatments might just as easily be handed down from father to son, or mother to daughter, as through guild training, so that much medical treatment was carried out by people with no formal training, but simply a reputation for effectiveness. Physicians, surgeons, and apothecaries sometimes objected to, in their words, these "quacks and charlatans" practicing medicine; these objections had more force once formal licensing procedures were instituted, with city councils and other governing bodies ordering unlicensed practitioners to stop dispensing medicine, or at least to stop charging if they did so. The complaints of professionals could not stop people from treating illness in their own homes, of course. Cookbooks, herbals, and household guides contained huge numbers of recipes for the treatment of everything from colds to the plague, and home remedies were the most common way of handling illness.

The reproducing body: childbirth and contraception

Childbirth also took place in people's homes. For many poor women and those who lived in isolated villages, childbirth was handled by female relatives and friends, and perhaps a woman known to be knowledgeable about the process of delivery. By the early sixteenth century, urban women in many parts of Europe could call on the services of a professional midwife, trained through an apprenticeship system and often licensed and regulated by the city or by church authorities. She was generally literate, and perhaps had read one of the many printed midwives' manuals available in most European languages, though most of her training was through assisting at actual deliveries. Her services would first be sought when a woman wanted to know whether she was really pregnant. Without home pregnancy tests and ultrasound screening, determining whether the cessation of menstruation, nausea, breast enlargement, and thickening around the middle were the result of pregnancy or illness was difficult. Only at quickening – that is, when the mother could feel the child move within her body – was a woman regarded as verifiably pregnant.

Like physicians, midwives varied in their techniques. Some midwives and mothers preferred to use a birthing stool, a special padded stool with handles which tipped the mother back slightly; other mothers lay in bed, kneeled, stood, or sat in another woman's lap. Midwives tended to intervene only if something was going wrong, usually a case of abnormal presentation. If the child was emerging feet or knees first (breech), it could usually be delivered, but if it emerged arm or face first it generally needed to be turned. Until the invention of the forceps, the best way to do this was to reach inside the uterus and grasp the feet, turning the child by the feet to effect a feet-first birth (this technique is termed podalic version). Midwives' manuals beginning in the sixteenth century recommend this, and records of births handled by professional midwives throughout the early modern period indicate they handled this technique successfully.

Until the mid-seventeenth century, and until the twentieth in many parts of Europe for most women, childbirth was strictly a female affair. The husband was not present unless his wife was dying, and male medical practitioners took little interest in delivery. Male physicians were only called in if the child or mother or both were dead or dying, so their presence was dreaded. This began to change in France in the mid-seventeenth century, where some male barber-surgeons began to advertise their services for childbirth as well, and the use of "man-midwives" came to be fashionable among the wealthy. At first the techniques of these men differed little from those of educated urban female midwives, for both read the same books and had the same concepts of anatomy and the birth process, but gradually the training of male midwives improved as they took part in dissections and anatomical classes, from which women were excluded.

Male midwifery spread to England, where, sometime in the seventeenth century, the forceps was invented by the Chamberlen brothers, who kept its design a family secret for nearly a century and then revealed it only to other male midwives. The forceps allows a midwife to grasp the head of a child which has become lodged in the birth passage and pull it out, a procedure that is not usually possible with the hands alone and had been accomplished earlier only on dead children with hooks stuck in their mouths or eyes. A higher level of training and more use of instruments made male midwives appear more scientific and "modern" to middle- and upper-class English and French women. Rural residents and lower-class urban dwellers retained a strong sense of the impropriety of male practitioners touching women in childbirth, and they could not pay the fees demanded by male midwives in any case. Male midwives were not very common in the early modern period in central Europe, and were not found at all in eastern and southern Europe, where female urban midwives were much more likely to be granted access to formal training in female anatomy and physiology than they were in France or England. In northern Italy in particular, midwifery schools were founded in the mid-eighteenth century to teach women anatomy, though most midwives continued to be educated through apprenticeship.

Childbirth was an event with many meanings: at once a source of joy and the cause of deep foreboding. Most women experienced multiple childbirths successfully, but all knew someone who had died in childbed and many had watched this happen. Using English statistics, it has been estimated that the maternal mortality rate in the seventeenth century was about 1 percent for each birth, which would make a lifetime risk of 5 to 7 percent. Women knew these risks, which is why they attempted to obtain the services of the midwife or other woman they regarded as the most skilled.

Many women also recognized that the dangers of childbirth might be intensified when children were born too close together, and they attempted to space births through a variety of means. Many nursed their children until they were over two years old, which acted as a contraceptive, for suckling encourages the release of the hormone prolactin, which promotes the production of milk and inhibits the function of the ovaries. They sought to abstain from sexual relations during the time of their monthly cycle, which was regarded as most fertile, though this "rhythm method," based on an incorrect view of the menstrual cycle, was even less effective than that practiced in the twentieth century. Couples practiced coitus interruptus, or used magical charms during sexual relations. Condoms made from animal intestines or bladders were available to those who could afford them by the mid-sixteenth century, but they were originally designed to protect men from venereal disease carried by prostitutes and were only slowly seen as a possible means of fertility control for married couples. As noted in chapter 2, some women used herbal mixtures, especially ones containing savin, rue, and pennyroyal, regarded as effective in preventing conception or causing the uterus to expel its contents, what was termed "bringing on the monthlies" or "inducing the menses." Medical texts and midwives' manuals often include recipes for such "menstrual regulators," in dosages probably strong enough to cause what would now be considered an early-term abortion in a pregnant woman, though it was difficult to control the amount of active ingredients such medicines contained.

Historians differ on how effective contraceptive or abortive measures would have been or how widely they were used. Limiting births was theoretically at odds with government aims of increasing population size, and there were occasional trials for using or providing abortifacients, but official response was sporadic. Laws prohibiting the distribution of birth-control information and devices were not passed until the later nineteenth century, at which point Pope Pius IX also declared that the fetus acquires a soul at conception rather than quickening.

The deviant body: infanticide, prostitution, and homosexuality

Contraception largely remained a private matter and not an issue of government concern in early modern Europe, but other sexual practices were clearly public issues. Unmarried women who became pregnant were viewed as guilty of fornication and thus merited punishment; if they miscarried or their infant happened to die, they were increasingly open to charges of infanticide. Before the sixteenth century, church and secular courts heard very few cases of infanticide, as jurists recognized that physicians could not make an infallible distinction between a stillbirth, a newborn who had died of natural causes, and one who had been murdered. Though there was no improvement in diagnostic techniques, this leniency changed in the sixteenth century, when infanticide became legally equated with murder in most areas of Europe and so carried the death penalty, often specified as death by drowning.

A French royal edict promulgated in 1556 carried this even further, requiring all unmarried women to make an official declaration of their pregnancy and decreeing the death penalty for any woman whose infant died before baptism after a concealed pregnancy or delivery, whether or not there was evidence of actual infanticide. A similar statute was passed in England in 1624 and in Scotland in 1690, and in various German states throughout the seventeenth century. Sometimes this surveillance of unmarried women bordered on the pornographic; an eighteenth-century German physician suggested, for example, that all unmarried women between the ages of fourteen and forty-eight should be viewed monthly at a public bath to see if their bodies showed any signs of pregnancy.

These stringent statutes were quite rigorously enforced in the sixteenth and seventeenth centuries; more women were executed for infanticide in early modern Europe than any other crime except witchcraft. In the Spanish Netherlands, women found guilty of infanticide were generally also accused of witchcraft – the reasoning being that only the devil could lead a mother to kill her child – and executed in gruesome ways, such as being impaled on a stake and then buried alive, or having the offending hand cut off before being drowned. In England the conviction rate went down after 1680 when women successfully argued that they had not intended to kill the child because they had prepared linen for it, or had killed it accidentally or through ignorance. Executions for infanticide or presumed infanticide also decreased in other parts of Europe in the eighteenth century, though the laws remained on the statute books. Whether this represented a decrease in the number of infanticides or only a change in enforcement is difficult to say, though there were more orphanages and foundling homes available for infants. The death rate at such places was extremely high, however, so that placing a child in them did not increase his or her life expectancy by much.

Selling sex for money was also increasingly criminalized. As we saw in chapter 6, during the sixteenth and early seventeenth centuries, licensed brothels in many cities were closed, and national statutes declared prostitution illegal. Rulers did not have the means to enforce these statutes, however, so illicit prostitution flourished, especially in ports and other growing cities and wherever large professional armies were housed. Many women combined occasional prostitution with other types of wage labor such as laundering, serving in taverns, or selling at the public market, and increasingly all unmarried poor women were suspected of prostitution. Religious and civic leaders regarded prostitutes as worse than other criminals, for they seduced other citizens from the life of moral order and discipline that authorities regarded as essential to a godly community. Women who sold sex, and women who simply engaged in sex outside of marriage, were "whores," and portrayed extremely negatively in sermons, popular plays, illustrations, and ballads. Sexual honor was a key element in women's social identity, so that calling someone or something a "whore" was a high insult. "Whore" continued to be used to describe religious opponents; in the words of an English anti-Catholic pamphlet from the 1680s, the Catholic Church was "a foul, filthy, old withered harlot . . . the great Strumpet of all Strumpets, the Mother of Whoredom."[4]

In the late seventeenth and early eighteenth century, large cities such as Paris and Amsterdam organized police forces, which monitored taverns and streets, arresting women suspected of selling sex. Women charged with prostitution were generally so poor that punishment by fine was impossible, so they were imprisoned, punished corporally and then banished from the area; in England this banishment occasionally included deportation to the colonies. Repeat offenders were sometimes executed, especially if they were also involved in other sorts of crime or had previously been banished and had broken their oath not to return to an area.

Prisons that housed prostitutes might also house other sorts of "fallen" women. In many southern European cities, women charged with fornication or unseemly flirting might be locked up, often in institutions dedicated to Mary Magdalene, the New Testament figure understood to be a repentant prostitute. Such houses also began to admit women who were regarded as in danger of becoming prostitutes, women whose husbands threatened them, poor young widows, or young women regarded as in danger of losing their sexual honor. The ordinances stated explicitly that the women admitted had to be pretty or at least have acceptable looks, for ugly women did not have to worry about their honor. Many of these asylums were started by reforming bishops, who also supported the establishment of orphanages and foundling homes (termed *ospizi* in Italy), in which unwed mothers were required to leave their children, and in which they might be required to work as wet-nurses for other infants along with nursing their own.

In such asylums, the women did not take vows and could leave to marry, but otherwise they were much like convents, with the women following a daily regimen of work and prayer. Some of them stressed penitence and moral reform while others were more purely punitive, closer to prisons than convents. This mixture of punishment and penitence may be seen very clearly in the Parisian women's prison of the Salpêtrière. In 1658, Louis XIV ordered the imprisonment there of all women found guilty of prostitution, fornication, or adultery, with release only coming once the priests and sisters in charge determined the inmate was truly penitent and had changed her ways. Imprisoning women for sexual crimes marks the first time in Europe that prison was used as a punishment rather than simply as a place to hold people until their trial or before

32 Onanism

Along with fornication, whoredom, and sodomy, masturbation (termed "the sin of Onan" from the biblical story of Onan who "spilled his seed on the ground" rather than have sexual relations with his brother's widow) was seen as a sin in sixteenth- and seventeenth-century Europe. Its punishment was left in God's hands, however, and it was never viewed as a source of physical harm. That changed in the eighteenth century. In 1715, an anonymous pamphlet with the long, self-explanatory title *Onania, or the heinous sin of self-pollution, and all its frightful consequences in both sexes considered, with spiritual and physical advice to those who have already injured themselves by this abominable practice* was published in London. It was republished and expanded in more than twenty editions, and widely read. One of its most avid readers was Samuel-August Tissot, a Swiss medical doctor, who published a number of medical treatises in Latin and French, several on the topic of what came to be known as "onanism." His *Onanism, or a physical discussion of the ailments produced by masturbation*, first appeared in Latin and then in French in 1760, with a new edition almost every year for the next twenty years, and translations into English, German, Italian, and Dutch. Tissot regards masturbation as a moral peril, but even more strikingly as a physical danger:

[It will cause in men] a general wasting of the machine; the weakening of all the corporal sense and all the faculties of the soul; the loss of imagination and memory; imbecility; contempt; shame; the resulting ignominy; the functions that are disturbed, halted, painful; long, deplorable, bizarre and disgusting illnesses; sharp and always renewed pains . . . a perceptible reduction of strength, of memory and even of reason; blurred vision, all the nervous disorders, all types of gout and rheumatism, weakening of the organs of generation, blood in the urine, disturbance of the appetites, headaches, and a great number of other disorders . . . The troubles experienced by women are just as explicable as those experienced by men. The humor they lose being less precious, less perfected than male sperm, its loss

does not perhaps weaken them as quickly, but when they indulge excessively, their nervous system being weaker and naturally more inclined to spasm, the troubles are more violent (*Onanisme*, 1764 edition).

Tissot reported on a young watchmaker he was called to treat who was "less a living being than a cadaver lying on straw, thin, pale, exuding a loathsome stench . . . sunk below the level of a beast, a spectacle of unimaginable horror, it was difficult to believe he had once belonged to the human race." Tissot could do nothing for him, and the young man died. To combat this peril, Tissot recommended milk, exercise, clean air, and cold baths, but primarily avoidance. Tissot's work was extremely influential, cited by physicians all over Europe during the century after it appeared, who added observations drawn from their own patients. His work formed the basis of the article on masturbation in the 1781 *Encyclopedia Britannica*; doctors devised metal rings, electrical alarms, and special garments to keep their patients from the "solitary vice"; and surgeons occasionally performed penile and vaginal surgery. Child care manuals advised mothers to tie children's hands. By the late nineteenth and early twentieth centuries, masturbation was linked with imperialism; young men had been given "a sacred trust for carrying on the race," wrote Lord Baden-Powell, the founder of the Boy Scouts, who warned "you are throwing away the seed that has been handed down to you as a trust instead of keeping it and ripening it for bringing a son to you later on" (*Scouting for Boys*, 1930). The anti-masturbatory campaign has sometimes been labeled a "panic" or a "hysteria," but it is important to recognize that it was promoted by highly educated physicians and scientists, not naïve villagers. Warnings about the dangers of masturbation were directed to, and accepted by, sophisticated urban residents, whose interest in new medical discoveries was a sign of their modernity.

(Quotations taken from Jean Stengers and Anne van Neck, *Masturbation: The History of a Great Terror*, trans. by Kathryn Hoffman [New York: Palgrave, 2001], pp. 65, 66, 70, 74, 146.)

---

deportation. Such prisons later became the model for similar institutions for men and young people – often specifically called "reformatories" – in which the inmate's level of repentance determined to a great degree the length of incarceration. (This, of course, is still true for prisons and "reform schools" today.) Thus the "Great Confinement" was clearly gendered, with women judged morally deviant imprisoned along with the mentally ill and vagrants.

Same-sex relations, termed "sodomy" or "buggery," were even more deviant than whoredom in the minds of many clerics and jurists, because they could never lead to procreation, and thus broke God's commandment to "be fruitful and multiply." They were therefore linked with heresy, and, as one German jurist commented, "such a monster [*Unmensch*] is called a heretic, and generally punished as a heretic, by fire."[5] These attitudes were shared by Protestant and Catholic authorities, but enforcement of sodomy laws was sporadic and selective, as was the enforcement of so many laws. Some authorities were less concerned about sodomy than about other types of sexual misconduct, because same-sex relations did not lead to a child who might create a public scandal or require public support. Most male homosexual relations seem to have occurred between a superior and inferior, such as an older man and a younger one, or a master and a servant. The dominant individual was generally married and heterosexually active, with his homosexual activities not viewed as upsetting the social order.

Alongside this age-based homosexuality, in the late seventeenth century homosexual subcultures began to develop in a few large cities such as London, Paris, and Amsterdam, with special styles of dress, behavior, slang terms, and meeting places. These networks brought together men of different social classes and backgrounds, but did not necessarily involve a dominant and subordinate partner. This was a new type of same-sex relationship, involving men interested only in other men, rather than the traditional structures in which the dominant male was also heterosexually active. Some men began to dress and act effeminately, at least in private, with wigs and clothing even fancier than those worn by most well-to-do men, and distinctive gestures. They met in special houses for sexual relations and socializing. In England such men were called "mollies," a word used originally for prostitutes, and the areas of town where mollies gathered were also frequented by female prostitutes and their customers. By the late eighteenth century, these effeminate men began to describe themselves as having a "condition" or "way of being" that was different from other men: as having what we might term a "homosexual identity."

The policing of homosexual activities could be intrusive, especially in cities. In London, the Society for the Reformation of Manners, founded in 1690 as a private group with a paid staff that would bring complaints regarding drunkenness, swearing, prostitution, and other moral offenses to the attention of authorities, organized raids on molly-houses. Police in Paris watched and kept records on men suspected of sodomy, using spies and informers, including clergy to spy on other clergy; typical punishment was being forced to stay awake for a few days in custody, though occasionally sterner measures were ordered. The persecution of sodomites was most severe in the Dutch Republic, where there was a major waves of arrests in the 1730s leading to interrogations with torture, secret denunciations, life-long imprisonments, and about 200 executions.

Women were not immune from sodomy accusations and trials, although there were only a handful in all of Europe during the early modern period. In part this was because, in the minds of most male authorities, true sexual intercourse involved penetration by a penis, so that female–female sex was not really sex. The cases that did come to trial generally involved women who wore men's clothing, used a dildo or other device to effect penetration, or married other women. The horror with which they were regarded sprang more from the fact that they had usurped a man's social role than that they had been attracted to another woman. Female–female desire was increasingly portrayed in poetry, drama, pornography, medical literature and the visual arts, however, sometimes coded as passionate friendship and sometimes as suspicious sexual deviance. Women themselves expressed powerful same-sex emotions in letters and poetry, though there is no evidence of the female equivalent of a molly-house.

The enforcement of many sexual laws was intermittent, and rarely applied to the upper classes, who continued to have extra-marital affairs of all types, generally with little social sanction. The "reformation of manners" did shape their extra-marital relations, however. Elite men sought the company of well-educated and refined women rather than streetwalkers; such women were generally dignified with the term "courtesan," a word that originated at the pre-Reformation papal court. Courtesans such as Veronica Franco (1546–91) became known for their poetry, while others, such as Ninon de Lenclos (1615–1705), were known for their connections to famous writers. Kings and high nobles often had an official mistress or two whose standing at court and family influence were enhanced, rather than lessened, through their sexual relations with the monarch. Jeanne-Antoinette Poisson, Madame de Pompadour (1721–64), was just such a *maîtresse en titre* to Louis XV of France, the third woman to have this title. She was an important patron of the arts and a skilled courtier as well as sexual partner, and her role eventually included choosing younger sexual partners for the king. Such courtesans were often glamorized in plays and poetry, and one, Françoise d'Aubigné, Madame de Maintenon (1635–1719), the last official mistress of Louis XIV of France, even became the wife of the king, though she was never named queen.

Extra-marital relations among the elite occasionally included same-sex ones, a situation that has been best studied for the French court. King Henry III (ruled 1574–89) visited courtesans when he traveled to Venice, but also wore women's clothing to balls and parties and surrounded himself with male favorites, his so-called *mignons*. Philippe d'Orléans (1640–1701), the brother of Louis XIV, regularly cross-dressed and had homosexual affairs, though he also married twice and had children with both wives.

The goings-on at court were avidly reported in scurrilous pamphlets and broadsides, though many of the stories they told were patently false. Marie Antoinette, the wife of Louis XVI, was accused in a series of pamphlets of being insatiable and debauched in her sexual desires, engaging in incestuous and lesbian affairs, and killing children. Paris police did not send spies to court or make arrests at the royal household, but this sexual demonization of Marie Antoinette, along with reports of her lavish spending, gambling, and seeming unconcern for the people of France, contributed to growing hostility toward the monarchy in the 1780s.

The body of any queen, and not just that of Marie Antoinette, was a matter of great public concern in early modern Europe, for only through that body – or that of another female relative – would a ruling dynasty continue. British writers during the reign of Queen Anne (ruled 1702–14), who had no children that lived to adulthood despite eighteen pregnancies, remarked – often in pamphlets published anonymously – on the problems created by depending on the bodies of women for political continuity. The body of a king was also a public body, which both represented the nation and was expected to father an heir. Political theorists, in fact, sometimes talked about the "king's two bodies," one his physical body that lived and died, and the other the body of the realm, which continued. Queens also had two bodies. Catherine II of Russia (ruled 1762–96), whose sexuality was as much a matter of gossip as Marie Antoinette's, had three children by several of her many lovers; only the one born while her husband was still alive was publicly acknowledged, however, and her husband was officially regarded as the father.

Today we might call this split between public and private life a distinction between the kingship and the king, but this division is sharper today than it was in the early modern period. In Robert Burton's *Melancholy*, kingdoms that were sick were best treated by reforms chopping off the diseased parts, while leaving the head intact. Burton wrote in 1621, however. By the middle of the eighteenth century, new anatomical ideas had their political counterparts. As in the treatment of the physical body, visible proof and logical argument, rather than divine will or inherited tradition, became for some thinkers the best means of deciding whether the head should stay on the body politic. For Hobbes, the original contract between rulers and ruled was unbreakable and unchangeable; in his own time and country, however, and elsewhere in Europe somewhat later, others were far less sure. Affirmations of the absolute power of kings were frequent and loud in the seventeenth and eighteenth centuries, as we will see in the next chapter, but those minuscule men that made up the body of the nation in *Leviathan* were not always willing simply to perform their allotted function.

Further reading

David George Hale, *The Body Politic: A Political Metaphor in Renaissance English Literature* (The Hague: Mouton, 1971), provides a solid, brief introduction to the issue.

Rebecca Earle, ed., *Epistolary Selves: Letters and Letter-Writers, 1600–1945* (Aldershot: Ashgate, 1999), examines the culture of letter-writing. Claire Tomalin has a fascinating new biography of Pepys: *Samuel Pepys: The Unequalled Self* (London: Knopf, 2002). For more general discussions of the development of ideas about the "self," see Dror Wahrman, *The Making of the Modern Self: Identity and Culture in Eighteenth-Century England* (New Haven: Yale University Press, 2004), and Jerrold Seigel, *The Idea of the Self: Thought and Experience in Western Europe since the Seventeenth Century* (Cambridge: Cambridge University Press, 2005).

Norbert Elias, *The Civilizing Process*, trans. Edmund Jephcott (Oxford: Oxford University Press, 2000), is an excellent new English translation and edition. For a wonderfully illustrated look at the development of civility and many of the other topics discussed in this chapter, see Roger Chartier, ed., *A History of Private Life*, vol. III: *Passions of the Renaissance*, trans. Arthur Goldhammer (Cambridge, MA: Harvard University Press, 1989), which includes material from the fifteenth through the eighteenth centuries. Further discussion of privacy can be found in Annik Pardailhé-Galabrun, *The Birth of Intimacy: Privacy and Domestic Life in Early Modern Paris* (Philadelphia: University of Pennsylvania Press, 1991). Michel Foucault's idea of the "Great Confinement" is developed especially in *Discipline and Punish: The Birth of the Prison*, trans. Alan Sheridan (New York: Vintage, 1979).

For general studies of orders and classes, see Susan Amussen, *An Ordered Society: Gender and Class in Early Modern England* (Oxford: Oxford University Press, 1988); James B. Collins, *Classes, Estates and Order in Early Modern Brittany* (Cambridge: Cambridge University Press, 1994); Steven Rappaport, *Worlds within Worlds: Structures of Life in Sixteenth-Century London* (Cambridge: Cambridge University Press, 1989). For the nobility and gentry, see Felicity Heal and Clive Holmes, *The Gentry in England and Wales 1500–1700* (Basingstoke, UK: Blackwell, 1994); Jonathan Dewald, *The European Nobility, 1400–1800* (Cambridge: Cambridge University Press, 1996); Ronald G. Asch, *Nobility in Transition: Courtiers and Rebels in Britain and Europe, 1550–1700* (London: Arnold, 2003). On citizenship, see Charlotte C. Wells, *Law and Citizenship in Early Modern France* (Baltimore: Johns Hopkins University Press, 1995). For the role of the family in urban society, see Katherine A. Lynch, *Individuals, Families, and Communities in Europe, 1200–1800: The Urban Foundations of Western Society* (Cambridge: Cambridge University Press, 2003).

For anatomy, see Roger French and Andrew Wear, eds., *The Medical Revolution of the Seventeenth Century* (Cambridge: Cambridge University Press, 1989). A more cultural approach is presented in Jonathan Sawday, *The Body Emblazoned: Dissection and the Human Body in Renaissance Culture* (London: Routledge, 1995). Clara Pinto-Correia, *The Ovary of Eve: Egg and Sperm and Preformation* (Chicago: University of Chicago Press, 1997), presents a fascinating and often funny look at an issue that greatly troubled early modern scientists. For medical treatments, see Margaret Pelling, *The Common Lot: Sickness, Medical Occupations and the Urban Poor in Early Modern England* (London: Longman, 1988); Carlo Cipolla, *Miasmas and Disease: Public Health and the Environment in the Pre-Industrial Age* (Cambridge: Cambridge University Press, 1995); Mary Lindemann, *Medicine and Society in Early Modern Europe* (Cambridge: Cambridge University Press, 1999); Colin Jones, *The Charitable Imperative: Hospitals and Nursing in Ancien Régime and Revolutionary France* (London: Routledge, 1989). Roy Porter, *Flesh in the Age of Reason: The Modern Foundations of Body and Soul* (New York: W. W. Norton, 2004), explores the development of new ideas about the moral, physical, and social self.

For childbirth, see Jacques Gélis, *History of Childbirth: Fertility, Pregnancy, and Birth in Early Modern Europe*, trans. Rosemary Morris (London: Polity Press, 1991), and Hilary Marland, ed., *The Art of Midwifery: Early Modern Midwives in Europe* (London: Routledge 1993).

For an excellent study of the incarceration of women, see Sherrill Cohen, *The Evolution of Women's Asylums since 1500: From Refuges for Ex-Prostitutes to Shelters for Battered Women* (New York: Oxford University Press, 1992). For women's sexual honor more generally, see Laura Gowing, *Domestic Dangers: Women, Words, and Sex in Early Modern London* (Oxford: Clarendon Press, 1996). On infanticide, see Peter C. Hoffer and N. E. H. Hull, *Murdering Mothers: Infanticide in England and New England, 1558–1803* (New York: New York University Press, 1981). Louis Crompton's massive *Homosexuality and Civilization* (Cambridge, MA: Belknap Press, 2003), includes extensive discussion of the early modern period, while Randolph Trumbach, *Sex and the Gender Revolution*, vol. 1: *Heterosexuality and the Third Gender in Enlightenment London* (Chicago: University of Chicago Press, 1998), focuses especially on new forms of same-sex relationships. Valerie Traub, *The Renaissance of Lesbianism in Early Modern England* (Cambridge: Cambridge

University Press, 2002), explores the representation of female same-sex desire in many different types of texts. Robert Jütte, *Poverty and Deviance in Early Modern Europe* (Cambridge: Cambridge University Press, 1994), looks at many types of social control, while Isabel V. Hull, *Sexuality, State, and Civil Society in Germany, 1700–1815* (Ithaca, NY: Cornell University Press, 1996), is an important broad-based discussion of the ways in which control of sexuality figured in the development of the modern state. Sarah Maza, *Private Lives and Public Affairs: The Causes Célèbres of Prerevolutionary France* (Berkeley: University of California Press, 1993), explores ways that public discussion of personal scandals involving monarchs and nobles politicized the French population.

 For more suggestions and links see the companion website www.cambridge.org/wiesnerhanks.

Notes

1 John Milton, *Of Reformation Touching Church-Discipline in England*, in *The Works of John Milton*, ed. Frank A. Patterson (New York: Columbia University Press, 1931–8), vol. III, pt. 1, pp. 47–8.
2 James I, "Speech of 1603," in *The Political Works of James I*, ed. Charles H. McIlwain (Cambridge, MA: Harvard University Press, 1918), p. 272.
3 Robert Burton, *The Anatomy of Melancholy*, ed. A. R. Shilleto, 3 vols. (London, 1896), vol. I, p. 87.
4 Quoted in Patricia Crawford, *Women and Religion in England, 1500–1720* (London: Routledge, 1993), p. 16.
5 Quoted and trans. in E. William Monter, *Ritual, Myth and Magic in Early Modern Europe* (Athens, Ohio: Ohio University Press, 1983), p. 118.

9 Politics and power, 1600–1789

In this painting from the Hall of Mirrors in Versailles, King Louis XIV of France stands before a map of Holland, giving orders to attack four strongholds in 1672, during one of his many wars. Charles le Brun (1619–90), the "first painter of the king" who created or supervised all artistic production at Versailles for several decades, depicts Louis and his generals in Roman garb, with Louis showing a distinct resemblance to the Roman emperor Augustus. Such classicized, grandiose scenes fit Louis's tastes, and were widely imitated when other rulers decorated their own palaces.

Timeline

1609	Muslims and Muslim converts expelled from Spain
1618–48	Thirty Years War
1648	Treaty of Westphalia
1642	English Civil War begins
1660	Restoration of Charles II
1652–4, 1665–7, 1672–8	Anglo-Dutch Naval Wars
1683	Ottomans besiege Vienna
1685	Louis XIV revokes Edict of Nantes
1688	William and Mary named rulers in England
1700–15	War of the Spanish Succession
1700–21	Great Northern War
1701	Rulers of Brandenburg-Prussia first declared kings
1703	Revolt in Hungary against Habsburg rule
1740–8	War of the Austrian Succession
1755–63	Seven Years War
1772, 1793, 1795	Partitions of Poland among Russia, Prussia, and Austria
1783	Treaty of Paris

IN 1678, Jacques Bénigne Bossuet (1627–1704), bishop of the city of Meaux in France, preacher and theologian at the court of Louis XIV (ruled 1643–1715), and tutor to the king's eldest son and heir (the *dauphin* in French) wrote an instruction book for his royal charge. Titled *Politics Drawn from the Very Words of the Holy Scripture*, it discussed the nature of royal authority, along with providing practical advice. "Monarchical authority comes from God," wrote Bossuet. "Royal authority is sacred...religion and conscience demand that we obey the prince. Royal authority is absolute...the prince need render account to no one for what he orders...even if kings fail in their duty, their charge and their

285

ministry must be respected...Princes are gods."[1] Bossuet was explaining, in terms even a boy could understand, the political theory known as the divine right of kings, which provided an intellectual justification for Louis XIV's moves to concentrate power in his own hands. The young dauphin Louis did not have to read very carefully, for he was surrounded by signs of royal power. The gigantic palace his father built at Versailles was decorated with paintings showing the king in heroic settings, and with mirrors, wall ornaments, and bas-reliefs decorated with Louis XIV's personal emblem, the sun, which the king himself described as "the most dazzling and most beautiful image of the monarch."[2] Versailles was also filled with nobles, church leaders, authors, and artists all fighting for royal favors: living demonstrations of the power of the Sun King.

Unfortunately for young Louis, he would never have the opportunity to test how well he had learned his lessons, for his father's authority was matched by his longevity. Louis XIV ruled for seventy-two years, outliving not only his son, but also his grandson. When he finally died in 1715, he was succeeded by his great-grandson, who, like the Sun King himself, came to the throne at the age of five.

The dauphin Louis was not the only one learning a lesson from Versailles, or from Bossuet. Five years after Bossuet wrote his instructions to the dauphin, a boy *did* inherit another European throne at the death of his father, though for a while he had to share it with his half-brother and half-sister. Like Louis XIV, this young monarch built a new capital and required nobles to follow certain rules of behavior, asserting that he would not "grant any rank to anyone until he performs a useful service to Us or to the state."[3] We do not know if this monarch read Bossuet's instructions, but he may very well have read other works by Bossuet, especially his histories. We do know that, as a young man, this monarch traveled to western Europe during the reign of Louis XIV, gathering ideas and individuals that would help him bring techniques of engineering, architecture, and military technology well known in Versailles, and in other western European cities, to his country. There was bitter opposition to all of his measures and many were imposed by force, but shortly after his relatively early death he was already known by the title we still use, Peter the Great (1672–1725), tsar of Russia.

Bossuet did not invent the divine right of kings, but built on the ideas of earlier thinkers. In 1609, James I of England proclaimed in a speech to Parliament, "the state of *Monarchy* is the supremest thing upon earth: For kings are not only God's Lieutenants upon earth, and sit upon God's throne, but even by God himself they are called Gods."[4] As we will see later in this chapter, civil war and revolution in England prevented James's successors from making good his words. In most of the other nation-states of Europe, however, monarchs attempted to make absolute royal authority a reality by enhancing the processes of centralization, military expansion, financial restructuring, and religious reorganization that had begun in the sixteenth century. Even in the smaller states of Italy and the Holy Roman Empire, dukes, counts, and princes tried to emulate the French model, issuing decrees and building palaces modeled on

Versailles. The Habsburg rulers of Austria-Hungary built Schönbrunn outside Vienna (begun in 1694), the Hohenzollern rulers of Brandenburg-Prussia, soon to elevate themselves to the title of kings of Prussia, built the Royal Palace in Berlin (begun in 1698), the dukes of Württemberg in southwestern Germany built Ludwigsburg (begun in 1704), and the dukes of Savoy built the palace of Stupinigi near Turin in Italy (begun in 1729). Even the prince-bishop of the German city of Würzburg, one of the twenty-six territories in the Holy Roman Empire ruled by independent bishops, decided he needed a residence and formal gardens that looked like Versailles. In all of these places, artists, architects, sculptors, tapestry-makers, composers, and poets created works that celebrated the rulers who paid for them.

Nineteenth-century historians, writing at a point at which most men in Europe had obtained the right to vote, looked back at political developments in the seventeenth and eighteenth centuries and were nearly as dazzled by the Sun King as Louis XIV's contemporaries. They proclaimed this an "age of absolutism," when rulers first in western Europe (especially France) and then in eastern Europe built up their personal powers, becoming "tyrants" or "despots" completely above the law. In tracing the rise of absolutism, they highlighted both political theory and actual measures imposed by rulers, and contrasted absolutist states such as France and Russia with "constitutionalist" states such as Britain or the Dutch Republic, where the monarchy had more limited powers. This intellectual model of a broad rise of absolutism contrasted with the more limited development of constitutional monarchy has been a powerful one in discussions of politics in the seventeenth and eighteenth centuries, and there is certainly evidence supporting it.

In terms of political theory, scholars have noted that, into the sixteenth century, various levels of government shared the power to make laws, impose taxation, and handle crises. The monarch was authorized to guide the "commonwealth" – the standard term for a large political entity – but only in the interests of the "common good," not in his own interests. The authority to do this emanated from God, but the monarch was understood to share this authority with other levels of government, whose authority was also God-given. The Reformation shattered this arrangement. Not only did it set different levels of government against each other in practice – Protestant city councils against Catholic kings, Catholic bishops against Protestant princes, Protestant law courts against the Catholic emperor – but it destroyed the idea of a smooth flow of authority and of a "common good." How could a Catholic king possibly be a mediator of God's will and sacred law for his Protestant subjects? Bossuet and other advocates of the divine right of kings provided one answer: sovereign power came from God, but only to a single monarch whose power was "absolute" and indivisible, shared by no other authority. In words attributed to Louis XIV, though he probably never said them, "I am the state" (L'état, c'est moi).

In terms of actions, historians have pointed to the ways rulers from Spain to Russia created new institutions of government, limited the powers of privileged social groups, expanded state activity in many realms of life, such as education and poor relief, and extended involvement in new areas, including health care, transportation and communication. Louis XIV stripped the title "sovereign court" from the *parlements*, the highest law courts of France, and created a new tax – the *capitation* – that the previously tax-exempt nobles and clergy would have to pay. In German-speaking lands, the rulers of both large and small states issued "police ordinances" (*Polizeiordnungen*) that regulated minute details of daily life. Peter the Great did as well, ordering men, women, and children above the level of peasant to adopt western dress, including "hats, jacket, and underwear."⁵ Russian men were to shave off their beards and moustaches, with fines set by social status ranging from 100 rubles for wholesale merchants to 1 copeck (one-hundredth of a ruble) for peasants, "to be collected at the town gates each time they enter or leave a town." Faculty at German law schools developed the idea of *cameralism*: that the state had the right – or indeed, the duty – to carry out policies that would enhance the well-being and tax-paying capacity of its residents. Bureaucrats trained in cameralist principles helped rulers in their close attention to all aspects of life; they promoted new crops such as the potato, collected statistics about longevity and health, and tried to develop industries such as silk-making. By the eighteenth century, rulers and their officials were actively involved in changing – or attempting to change – areas of life that had previously been the province of the church, the family, or local organizations such as guilds, enhancing their authority in the process.

More recent scholarship has pointed out that these changes in theory and practice did occur, but they were much more limited than earlier historians had assumed. In terms of political theory, even the most vigorous supporters of the divine right of kings regarded the authority of the king as subject to the laws of God and to what they termed "natural law." Bossuet declared that royal authority is sacred and absolute, but in the same work he also asserted that it is neither godless nor lawless, and is also "paternal" and "subject to reason." The paternal nature of the king's authority was generally used to make it appear stronger and more natural. "By the law of nature," stated James I to Parliament, "the king becomes a natural father to all his lieges at his coronation."⁶ Criticism of monarchs could also be couched in paternal language, however. Pamphlets directed against the crown during the revolt known as the Fronde in seventeenth-century France, for example, justified their opposition by asserting that the king was not properly fulfilling his fatherly duties. They did not call for a reduction in his powers, however, but wanted him to act like a more responsible father. Advocates of limited monarchy were thus not the only ones to set limits on royal power.

Existing political structures put even more limits on the level of actual control even the most "absolute" monarch could impose. Many states had been built up through the gradual assembly of different provinces, and each province often had different civil and criminal legal systems, local representative assemblies, taxation structures, and even weights and measures. Making these more uniform was often a goal, but very difficult in practice. Civil law, which regulated the private relations between individuals on such matters as inheritance and the exchange of property, was based on custom as well as written codes, and was thus nearly impossible for monarchs to change. Nobles still held considerable military and financial power, and in many areas of Europe met regularly in representative bodies where they could make their wishes known. Like private law, their privileges, and those of other groups such as the clergy or the citizens of towns, were regarded as "customary" and thus very difficult to alter. Louis XIV might create a *capitation* paid by every person, and other rulers might invent similar new taxes, but they could not simply do away with the huge range of privileges established by custom. The most successful monarchs collaborated with aristocrats and other privileged groups on projects that enhanced both royal and elite prestige. "Absolutism" was a joint venture, with the most effective rulers generally co-opting, rather than crushing, traditional elites. Those elites remained the dominant group in the more "constitutionalist" states of Britain and the Netherlands as well, creating similarities across Europe rather than a sharp dichotomy between limited and absolute monarchy.

Legal variations and customary privileges provided significant limitations to absolutism, and geographic and cultural realities created even more. It would have taken a traveler three weeks to cross a large country like France in 1600, so royal orders were slow to communicate, and in many states they would need to be translated into local dialects, or even into different languages, in order to be understood. They were also hard to enforce. Maria Theresa (ruled 1740–80), the ruler of the Habsburg territories in central Europe, ordered the creation of grammar schools in every parish in 1774, but parents in Hungary refused to enroll their children, and she had no way to force them to comply. Peter ordered men to shave their beards and dress in western clothing, but enforcing this across the vast territories of Russia was impossible. Such dissonance between proclamations and orders emanating from the capital and what actually occurred was repeated in every state in Europe. In many of those states, orders that came from centralizing rulers also provoked vehement reactions, leading to mob violence, localized urban and rural revolts, regional upheavals, and in some cases nationwide civil wars.

33 The "crisis of the seventeenth century"

During the middle of the seventeenth century, there were violent revolts against existing regimes in England, France, Catalonia (northern Spain), Portugal, and Naples. These nearly simultaneous challenges to existing regimes led historians in the middle of the twentieth century to propose that there was a "crisis of the seventeenth century" involving much of Europe. The conceptualization of a "crisis" was expanded to include more political upheavals, along with certain striking economic, intellectual, and social developments. Some scholars, including the British historians Eric Hobsbawm and H. R. Trevor-Roper, suggested that there was a "general crisis" that involved continent-wide patterns of change in all aspects of life, which may have started in the early sixteenth century. Other historians wondered whether it made much sense to call something that went on so long a "crisis," which generally suggests a short period of extreme distress followed by some sort of resolution. (The word "crisis" was originally used in medicine, and meant the point in a disease at which the patient suddenly begins to get significantly worse or better.) In the 1980s the American historian Theodore K. Rabb suggested that "struggle for stability" was a better term, though others pointed out that this phrase could be used to describe certain historical eras in many places, not simply the seventeenth century in Europe. Despite criticisms, however, both the notion of a "crisis of the seventeenth century" and of a "struggle for stability" still shape some scholars' understanding of this period.

 For additional chapter resources see the companion website www.cambridge.org/wiesnerhanks.

The aims of European rulers in the seventeenth and eighteenth centuries far exceeded what they could actually do, and could also work at cross-purposes to one another. Opening schools or taking them over from the church allowed greater control of the education of one's subjects, but cost money, as did the bureaucracy needed to oversee other royal projects. Building fabulous palaces or better roads enhanced royal prestige, but could be enormously expensive. Defending or expanding one's territories offered the greatest possibilities for personal and national aggrandizement, but could also bring bitter disappointment and financial ruin. The possibilities war offered were too great to ignore, however, so that all political developments in these centuries played themselves out against a backdrop of nearly constant warfare.

Warfare and alliances

The history of Europe in the seventeenth and eighteenth centuries is often told in terms of a series of wars. Some of these wars came to have specific names, and some did not; some of them involved long-standing conflicts over trade and territory that flared into actual warfare from time to time but simmered continuously. There were general Europe-wide wars, such as the Thirty Years War of 1618–48. There were regional wars, civil wars, naval wars, and wars about who would succeed to various thrones when rulers died childless or without male heirs. There were revolts against rulers, particularly in the 1640s to 1660s, which first led historians to call this a time of "crisis." Wars that started in the New World came to involve Europe, including the war for American Independence (1775–83), which eventually included England, France, Spain, and the Netherlands. European wars also spread outward, including the Seven Years War (1755–63), which came to be fought in North America (where it was called the French and Indian War) and India, as well as in Europe.

Most of these wars involved frequently shifting alliances, some of them open and some of them secret. They were often ended by treaties involving only some of the participants, so war in one theatre dragged on after fighting stopped elsewhere, with rulers shifting their armies and navies. The treaties of Nijmegen in 1678 to 1679, for example, which ended one of the many wars that pitted France and its allies against the Netherlands and its allies, were actually six different peace treaties, all separately brokered.

This pattern of shifting alliances and complex treaties was set by the Thirty Years War, which many historians see as the first "modern" war in terms of tactics, organization, and level of devastation. As noted in chapter 5, the Thirty Years War can also be seen, at least in its initial stages, as round 3 in the series of religious wars that resulted from the Reformation. Round 1 had ended with the Peace of Augsburg in 1555, and round 2 with Henry IV of France allowing French Protestants limited freedom of worship, and a truce in 1609 between the Netherlands and Spain.

The Peace of Augsburg ended religious wars in central Europe for over fifty years, but it was an uneasy peace. The terms of the treaty recognized only Lutheranism and Catholicism as allowable denominations, but in the second half of the sixteenth century Calvinism was more dynamic. Some states became Calvinist, ignoring the terms of the treaty. A few bishops converted from Catholicism to Lutheranism, taking their territories with them, to the dismay of the Catholic Church. Jesuit preachers and scholars converted Lutheran princes back to Catholicism, and territories sometimes switched denominations with every generation, as rulers backed whatever religion their father had opposed. In 1608, Lutheran rulers formed a military alliance called the Protestant Union, and in the following years Catholics responded with the Catholic League.

Dynastic considerations mixed with religion to turn this tense situation into open warfare. Dismayed at the failure of his efforts to secure religious unity, Emperor Charles V had abdicated in 1556, dividing his vast holdings between his son Philip II (who got Spain, the Netherlands, and the Spanish empire) and his brother Ferdinand I (who got Austria and other central European holdings, and the title of Emperor). The Habsburg family was thus divided into a Spanish and an Austrian branch, though both supported each other and were firmly Catholic. In 1617, Ferdinand of Styria, a Habsburg cousin, was chosen king of Bohemia (in what is now the Czech Republic), an area that had rejected the Catholic Church a century before Luther and was overwhelmingly Protestant. When Ferdinand began to close Protestant churches, Bohemian officials objected, and threw two of his representatives out of the window in Prague. They did not die – depending on your point of view, they were saved either by angels or by a pile of manure – but the incident led to civil war in Bohemia.

Armies of the Catholic League and the Protestant Union joined the fight, and in the first years the Catholics were overwhelmingly successful. Ferdinand, who had meanwhile become Holy Roman Emperor with the title Ferdinand II (ruled 1619–37), wiped out Protestantism in Bohemia with forcible conversions. He appointed a wealthy Bohemian nobleman, Albrecht of Wallenstein (1583–1634) as general of the imperial armies, who continued scoring victories against Protestants, including not only German troops but also those sent by the king of Denmark. Wallenstein was an effective leader and ruthless entrepreneur, raising an army – by forcible conscription as well as promises of pay – that eventually numbered over 100,000, supplying them through extortion and confiscation. It looked as if Ferdinand might be able to accomplish what had eluded his great-uncle Charles V: the creation of a large, strong Catholic state in central Europe under Habsburg rule. In 1629 he passed the Edict of Restitution, which forbade Calvinism and ordered all lands that had become Protestant since 1552 to revert to Catholicism.

The prospect of a strong Empire under Habsburg domination frightened not only Protestants in Europe, but also Catholic opponents of Habsburg power, especially France. In the early 1630s, well-disciplined and well-armed Swedish troops, under the leadership of King Gustavus Adolphus (ruled 1611–32) and bankrolled by the French, successfully defeated Catholic forces several times, though Gustavus Adolphus died at the Battle of Lützen. Wallenstein was accused of conspiracy with the French, and was assassinated at the emperor's orders. Ferdinand II decided to dissolve the Catholic League and make peace with the German Protestant princes, but this Peace of Prague (1635) did not satisfy either the Swedes or the French. France sent troops against those of the emperor and his Habsburg cousins in Spain; Spanish forces were defeated in naval battles with the Dutch and by the Portuguese, who revolted against Spanish rule in 1640 and declared themselves an independent country again. The war had become a Europe-wide war, with territorial aims now more important than religious allegiances.

Each side won battles, but was not able to exploit its victories, and the war dragged on, with devastating effects. Troops were often recruited by independent military contractors, of which Wallenstein had been the most successful, with promises of pay and plunder, and little training or discipline. There were no clear lines of battle, so that these mercenary armies indiscriminately burned crops and villages and killed animals and people. Hunger and disease, including dysentery, plague, and syphilis, accompanied the troops and the refugees who fled from place to place. Some historians estimate that at least one-quarter and perhaps as many as one-third of the population of the Empire died during the course of the war, though total devastation was localized. Such civilian losses would not be matched again until the wars of the twentieth century. Finally, in 1645 negotiations were begun in two cities in the German province of Westphalia, but it took three years for the terms of a peace treaty to be agreed upon, with armies sporadically fighting and living off what was left of the German countryside during that time.

The resulting Peace of Westphalia recognized certain political realities in Europe, but did not lead to lasting peace. It recognized the United Provinces of the Netherlands and Switzerland as fully independent, and made the larger principalities within the Holy Roman Empire effectively sovereign, though the Empire itself also continued to exist. France gained territory on its eastern border, and Sweden gained most of the German North Sea coastline, which enhanced the prestige of the monarchy in both countries. Territorial rulers in the Empire were given the right to choose the religion of their territories, with Calvinism joining Catholicism and Lutheranism as an acceptable choice. There were more than a hundred other clauses, largely confirming various princes' rights over certain territories, though occasionally stipulating transfers of land or new titles. The religious lines of division in central Europe were largely fixed, with most of northern Germany Protestant and most of southern Germany Catholic. The Habsburgs largely retained their family holdings and claims on the imperial title. As it had in the sixteenth century, the basic conflict in Europe continued to pit France against the Habsburgs, especially as the Peace of Westphalia had not included stipulations about the war between France and Spain, which continued.

The Thirty Years War set the pattern for later wars in many ways, but it also provided lessons about what not to do for more astute military commanders

Map 10. Europe after the Peace of Westphalia, 1648.

and political leaders. The biggest problem was logistical, not tactical, for supply systems could not keep up with troops. Roads were primitive or nonexistent and rivers could not be found everywhere. Armies had to stop every three or four days to let the millers and bakers who accompanied the troops catch up and bake the rough bread that was the soldiers' standard ration, and let the wagons with tents and other supplies catch up. Looting supplies from the surrounding countryside only worked for a short time, for farmers in most parts of Europe lived near subsistence level themselves and had little food to spare. In fact the most impressive aspect of Ottoman armies – which were not involved in the Thirty Years War, although they were in other seventeenth-century conflicts – was not their enormous size, but the relatively effective way they were supplied. Even the Ottomans could not sustain large armies in the field for many months, however, and shorter wars with limited objectives were more likely to produce clear-cut outcomes than those that dragged on for years.

Even these shorter wars – of which there were many in the 150 years after the Peace of Westphalia – were fought with larger and more deadly standing armies, however. By the middle of the eighteenth century, Brandenburg-Prussia,

34 Warfare at sea

Improved training and increasing specialization affected warfare at sea as well as on land. During the sixteenth century, most states relied on merchant ships temporarily armed with a few cannon for their naval battles, but it became increasingly clear that specialized gun-armed warships and merchant ships built to carry a substantial number of guns were more effective. Between 1652 and 1678, the English and the Dutch fought a series of wars for control of the English Channel and the North Sea, which involved larger and larger sailing ships armed with heavier guns, arranged in a formal line of battle and firing continuously. Such tactics required professionally trained officers, well-drilled gun crews, and disciplined sailors who could maintain clear battle lines.

In the eighteenth century, the Dutch preferred neutrality, concentrating on defending and supplying their worldwide trading network. The British continued to expand their navy, becoming the world's dominant sea power; measured in terms of total weight, the British navy in 1790 was almost ten times what it had been in 1650, a figure that reflects both the greater number and the larger size of ships. The French and the Spanish also built up their battle fleet strength, largely to challenge Britain in the Atlantic, while in the Baltic, Denmark, Sweden, and Russia expanded their navies. By the end of the eighteenth century the Russian navy was the third largest in Europe (after Britain and France), confronting the Ottomans in the Black Sea and the Mediterranean as well as the Scandinavian states in the Baltic.

one of the larger states in Germany, tried to sustain a permanent army of about 80,000 troops with a population of perhaps 3.5 million; during the Seven Years War, this army increased to almost 150,000, or about one-quarter of all adult males. Most eighteenth-century armies were equipped with reliable flintlock muskets that no longer needed a separate match to fire, bayonets on the end of those muskets, and more accurate and mobile artillery. The best-supplied soldiers had cartridges in which shot was prepackaged with gunpowder, and the best-disciplined had spent long periods training and drilling. These technical improvements increased battlefield casualties significantly, with losses sometimes approaching one-quarter of all the troops deployed in the field. Better weapons, bigger armies, longer training, and fuller supply systems all significantly increased the costs of warfare. Pressures of war finance enhanced the power of some monarchs, including those of Brandenburg-Prussia, while derailing the expansion of royal power elsewhere, most dramatically, as we will see below, in England.

The development of colonial empires and international trade meant that European wars in the later seventeenth and eighteenth centuries often spread beyond Europe itself. (In some ways, the Thirty Years War can be seen as the last "pre-modern" war as well as the first "modern" one, because it was at least initially motivated by religion and was limited to Europe.) In the Anglo-Dutch wars, British ships attacked Dutch holdings in Africa, the West Indies, and North America, eventually gaining New Amsterdam, which was renamed New York. During the 1630s, the Dutch challenged the Portuguese in Brazil, and the British captured part of French Canada, though they later gave it back. During the War of the League of Augsburg (1689–97), French and British colonists in North America massacred each other, while during the War of the Spanish Succession (1701–13), the British attacked Spanish forts in Florida and the French attacked Portuguese Brazilian ports. The colorfully named War of Jenkins' Ear between Spain and Britain (1739–48) started after an English sea captain appeared before Parliament with his ear, claiming it had been cut off by Spanish authorities boarding his ship in the Caribbean. During the War of the Austrian Succession (1740–8), French ships captured British-held Madras in India, while British colonists captured Louisburg in Canada from the French.

The Seven Years War (1755–63) was so global in scope that it could almost be called the first "world war," involving conflict in North America, the Caribbean, the Pacific, and India as well as Europe. As in other early modern wars, logistical problems proved as important as battlefield losses in determining the final results.

The Seven Years War also involved new lines of alliance and hostility that reflected changing realities of power. During the sixteenth and seventeenth centuries, the major line of antagonism in Europe was hostility between France and the Habsburgs. As we saw in chapter 3, this had resulted in wars in Italy, Switzerland, Spain, and elsewhere, and in France coming in on the side of the Protestants during the Thirty Years War. As the British navy and British colonial holdings expanded during the seventeenth and early eighteenth centuries, however, France worried increasingly about British power, while Britain worried about France, which was the strongest and wealthiest country in Europe in the seventeenth century. After 1688, as we will see in more detail below, monarchs in Britain came from the ruling houses of two medium-sized states in the Netherlands and Germany, so they had continental territories to defend. The Austrian Habsburgs continued as the strongest power in central Europe, but by the middle of the eighteenth century they were increasingly worried about Prussia, a state made up of scattered territories within and to the east of the Holy Roman Empire, whose rulers were establishing an enormous and well-disciplined army. Russia, which had played no role in the religious and dynastic controversies of the sixteenth and seventeenth centuries, was also worried about Prussia, and had expansionary plans of its own.

This complicated scenario led, in 1756, to Great Britain making an alliance with Prussia, to which France, Russia, and the Austrian Habsburgs responded with a triple alliance. War broke out between France and Britain in North America, in part because settlers from both countries were staking out claims in the Ohio Valley, and between all the allies in Europe. In terms of economic might and military manpower, the triple alliance was much stronger than Prussia, but the ruler of Prussia, Frederick II (ruled 1740–86; known as Frederick the Great), was a brilliant military strategist who understood how to use different types of troops – infantry, cavalry, and artillery – very effectively. He attacked Austria, and his opponents were slow to respond and did not cooperate with one another. British blockades of French ports and victories over the French fleet in naval battles meant that France could not resupply its forces in either North America or eastern Germany, and in 1760 the French governor surrendered all of Quebec to the British. Spain joined in on the side of France, and the British captured both Spanish and French colonies, including Cuba, the Philippines, French islands in the Caribbean, and French forts in Africa and India. Two separate peace treaties finally ended the war in 1763, with France losing most of its overseas colonies, Spain ceding Florida to England but gaining back Cuba and the Philippines, and Prussia being confirmed in its takeover of the territory of Silesia from Austria.

Map 11. Europe in 1763.

In contrast to the Thirty Years War, the Seven Years War was truly "modern": fought over territory and trade by professionally trained and relatively well-supplied troops, with naval operations and new military technology used effectively. The treaties of 1763, however, were no more successful than the Peace of Westphalia in ending hostilities for very long. Prussia and Austria went to war again in 1778 over who would inherit the throne of Bavaria, a large state that bordered Austria in the southern part of the Holy Roman Empire. In the same year France entered the American Revolution on the side of the colonists, and later Spain and the Netherlands did as well. The Treaty of Paris in 1783 that recognized the independence of the thirteen British North American colonies transferred other colonial territories – Tobago and Senegal – from Britain to France and reaffirmed Spanish rights over Florida. (Spain ceded Florida to the United States in 1819.) Just a few years later, however, the French Revolution and its aftermath would once again set most of the powers of Europe against each other.

By their very nature, wars generally involve external relations between states. Those relations – and success or failure in war – were shaped by internal political developments in the countries and empires of Europe. The internal political history of each state is somewhat distinct, so that the following sections look at different countries separately. There are certain themes that we can follow in all – or at least most – of them: an expansion of centralized authority, whether held by a monarch alone or shared by a representative body; the continued development of government bureaucracy; and the pursuit of territorial power and colonial wealth.

France

Along with war, the other constant in European politics of the seventeenth and eighteenth centuries was the dominant power of France. Except for Russia and the Ottoman Empire, France was the largest state in Europe geographically, and its population was by far the largest outside the Ottoman Empire; in 1620 it had about twenty million people, which was four times the population of England, and twice that of Spain or Russia. In the sixteenth century Ottoman and Spanish armies were the largest in Europe, but by the seventeenth century the largest army belonged to France.

Though Bossuet was the most eloquent defender of royal authority, and Louis XIV its most famous exemplar, the kings of France had already begun an expansion of central power before Louis's accession. In 1598 Henry IV issued the Edict of Nantes, which declared that France was officially a Catholic country but that Calvinist Protestants (Huguenots) would have the right to practice their faith and maintain military garrisons in 150 towns. Assisted by his Protestant chief minister, Maximilian de Béthune, duke of Sully (1559–1641), Henry IV tackled other problems as well, restoring public order, overhauling government finances, lowering taxes on the peasants somewhat, and supporting measures that encouraged trade. He expanded the sale of royal offices begun by his predecessors, and made royal officials pay an annual tax, the *paulette*, if they wanted their offices to remain hereditary.

Henry's toleration of Protestantism was too much for some, and in 1610 he was stabbed in the streets of Paris by a fanatical Catholic assassin; the monarchy passed to his son Louis XIII (ruled 1610–43), who was only eight. Actual power was held by the queen-mother, Henry IV's second wife Marie de' Medici (1573–1642), and various high nobles. Different factions rose and fell in favor and influence, but by the 1620s the most powerful figure was Armand-Jean du Plessis, a nobleman and bishop who was made Cardinal Richelieu (1585–1642). Shrewd and extremely able, Richelieu became chief minister, and succeeded in keeping the forces threatening the power of the monarchy in balance. Always acting in the name of the king, he further limited the independent power of the high nobility, rewarding those who supported him with high offices, military commands, and advantageous marriage alliances, while sending those who opposed him into exile or even executing them. The list of exiled nobles eventually included the queen-mother herself, who had demanded her son dismiss Richelieu but instead ended up spending the rest of her life outside France. Richelieu used cultural patronage to support royal power, recruiting writers to defend crown policies in print through newsletters, gazettes, and histories. In 1635 he gave official support to the Académie Française, a society of writers and philologists intent on standardizing the French language, which would provide a cultural counterpart to political measures of centralization.

Richelieu extended the power of royal officials called *intendants*, who were appointed directly by the monarch so that they did not own their offices, and were almost always members of the newer *noblesse de robe*. Each intendant had authority over a certain district, collecting taxes, recruiting men for the army, ordering soldiers to be billeted with families, regulating economic activities, administering local courts, and enforcing royal decrees. Intendants could not be native to the district in which they operated, so they had no independent base of power; their activities worked to build up the power of the centralized state and further weaken the regional nobility. They were assisted by deputies who did much of the actual work and understood local power relations, so that these too could be used to royal advantage. Louis and Richelieu also asserted stricter controls over the Huguenots, continuing to allow them freedom of worship but forbidding them from maintaining fortified towns. They successfully besieged the Atlantic port city and Protestant stronghold of La Rochelle when its inhabitants objected, pulling down its walls and suppressing the municipal government.

Foreign policy under Louis and Richelieu was marked by continued opposition to Habsburg power, which led France into war in Italy and Spain, and into the Thirty Years War, first backing Sweden and then as a combatant. The financial drains of these wars were enormous; rising taxes and grain shortages led to popular rebellions and collective violence in cities and rural areas. Peasants in the Angoumois region of southwestern France, for example, killed or drove off royal tax collectors in 1636, burning their houses and refusing to pay higher taxes or the costs of garrisoning troops. A manifesto issued in the name of the peasants ordered "all inhabitants of each parish to arm themselves according to their means and to be well supplied with lead and powder," and specifically requested local nobles to "provide arms and march in our defense."[7] With much of its military away fighting in Germany, the royal government initially made some concessions to this regional opposition, though the following year royal troops returned, defeated the peasants, and executed their leaders.

Rebellions against the monarchy and its policies culminated in the 1640s, after the death of Richelieu in 1642 and Louis XIII the following year. The situation was much the same as it had been a generation earlier: the new king, Louis XIV, was only a child, and real power was held by the queen-mother, Anne of Austria (1601–66), together with a cardinal and chief minister, Jules Mazarin (1602–61). The rebellions, known as the Fronde, shook the monarchy, but were never intended to topple it; the focus of the rebellion was Mazarin, who was described as an evil foreigner building up his own power and leading the queen and young king to neglect the true interests of the country. At

Mazarin's death, Louis decided to rule without a chief minister, taking over the day-to-day operation of government himself in what would be the longest reign in the history of Europe.

Louis was hard-working, suspicious, and cautious, supporting measures that worked toward greater uniformity in law and practice. He read the dispatches of ambassadors, officials, and spies, and supervised all aspects of the military, personally appointing all officers down to the rank of colonel. Careful not to give the nobility or other influential individuals a chance to come together outside his presence, he never called a meeting of the Estates General. He frequently backed projects where royal and noble interests merged, however, such as the building of canals. He recognized that the most sensible solution to France's financial problems – taxing the nobility – was politically impossible, so he supported commercial activities that would bring in wealth. He and his controller-general of finances, Jean-Baptiste Colbert (1619–83), subsidized the production of cloth, steel, and firearms, gave bonuses to ship-builders, expanded the merchant marine, organized guilds in many industries, established trading companies, and developed preferential policies on immigration, imports, and exports. Colbert sent peasants as settlers to New France in North America, and supported explorations in the American interior, including that of Robert la Salle (1643–87), who claimed the delta of the Mississippi River for France in 1684, naming it, not surprisingly, "Louisiana."

Louis's desire for unity and uniformity in his realm extended to matters of religion. Huguenots were increasingly deprived of their political rights, barred from many professions, ordered to quarter more troops in their households, and sometimes forced to undergo Catholic baptism. They were officially forbidden to emigrate to New France – though some did – a policy that contrasted with that of

35 The Fronde

In the 1630s, France joined the forces opposing the Habsburgs in the Thirty Years War, first financially supporting Swedish actions and then sending in French troops. The costs of the war meant government expenditures doubled between 1630 and 1640, and the government attempted to establish new means of raising revenue. In 1648, Queen Anne and her chief minister Cardinal Mazarin tried to force the *parlement* of Paris, the most prestigious and influential court in France, to accept new taxes. They refused, the queen arrested some of their leaders, and the populace of Paris reacted with violence. Civil order completely collapsed and mobs threatened the royal family, breaking into the palace and forcing them to flee the city. Several months later the queen made peace with the rebels in Paris, which calmed the city for a while, but the situation in many provinces was very unstable. Local *parlements* refused to send any taxes to the capital, and a series of revolts and civil wars broke out from 1648 to 1653. Together these disturbances became known as the Fronde, a word that means "slingshot" in French and was derived from the weapons that poor children used to throw mud against the coaches of the rich. *Frondeurs* did include poor urban workers and peasants protesting high taxes, but also many groups armed with far more than slingshots and mud. High nobles led many of the provincial rebellions against royal officials, arguing that they were attempting to restore structures of power to what they had been before Richelieu. Royal intendants, meant to be the enforcers of absolutism, became part of the resistance, demanding that the crown pay more attention to their interests. Thousands of pamphlets, written by well-educated political writers, not peasants, accused Mazarin, who was Italian, of treachery; some included the queen-mother, born the daughter of the Habsburg king of Spain, in their denunciations of the influence of evil foreigners.

The very breadth of the Fronde was part of the reason it did not succeed, however, as the rebels were never able to unify their plans or aims. Mazarin played one faction off against the others and used loyalty to the young king as a tool to counter the rebels. In 1651, at the age of thirteen, Louis was declared ruler in his own right – that is, no longer under the regency of his mother – and much of the rebellion disintegrated. Most of the leaders were pardoned, and Mazarin was even exiled for brief periods, though he eventually returned and continued to lead the government until his death in 1661. The dramatic and frightening events of the Fronde had deeply influenced Louis, however, who hated revolts, hated Paris, and favored anything that encouraged order and enhanced his own regal power.

England, where the rulers were happy to let religious malcontents such as Puritans and Quakers leave the country. In 1685, Louis formally revoked the Edict of Nantes, ordering Protestant churches and schools closed and Protestant clergy to leave the country. Protestant lay people were ordered to convert and forbidden to emigrate, though tens of thousands of them did, fueling hatred of Louis in northern Europe. Inside France, however, Louis won wide praise for this action, especially among the nobility. In some areas of France, the emigration of Huguenots meant a loss of substantial numbers of skilled people (and their taxes), but overall this did not have a dramatic effect on economic development.

The French economy could survive the loss of Huguenot knowledge and skills, but it could not absorb the ever-expanding costs of Louis XIV's wars. Pushing northeastward, he invaded the Spanish Netherlands and the United Provinces, ultimately gaining some Flemish towns and the area of Franche-Comté. In the 1680s, he seized the city of Strasbourg, and sent his armies into the province of Lorraine. Though his army was gigantic and well-trained, the efforts of his opponents and his inability to squeeze any more money out of the taxable portion of the French population prevented him from annexing any more territory. A series of bad harvests caused starvation, disease, and depopulation in many parts of France, leading to renewed peasant revolts in the 1690s. These problems halted Louis's military adventures only briefly, for the last years of his reign were taken up with trying to secure the throne of Spain for his grandson Philip when the ruling Habsburg king died childless, in a war that became known as the War of the Spanish Succession. (Louis XIV's mother, and thus Philip's great-grandmother, was the daughter of one Habsburg king of Spain, and Louis XIV's wife, who was Philip's grandmother, was the daughter of another.) In this he was successful, and Philip became the first Bourbon king of Spain, but only after extended war and a peace treaty that specified that the crowns of France and Spain were never to be held by the same member of the Bourbon family. The treaty also gave far more land to the Austrian Habsburgs than to France. All of Louis's military efforts had gained relatively little territory and had financially exhausted the country; his subjects greeted his death with relief.

Louis's successors, his great-grandson Louis XV and his great-great-grandson Louis XVI, engaged in warfare on a scale slightly more limited than Louis XIV, but still ruinously expensive. The nobility saw the constant need for more revenue as an opportunity to reassert their dominance after decades of subservience to the Sun King. The *parlement* of Paris and other regional *parlements* challenged all attempts by the monarchy to impose emergency or regular taxes, using their traditional privileges increasingly as a basis from which to push for the right to approve all taxes and limit the power of the monarchy. The *parlements* reasserted their right to review royal decrees before they became law. Louis XV (ruled 1715–74) disbanded the *parlements* in an attempt to crush his opposition, who increasingly portrayed themselves as representing the entire French nation. Louis and his ministers were attacked in anonymous pamphlets as degenerate despots. His attempts at reform and modernization, including a reorganization of the judiciary, were often short-lived and vacillating. Louis XVI (ruled 1774–92) reinstated the *parlements*, a measure widely supported by public opinion, and promoted trade and industry. He would not agree to other measures of reform, however, and France drifted toward political upheaval.

Spain and Portugal

The costs of a huge army and an expansionary foreign policy led to revolts and political crises in Spain as well as France. In the sixteenth century, Spain was the wealthiest and most powerful country in Europe, conquering Portugal in 1580 and ruling an empire that stretched around the world. Gold and silver from New World mines poured into Spain, and Spanish oil, wine, and wool were exported to the colonies. Serious problems were already in evidence by the end of the century, however. Spanish armies had not been able to quash the revolt in the Netherlands, and in 1609 Philip III (ruled 1598–1622) recognized the independence of the northern part of the Netherlands as the United Provinces. Dutch and English ships took over much of the trade with the Spanish colonies, and Spanish attempts to prohibit this were futile. Central and South American mines gradually produced less metal, and the Indians and Africans forced to work in them died of disease and malnutrition. Royal expenses continued to increase, so much so that the crown declared bankruptcy five times between 1590 and 1680. Declaring bankruptcy cancelled debts in the short term, but only heightened the crisis, as new loans to keep the government afloat could only be secured at higher and higher rates of interest, thus transferring more wealth to the bankers and merchants (many of them outside Spain) who were willing to risk loaning money to the government.

Like the old French nobility, Spanish aristocrats disdained commercial ventures as vulgar and lived off the rents of their lands. Their hostility to change and devotion to past military glories were stronger than those of nobles elsewhere, however, largely preventing the ennobling of new families through service as judges or officials. Though wealthy commoners could increasingly buy noble titles, they expected after doing so to live off rents, not hold a legal or government position that would require actual work. The exclusivity of the nobility was further enhanced by the obsession with "purity of the blood" – having no Muslim or Jewish ancestors – for converts included the sort of well-educated urban professionals that in other parts of Europe were becoming state bureaucrats and royal administrators. In 1609 to 1611, over 200,000 Muslims and Muslim converts were expelled to North Africa, further reducing a population that had already declined significantly because of famine and epidemic disease. Spanish nobles saw no way other than raising rents to increase their income and pay for imported luxuries, but this came at the same time as the government was increasing taxes; the peasants often had no surplus to sell and could not pay, abandoning their lands and drifting into cities or becoming vagabonds. The middle class was tiny, and there was little support for programs to develop industry or improve agricultural productivity.

The Spanish nobility did back the crown in its military ventures, but these only brought further debt. Spain entered the Thirty Years War on the side of its Habsburg cousins, which allowed Portugal to revolt against Spanish rule in 1640 and regain its independence. The northern Spanish province of Catalonia revolted the same year, a war that dragged on for fifteen years, though ultimately Spain recovered the province. Spain and France continued fighting after the Peace of Westphalia, with Spain eventually compelled to give up large territories to France.

In recent years, historians have emphasized that the decline of Spain from its sixteenth-century heights of power was not as uniform as earlier historians had held. Philip III was long criticized for ruling through royal favorites and officials, but this may have represented his recognition of the realities of governing a huge and far-flung empire, rather than being simply a sign of weakness or incompetence. The establishment of the Bourbon dynasty with Philip V (ruled 1700–46) did lead Spain to become a fully unified country, with its capital in Madrid. In the middle of the eighteenth century Charles III (ruled 1759–88) began a few programs of reform, which stabilized the economy somewhat and reduced government debt. Population and industry grew, especially in rural areas away from the capital. These measures were opposed by the nobility and the church, however, and this opposition combined with further involvement in wars abroad meant that government finances remained chaotic.

Portugal was under Spanish Habsburg rule from 1580 to 1640, when opposition led to the proclamation of an independent Portuguese monarchy under John IV (ruled 1640–56). He left several sons, the younger of whom, at nineteen, ousted his older brother in a coup, ruling as regent until the older brother died in prison, when he took over officially as Peter II (ruled 1683–1706). Because of the rather questionable way he had come to the throne, Peter shared power with the high nobles, whose support he needed; he also made strategic marriage alliances with many of Europe's ruling houses. Portugal became involved in the War of the Spanish Succession, during which parts of the country were left in ruins, but otherwise largely stayed out of international conflicts. During the long reigns of John V (ruled 1706–50) and Joseph I (ruled 1750–77), Portugal benefited from gold flowing in from Brazil. The kings built churches and palaces in imitation of Louis XIV, and brought in a series of reforming ministers. After the city of Lisbon was devastated by an earthquake in 1755, the most dynamic of those ministers, Sebastião José de Carvalho e Melo (1699–1782), usually known as the marquis de Pombal, consolidated his power in the interests of centralized control and sounder economic policies. He limited the independent power of the nobility and greatly reduced the power of the church in both Portugal itself and its empire. He dramatically shrank the Inquisition, and in 1759, under Pombal's direction, Portugal and its colonies expelled the Jesuits.

British Isles	France	Spain	Portugal
1603–25 James VI/I	1589–1610 Henry IV	1598–1621 Philip III	1598–1621 Philip II
1625–49 Charles I	1610–43 Louis XIII	1621–65 Philip IV	1621–40 Philip III
1649–60 Interregnum	1643–1715 Louis XIV		1640–56 John IV
1660–85 Charles II		1665–1700 Charles II	1656–67 (1683) Alfonso VI
1685–8 James II			
1688–1702 William and Mary			(1667) 1683– 1706 Peter II
1702–14 Anne		1700–46 Philip V	1706–50 John V
1714–27 George I	1715–74 Louis XV	1746–59 Ferdinand I	
1727–60 George II		1759–88 Charles III	1750–77 Joseph I
1760–1820 George III	1774–92 Louis XVI	1788–1808 Charles IV	1777–1816 Maria I

Fig. 21. Rulers of western Europe, 1600–1789.

The British Isles

In 1603, Queen Elizabeth died after ruling for almost fifty years, and the English throne was inherited by her distant cousin James Stuart (1566–1625), the son of Mary Queen of Scots, who had already been king of Scotland for thirty-five years. James had come to the Scottish throne as an infant, and had been raised by advisors who accepted Calvinist theology and supported the Scottish Presbyterian church structure, in which power was held by elected councils, called presbyteries, rather than by appointed bishops. He gained an excellent education, but also developed a strong sense of the divine right of kings; as we saw above, in a speech to the English Parliament shortly after he assumed the throne, James described himself as their "natural father," responsible only to God. His audience in Parliament, especially the House of Commons, did not agree. During Elizabeth's reign, they had gone beyond discussing and approving taxes to raising other issues of policy, and they were clearly not willing to accept any lessening in their role.

James inherited Elizabeth's problems, but boasted none of her tactical political skills. Like all early modern monarchs, Elizabeth used patronage very lavishly, rewarding favorites with positions and offices – and often the income that went with them – for their service. Those who hoped for advancement flocked to London and to the court in the same way French aristocrats later would to Versailles. Patronage seekers included some of the great nobles, who held seats in the House of Lords, but also the lower-level nobility – what in England are usually termed "gentry" – and wealthy merchants and professionals, all of whom were represented in the House of Commons. In contrast to France and Spain, English nobles and gentry did not look down on commercial ventures, and they were not tax-exempt. Both gentry and urban merchants gained economically from England's overseas trade, and also invested in new commercial ventures at home, gradually gaining more land and wealth than the high nobility. Members of the House of Commons were better educated as well as wealthier by the seventeenth century, and they were intent on making sure that they had a voice in determining the taxes they were obliged to pay and other matters of public policy.

Some of the gentry and many urban residents, especially in London, were also dissatisfied with the Church of England established by Henry VIII and affirmed by Elizabeth. They thought that the church, with its hierarchical structure of bishops and elaborate ceremonies, was still too close to Roman Catholicism, and they wanted to "purify" it of what they saw as vestiges of Catholicism. These "Puritans," as they became known, had become increasingly vocal toward the end of Elizabeth's reign, and they expected James, who had been raised in Presbyterian Scotland, to support them. Instead he viewed the hierarchy of bishops as a key support for royal power, stating flatly, "no bishop, no king."

The war with Spain had left England deeply in debt at James's accession, and the struggle to pay off these debts gave the House of Commons the leverage it needed to expand its powers. The first three decades of the seventeenth century saw a running battle between the Commons and the king. The Commons gradually gained the right to discuss foreign policy as well as taxation, and refused to approve the union of Scotland and England. These disputes continued under James's son, Charles I (ruled 1625–49), and in 1629 Charles dissolved Parliament and resolved to rule on his own. He financed his government by expanding existing taxes in ways that most people considered illegal, such as charging inland areas as well as port cities special "ship money" for defense. His archbishop of Canterbury, William Laud (1573–1645), tried to force all English churches to adopt more elaborate ceremonies and services or risk punishment through a newly established "Court of High Commission."

Laud's measures were deeply unpopular in many parts of England, but he provoked even greater opposition when he tried to introduce a new prayer book in Scotland, where the church had been Calvinist in theology for more than seventy-five years. The Scots revolted and invaded England, and in 1640 Charles was forced to call Parliament to pay for an army to fight the Scots. This Parliament, called the "Long Parliament" because it met for thirteen years, was dominated by men with long-standing grievances against the king, and refused to trust him with an army without drastically limiting his power to use that army. It passed an act ruling that the king had to call Parliament at least once every three years, and prohibiting any king from dissolving a Parliament without its approval. It abolished the Court of High Commission and other separate royal courts, and impeached Archbishop Laud. It discussed depriving the bishops of their votes in the House of Lords, and even doing away with the episcopal structure completely. Charles met these demands, as he was faced with both the Scottish invasion and a rebellion in Ireland, in which English Catholics often joined with their Gaelic co-religionists against Protestant Scottish and newer English immigrants. Some members of the House of Commons wanted to go further, however, and give Parliament control over the army, the church, and the appointment of all judges and officials. Charles refused, and also maneuvered to take back some of the measures he had already agreed upon. He began to recruit a separate army from among the nobility and gentry who were loyal to him, and gradually the country split into two camps: the parliamentarians and the royalists, with some moderates in between. England headed toward civil war in what would be the only full-scale revolution in Europe in the seventeenth century.

Looking back at this dramatic period of English history, historians have tried to determine what would make people join one side or the other. The lines were often confusing, but there are some definite trends. Religion was a major factor; in general, Puritans seeking further reformation of the Church of England were parliamentarian, though there were also some Puritans who supported the monarchy. Many people worried that the king planned to return the country to allegiance to Rome. Region also played a role; the south and east of England, including the city of London, tended to support Parliament, while the north and west backed the king. This meant that the more cosmopolitan, richer, and densely populated parts of the country opposed the king. Parliamentarians were also somewhat older; they nostalgically remembered (or imagined) what life had been like under "Good Queen Bess," and thought that the "foreign" Stuarts had broken with these "English" traditions of monarchy. Sometimes the lines reflected local and personal conflicts; as in the Reformation, rivals in various localities took opposing sides, each hoping to gain land or power if the other side lost. Also as in the Reformation – and in later revolutions throughout the world – printed pamphlets whipped up support, with each side portraying the other as foolish or evil. Censorship and other restrictions on publication were not enforced during the chaos of the 1640s, and a wide range of authors took the opportunity to publish political and religious works that might otherwise have been banned.

Those works include many that offered radical plans for change, which were also discussed orally in businesses, houses, and other meeting places. A group who called themselves Levellers, primarily members of the army, advocated abolishing the House of Lords and extending the vote to all adult males, instead of only those with a certain amount of property; this political egalitarianism disturbed most members of Parliament. Radical religious groups such as the Ranters preached that God was in everyone, so that people should listen to the Jesus Christ inside themselves rather than to ministers in church buildings. Under the leadership of George Fox (1624–94) and his wife Margaret Fell Fox (1614–1702), the Society of Friends – called "Quakers" by their detractors because they sometimes shook when "moved by the spirit" – also stressed equality among Christians, going so far as to suggest that women should have the right to preach and minister to others if they had the spirit. All of these ideas were spread by word of mouth, as Quaker preachers and Leveller orators spoke on street corners and town squares, and also communicated through posters, pamphlets, and cheap books.

Fighting began in the summer of 1642, and was generally indecisive for several years. In 1645, Oliver Cromwell (1599–1658), a member of the gentry and a leader in the House of Commons, convinced Parliament to create a completely reorganized army, the New Model Army, with himself in command.

36 Gerrard Winstanley and the True Levellers

Gerrard Winstanley (1609–76) was a laborer and clothing maker who began having religious visions in 1649 telling him that the earth should be held in common. He wrote a series of pamphlets laying out his views, becoming the leader of a community of like-minded people calling for an end to private property. They called themselves True Levellers, though their detractors called them Diggers because they demonstrated their aims in a sort of street theatre, tearing down hedges and digging up fields that had previously been held in common by villages but were now owned by gentry. The True Levellers offered social criticism far more radical than the generally property-owning members of the House of Commons would accept, and they were forced to stop their actions. Winstanley used religious, moral, and political grounds in arguing his ideas:

In the beginning of time the great Creator made the earth to be a common treasury, to preserve beasts, birds, fishes and man, the lord that was to govern this creation . . . Not one word was spoken in the beginning that one branch of mankind should rule over another . . . But selfish imaginations . . . did set up one man to teach and rule over another. And thereby . . . man was brought in to bondage, and became a greater slave to such of his own kind than the beasts of the field were to him. And hereupon the earth . . . was hedged into enclosures by the teachers and rulers, and the others were made . . . slaves. And that earth that is within this creation made a common

storehouse for all, is bought and sold and kept in the hands of a few, whereby the great Creator is mightily dishonored, as if he were a respecter of persons, delighting in the comfortable livelihood of some and rejoicing in the miserable poverty and straits of others. From the beginning it was not so . . . The poorest man hath as true a title and just right to the land as the richest man . . . True freedom lies in the free enjoyment of the earth . . . If the common people have no more freedom in England but only to live among their elder brothers and work for them for hire, what freedom then have they in England more than we can have in Turkey or France? . . . All laws that are not grounded upon equity and reason, not giving a universal freedom to all . . . ought to be cut off with the King's head . . . Wheresoever there is a people . . . united by common community of livelihood into oneness, it will become the strongest land in the world; for then they will be as one man to defend their inheritance . . . Whereas on the other side, pleading for property and single interest divides the people of a land and the whole world into parties, and is the cause of all wars and bloodshed and contention everywhere . . . But when once the earth becomes a common treasury again, as it must . . . then this enmity of all lands will cease.

(From G. H. Sabine, *The Works of Gerrard Winstanley* [Ithaca, NY: Cornell University Press, 1941], pp. 251–4, 288.)

Cromwell whipped the army into a fervor with sermons and hymns, paid it very well, and turned it into a formidable fighting force. Charles was forced to surrender, but the Commons quarreled about what to do next. Cromwell captured the king, and dismissed those members of Parliament who disagreed with him. The remaining members of Parliament (sometimes called the Rump Parliament), abolished the House of Lords, tried Charles for high treason and executed him, to the horror of most of Europe and much of England.

This left Oliver Cromwell master of England, and the army as the most powerful political institution. It passed a constitution, called the Instrument of Government (1653), which made Parliament supreme, but gave Cromwell executive power, with the office of Lord Protector. Cromwell declared that the state of emergency necessitated him having even more power; he dissolved Parliament, proclaimed quasi-martial law, and ruled as virtually a military dictator, dividing the country into twelve districts ruled by major-generals. He was ruthless against the rebellion in Ireland, crushing it and further enhancing Irish hatred of the English; by 1659 Catholics owned less than 10 per cent of the land in Ireland. Officially Cromwell was tolerant in religion (in England), allowing all Protestant Christians the right to worship freely and welcoming Jews back into England after centuries of exclusion, but in practice he enforced measures supported by Puritans, such as closing the theatres and forbidding sports.

Wide discussion of plans for change among radical groups, and other sorts of social turmoil, made Cromwell more intent on maintaining order and control. He banned newspapers, hired innkeepers as spies, and ordered the postal system to open and read all letters. Such measures widened the opposition to his rule, and conspirators gathered around the young Charles, the son of Charles I, who was safely in France. Cromwell appointed his own son Richard – popularly known as "Tumbledown Dick" – as his successor, but after Cromwell's death in 1658 factions were divided about what to do next and Parliament instead backed the restoration of the Stuart monarchy. Most people were weary from years of disruption, and in 1660 Charles returned from France as Charles II. Along with the monarchy, the House of Lords, the established Anglican Church with its hierarchy of bishops, and the courts of law were all restored. Religious dissent was repressed, and those who refused to receive communion in the Church of England could not vote, hold public office, attend university, or preach. Not surprisingly, Charles had good relations with the Parliament that had brought him back; he regained the right to summon Parliament by agreeing to do so regularly. He ruled through a group of advisors who were also members of Parliament. Known as the "Cabal" from the first initials of their names, they formed a group of chief advisors that later came to be called a cabinet of ministers.

In return for having its right to approve taxes assured, Parliament informally agreed to provide Charles with enough revenue to run the kingdom, but it did not, and Charles turned to the wealthiest state in Europe to make up the difference: France. In a secret agreement with Louis XIV, Charles received a huge annual subsidy in return for support against the Dutch, and a promise that he would gradually return England to Catholicism. The treaty did not stay secret for long, and England was swept by anti-Catholic hysteria, made more powerful by the fact that Charles had no legitimate heirs, so that on his death the throne would pass to his openly Catholic brother James. Parliament attempted to pass legislation that would have prevented the throne from going to a Catholic, but this never became law.

James did succeed his brother, appointed Catholics to important positions, and granted religious toleration. There was a renewal in the tug-of-war over the limits of royal and Parliamentary power. When James's second wife gave birth to a son – thus assuring a Catholic dynasty – a group of leaders in the House of Commons offered the throne to James's Protestant daughter Mary and her husband William, a Dutch prince from the House of Orange-Nassau, who also happened to be a grandson of Charles I. In 1688 William invaded England with a small force, James II and his wife and young son fled to France, and Mary and William were named joint rulers by Parliament. They explicitly recognized that sovereignty was shared by monarch and Parliament, and agreed to a Bill of Rights that, among other provisions, forbade royal interference in the making or enforcement of laws and the creation of a standing army during peacetime. They allowed limited religious toleration, though hostility to Catholicism was enshrined in laws that required all future monarchs to be members of the Protestant Church of England, and allowed only Protestants to own firearms.

This coup, bloodless in England though not in Scotland and Ireland, was later called the "Glorious Revolution." It assured the political power of the gentry, that 2 percent of the population perched socially between the tiny group of high nobles and the rest of the population. Despite the restoration of the House of Lords, the House of Commons was the most powerful half of Parliament, and the majority of members were gentry, along with merchants, lawyers, and professionals who often married into gentry families; this small elite controlled England's policies and institutions into the twentieth century. William brought England into various continental alliances against Louis XIV, and the expenses of war led to the establishment of a regular program for paying off the national debt, financed through the Bank of England, which was founded in 1694. Military campaigns included several in Ireland, where the supporters of James II were eventually defeated, and a series of harsh penal laws were enacted against Catholics, further reducing Catholic landhold-ing. William also authorized a massacre of the leaders of one of the Scottish clans, and opposition to English rule in Scotland simmered, though the two countries were officially united in 1707 with the Union of Parliaments, which provided that Scotland would send members to the House of Lords and the House of Commons in London instead of having its own Parliament. (Scotland reestablished a separate representative assembly in 2000.) Scotland, England, and Ireland were declared the "United Kingdom of Great Britain."

William and Mary, who had no surviving children, were succeeded by Mary's sister Anne (ruled 1702–14), who also had no surviving children, despite eighteen pregnancies. At Anne's death, the crown passed, with Parliament's approval, to Anne's distant cousin George, the ruler of the small German principality of Hanover. Groups in Scotland favoring James, the son of James II, who had grown to be a young man in France, revolted. This uprising in favor of the Stuarts – termed "Jacobite" from the Latin form of James's name – was suppressed, as was a similar uprising in 1745 which sought to bring back James's son Charles ("Bonnie Prince Charlie").

The Hanoverians, almost all of whom were named George, ruled Britain into the nineteenth century, with more and more executive power moving into the hands of their chief officials, who came to be called Prime Ministers; in this the model was set by the brilliant Robert Walpole (1676–1745) who was the Prime Minister for both George I and George II. George I (ruled 1714–27) and his son George II (ruled 1727–60) were more interested in Hanoverian interests than British ones, and spent much of their time in military campaigns on the continent. They had difficult relations with one another, though both were competent and pragmatic, allowing the further development of political structures, including rival political parties, the Whigs and the Tories. Toward the end of George II's reign, national policy was directed by William Pitt the Elder (1708–78) who managed British successes in the Seven Years War. Under Pitt's leadership, Britain became the dominant European power in North America and south Asia. Part of British North American holdings were lost in the American War of Independence, but British sea power remained formidable.

The Dutch Republic

The tumultuous nature of England's path to a limited monarchy sometimes benefited its neighbor – and often rival – across the Channel, the Republic of the United Provinces of the Netherlands, the seven northern provinces of the Netherlands that had won their independence from the Spanish Habsburgs in the late sixteenth and early seventeenth centuries. (This long official name is shortened in various ways: the United Provinces, the Netherlands – which means "low countries" – and the Dutch Republic all refer to the same political entity; "Dutch" is a variant of the word "Deutsch," meaning German. This area is also sometimes called "Holland," the name of its westernmost province, whose provincial capital, The Hague, became the capital of the country.) Individuals and groups who opposed Stuart or Cromwellian rule were welcome in the tolerant Netherlands, as were those fleeing religious or political persecution in other parts of Europe. The French philosopher René Descartes lived most of his adult life in the Netherlands, where he felt freer to write and publish than he did in France. The English philosopher John Locke published many of his important works while living in the Netherlands during the 1680s, where he shared the streets of Dutch cities with French Protestants who had left France after Louis XIV had revoked the Edict of Nantes in 1685. Thousands of Jews from the Iberian peninsula, especially from Portugal, emigrated to

Amsterdam, where in the 1670s they built what is still the largest synagogue in the world outside Israel, a beautiful building that is still in use today. All of this immigration dramatically increased the size of Dutch cities – Amsterdam's population grew from 30,000 in 1570 to 200,000 in 1700 – and provided a basis for economic prosperity that was the envy of the world.

Politically, the successful war with Spain left the United Provinces without a clear monarch, and the representative assemblies, called Estates, in each of the seven provinces determined that they liked things this way. They sent representatives to a centralized assembly, the Estates General, which met in The Hague and decided matters of foreign policy and war, though its decisions had to be ratified by each provincial Estate. The Estates General appointed an administrator, called the *stadholder*, for each province. During the seventeenth and eighteenth centuries the same individual was generally chosen as the *stadholder* in all seven provinces, all of them descendants of William the Silent from the house of Orange-Nassau, the nobleman who had led Dutch armies against the Spanish and been assassinated in 1584. This situation might have led to the establishment of a centralized monarchy, but it did not, as real power in both the Estates General and the provincial Estates was held by wealthy merchants and financiers called "regents." The regents resisted any move that would have turned their confederation into a unified state or made the office of *stadholder* more like that of a king. One of these *stadholders*, William III (held office 1672–1702) was the man invited to take over the English throne in 1688, together with his wife Mary, but this brought no major changes in the Dutch political system. William did end a series of commercial wars between the Netherlands and England – instead uniting England and the Netherlands against France – but on his death (with no heirs) the Netherlands simply operated without a *stadholder* for nearly fifty years, with the Estates General making all political decisions.

This political independence was facilitated by amazing commercial prosperity. Even during the Thirty Years War, the Dutch acted as middlemen for trade, especially in raw materials such as grain, metals, and timber from the Baltic, and fish from the Atlantic and Scandinavia. As we saw in chapter 6, the Dutch invented and then mass-produced new types of boats to carry merchandise, developed new types of processes to transform raw materials into finished products, and created new types of financial institutions to handle the money pouring in. All of these ventures could be extremely profitable for merchants, and created a higher standard of living for peasants and artisans in the Netherlands than anywhere else in Europe. Dutch success was often regarded as an enviable mystery by merchants in other parts of the world. By the middle of the seventeenth century, many countries in Europe attempted to exclude Dutch merchants with policies favoring their own ships and traders, including restrictive tariffs, subsidies, prohibitions, and at times outright commercial warfare. Such measures were not initially successful, but gradually Dutch prosperity lessened, particularly with losses of men and money in the War of the Spanish Succession in the early eighteenth century.

Fig. 22. Jan Vermeer's (1632–75) painting of a young woman sipping a glass of wine captures the elegance of a well-to-do Dutch household, with a tapestry tablecloth, a landscape painting in a gilt frame, a stringed cittern on a carved chair, and printed song books. The artist may be providing a bit of social commentary by including the allegorical figure of Temperence – an emblem of moderation – in the ornate stained-glass window.

Dutch achievements were a mystery to contemporaries in other parts of Europe, but historians differ in their explanations of Dutch success. Because the majority of leading regent families were Calvinist, the original explanations linked Dutch successes to Calvinist theology and principles of thrift and frugality. The problem is that the Dutch were hardly thrifty, but spent money on elaborate dinners, imported carpets, brass chandeliers, oil paintings of their families and houses, and (most famously) ever more exotic types of cultivated tulips. Such luxuries were paid for by hard work, however, and accompanied by a sense of social responsibility. The Dutch supported orphanages, hospitals, old-age homes, and almshouses, all directed by boards of men and women from regent families. Spending money on luxuries made in the Netherlands or imported in Dutch ships just returned wealth back into the economy, so that their own willingness to spend explains some of Dutch prosperity. Religious toleration – unique in the Europe of the seventeenth century – explains more of it, as this attracted people and capital to Dutch cities. What we might call "social toleration" also played a role, for it was far easier for successful and intelligent artisans or lesser merchants to rise in stature, gaining local or even provincial offices and marrying into regent families, than it was for commoners in countries of Europe dominated by aristocracies to move into the highest circles of power.

The Ottoman Empire

While Dutch successes provided luxury for some, and decent food, clothing, and housing for most, in eastern Europe only the elites flourished. Most states in eastern Europe were ruled by dynasties that considered their realms as simply large estates to be exploited and expanded, and which were dependent on the higher nobility for money and troops. As we saw in chapter 6, noble landowners reintroduced serfdom in much of eastern Europe in the sixteenth and seventeenth centuries, passed laws that hindered the growth of cities or the development of new forms of production, and maintained their own freedom from taxation and other privileges. Their economic and legal privileges were generally enhanced during the seventeenth and eighteenth centuries by rulers who depended on the nobles to be officers in their growing armies and officials in their expanding bureaucracies. These rulers created absolutist states – most of which lasted until World War I – not by limiting the power of nobles, but co-opting it.

The largest state in eastern Europe in 1600 was the Ottoman Empire, with Istanbul by far the largest city in Europe. (Historical demographers estimate that the two largest cities in the world in 1600 and 1700 were Beijing and Istanbul, both with populations of about 700,000.) Ottoman holdings stretched around the eastern Mediterranean to North Africa and down the Tigris and Euphrates to the Persian Gulf; all of the area around the Black Sea was controlled directly by the Ottomans or by states that paid tribute to the sultan. In theory, Ottoman sultans were absolute monarchs, appointing local leaders, making political decisions, and directing the army and navy. In practice, as the empire grew, more of the day-to-day administration was handled by officials, under the leadership of a grand *vizier*, a position that became heritable. The sultans themselves rarely left their extensive palaces, where they were surrounded by wives, concubines, servants, and officials who followed elaborate rituals in their interactions with the ruler. Complex protocol also marked Louis XIV's court at Versailles, but Louis personally oversaw political and military affairs, whereas most sultans did not, growing ever more distant from the realities of their subjects' lives.

The Ottoman Empire was built through military expansion, and the Janissaries – troops forcibly conscripted from Christian or Muslim families – became increasingly important politically as well as on the battlefield. There was no clear line of succession in Islamic law, so that various sons, nephews, and other male relatives of the ruling sultan might all claim the throne. In early Ottoman practice, many of these royal princes had been given adminis-trative or military positions with real duties, but by the seventeenth century most of them were also more or less imprisoned in the palace, so that they were not prepared for the challenges of rule. The death of every sultan was followed by intrigue and often warfare among claimants to the throne, with each faction backed by powerful Janissaries and officials. The huge bureau-cracy needed to run the enormous empire became increasingly corrupt, with local officials regarding the provinces under their authority as territories to be exploited rather than parts of a whole.

In the fifteenth and sixteenth centuries, the Ottomans developed the most effective army in Europe in terms of both weaponry and supply systems, along with a huge war fleet of armed galleys that controlled the Mediterranean. In the late sixteenth and seventeenth centuries, other European powers built on Ottoman advances, and developed lighter and more mobile field artillery, as well as sailing ships that were faster and sturdier than rowed galleys. Much of the Ottoman fleet was destroyed by a combined fleet of European powers at the Battle of Lepanto in 1571. Though the fleet was rebuilt within a year, and the Ottomans took Tunis in North Africa from the Spanish in 1574, they no longer dominated trade in the Mediterranean, but shared it with Venetian and later Dutch and English merchants.

On land, Ottoman armies were split between fighting the Safavid Empire in Persia to the east and maintaining their hold in Europe. The collapse of the Safavids in the seventeenth century allowed the Ottomans to turn their attention fully to Europe, and they mounted a huge campaign against the Habsburgs, making an alliance with two other Habsburg enemies, Protestant nobles in Hungary and Louis XIV. The Ottomans besieged Vienna in 1683, but German and Polish armies rescued the city, and then continued to push the Ottomans out of most of Hungary and Transylvania (part of present-day Romania). Despite these losses, Janissaries and other officials who dominated the Ottoman court blocked political, military, or economic reforms; tax rev-enues declined, agricultural and technological innovations developed else-where were not adopted, and Ottoman society stagnated.

Habsburg lands

The main beneficiary of the decline of Ottoman power was the Austrian Habs-burg dynasty, which controlled a complex group of territories in central and eastern Europe, some of them within the Holy Roman Empire and some outside it: the German-speaking provinces of Austria, Tyrol, Styria, and several smaller territories, along with Czech-speaking Bohemia, Moravia, and Hungarian-speaking Hungary. The Thirty Years War, much of which was fought on Habsburg lands, left these territories depopulated and impoverished, and made it clear that the Empire would not be united in religion or transformed into a strong state. It also left the Habsburgs in clearer control of many of their holdings, and though they continued to be regularly elected as Holy Roman

Emperors, they concentrated on their own family lands. They expanded their power by imposing new taxes, organizing permanent standing armies, and reducing the power of local nobles or representative institutions. In Bohemia, for example, the native nobility, most of whom were Protestant, were defeated militarily in the Thirty Years War, and the victorious Habsburg rulers gave much of their land to the few Catholic nobles or foreign mercenary commanders. This new nobility helped the Habsburgs centralize their rule, impose harsher controls on peasants, and wipe out Protestantism, the latter with the assistance of Jesuits brought in to open schools. The Habsburgs carried out similar measures in their German-speaking holdings, and then turned to Hungary, the largest of their territories.

Hungary had been divided between the Ottomans and the Habsburgs after the Battle of Mohacs in 1526, but before then it had been an independent state for several centuries. Throughout the period of foreign rule, it maintained a sense of national identity largely centered on its distinctive language. Many Hungarians living under the relatively tolerant Ottomans became Protestant, or even Unitarian, or members of other more radical religious groups. In the late seventeenth century, Habsburg forces drove the Ottomans out of most of Hungary, and attempted to re-Catholicize the whole country and consolidate their rule. Hungarian nobles revolted several times, and in 1703, when the Habsburgs were engaged in the War of the Spanish Succession, they organized a major patriotic uprising under the leadership of Prince Francis Rákóczy II (1676–1735). The rebellion was defeated, but the Habsburgs were forced to allow the Hungarian nobility to retain their traditional privileges, and Hungary did not simply become part of a unified Habsburg state. Except for this, the War of the Spanish Succession was a great boon for the Austrian Habsburgs, who gained the southern part of the Netherlands, along with Spanish Habsburg holdings in Italy, though the latter proved to be temporary.

The Austrian Habsburgs had their own succession problems, however. The Habsburg Emperor Charles VI (ruled 1711–40) had no sons, and imperial law officially prohibited the emperorship passing to a woman. (This law was based on the Salic Law – which also excluded women from the throne of France – believed in the eighteenth century to be an ancient law of the Franks dating from the seventh century. Historians have recently demonstrated that it was concocted much later, when French lawyers sought to exclude both women and heirs who had inherited through the female line during a succession controversy.) Charles issued a Pragmatic Sanction, or imperial decree, allowing his eldest daughter to inherit, and got a number of states within the Empire and most other European countries to agree to this. At his death, however, several of these reneged on their promises and attacked Austria, claiming parts of the territories of his eldest daughter Maria Theresa (ruled 1740–80) in what became known as the War of the Austrian Succession. She was forced to give up the province of Silesia to a new power on the scene, Prussia, but was recognized as the legitimate ruler of Austria, Bohemia, and Hungary. Her husband, Francis I of Lorraine, became the emperor, an office that later passed to their son, who became Emperor Joseph II (ruled 1765–90). Maria Theresa and Joseph II further

Sweden	Denmark/ Norway	Poland	Austrian Habsburgs	Russia	Ottoman Empire
1604–11 Charles IX	1588–1648 Christian IV	1587–1632 Sigismund III	1576–1612 Rudolf II	1598–1605 Boris Godunov	1595–1603 Mehmet III
1611–32 Gustavus Adolphus		1632–48 Vladislav VII	1612–19 Matthias	1605–13 Time of Troubles	1603–17 Ahmed I
1632–54 Christina			1619–37 Ferdinand II	1613–45 Michael Romanov	1617–18 1622–23 Mustapha I
1654–60 Charles X	1648–70 Frederick III	1648–68 John II Casimir	1637–57 Ferdinand III	1645–76 Alexis I	1618–22 Osman II 1623–40 Murad IV
1660–97 Charles XI	1670–99 Christian V	1669–76 Michael Wisniowiecki	1658–1705 Leopold I	1676–82 Theodore III	1640–8 Ibrahim I 1648–87 Mohamed IV
1697–1718 Charles XII		1674–96 John III Sobieski		1682–9 Ivan V	1687–91 Suleiman I 1691–5 Ahmed II
1718–20 Ulrika	1699–1730 Frederick IV	1697–1733 Augustus II	1705–11 Joseph I	1689–1725 Peter I	1695–1703 Mustapha II
1720–51 Frederick			1711–40 Charles VI	1725–27 Catherine I 1727–30 Peter II	1703–30 Ahmed III 1730–54 Mahmud I
	1730–46 Christian VI	1734–63 Augustus III		1730–40 Anna	1754–57 Osman III
1751–71 Adolphus Frederick	1746–66 Frederick V		1740–80 Maria Theresa	1741–62 Elizabeth	1757–74 Mustapha III
1771–92 Gustavus III	1766–1808 Christian VII	1764–95 Stanislas Poniatowski	1765–90 Joseph II	1762–96 Catherine II	1774–89 Abdul Hamid I

Fig. 23. Rulers of northern, eastern, and central Europe, 1600–1789.

strengthened the centralized bureaucracy, reformed the tax system so that even nobles had to pay some taxes, and limited the independent power of the papacy in Austria.

Brandenburg-Prussia

The combatants in the War of Austrian Succession, and the subsequent Seven Years War in which Austria tried unsuccessfully to regain Silesia, involved some countries that had been major powers in Europe for centuries, but also one that was quite new: Brandenburg-Prussia. In the fifteenth century, two branches of the Hohenzollern family ruled various scattered territories in the northern part of central and eastern Europe, the largest of which were Brandenburg – officially called an "electorate" because its ruler was one of the seven people who elected the Holy Roman Empire – and Prussia, a duchy on the Baltic that had earlier been ruled by the Teutonic Knights. These two states were separated from one another by part of Poland, and other Hohenzollern holdings were even more distant. Brandenburg was poor, and its population was devastated in the Thirty Years War. During the course of the war the Elector of Brandenburg inherited Prussia and the rest of the Hohenzollern holdings when one branch of the family died out, and toward the end of the war this office passed to the very talented Frederick William (ruled 1640–88).

Frederick William, dubbed the "Great Elector," and his successors, who had themselves crowned kings of Prussia starting in 1701, followed a distinctive path toward building an absolutist nation-state. Frederick William forced the Estates of his various territories to grant him permanent taxation rights, promising in return that the nobles who dominated the Estates would be free to deal with their peasants as they wished and pay lower taxes. (The latter promise was broken by his successors.) He used the money to build a huge army, in which soldiers also served as tax-collectors and policemen, so that any opposition to his measures was easily crushed. He steadily increased taxation to pay for the army, and supported measures that would improve the tax base, such as encouraging industry. Prussia learned from the experience of the Netherlands about the economic benefits of religious toleration, so welcomed French Huguenots and other refugees, many of whom became soldiers in the Prussian army.

Frederick William's grandson, also named Frederick William (ruled 1713–40) took devotion to the army to new heights. He always wore a military uniform, and surrounded himself with a platoon of very tall soldiers, who were recruited by his agents from throughout Prussia and elsewhere in Europe, sometimes by force. He drilled troops himself, and was fanatically obsessed with discipline, beating soldiers who did not meet his standards. His troops became the terror and the model for those in other countries, so feared for their skills that Frederick William actually needed to use them relatively rarely, accomplishing more of his objectives by diplomacy than force. Frederick William expected martial values to shape all of Prussian society, not just the army, autocratically demanding the obedience "with life and limb, with house and wealth, with honor and conscience" of his subjects. He supported compulsory primary education and broadened technical training because these would provide better soldiers, and rewarded officials who were efficient with high positions, even if they were commoners. He did not neglect the nobles, called *Junkers*, giving those who supported him positions as officers in the army, where they would have nearly absolute control over their soldiers in the same way as they did over the peasants on their estates. Prussian society in and out of the army became highly disciplined, with obedience and order the most prized virtues.

Frederick William's son Frederick II ("the Great") built on his father's example in many ways, further expanding education, demanding honesty and hard work of his officials, promoting improvements in agriculture and industry, and personally leading his troops. He used the huge Prussian army more than his father had, doubling the population of the country by taking Silesia from Austria, and warding off attempts by the combined forces of France, Austria, and Russia to conquer Prussia during the Seven Years War.

Sweden and Poland

Prussian success at creating a strong state depended on a line of soldier-kings, and for a brief period Sweden under the Vasa dynasty – which also ruled Finland – followed this pattern as well. Gustavus Adolphus, the most dynamic of these kings, came to the throne as a teenager, when Sweden was fighting Denmark, Poland, and Russia. He was largely victorious in these wars, gaining control of a number of Polish and Russian ports and dominating trade in the Baltic. He created a more systematic bureaucracy, opened primary and secondary schools supported by the government, and promoted trade and shipping. After significant victories by the emperor's forces, Gustavus Adolphus entered the Thirty Years War on the side of the Protestants, pressing all the way into southern Germany with his troops, some of whom had been forcibly conscripted in what was Europe's first nationwide draft. He died on the battlefield, but his very able chancellor Axel Oxenstierna (1583–1654) kept command of the army, and Sweden gained a huge amount of territory, becoming the most powerful state in northern Europe, despite the fact that the population of Sweden itself was tiny, only a million in comparison with France's twenty million.

Gustavus Adolphus paid for his wars by selling royal lands to wealthy nobles, though this was a short-sighted solution, as it made the land tax-free. Nobles also received salaries or pensions for serving as army officers, and after the king's death, they asserted their power and privileges. Swedish political history for the next two hundred years saw a series of such noble bids for power, alternating with periods in which kings tried to become absolutist on the French or Prussian model. What made the Swedish case distinctive was the fact that peasants were also active players in this struggle. In the later seventeenth century, Swedish kings forced the higher nobility to give back about half the land they had bought, and then sold it to peasants and lesser nobles, making it taxable. These groups then provided support for the monarch in his moves to assert more centralized control, at least until King Charles XII (ruled 1697–1718), led an army against the Danes, Poles, and Russians in the Great Northern War. Defeated as much by the Russian winter as by actual battles, as Napoleon and Hitler later would be, Sweden lost all of its Baltic possessions. Charles escaped to Istanbul, where he spent several years trying, unsuccessfully, to make an alliance with the Ottomans. On finally returning to Sweden he was shot in the head, perhaps by one of his own troops.

The assassination of Charles XII ushered in what Swedish historians call the "Age of Freedom," a fifty-year period in which the Swedish national assembly, called the *Riksdag*, ruled the country. The *Riksdag* was the only assembly in Europe that included a house with peasant representatives, though the nobles, clergy, and townsmen who made up the other three houses were suspicious of the peasants and often held secret meetings that excluded them. This was a prosperous period economically for Sweden, and the *Riksdag* encouraged science and manufacturing; in 1731 it chartered the Swedish East India Company to expand trade with China and Southeast Asia. Disastrous losses in still more wars, however, first against Russia and then Prussia, provided an opportunity for a reassertion of royal control. Gustav III (ruled 1771–92) restored absolutist government in 1772 with a *coup d'état*, throwing the leaders of the *Riksdag* in prison. Gustav also died by assassination, his successor was forced to abdicate after military losses, and the Swedish nobility chose the next several kings, much as the English gentry had engineered the choice of monarchs several times in the seventeenth century. By this point Sweden had lost Finland and all of its other Baltic territories to Russia, and was no longer a major power; the Swedish East India Company went bankrupt in 1813.

Poland experienced similar struggles between the nobles and the kings for political dominance, but here the noble class, called the *szlachta* (pronounced shlahta), was completely successful. In the sixteenth century, the *szlachta* affirmed its right to elect the kings of Poland, and throughout much of the seventeenth century it elected younger members of the Vasa family who had married into the existing Polish dynasty and whose older brothers or cousins ruled Sweden. The seemingly endless wars between Poland and Sweden were thus due in part to family jealousies and conflicts. Warfare in the seventeenth century was generally disastrous for Poland, which lost the Baltic areas to Sweden and the Ukraine to Cossacks, cavalry warriors who lived in independent self-governing communities north of the Black Sea, many of them former serfs who had fled Russia. The Cossacks – the word comes from the Turkish word for robber or adventurer – used the opportunity to murder tens of thousands of Jews, asserting the Jews were agents of Polish oppression. Under the leadership of an able military leader elected king, John III Sobieski (ruled 1674–96), Polish troops were key to the defeat of the Ottomans outside Vienna, but Sobieski could not use these military successes to obtain more power for the monarchy or to reform the way the Polish parliament (*sejm*) operated. The *sejm* itself was paralyzed by the practice of the *liberum veto*, which allowed a single member to defeat any measure.

The eighteenth century saw a string of devastating wars on Polish soil, some involving foreign combatants and others primarily civil wars, with foreign powers intervening on the side of one faction or another. Between 1768 and 1772, Russian armies won a series of victories against the Turks, which alarmed Austria, which began making preparations to invade Russian-held territory.

37 The memoirs of Jan Pasek

Jan Chryzostom Pasek (1636?–1701) was a member of the Polish lower nobility and an army officer who fought in wars against Sweden and Muscovy in the 1650s and 1660s. Toward the end of his life, he began composing memoirs in which he always portrayed himself as the hero; they provide dramatic stories about battles, but also small details about the realities of military life, including the importance of horses and of maintaining social distinctions. This is from a description of one battle with Muscovite troops near Minsk in 1660.

Our army set forth, with God as our aid, in order to gain an early start at this play. On this march, everyone performed his own devotions – songs, hours [prayers to the Virgin Mary]; our chaplains, riding on horseback, heard confessions. Everyone was making himself as ready as he could for death . . . Just opposite our right flank at the crossing was a manorial farm, stockaded; Muscovy, anticipating we would try our luck there, had garrisoned within several hundred foot [-soldiers] with four small cannons. They concealed themselves until we were struggling out of that marshland onto solid ground; only then did the Muscovite infantry move out. Now do they give fire, now do they scorch us from the cannons, balls fly like hail, felling many of our men; others are shot down by musketfire. Nevertheless, we charged them at full tilt, knowing we had to unless all were to perish, should we turn our backs. And now, having jostled blindly into the fire, we mingled with them like wheat and chaff, for there was little else to do.

Then did a fierce massacre take place in that crush; the worst were the battleaxes. Yet a quarter of an hour did not go by, from the moment we tangled with them, before we had slain them all, so that not a single one escaped, we being in the open field; there were 100 corpses it was said. Our men also suffered, some were killed, some wounded; my bay [horse] was shot in the chest under me, smashed in the head with a battleaxe, another time in the knee. I would have used him still, if not for that knee-wound. Such luck I had with horses in the army, that I can't recall ever selling one, after having paid dear for him; every one of them was either injured, or died, or was killed; this ill-luck drove me from the army. For I would be a soldier now, and would have been all this time, except that my father no longer had the means wherewith to buy horses, and I, too, was disgusted by this ill-luck; many a time I'd shed tears over it. I changed mounts then, switching to my grey horse, having bid my retainer [i.e. the servant who accompanied him] who was riding it, to wander back on foot across the river; but he soon overtook me, riding a captured horse, a better one than that upon which I was seated . . . the mercenary cavalry opened heavy fire on us, whereas our men fired back seldom, having already used up their charges on the infantry; besides, we lacked the time to reload. Thus, I always say that a loaded musket is most useful while advancing on the enemy, but once armies are locked in combat, reloading can but seldom be accomplished – the saber's the main thing here. Only sabers are effective when it's man against man, this one against that, that one against this . . . Now we were slaughtering them like sheep. Had I but one retainer with me then, he could have had his choice of the handsomest steeds, for the superior officers were being cut down, and whatever was elegant was on horseback. What can you do if your rascal of an attendant is most alert when his master is at the bottle, but nowhere to be seen when in battle! Nor is it very much in style for a cavalier to be holding the reins of a second horse; if there is no one around to hand it to, then he who values his dignity will prefer not to take it at all.

(From *Memoirs of the Polish Baroque: The Writings of Jan Chryzostom Pasek, A Squire of the Commonwealth of Poland and Lithuania*, ed. and trans. Catherine S. Leach [Berkeley: University of California Press, 1976], pp. 67, 68, 69, 71. Reprinted with permission.)

Fearing a resumption of Europe-wide fighting just five years after the treaty that ended the Seven Years War, Frederick the Great of Prussia proposed that instead of gaining land from the Ottoman Empire, Russia should be given part of Poland. This expansion of Russian holdings would be balanced by similar expansions in Prussia and Austria, as they also would take parts of Poland. The deal was agreeable to all three powers, and Poland lost half its population in this partition, with the Polish king and parliament unable to do anything about it. Political reforms and national revolutions were also unable to stop two further partitions in 1793 and 1795, and Poland disappeared from the map of Europe.

Russia

By the eighteenth century, the map of Europe, as well as people's mental understanding of "Europe," included a large space for Russia. Ivan IV ("the Terrible"), who ruled for fifty years in the middle of the sixteenth century, used special black-clad troops to arrest and kill hundreds of high nobles (called "boyars") and their families and servants. He confiscated their estates and gave about half the land to lower-level "service nobility" who had shown their loyalty to him; the rest he reserved as his personal domain, called the *oprichnina*. These new nobles, and Ivan himself, increased the demands on the serfs bound to their estates, which drove many to flee to the thinly populated areas on the borders of Ivan's ever-expanding state, where they joined Cossack groups. Ivan's autocracy extended to trade and industry, as he and subsequent rulers turned mines, commercial activities, and production into royal monopolies, which kept cities small and prevented the type of commercial expansion that was enriching urban residents in London and Istanbul.

Ivan's death was followed by a period of social unrest the Russians called the "Time of Troubles," which saw various factions fighting and murdering to gain the throne, a series of pretenders claiming to be one or other of the murdered princes, the Polish occupation of Moscow, and revolts by Cossacks and peasants. Boyars and service nobility met together in a national assembly (*zemski sobor*) and elected a grandnephew of Ivan, Michael Romanov (ruled 1613–45), as tsar, establishing a dynasty that would rule until the Russian Revolution in the early twentieth century. The *zemski sobor* did not use this opportunity to limit royal power, however, the way the Polish *sejm* did when electing kings, or as the English Parliament would do later in the century when it brought in William and Mary. Michael was not especially capable, but his advisors were very skillful at winning the allegiance of the nobles by granting them still further privileges at the expense of the peasants and townspeople. In 1649, the nobles agreed to a new code of law that completely bound the serfs to the land. Through diplomacy and annual payments, Michael's advisors were even able to make an alliance with the Ukrainian Cossacks, who became loyal troops in the tsar's army and played an important role in expanding the authority of the tsar, especially in Siberia. In 1670–1, nobles and Cossacks aided the tsar in defeating a major peasant rebellion, though this was led by poorer Cossacks who had not benefited from the tsar's arrangements. After this, the tsars felt strong enough not to bother calling the *zemski sobor* again.

Disputes between heirs to the throne might have plunged Russia into a second time of troubles in the 1680s, but an unusual arrangement of two young half-brothers sharing the throne, guided by their older sister, averted this. The youngest of those brothers was Peter I, who in 1689, at age seventeen, dismissed his sister and half-brother and took over personal rule. Peter determined to make Russia even larger and stronger than it was, and decided the best way to do this was through war; Russia was at war on one or more of its borders every year of Peter's reign except one. As a boy, Peter studied western technology and warfare, and as a young man – after he had already fought major battles against Ottoman holdings on the Black Sea – he traveled to European cities to gain a better understanding of production processes and to make allies. The story told later was that he traveled incognito, but it is difficult to imagine how a six foot seven Russian accompanied by 250 officials could have blended into the streets of London or Amsterdam. He did travel without the normal ceremonies that would have interfered with his actually learning anything, however, and he returned home full of plans.

Seeking to gain a port on the Baltic, in 1700 Peter ordered an attack on Sweden, also ruled by a teenaged king, Charles XII. The well-disciplined Swedish army quickly defeated Russian troops, and Peter immediately began a drastic program to reorganize and modernize the army. He promoted anything that would enhance military effectiveness. Following the Swedish model, he introduced conscription, but on a huge scale. All nobles, whether *boyar* or service nobility, would be required to serve for life in the army or the government bureaucracy. Hundreds of thousands of peasants were also drafted for life, to serve as the footsoldiers who would be the core of this huge army. Thousands of other peasants were drafted to work in mines and factories, producing cannon, uniforms, muskets, wagons, and anything else the army needed. On the land, peasants were required to plant new crops that could feed soldiers and themselves, especially potatoes. War requires money, so Peter tripled taxation, spending, as Louis XIV had, at least three-quarters of all revenues on war. Effective war requires technically competent troops and well-trained leaders, so Peter opened schools and universities. He brought in Dutch, German, English, and French experts to provide advice on technology and tactics, and hired Western architects to design a new capital where the Neva River empties into the Baltic. This city, which he named – unsurprisingly – St. Petersburg, was also built with conscripted labor; historians estimate that it took hundreds of thousands of laborers to build its streets, canals, houses, bridges, palaces, churches and fortresses in the swamps and marshes of the Neva. Western ideas trickled into Russia with these more frequent contacts, but only to a small group of educated nobles. For the vast majority of Russians, Peter's moves only enhanced their misery.

Seen in the light of his own aims, Peter's autocratic reforms were effective. Russian troops defeated the Swedes in later battles, gaining large areas along the Baltic, and later in the eighteenth century they took the north coast of the Black Sea and much of Poland, building a large navy to defend their holdings. Peter's placement of talented foreigners in positions of authority eventually reached levels that even he had not anticipated, however. His daughter Elizabeth (ruled 1741–62) married her weak and stupid son Peter to a German princess from a tiny principality, whose mother was loosely related to the Romanovs. On converting to Russian Orthodoxy, the princess took the name Catherine, studied Russian and French, and won powerful allies at court, including her noble lover Gregory Orlov and his officer brothers. Her husband became tsar as Peter III (ruled 1762), and his admiration for Frederick the Great led him to call off the Russian attack on Prussia. This was all the pretext Catherine and the Orlovs needed, and they had Peter arrested; the Orlovs killed him, and Catherine became ruler. A serious revolt by the Cossacks under the leadership of Emelian Pugachev in 1773–5 led Catherine to conclude that reforms were needed to strengthen the role of royal officials in the provinces, improve agriculture, and enhance civil order, and she issued a series of new laws, which later commentators dubbed "legislomania."

Catherine – later, like Peter, called "the Great" – could have read the works of Bishop Bossuet in their original French, and believed as firmly as he had a hundred years earlier in the divine, absolute, and paternal nature of royal authority. (She understood "paternal" to include female rulers who looked after their subjects as good parents cared for their children.) Her understanding of reason – Bossuet's fourth ground for supporting the rule of kings – was quite different than his, however, for the intervening century had seen writers, thinkers, and intellectuals debating the role of reason in all areas of life, not just politics. Catherine corresponded directly with many of these thinkers, invited them to her court, and sent them money. They in turn praised her as "enlightened," a word they used for themselves, and an increasingly important standard among educated Europeans for viewing and judging the world in the eighteenth century, as we will see in the next chapter.

Catherine was not the only ruler to consider herself, or be considered, "enlightened." Beginning in the 1760s, rulers in Russia, Prussia, Austria, Spain, Sweden, and some of the smaller states in Germany and Italy began programs of reform that were based in part on the desire to continue concentrating authority in their own hands and expanding the military might and economic base of their states, but also on a desire to improve the lives of their subjects. They increasingly regarded these aims as integrally related.

The reforms of "enlightened" monarchs shaped many realms of life. In government and administration, they often reorganized bureaucracies in an attempt to make them more coherent and speed up the implementation of state policy. Many of them set up an examination system for civil servants, so that at least some state offices were held by men who had obtained them through their merits and abilities rather than simply purchasing them. They tried to unify and codify the body of laws in their dominions and make the judicial process shorter and simpler. The use of judicial torture was restricted, and cruel methods of execution such as death by drowning were abolished, though penalties for crimes remained harsh; in fact, those for property crimes such as theft grew harsher, sometimes involving deportation or hard labor in a workhouse.

In economics, enlightened rulers developed protectionist policies in regard to imports and invested in some industries, with an eye to building up the manufacturing capacity of their own states. They tried to reduce the ability of independent groups such as guilds to regulate production, or of cities or provinces to charge tolls on trade within the country. They were very concerned about agriculture, promoting projects that would increase the amount of land under cultivation or introduce new crops, such as the potato. They tried to reform the tax structure; in many places this meant taxing the clergy or taking over church lands. Occasionally they even taxed the nobility, though this generally happened only as a last resort, not as a matter of policy. They supported the establishment of schools, especially those that were oriented toward vocational and technical education, though they also supported elementary schools that taught basic reading and writing; the first legislation regarding compulsory schooling in Europe was in Prussia in 1763. Rulers also supported institutions that cared for orphans, invalids, the elderly, and military veterans, and tried to curtail the harassment of peasants by their landlords. They generally did not end serfdom as a labor system, but attempted to limit those aspects that reduced agricultural productivity or made peasants completely unfit for military service. In the 1780s Joseph II of Austria-Hungary did abolish serfdom, though the obligations of the peasants to their landlords – which were primarily paid in cash by this point, not labor services – were simply transformed into tax obligations to the state.

State-sponsored schools competed with those of the church, and rulers limited the independent powers of the church in other ways as well. In Catholic countries, rulers asserted greater control of church appointments or restricted the special privileges of the clergy, such as being tried for crimes in separate courts. In Austria, Joseph II dissolved many of the monasteries, arguing that their residents were idle parasites, and that their property would be better used to support secular schools and charitable institutions. In many countries, rulers abolished the Jesuit order. Religious minorities were accorded at least limited formal toleration, which was even extended to Jews in some places at the very end of the century. Such measures were often financially advantageous, as they boosted the economy by encouraging the immigration of skilled workers. They were also a clear sign that the church was to be simply one institution among many whose purpose was to support the state, not a separate body with powers that rivaled those of the ruler.

Late-eighteenth-century absolutist rulers were better able to achieve their aims than those a century earlier, though their plans still far exceeded their abilities to bring them about. In their reforms, enlightened rulers were motivated by humanitarian concerns about the welfare of their subjects, but even more by pragmatic considerations about the strength of the state as a military and economic unit and the preservation of the political integrity of monarchical absolutism. They did not see these goals as antithetical, however, but as closely linked, for healthy, prosperous, contented subjects would work more, have more children, and be able to pay more taxes. Louis XIV may have understood himself to *be* the state, and certainly thought that he ruled by divine right. Frederick II of Prussia declared that he was simply "the first servant of the state," whose power was justified by the well-being of his subjects. Neither Louis nor Frederick expected their subjects to disagree, but, as we will see in the following chapter, by the last decades of the eighteenth century, some individuals in France and Prussia and other parts of Europe were not so sure that absolutism, or even limited monarchy, could ever truly be "enlightened."

Further reading

Accounts of absolutism and its limitations include William Beik, *Absolutism and Society in Seventeenth-Century France: State Power and Provincial Aristocracy in Languedoc* (Cambridge: Cambridge University Press, 1985); Valerie A. Kivelson, *Autocracy in the Provinces: The Muscovite Gentry and Political Culture in the Seventeenth Century* (Stanford: Stanford University Press, 1996).

Many points of view of the "crisis of the seventeenth century" can be found in Trevor Ashton, ed., *Crisis in Europe, 1560–1660* (New York: Basic Books, 1965), and Geoffrey Parker and Lesley M. Smith, eds., *The General Crisis of the Seventeenth Century*, 2nd edn (London: Routledge, 1997). Theodore Rabb's reconceptualization of the issue is *Struggle for Stability in Early Modern Europe* (Oxford: Oxford University Press, 1975). A very recent collection that returns to these issues is Philip Benedict and Myron P. Gutmann, eds., *Early Modern Europe: From Crisis to Stability* (Dover: University of Delaware Press, 2006).

For discussions of the role of warfare and its funding in the rise of states, see John Brewer, *The Sinews of Power: War, Money, and the English State, 1688–1783* (Cambridge, MA: Harvard University Press, 1990); Charles Tilly, *Coercion, Capital, and European States A.D. 990–1990* (Oxford: Oxford University Press, 1990); Brian M. Downing, *The Military Revolution and Political Change: Origins of Democracy and Autocracy in Early Modern Europe* (Princeton: Princeton University Press, 1992); Rhoads Murphey, *Ottoman Warfare, 1500–1800* (New Brunswick, NJ: Rutgers University Press, 1999); Robert I. Frost, *The Northern Wars: War, State, and Society in Northeastern Europe, 1558–1721* (Harlow, UK: Longman, 2000); H. M. Scott, *The Emergence of the Eastern Powers, 1756–1775* (Cambridge: Cambridge University Press, 2001). The standard account in English of the Thirty Years War is Geoffrey Parker, ed., *The Thirty Years War*, 2nd edn (London: Routledge, 1997).

There are many works on various aspects of the English Civil War. Two examinations of its causes are Christopher Hill, *Intellectual Origins of the English Revolution Revisited*, rev. edn (Oxford: Clarendon Press, 1997), and Ann Hughes, *The Causes of the English Civil War*, 2nd edn (Basingstoke, UK: Palgrave-Macmillan, 1998). David Scott, *Politics and War in the Three Stuart Kingdoms, 1637–1649* (Basingstoke, UK: Palgrave-Macmillan, 2003), provides a good narrative, while Jonathan Scott, *England's Troubles: Seventeenth-Century English Political Instability in European Context* (Cambridge: Cambridge University Press, 2000), examines the impact of events in England on the rest of Europe. Christopher Hill, *The World Turned Upside Down: Radical Ideas during the English Revolution* (New York: Viking Press, 1972), remains the best analysis of all of the radical groups. For later developments, see Eveline Cruickshanks, *The Glorious Revolution* (Basingstoke, UK: Palgrave-Macmillan, 2000), and Gerald Newman, ed., *Britain in the Hanoverian Age, 1714–1837* (New York: Garland, 1997).

On the Netherlands, Jonathan I. Israel, *The Dutch Republic: Its Rise, Greatness and Fall, 1477–1806* (Oxford: Oxford University Press, 1995), is a solid political history, while Simon Schama, *The Embarrassment of Riches: An Interpretation of Dutch Culture in the Golden Age* (New York: Vintage, 1997), looks more broadly at Dutch culture.

General studies of France include William Doyle, ed., *Old Regime France* (Oxford: Oxford University Press, 2001) and Sharon Kettering, *French Society, 1589–1715* (Harlow, UK: Longman, 2001). On the Fronde, the authoritative work is Orest Ranum, *The Fronde: A French Revolution, 1648–1652* (New York: W. W. Norton, 1993). John B. Wolf, *Louis XIV*

(New York: W. W. Norton, 1968), remains the best biography in English of this dramatic monarch. For Spain, see John Lynch, *Bourbon Spain, 1700–1800* (Oxford: Oxford University Press, 1989).

Studies that investigate political changes at a more local level include David Underdown, *Fire From Heaven: Life in an English Town in the Seventeenth Century* (New Haven: Yale University Press, 1992), William Beik, *Urban Protest in Seventeenth-Century France: The Culture of Retribution* (Cambridge: Cambridge University Press, 1997); Wayne te Brake, *Shaping History: Ordinary People in European Politics, 1500–1700* (Berkeley: University of California Press, 1998); John Morrill, *Revolt in the Provinces: The People of England and the Tragedies of War, 1630–1648* (London: Longman, 1999).

For northern and eastern Europe, see D. G. Kirby, *Northern Europe in the Early Modern Period: The Baltic World, 1492–1772* (London: Longman, 1990); Simon Dixon, *The Modernization of Russia, 1676–1825* (Cambridge: Cambridge University Press, 1999); Nancy Shields Kollman, *By Honor Bound: State and Society in Early Modern Russia* (Ithaca, NY: Cornell University Press, 1999); Charles Ingrao, *The Habsburg Monarchy, 1618–1815*, 2nd edn (Cambridge: Cambridge University Press, 2000); Donald Quataert, *The Ottoman Empire, 1700–1922* (Cambridge: Cambridge University Press, 2000); Philip G. Dwyer, ed., *The Rise of Prussia 1700–1830* (Harlow, UK: Longman, 2000).

On enlightened absolutism, John Gagliardo, *Enlightened Despotism* (New York: Harlan Davidson, 1967), remains the standard analysis, while Hamish Scott, ed., *Enlightened Absolutism: Reform and Reformers in Later Eighteenth-Century Europe* (London: Macmillan, 1990), presents a series of essays about different countries. James Van Horn Melton, *Absolutism and the Eighteenth-Century Origins of Compulsory Schooling in Prussia and Austria* (Cambridge: Cambridge University Press, 1988), looks at one area of concern for rulers, while Marc Raeff, *The Well Ordered Police State: Social and Institutional Change through Law in the Germanies and Russia* (New Haven, CT: Yale University Press, 1983), remains an important, and highly critical, analysis of legal changes.

 For more suggestions and links see the companion website www.cambridge.org/wiesnerhanks.

Notes

1 From Richard H. Powers, ed. and trans., *Readings in European Civilization Since 1500* (Boston: Houghton-Mifflin, 1961), pp. 129, 130.

2 Quoted in Steven G. Reinhardt and Vaughn L. Glasgow, eds., *The Sun King: Louis XIV and the New World* (New Orleans: Louisiana State Museum Foundation, 1984), p. 181.

3 Peter the Great, Table of Ranks, quoted in Richard Lim and David Kammerling Smith, *The West in the Wider World: Sources and Perspectives*, vol. II (Boston: Bedford, 2003), p. 100.

4 James I, "Speech of 1609," in *The Political Works of James I*, ed. Charles Howard McIlwain (New York: Russell and Russell, 1965), p. 307.

5 Peter the Great, Decrees on Western Dress and Shaving, 1701 and 1705, quoted in Lim and Smith, *The West*, p. 99.

6 James I, *Political Works of James I*, p. 307.

7 Archives Nationales de France, U793, fo. 88, trans. and quoted in Merry E. Wiesner, Julius Ruff, and Bruce Wheeler, *Discovering the Western Past: A Look at the Evidence*, 5th edn (Boston: Houghton-Mifflin, 2003), p. 332.

10 Cultural and intellectual life, 1600–1789

nubem pellente Mathefi
Clauftra patent cœli, rerumq; immobilis ordo,
Jam fuperùm penetrare domos, atq; ardua cœli
Scandere, fublimis genij conceffit acumen. D'. Hal-
ley.

THE

MATHEMATICAL

PRINCIPLES

OF

Natural Philofophy.

By Sir *ISAAC NEWTON*.

Tranflated into *Englifh* by ANDREW MOTTE.

To which are added,

The Laws of the MOON's Motion, according to Gravity.

By JOHN MACHIN *Aftron. Prof. Grefh*. and *Secr. R. Soc.*

IN TWO VOLUMES.

LONDON:
Printed for BENJAMIN MOTTE, at the *Middle-Temple-Gate*, in *Fleetftreet*.
MDCCXXIX.

The title page and frontispiece illustration of an English translation of Isaac Newton's *Principia*, published in 1729, two years after his death. The illustration shows a man in classical dress seated in the clouds, with the nude figure of a woman holding a compass standing in front of him and the solar system below. Nude women, sometimes explicitly labeled "Nature revealing her secrets," often appear in heroic illustrations of major scientific thinkers or their ideas.

Timeline

1543	Copernicus publishes *On the Revolutions of the Heavenly Bodies*
1610	Galileo publishes *The Starry Messenger*
1620	Bacon publishes *New Instrument*
1635	Académie Française founded
1637	Descartes publishes *Discourse on Method*
1660	Royal Society of London founded
1661	Palace of Versailles begun
1667	Milton publishes *Paradise Lost*
1687	Newton publishes the *Principia*
1748	Montesquieu publishes *The Spirit of the Laws*
1752–72	Diderot and d'Alembert publish the *Encyclopédie*
1759	Voltaire's *Candide* published anonymously
1762	Rousseau publishes *Emile: Or, On Education*
1786	Mozart composes *The Marriage of Figaro*
1789	Lavoisier publishes *Elementary Treatise on Chemistry*

In 1550, the Italian art historian Giorgio Vasari, who coined the word Renaissance, described the painters, sculptors, and architects of his era in a series of biographies as "rare men of genius." One hundred and seventy-five years later, another cultural commentator, the English poet Alexander Pope (1688–1744), extended this judgment to a mathematician and physicist, Isaac Newton (1642–1727), offering a brief couplet as part of the outpouring of eulogies right after Newton's death:

> Nature, and Nature's laws lay hid in night,
> God said *Let Newton be!* and all was *Light.*

Newton himself was not so sure about this, writing in a letter to fellow scientist Robert Hooke in 1675, "If I have seen further [than certain other men] it is by standing upon the shoulders of giants." In terms of intellectual development, the period from Vasari's biographies to Pope's poem is often referred to as the "Scientific Revolution," a phrase invented in the nineteenth century to label this time of change in the way learned individuals approached, conceptualized, and studied the natural world. Like the Renaissance, the Scientific Revolution is not an event with a specific beginning and end, but a series of developments. Whether these changes were as Pope envisioned – sudden bursts of genius that altered everything – or as Newton described them – steady advances that built on earlier ones – is still a matter of debate, however.

Among recent scholars, one of the most influential voices arguing in favor of dramatic change was the philosopher and physicist Thomas Kuhn (1922–96). In *The Structure of Scientific Revolutions* (1962), Kuhn proposed that people studying the natural world (what we would now term scientists) work within a specific world view until there is too much data that contradicts that world view, but no one theory that explains all the contradictions. At that point, someone – often from outside the establishment in which scientists normally work – proposes a radically different world view, what Kuhn calls a "paradigm shift." This new paradigm does not just add to earlier knowledge, but makes people who accept it view the world in a completely new way. Kuhn uses a number of scientific developments from the sixteenth through the eighteenth centuries as examples of such paradigm shifts, the most dramatic of which was the shift from an earth-centered to a sun-centered view of the cosmos. Since then, other historians of science have argued that Kuhn overemphasized big changes. The major thinkers of the Scientific Revolution, they point out, continued to accept many ideas because they appeared in ancient sources, and built on the work of medieval scientists. Kuhn's argument has been very powerful, however, and his phrase "paradigm shift" is now so pervasive in business, government, and other realms of life that it has become a joke, particularly when coupled with "thinking outside the box."

Whether we call it a paradigm shift or not, the idea that there was a radical break in the world view of educated Europeans in the seventeenth and eighteenth centuries is a powerful one, and extends beyond the realm of science. Pope uses the word "light" to praise Newton because many of Newton's discoveries involved light and optics, and because Pope saw him as setting a pattern in which the "light of reason" is used to explore the universe. Thinkers in the eighteenth century described their enterprise as "Enlightenment," whose principles the German philosopher Immanuel Kant (1724–1804) summarized in 1784 in the phrase: "*Sapere aude*! [Dare to know!] Have the courage to use your *own* understanding!"[1]

The Enlightenment was a self-conscious intellectual movement in the same way as the Renaissance had been. Renaissance thinkers envisioned themselves as part of a rebirth of classical culture, while Enlightenment thinkers asserted that knowledge could free them *from* the ancient past. The "light of reason," they argued, could be used against the darkness of prejudice, superstition, blind belief, ignorance, tyranny, and injustice. The classical past was not uniformly rejected, as architects, writers, and even political theorists used Greek and Roman models for their works, but it was to be emulated selectively and deliberately, and not regarded as superior. This questioning of received wisdom extended to the realm of religion, as thinkers challenged the cultural and institutional authority of the Christian churches and criticized many beliefs and practices as "superstition."

Thinkers in the Enlightenment – those in France called themselves *philosophes* – regarded the development of science as one of the most important sources of their own intellectual liberation, and also looked to the writings of several seventeenth-century thinkers who emphasized the role of reason and observation as challenges to received wisdom, including René Descartes and John Locke. They took ideas and methods from the realm of the natural sciences and applied them to the social sciences, seeking to find rules and laws that applied to human beings in the same way that the law of gravity or other of "Nature's laws" applied in the physical world. This search for order did not lead to a single ideology, for there was great diversity of opinion on a range of issues, but general consensus around a set of common values: reason, religious toleration, progress, liberty, utility, and skepticism toward traditions and dogmas.

The Scientific Revolution and the Enlightenment were not the only intellectual and cultural developments in seventeenth- and eighteenth-century Europe, which also saw new forms and themes in art, literature, and music. All of these were supported by the centralizing monarchs we discussed in chapter 9, for intelligent rulers recognized that having educated and talented writers, scientists, philosophers, musicians, and artists at their courts only enhanced their stature. In return for flattering dedications in scientific or philosophical works, defenses of their policies, effusive poems of praise, and larger-than-life individual and family portraits, rulers – and also wealthy churchmen and nobles – provided pensions in cash, positions as tutors, offices at court or ecclesiastical benefices.

Along with this traditional system of patronage, however, new social and cultural institutions developed through which ideas were exchanged, and writers, artists, and thinkers were supported. Some of the institutions were formal, including scientific and literary societies, journals and newspapers, and clubs or lodges that one paid to join. Many of them were more informal, including salons, coffeehouses, and taverns. These new institutions operated outside the traditional intellectual centers of courts, churches, and universities, and created what the German philosopher and historian Jürgen Habermas called the "public sphere," which provided both an audience for new ideas and a place where those ideas were often germinated.

Cultural institutions

The "public sphere" as Habermas envisioned it developed fully in the eighteenth century, but it built on earlier formal and informal groups of people who gathered together to talk, argue, and debate. In the cities of the Italian Renaissance, humanists thought of themselves as belonging to the "Republic of Letters," a phrase they invented that came to mean those who engaged in learned exchange of all types, both oral and written. The most formal of these were learned academies and societies, originally devoted to studying the classics, but by the end of the sixteenth century often with the broader goals of encouraging learned conversation on many topics. Many academies were short-lived private gatherings, but several gained royal patronage and grew into national academies, usually with a very limited number of members. The Académie Française, for example, which focused on French language and culture, was founded in 1635 by Cardinal Richelieu and Louis XIII and still exists today.

During the seventeenth century, academies specifically devoted to the study of nature and science were founded in Rome, Florence, Paris, London, and elsewhere. The Royal Society of London (founded 1660) collected specimens for study, supported experiments using new types of instruments such as the air pump and the barometer, and published reports. The Academy of Science in Berlin, founded in 1700 by the German philosopher and mathematician Gottfried Wilhelm Leibniz (1646–1716) for the Electress Sophie Charlotte, supported astronomical and other types of scientific study. In the middle of the eighteenth century, some new learned societies saw their mission as (in the words of the Royal Dublin Society, founded in 1731) "promoting husbandry, manufactures, and other useful arts." They wanted to apply learning to practical problems and make knowledge available to a broader public, so they published their findings in the vernacular, not Latin.

Learned societies, first in Italy and then elsewhere, put together permanent collections of natural objects: what we would today call museums of natural history but were then usually termed "chambers of wonders" or "cabinets of curiosities." These contained strange things found locally – unusual specimens of plants, animals born with birth defects (preserved in jars or mounted and stuffed), fossils, beautiful geological formations such as geodes – and objects brought in from European voyages around the world. Collections were initially private, but many were gradually opened to the public; as Robert Hooke (1635–1703), the first curator of the collection of the Royal Society in London commented, viewing a collection offered visitors opportunity to "peruse, and turn over, and spell, and read the Book of Nature." As museums do today, the founders of these collections sought wealthy patrons who could provide permanent buildings and the resources to obtain still more objects; Peter the Great amassed a huge collection, specializing in archeological finds from Siberia and central Russia. Along with the "wonders of nature," collections included art and artifacts from Europe's past and from different parts of the world, jumbling together human-produced and natural objects in an effort to awe and astonish. Visitors discussed what they had seen or wrote about it in letters and essays. Some collections issued printed catalogs, so that even those who could not afford to visit could know the wonders they contained. Wealthy young men, especially from England, visited collections as part of their "Grand Tour" of the cultural and intellectual centers of Europe, designed to give them polish and sophistication.

The members of one learned society, the Academy of Linceans (that is, of the lynx), whose most famous member was the Italian scientist Galileo Galilei, decided to make a pictorial record of all of nature. They traveled all over Europe, making drawings of materials in collections. Many of these collections became the foundation of later national museums, and by the last half of the eighteenth century a few of these began organizing their holdings in ways that emphasized the order rather than the exuberance of nature.

Learned societies and museums were only some of the places where discussion flourished in European cities. The Society of Freemasons, a fraternal voluntary association whose exact origins are disputed, established lodges first in England and then on the continent, where members gathered to discuss politics as well as science and learning. In Edinburgh, discussion groups met at the universities, in private homes, and in the city's many taverns – one estimate is six hundred drinking establishments in a town of only forty thousand people. Individuals in Paris established clubs called *musées* in the late eighteenth century, in which people paid a fee to hear lectures, watch or perform scientific experiments, and participate in discussions on a range of issues. Several of these had hundreds of members; fees were too high for artisans or workers, but lawyers, officials, shop-owners, and even a few middle-class women joined. Societies and clubs devoted to "progress" and the "useful trades," and lodges of Freemasons, sprang up in European colonial cities like Philadelphia and Rio de Janeiro as well, whose members were in frequent contact with European thinkers.

Members of these learned societies and others interested in literature and learning discussed their ideas orally or in letters, and by the late seventeenth century circulated them in printed journals, such as Pierre Bayle's *News from the Republic of Letters* (1684). The English journals *The Tatler* (1709–11) and *The Spectator* (1711–12), edited by the playwright Richard Steele and the poet Joseph Addison, had circulations in the tens of thousands, which meant they were read by far more people than just a small elite. They included essays by their editors, commentary on theatrical productions, and a skillful mixture of society news and social criticism. Readers were encouraged to respond, and their letters were printed, so that the circle of authors as well as readers expanded. Similar literary journals appeared later in the eighteenth century in Germany, Italy, and the Netherlands.

In many European states journals and books that included material too critical of the church or the government were often censored or banned, but such efforts were not very effective at limiting the spread of ideas. Philosophical and political works in many languages were published in tolerant Amsterdam or in Switzerland, and then smuggled to eager readers, while works that criticized or satirized political figures and religious authorities were easily available with a word to the right bookseller.

Along with journals, newspapers were an important element in the circulation of ideas. A regular postal service allowed printed publications to be delivered on a set schedule, and the first printed newspaper appeared in Germany in 1605. Newspapers soon appeared in other central and western European countries, and by the eighteenth century there were a few daily newspapers in larger cities, and weekly or twice-weekly papers elsewhere. They were generally sold by subscription, and initially contained little or no advertising, as businesses did not see the point of paying to market their products. Coffeehouses, taverns, wine-shops, and cafés *did* see the point of providing newspapers for their patrons to read, so that a single subscription was often read by many people, provoking animated discussion. Rulers recognized that the press could be a powerful force; they required publishers to get a license, fed information about laws and government activities to them, and routinely censored unflattering news. Besides their local newspapers, educated people often read and discussed international French-language newspapers printed in the Netherlands.

At about the time that national scientific academies were being founded, elite women in Paris created a more informal and private institution that would allow them greater access to the "Republic of Letters" – the salon. Salons were gatherings of men and women for formal and informal discussion of topics decided upon by the women who ran them, held in the drawing rooms (*salons* in French) of their own homes. The *salonnière*, or salon hostess, selected the guests, determined whether the conversation on any particular night would be serious or light, and decided whether additional activities such as singing, poetry readings or dramatic productions would be part of the evening's offerings. She took what she did seriously, preparing herself by reading and practicing letter-writing and conversational skills. *Salonnières* did not have any official public or academic role, but the approval of certain salon hostesses was often an unofficial requirement for a man to gain election to the Académie Française, the highest honor for a French intellectual or writer. (No woman was elected to the Académie Française until 1979, and there were only a handful of women in any European national academy; the first woman was elected as a full member to the British Royal Society in 1935.) Writers such as Jean-Jacques Rousseau (1712–78) warned that salons were "feminizing" French culture and weakening the country's military and work ethic. In the later eighteenth century, salons became important institutions in the development and dissemination of philosophical and political ideas associated with the Enlightenment. They were places where wealthy nobles, professionals, and members of the clergy who were interested in new ideas or cultural forms met less-well-off writers and artists. English and German women also created salons on the French model; those in Germany were one of the few places where Christians and Jews could mix.

Though rulers and church leaders were still important shapers of culture, the institutions of the "public sphere" – learned societies, literary journals, newspapers, salons, and clubs – helped create what we now call "public opinion," a force that became more powerful as the eighteenth century progressed. Public opinion was shaped by the tastes of elites, but also by those of more ordinary people, and increasingly determined which artistic and literary genres and styles would be judged praiseworthy, and which political ideas and plans should be accepted or rejected. Many artists, writers, and composers continued to get commissions from aristocratic patrons, but others depended on selling their work to a middle-class public through galleries, art shops, book stores, or subscriptions. Middle-class urban households often had more disposable income in the eighteenth century than they had had in the sixteenth, and the consumer goods they purchased included books, engravings, paintings, musical instruments, and music to play on them.

The men and women who gathered in societies, academies, clubs, and salons embraced science as well as other interests. Like Pope – who was a favorite of discussion groups in London – they saw new developments in science as a proper basis for all knowledge and something that all educated people should understand. They regularly purchased popularizations of scientific works, which sought to explain both the basis and the impact of new ways of understanding the world.

Ancient authorities and new methods

In the later Middle Ages, learned study of the natural world, usually termed "natural philosophy," had gone on primarily in Europe's universities, where it was seen as an appropriate part of understanding the glory of God. Such study revolved around ancient Greek ideas and texts, particularly those of Aristotle and Ptolemy. Aristotle (384–322 BCE) viewed the cosmos as centered on a motionless earth, with the planets (including the moon and sun) revolving around it in fixed spheres made up of a crystalline substance, and the fixed stars at its outer perimeter. The planets moved, he thought, in exactly circular orbits at a uniform speed, and were perfectly round bodies made of ether, a substance completely different from the four terrestrial elements – earth, air, fire, and water. Above the moon – the heavenly body closest to earth – the cosmos was changeless, so that objects that did change in the skies, such as comets and meteors, must be closer than the moon. Things on earth did change, and each element had a tendency to move in a specific direction; things made primarily of the element earth tended to move toward the center of the earth, while water flowed sideways around the earth and air went upward. The earth was round, the perfectly spherical center of a perfectly spherical cosmos.

There were problems with Aristotle's view. For one, it did not fit with the motions of the planets observable from earth – the planets often appear to move backwards or reverse direction – but this was solved in the second century by Ptolemy (c. 100 – c. 165 CE), a Greek astronomer working at Alexandria. Ptolemy held that the moon, sun, planets, and stars move around the motionless earth at various rates of speed in spiral-like paths he called epicycles. Based on observation, he calculated the epicycles of the major heavenly bodies, and the Ptolemaic system gained wide and long-lasting acceptance.

The rediscovery of Greek writings other than those of Aristotle and Ptolemy led scholars in a different direction. In the fifteenth and sixteenth centuries, the works of Pythagoras (*c*.582 – *c*.496 BCE), Plato (*c*. 428 – *c*. 348 BCE), and Archimedes (*c*. 287 – *c*. 212 BCE), were copied, translated, and ultimately printed. All of these ancient writers emphasized the importance of mathematics as the underlying structure of the universe, an idea that was echoed by their later admirers. Johannes Kepler (1571–1630), a German astronomer who calculated the laws of planetary motion, wrote: "Geometry, which before the origin of things was coeternal with the divine mind and is God himself … supplied God with patterns for the creation of the world."[2] Kepler and other scholars saw the mathematical patterns of the universe as a mystical harmony, created by God and ultimately understandable to humans.

38 Alchemy and the history of science

The nineteenth-century historians of science who developed the idea of a "Scientific Revolution" often tried to ignore the alchemical and magical interests of the thinkers they championed, but most major figures in the Scientific Revolution believed firmly in alchemy, astrology, and other what are now often judged to be fringe occult beliefs. In his work on the motion of the planets, Kepler hoped to discover the mystical proportions underlying the universe and an explanation for how the heavenly bodies influenced human life. The Danish astronomer Tycho Brahe (1546–1601) constructed an advanced observatory and kept careful records of the skies, and also had an alchemical laboratory with multiple ovens for cooking and distilling plants and minerals to gain their spiritual essence. The Irish chemist Robert Boyle (1627–91) developed laws about the behavior of gases and disproved the theory that air, earth, fire, and water were the basic elements, asserting instead that everything was made of very small particles in motion, which he called "corpuscles." In long laboratory reports written in code, Boyle also reported to have witnessed elixirs that turned lead into gold and gold into lead. Isaac Newton collected Hermetic and alchemical texts, and spent decades trying to discover or manufacture a substance that would cause metals to grow or transform. His extensive writings on alchemical and spiritual subjects led the British economist John Maynard Keynes, who bought Newton's papers in the mid-twentieth century, to declare that "Newton was not the first of the age of reason … he was the last of the magicians." For all of these thinkers, the universe was not only to be comprehended, but manipulated and controlled, and alchemy offered the best opportunity for this.

 For additional chapter resources see the companion website www.cambridge.org/wiesnerhanks.

Among the ancient texts rediscovered in the fifteenth century was a body of writings attributed to Hermes Trismegistus, a god-like Egyptian sage thought to have lived at the time of Moses. These Hermetic writings – now known to have been written in the second and third centuries CE – were revered as ancient wisdom, and offered suggestions on how to exploit the hidden divine powers of minerals, plants, the planets, and other natural objects. Through processes of distillation, heating, and sublimation (cooking something to a gaseous state and then resolidifying it), these hidden powers could be tapped to transform lead into gold or cure disease and prolong life, practices usually termed alchemy.

The Swiss physician Theophrastus Bombastus von Hohenheim, who called himself Paracelsus (1493?–1541), fully embraced the Hermetic tradition, as did many other scientists, who sometimes linked Hermeticism with Christian ideas about the power of angels. Paracelsus rejected the Aristotelian elements and the Galenic notion that disease is caused by an imbalance of bodily humors, and introduced the use of drugs made from small doses of purified minerals, especially sulfur, antimony, and mercury. Hoping to find one powerful agent – often called the "philosopher's stone," or the "elixir of life" – that was capable of healing all illnesses and transforming all less perfect substances into more perfect ones, Paracelsus and other alchemists experimented with ways to extract pure elements (termed *magisteria*) and divine essences (termed *arcana*).

With its peculiar properties as a metal that is liquid at normal room temperature, mercury was often part of alchemical theories, as was gold distilled in various liquids so that it was drinkable (*aurum potabile*).

Alchemists such as Paracelsus were rooted in ancient texts, but they were innovative in their methods, advocating experimentation as the best way to discover the hidden properties of various substances. They were often the earliest to make extensive use of what was later called the "scientific method," in which a hypothesis to explain a phenomenon is developed, tested, the results recorded and measured, and the hypothesis confirmed, rejected, or modified. They invented equipment still used in laboratories today, such as beakers and balance scales, and discovered new ways of producing chemical changes, such as the application of acids and alcohols.

The development of the scientific method is often associated with the English philosopher and statesman Francis Bacon (1561–1626), who took his inspiration and procedures straight from alchemy. In *The Advancement of Learning* (1605) and *Novum Organum* (New Instrument, 1620), Bacon rejected earlier claims of knowledge as based on faulty reasoning, and called for natural philosophy that began with the empirical observation of many similar phenomena. Those studying the phenomena would then use their powers of reason to propose a generalized explanation or hypothesis for the phenomena, a process called induction. This generalization would then be tested with further empirical and inductive inquiry. Like any good alchemist, Bacon was a firm believer in the practical value of science in promoting human progress and greater control of nature. He called for national support for scientific investigations, which led the founders of the English Royal Society in 1660 to see him as an inspiration.

Experimentation was very important in the study of material substances. George Ernst Stahl (1660–1734), a German chemist and physician, proposed that combustion and other processes resulted in the release and absorption of a substance he called phlogiston. The phlogiston theory led other chemists to study gases – what they called "airs" – and in the middle of the eighteenth century carbon dioxide and hydrogen were both identified as substances different than the air that surrounds us. In the early 1770s, the Swedish apothecary Carl Wilhelm Scheele (1742–86) and the English cleric and theologian Joseph Priestley (1733–1804) both discovered an air in which substances burned more easily. Viewing his discovery within the context of the phlogiston theory, Priestley called it "dephlogisticated air."

The French chemist Antoine Lavoisier (1743–94) performed similar experiments, but interpreted the results differently. He recognized that the same substance allows for combustion, the action of acids, and respiration in living things, and called this substance "oxygen." Lavoisier's oxygen theory came to replace the phlogiston theory, particularly as Lavoisier made it part of a radically new way of discussing chemical compounds and processes in his *Elementary Treatise on Chemistry* (1789), the first modern textbook on chemistry. Like Bacon, Lavoisier regarded science as a way of providing solutions to real-world problems, and he experimented on crop rotation, the quality of drinking water, the military and scientific use of balloons, and the production of gunpowder.

He also proposed reforms for the French economy and prison system, but his involvement in tax-collection ultimately outweighed his contributions and he was sent to the guillotine during the French Revolution.

The revolution in cosmology

While Priestley and Lavoisier developed their ideas in the realm of chemistry through experimentation, the most dramatic developments in early modern science often came from applying mathematics and philosophical principles to the physical world. Verification came later, sometimes much later when instruments were invented and methods developed that would allow an idea to be tested through observation and experiment. The prime example of this is the proposal by Nicolaus Copernicus (1473–1543), a Polish priest, lawyer, church official, painter, and astronomer, that the sun, not the earth, was the center of the universe. Copernicus became interested in astronomy and mathematics while he was a student, and put the two of them together in proposing a heliocentric system, with the earth rotating on its axis while revolving around the sun, first in an anonymous treatise and then at the very end of his life in *On the Revolutions of the Heavenly Bodies* (1543). Copernicus proposed this idea as a "mathematical hypothesis," but he clearly felt it was valid, not because he had physical proof, but because it was far simpler than Ptolemy's system in terms of the geometry involved in calculating planetary motion. This desire for simplicity, reinforced by Platonic ideas about perfect mathematical forms, meant Copernicus retained circular orbits for the planets, as the circle was the most perfect form.

Copernicus's work was discussed by astronomers, but it created no great stir, especially as it also created problems – if the earth was not the center of the universe, why did objects fall? And if it rotated, why did objects thrown into the air not land west of where they were thrown? The Aristotelian world-view was gradually challenged by others, however. From his observatory, Tycho Brahe saw and measured the appearance of a supernova and a comet in the 1570s, proving that these could not be below the moon and that the heavens did indeed change. Accepting Copernicus's idea of a heliocentric universe was too much for Brahe, however, and he posited a complicated double-centered universe, with the planets traveling around the sun, and the sun, moon, and stars revolving around a motionless earth. Using Brahe's data, Johannes Kepler proposed in 1609 that the sun was indeed the center, but that the planets moved in elliptical orbits around it at speeds that varied according to the distance the planet was from the sun. He figured out the exact proportions of speed and distance – what were later called the "laws of planetary motion" – and asserted that these applied to all the planets, including the earth. In Kepler's conceptualization, the planets circling the sun were a system distinct from the rest of the universe, clearly breaking with the Aristotelian notion of a unified cosmos, just as his elliptical orbits challenged Aristotelian (and Copernican) concepts of perfectly circular forms.

Brahe's and Kepler's observations had all been done with the naked eye, but the invention of the telescope by Dutch opticians in the early seventeenth century allowed for closer observations. On hearing about the Dutch invention, Galileo built his own telescope and used it to study the sky. Galileo was a tutor and later professor of mathematics at the universities of Pisa and Padua, where he was expected to teach courses in astronomy. Studying astronomical theory convinced him that Copernicus was right, and his telescopic discoveries offered evidence that Aristotle's understanding of the universe was wrong. The moon was not a perfectly round sphere that glowed, but was pitted like the earth and simply reflected light; the sun was not changeless, for sunspots moved across its surface. The earth was not the only center of rotation, for the planet Jupiter had *four* moons, a dramatic discovery that Galileo highlighted in *The Starry Messenger*, published in 1610. In this lively account, which the title-page describes as "unfolding great and very wonderful sights," Galileo named the moons of Jupiter the "Medicean Planets," in honor of the ruling Medici family of Florence. He wrote that this was the best possible tribute, for "all human monuments ultimately perish through the violence of the elements or by old age." Galileo's bid for patronage paid off, and Cosimo de' Medici, the Grand Duke of Tuscany, named Galileo his personal mathematician and brought him to Florence, where he continued his investigations of the heavens, and also turned his attention to the mechanics of motion on earth.

Galileo had a forceful personality and was always willing to engage in controversy. In 1615, he wrote a letter to Cosimo's mother, the Grand Duchess Christina, in which he argued that Copernican theory was consistent with biblical teachings, and in any case "the intention of the Holy Ghost is to teach us how one goes to heaven, not how heaven goes." The letter was circulated widely, a complaint was made to the Roman Inquisition, and Galileo was ordered not to

39 Letters Between Kepler and Galileo, 1597

Though published writings and scientific societies were important in spreading new ideas, people interested in science also communicated through personal letters, where they often felt freer to discuss their conclusions and theories openly. In this exchange, Kepler urges Galileo to publish his views; it would be more than a decade before Galileo took his advice.

Galileo to Kepler, August 4, 1597, Padua
I received your book, most learned sir ... So far I have read only the introduction to your work, but I have to some extent gathered your plan from it, and I congratulate myself on the excellent good fortune of having such a man as a comrade in the pursuit of truth. For it is too bad that there are so few who seek the truth and so few who do not follow a mistaken method in philosophy ... I have written many direct and indirect arguments for the Copernican view, but until now I have not dared to publish them, alarmed by the fate of Copernicus himself, our master. [Copernicus died peacefully in his bed; Galileo is here referring to the ridicule he mentions in the next sentence.] He has won for himself undying fame in the eyes of a few, but he has been mocked and hooted at by an infinite multitude (for so large is the number of fools).

Kepler to Galileo, October 13, 1597, Graz
I received your letter of August 4 on September 1. It gave me a twofold pleasure, first, because it sealed my friendship with you, the Italian, and second, because of the agreement in our opinions concerning Copernican cosmography ... You advise us, by your personal example, and in discreetly veiled fashion, to retreat before the general ignorance and not to expose ourselves ... But after a tremendous task has been begun in our time, first by Copernicus and then by many very learned mathematicians, and when the assertion that the earth moves can no longer be considered something new, would it not be much better to pull the wagon to its goal by our joint efforts, now that we have got it under way, and gradually, with powerful voices, to shout down the common herd, which really does not weigh arguments very carefully?

("Comrades in the Pursuit of Truth", trans. Mary Martin McLaughlin in James Bruce Ross and Mary Martin McLaughlin, eds., *The Portable Renaissance Reader*, pp. 597–9. Copyright 1953, renewed 1981 by Viking Penguin Inc. used by permission of Viking Penguin, a division of Penguin Group [USA] Inc.)

"hold or defend" Copernican theory, though he could "discuss it as a mathematical supposition"; this prohibition was soon extended to all authors. Galileo was chastened for a while, but in 1632 he published a long synthesis of his astronomical observations, the *Dialogue concerning the Two Chief World Systems, Ptolemaic and Copernican*. Galileo structured this as a dialogue between advocates of each system and claimed he was providing a balanced argument, but gave his inept Aristotelian the name Simplicio, and made his own position clear in the final discussion. Summoned again to Rome, Galileo was forced to recant, and was sentenced to life imprisonment; he spent the rest of his life under house arrest, though this did not stop him from publishing a further defense of new scientific ideas in many fields.

In an older view of the history of science, the trial of Galileo was part of a long battle between religion, especially Catholicism, and science, in which science, or at least Galileo, was finally vindicated in 1992 when Pope John Paul II publicly admitted the church had made a mistake in condemning him. Most historians of science today find the story to be more complicated, as Galileo had many supporters within the Catholic church, especially among Jesuits, and both personal and political issues were involved in the 1633 condemnation. Catholics and Protestants varied in their acceptance of the Copernican system and other new ideas, and it is clear that most scientists regarded their religious beliefs as essential to their scientific work.

Mathematics, motion, and the mind of God

Cosmology was not the only field of inquiry in which mathematical speculation led to radically new ideas. The French mathematician and philosopher René Descartes (1596–1650) agreed with traditional teachings that everything depends on the power of God, but he also asserted that God created the world according to mathematical principles. Humans could perceive one perfect and infinitely powerful being, Descartes reasoned, only if that being actually existed and had created them. Along with this intuition about God, Descartes wondered what else we could know for sure. Earlier writers such as Michel de Montaigne (1533–92) had puzzled over this question of the foundation of knowledge – a branch of philosophy known as epistemology – noting that established authorities such as Aristotle had been proven wrong, and that sense perceptions and empirical observations might be deceiving. Montaigne remained skeptical about whether true knowledge is ever possible, but Descartes decided that what we can know for certain is that we exist as thinking beings, a philosophical position called rationalism. He captured this in the *Discourse on Method* (1637) in the phrase "I think, therefore I am" (in Latin, *Cogito ergo sum*).

From these two conceptions – God and self – the existence of the rest of the universe and its laws could be posited by applying logical principles, a process called deduction. In Descartes's philosophical system, known as Cartesianism or

Cartesian dualism, the world consists of two basic substances, matter (or body) and mind (or spirit), each of which can exist, at least theoretically, without the other. Humans are a union of these two substances, but there is nothing material about the mind, and nothing spiritual about the body or any other material objects, which only move when acted upon by some outside force. Descartes thought that all motion could be explained as a result of invisibly small particles pushing an object, a completely mechanical explanation. Though he thought even gravity and magnetism operated this way, some of his followers put greater emphasis on God as the ultimate cause of all events and actions in the universe; God was thus the Prime Mover.

For Isaac Newton, the natural world provided unambiguous evidence for certain religious ideas. An aloof and intense young man, Newton was a student and then professor of mathematics at Cambridge, where he studied the new concepts of mechanics and cosmology, and built the first working reflecting telescope. He developed the calculus, a branch of mathematics that allows calculations involving rates of change, varying quantities, and curved figures, that would ultimately underlie modern physics and engineering as well as mathematics. In the 1670s Newton studied the nature of light, and also studied the Bible and the writings of the early Christian church, because he was expected to be ordained as a clergyman in the Anglican Church as a condition of his position at Cambridge. His views on optics were published by the Royal Society, but his views on religion were far too dangerous to be shared publicly. He decided that the doctrine of the Trinity, in which the Father, Son, and Holy Spirit are equally part of a triune God, was not part of the early church, but invented in the fourth century; the ultimate God was one, not three, though Christ was divine. Denying the Trinity was heresy and also illegal, so that Newton kept his religious writings private, and got special dispensation to remain at Cambridge without being ordained. He continued to write extensively on religious and alchemical topics, however, though these works were not published.

In 1687, Newton published his most important work, the *Philosophiae Naturalis Principia Mathematica* (Mathematical Principles of Natural Philosophy, usually just called the *Principia*). The *Principia* provided mathematical descriptions of the laws of motion and the operation of gravity. This book brought together Galileo's discoveries about motion on earth and Kepler's discoveries about motion in the heavens, developing universal laws that applied anywhere, expressed in mathematical terms. All bodies attract one another across empty space, with the force of attraction dependent on the size of the bodies and the distance between them (universal gravitation), and all bodies continue to move or not move unless an outside force acts on them (inertia). Though few people could actually understand it, the *Principia* was immediately recognized as a work of genius, and Newton was rewarded with a position as Master of the Royal Mint, in charge of issuing coins and bills and preventing counterfeiting. Newton's public fame and status continued to grow. He was elected to Parliament several times, and elected president of the Royal Society in 1703, a position he held until his death. He was given a magnificent state funeral and was buried alongside kings and other notables in Westminster Abbey.

In the *Principia* Newton described *how* gravity operated, but not *why*, and the idea that one body could attract another across empty space was initially unacceptable to many continental thinkers. By the middle of the eighteenth century, however, Newton's ideas had triumphed, and other scientists began to apply his theorems to the study of heat, light, magnetism, and electricity. His followers wrote popular works explaining Newtonian science in terms that educated people who were not mathematicians could understand, several labeled "Newton for the Ladies" or something similar. This fueled the idea, as Pope expressed succinctly in his couplet, that Newton had once and for all explained the mechanism of the universe.

Developments in science shaped philosophy, and also other realms of life. In politics, finance ministers and other officials used more quantitative methods of administration; governments began to take statistical surveys, attempting to calculate aggregate figures for things like population growth, manufacturing output, income, and imports and exports. This would allow more effective application of mercantalist principles, officials reasoned, and also provide a sort of unified picture of the nation to parallel Newton's unified picture of the cosmos. In literature, writers began to use scientific terms more widely in all types of prose, and some advocated a simpler and plainer style, more in line with what they saw as a scientific emphasis on clarity and logic. As Pope put it in another couplet:

> Words are like leaves, and where they most abound
> Much fruit of sense beneath is rarely found.

Not everyone was convinced of the value of science, however. In 1726, the year before Newton's death, Jonathan Swift (1667–1745) published *Gulliver's Travels*, in which his fictional traveler goes to Laputa and Lagado, where scientists are working on extracting sunbeams from cucumbers, converting ice into gunpowder, building houses from the roof downward, and preventing the growth of wool on sheep. All of these satires are based on proposals being discussed by the Royal Society at the time Swift was writing. Swift was not alone in pointing out that actual scientific discoveries did little to improve the lives of most people. Newtonian ideas about motion helped gunners to fire their artillery more accurately, but in general scientific ideas had few practical effects on technology until the very end of the eighteenth century.

Reason, knowledge, and property

Mathematics, abstract reasoning, and experimentation all provided tools for studying the natural world in the seventeenth century, and they also provided tools for thinkers contemplating the place of humans and God in that world, and the limits of human knowledge. Descartes based all knowledge on our intuition about God's existence and understanding of ourselves as thinking beings, but other philosophers had different ideas.

Baruch Spinoza (1632–77) was born to Jewish parents in Amsterdam, but his freethinking and unorthodox views led him to be thrown out of the Jewish community. He traveled from town to town, making a living as a lens-grinder, an occupation that cut his life short because he steadily breathed in glass dust. Hostility to his earliest published works and political instability in the Netherlands led him to withhold his writings from publication, and his main work, *Ethics*, was only published after he died. In *Ethics* (1677), Spinoza argues that there is really only one substance in the universe. That substance is God. God and Nature, Creator and creation, mind and matter are all the same, a position called pantheism, which Spinoza demonstrated through logical geometrical proofs and theorems. Our sense of remoteness from one another or separation from God is an illusion, he asserted, and our immortality is certain, as the One Substance is eternal. Whatever happens is destined to happen – a position called determinism, akin to Calvin's idea of predestination – but because God and the universe are one, we can be confident that things happen for a reason. We do not have free will, but if we understand our place in nature, we can achieve freedom of mind and an intellectual love of God, a state Spinoza calls bliss. This bliss, this sense of oneness with God and other people, is vastly superior to any other emotion, which Spinoza urges us to control.

The German philosopher Gottfried Wilhelm Leibniz met Spinoza, and built his own philosophical system on Spinoza's ideas, though their lives were dramatically different. In his long life, Leibniz corresponded and visited with thinkers, rulers, and statesmen all over Europe, serving as a diplomat in Paris and the official historian and librarian for the dukes of Brunswick. He invented the calculus independently of Newton, and sought to apply Cartesian rational principles to law, theology, and politics as well as scientific issues. He was fascinated by Chinese learning, corresponding with Jesuits who had been in China and writing a knowledgeable book praising Chinese culture. Leibniz accepted Spinoza's notion that everything happens for a reason, and because all reasons are God's and God is good, everything must happen for a good reason. The world as it exists is only one of many possible worlds, but because it is what God has chosen, it is the best of all possible worlds. Suffering and evil are the result of our not understanding God's reasons.

Leibniz was ruthlessly satirized in the French author Voltaire's anonymous novel *Candide or Optimism* (1759) in which the young hero Candide, accompanied by his Leibniz-quoting tutor Pangloss, experiences a series of dreadful events, including shipwrecks, trials by the Inquisition, starvation, flogging, and the Lisbon earthquake of 1755, which was followed by a tsunami and fire. No matter what happened, Pangloss responds with "everything is for the best in this best of all possible worlds," until finally by the end Candide decides that simple work is the only real escape. "All that is very well," he says in the last words of the book, "but let us cultivate our garden."

While Descartes, Spinoza, and Leibniz viewed abstract reason as the best tool for understanding the world, the English philosopher and political theorist John Locke (1632–1704) picked up on Francis Bacon's emphasis on experience, observation, and sense perceptions as the true basis of knowledge. In *An Essay Concerning Human Understanding* (1690) Locke argued that the mind at birth is a blank tablet (*tabula rasa*) with no innate ideas. All knowledge is derived from actual experiences, a position called empiricism or experientialism; education was thus extremely important, for only through education could the mind reach its fullest potential. Locke's empiricism was not absolute, however, for he did make room for both reason and faith in the acquisition of knowledge.

Reason, experience, and divine will were not only the sources of human understanding for Locke, but also the proper bases for government. In *Two Treatises on Government* (1690), Locke challenged both Robert Filmer (1588–1653), whose *Patriarcha* based the divine right of kings on the patriarchal power given to Adam by God, and Hobbes, who viewed the original "contract" by which monarchs had been given authority in return for order as immutable. Locke did not see the family and political society as analogous; property, not fatherhood, was the proper basis of political authority. God had given the world to humans in common, and individual property derived from applying labor and talents to that common inheritance; the state of nature was not, as it was for Hobbes, "solitary, poor, nasty, brutish and short," but rather pleasant. Individuals had not formed a contract with governments to avoid chaos, but simply to better assure protection for their property. Monarchs who did not do this, or who applied their powers in capricious or arbitrary ways, could justifiably be overthrown.

Locke uses the word "property" in several senses. Narrowly, he takes it to mean land, goods, and money. Only those who owned property, he argued, could be free enough to make political decisions without being influenced by others, an idea that fitted well with the political realities of England in the late seventeenth century, and provided justification for limiting voting rights in national elections to property-owning males until the nineteenth century. (In a few local elections in some areas of Britain and eventually in some British colonies in North America, unmarried and widowed female property owners were allowed to vote. Laws that eliminated property ownership as a requirement for voting in the nineteenth century used the word "male," thus explicitly excluding women on the basis of their gender.) More broadly, Locke uses property to mean "life, liberty, and estate," which he describes, somewhat vaguely, as "natural rights" given to humans by God. Tyrannical monarchs could thus be legitimately opposed when they failed to protect individuals' property, but also when they failed to uphold these broader natural rights.

Natural rights and their limits

The concept of natural rights as defined by Locke and other political theorists was enormously important for the eighteenth-century thinkers of the Enlightenment. They prepared translations, commentaries, and popularizations of works of political theory, and rights joined reason as a topic for discussion in academies, salons, and coffee-houses. Denis Diderot, one of the editors of the massive compendium of knowledge known as the *Encyclopédie*, contributed to critiques of the slave trade, while the French mathematician and philosopher Marie Jean Antoine Nicolas Caritat, marquis de Condorcet (1743–94), called for broader political representation and the extension of human (though not political) rights to women, non-Europeans, and Jews. Their works were read, and ideas accepted, in European communities outside Europe. "All men are created equal," wrote Thomas Jefferson (1743–1826), in the first words of the American Declaration of Independence, "endowed by their creator with certain inalienable rights: life, liberty, and the pursuit of happiness."

Enlightenment thinkers also built on Locke's ideas about the role of experience and the value of education. The Scottish philosopher and historian David Hume (1711–76) wrote essays and popular philosophical works he titled "Enquiries," advocating the teaching of analytical skills and a wide array of subjects. Hume was a thoroughgoing empiricist, holding that all ideas are based on experience; ideas about things we have never experienced come simply from combining impressions in new ways. Because all we have are sense impressions, we can never really know the substance of anything, and our "deductions" about the world are really no more than beliefs, ultimately unverifiable; nature provided models of probability, not absolute certainty. Hume did argue that we are all born with a capacity for sympathy toward others and common sense about the way the world operates and the way we should behave. These "natural" sentiments, combined with education, will allow us to build ethical political and social systems whether or not we can know anything for certain. Condorcet agreed with Hume about the value of education, though he was far less skeptical about people's ability to achieve true knowledge and more confident about human progress. "The number of men destined to push back the frontiers of the sciences by their discoveries will grow in the same proportion as universal education increases," he wrote in *Sketch for the Historical Picture of the Progress of the Human Mind* (1794), which will in turn lead to "the general welfare of the human species," and the "indefinite perfectibility of mankind."

Science also provided a ready model for philosophical works. In *The Spirit of the Laws* (1748), which many historians see as the single most influential Enlightenment text, Charles de Secondat, baron de Montesquieu (1689–1755), sought to construct social science based on the methods of natural science – experiment, observation, deduction, and rational inquiry. "The material world has its laws," he wrote, "the intelligences superior to man have their laws, the beasts their laws, and man his laws." Montesquieu studied governments and societies throughout time and around the globe, trying to deduce general laws from these empirical observations. He asserted that there was no liberty and no assurance of rights without law, and decided that the best form of government was one in which the legislative, executive, and judicial powers of government were separated and held in balance. Montesquieu's ideas shaped the writing of the United States constitution, and in 1811 Jefferson translated a French commentary on Montesquieu's text. *The Spirit of the Laws* was thus influential on both sides of the Atlantic, serving as a foundation for later developments in the writing of history and the conceptualization of economics as well as the creation of political systems.

While Montesquieu was primarily interested in human laws, others explored the relationship between God's laws and those of nature. God had first established physical and moral laws in creating the universe, but then, in the minds of many Enlightenment thinkers, he largely left it alone. This idea, called deism, starts with the ideas of Descartes and Newton, but accords God a much less active role than they did; God was the clockmaker, in a widely used analogy, and the clock he created was so perfect it never needed adjustment. The laws of nature would ultimately be discovered, argued many Enlightenment writers, because God, who had endowed humans with reason, would not have made a universe so complex that humans could not understand it. Hume went even further, arguing that our perceiving the world as large and complex does not prove it was made by an intelligent creator, for it could have come into existence by accident.

God remained far more than a clockmaker in the writings of other Enlightenment thinkers. Moses Mendelssohn (1729–86), a philosopher, biblical scholar, literary critic, and Jewish community leader in Prussia, accepted Enlightenment ideas about the importance of reason, using these to develop a Jewish philosophy of religion. Though he observed traditional religious practices, he was also part of the *Haskalah* (a Hebrew word meaning Enlightenment), a cultural movement that advocated reforming and modernizing Jewish education and ways of life. Mendelssohn also advocated civil rights for Jews, and produced a new translation and commentary on the first books of the Hebrew Bible.

Nature not only provided a model for human society, but shaped it, according to many Enlightenment thinkers. Reflecting on his observations, Montesquieu decided that there are three basic types of government: despotisms, monarchies, and republics. The latter, in which leaders are chosen by the people, was the best, but only possible for people who lived in cold or moderate climates, where people "have a certain vigor of body and mind, which renders them patient and intrepid, and qualifies them for arduous enterprises." Especially in places with moderate climate – of which France was the best example – there was "a genius for liberty that renders every part extremely difficult to be subdued and subjected to a foreign power, otherwise than by the laws and the advantage of commerce." By contrast "the effeminacy of the people in hot climates has almost always rendered them slaves ... Power in Asia ought,

40 The *Encyclopédie*

Written collections of information date back to ancient Greece and China, but the form of the modern encyclopedia, with an alphabetic arrangement, cross-references, many authors, and bibliographies, was set in the eighteenth century. Ephraim Chambers, an English mapmaker, published a two-volume *Cyclopaedia, or the Universal Dictionary of Arts and Sciences*, in 1728. It sold very well, and a French publisher commissioned two close friends, the writer Denis Diderot (1713–84) and the mathematician Jean le Rond d'Alembert (1717–83), to begin work on a translation. This grew into the twenty-eight-volume *Encyclopédie (Encyclopedia or Reasoned Dictionary of the Sciences, the Arts, and the Crafts)*, written by more than 150 contributors and published over the period 1751–72, with seven more volumes added later. In his article about the *Encyclopédie* itself, Diderot succinctly captures Enlightenment ideas about the power of knowledge and the responsibility of each generation to pass on what it knows:

> The purpose of an encyclopedia is to collect knowledge disseminated around the globe; to set forth its general system to the men with whom we live, and transmit it to all who will come after us, so that the work of preceding centuries will not become useless to the centuries to come, and so that our offspring, becoming better instructed, will at the same time become more virtuous and happy, and that we should not die without having rendered a service to the human race … We do not know how far a given man can go. We know even less how far the human race would go, what it would be capable of, if it were not halted in its progress …
>
> One consideration above all must not be lost sight of, and that is that if man or the thinking, observing being is banished from the face of the earth, this moving and sublime spectacle of nature is nothing but a sad and silent scene … It is the presence of man that gives interest to the existence of beings …
>
> I have said that only a philosophical century could attempt an *encyclopedia*; and I said this because this work everywhere requires more boldness of mind than is normally possessed in centuries of cowardly taste. One must examine and stir up everything, without exception and without cautiousness … We must trample underfoot all that old foolishness; overturn barriers not put there by reason; restore to the sciences and arts their precious liberty.

(Denis Diderot, "Encyclopedia [Philosophy]," trans. Philip Stewart, from *Encyclopedia of Diderot and d'Alembert Collaborative Translation Project*, at http://www.hti.umich.edu/d/did. Reprinted in Dena Goodman and Kathleen Wellman, eds., *The Enlightenment* [Boston: Houghton Mifflin, 2004], pp. 14, 16, 19, 20.)

then, to be always despotic, for … there reigns in Asia a servile spirit, which they have never been able to shake off … Africa is in a climate like that of the south of Asia, and is in the same servitude."[3]

This servile spirit extends to domestic relations as well as political ones, for in hot climates women marry at a young age when "their reason never accompanies their beauty … [so that] these women ought then to be in a state of dependence." In temperate climates, women marry later, so "they have more reason and knowledge at the time of marriage," though never so much that they should dominate their husbands, for "it is contrary to reason and nature that women should reign in families." Montesquieu sees dire consequences if Parisian norms for women's behavior were introduced into the warmer climates of Asia or Africa:

> Let us only suppose that the levity of mind, the indiscretions, the tastes and caprices of our women, attended by their passions of a higher and a lower kind, with all their active fire, and in that full liberty with which they appear amongst us, were conveyed into an eastern government, where would be the father of a family who could enjoy a moment's repose? The men would be everywhere suspected, everywhere enemies; the state would be overturned, and the kingdom overflowed with rivers of blood.[4]

For Montesquieu, the possibility of liberty based on reason was thus in-fluenced by climate and gender, an idea shared by many other eighteenth-century thinkers, including Adam Smith. Climate and gender were also re-lated, as can be seen in Montesquieu's reference to the "effeminacy" of people in hot climates. European travel literature and cultural comparisons based on this literature almost always discuss the scanty clothing of indigenous peo-ples, which was viewed as a sign of their uncontrolled sexuality. Hot climate – which we would probably view as the main influence on clothing choice – was itself regarded as leading to greater sexual drive and lower inhibitions. Indigenous peoples were often feminized, described or portrayed visually as weak and passive in contrast to the virile and masculine conquerors, or they were hypersexualized, regarded as animalistic and voracious (or sometimes both). Racial hierarchies became linked with those of sexual virtue, especially for women, with white women representing purity and non-white women lasciviousness.

The world's three zones – torrid, temperate, and frigid – were both climatic and sexual, with this schema linked to the advancement of civilization. "No people living between the tropics," wrote Hume in *Political Discourses* (1752) "could ever yet attain to any art or civility." Hume considered the differences between groups of people more fully in *Of National Characters* (1753), and decided that it was not climate alone that shaped these, but skin color:

> I am apt to suspect the negroes and in general all the other species of men (for there are four or five different kinds) to be naturally inferior to the whites. There never was a civilized nation of any other complexion than white, nor even any individual eminent either in action or speculation. No ingenious manufactures amongst them, no arts, no sciences . . . Such a uniform and constant difference could not happen, in so many countries and ages, if nature had not made an original distinction betwixt these breeds of men.[5]

Such racist ideas were not especially new, as European Christians and Arabic Muslims had used African "barbarity" as justification for the slave trade since the fourteenth century, but Hume rooted his ideas not in religion – whose authority he rejected – but in "nature." He described his observations as based on empirical study, the same methods used by his contemporaries exploring the physical world, but they were not; Hume spent much time in Paris, but did not leave Europe. In the nineteenth century, however, scientific methods of measuring and experimentation *were* used to affirm the racial differences Hume (and others) posited.

Nature had not only created distinct and permanent differences between the races for many Enlightenment thinkers, but also between the sexes. Women and men who were part of the "Republic of Letters" argued about women's intellectual capacities, moral virtues, and proper social role. Some, such as Voltaire's close friend and patron Emilie du Châtelet (1706–40), who translated Newton's *Principia* into French, held that women's unequal and limited educa-tion was responsible for women's lesser contributions in science and philoso-phy. Condorcet agreed, arguing that "among the progress of the human mind that is most important for human happiness, we must count the entire de-struction of the prejudices that have established inequality between the sexes, fatal even to the sex it favors."[6] Others were less sure, arguing that women's lack of achievement was the result of a smaller capacity for reason, and that men and women were fundamentally different in their basic natures. Women might have moral superiority to balance their intellectual inferiority, but the proper sphere for demonstrating that morality was the private sphere of the family, not the public world of politics. Even Condorcet sees the primary ben-efit of treating men and women equally as the "greater happiness of families, and … the spread of the domestic virtues, the first foundation of all other virtues."[7]

The most influential voice arguing for women's and men's radically different natures was the philosopher Jean-Jacques Rousseau, who commented that "a perfect woman and a perfect man ought not to resemble each other in mind any more than in looks."[8] Rousseau was born in Geneva, in French-speaking Switzerland, and came to Paris intent on making his intellectual mark. Success eluded him as a young man, and he grew suspicious of his *philosophe* friends and the salon hostesses who supported them. He also began to doubt Enlight-enment belief in reason and progress, attacking rationality and culture for destroying human freedom and corrupting humanity. In his treatise *Emile: Or, On Education* (1762), Rousseau calls for education that removes children from the corrupting influences of cities, and places boys under a wise tutor who will understand them and guide their interests. Most of the book – which be-came one of the most widely read books on education throughout the world – discusses the education of Emile, the boy at its center, but the last chapter turns to the education of Sophie, the girl destined to be Emile's wife. "Woman," Rousseau declares, "is made specially to please man … and to be subjugated." Her education was to focus on purity, virtue, and "the cares of her household," though she should gain some knowledge, for "how [else] will she incline her children toward virtues she does not know?" Rousseau did not use his own children to test his ideas; he had five, by the illiterate seamstress who lived with him and whom he eventually married, but he sent them to orphanages.

For Rousseau – as for most early modern political thinkers – marriage was a contract between partners understood to be unequal. In *The Social Contract* (1762), written in the same year as *Emile* and one of the most influential works of political philosophy in Western history, Rousseau also considered contracts more broadly. In contrast to Hobbes and in agreement with Locke, Rousseau saw early human society as basically good; in contrast to Locke, and in agree-ment with Hobbes, he saw it slowly degenerating as private property increased inequality and competition. At this point, the wealthy and powerful forced the weak to agree to laws and political structures that reinforced their dominance. The only way out of this was for individuals to join together in a social con-tract, in which they agreed to submit to what Rousseau terms the "general will of the people." By this he means not a majority vote, but what the community of citizens would unanimously agree to if everyone had complete information, good sense, and public spirit. Objecting to this "general will" would mean someone was putting his or her "particular will" above the common good, so that "whoever refuses to obey the general will shall be compelled to do so by the whole body." Because it is the general will that assures freedom from the tyranny of one individual or from chaos, this means that people "will be forced to be free." Rousseau was clearly not setting out a practical plan for political change, though his ideas were later used by both democratic revolutionaries and dictators, all of whom claimed to be representing the true "general will."

Rousseau has been seen as both a key Enlightenment thinker and a strong voice against the Enlightenment, just as the Enlightenment itself has been seen as both a liberating movement that led directly to the revolutions of the later eighteenth century, and an authoritarian movement whose motto – "dare to know" – led science and the state to be elevated above all else, a quality found in twentieth-century fascism. Most historians and philosophers situate themselves between these two extremes when evaluating the legacy of the Enlightenment. They point out that the Enlightenment thinkers did not advocate political revolution, but were more concerned on a practical level with achieving limited civil rights such as freedom of religion or freedom of expression. Documents that emerged from late-eighteenth-century political revolutions, however, including the American Declaration of Independence and the French Declaration of the Rights of Man and Citizen, were written in the language of "natural rights" that was developed by Locke and expanded by Enlightenment thinkers. Most Enlightenment thinkers did not contemplate extending natural rights or civil liberties to anyone other than white male property owners, and viewed Europeans as more rational and productive than non-Europeans, thus providing support for colonial inequities. Nineteenth-, twentieth-, and twenty-first-century movements advocating the expansion of rights to many different groups, however, have found Enlightenment concepts useful.

Literature and drama

Scientists, philosophers, and political theorists in the seventeenth and eighteenth centuries did not limit themselves to formal treatises or learned articles, but also wrote poetry, fiction, plays, satires and other imaginative works. Francis Bacon wrote *The New Atlantis* (published in 1627 after his death), describing an imaginary island called Bensalem where families headed by fathers with absolute power devote themselves to science. Galileo wrote poetry and plays, and attempted to map hell as described by Dante in the *Inferno* in the same way as cartographers were mapping real landscapes. Montesquieu first gained attention with the witty and satirical *Persian Letters* (1721), in which two fictional Persian aristocrats on a visit to Paris comment on French social life, religious practices, literary skills, and political activities. Diderot wrote novels, including *The Nun* (1760) and *Jacques the Fatalist* (1773), along with plays that called for greater realism in staging and acting, a call taken up by later playwrights.

These works were often very popular and sold widely, another way in which new scientific and philosophical notions were shared.

Political events as well as scientific and philosophical currents shaped literature. In Germany, the horrors of the Thirty Years War were captured in Hans Jakob von Grimmelshausen's *The Adventurous Simplicissimus* (1669) and several sequels. These tell the story of a naïve young man caught up in the horrors of the war; like Candide, Simplicissimus finally finds peace by retreating from the world. Grimmelshausen's sympathetic hero, linguistic skills, searing social criticism, and black humor made his works popular with nobles and middle-class readers, though they also commented on his graphic violence.

Political developments in seventeenth-century England had direct effects on literature, particularly drama. In the first decades of the seventeenth century, public theatres increasingly offered tragicomedies – serious plays with happy endings – while elaborate masques with stage scenery, lavish costumes, and complex musical scores were performed at court. With the outbreak of the Civil War in 1642, the public theatres were closed, though private performances continued, especially of "closet" dramas designed to be read rather than staged. With the restoration of the monarchy in 1660, the theatres opened again, and audiences flocked to satirical "comedies of manners" that both criticized and celebrated excessive behavior, and to heroic tragedies with flowery speeches and violent action. Female parts were increasingly played by women, and particular actors or actresses became wealthy celebrities. English prose fiction and poetry also reflected political, social, and economic changes. During the Civil War period, royalist sympathizers masked their praise of kings and nobles in fantasy romances focusing on gallant aristocrats, while ballads and popular poems satirizing rulers and government ministers circulated orally, in manuscript, or as single-page printed broadsheets. Such works continued after the Restoration, though they were sometimes a bit more muted; John Dryden's political satire *Absalom and Achitophel* (1681), for example, depicts enemies of the future James II as evil biblical characters.

John Milton (1608–74) wrote a number of political works, including an attack on censorship in *Areopagitica* (1644), a defense of the lawfulness of executing the king in *Eikonoklastes* (1649), and a condemnation of the imminent restoration of the monarchy in *The Ready and Easy Way to Establish a Free Commonwealth* (1660). He served as a government official during the period of Parliamentary rule – keeping his position after he grew blind – and was imprisoned briefly after 1660, but was allowed simply to retire from court. Milton's greatest work is the epic poem *Paradise Lost* (1667, revised 1674), which addresses basic questions about freedom and evil as it tells the story of creation, Satan's rebellion against God, and the fall of Adam and Eve.

Issues surrounding the slave trade emerge in *Oroonoko, or the History of the Royal Slave* (1688), by Aphra Behn (c. 1640–89), the first woman in England to make her living by writing. Behn tells the story of an African prince who leads a slave rebellion in the South American colony of Surinam. Behn had lived in Surinam as a young woman, and used her experiences to provide details about the natural setting and the slave system. Behn and others were gradually creating a new literary form, the novel, which involves a long and complex plot that develops through the thoughts and actions of distinctive characters. Daniel Defoe's *Life and Strange and Surprising Adventures of Robinson Crusoe* (1719) and Swift's *Gulliver's Travels* were other early novels that incorporated overseas voyages into their stories, as did *Candide*.

Spanish literature of the seventeenth century – that "Golden Age" in the eyes of literary scholars – is less overtly political than English literature. It includes the hundreds of plays of Lope de Vega, which often blend tragic, romantic, and comic elements. Pedro Calderón de la Barca (1600–81) also wrote many plays about noble honor and cloak-and-dagger intrigue, but became best known for his more serious works, including about seventy *autos sacramentales*, allegorical religious dramas on the theme of the Eucharist. These plays were performed during the Feast of Corpus Christi outdoors on wagons or more permanent stages, by troupes of professionals hired by church or city officials. In many of his *autos sacramentales*, Calderón tackles the issue of the limits of human understanding that so concerned Descartes, Locke, and Calvinist theologians; he resolves it by advocating unquestioning obedience to the monarch and intense devotion to the Catholic Church. Not surprisingly, this made Calderón very popular at court, where his plays were staged as costly and elaborate spectacles; after the death of his mistress, he became a priest, and later the royal chaplain. His plays, and those of Lope de Vega, continued to be performed throughout the eighteenth century, although in 1765 church authorities in Madrid forbade Corpus Christi performances as they thought people were attending more for the increasingly bawdy comical interludes than the main devotional play.

In France, political themes were portrayed in poetry and drama that emphasized the importance of the will, duty, and honor, a movement often termed "classicism." Classical poets such as François de Malherbe (1555–1628) wrote clear and forceful lyrics on moral and patriotic subjects, as did the playwright Pierre Corneille (1606–84), whose fearless but remorseless heroes are often taken from Roman history. Jean Racine (1639–99) also adapted Greek and Roman subjects for his tragedies, with larger-than-life heroes and heroines brought down by passions and internal conflicts they cannot control. Racine used simple and austere language and well-organized plots to drive along the downfall of his characters. He wrote several plays specifically for certain actresses or the girls' school of St. Cyr, and the depth and complexity he gave to the doomed figure at their center has made them popular roles for stage actresses ever since. Molière (1622–73), the stage name of Jean Baptiste Poquelin, turned human failings into comedy instead of tragedy in plays that are still widely performed. An actor, theater manager, and director as well as playwright, Molière favored plots that mocked social pretentions and religious hypocrisy, but in an amusing and good-natured way. Several of his plays, including *Tartuffe* (1664), were banned by officials of the French church, though Molière himself was protected by King Louis XIV and his brother, the duke of Orléans.

In the eighteenth century, Enlightenment values often emerge in plays and novels. The French author Françoise de Graffigny (1695–1758) published *Letters of a Peruvian Woman* (1747) in which a fictional Peruvian princess, Zilia, captured and brought to France, comments on the hypocrisy she sees in French culture and the limitations in the way young women were raised. Graffigny embeds her social commentary in a dramatic story of lovers' separation, exile, and romantic conflict, and the novel became a best-seller in several languages. The German playwright and philosopher Gotthold Ephraim Lessing (1729–81) created characters with which his audience could identify, centering his tragedies and comedies on realistic middle-class people rather than ancient kings or mythical heroes. In his plays and other works, Lessing considers central Enlightenment issues such as the role of reason in religion and the value of toleration; his last and most famous play, *Nathan the Wise* (1779), argues that the three major Western religious traditions – Judaism, Christianity, and Islam – agree more than they differ on moral values and basic teachings. Lessing based the main character in this play on his lifelong friend Moses Mendelssohn. The French playwright Pierre Augustin Caron de Beaumarchais (1732–1799) wrote the satirical comedies *The Barber of Seville* (1775) and *The Marriage of Figaro* (1784), both of which use the witty, irreverent barber Figaro to satirize aristocratic privilege. Both of these plays became the basis for later operas that are now part of the standard opera repertoire: Wolfgang Amadeus Mozart's *The Marriage of Figaro* (1786) and Gioacchino Rossini's *The Barber of Seville* (1815).

Lessing was not the only author to create sympathetic characters in ordinary circumstances who triumphed over misfortunes or were just as doomed by their own flaws as Racine's classical protagonists. The heroine in Samuel Richardson's *Pamela: or, Virtue Rewarded* (1740–1) is hired as a servant by a man who is her social superior; he tries to rape her – a scenario that, according to court records in cases of pregnancy outside wedlock, was very common in real life – but she resists. Over the course of the very long novel, written in the form of letters, he is convinced by the virtuousness of the heroine that he should marry her instead. Richardson's novel became wildly popular, inspiring Pamela dolls and other merchandise, though it also led several novelists to write parodies that skewer its ideas about virtue, including Eliza Heywood's viciously satiric *Anti-Pamela* (1741) and Henry Fielding's pointed yet very funny *Shamela* (1741).

Toward the very end of the eighteenth century, playwrights and poets in Germany associated with what they called the *Sturm und Drang* (Storm and Stress) literary movement both extended and opposed Enlightenment ideas, in a similar way to what Rousseau was doing in France. Plays such as Friedrich Schiller's *The Robbers* (1781) brashly called for immediate reforms and greater liberty, radicalizing Enlightenment ideas. At the same time, the writer, folklorist, and philosopher Johann Gottfried von Herder (1744–1803) defended German tastes for the emotional and extreme against French classicism and rationalism, arguing that each cultural group was unique and that there was no such thing as universal reason.

Art and architecture

Art and architecture in the seventeenth century is full of the same fascination with the natural world that led to the creation of learned societies and collections of curiosities. Much of it is also a celebration of the power of strong leaders, both secular rulers and church officials, who ordered, paid for, and sometimes helped design gigantic paintings and buildings. The word usually used to describe seventeenth-century art, architecture, and music is "baroque," which may be derived – the origins are debated – from the Portuguese word for a pearl that is deformed and not perfectly round, *barroco*. The word was first used in the middle of the eighteenth century as a term of criticism to describe art that was exaggerated, emotional, confused, twisted, and theatrical. This baroque style was a decline, in the eyes of its eighteenth-century critics, from the classical forms prized and emulated in the Renaissance and early seventeenth century, and favored again in their own day. Even worse, in some eyes, was "rococo," a term first coined by late-eighteenth-century artists to dismiss art and architecture from the early eighteenth century that they judged overly fussy, busy, precious, and decorative. Since the words were invented, art historians and cultural critics have debated what was and what was not "baroque" or "rococo," and whether these terms should be used at all. They still prove useful to describe certain trends and style, however, though they have lost their distinctly pejorative sense; whether you like baroque, rococo, or classicism – or all three – is a matter of personal taste.

Art later labeled baroque first appeared in Rome in the late sixteenth century, when the papacy, the Jesuits, and other patrons encouraged art that was more emotional, powerful, and exciting than the orderly and often symmetrical art of the Renaissance. Dramatic art would glorify the reformed and reinvigorated Catholic Church, appealing to the senses and proclaiming the power of the church to all who looked at paintings or sculpture or worshiped in churches. Secular rulers, especially in Catholic Europe, recognized that this grand style would express the authority of the state as easily as that of the church, and built magnificent baroque palaces set in elaborate gardens with cascading fountains, trees trimmed into fanciful shapes, and artificial grottoes lined with shells, fossils, and other interesting natural objects. Louis XIV's palace of Versailles (begun in 1661), sits in the middle of just such gardens; it has about 1,300 rooms, including the huge Hall of Mirrors decorated with paintings glorifying the king's achievements, one of which is the frontispiece in chapter 9.

Baroque architecture was designed with large numbers of columns, sweeping curved forms, and ornate decoration, while baroque sculpture pulls the viewer into the scene with a tremendous sense of movement, strong feelings, and realistic features. Baroque painting tends to display large-scale dynamic forms and intense emotions, with strong contrasts between light and dark

Fig. 24. Statues of powerful popes and leaders of the church top the huge colonnade created by Gian Lorenzo Bernini (1598–1680), the most influential Italian baroque sculptor and architect, enclosing the courtyard outside St. Peter's Basilica in Rome. The courtyard was designed in a keyhole shape to represent the welcoming arms of the church, and contains two fountains, a common feature in baroque architecture.

(called "chiaroscuro"); the figures are often arranged diagonally to heighten the drama. Painters and their patrons in different parts of Europe favored different subjects and styles, however, so that there are striking variations in paintings that are all labeled "baroque."

In Italy, Michelangelo da Caravaggio (1573–1610) used people who looked like village peasants or artisans when portraying traditional biblical figures, sometimes offending the church officials who had commissioned his paintings with these unidealized and unorthodox interpretations. He often cloaked his figures in shade penetrated by a bright light from an unknown source, combining this technique – called "tenebrism" – with gestures and facial expressions designed to capture the exact moment of a startling event, such as the conversion of St. Paul or the beheading of John the Baptist. Artemisia Gentileschi (1597–?1651), who learned to paint from her father, was one of the many painters inspired by Caravaggio's revolutionary vision, frequently portraying powerful biblical or classical heroines at a particularly tense moment. The influence of Caravaggio appears in many Spanish painters, including Francisco de Zurbarán (1598–1664), whose intense pictures of meditating monks and saints seem to be both real people and ethereal models to be venerated. Diego Velázquez (1599–1660), the official court painter to King Philip IV of Spain for nearly forty years, also uses dramatic lighting and bold colors in his many portraits of royal family members.

Artists working in the Netherlands, especially Rembrandt van Rijn (1606–69) also showed deep insight in their work, capturing individual personalities often engaged in introspection. These qualities emerge most clearly in the series of about a hundred etched, drawn, and painted self-portraits that Rembrandt made throughout his life, fashioning his visual legacy to match Vasari's judgment that painters were "rare men of genius." Rembrandt did not spend all his time gazing inward, however, for he also received commissions for individual and group portraits, primarily from wealthy middle-class urban residents. Rembrandt and his contemporaries Franz Hals (1580?–1666), Jan Vermeer (1632–75) and others are often called the "Dutch masters," most of whom perfected one type of painting, such as portraits, seascapes, still-lifes, or the intimate domestic scenes of women reading, children playing, or families eating called genre paintings. Many of these paintings were not done for specific patrons, but sold at fairs or increasingly at the shops of professional art dealers, who produced catalogs describing their wares. Art shops became gathering places for those interested in new cultural forms, and art dealers also bought and sold antiquities and imported artifacts along with locally produced paintings, prints, and drawings. In the eighteenth century, reproductions of famous works, offered at a price middle-class people could afford, were sold in shops in every city, while lesser-known artists sold their works at street fairs and markets.

In terms of reputation and commissions, the most successful seventeenth-century artist was Peter Paul Rubens (1577–1640), who used every square inch of his gigantic canvases to glorify royal power when this was desired by his patrons. His paintings of events from secular and Christian history

Fig. 25. Artemisia Gentileschi, *Judith Beheading Holofernes* (*c.* 1620), a biblical story that she painted a number of times for various patrons. Gentileschi's paintings of women have been read as clues to her personal life and psychological make up, but they are better seen as demonstrations of her skills at portraying women and capturing the baroque dramatic style.

and from mythology are crammed with writhing muscular men, fleshy semi-nude women – a body type later dubbed "Rubenesque" – and chunky smiling cherubs, even when the main subject is a saintly miracle or a royal wedding. Rubens ran a huge workshop, and his pupils and assistants did much of the actual painting after the master had designed the composition and provided oil sketches as models, with Rubens returning at the end to add a line or spot of color here and there. Rubens oversaw the mass production of prints and tapestries based on his paintings, organized pageants in which his paintings

Fig. 26. Rembrandt, *Self-portrait in Oriental Costume* (1631). This is the only full-length self-portrait of the many that Rembrandt painted, and he added the dog later as he was apparently dissatisfied with how he had painted the feet. Like many people, Rembrandt was fascinated with the Asian products readily available in Dutch ports, and painted many portraits of men, including his father, dressed in turbans.

served as backdrops, and served as a diplomat in warring post-Reformation Europe. After one of these missions – to Madrid trying to broker a treaty between Spain and England – he was knighted by Charles I of England.

Among Rubens's many apprentices was Anthony Van Dyck (1599–1641), who became the court painter to Charles I. Van Dyck's elegant and refined portraits of the royal family set a pattern for flattering portraits of the wealthy and powerful, later followed by the English painters Thomas Gainsborough (1727–88) and Joshua Reynolds (1723–92), two of the founders of the Royal Academy of Arts.

By the end of the seventeenth century, Paris began to rival Rome and Amsterdam as an artistic capital. Though in terms of scale Louis XIV's architectural projects are often seen as baroque, in terms of style Louis favored a slightly more restrained look that became known as classicism, typified by the dignified, serious mythological and biblical scenes of Nicolas Poussin (1594–1665). After Louis's death in 1715, however, French aristocrats decorating their houses in Paris and villas in the country increasingly favored the light, delicate, and highly ornamented style later called rococo. They painted interiors and exteriors pink, yellow, and aqua, adding embellishments made of plaster, shells, and artificial marble. For the walls they purchased paintings of games, shepherdesses, or couples courting, lighthearted subjects of which Antoine Watteau (1684–1721) was the undisputed master. From France, rococo spread to southern Germany and Austria, where palaces, churches, and even monasteries were built in this intricate style, with mythological goddesses mixed in with Christian saints.

Rococo never became very popular in England or Italy, where architects and sculptors – and their patrons – continued to prefer more classical styles, taking their inspiration from the sixteenth-century Italian architect Andrea Palladio (1508–80). Palladian style, also called neo-classical, used simpler forms such as the square and circle rather than curves and swirls, and favored white rather than the bold colors of baroque or the pastels of rococo. (The preference for white was in part an imitation of classical statuary, which was dug up in great quantities after the discovery of the buried Roman cities of Pompeii and Herculaneum in the middle of the eighteenth century. We now know that most classical statuary was originally brightly painted.) Neo-classical buildings and statues appeared in country houses and city squares in Britain, and then in other countries of Europe and the British colonies as well. White domed and pillared neo-classical buildings form the heart of Washington DC today, and many North American government buildings have also been designed in this very familiar style.

Music

Like art and architecture, baroque music is filled with strong contrasts, sweeping emotion, and dynamic movement, qualities that can best be seen in opera, an art form that emerged in Italy in the late sixteenth century. Opera was usually performed outside and it often involved elaborate stage sets, so that it combined painting, sculpture, and architecture with singing, instrumental music, and dance. Claudio Monteverdi (1567–1643), who also wrote songs for two or more voices called madrigals, composed some of the earliest operas, basing them on classical stories. They included passages for a chorus, but highlighted soloists singing recitatives that carried the plot forward, and dramatic, fanciful arias in which soloists showed off their vocal skills and expressed their feelings. Monteverdi was the court composer for the ruling houses of various Italian city-states, and in 1637 he became the composer for the first public opera house, the Teatro San Cassiano in Venice.

By the end of the seventeenth century, Italian-style operas were being written and performed in many European countries, often in Italian no matter what the native language of the composer or the audience was. Rulers and nobles spent huge amounts of money on special effects, using fireworks, real cannon, and live horses, for example, to depict gods traveling across the sky. Some of these were serious operas based on classical stories, while others were comic opera, called *opera buffa*. Opera buffa developed out of the comic skits known as *intermezzi* that were originally performed in between acts of serious operas. The characters were normal people – peasants, merchants, servants, soldiers – rather than the larger-than-life heroes and heroines of serious opera. The plot often involved some sort of humorous situation involving love, money, or a combination of the two, making them appealing to a wide range of audiences.

Italy was the most dynamic center for music, and attracted composers and musicians from all over Europe who learned and then built on Italian musical forms. The German composer George Frideric Handel (1685–1759) was a child prodigy, appointed as organist at the cathedral in Halle, his birthplace, when he was twelve. He studied in Italy, then moved to England, where he was one of the first to compose and stage operas, sung in Italian, which became popular with both the nobility and middle-class urban residents. Later in life Handel concentrated on oratorios, complex dramatic compositions for singers and instruments with sacred themes, performed in English and without staging, of which *The Messiah* (1742), and especially its "Hallelujah" chorus, is the best known. Immediately popular during Handel's lifetime – the composer himself conducted at least thirty performances – *The Messiah* is now performed annually by many amateur and professional choruses, including scores of sing-along versions, often for charity, as was Handel's original performance.

Handel's contemporary Johann Sebastian Bach (1685–1750) is often considered the greatest baroque composer, writing hundreds of complex works that featured the new techniques of counterpoint – playing two or more melodies at one time – and fugue, in which different instruments repeat the same melody with slight variations. Bach also began his musical career as the organist in a Lutheran church, and worked for the rulers of various small German states as court composer and director of music. He founded a musical dynasty, with four of his sons becoming distinguished composers. Bach was an intensely religious man; like Luther, he believed that music could convey deep spiritual truth and bring people to God, and he often worked hymns into his compositions. Many of his contemporaries thought his works were too elaborate, however; Bach's posthumous reputation as a composer far outweighs that of his lifetime, when he was more appreciated as an organist.

Handel had great commercial success, and Bach had a series of ever more prestigious permanent positions, but other composers failed at both the traditional forms of cultural patronage and the newer, more commercial structures. The most spectacular failure was the Austrian composer Wolfgang Amadeus Mozart (1756–91). The son of an orchestra director, Mozart was playing and composing for the Austrian court by the time he was five. His father trotted him and his sister around on concert tours through much of Europe before they were ten. Mozart became an international phenomenon, composing and giving court and public performances. He decided not to take a permanent position as a court composer, but try his hand in Vienna as a free agent, composing on commission. Mozart composed twenty-two operas in Italian and German, including *The Marriage of Figaro* (1786) and *The Magic Flute* (1791), over forty symphonies, masses, concertos, serenades, and other types of sacred and secular music. Some of his works, especially his operas, were witty and musically inventive, though his sacred music, especially the Requiem Mass he was composing at the time he died, was grave and profound. Mozart's compositions did not give him the income or fame he craved, however, and he died in poverty at the age of thirty-five. He would no doubt be amazed at the millions of dollars now spent every year in his home town of Salzburg on festivals and tours in his honor, with visitors all munching on foil-wrapped chocolate balls decorated with his picture (*Mozartkugeln*).

Among Mozart's many compositions were musical forms new in the eighteenth century and designed for public performance. These included string quartets, sonatas for piano (an instrument that was new, and that Mozart helped make popular), solo vocal works that showed off the virtuosity of performers, and symphonies. The undisputed master of these forms was Franz Joseph Haydn (1732–1809), who was the music director for a wealthy noble family for much of his life, but in his later years achieved smashing commercial success in London and Vienna, composing and conducting for public performances in theatres, concert halls, and gardens. People flocked to hear music they were already calling "classical," a demand that inspired the composition of hundreds of string quartets and over a thousand symphonies in the eighteenth century alone.

Composers were often innovators in terms of instruments as well as compositions. Bach helped design larger and more complicated pipe organs, while the Italian composer Antonio Vivaldi (1678–1741) and others refined string instruments. Among the violins and cellos that Vivaldi owned were several made by Antonio Stradivari (1644?–1737), whose instruments are still prized by musicians and audiences today, selling for hundreds of thousands of dollars when they come up for sale, which is rarely. Violin makers, musicians, chemists, and physicists have tried to figure out what gives Stradivarius instruments their special sweet sound – the varnish? the wood? the proportions? a secret ingredient? – but have come to no agreement. They do know that many survived later modification, designed to produce more volume as concert halls got larger, without losing that sound, and more recently survived restoration to their original set-up as musicians have tried to achieve a more authentic baroque sound.

41 Castrati

Parts for high voices were sometimes sung by women, despite official prohibitions, and sometimes by castrati, men who had been castrated when they were boys so that their larynx and vocal cords did not grow, as normally happens in puberty. Castrati first sang in cathedral choirs in Spain and Italy, where their huge vocal range – often more than four octaves – made them more prized than boys or men singing falsetto; the Sistine Chapel Choir was especially known for its castrati. These skills translated well to opera, where castrati sang both female roles and those of the male heroic lead, which were often written specifically for the combination of brilliant technique, enormous vocal range, and great power that castrati developed through years of training. Some of Handel's operas and those of his Italian contemporaries feature parts written for particular castrati, who apparently further embellished the melodic line to show off their virtuosity. (When these operas are performed today, such parts are taken by women or countertenors.)

Some castrati, such as the Neapolitan Carlo Broschi, who took the name Farinelli (1705–82), became international stars, with fans wearing medallions with their portraits and following them from concert to concert. Farinelli sang to great acclaim in Rome, Vienna, London, and Paris, and spent twenty years in Madrid, where the queen arranged for him to sing every night to King Philip V in the hopes that this would cure the king's severe depression. (It did not.) Such fame led some poor parents to castrate their sons in the hopes that this might prove a way out of poverty, but there is no assurance that castration will produce a gorgeous voice, and most castrati were at best members of cathedral choirs or opera choruses rather than wealthy superstars. By the end of the eighteenth century, though castrati still appeared regularly in operas, female roles were being sung more often by women, and composers such as Mozart were pitching the parts of male leads slightly lower, so they could be sung by tenors. The last known castrato sang publicly in the early twentieth century.

The complexity of baroque and classical music made it increasingly difficult for untrained musicians to sing or play, and courts, churches, and cities hired professional composers and performers. Sometimes these were highly specialized. Vivaldi, for example, worked as the violin master for one of the girls' orphanages in Venice known for its excellent chorus and orchestra. These *Ospedali grandi* put on regular performances, and talented girls who were not orphans were taken on as day students to develop their musical skills. Such opportunities were rare, however, for the Catholic Church officially opposed women singing polyphonic music or playing instruments. In 1686 Pope Innocent XI extended this prohibition, forbidding all women from learning music for any reason "because it is completely injurious to the modesty that is proper for the [female] sex."[9] Though such edicts were ignored in Venice, elsewhere they limited women's access to music, and court and city orchestras, even in Protestant areas, hired only men.

Women continued to play music in their own homes, however, and singing or playing an instrument became a suitable "accomplishment" for middle- and upper-class young ladies, making them more attractive in the marriage market. As the author of a 1722 conduct book put it, "Music refines the Tastes, polishes the Mind; and is an Entertainment that preserves them [young women] from the Rust of Idleness, that most pernicious Enemy to Virtue."[10] Men who were not professional musicians also played privately, as the extract from Pepys's diary in chapter 8 shows. Music publishers produced simplified versions of complex compositions that could be played more easily by amateurs, sometimes with separate parts printed directly onto tablecloths so that families or friends sitting around a table could each play a part.

Restrictions on women performing in public never applied to dance, and ballet involving men and women gradually joined musical performance as a professional enterprise watched by an audience, rather than something done by amateurs. In the sixteenth century, Catherine de' Medici, the queen of France, made dancing a more important part of court life, hiring an Italian dancing master to train her court ladies and gentlemen to perform elaborate spectacles with dancing, lavish costumes, and scenery. Louis XIV continued these court entertainments, and also founded the Royal Academy of Dancing and later the Paris Opera to provide serious training for professional dancers. His dancing master, Pierre Beauchamp (1636–1705) codified many of the steps used in ballet, including the five basic positions of the feet. In the eighteenth century, professional dancers began to perform in theatres as well as at court, shortening and simplifying their costumes so people could see their movements better, and eliminating singing and speaking from their performances. The movements, bodies, and faces of the dancers should tell the story, argued influential dance masters and choreographers, and ballet schools were established in many European capitals, including the Russian Imperial Ballet of St. Petersburg.

In their swirling, dramatic forms, baroque art, architecture, and music might seem to be the opposite of the emphasis on reason that marked the Scientific Revolution and the Enlightenment, and to some degree they are. We can find some overarching themes in all the intellectual and cultural developments of the seventeenth and eighteenth centuries, however. Scientists, philosophers, writers, artists, and composers, and the people who read, saw, heard, and discussed their works in clubs, coffeehouses, and salons, were interested in issues of order and structure. What were the underlying structures of the universe? Of human society? Of the individual? How did people learn these? How could natural structures be reproduced, or enhanced? Should they be? How could social structures be improved? Should they be? Could disorderly things be made orderly? Were there limits to human nature, or were individuals infinitely improvable? All individuals, or just some? Were there limits to human knowledge and understanding? If so, who or what set those limits? The answers to many of these questions had long been provided by religious authorities, but, as we will see in the next chapter, religious institutions were themselves deeply split by concerns about structure and order in these centuries.

None of these questions provoked a uniform answer, but by the end of the eighteenth century the number of people thinking, talking, and writing about them, at least in the larger cities of Europe, was far greater than had been the case two centuries earlier. This expansion of what Renaissance humanists called the "Republic of Letters" did not include the vast majority of the European population, who remained agricultural producers living in villages, but it was an important part of the creation of what was later termed "middle-class" culture. This broadening was also accompanied by a growing split between professional and amateur. Though there were many popularizations of scientific and philosophical works, scientific advances increasingly required expensive equipment and an understanding of mathematics beyond the reach of most people. Musical forms such as the opera or the oratorio were not for singing or playing at home. People did share in such things, but as audiences, not participants. These two trends – broadening and professionalization – are actually linked, because both created a larger market for many types of cultural products. By the end of the eighteenth century, culture was a commodity to be purchased, through paintings for a sitting room, tickets to performances, subscriptions to journals, or visits to museums. The "Republic of Letters" had become the "marketplace of ideas," a new metaphor appropriate in an increasingly commercialized world.

Further Reading

Thomas Kuhn's *The Structure of Scientific Revolutions* (Chicago: University of Chicago Press, 1962), is brief and very readable, as is Peter Dear's *Revolutionizing the Sciences: European Knowledge and its Ambitions, 1500–1700* (Princeton: Princeton University Press, 2001), which explores continuities between seventeenth-century and earlier science. Jürgen Habermas, *The Structural Transformation of the Public Sphere: An Inquiry into a Category of Bourgeois Society,* trans. Thomas Burger and Frederick Lawrence (Cambridge, MA: MIT Press, 1989), is a bit more ponderous.

   Studies of new cultural institutions include James E. McClellan III, *Science Reorganized: Scientific Societies in the Eighteenth Century* (New York: Columbia University Press, 1985); Margaret C. Jacob, *Living the Enlightenment: Freemasonry and Politics in Eighteenth-Century Europe* (New York: Oxford University Press, 1991); Elizabeth L. Eisenstein, *Grub Street Abroad: Aspects of the French Cosmopolitan Press from the Age of Louis XIV to the French Revolution* (Oxford: Oxford University Press, 1992); Dena Goodman, *The Republic of Letters: A Cultural History of the French Enlightenment* (Ithaca, NY: Cornell University Press, 1994); Geoffrey V. Sutton, *Science for a Polite Society: Gender, Culture, and the Demonstration of Enlightenment* (Boulder: University of Colorado Press, 1995); Paula Findlen, *Possessing Nature: Museums, Collecting and Scientific Culture in Early Modern Italy* (Berkeley: University of California Press, 1996); James van Horn Melton, *The Rise of the Public in Enlightenment Europe* (Cambridge: Cambridge University Press, 2001); David Freedberg, *The Eye of the Lynx: Galileo, his Friends, and the Beginnings of Modern Natural History* (Chicago: University of Chicago Press, 2003).

   Brief general surveys of the Scientific Revolution include Steven Shapin, *The Scientific Revolution* (Chicago: University of Chicago Press, 1998), which argues that there wasn't one, and John Henry, *The Scientific Revolution and the Origins of Modern Science,* 2nd edn (Basingstoke: Palgrave-Macmillan, 2002), which argues that there was. Margaret J. Osler, ed., *Rethinking the Scientific Revolution* (Cambridge: Cambridge University Press, 2000), includes articles that take both positions. For the culture of science, see Lisa Jardine, *Ingenious Pursuits: Building the Scientific Revolution* (London: Anchor, 2000). On magic and alchemy in science, see Paolo Rossi, *Francis Bacon: From Magic to Science* (London: Routledge, 1968), and Charles Webster, *From Paracelsus to Newton: Magic and the Making of Modern Science* (Cambridge: Cambridge University Press, 1982). On Newton, see Michael White's very readable biography, *Isaac Newton: The Last Sorcerer* (London: Perseus Group, 1999). On issues relating to women and science, see Londa Schiebinger, *The Mind Has No Sex? Women in the Origins of Modern Science* (Cambridge, MA: Harvard University Press, 1989).

   The most authoritative studies of seventeenth-century political philosophers remain the works of Quentin Skinner: *The Foundations of Modern Political Thought,* 2 vols.

(Cambridge: Cambridge University Press, 1978), and *Visions of Politics*, 3 vols. (Cambridge: Cambridge University Press, 2002).

Dorinda Outram, *The Enlightenment* (Cambridge: Cambridge University Press, 1995), provides a solid one-volume introduction to the topic, while John W. Yolton, *The Blackwell Companion to the Enlightenment* (Oxford: Blackwell, 1992), includes articles on all aspects of the Enlightenment, with extensive lists of additional reading. Peter Gay, *The Enlightenment: An Interpretation*, 2 vols. (New York: W. W. Norton, 1966 and 1969) remains an important work from the perspective of intellectual history. Roy Porter, *The Creation of the Modern World: The Untold Story of the British Enlightenment* (New York: W. W. Norton, 2001), is a massive study that includes an excellent discussion of culture and politics. For critiques of the Enlightenment and its legacy, see James Schmidt, ed., *What is Enlightenment? Eighteenth-Century Answers and Twentieth-Century Questions* (Berkeley: University of California Press, 1996), and Peter Hulme and Ludmilla Jordanova, *The Enlightenment and its Shadows* (London: Routledge, 1990). For women and the Enlightenment, see Samia I. Spencer, ed., *French Women and the Age of Enlightenment* (Bloomington: Indiana University Press, 1984).

On the changing culture of art and music, see Thomas E. Crow, *Painters and Public Life in Eighteenth-Century Paris* (New Haven: Yale University Press, 1985); Simon McVeigh, *Concert Life in London from Mozart to Haydn* (Cambridge: Cambridge University Press, 1993); John Butt, *Music Education and the Art of Performance in the German Baroque* (Cambridge: Cambridge University Press, 1994); James H. Johnson, *Listening in Paris: A Cultural History* (Berkeley: University of California Press, 1995); Pamela H. Smith and Paula Findlen, eds., *Merchants and Marvels: Commerce, Science, and Art in Early Modern Europe* (New York: Routledge, 2002).

 For more suggestions and links see the companion website www.cambridge.org/wiesnerhanks.

Notes

1 Immanuel Kant, "An Answer to the Question: What is Enlightenment?" (1784), in James Schmidt, ed. and trans., *What is Enlightenment? Eighteenth-Century Answers and Twentieth-Century Questions* (Berkeley: University of California Press, 1996), p. 58.

2 Johannes Kepler, *The Harmony of the World* (1619), trans. E. J. Aiton, A. M. Duncan, and J. V. Field, *Memoirs of the American Philosophical Society*, vol. ccix (Philadelphia: American Philosophical Society, 1997), p. 304.

3 Montesquieu, *The Spirit of the Laws*, book 17, "How the laws of political servitude bear a relation to the nature of the climate," at http://www.constitution.org/cm/sol_11_17.htm#002

4 Ibid., book 16.

5 David Hume, "Of National Characters," in *The Philosophical Works of David Hume* (Boston: Little, Brown and Company, 1854), vol. III, p. 228.

6 Condorcet, *Sketch for a Historical Picture of the Progress of the Human Mind*, from *Modern History Sourcebook*, ed. Paul Halsall, at http://www.fordham.edu/halsall/mod/condorcet-progress.html.

7 Ibid.

8 Jean-Jacques Rousseau, *Emile*, trans. Allan Bloom (New York: Basic Books, 1979), p. 358.

9 Translated and quoted in Jane Bowers, "The Emergence of Women Composers in Italy, 1566–1700," in Jane Bowers and Judith Tick, eds., *Women Making Music: The Western Art Tradition, 1150–1950* (Urbana, University of Illinois Press, 1986), p. 139.

10 John Essex, *The Young Ladies' Conduct: Or Rules for Education* (London, 1722), p. 85.

11 Religious consolidation and renewal, 1600–1789

William Hogarth (1697–1764), *Hudibras and Ralpho in the Stocks* (1726), one of twelve illustrations that Hogarth produced for *Hudibras*, a satirical mock-epic poem poking fun at the Puritans written by Samuel Butler (1610–80) during the Restoration. Many people supported the goals of Puritans and others who called for moral rigor and personal piety, while others, including Butler, opposed strong religious fervor that, as the opening of the poem reads, "made them fight, like mad or drunk, For Dame Religion."

Timeline

1555	First Jewish ghetto established in Italy
1563	England and Scotland make witchcraft a civil crime punishable by death
1581	Jewish Council of the Four Lands established in Poland
1589	Metropolitan bishop of Moscow declared a patriarch
1631	Netherlands States General grants official toleration to several versions of Calvinism
1650s	George Fox founds the Society of Friends
1653, 1656, 1713	Papal bulls condemn Jansenism
1667	Reforms in Russian Orthodoxy lead to split with Old Believers
1675	Philipp Spener publishes *Pia desideria*
1685	Louis XIV revokes the Edict of Nantes
1689	English Parliament agrees to limited religious toleration
1721	Peter the Great abolishes the Moscow patriarchate
1738	John Wesley begins preaching in England
1773	Pope Clement XIV suppresses the Jesuit order
1774	Mother Ann Lee leads the Shakers to America
1780	Joseph II begins closing the monasteries in Austria

"WHAT did you learn about salvation and the Bible in church today?" a mother asks in *Spiritual Conversation Between a Mother and Child About True Christianity*, a satirical poem published in Amsterdam in 1650. "Nothing," the child answers. "About the prophets and Revelation?" "Nothing." The mother then launches into a harsh critique of the clergy's monopoly of religious discussion despite their lack of spiritual understanding:

> No one is allowed to contradict him
> Even if he says that crooked is straight
> And black is white. He must be right.

The author of this poem, Anna Owen Hoyer (1584–1655), is certainly not the household name that Martin Luther is, but her writings and her life can serve as a mirror for understanding key religious developments in the seventeenth and eighteenth centuries as fully as his can for the sixteenth. She attacked clergy in an established state church – in her case, the Lutheran church of her native Schleswig-Holstein in northern Germany – for laxness, pride, greed, and empty formalism, calling them "devil pastors" and even blaming them for the Thirty Years War. She advocated churches that did not have close relations with a state, and called on lay people to develop practices that met their spiritual needs better than the state churches did. She met with a small group of like-minded individuals, and they were forced to flee religious persecution, eventually finding refuge far from home. Her enemies were equally harsh in their language, describing women such as Hoyer as the "false prophetesses, quacks, fanatics and other sectarian and frenzied female persons through whom God's church is disturbed."[1]

Hoyer, and many others like her, was responding to developments in European Christianity that might be seen as signs of strength and success. From the late sixteenth century, Lutheran, Calvinist, and Catholic university professors and theologians created and defended elaborate theological systems that drew clear lines of difference between the Christian confessions. Such systems are often called "confessions" or "orthodoxies," the latter a word of Greek origin that Christians had long used to mean "true belief." Western European orthodoxies are spelled with a small "o" to distinguish them from Orthodoxy, the term used to describe the Christian churches of eastern Europe, such as Greek Orthodoxy, Russian Orthodoxy, Serbian Orthodoxy, and so on (these also developed their own "orthodoxies," to some extent). Highly educated clergy dominated intellectual life in many cities, and in Lutheran and Calvinist areas important preaching positions and chairs of theology were often handed down from father to son, or from father to son-in-law, creating virtual clerical dynasties. Village priests and pastors received more thorough training than they had before the Reformations, and were expected to communicate orthodox religious ideas to their parishioners through sermons and teaching, in the process of strengthening the religious understanding and adherence historians have more recently termed "confessionalization."

Confessional unity was a matter of secular law, not simply religious practice. Though the Thirty Years War convinced most people that religious unity was not possible in Europe as a whole, it did not convince many religious or political leaders of the virtues of toleration within one territory. English Puritans who were too vocal in their opposition to bishops and elaborate ceremonies during the early reign of King Charles I were persecuted, but many of those same individuals later backed harsh laws against Catholics and radical Protestants. This happened at exactly the same time as King Louis XIV of France was intensifying punitive measures against Protestants, and Russian tsars were persecuting "Old Believers," clergy and lay people who did not agree with changes in liturgy, prayers, and rituals ordered from above. In 1689, the English Parliament and the rulers William and Mary did agree to limited religious toleration, a policy that had already served the merchants who controlled the Netherlands well. Only in a few German and Dutch cities did people of more than one Christian confession have equal political and legal rights, however, a situation that did not begin to change until the very end of the eighteenth century. In 1731, in fact, the Catholic archbishop of Salzburg ordered thousands of Protestants in his territory into exile, giving them eight days' notice; Prussian officials resettled many of them in Prussian territory, though some ended up as far away as the British colony of Georgia. Every state in Europe had secular laws against witchcraft and sorcery, and secular officials were just as active in hunting and executing witches as members of the clergy.

Confessional standardization and religious coercion created established state churches that were powerful institutions, but increasing numbers of people began to think that these churches had lost their spiritual vigor and encouraged empty conformism. Like Anna Hoyer, they turned to groups that emphasized personal conversion, direct communication with God, interior individual piety, and moral regeneration. Some of these groups, such as the Levellers who advocated communal ownership of property in Civil War England, survived only briefly and had little long-term impact. Others, such as the Quakers, became involved in social and political changes in both Europe and European colonies. Others, such as the Moravians in central Europe or the Methodists in Britain, became institutionalized as separate denominations. Still others, such as the Jansenists in the Netherlands and France or the pietists in Germany and Scandinavia, shaped the existing Catholic and Protestant churches. Catholicism, Lutheranism, and Calvinism all came to include individuals who regarded personal piety and an active devotional life, as well as services and rituals, as central to Christian spirituality.

Though it has been more extensively studied for western European Christianity, the interiorization of religion, emphasis on personal piety, and hostility to established churches also included Eastern Orthodoxy, Judaism, and, to some degree, Islam in the Ottoman Empire. Old Believers in Russia opposed changes in liturgy and ritual made by the state church, and in the eighteenth century formed large communities that followed strict rules of piety and behavior. Jews focused on the mystical teachings of the cabala as a guide to morality, and in the eighteenth century supported the vibrant emotional spirituality of Hasidism. Within Islam, Sufi shrines and brotherhoods offered the possibility of intense religious devotion without years of study of the Qur'an. Thus, in terms of religious life, the seventeenth and eighteenth centuries saw both a continuation of the process of consolidation begun in the sixteenth century and calls for renewal that highlighted the shortcomings of established churches.

Established Protestant state churches

The close relationship between church and state can best be seen in the Lutheran states of Germany and in Scandinavia. Here rulers controlled every appointment to higher church positions, set clerical salaries, and oversaw all practical matters involving the church. They saw the church not simply as an institution for sustaining and expressing faith, but also as an agency of public policy, requiring clergy to publish official decrees and recruit for the army. Those pastors who refused, or who argued that the church should play an independent role, were dismissed from their positions or given minor rural posts where they could have little influence and had only a precarious income.

Because the clergy could not be intellectually, financially, or politically independent, many turned their attention to theological controversies, hurling invectives at those who disagreed with them on such issues as the exact way in which the Bible was divinely inspired, and developing a rigid Lutheran orthodoxy. They criticized those who disagreed with them, or who suggested that certain points of theology might not be essential to salvation. Sermons became occasions for pastors to show off their knowledge of obscure theological points rather than provide moral guidance. A seventeenth-century Lutheran sermon on Matthew 10: 38, for example ("Even the very hairs of your head are numbered"), did not focus on the larger meaning of this verse – divine concern for all aspects of human life down to the smallest detail – but on the origin and correct care of hair, other biblical references to hair, and the hairstyles proper to good Lutheran men and women.

Calvinists engaged in intense theological debates as well, expanding Calvin's already comprehensive theological system into very detailed statements of faith. In the Netherlands, theological controversy centered on the exact nature of predestination. The more conservative faction, called Gomarists, argued that before the beginning of the world, God had decided who would have faith and who would not, so that an individual's going to heaven or hell was a matter of God's *will.* The less conservative faction, called Arminians or Remonstrants, argued that before the beginning of the world, God had decided to send Christ as the redeemer; God knew, but did not decide, what each person's response would be, so that predestination was a matter of God's *knowledge.* In 1618, just as the Thirty Years War was breaking out, the Dutch States General called for an international conference of Calvinists to decide this matter. This meeting, called the Synod of Dort, took a very conservative position on the disputed issues and condemned all those who disagreed. For a decade or so, leaders of the opposition were exiled or executed, but in 1631 the States General changed its mind about the wisdom of this, and granted official toleration to a range of Calvinist opinions. This was the first step in an expanding pattern of toleration that would eventually extend even to non-Christians, and play a significant role in Dutch prosperity and cultural advance. Once they had established this general pattern, however, neither the States General nor the *stadholders* in the

Netherlands intervened in the operation of the church in the ways Lutheran princes did in Germany.

In England, disputes about the structure and theology of the established state church were one of the causes of the Civil War in the 1640s. At the beginning of the seventeenth century, all adults were supposed to be members of the official Church of England, attend church, and pay their church taxes. All teachers and tutors were licensed by bishops, who also censored books and could excommunicate those who did not conform. Bishops had seats in the House of Lords, and many also had other positions in the royal government. Church services were in English, clergy were allowed to marry, and the official position on most theological points was clearly Protestant, but many people thought that there were still too many "popish" holdovers. They supported measures they thought would "purify" the Anglican church – for this they were given the name "Puritans" – and bring it theologically closer to continental Calvinism with its emphasis on predestination and personal piety.

Puritans wanted clergy who were both learned and godly, and frowned on "frivolous" pastimes such as dancing or cards, as these wasted time better spent in reading Scripture or praying. Every waking hour could be improved by greater concentration on spiritual matters: family devotions should start and end each day, work should be done in a reverent spirit so that it better pleased God, free moments or hours should be used in self-examination and exploring one's conscience. In terms of church structure, Puritans had widely varying opinions. Some were willing to stick with bishops as long as incense, elaborate clerical dress, and complex worship services were dropped. Others wanted to follow the Calvinist model of the Scottish Kirk, with meetings of lay elders called presbyteries given the most power. Others, who came to be called "independents," wanted each congregation relatively independent in terms of doctrine and structure. A few even wanted no state church at all.

James I did not give in to any Puritan demands and affirmed the existing church structure. He instructed a group of scholars to develop a new translation of the Bible that would be more faithful to the original Greek and Hebrew than the existing English Bibles, resolve certain disputed points of translation, and support the understanding of Christian theology and church structure accepted by the Church of England. The resulting Authorized Version – often called the King James Version – was accepted only slowly in England, but eventually came to be the standard Bible in most English-speaking areas, and had a tremendous influence on religious and secular English-language literature.

Puritans responded to James's support of the Church of England by gradually developing alternative institutions, as well as continuing to push for reforms. Wealthy individuals, especially in London, paid unofficial "lecturers" to preach and teach, which James came to see as seditious. They organized what were known as "gathered" churches in their own homes where individuals prayed and read the Bible, often without a member of the clergy present. Puritans viewed prayer as an active force that could influence state affairs, so they prayed privately and publicly for certain political changes, and were firmly convinced that prayer aided one's family, community, and political allies. As we saw above, Puritans hoped to convert the entire Church of England to their way of thinking, but when it became clear this was not going to happen, they turned increasingly inward and concentrated more on personal conversion than on institutional change. Some Puritans left England for the Netherlands, where they rarely ran into difficulties with authorities as their aims and practices blended well with the Calvinist traditions that were dominant there. About a hundred of these people left the Netherlands for British North America in 1620, and shortly afterwards other Puritans emigrated directly from England; at Plymouth and Massachusetts Bay, these groups established Puritanism as the official state church, and in turn persecuted dissident groups such as the Quakers.

Puritans who stayed in England increasingly made their opinions known in Parliament as well as their houses and streets, which led, as we traced in chapter 9, to war, and eventually to rule by Oliver Cromwell. Cromwell – along with most of the army – was basically an independent, but he had no comprehensive plan for a new church structure, so religious measures were gradual and piecemeal. Bishops were deprived of their positions, compulsory attendance at church was dropped, and church courts ceased to function, though the army leaders who actually governed England carried out some of their functions and enforced social policies many Puritans supported, such as banning cock-fights, closing disorderly ale-houses, and shutting theaters. Puritan leaders in Parliament briefly established a presbyterian form of church and drew up a long statement of faith called the Westminster Confession that largely agreed with the Synod of Dort on its main points of theology. Cromwell did not support these moves, however, and the disorder of the civil war made enforcing anything difficult, so a strictly Calvinist state church in England was never really established.

The restoration of the monarchy in 1660 also restored the Church of England with its bishops, and laws were passed against Catholics and anyone who refused to conform to the Church of England. Such Nonconformists – often called "dissenters" – were forbidden to hold private religious meetings and were banned from public office, while Nonconformist ministers were stripped of their positions and incomes. The Toleration Act of 1689 allowed Nonconformists to have their own ministers and places of worship, but it still prohibited them, as well as Catholics, from attending universities. Nonconformists responded by developing their own places of higher education, which in the eighteenth century became much more vigorous places of intellectual exchange than the allegedly stuffy and elitist halls of Oxford and Cambridge. Restrictions on Nonconformists eased slowly throughout the eighteenth century, though those on Catholics remained longer. Catholics in all of Britain – including Ireland – were prohibited from sending their sons abroad to be educated, passing their lands to a single heir, or serving in Parliament. As voting rights were slowly expanded, Catholics were explicitly prohibited from voting in 1728. Toward the end of the eighteenth century, a series of measures gradually began to lift these restrictions, though the first of these provoked the Gordon riots in 1780, when a huge crowd marched on Parliament and destroyed Catholic churches, chapels, and homes. Complete religious toleration was later adopted in the United Kingdom, though the Church of England remains the official state church today, with the reigning monarch as its official head.

Church and state in Catholicism

Within Catholicism, the relationship between church and state in the development of a rigid system of belief was somewhat different than in Protestant countries, as the pope was both the head of a "state" – a political unit stretching across central Italy – and the universal head of the Roman Catholic Church. In the middle of the sixteenth century, the Council of Trent affirmed the power of the papacy, and late-sixteenth-century popes created a strong bureaucracy and centralized institutions that paralleled, and in some cases served as a model for, those developing in nation-states. By the late seventeenth century, this consolidation of papal authority increasingly conflicted with the power of both local bishops and secular rulers.

Spanish monarchs controlled church appointments, limited papal tax collection, reserved the right to approve papal bulls before they could be published, and directed the Spanish Inquisition. The Inquisition was successful at combating any sign of heresy at the Spanish universities, but this also stamped out any free inquiry, and Spanish universities languished. Despite the Council of Trent's call for improvements in clerical education, most priests in Spain had little opportunity to obtain more than rudimentary training. Spain had more priests and monks as a percentage of the population than any other Catholic country, but most of them were not interested in intellectual pursuits.

Monarchs also increased their control over the Catholic Church in France. As we traced in chapter 9, Louis XIV, seeking to make his realm more uniform, gradually made it more difficult to be a Huguenot. In 1685, these repressive policies culminated in the revocation of the Edict of Nantes, and thousands of Huguenots fled. Louis hoped this would also be a way of demonstrating his Catholic loyalty to the pope, for in other ways he was taking measures to limit papal power. These built on a long-standing tradition of hostility to papal authority within the French church, called "Gallicanism," that began when the papacy moved to Avignon in southern France in the fourteenth century. During the Avignonese papacy, all the popes were French, but when the papacy returned to Italy, almost all the popes were Italian. By the time of Louis XIV, all the popes had been Italian for more than a century – and would continue to be so until the election of John Paul II in 1978 – and the king and many of the French clergy saw the pope primarily as an Italian prince, not the leader of an international church.

The French church refused to accept any of the decrees of the Council of Trent that dealt with church–state relations, and in the seventeenth century the French bishops declared that they were superior to the pope when they met in a council. They largely supported the king in his declaration that he did not have to submit to papal authority in ecclesiastical matters. The popes objected, but they could do nothing about the growing royal influence on church personnel, or state involvement in matters that had previously been the province of the church, such as education and marriage.

The clergy and the monarchs in France did not always agree about how and why papal power should be limited, however, and theological issues were closely interwoven with political concerns. As was true throughout Catholic Europe, the French clergy were very diverse, ranging from bishops and archbishops who were nobles down to very poor parish priests. The church owned a huge amount of land, none of which was taxed, so that high church officials were economically independent of the crown, but parish clergy were totally controlled by their bishops. During the seventeenth century, increasing numbers of people began to feel that the church hierarchy was too focused on monetary concerns and the outward observance of ritual. They called for spiritual regeneration, ethical earnestness, and deep piety, taking the name for their movement from Cornelius Jansen (1585–1638), the bishop of Ypres in the Spanish Netherlands. Particularly in his posthumously published work *Augustinus* (1642), Jansen advocated greater personal holiness, lay reading of and meditation on Scripture, lay participation in church services, and scrupulous attention to morality. Jansenism won converts among middle-class townspeople, intellectuals, rural clergy, and even a few convents and members of the nobility. Its most famous follower was the mathematician Blaise Pascal (1623–62) who became convinced that philosophical reasoning was not sufficient to understand God.

Jansenist ideas led to attacks on the Jesuits, some of whom had developed a system of penance they termed "probabilism," which held people were free to follow their own consciences if they had any moral doubts about an action. No confessor could judge something invariably a mortal sin or refuse to grant absolution, which made probabilists popular confessors and confession an increasingly frequent and important part of people's religious lives. By contrast, Jansenists held to inflexible moral principles, and suggested people confess and take communion less frequently, thus reducing the role of confessors and other clergy over their congregations.

Two papal bulls in 1653 and 1656 condemned some of the ideas contained in *Augustinus*, and in 1661 Louis XIV ordered all members of the French church to sign a statement indicating their adherence to the bulls. Many refused, including the nuns at the convent of Port-Royal, which, under the leadership of abbess Angélique Arnauld (1591–1661), had become the spiritual center of Jansenism in France, renowned for its piety and discipline. A truce with the papacy quietened the debate for several decades, but in 1705 the Port-Royal nuns were ordered to accept another anti-Jansenist papal bull. They again refused, and in 1709 Louis XIV demolished the convent and banished the nuns to other houses.

The writings of the Port-Royal nuns became part of a body of Jansenist literature that continued to circulate, and the fight over Jansenism continued. Though some Jansenist priests fled France, Jansenist laity continued to hold underground prayer meetings. Jansenism continued to shape the religious life of many men and women in France, encouraging them not only to become literate but to become frequent readers, and to develop their children's spiritual lives through family devotions. Salvation was not something to be left in the hands of the clergy, but to be sought through personal piety and prayer, an idea that spread among many Catholics outside France as well. In 1713 Pope Clement XI condemned the main ideas of Jansenism again in the bull *Unigenitus*, which led to a schismatic Catholic church being founded in Utrecht. The French church continued to debate theological issues raised by Jansenism, and the proper level of papal power, right up to the Revolution.

Conflicts about church and state also emerged in German-speaking Catholic areas. There was no unified German state to oppose the power of the papacy, but several German theologians wrote works that built on Gallican ideas. In 1763, the auxiliary bishop of Trier Nikolaus von Hontheim (1701–90), writing under the pen name "Justinus Febronius," attacked the papacy and called for a conciliar church structure and a stronger role for the secular ruler in church affairs. Febronianism was condemned by the pope, but won support in Germany, where both Catholic secular territorial rulers and prince-bishops, modeling themselves on Louis XIV, sought to restrict the power of the pope in their domains.

42 Quietism

Along with Jansenism, what came to be known as Quietism also led to controversy within Catholicism. Quietism was based on the ideas of the Spanish theologian Miguel de Molinos (1628–96), whose *Spiritual Guide* (1675) advocated losing one's individual soul in God, reaching inner peace through prayer and pure disinterested love of God. Any visible religious activity, including attendance at services or even ascetic discipline, took one away from this passive contemplation. Molinos was arrested by the Inquisition, which argued that his teachings were leading people to neglect morality and reject the authority of the church. At his trial, Molinos refused to defend himself, which his followers interpreted as Quietism in action and his opponents as a sign of his guilt. The pope decided not to make a martyr out of Molinos, and imprisoned him for the rest of his life instead of executing him. Quietist ideas spread to France, where Jeanne-Marie Bouvier de la Mothe Guyon (1647–1717) became the center of a group of intensely religious individuals, several of whom were mystics. Madame Guyon felt herself called to spread this mystical method of turning inward, and in 1685 published *A Short and Easy Method of Prayer*. Her ideas attracted women and men, including high church officials such as archbishop of Cambrai François Fénelon (1651–1715), who wrote that he had learned more from her than any theologian. Madame Guyon was imprisoned several times and Fénelon was silenced and exiled from Paris on the orders of Bishop Bossuet, the most powerful cleric in France. Bossuet was particularly incensed about the idea of a mystical "pure love" and the lack of concern for external religious structures that emerged in their writings; if such ideas spread further, wrote Bossuet, they would lead to an intolerable lack of respect for authority. After Madame Guyon died, her writings were translated and printed in the Netherlands and England; in translation they became popular with Methodists in Britain and North America. They are available in paperback versions from many Christian publishers today, advertised for their guidance in prayer and spirituality, not as historical documents.

 For additional chapter resources see the companion website www.cambridge.org/wiesnerhanks.

In Austria, the Habsburg rulers remained Catholic, but felt they had the responsibility to oversee all aspects of religion. The church, in their view, was simply one arm of government, there to assist rulers improve the lives of their subjects, but not to play an independent role. Joseph II issued an Edict on Idle Institutions (1780) closing hundreds of monasteries and using their property to provide better incomes for rural priests, state-controlled seminaries, and more secular schools. The following year he issued an edict of religious toleration for Protestants and Jews, and later called for civil marriages and funerals. These policies of limiting the economic and cultural power of the Catholic Church are often called "Josephinism," with Joseph commenting at one point that he viewed service to God as the same as service to the state.

Though in the later seventeenth and early eighteenth centuries the Jesuits were successful in convincing both the papacy and the French monarchy to condemn Jansenism, by the middle of the eighteenth century the Jesuits were increasingly seen as reactionary and obscurantist. "Enlightened" Catholic rulers resented their autonomy. Education became one flashpoint. In the sixteenth and seventeenth centuries, Jesuit schools were the best in Europe, and extremely effective tools in the Catholic Reformation, but by the eighteenth century they had declined, and the education they offered was viewed as antiquated. Jesuit interference in the exploitation of indigenous peoples by colonial powers, and the acceptance of non-European rituals by Jesuit missionaries, also provoked controversy. Reports of native converts continuing to wear Brahmin insignia in India or bowing to ancestral shrines in China led members of other orders (and some Jesuits themselves) to claim that Jesuits were promoting a watered-down understanding of the Catholic faith. Diplomacy was a third area of conflict, with Jesuit confessors and envoys accused of diplomatic intrigue, or of being agents for internationalism at a time of growing nationalism. A fourth line of criticism was economic, for like all church bodies, Jesuits paid no taxes, despite huge wealth. Anti-Jesuit propaganda fueled this opposition, dragging up old issues and accusing the Jesuits of being behind the regicide of King Henry IV of France in 1610.

All these problems led secular rulers in Europe to suppress the Jesuits – Portugal led the way in 1759, with France following in 1764 and Spain in 1767. Rulers pushed for the election of a pope who agreed with them or would bend to their will, and Clement XIV (pontificate 1769–1774) was elected. He universally suppressed the order in 1773, ostensibly for colluding with the French king, supporting probabilism and the power of free will, and participating in ancestor worship in China.

The suppression of the Jesuits was not effective everywhere. Jesuits in the Russian part of Poland were protected by Catherine the Great, and a novitiate and headquarters survived there. The effects of the disbanding of the Jesuits were felt immediately in education and missionary work, however. Pope Pius VII lifted the ban in 1814, but this did not reverse the declining influence of the papacy in most Catholic countries since the days of the Council of Trent.

Opposition to state church orthodoxy: spiritualism and pietism

Within Protestantism, opposition to state churches began as early as the Reformation itself, among groups such as the Mennonites, Hutterites, and other radicals who advocated a voluntary church of believers with no relation to the state. In the sixteenth century, as we saw in chapter 5, radical groups were persecuted by Catholics and magisterial Protestants, and many fled to areas that were more tolerant, such as Moravia, Silesia, Transylvania, and other parts of eastern Europe. The disruption of the English Civil War allowed radical and dissenting groups to flourish in England for a brief period, but the Restoration brought renewed suppression by royal and Anglican authorities. Some English groups and other radicals migrated to the Netherlands, eastern Europe, or Britain's New World colonies.

In the seventeenth century, several groups continued the emphasis on inner devotion that had characterized some of the earlier radicals, downplaying the importance of the Bible, an ordained clergy, outward ceremonies or sacraments, higher education, and sometimes reason. These groups are often called "spiritualists," of which the most organized was the Society of Friends, called the Quakers, founded by George Fox during the 1650s. Fox had a powerful conversion experience, which he described as receiving the Inward Light of Christ, and he regarded this contact with the divine as open to all people. Quakers had no ordained clergy or formal services, but worshipped in silence until someone was moved by the spirit to speak or pray; decisions were made communally, by discussing a matter until an agreement was reached. They refused to pay tithes, swear oaths, or show deference to their superiors; they dressed simply and addressed each other as "thee" and "thou," the older and less formal version of "you," to signify their rejection of hierarchy and their distinctiveness from others. Early Quakers were often very vocal in their rejection of other forms of worship, disrupting services they saw as ungodly.

Quaker men and women preached throughout England and the English colonies in the New World, and were active as missionaries also in Ireland, continental Europe, and occasionally elsewhere in the world. They were whipped and imprisoned, and often wrote apocalyptic prophecies or "encouragements" for co-believers while in prison. Many Quakers moderated their position with the accession of William and Mary in 1688 and the Toleration Act of 1689, agreeing to pay tithes and moving out of politics. Both British and American Quakers continued to be involved in social action, however, and were among the founders and leaders of the international antislavery and women's rights movements.

Other spiritualist leaders never achieved the level of organization that Fox did, and their groups remained much smaller than the Quakers. Jakob Boehme (1575–1624), a German cobbler, began having mystical visions as a young man, which gained him admirers but also brought him to the attention of the Lutheran authorities. His visions, which he wrote down in a series of works, mixed together Christian themes with ideas from magic and alchemy to develop a complex theory of the dialectical emergence of the world from chaos into being through God's power. His language about "virgin wisdom," the eternal womb of God, and the power of intuition to hear the sympathetic vibrations of God's emergence in nature, often confused the theologians who were trying to determine whether his ideas were heresy or not. What seemed more clearly dangerous was Boehme's rejection of the importance of the Bible, and his stress on the freedom of the spirit and direct revelation. The town council where Boehme lived ordered him to stop writing, an order he followed for a while, but toward the end of his life writing streamed from his pen. Many of his works were published later in the Netherlands and England, where they influenced Fox and many other religious thinkers; they were also important to Romantic poets, including William Blake, and later German philosophers, including Georg Friedrich Hegel.

Jane Lead (1623–1704) was one of those who read Boehme, writing that true religious knowledge came only through turning inward and finding one's own inner light. She organized a circle of like-minded people called the Philadelphian Society, urging them to seek the "virgin wisdom of God" and not go "whoring after Lord Reason." Jean de Labadie (1610–74), a French ex-Jesuit, and Antoinette Bourignon (1616–80), a French mystic, also developed spiritualist ideas, writing that spiritual rebirth was more important than baptism, so that Jews and Muslims might also be blessed and resurrected. They gained a small group of followers, usually called Labadists, and were forced from France to Flanders, then to Germany, and finally to the Danish-controlled city of Altona and to the Netherlands, which provided a refuge for Philadelphians and Quakers as well. By the late seventeenth century, the Netherlands was the most tolerant part of Europe, so that it was also the most common place of publication for the works of radical religious thinkers.

Though Boehme and Lead were suspicious of reason, not all spiritualists were anti-intellectual. Some of them carried on the tradition of the Italian reformer Fausto Sozzini, who had emphasized the links between reason and revelation. The Swedish nobleman Emanuel Swedenborg (1688–1772), for example, edited the first Swedish scientific journal, and was interested in geology and cosmology. He investigated the lobes of the brain, deciding that the soul was located in the cortex, and combined scientific and religious speculation to explain the origins of the world. Like Fox, Boehme, and Madame Guyon, he had a mystical vision he regarded as a direct message from God about true reality; this vision would usher in a new age of the spirit, he wrote in his many works, in which all that exists would be shown to be simply a reflection of God. Swedenborg had few followers during his lifetime, but after he died the Church of the New Jerusalem based on his writings was founded in London; there are small groups of Swedenborgians still around today, most of them in North America.

Except for the Quakers, most of the spiritualist groups remained very small. A much larger movement, and one that did not break totally with state churches, was pietism, a word that originated as a term of ridicule and derision but, like Yankee, was later used positively by those who had been so labeled. Different pietists had different specific aims, but in general pietists wanted to build a meaningful religious fellowship *within* the state church through devotion, moral discipline, and personal religious experiences. Puritanism in England is similar to pietism, as it also emphasized personal conversion, voluntary prayer meetings, and rigorous moral standards.

Lutheran pietism developed late in the seventeenth century. The German pastor and theologian Philipp Spener (1635–1705) set up Bible study groups that he called "colleges of piety" in Frankfurt during the 1670s, and in 1675 published *Pia desideria*, which outlined a program for the enhancement of piety through reforming the seminaries, charitable activities, and prayer circles for lay people. Spener called for preachers to emphasize the word of God in their sermons instead of complicated doctrinal issues, and to provide evidence of their own personal spiritual regeneration as well as their theological training before being given a position. He never directly attacked any Lutheran doctrine, but the orthodox Lutheran theologians at the University of Wittenberg and elsewhere decided he was a Calvinist, as he emphasized sanctification – holiness of life, achieved through the power of God – more than justification by faith. Spener was forced to leave first Frankfurt and then Dresden. Despite – or perhaps because of – this opposition, lay people organized and joined colleges of piety in many German cities, and other Lutheran pastors also began to advocate similar ideas. August Francke (1663–1727), a pastor in Leipzig, was forced to step down from his position for his emphasis on spiritual conversion and lay involvement; he joined Spener at Halle in Brandenburg – the most tolerant state in Germany – where they established a new university.

The University of Halle became the largest divinity school in Germany, and its graduates set up orphanages, schools, and study groups. They were the first Protestants to engage in missionary activity; in 1707, the king of Denmark sent two graduates of Halle to the Danish colony of Tranquebar in India, and soon pietist Protestant missionaries were in Lapland, Greenland, and colonial America. Lutheran pietists varied in their reaction to political changes. Some of them were politically passive, while those in the expanding state of Brandenburg-Prussia played an important role in the establishment of the bureaucratic absolutist state.

Moravians and Methodists

Though Spener and Francke did not break officially from state–church Lutheranism, the pietest movement in Germany did lead to the creation of a new denomination, the Unity of Brethren, usually called the Moravians. Count Nicholas von Zinzendorf (1700–60), a German nobleman, studied at Halle, and later encountered a group of radical Protestants who had been forced to flee their homeland in Moravia – now part of the Czech Republic – by Catholic authorities. Zinzendorf gave them asylum at his estate in Herrnhut in Moravia, and later joined the group himself. Like the Quakers, the Moravians had distinctive dress and speech. Their hymns, writings, and ceremonies emphasized a mystical union with Christ, and were often very physical and sensuous, full of images of bathing in the wounds of Christ and even celebrating Christ's penis as a symbol of his full humanity.

Zinzendorf had originally wanted the Herrnhut community to be simply a group within the Lutheran Church that encouraged deeper religious sensibilities, but they became instead a separate body. Zinzendorf was banished from Germany for more than ten years and traveled to England and America to set up Moravian congregations. (Bethlehem and Nazareth in Pennsylvania began as Moravian colonies, as did Salem in North Carolina.) Other Moravian missionaries traveled to Africa, India, the Caribbean, and South America; the small Moravian church may have supplied half of the Protestant missionaries active in the world in the eighteenth century.

The strong faith of Moravian missionaries made a deep impact on a young English pastor, John Wesley (1703–91), on his way to Georgia to preach to colonists and Native Americans. Wesley's father Samuel was a minister in the Church of England, and his mother Susanna provided religious and moral teachings to all of her nineteen children. Wesley attended Oxford, where he and his brother Charles formed a religious group that read the Bible for several hours each day, took communion frequently, visited prisons and the poor, and pledged to live a moral life. They were ridiculed by other students as a "holy club" or as "Methodists" who proposed a method of achieving sanctification and spiritual perfection.

Wesley was ordained, and decided to go to America; while on shipboard he met a group of Moravians, who showed great courage by singing hymns through a violent storm. Wesley was completely unsuccessful in Georgia; his white congregation hated him, and Native Americans were not the noble savages he had expected them to be. He came to doubt his own faith, and returned to England bitter and uncertain. There he worshipped with a small group of Moravians, and had a conversion experience in which his "heart [was] strangely warmed" with "trust in Christ."

Wesley joined George Whitefield (1714–70), a former member of his "holy club" at Oxford, preaching in the open to large crowds of people, especially in the growing factory and mining towns that often lacked churches or schools. They often preached three or four sermons a day, to which people responded by crying, moaning, and shouting. In some cases sermons led to riots, sometimes instigated by thugs paid by local Anglican ministers or landowners; Wesley, a small man, became known for his physical courage and absolute fearlessness. He and Whitefield separated because of theological and personal differences, but the movement grew, and lay people as well as ordained ministers began to preach. Wesley originally opposed this, but slowly accepted lay preachers as necessary in this time of deep spiritual need. He organized his followers into small groups called "classes" for weekly meetings led by lay leaders; a group of classes formed a "circuit" led by a superintendent, and circuits met together in an annual conference. This structure gave leadership opportunities to quite ordinary people, including women, and also kept members in line, as they had to give an account of their journey toward perfect Christian love to the group each week.

Wesley saw all of these activities as a supplement to normal Anglican services, and never officially broke with the Anglican Church. Anglican bishops refused to ordain his preachers, and Anglican clergy refused to give communion to people known to be Methodists. In the 1780s, Wesley broke with Anglican rules that allowed only bishops to ordain new ministers, and ordained several men to serve in the newly independent British colonies in America and in Ireland. By the time of his death, Methodism was becoming a separate church, and it later grew into the largest Protestant denomination in the English-speaking world. Wesley himself was politically conservative – he opposed both the American and French revolutions – but Methodists gradually came to support humanitarian causes such as the abolition of slavery, prison reform, temperance, and public education, which had political implications. They still tended to emphasize personal regeneration and holiness more than political or social change, however, which led many leaders in the trade union movement to despise the Methodists for what they saw as patronizing and placating workers. In many parts of Europe by the nineteenth century, urban working-class people were divided between conservative Methodists and other pietists and more radical trade unionists; both offered Sunday group activities, and people chose the church or the union hall.

43 Methodist hymns

Hymns were extremely important in Methodism, both for teaching basic ideas to people who could not read and for deepening spiritual commitment and enthusiasm. John Wesley's brother Charles (1707–88) wrote hundreds of hymns, including "Hark the Herald Angels Sing," many of which were later used by other denominations as well. This hymn by Charles, from one of the earliest Methodist hymnals, focuses on the power of redemption available to all and the proper response to God's grace.

"O for a Thousand Tongues to Sing" (1740)

O for a thousand tongues to sing
  My dear Redeemer's praise,
The glories of my God and King,
  The triumphs of his grace.

My gracious Master and my God
  Assist me to proclaim
And spread through all the earth abroad
  The honors of thy Name,

Jesus! The Name that charms our fears
  And bids our sorrow cease;
'Tis music in the sinner's ears,
  'Tis life and health and peace.

He speaks; and listening to his voice
  New life the dead receive,
The mournful broken hearts rejoice,
  The humble poor believe.

Hear him, ye deaf, ye voiceless one,
  Your loosened tongues employ;
Ye blind, behold your Savior comes,
  And leap, ye lame, for joy!

Glory to God and praise and love
  Be now and ever given
By saints below and saints above,
  The Church in earth and heaven.

 For additional chapter resources see the companion website www.cambridge.org/wiesnerhanks.

Gender issues in western Christianity

Many of the spiritualist and pietist groups regarded personal religious devotion as more important than theological training or holding an official clerical position in determining who was properly called by God, so that women often played more important roles than they did in the official state churches. Johanna Eleonora Petersen (1644–1724) organized several pietist circles and wrote a huge number of tracts, including a commentary on the Book of

Revelation. Erdmuthe von Zinzendorf (1700–56) was largely responsible for the financial security and day-to-day operations of her husband's colony of Moravian Brethren at Herrnhut in Germany, and handled missionary work in Denmark and Livonia. Susanna Wesley, John and Charles's mother, held meetings with hundreds in attendance at which she read sermons and discussed religious issues, and other Methodist women preached and ran weekly meetings.

The Shakers – officially the United Society of Believers in Christ's Second Appearing – a spiritualist group that began in the 1740s around Manchester in England, came under the leadership of the visionary and mystic Ann Lee (1736–84). Lee's followers regarded her as the second coming of Christ; God, in their eyes, was both female and male, so Christ's second coming would have to be in a female body. Her visions also told her that sexuality was depraved, and her followers swore celibacy and chastity. She and her followers were severely persecuted, and in 1774 she led eight of them to the American colonies; persecution continued and she died as the result of beatings. Despite – or perhaps because of – their advocacy of celibacy, the Shakers continued to win followers; at their peak, in about 1830, American Shakers may have numbered 6,000 people.

The Shakers were not the only radical or pietist group to develop unusual ideas about sexuality or distinctive systems of marriage. Such groups did not regard marriage as a sacrament – most rejected the idea of sacraments completely – but they placed more emphasis on its spiritual nature than did Lutherans or Calvinists. Marriage was a covenant – a contract – between a man and a woman based on their membership in the body of believers, and thus was linked to their redemption. Because of this the group as a whole or at least its leaders should have a say in marital choice, broadening the circle of consent far beyond the parental consent required by Luther, Calvin, and other less radical reformers. Quakers who wished to marry had to produce a certificate stating that both parties were Quaker, or risk expulsion. Moravians in Pennsylvania were segregated by sex until marriage; when a man wished to marry, he came to the Elders' Conference, which proposed a possible spouse. Three colored ballots standing for "yes," "no," and "wait" were placed in a box, and one was drawn, which was regarded as the "Savior's decision."

To their adherents and supporters, the actions of female leaders were heroic signs of God operating through the least of his creatures, and unusual structures of marriage highlighted a distinction from the rest of the "fallen" world. To their opponents, the women's actions and the strange marriage rules were proof of a group's demonic or at least misguided nature. Among the "errors, heresies, blasphemies and pernicious practices of the sectaries," described by Thomas Edwards in *Gangraena* (London, 1646), a long tract against those who opposed state churches, was the fact that they allowed women to preach. Johann Feustking, a German theologian, turned his attention entirely to women in *Gynaeceum haeretico fanaticum* (Frankfurt and Leipzig, 1704), spending 700 pages describing, as his full title reads, the "false prophetesses, quacks, fanatics and other sectarian and frenzied female persons through whom God's church is disturbed." Methodists were ridiculed for allowing female preaching, and often criticized in gendered language – as "silly women" – because the testimony of all followers seemed overly emotional and sentimental. Individuals claiming to be divinely inspired, whether female or male, were "enthusiasts" whose practices, in the eyes of their more restrained critics, were both theologically suspect and medically dangerous.

In the later eighteenth century, especially in France, Catholicism was also condemned for allowing women to be too influential. Philosophers criticizing the power of the Catholic Church over education, marriage, charities, and other aspects of culture decried an alliance between women and priests in which emotion and "blind" faith were prized and reason was excluded. After the French Revolution, they pointed to women's actions during the conflict – hiding priests who refused to sign oaths of loyalty to the government, attending illegal worship services, and organizing prayer-meetings and processions – as signs of this feminine weakness for "superstition."

Historians of Christianity in the late nineteenth century often attempted to be more "objective" and "scientific," which meant that they highlighted official institutional and intellectual developments and paid less attention to popular devotional practices or individuals outside the mainstream. Like their colleagues in the newly professionalizing field of secular history, they often left women out of the story. Pietist and Methodist historians who did include women such as Johanna Petersen, Erdmuthe von Zinzendorf, or Susanna Wesley in their histories were careful to describe them as "helpmates."

Over the last thirty years, however, many scholars have returned to a position closer to Edwards and Feustking than to nineteenth-century church historians. They see the seventeenth and eighteenth centuries as a period in which Christianity in many parts of Europe – and not simply that of "sectaries," "fanatics," or "enthusiasts" – offered new avenues of religious creativity and activism for women. Even within the state churches, women bought many more devotional books than men, joined confraternities and prayer groups in record numbers, and wrote religious books that were read by both women and men. Whether in sectarian groups or state churches, women rarely broke with religious traditions that privileged men and instructed women to be obedient and subservient, but their independent actions provided a more ambiguous message. This "feminization of religion," as it has been termed, continued into the nineteenth century, with religion increasingly viewed, along with the family, as part of the female sphere.

Eastern Orthodoxy

Relations between church and state in early modern eastern Europe followed two general patterns. With the expansion of the Ottoman Empire in the fifteenth and sixteenth centuries, Christians in Greece, the Balkans, and the rest of southeastern Europe came to live under Muslim rule; Orthodoxy, Catholicism, and other Christian denominations were tolerated, but the official religion was Islam. In Russia, Orthodoxy was the state religion, with its religious leader in Moscow; church and state were expected to work together, and both came under the increasing control of the tsar.

In the middle of the fifteenth century, the Byzantine emperor and the patriarch of Constantinople appealed for western help against Turkish advances, even agreeing to a union of the eastern and western churches under the pope. This agreement dissolved with the Ottoman conquest of Constantinople in 1453. The patriarch fled the city, but Sultan Mehmet II allowed the bishops to elect a new patriarch, whom he personally invested with the symbols of office. Mehmet permitted Christian services to continue in about half the churches in the city, while the other half, including the Hagia Sophia, the largest church in the city, were turned into mosques. He gave the patriarch civil and religious authority over all Christians under Ottoman rule, not only those in Greece, but also those in the Balkans, Syria, Palestine, and eventually Egypt. Christians were understood to belong to a semi-autonomous community called the *millet*, which followed Christian law in terms of marriage, divorce, and other matters. These measures increased the power of the patriarchs, but also increased their dependence on the sultan; those who did not implement government policies were quickly removed from office. Ottoman officials also realized that they could demand gifts or bribes from candidates for the patriarchy or regional bishoprics, so encouraged quick successions; during the seventeenth century, the position of patriarch changed hands sixty-one times, though many individuals held the position more than once.

The patriarchs and their clergy were in charge of collecting taxes from the Christian *millet*, taxes that were heavier than those paid by Muslims, and they often turned to secular officials to do the actual work for them. Some of these officials, call *Phanariots* from the section of Istanbul where they lived, grew very wealthy, investing in international trade and sending their sons to study at western European universities. Phanariots gained the right to rule in eastern European areas such as Moldavia and Walachia, where they founded Greek-speaking schools and intermarried with the local nobility. The dominance of Greek lay and church officials frequently led to resentment, particularly when patriarchs tried to increase uniformity in worship and imposed a Greek liturgy on Orthodox Christians who were used to using Serbian, Rumanian, Bulgarian, or other languages.

During the sixteenth century, both sides in the Reformation attempted to get the Orthodox Church to weigh in supporting their religious position. Philipp Melanchthon, Luther's follower and associate, translated the Augsburg Confession into Greek and sent it to the patriarch for comment. A response was not forthcoming until years later, long after Melanchthon's death, and it highlighted the many areas where Lutheran and Orthodox understandings differed: faith and good works, the number of sacraments, the nature of the Eucharist, the worship of saints and the Virgin Mary. In the seventeenth century, the patriarch Cyril Lukaris (1572–1638) became very interested in Calvinist ideas, learned through discussions with Dutch diplomats in Istanbul and correspondence with Dutch ministers. He wrote a Confession of the Orthodox faith that was quite Calvinist in tone, which so alarmed both the French ambassador and

Jesuits in Istanbul that they persuaded the sultan to have him strangled. Cyril's confession was condemned as heretical, but it inspired other Eastern Orthodox theologians to write their own, and by the late seventeenth century there were several approved Orthodox statements of faith. These tended to be less detailed than those worked out by western Christian denominations, as the Orthodox Church held that divine mysteries could and should not be described in precise detail.

Rituals, and not official statements, were at the heart of Orthodoxy for the vast majority of believers. They attended regular Sunday services, venerated holy icons, participated in ceremonies to mark the stages of life and the change of seasons, and went on processions to celebrate holidays. Communities often chose their own priest from among the married men of the village; he went off for a few months to a monastery to learn the services, and then returned to take up both his family and clerical duties. Monks and nuns devoted themselves more to prayer than to intellectual accomplishments, and some were greatly venerated by local lay people for the rigor of their prayer schedule. Monasteries and convents – of which there were many in the Ottoman Empire – often owned icons understood to be miracle-working, so were places of pilgrimage as well as residences.

Even before the Reformation, some groups in eastern Europe had received permission to use their own language and rituals, and accept married clergy, but still be considered Catholic, as long as they swore allegiance to the pope. Such groups, called Uniates or Eastern Rites Catholics, had developed first in Poland-Lithuania; in the partitions of Poland in the late eighteenth century roughly half of Poles were Roman Catholic, and most of the rest were Uniates who used Greek or Church Slavonic instead of Latin in their services. Uniates were a sizable minority in Hungary, and in Croatia and Dalmatia, where there were conflicts between Latin and Uniate church hierarchies.

The religious situation in the Balkans became even more complicated with the various advances and retreats of the Habsburgs and Ottomans in the seventeenth and eighteenth centuries. In Bosnia and Albania, most of the population had converted to Islam, but in the rest of the Balkans Christians of various denominations predominated. Jesuit and Franciscan missionaries often accompanied Habsburg conquests, seeking to firm up loyalty to Rome; the Orthodox hierarchy responded by stressing its differences from Rome, and requiring Christians baptized in the west to be re-baptized in order to join the Orthodox Church. (This was not required by Catholics or Protestants in western Europe, who decided to accept baptism and marriage celebrated by the other as fully valid.)

This policy made life difficult for Uniates, who sometimes migrated to areas they hoped would be more hospitable. In 1690, for example, 3,600 Uniate families left Serbia, where Orthodoxy predominated, for lower Hungary. Their Uniate bishop led them, but discovered when he got to Hungary that the Roman Catholic Church there was less than welcoming. Religious conflicts in Hungary and the Balkans thus involved disputes among Orthodox, Roman Catholic, Uniate, and in some places Protestant, Christians, as well as between Christians and Muslims. War led to the displacement and migration of many of these groups, further complicating religious and ethnic divisions, and setting the stage for long-lasting ethnic conflicts.

The largest Orthodox community in the east was that of the East Slavs, who had adopted Christianity in the tenth century. By the fifteenth century the most powerful state in eastern Europe was the principality of Muscovy, with its capital at Moscow, which also served as the center of the Russian church. The head of the Russian church, called the metropolitan, was initially appointed by the patriarch of Constantinople, but with the fall of Constantinople to the Turks in 1453 metropolitans became largely independent. The Turkish conquest left Moscow as the only major city in the east to be ruled by a Christian prince, which many Russians interpreted as the will of God. In their minds, God had clearly punished the Greek Orthodox Church for making an agreement with Rome, and now that the "second Rome" – Constantinople – was under infidel rule, Moscow was destined to be the "Third Rome." The princes of Muscovy began using the title "tsar," Russian for caesar, and asserted that they had God's blessing in their conquest of other Russian princes. In 1589 Muscovite political and religious authorities pressured church leaders throughout the east to declare the metropolitan of Moscow a patriarch, which gave him a status equal to the pope in Rome and the patriarch of Constantinople.

As had the leaders of the Byzantine church, the patriarchs of Moscow saw the proper relationship between church and state as harmonious. The church controlled private family matters such as marriage and wills, and owned vast estates with villages and serfs, but it was not politically powerful. The tsar generally stayed out of doctrinal matters, though he often determined who would be appointed to high church offices. In 1551 the Russian church issued a law code known as the *Stoglav* ("Hundred Chapters") that paralleled a recent law code of the tsar and largely reiterated earlier statements relating to proper rituals, beliefs, and practices. This document and other works emanating from church officials were not very theological, as the Orthodox Church held that the essence of God is ultimately unknowable – a type of theology termed "apophatic" – so that positive statements about God's nature risk being blasphemous. In fact, critical analysis of texts and theological innovations were specifically condemned, and intellectual debates about such matters as the nature of the Eucharist or the interpretation of certain biblical passages were unknown in the Russian church. The church held that because faith is unchanging and eternal, no church body has the right to alter doctrine or sacraments. A complete Russian Bible was not even available until the 1490s, and the translators – working from Greek texts – had few debates, because "books are created by the Holy Spirit," in their opinion, not by translators.

Disastrous Russian losses to Polish and Swedish armies in the early seventeenth century, and other problems in this "Time of Troubles," led both church and government leaders to wonder whether God had abandoned Russia in the same way he had earlier abandoned the Greeks. Tsar Aleksei (ruled 1645–76) and some church officials increasingly thought that this had happened because the Russian church had strayed from "true" Christian practice in its rituals, which were the center of Russian church life. Under the leadership of Bishop Nikon (1605–81), whom Aleksei promoted to patriarch in 1652, the church outlawed rituals that seemed to contain non-Christian elements or promote carnivalesque celebrations, and passed measures to make services more uniform. It instituted modest reforms in church liturgy, prayers, and rituals, such as using three fingers for the sign of the cross instead of two and spelling the name of Jesus in a new way, which made Russian practice more like that of the Greek and Ukrainian Orthodox Churches. These changes were formalized in the Moscow Church Council of 1666–7, and those who did not accept them were excommunicated.

The reforms were opposed by those who wanted to stay with traditional practices, later termed Old Believers, and by local church officials who opposed Nikon's centralizing measures. Some groups of Old Believers opened new religious communities and held services that followed the old rituals, while others were convinced that the changes were the work of the Anti-Christ and that the Apocalypse was at hand, so in 1688 they did not plow their fields and lay in white shrouds in coffins. Because they cast the tsar and the government as the "spirit of the Anti-Christ," and refused to serve in the army, obey central directives, or pay taxes, Old Believers were subjected to persecution, often in the form of military campaigns. Some Old Believers chose the route of martyrdom, usually by

44 Peter the Great's marital policies and the Russian Orthodox Church

Peter the Great's political ambitions resulted in nearly constant warfare, and so he favored anything that would increase the Russian population. Peter was convinced that unhappy marriages produced fewer children, so in 1722 he added his voice to that of the Orthodox Church forbidding forced marriages at all social levels, including landlords arranging the marriages of their serfs. He criminalized infanticide, opening orphanages for babies born out of wedlock, and, with an eye to both procreation and Western models, criminalized male homosexual activity. He continued the policy, begun in the fifteenth century, of requiring priests to marry and ordering them to retire if their wives died.

Peter also wanted to modernize Russian gender norms and marriage practices. In the sixteenth and seventeenth centuries, it had become customary in Russia to protect the honor of elite women, especially marriageable daughters, by secluding them in the *terem*, separate women's quarters. Although women in the *terem* could carry out economic activities and invite guests, they rarely appeared in public. Peter required that elite women abandon the *terem*, and appear at public social gatherings, mingling with men. He ordered men and women of the elite to dress western style, and required all men to shave their beards in defiance of Orthodox tradition; well-to-do women were to don the corsetted gowns and adopt the bare-headed coiffures of the west.

Popular rituals that stressed female purity, such as showing the bride's bloody sheets or nightgown after the wedding night, were prohibited, and women who bore children out of wedlock were not to be forced to marry the father of their child, though they were allowed to. (As in western Europe, children conceived or even born out of wedlock in rural areas generally brought little dishonor if their parents subsequently married.) Peter regarded marriages between social equals as preferable, and so required spouses to be of the same social class. Religious differences, on the other hand, were not an issue; over the objections of the church, he allowed marriages between spouses of different Christian denominations, demanding only that the children be baptized into the Orthodox faith. Because Peter saw no purpose in wasting human resources on monastic life, he forbade physically capable men and women of childbearing years from taking vows.

self-immolation, while others fled to the fringes of the enormous Russian Empire or even abroad. The small groups that survived copied the letters and writings of their martyred leaders, crafting them into heroic stories and creating an Old Believer identity.

The modest adoption of western practices that so horrified Old Believers paled in comparison with those demanded by Peter the Great. As we saw in chapter 9, Peter was intent on modernizing and westernizing Russia, in order to make it a larger, more powerful, and more centralized state. An independent church did not fit this vision, and when the patriarch died in 1700, Peter prevented the election of a new one. In his church reform of 1721, Peter abolished the office of patriarch and instead established a committee, the Holy Synod, as the church's ruling body, headed by a lay official he appointed. This effectively made the church a department of the secular government. With the endorsement of the church hierarchy, Peter required parish priests to keep records of births, baptisms, marriages, and deaths. These records allowed the state to determine men's status for taxation and military service.

Although the church and state of Peter's era issued many new regulations, it proved much more difficult to alter ingrained attitudes and behavior. Church leaders complained about peasants' ignorance of Christian teachings, but made little concrete effort to remedy it. Peter and his successors opened seminaries for the training of clergy, but these stressed Latin rather than Greek, Russian, or Church Slavonic, so the priests and monks who emerged were ill-prepared to serve their congregations. Rules concerning entrance into monasteries and convents were relaxed, and displaced widows in particular sought this alternative, though monasteries gradually lost landed wealth. Catherine the Great speeded up this transfer of land from monasteries to the government, and placed the appointment of all offices of the church under state control.

During Peter's reign, large numbers of peasants moved to Old Believer communities to avoid army recruitment, higher taxes, and imposed social changes; by 1800 there were several million Old Believers in communities on Russia's southern and western borders and in Siberia. They grew increasingly separate from the rest of Russian society, dressing distinctively, prohibiting alcohol, tobacco, and tea, opening schools, limiting contact with outsiders, and developing a theology distinct from Russian Orthodoxy. In many ways they were similar to spiritualist and pietist groups in western Europe, with a strong sense of religious devotion and practical piety. Old Believer communities were sporadically persecuted, but eventually Catherine the Great allowed them a degree of tolerance, though they had to pay twice the taxes that members of the state church did.

Witchcraft

The cooperation of state and church authorities in the establishment of official Christian churches in the centuries after the Reformation was also evident in trials for witchcraft, which reached their peak in Europe in the late sixteenth and early seventeenth centuries. Because so many records have been lost or destroyed, it is difficult to make an estimate for all of Europe, but most scholars agree that during the sixteenth and seventeenth centuries somewhere between 100,000 and 200,000 people were officially tried for witchcraft and between 40,000 and 60,000 were executed. Between 75 and 85 percent of these were women, though the gender balance varies widely in different parts of Europe. The reasons for this predominance of women are complex: women were viewed as weaker and so more likely to give in to the devil's charms or use scolding and cursing to get what they wanted; they had more contact with areas of life in which bad things happened unexpectedly, such as preparing food or caring for new mothers, children, and animals; they were associated with nature, disorder, and the body, all of which were linked with the demonic. Europeans took their notions of witchcraft with them to the New World: a few people, most of them women, were executed for witchcraft in the European colonies in North America. In the Andean region of South America, older native women who had fled to mountainous areas and refused to become Christians were charged with witchcraft and idolatry. Some European thinkers even blamed witchcraft on the explorations, asserting that demons had decided to return to Europe from the Americas once Christian missionaries were there, and so were possessing and seducing many more people than they had in the Middle Ages.

Anthropologists and historians have demonstrated that nearly all pre-modern societies believed in witchcraft and made some attempts to control witches, who were understood to be people who use magical forces to do evil deeds (*maleficia*). Witches themselves often believed in their own powers, which could serve as a way to earn a living or gain influence over their neighbors. In the later Middle Ages, however, many educated Christian theologians, canon lawyers, and officials added a demonological component to this notion of what a witch was. For them, the essence of witchcraft was making a pact with the devil, a pact that required the witch to do the devil's bidding. Witches were no longer simply people who used magical power to get what they wanted, but people used by the devil to do what *he* wanted. This demonological or Satanic idea of witchcraft was fleshed out, and witches were thought to engage in wild sexual orgies with the devil, fly through the night to meetings called sab-bats which parodied the mass, and steal communion wafers and unbaptized babies to use in their rituals. Some demonological theorists also claimed that witches were organized in an international conspiracy to overthrow Christian-ity, with a hierarchy similar to the hierarchy of angels and archangels that Christian philosophers had invented. Witchcraft was thus spiritualized, and witches became the ultimate heretics: enemies of God.

The earliest trials involving this new notion of witchcraft as diabolical heresy were in the 1430s in the area around Lake Geneva in Switzerland and France, and in 1484 Pope Innocent VIII (pontificate 1484–92) authorized two German Dominicans, Heinrich Krämer (*c.* 1430–1505) and Jacob Sprenger (*c.* 1436–95) to hunt witches in nearby areas of southern Germany. Krämer oversaw the trial and execution of several groups – all of them women – but local authorities objected to his use of torture and his extreme views on the power of witches, and banished him. While in exile, he wrote a justification of his ideas and methods, the *Malleus maleficarum* (*The Hammer of [Female] Witches*), published in 1486. The *Malleus* pays particular attention to the sexual and gendered nature of witchcraft:

> As for the first question, why a greater number of witches is found in the fragile feminine sex than among men ... the first reason is, that they are more credulous, and since the chief aim of the devil is to corrupt faith, therefore he rather attacks

them ... the second reason is, that women are naturally more impressionable, and ... the third reason is that they have slippery tongues, and are unable to conceal from their fellow-women those things which by evil arts they know ... But the natural reason is that she is more carnal than a man, as is clear from her many carnal abominations ... To conclude. All witchcraft comes from carnal lust, which is in women insatiable.[2]

The *Malleus* also provided practical advice for future witch-hunters, advising them how to recognize and question witches, and recommended that secular authorities work with inquisitors in prosecuting witches. Later demonological works were not as deeply misogynistic as the *Malleus*, but the stereotype of the witch that developed across much of Europe was female.

Secular rulers north of the Alps increasingly agreed with Krämer about their role, and passed witchcraft statutes authorizing the death penalty if witches harmed people through magic or sorcery. These civil witchcraft laws, such as the criminal code of the Holy Roman Empire from 1532 or the English and Scottish witchcraft statutes of 1563, tend to focus more on *maleficia* and less on pacts with the devil, though in actual trials the influence of *Malleus* and other works of demonological theory is evident, at least in central Europe. Witch trials died down somewhat during the first decades after the Protestant Reformation, when Protestants and Catholics were busy fighting each other, but they picked up again more strongly than ever in about 1570. Most of them were handled by civil authorities, though the German prince-bishops – who were both religious and secular authorities in their bishoprics – were among the most active witch-hunters.

Though at the popular level people continued to be primarily concerned with the *effects* of a witch's powers while at the learned level they were concerned with the *origins* of them, learned ideas gradually began to infiltrate popular understanding of what it meant to be a witch. Illustrated pamphlets and broadsides portrayed witches riding on goats or pitchforks to sabbats where they engaged in anti-Christian acts such as spitting on the communion host and sexual relations with demons. Though witch trials were secret, executions were not; they were public spectacles witnessed by huge crowds, with the list of charges read out for all to hear. By the late sixteenth century, popular denunciations for witchcraft in many parts of Europe involved at least some parts of the demonic conception of witchcraft, and suspects confessed to night-riding and attending sabbats. In areas of Europe in which the demonic concept of witchcraft never took hold, such as Finland, Iceland, Estonia, and Russia, there were no large-scale hunts. In Finland and Estonia about half of those prosecuted for witchcraft cases were male, and in Iceland and Muscovite Russia the vast majority of those prosecuted were men charged with sorcery or with harming people or animals.

Along with witchcraft statutes, other legal changes also played a role in causing, or at least allowing for, massive witch trials. One of these was a change from an accusatorial legal procedure to an inquisitorial procedure. In the former, a suspect knew the accusers and the charges they had brought, and an

Fig. 27. Witch flying off to a sabbath on a winged goat, while other witches look on, from F. -M. Guazzo, *Compendium Maleficarum*, 1610. Pamphlets describing witch trials and demonology were often illustrated, and artists frequently copied one another, which helped spread stereotypes. This is from an Italian guide to witches; the dress of the female and male witches is quite elegant, and different from what most people accused of witchcraft could have afforded.

accuser could in turn be liable for trial if the charges were not proven; in the latter, legal authorities themselves brought the case. This change made people much more willing to accuse others, for they never had to take personal responsibility for the accusation or face the accused's relatives. Inquisitorial procedure involved intense questioning of the suspect, often with torture; areas in Europe that did not make this change saw very few trials and almost no mass panics. Inquisitorial procedure came into Europe as part of the adoption of Roman law, which also (at least in theory) required the confession of a suspect before she or he could be executed. This had been designed as a way to keep innocent people from death, but in practice in some parts of Europe it led to the adoption of ever more gruesome means of inquisitorial torture. Torture was also used to get the names of additional suspects, as most lawyers trained in Roman law firmly believed that no witch could act alone.

The use of inquisitorial procedures did not always lead to witch hunts, however. The most famous Inquisitions in early modern Europe, those in Spain,

Portugal, and Italy, were in fact very lenient in their treatment of those accused of witchcraft: the Inquisition in Spain executed only a handful of witches, the Portuguese Inquisition only one, and the Roman Inquisition none, though in each of these areas there were hundreds of cases. Inquisitors firmly believed in the power of the devil and were no less misogynistic than other judges, but they doubted very much whether the people accused of doing *maleficia* had actually made a pact with the devil that gave them special powers. They viewed them not as diabolical devil-worshippers, but as superstitious and ignorant peasants who should be educated rather than executed. Their main crime was not heresy, but rather undermining the church's monopoly on supernatural remedies by claiming they had special powers. Thus Inquisitors set witchcraft within the context of false magical and spiritual claims, rather than within the context of heresy and apostasy, and sent the accused home with a warning and a penance.

Though there were "witch-hunters" like Krämer or the self-proclaimed English witch-finder Matthew Hopkins in the 1640s who came into areas specifically to hunt witches, most witch trials began with an accusation of *maleficia* in a village or town. Individuals accused someone they knew of using magic to spoil food, make children ill, kill animals, raise a hailstorm, or do other types of harm. Local studies have shown that kinship stresses often played a role in these initial accusations, for tensions over property, stepchildren, or the public behavior of a relative or in-law were very common in early modern families. Household or neighborhood antagonisms might also lead to an accusation. The *Malleus* warned that midwives were prone to witchcraft, but actual accusations against them were not especially numerous. Women who took care of infants and new mothers were more common targets, charged with killing the child or drying up the mother's milk.

Women number very prominently among accusers and witnesses as well as those accused of witchcraft because the actions witches were initially charged with, such as harming children or curdling milk, were generally part of women's sphere. Women also gained economic and social security by conforming to the standard of the good wife and mother, and by confronting women who deviated from it. Women accused of witchcraft were often argumentative, willful, independent, and aggressive; as the indictment of Margaret Lister in Scotland in 1662 put it, she was "a witch, a charmer, and a libber."[3] The last term carried the same connotation and negative assessment of "liberated woman" as it does today.

Very often the incident that led to the charge was not the first, but for some reason the accuser decided no longer to tolerate the suspect's behavior. Once a first charge was made, the accuser often thought back over the years and augmented the current charge with a list of things the suspect had done in the past. The judges then began to question other neighbors and acquaintances, building up a list of suspicious incidents that might stretch back for decades. Historians have pointed out that one of the reasons those accused of witchcraft were often older was that it took years to build up a reputation as a witch. Fear or a desire for the witch's services might lead neighbors to tolerate such actions for a long time, and it is difficult to tell what might finally drive them to make a formal accusation.

At this point, the suspect was brought in for questioning by legal author-ities, and in many parts of Europe we have detailed records about these tri-als. They have been used by historians to study many aspects of witchcraft, but they cannot directly answer what seems to us an important question: did people really practice witchcraft and think they were witches? They certainly confessed to evil deeds and demonic practices, sometimes without torture, but where would we draw the line between reality and fantasy? Clearly people were not riding through the air on pitchforks, but did they think they were? Did they actually invoke the devil when they were angry at a neighbor, or was this simply in the mind of their accusers? Trial records cannot tell us, and historians have answered these questions very differently, often using insights from psychoanalysis or the study of more recent victims of torture in their explanations.

Though we cannot determine the extent to which people actually practiced witchcraft, we know that there were great regional differences in the likely outcome of a trial. As noted above, in southern Europe all cases of witchcraft were handled by the Spanish, Portuguese, or Roman Inquisitions, which most often simply dismissed them. In Europe north of the Alps and Pyrenees, the initial accusation might also be dismissed if the judges regarded the evidence as questionable; one set of figures from the Home Assize Circuit court in England shows 513 persons accused of witchcraft between 1559 and 1736, of whom 200 were convicted and 109 hanged, with the percentage of convictions and executions declining throughout the period. At the same time, when an English judge asked some of his German counterparts how a person accused of witchcraft could escape conviction, they could not think of a way to answer him.

Sexual relations with the devil rarely (and in some parts of Europe, espe-cially Scandinavia, never) formed part of popular ideas about witchcraft, but questioning and torture were in the hands of learned authorities, who were generally more versed in demonological theory, and had often read the *Malleus* with its intense concerns about sex. During the course of questioning, judges and inquisitors sought the exact details of a witch's demonic sexual contacts. Suspects were generally stripped and shaved in a search for a "witch's mark" or "pricked" to find a spot insensitive to pain. In central Europe and Scotland accusations of sex with the devil were generally limited to women, while in France demonologists thought witches of both sexes engaged in sexual inter-course with the devil, and accused witches of both sexes were questioned about such activities.

Once the initial suspect had been questioned, and particularly if he or she had been tortured, the people that had been implicated were brought in for questioning. This might lead to a small hunt, involving from five to ten victims, which was most common in Scotland and parts of Switzerland and Germany. Small hunts grew into large-scale panics occasionally in England (in the 1640s with Matthew Hopkins) and Sweden (beginning in the province of Dalarna during the period 1668–76), but most often in the part of Europe that saw the most witch accusations in general – the Holy Roman Empire, Switzerland, and parts of France. There are a number of possible explanations for this: much of this area consisted of very small governmental units, which were jealous of each other and after the Reformation were divided by religion. The rulers of these small territories often felt more threatened than the monarchs of western Europe, and were largely unhindered in their legal or judicial moves by any higher authority. The parts of France that were under the tighter control of the French monarchy and the appeals court of the *parlement* of Paris saw far fewer large witch-hunts than the areas that bordered Switzerland or the Empire. Many of the deadliest hunts were in the prince-bishoprics in the Empire, such as Trier, Mainz, Würzburg, Ellwangen, Bamberg, or Cologne, where bishops saw persecuting witches as a way to demonstrate their piety and concern for order; in one hunt in Ellwangen, over 400 people were executed between 1611 and 1618, and one of the bishops of Bamberg later acquired the nickname the "burning bishop of Bamberg."

Areas in which the learned stereotype of witchcraft as a devil-worshipping international conspiracy was never fully accepted, including England, the northern Netherlands, and Scandinavia, had a more restricted use of torture and few mass panics. (Torture and demonology were linked, as torture was generally used primarily to find out a witch's accomplices and learn the details of the demonic pact; it was employed most by those convinced of the reality of massive numbers of witches and in turn led to the denunciation of as many other people as the judges thought necessary, for torture was stopped only when the accused supplied what the judges thought was a sufficient number of names.) Witches were also tried by jury in England, which some analysts see as leading to milder sentences, though jury trials did not have this effect in Denmark.

Large-scale panics might begin in a number of ways. Many were the outgrowths of smaller investigations, in which the circle of suspects brought in for questioning simply continued to grow unchecked. Some were also the result of legal authorities rounding up a group of suspects together, and then receiving further denunciations. They often occurred after some type of climatic disaster, such as an unusually cold and wet summer, and came in waves. Panics spread in southern Germany and eastern France in the 1570s, 1590s, 1610s and 1660s, the last spreading as far north as Sweden. In large-scale trials a wider variety of suspects were taken in – wealthier people, children, a greater proportion of men. Mass panics tended to end when it became clear to legal authorities, or to the community itself, that the people being questioned or executed were not what they understood witches to be, or that the scope of accusations defied credulity. Some from their community might be in league with Satan, but not this type of person and not as many as this.

In many ways it was similar skepticism that led to the gradual end of witch-hunts in Europe. Even in the sixteenth century, a few individuals, including the German physician Johann Weyer (1515–88) and the English gentleman Reginald Scot (1538?–99) questioned whether witches could ever do harm, make a pact with the devil, or engage in the wild activities attributed to them. In 1631, the Jesuit theologian Frederick Spee (1591–1635) questioned whether secret denunciations were valid or torture would ever yield a truthful confession. These doubts gradually spread among the same type of religious and legal authorities that had so vigorously persecuted witches. By the end of the sixteenth century, prosecutions for witchcraft were already difficult in the Netherlands, Bavaria, and the area under the jurisdiction of the *parlement* of Paris; the last official execution for witchcraft in England was in 1682, and by then trials were increasingly rare even in the Holy Roman Empire. Witchcraft trials were prohibited in France in 1682, England in 1736, Austria in 1755, and Hungary in 1768. Sporadic trials continued into the late eighteenth century in other areas, but by then people who thought themselves witches were more likely to be regarded as deluded or mentally defective, meriting pity rather then persecution, even by people who still firmly believed in the devil. At the popular level, belief in the power of witches often continued, but this was now sneered at by the elite as superstition, and people ceased to bring formal accusations when they knew they would simply be dismissed.

Judaism

Along with persecuting witches, Christian authorities also persecuted Jews. Jewish life in the early modern period was profoundly shaped by repression, restriction, and in some cases expulsion at the hands of Christian society, though also by economic and intellectual innovation. The center of Jewish culture and the majority of the Jewish population in Europe moved eastward. After Ferdinand and Isabella ordered all Jews to leave Spain or convert in 1492, many Sephardic Jews – who took their name from *Sepharad*, the Hebrew name for Spain – fled across the borders to Portugal and Navarre. Those who converted and their descendants (termed *conversos* or "New Christians") were frequently targets of the Spanish Inquisition, which investigated and prosecuted converts suspected of secretly engaging in Jewish practices or maintaining Jewish beliefs. Portugal expelled the Jews in 1496 and Navarre in 1498, but the Portuguese Inquisition was not as well established as the Spanish, and it was safer to be a *converso* in Portugal than in Spain, at least until the Portuguese Inquisition was intensified in 1579 and Portugal united with Spain in 1580.

Many Sephardic Jews migrated further, to cities in the Low Countries that were more open, or to Italy, where some city rulers invited Jews in to help expand foreign trade, though placating local Christians by segregating the Jews in walled ghettoes. Between 1555 and 1779, twenty-three ghettoes were established in northern Italy, pulling in populations from Spain, the Spanish-ruled territories in Italy, the Papal States (where Jews were banned in 1569), and elsewhere in Europe. Such bans were not always enforced, but the sixteenth and seventeenth centuries saw individuals, families, and whole communities moving from one place to another in a diaspora that involved disruption and loss of property, but also created personal and familial connections across broad areas. Jews became important merchants for New World products like tobacco and sugar, whose trade was usually not restricted by guild rules, and in furs and grain. In the middle of the seventeenth century, Jewish financiers became important to many rulers in western and central Europe as military suppliers and bankers. These "court Jews," as they were known, such as Samuel Oppenheimer (1630–1703) and Joseph Süss Oppenheimer (1698–1738 – known as "Jew Süss"), were indispensable to the rulers they served, but also very vulnerable; Samuel was killed by an angry mob in Vienna and Joseph was executed.

Many Jews went to the eastern Mediterranean, where the Ottoman sultans welcomed Jewish skills. Within the Ottoman Empire, Jews, like Christians, had their own *millet*, with the right to maintain their own laws regarding marriage, morals, and religious practices. The Jewish community was linguistically and culturally diverse: Greek Jews spoke Greek, Middle Eastern Jews spoke Arabic, and Sephardic Jews spoke Spanish. This Spanish later evolved into a distinct language called "Judezmo" or "Ladino," written in Hebrew letters and taking in Greek and Turkish words. Jews were a significant share of the population in Constantinople and an even larger share of that in Salonika, where they set up the first printing presses in the Ottoman Empire. Jewish scholars in Salonika produced scientific and legal works, commentaries on the cabala (alternatively spelled kaballah), and a tri-lingual edition of Hebrew Scripture.

Central European Jews – called *Ashkenazic* from the Hebrew word for the Rhineland area – also migrated eastward, pushed by persecution and pulled by the more welcoming policies of the rulers and nobles of Poland-Lithuania. They were hired by nobles to manage vast estates and the serfs that lived on them, and to populate areas that were thinly settled, including Lithuania and the Ukraine. Like Sephardic Jews in the Ottoman Empire, Ashkenazic Jews carried their language with them; they spoke a German that gradually evolved into Yiddish, written in Hebrew letters but sounding quite similar to German. Ashkenazic immigrants opened religious academies in Lublin, Poznán, and Kraków, which became centers of scholarship on the Talmud. In 1648, peasant discontent about oppressive economic conditions combined with Ukrainian Cossack resentment at Polish rule in a violent rebellion led by the Ukrainian Bohdan Khmelnytsky (1595–1657). About a quarter of the Jews – perhaps as many as 40,000 people – were killed, the largest such massacre until the twentieth century, and many more migrated westward, though Poland continued to have the greatest concentration of Jews in Europe.

Rulers gave Jewish communities autonomy in many aspects of life, and they developed self-governing institutions from the local to the international level. At the local level, a legitimate Jewish community required a group of ten adult males for obligatory prayers (*minyan*), a cemetery, a kosher slaughterer, and a ritual bath (*mikvah*). Communities elected councils and officers, and often hired a rabbi for spiritual leadership, though rabbis did not play an essential role in rituals. They established civil and religious courts, systems of taxation, charities for the poor, and burial societies to provide for funerals and prayer (*hevrahs*). Official positions, public prayers, and formal schooling were generally limited to men, though there were a few women's *hevrahs* run by the women themselves. Women developed special voluntary prayers in Yiddish (*thkines*) for biological and cultural events particularly important for women, including menstruation, pregnancy, childbirth, baking bread, or visiting cemeteries, which transformed folk rituals not mentioned in Jewish law, such as making candles for Yom Kippur, into true religious duties.

Local communities sometimes sent representatives to regional councils or rabbinic synods, and in 1581 the Polish crown established the Council of the Four Lands, a parliamentary body of rabbis and lay officials that met annually or biannually to set general policies for Jews in all the territory it ruled. This lasted until it was dissolved by the Polish parliament in 1764, and shortly afterwards Jewish life, like everything else in Poland, came under the Prussian, Russian, and Austrian rule when Poland disappeared with the partitions.

Jewish life centered on the observance of Jewish law (*halakhah*), which was fundamentally based on Mosaic law and also on the Talmud, a large work of legal commentary and rabbinic interpretation compiled in the sixth century CE in Babylonia. Talmudic principles were further expanded, interpreted, and adapted to specific circumstances in *responsa* literature, which were answers from leading scholars to questions from local rabbis or communities about the proper application of legal principles. The disruptions, migrations, and resettlements of the early modern period provided plenty of issues to be discussed, and some Jewish legal authorities sought to codify the increasingly large body of Jewish law in a way that would provide more helpful practical guidance. (This was at exactly the same time as Christian jurists and legal scholars in western Europe were advocating the adoption of the more organized Roman law instead of a jumble of local law codes.) First Sephardic and then Ashkenazic rabbis systematized legal commentary, though they also tried to retain flexibility in its application to specific local situations.

Along with *halakhah*, many rabbis and ordinary Jews increasingly celebrated the cabala, Jewish mystical texts that originated in the twelfth and thirteenth

45 Jewish Messianism

Jewish scholars and ordinary people sometimes interpreted the events, upheavals, and persecutions of the early modern period as signs that the redemption of the Jews and the coming of a Messiah (from the Hebrew for "anointed") as prophesied in biblical texts was near. Charismatic individuals emerged as messianic leaders, of whom the most important was Shabbetai Tzevi (1626–76), a rabbi born in Smyrna in southern Turkey. Tzevi studied Jewish law and mysticism, and came to believe that he was the messiah foretold in Scripture. He traveled around the Ottoman Empire gaining adherents, and rumors of his miracles and his message spread throughout Europe among both Jews and Christians, feeding on apocalyptic predictions centering on the year 1666. He publicly declared he was the Messiah in 1665, and masses of people flocked to the area near Istanbul where he was living, while others waited for his signal to journey to the Holy Land. Leaders from Jewish communities all over Europe took him very seriously, offering prayers for him and sending him money.

The sultan grew increasingly worried about what could happen and imprisoned Tzevi; in 1666 Tzevi agreed to convert to Islam instead of being executed. This split his followers; some argued that this was all part of his plan and converted to Islam as well, while others denounced him. Even after he died, his followers kept the Shabbetai movement alive with predictions that he would return, worshipping as a secret group that seems to have blended Jewish and Muslim teachings. In the eighteenth century, a Polish merchant named Jacob Frank (1726–91) claimed to be the reincarnation of Shabbetai Tzevi, and acquired hundreds of followers, adding Christian teachings to the Shabbetai blend. He was eventually baptized as a Christian and gained the favor of Maria Theresa, who thought he could spread Christianity among Jews. The Frankist sect disappeared quickly and had little long-term impact, though the Shabbetai movement itself split Jewish communities in both Ottoman and Christian Europe for centuries.

centuries in Spain and southern France, but looked back to much older traditions. Cabalistic writings and practices spread throughout the Mediterranean and into Europe with the diaspora of Spanish Jews, and were among the earliest printed works in Hebrew. The cabala offers mystical understandings of the nature of God, the origins of evil, the meaning of religious texts and ceremonies, the parts of the human soul, and a range of other topics. In the sixteenth and seventeenth centuries, cabalists such as Isaac Luria (1534–72) developed systems of spiritual practices, mystical ceremonies, and guides to behavior based on the cabala. Groups studying and practicing cabala were organized in many Jewish communities devoted to intense prayer, moral behavior, interior individual piety, and the study of sacred texts; they were thus very similar to pietist groups that were emerging at the same time within Christianity.

In the eighteenth century, Judaism developed in different directions. *Haskalah* (from the Hebrew word for intellect or enlightenment), an intellectual and religious movement centered on Germany and Poland, advocated the critical study of religious texts and history, expanded secular education, and more integration into non-Jewish society. This modernization of traditional Jewish beliefs and practices led to both more assimilation and more intense interest in Jewish identity; the latter gradually grew into Zionism, the Jewish nationalist movement, and greatly influenced the founders of the state of Israel. At roughly the same time in the Ukraine, Rabbi Israel ben Eliezer (1700–60), also known as the Baal Shem Tov or Besht, developed a more emotional form of piety that centered on prayer, singing, movement, and joyful worship as well as mysticism to achieve communion with God. His movement, called Hasidism from the Hebrew word for "loving kindness," emphasized sincere faith in the omnipresent power of God, and eventually spread to the majority of Jews in Eastern Europe.

Extending civil rights to Jews became a matter of public discussion and political debate in the later eighteenth century. Prohibitions banishing Jews were overlooked, and Jews began to move back into western Europe. In Britain, Parliament passed the Jew Bill of 1753, which allowed foreign-born Jews to become naturalized citizens. This led to a huge public outcry, however, and the measure was repealed the following year; Jews in Britain did not gain full civil rights until the nineteenth century. In 1782, Joseph II issued a "Patent of Toleration for the Jews of Lower Austria," granting Jews civic equality, though much Habsburg territory remained officially closed to Jews, and Jews continued to pay heavy taxes. Jews were given permission to settle in all parts of France in 1784, and were granted rights as citizens during the French Revolution.

Islam

The Ottoman Empire was not only a major center of Jewish life in Europe in the early modern period, but, after the conquest of Granada by Christian forces, the most important center of Muslim life in Europe as well. Christians and Jews in the Ottoman Empire had their own courts for handling internal affairs, but anything that involved Muslims would come before a Muslim court. In the early Ottoman Empire, men wishing to study Islamic law (*shari'a*) or theology had to go to Damascus or Cairo, but beginning in the middle of the fifteenth century religious colleges (*madrasas*) were attached to mosques, supported by income from land in the area. The most important of these were those established by the sultans; those who hoped to gain a judgeship in a large city or a position as an imam at any important mosque needed to attend one of these elite colleges. Judges ruled on specific cases and interpreted both religious and secular law, and they also enforced the sultan's decisions.

The decision of judges applied only to the case at hand; if a broader ruling was desired, people turned to muftis, religious officials with the authority to issue fatwas, or legal opinions that were universally binding. The chief mufti of the Ottoman Empire was a powerful individual, usually drawn from a small handful of families. His opinions had to be put in force by a decree of the sultan, but sultans also turned to the chief muftis for opinions about political issues and muftis became important advisors to the court. Though officially Islam does not have a chief figure of authority akin to the pope, by the later sixteenth century the chief mufti was understood to be the head of the religious-legal establishment, and his office regularly issued fatwas on many aspects of life.

Formal education in law, theology, or the Qur'an was one avenue to religious understanding in the Muslim world, but direct revelation was another. Beginning in the eighth century, Muslim mystics, termed Sufis, taught that divine revelation could come to certain holy individuals, especially those saints who could fully lose themselves in God. This radically different line of thought could have developed into a separate branch of Islam, but most Sufis taught that those who gained knowledge of God through mysticism still had to obey the shari'a, and Sufism became part of orthodox Islam, in both its Shi'a and Sunni branches. Sufis were often wandering ascetics, venerated for their wisdom and austere lifestyle. Religious orders or brotherhoods (*tariqas*) were established dedicated to specific Sufi saints, which, like Christian monasteries, came to own property.

Many Muslims belonged to a Sufi order, and some orders included women, providing a religious community and role not available elsewhere in Islam. There were many different Sufi orders in the Ottoman Empire and elsewhere in the Islamic world, and they often split and recombined over the centuries. Each group had its own rituals and ceremonies, often involving music and the recitation of sacred texts. Some orders, such as the Bektashis, were popular among rural people; they spread Turkish religious poetry, broadened the understanding of Islam among villagers, and provided places for people to stay while traveling. There was no organized plan for conversion in the Ottoman Empire, though over the years peasants in many areas gradually turned to Islam, more as the result of contact with orders such as the Bektashis than with learned theologians in Istanbul. Not all Sufi orders were rural ascetics, however. Devotion among the Mevlevi order focused on sacred texts in Persian

Fig. 28. An engraving from about 1720 by the French artist Gérard Jean-Baptiste Scotin (1690–1745?), titled *Dervishes in their temple after the dance.* Western Europeans were fascinated by Sufi brotherhoods, especially the Mevlevis with their mystical dances.

and on dancing to produce a state of ecstasy until one was "a drop of wine in the ocean of God's love." (Western Europeans referred to them as "whirling dervishes," from the Persian word "darvish," which means an ascetic.) Mevlevi orders thus taught the Persian language, poetry, and music; many of the most important poets and composers in the Ottoman Empire were Mevlevis.

Sufi saints were the focus of popular devotion; as in Christianity, people read or heard stories about their lives and miracles, prayed to them for assistance, and made pilgrimages to their shrines. Some Sufi shrines had, in fact, been Christian shrines earlier, and a few places were sacred to both Christianity and Islam, such as the shrine on the Greek island of Levitha, honored by Catholic and Orthodox Christians as a site sacred to the dragon-slayer St. George and by Muslims as a site associated with Koç Baba, a spiritual leader also regarded as a killer of mythical beasts. Learned imams sometimes objected to the emotional rituals and pilgrimages favored by Sufis and their adherents, arguing that they led people away from the essentials of Islam. Sufi brotherhoods provided important social links, however, and their ceremonies were generally more popular than the more formal and reserved services in mosques. For these reasons, and because many sultans and other powerful people were members of Sufi brotherhoods, opposition to Sufi teachings rarely had much effect and most imams did not press the issue.

This toleration of a range of religious practices did not extend to Shi'ites, however. The Ottomans – who were Sunni – saw Shi'ites as linked to the Shi'ite Safavid dynasty in Iran, and so as political opponents as well as heretics. They arrested and charged people with being Safavid sympathizers, testing their loyalty by demanding they say Sunni prayers and affirm the early caliphs as the true successors to Muhammad. (Sunnis believe that the earliest caliphs were legitimate successors to the Prophet, while Shi'ites believe that leadership can only pass through a blood relative of Muhammad.) In 1537, Süleyman I ordered that mosques should be built in every village and that all men should be expected to attend prayer services regularly. He, and later Ottoman rulers, did not inquire closely into people's beliefs, however, and as the Safavids declined in power in the seventeenth century investigations and trials decreased. In general, the Ottoman Empire was tolerant of a wider range of beliefs and practices within Islam than most Christian states of different variants of Christianity, and certainly more accepting of those who followed other religions.

The eighteenth century is often described as a time of growing secularism in Europe, when religion became less important in people's lives. This is true for some individuals, especially among educated elites in western European cities; a few Enlightenment philosophers and more ordinary folk even declared they were atheists, and no longer believed in a god at all. For most Europeans, however, religious devotion, expressed through individual actions such as prayer or communal activities such as worship services, remained strong. In fact, movements such as Methodism, Jansenism, pietism, and Hasidism had made religion *more* rather than less important in many people's lives. The significance of religion would become very evident in the opposition to the French Revolution, and in the broad support for Christian missionary endeavors, which by the nineteenth century had transformed Christianity into a genuinely world religion.

The religious landscape of Europe was more diverse by the end of the eighteenth century than it had been two hundred years earlier, however. Every country of Europe still had an official state church in 1789, but limited toleration meant people of different faiths, or at least different denominations within Christianity, often lived in the same village or neighborhood. Within many denominations there was also a wide spectrum of belief and practice, from those who attended services only for holidays and family events, to those for whom faith shaped every activity. Religion was not the only area of life where the experiences of Europeans in 1789 were more diverse than in 1600, however, for, as we will see in the next chapter, economic changes were transforming the physical and social landscape at the same time as religious movements were transforming the spiritual panorama.

Further reading

There are several good general introductions to Christianity in this era: W. R. Ward, *Christianity under the Ancien Régime, 1648–1789* (Cambridge: Cambridge University Press, 1999); Gerald R. Cragg, *The Church and the Age of Reason, 1648–1789* (London: Penguin, 1990); Nigel Aston, *Christianity and Revolutionary Europe, 1750–1830* (Cambridge: Cambridge University Press, 2004). Ted A. Campbell, *The Religion of the Heart: A Study of European Religious Life in the Seventeenth and Eighteenth Centuries* (Columbia: University of South Carolina Press, 1991), presents a positive view of individuals and groups that emphasized interior religion, while Michael Heyd, *Be Sober and Reasonable: The Critique of Enthusiasm in the Seventeenth and Early Eighteenth Centuries* (Leiden: E. J. Brill, 1995), surveys those who were hostile. Craig Harline, *Miracles at the Jesus Oak: Histories of the Supernatural in Reformation Europe* (New York: Doubleday, 2003), looks at popular beliefs and practices in the sixteenth and seventeenth centuries.

For continental Protestantism, see Bodo Nischan, *Prince, People, and Confession: The Second Reformation in Brandenburg* (Philadelphia: University of Pennsylvania Press, 1994); Philip Benedict, *Christ's Churches Purely Reformed: A Social History of Calvinism* (New Haven: Yale University Press, 2002). For Catholicism, see R. Po-chia Hsia, *The World of Catholic Renewal, 1540–1770* (Cambridge: Cambridge University Press, 1998).

Religious developments in seventeenth-century England have been the focus of wide research. Representative studies include Stephen Brachlow, *The Communion of Saints: Radical Puritan and Separatist Ecclesiology, 1570–1625* (Oxford: Oxford University Press, 1988); Phyllis Mack, *Visionary Women: Ecstatic Prophecy in Seventeenth-Century England* (Berkeley: University of California Press, 1992); Tom Webster, *Godly Clergy in Early Stuart England: The Caroline Puritan Movement, 1620–1643* (Cambridge: Cambridge University Press, 2003). In France, several good new studies have focused on Jansenism: William Doyle, *Jansenism: Catholic Resistance to Authority from the Reformation to the French Revolution* (London: St. Martin's, 2000); Ephraim Radner, *Spirit and Nature: A Study of 17th Century Jansenism* (London: Herder and Herder, 2002).

Carter Lindberg, *The Pietist Theologians: An Introduction to Theology in the Seventeenth and Eighteenth Centuries* (London: Blackwell, 2004), provides just what its title promises, as does Frederick Herzog, *European Pietism Reviewed* (Princeton: Princeton Theological Monograph Series, 2003). Relations between pietism and political developments have been explored in Mary Fulbrook, *Piety and Politics: Religion and the Rise of Absolutism in England, Württemberg and Prussia* (Cambridge: Cambridge University Press, 1983), and Richard L. Gawthrop, *Pietism and the Making of Eighteenth-Century Prussia* (Cambridge: Cambridge University Press, 1993). On the Moravians, see Colin Podmore, *The Moravian Church in England, 1728–1760* (Oxford: Oxford University Press, 1998), and on Methodism, see David Hempton, *Methodism: Empire of the Spirit* (New Haven: Yale University Press, 2005). There are several recent very interesting biographies of Wesley, including Henry Abelove, *The Evangelist of Desire: John Wesley and the Methodists* (Stanford: Stanford University Press, 1992), and the comprehensive Henry D. Rack, *Reasonable Enthusiast: John Wesley and the Rise of Methodism* (London: Epworth, 2002).

Timothy Ware, *The Orthodox Church*, 2nd edn (Harmondsworth: Penguin, 1993) provides a good introduction to the entire history, as well as the doctrine and rituals, of the Orthodox Church. Two collections of articles provide some of the newest research on religion in early modern Russia: Samuel H. Baron and Nancy Shields Kollmann, eds., *Religion and Culture in Early Modern Russia and Ukraine* (DeKalb, IL: Northern Illinois University Press, 1997), and Valerie A. Kivelson and Robert H. Greene, eds., *Orthodox Russia: Belief and Practice under the Tsars* (University Park, PA: Pennsylvania State University Press, 2003).

Brian Levack, *The Witch-Hunt in Early Modern Europe*, 2nd edn (London: Longman, 1995), presents a good overview of witchcraft in this era. More specialized studies include Robin Briggs, *Witches and Neighbors: The Social and Cultural Context of Early Modern Witchcraft* (New York: Penguin, 1996); Stuart Clark, *Thinking with Demons: The Idea of Witchcraft in Early Modern Europe* (Oxford: Oxford University Press, 1997); and Lyndal Roper, *Witch Craze: Terror and Fantasy in Baroque Germany* (New Haven: Yale University Press, 2004).

John Edwards, *The Jews in Christian Europe 1400–1700* (London: Routledge, 1988), and Anna Foa, *The Jews of Europe after the Black Death*, trans. Andrea Grover (Berkeley: University of California Press, 2000), explore many aspects of Jewish life. Isadore Twersky and Bernard Septimus, eds., *Jewish Thought in the Seventeenth Century* (Cambridge, MA: Harvard University Press, 1987), presents original sources and analyses.

J. Spencer Trimingham, *The Sufi Orders in Islam* (Oxford: Oxford University Press, 1998), is a general overview of all the orders, while Shems Friedlander, *The Whirling Dervishes* (Binghamton: State University of New York Press, 1992), is a discussion of the Mevlevi order by a scholar who is himself a Mevlevi. The older Norman Itzkowitz, *Ottoman Empire and Islamic Tradition* (Chicago: University of Chicago Press, 1972), provides a solid discussion of religion and politics.

 For more suggestions and links see the companion website www.cambridge.org/wiesnerhanks.

Notes

1 Johann Feustking, *Gynaeceum haeretico fanaticum* (Frankfurt and Leipzig, 1704), title page (my translation).
2 *Malleus maleficarum* (1486), trans. and quoted in Alan C. Kors and Edward Peters, eds., *Witchcraft in Europe 1100–1700: A Documentary History* (Philadelphia: University of Pennsylvania Press, 1972), pp. 114–27.
3 Quoted in Christina Larner, *Witchcraft and Religion: The Politics of Popular Belief* (Oxford: Basil Blackwell, 1984), p. 85.

12 Economics and technology, 1600–1789

Un Caffetier. Ein Cave Schenck.

1. Une boëtte à thé. 1. eine The Büy. 2. une Caffétiere. 2. eine Caffe Kanne. 3. des coupes pour le sucre.
3. Zücker schälen. 4. Theers. 4. The kanten. 5. Chocolatiere. 5. Chocolat Kane. 6. flacons aux liqueurs et verres.
6. Rosoli fläschel u Gläßer. 7. Rouleaux de tabac. 7. Dübacth.
Cum Priv. May. 8. pipes. 8. Dübacthopfeiffen. Martin Engelbrecht excud. A.V.

A coffee vendor in about 1730, from a collection of engravings of artisans and artists
published by Martin Engelbrecht. The vendor carries a steaming pot of chocolate, with
a tea box on his head, a coffee pot on his arm, and cups on his belt. He smokes a pipe
with another product new to European consumers – tobacco. The artist highlights the
exotic allure with background scenes of Chinese and Arabic men smoking and
drinking stimulating beverages.

Timeline

1630s	Major draining of the English fens begins
1647	Revolt of Naples against government tax policies
1649	Serfs completely bound to the land in Russia
1665–6	Major outbreak of the plague and the Great Fire in London
1712	Thomas Newcomen develops the steam engine
1720	Mississippi and South Sea bubbles of stock speculation
1760s	Richard Arkwright develops the spinning frame
1760s	James Watt improves the steam engine
1775	Flour War protests in France against rising prices

G LICKL bas Judah Leib advised her husband on business matters while bearing and raising their twelve children. At his death, she took over the whole business, rescuing her eldest son from repeated bankruptcies, and expanding into new markets:

> I had a manufactory for Hamburger stockings, many thousands worth of which I turned out for my own account ... I procured wares from Holland, I bought nicely in Hamburg as well, and disposed of the goods in a store of my own. I never spared myself, summer and winter I was out on my travels, and I ran about the city the livelong day. What is more, I maintained a lively trade in seed pearls. I bought them from all the Jews, selected and sorted them, and then resold them in towns where I knew they were in good demand.[1]

Glickl was in many ways highly unusual. She was a woman operating in a man's world, running a factory, traveling to trade fairs and markets, and handling large amounts of merchandise, including luxury goods such as pearls, jewels, and gold lace. In this her Judaism proved an advantage. Because Jews were prohibited from staying in most inns run by Christians, they often had networks of friends with whom women could stay safely, and because Judaism prized the life of a scholar more than that of a merchant, Jewish women were often freer to run businesses than their Christian neighbors. Even more unusually, as we saw in chapter 8, Glickl decided to recount her life story for her children and grandchildren.

Her memoirs are unique, but her activities reflect some of the most important economic developments of the seventeenth and eighteenth centuries.
She ran a "manufactory" making stockings, in which many workers gathered
together in a single location owned by a capitalist investor to produce one type
of textile product, for which they were paid wages. The production of thread,
cloth, and clothing on an ever larger scale was at the heart of Europe's economic expansion in this era. The other booming sector of the economy was
trade. Glickl traded in pearls, which came from South and Southeast Asia to
northern European cities such as Amsterdam and Hamburg. They were handled first by wholesale brokers, who may have financed the voyage, then by
middlemen – or in Glickl's case middlewomen – and then retail dealers. The
retail dealers sold them to embroiderers, goldsmiths, tailors, and other artisans who used pearls, gems, and semi-precious stones in jewelry, clothing,
tableware, clerical vestments, communion goblets, and household items purchased by wealthy Europeans. International merchants were usually male, but
retail trade tended to remain a family business, in which women sometimes
had opportunities to work on their own.

Increases in production and trade provided Europeans, including many with
moderate incomes, with cheaper and more diverse consumer goods of all types.
From Europe's overseas colonies came new foodstuffs such as sugar, chocolate,
tea, and coffee, new types of fabrics such as calico, and new types of household
goods, such as lacquerware and the porcelain that came to be known as "china."
Spices such as cinnamon and pepper grew so affordable that they were no
longer a mark of status and their consumption declined; instead people who
wanted to be elegant used perfumed waters such as rose water or orange-flower
water as flavorings in pastries and sauces. The fashionable drank coffee and hot
chocolate in coffeehouses and cafés, of which there were about six hundred
in Paris by 1750. Brewing and drinking tea became part of the lives of city
residents in some countries, especially England, and even domestic servants
bought their own teapots. Servants, and other relatively poor people, chose
to spend their income on other "frivolous" consumer goods as well, such as
tobacco, lace collars and cuffs, mirrors, parasols, sugared cakes, Chinese tea
sets, and hats. Middle-class people bought more and fancier clothing and home
furnishings, paying attention not only to quality and price but also to changing
styles, which they learned about through printed works and shop displays. They
paid for paintings that showed off their possessions, both interior scenes of
well-furnished homes and still lifes with elaborate flower arrangements, glass
dishes, clocks, mirrors, and books.

As tea and coffee became common drinks for the daytime, Europeans
increased their consumption of stronger alcoholic drinks as well. Beer, ale,
wine, and hard cider had long been the most common beverages for all social
classes, but in the seventeenth century distilled liquors became widely available
as well. Every wine-producing area began to distill brandy and sweet liqueurs,
while rum made from sugarcane poured in from the West Indies and brandy

made from fruits such as apples, pears, plums, and cherries was produced and sold locally. Improvements in the distillation of grains helped distilled liquors compete with brandy in terms of price, and whisky, gin, and vodka became more common beverages, especially for poorer people. In England, the government decided that distilling gin was a way to use up poor-quality grain, so let anyone distill and sell it; by 1740, the production of gin was six times that of beer, with thousands of gin-shops in London alone. Gin-drinking was seen as the root of many social problems, however, and in 1751 the government limited the sale to licensed dealers, although illegal production and sales continued.

In their analyses of economic systems, historians have traditionally regarded production as the most important variable, with trade as a secondary factor and consumption – the purchasing and use of the goods produced and traded – a distant third. They viewed the transformation of the European economy into its "modern" commercial form as the result of technological and organizational changes that dramatically increased the supply of goods and sharply reduced prices. In part because consumption plays such an important role in today's post-industrial economy, however, historians are now paying greater attention to the role of the consumer in times past. Europe's economic growth was fueled by changes in production, and also by international trading ventures and the development of colonial empires, a subject we will take up in chapter 13. It was also fueled by a growing demand for consumer goods within Europe itself, as people living in some parts of Europe decided that certain consumer goods were so desirable they were worth working longer hours to obtain. This "industrious revolution," as the economic historian Jan de Vries has termed it, produced a more comfortable standard of living for people in some parts of Europe, and prompted technological and organizational change.

These changes were very uneven, for in many parts of Europe, working longer and harder would not have brought any improvement in people's lives, while in other areas improvements for some people led to decreases in the quality of life for others. Consumer demand brought economic change even to parts of Europe where the only consumers were members of the aristocratic elite, however. These changes occurred in cities where merchants like Glickl bought, sold, and manufactured merchandise, but also in the countryside.

Agriculture change and rural protests

In 1600, European agricultural productivity was not much different than it had been two centuries earlier: about five bushels of grain per bushel sown in fertile areas, roughly one-tenth of the average yield today. Yields were even lower on poor soil or during the all too frequent droughts, late frosts, or heavy rains. The percentage of the labor force employed in food production was only slightly less than it had been centuries earlier, about two-thirds of the working population. During harvest, when armies of men, women, and children were needed to cut, gather, and stack grain, and then thresh it to separate the kernels from the stalks, even more people worked in the countryside. Two centuries later, these numbers had still not changed very much when looking at Europe as a whole. Only when mechanical reapers and threshers, steel plows, and other agricultural machinery gained widespread use in the nineteenth and twentieth centuries did the numbers of people employed in agriculture plummet, and only with chemical fertilizers did yields skyrocket.

Aggregate numbers hide great regional variations, however, for during the seventeenth and eighteenth centuries agriculture in some parts of Europe underwent tremendous changes. These included new crops and crop rotation schedules, altered patterns of land ownership, selective breeding of stock and plants, and increases in the amount of land put under cultivation through the draining of marshes and coastal areas and the clearing of woodlands. In areas where these changes were introduced, first the Netherlands and then England, agricultural workers produced between 50 and 175 percent more than farmers elsewhere. This meant that there was more surplus to sell, and in both places governments and private investors encouraged the building of canals to get produce to local and regional markets, and in some cases into ships carrying goods internationally. That surplus also allowed many rural residents to purchase consumer goods those ships brought in, or to make further improvements to their property.

In many of these developments, the Dutch led the way, combining technological and organizational innovations to improve agriculture just as they used them to speed up the production of ships and textiles. By the fourteenth century, the Netherlands – including both Flanders and what later became the Dutch Republic – was one of the most urbanized parts of Europe, which created a steady demand for agricultural products. As we saw in chapter 6, this led farmers to work their land more intensively, and to experiment with crop rotation patterns that would lessen the amount of time land needed to be left fallow. They discovered that planting legumes such as beans, peas, alfalfa, or clover actually made the soil richer, increasing the next year's grain crop from that land. Agricultural scientists would later learn that this effect resulted from legumes converting atmospheric nitrogen into the soil nitrates needed by grain crops, but farmers experimented with crop rotations long before anyone understood the chemistry behind them. In the eighteenth century farmers added turnips and potatoes to their rotation patterns, and often increased the frequency with which they grew hay. These crops increased the amount of food available for animals, allowing rural residents to build up their herds of sheep and cattle and feed them over the winter instead of slaughtering most of them in the fall. Farmers in the Netherlands experimented with livestock breeding as well as crop rotation, cross-breeding cattle to select for those that would produce more or higher-quality milk or meat. Dutch butter and cheese became known throughout Europe and beyond. More and bigger animals meant more manure for fertilizer, which improved the productivity of the fields even further.

Along with more intensive use of existing land, the Dutch also created new land. They built dikes and walls out into the sea along their shallow coast, and then drained the land behind the walls. The average elevation of the already Low Countries grew even lower with such large-scale drainage projects, in which new fields, called polders, were bordered by ditches and canals, the largest of which could be used for transport. (Today 27 percent of the Netherlands, with 60 percent of its population, lies under sea level, and the maintenance of sea walls is an important national issue.) Pumps powered by windmills helped keep the land dry.

This process of draining could also be used for marshes and swamps, and by the seventeenth century landowners and rulers in other parts of Europe were hiring Dutch engineers to carry out similar projects. They built canals and reclaimed land for Italian princes, French cities, and the Spanish crown, and built mines in Poland, Russia, and other Baltic areas. In 1619, King Gustavus Adolphus decided he needed a city on the west coast of Sweden that was well fortified to fend off Danish attacks. He used Dutch plans for canals and fortifications and hired Dutch engineers and workers to construct this city of Göteborg (Gothenburg), which they modeled on the Dutch colony of Batavia on the island of Java (now Jakarta in Indonesia). The majority of the first city council was Dutch, and in 1731 Göteborg became the home of the Swedish East India Company, modeled on the similar Dutch company.

Dutch innovations found their readiest market in England, where landlords were already enclosing fields and common lands to create sheep-runs, selling their wool to the growing textile industry. Enclosed fields, controlled by a single owner rather than a village community, could be easily planted in an innovative rotation pattern if the owner thought this would be even more profitable than wool. Viscount Charles Townshend (1674–1738) was an advocate of such changes; he had seen what the Dutch could do while serving as English ambassador to the Netherlands, and he returned to his huge estates extolling the virtues of new crops and methods. He advocated a four-field system of crop rotation, with each field planted successively in two kinds of grain, legumes, and turnips; each of these crops either adds nutrients to the soil or absorbs nutrients differently, so that no land has to be left fallow. This system was already being used by some farmers in England, and Townshend encouraged the farmers who leased his lands to adopt it, which led his fellow landowners to nickname him "Turnip" Townshend.

Sowing grain – which formed the bulk of the European diet – was done through scattering seeds by hand, and various inventors tried to build machines that would put the seeds in the soil in a regular pattern instead of haphazardly on top of it. Jethro Tull (1674–1741), the son of a gentleman farmer, developed the first mechanical seed drill that worked. Drawn by horses, his seed drill made rows of small trenches in the soil and dropped seeds in to them, using less seed than sowing by hand. Tull's seed drill is seen as the ancestor of modern farm machinery because it was the first successful agricultural machine with inner moving parts. It was complicated and expensive, however, and seed drills were not widely adopted until the early nineteenth century. Tull also invented a horse-drawn hoe for weeding and modified existing plow designs, but none of these brought him great success. He ended his days unhappily on the estate he had hopefully named Prosperous Farm, a title that turned out to be more ironic than accurate.

Many innovators were aristocrats or gentry who had the wealth and leisure to contemplate new methods, but some were individuals who actually worked the land themselves. Robert Bakewell (1725–95), born into a family of tenant farmers, traveled around Europe observing agricultural methods. He experimented with flooding fields to improve hay yields and built special stalls for cattle in which they would not lie in their own manure, which kept them healthier, yielded more manure for fertilizer, and lessened the amount of straw needed for bedding, thus increasing the straw available for animal feed. He was especially interested in intensive selective breeding, and separated males from females in his herds so that he could breed specific individuals. He bred cattle and sheep that produced more meat, as did other experimental farmers, turning beef and mutton from foods for the upper classes into staples of the English diet.

Landowners in England also emulated Dutch techniques of gaining new land. They brought in Dutch engineers and technicians to design and build drainage projects in the marshy areas of eastern England called the fens, turning them from low-intensity use into high-intensity fields. Woods and hillsides were also cleared and planted in clover or turnips, which could grow on poor soil and provide still more food for animals. All of these changes created an agricultural system that was sustainable over the long haul and produced a steadily increasing amount of food.

Changes in rural life were gradual, but their cumulative result could be very disruptive. When fields were enclosed, land that had been held in common by the whole village became the property of one individual or one family; individuals were supposed to receive land in proportion to their share of the open fields, but large landowners often got a disproportionate share of the better land. This was particularly true after 1750, when enclosure was more often by Act of Parliament than by an agreement among local landowners. Enclosed property often included not just existing fields, but also woods and scrub areas where poorer people raised a few pigs or geese, and gathered nuts, coal, stone and firewood for their own use or to augment their meager incomes. Enclosure, and sometimes even the rumor of impending enclosure, sparked protests, threats, and occasionally riots. In 1631, for example, a crowd of several thousand people gathered in Gloucestershire to protest the sale of royal forests to entrepreneurs for subdivision; the crowds destroyed fences, burned down the houses of the encloser's agents, and finally burned an effigy of the encloser himself, Sir Giles Mompesson. In 1753, armed crowds

46 The draining of the English fens

The English fens, huge low-lying wetlands similar to the American Everglades, were home to a distinctive culture in which people supported themselves by fishing, hunting, cutting willow for furniture, and cutting peat – the thick layer of sphagnum moss that covered much of the fens – to sell for fuel. Parts of the fens were so wet that people worked on stilts, though higher and dryer areas held villages, towns, and the city of Ely. In the 1630s, the earl of Bedford and a group of venture capitalists – "adventurers" as they were then known – hired Cornelius Vermuyden, a Dutch engineer, to start a major drainage project. If it worked, the investors would receive thousands of acres of new and very fertile farmland. Fen-dwellers protested the loss of their livelihood, and there were violent riots, especially during the 1640s – the time of the English Civil War – when their concerns were linked with other political and social grievances. An unknown author put the complaints of the fen-dwellers into verse:

> Come, brethren of the water, and let us all assemble,
> To treat upon this matter which makes us quake and tremble,
> For we shall rue it, if't be true, the Fens be undertaken,
> And where we feed in fen and reed, they'll feed both beef and bacon.
>
> Behold the great design, which they do now determine,

Will make our bodies pine, a prey to crows and vermin;
For they do mean all fens to drain and waters overmaster;
All will be dry and we must die, 'cause Essex calves want pasture.

The feathered fowls have wings to fly to other nations,
But we have no such things to help our transportations;
We must give place (oh grievous case!) to horned beasts and cattle,
Except that we can all agree to drive them out by battle.

(Cited in William Dugdale, *The History of Imbanking and Draining of Divers Fens and Marshes* [1661].)

Investors and agricultural improvers scoffed at such protests. In *The English Improver Improved* (1652), Walter Blith wrote "As to the draining, or laying dry the fens: those profitable works, the Commonwealth's glory, let not curs snarl, nor dogs bark thereat." Both draining and protest riots continued, though by 1850 there were very few people who made their living in traditional occupations, and by 1950 99 percent of the fens had been drained. In the last several decades, with worldwide recognition of the ecological value of wetlands, conservationists have been working to restore a small part of the fens to their original state and provide habitat for wetland plants and animals.

 For additional chapter resources see the companion website www.cambridge.org/wiesnerhanks.

broke into the area where a noble landowner had begun raising rabbits for the urban market, killing thousands of the animals they believed destroyed grazing lands.

Such protests did not stop changes in the countryside. Rural residents with small amounts of land were often forced to sell once they had lost their rights to use common lands, increasing the number of landless. They then hired themselves out as servants or day laborers to larger landowners, for root crops, hay, and specialized market crops were all very labor-intensive, increasing the demand for workers in the countryside at all times of the year, not simply during the grain harvest. Intensified stock-raising and enclosed fields meant animals were often fed all year in stables rather than being allowed to range freely. This created constant work, especially for women, for feeding animals was viewed as a woman's task. Historians estimate that by 1700 there were about two landless agricultural laborers for every independent farmer in England, and this proletarianization of the rural population continued in the eighteenth century. By 1800, more of the rural population in England were completely landless wage workers than elsewhere in western Europe.

As in many parts of Europe, aristocratic landholders in England owned vast estates, but they often rented out much of their land to large-scale tenant farmers. The noble landowner then paid for improvements while the tenant farmer and hired laborers did the actual work fencing fields, felling trees, manuring soil, and breeding livestock. Tenant farmers, and wealthier peasants who owned fairly large farms in both England and the Netherlands, were the real entrepreneurs, developing technical expertise that led to farm improvements and adopting new products with changing demand and market conditions. The number of independent peasant farmers declined slowly in England as many found it advantageous to sell their lands to large landowners and then lease them back as tenant farmers, but they never completely disappeared.

Agricultural practices changed more slowly in other parts of Europe than they did in the Netherlands or England. In eastern Europe, the institutions of serfdom established in the sixteenth century became even more onerous, with serfs bound completely to the land in Russia in 1649 and living in similar circumstances elsewhere. Aristocrats held estates with thousands of acres, though they often calculated their landed resources in terms of serfs rather than acres because the number of workers available to them was the most important determinant of total output. They took little interest in improving productivity, however, for they were operating on such a large scale that even with a high ratio of labor per acre and very primitive methods they were still able to produce a marketable surplus for export. Spanish landowners were similarly uninterested in agricultural innovation. High taxes and rents drove many peasants to sell their land to nobles, who sometimes chose to raise sheep for the international wool trade, but did so with traditional methods of transhumant sheepgrazing, not intensive stock-raising.

In most of western Europe, much of the land was held by peasant proprietors with very small holdings, and even the larger landowners – nobles, townspeople, monasteries, church officials – did not own more than 1,000 acres. Local aristocrats often charged various dues and fees on peasant property, or for certain services, such as milling grain, and regional or central governments charged taxes. As we saw in chapter 6, during the sixteenth century these fees and taxes often went up, forcing some peasant proprietors to sell their land and become tenant farmers or agricultural workers. Even for peasants who were able to keep their land, higher taxes and dues meant they had little surplus to experiment with new crops or techniques, and little incentive to change, as that would simply have meant an even higher tax burden. This meant that except in a few areas, such as the district around Paris, the German North Sea coast, and some parts of northern Italy, yields did not go up as they did in the Netherlands and England. There was some enclosure of common lands, but relatively little. There were few canals or roads for the transport of agricultural products, so that even in areas with specialized agriculture, such

Fig. 29. Domenico Gargiulo's (1612–79) dramatic painting of the Revolt of Naples in 1647, which began as a protest against a new tax on fruit, and escalated into a nine-month revolt. Armed crowds took control of the city under the leadership of a fishmonger named Masaniello (shown here addressing the crowd), burned storehouses and government offices, and killed financiers and tax collectors. Masaniello was later murdered on the order of the Spanish governor, and the power of elites in the city over the countryside was strengthened.

as the wine-growing parts of Italy or France, peasants still needed to produce enough grain to sustain themselves. Wine or olives or silk thread were valuable enough to carry to market, but grain was generally too expensive for peasants to buy if it had to be transported. During years with poor harvests, rural crowds also tried to prevent grain from being taken away to nearby cities by blocking roads or waterways. This happened in the regions that supplied London in the 1630s and those that supplied Rome in the 1640s; in the latter instance, crowds grew so violent that they killed the local papal governor and burned down his residence.

Rising grain prices in the eighteenth century actually made the situation worse instead of better. As they had in the sixteenth century "price revolution," wheat prices rose throughout the century, especially in France. Peasants and other landholders responded by planting as much wheat as they possibly could rather than legumes or crops for animal consumption. Wheat strips nutrients from the soil very quickly, however, so that yields per acre went down, especially as there was not enough livestock to produce the necessary nitrogen-rich manure. This led to higher prices, and created a vicious cycle of even *more* wheat being planted. Most French peasants still had to buy some grain to survive, so they suffered more than they gained from the rise in prices. In 1775, a year with crop failures in many parts of France, crowds protesting rising prices gathered in hundreds of towns; they seized wheat, flour, and bread, sometimes for their own use and sometimes to force sales at prices they thought were reasonable, what was known as the *taxation populaire*. These violent actions, later called the Flour War, were eventually put down only when the monarchy brought in 25,000 troops.

The French monarchy responded to these problems by alternately regulating and de-regulating the grain trade, but this vacillation, combined with harvest shortfalls, created more dislocation and unrest. The harvest of 1788 was again very meager, bread prices soared, and riots broke out in many towns in late 1788 and 1789. The most dramatic of these was in Paris, where on July 14 crowds stormed the Bastille, a fortress and prison in the center of the city, looking for weapons. At the same time, peasants in the countryside ransacked the houses of their noble landlords, reoccupied common lands, and burned documents that recorded their taxes and dues. The inability to produce enough food at prices that people could afford became a political as well as an economic matter, and an important ingredient in the French Revolution.

Population growth

What caused the rise in food prices in the eighteenth century? Contemporaries often blamed "hoarders and speculators," and killed individuals suspected of withholding grain or flour from the market. Bad harvests and difficulties in getting large amounts of grain from one place to another were more significant factors than the actions of real or imagined speculators, however. Even more

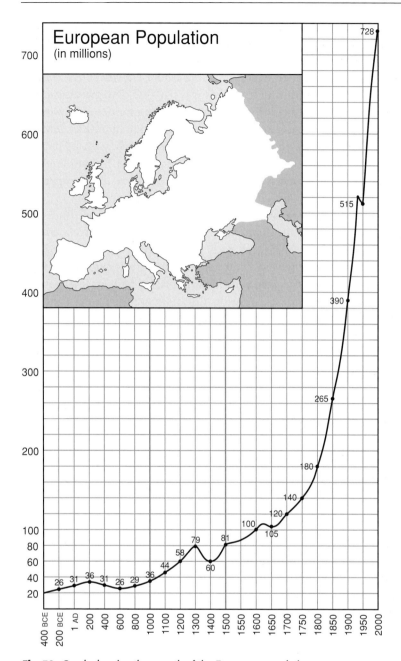

Fig. 30. Graph showing the growth of the European population.

important was a steady growth in population, especially after mid-century. The slow growth of the European population in the sixteenth and seventeenth centuries – an increase of about 20 percent over each century – turned sharply upward, with the population of Europe as a whole nearly doubling from 1750 to 1850. As in the sixteenth century, more people meant a greater demand for food, and thus higher prices (see figure 30).

This explanation only leads to a second question: why did the population go up? Historical demographers have analyzed all kinds of records to determine the reasons for this dramatic upsurge. They studied age at marriage, wondering if people were marrying earlier, which in an era before effective birth control meant they were having more children. This was true in a few places, such as England, where in many areas there were more opportunities for rural women to gain paid employment at a young age and so start saving money for dowries earlier. England experienced the fastest demographic growth, with its population tripling, from 5.8 million in 1750 to 16.6 million in 1850. In both England and Europe as a whole, however, declining death rates were more important than rising birth rates as a cause of population increase.

Why death rates went down – thus making life expectancy go up – is a complicated question, and historians point to a number of interrelated factors. Though public health measures such as improving the quality of the water supply and building sewer systems for waste were less effective than their builders hoped, they did help reduce outbreaks of typhoid fever, dysentery, and other intestinal diseases. (Intestinal diseases are the seventh leading cause of death worldwide today, mostly in parts of the world that continue to lack clean water or adequate sewers.) Draining swamps and marshes reduced the fly and mosquito population, which lessened outbreaks of malaria. Contagious diseases tend to hit infants and children particularly hard, so that the slight reduction in their occurrence decreased infant and child mortality faster than the mortality of adults. Improved child-rearing practices, including longer nursing and more frequent changes in clothing, may have also lessened child mortality.

Most contagious diseases grew only slowly less virulent, but the bubonic plague disappeared from western and central Europe in the eighteenth century. There were serious plague epidemics throughout the seventeenth century, including a devastating outbreak in London in 1665 to 1666 that may have killed more than 100,000 people. An outbreak in southern France also killed a similar number in 1721, but this was the last appearance of the plague west of the Ottoman Empire. The *cordons sanitaires* that had first been set up around uninfected cities were extended to whole regions. Ships traveling from Syria or the Ottoman Empire were forced to wait before unloading cargo or passengers, and the border between Ottoman and Habsburg territories along the Danube was patrolled with an eye to disease control. Such quarantine measures could not be foolproof, of course, given the amount of trade and smuggling, but they helped.

Changes in building styles, including wider streets and housing made of brick, stone, or other sturdy materials that were more difficult for rats and other vermin to enter, may have also helped end the plague and lessen other contagious diseases. In London, 80 percent of the city was destroyed in the Great Fire of 1666, just a few months after the plague had died down. Many residents interpreted the conjunction of the two events as a clear sign of God's wrath, but the fire allowed the city to be rebuilt in a slightly less crowded pattern. Some medical historians have suggested that changes in the nature of the rat population or in rats' immunity to the disease might also have played a role in ending the plague in western Europe. Epidemiologists are not sure why similar changes did not have the same impact in eastern Europe and the Near East, however, so the disappearance of the plague remains somewhat of a mystery.

Many contagious diseases, including diphtheria, whooping cough, tuberculosis, and measles, remained common, sometimes flaring up into epidemics that killed thousands of people. Smallpox proved to be the most deadly of the European diseases carried to the New World, and remained a killer in Europe throughout the eighteenth century; the inoculation procedures discussed in chapter 8 were limited to some parts of the Ottoman Empire and England, and had little impact on the population of Europe as a whole. Epidemic typhus, a disease spread by fleas, lice, ticks, and mites, actually increased in Europe during the eighteenth and nineteenth centuries, especially in crowded cities and among war refugees.

In addition to a slow decrease in the rates of death from contagious diseases, new foods and changes in eating patterns may also have increased longevity. Ever larger fishing fleets brought back thousands of tons of fish from the Grand Banks of the Atlantic, which was sold fresh, pickled, salted, and smoked, increasing the amount of protein in people's diets. More farm animals meant more meat, especially in northern Europe, which was already one of the most carnivorous parts of the world. Climatic conditions improved slightly after a cooling trend in the seventeenth century, which brought increases in grain production and fewer disastrous harvests. Increased planting of vegetables, including spinach, asparagus, lettuce, artichokes, peas, and green beans, helped to vary and enrich people's diets. Sunflowers, brought by the Spanish from South America, joined olives in southern Europe as a source of cooking oil, and corn (maize), also brought from Mexico, became popular in Spain, Italy, and the Balkans. During the seventeenth century, Europeans recognized that the tomato, another New World plant, was not deadly, and began planting it as a food crop as well as a garden ornamental.

Suspicion of the tomato came in part because of its relationship to deadly nightshade, a highly poisonous plant, and the most important New World foodstuff was another relative of nightshade, the potato. Potatoes originated in the Andes, and Spanish sailors carried – and ate – them on their way back to Europe. There they met great disdain. Potatoes were not mentioned in the Bible and grew underground, so they were seen as vaguely demonic, and people hated the way they tasted. Potatoes, like turnips, were fine for animals (and slaves in the New World), but not people in Europe. This lack of interest changed slowly when people realized they could be grown on extremely poor soil and were easy to harvest and store; a field planted with potatoes could feed two or three times the number of people that could be fed by the same field planted with grain. By the late seventeenth century, potatoes were an important crop in the Netherlands, Switzerland, and Ireland, where they fed both animals and people. Agricultural historians estimate that, by 1800, the Irish diet included an average of ten potatoes per person per day, or 80 percent of people's caloric intake, not including the milk, cheese, and meat that came from animals fed on potatoes.

The rulers of Prussia, especially Frederick the Great, recognized potatoes would grow equally well in the cool summers and sandy soil of Prussia, and ordered farmers to plant them, as did the kings of Sweden and Norway. The War of the Bavarian Succession in 1778–9, between Prussia and Austria, has been nicknamed the "Potato War" because the primary tactic involved gaining the food supply of the opposite side rather than actual battles, and Prussian troops spent their time harvesting potatoes. Antoine-Auguste Parmentier (1737–1813), a French army doctor and agronomist who had been imprisoned by the Prussians during the Seven Years War, promoted potato cultivation in France, convincing Marie-Antoinette, so the story goes, to wear potato flowers in her hair and inviting local notables to all-potato dinners. (There are several soups and side dishes named in his honor, all containing potatoes.)

Potatoes are actually more nutritious than grain because they have higher vitamin and mineral content. The potato crop is also more reliable year to year, as it is less likely to be destroyed by hail, drought, or unexpected early frosts. (Like grain, potatoes are subject to blight; the worst blight was in the 1840s, which destroyed the crops in many European countries, most famously in Ireland, where more than a million people died of famine and disease, and a quarter of a million emigrated.) The harvest is thus more regular year to year, which evens out the available food supply.

Changes in the nature of warfare may also have reduced death rates. The devastation of the Thirty Years War led military and political leaders to put more emphasis on provisioning their troops, which lessened the amount of food and other supplies that armies would confiscate from the countryside through which they moved. Armies were larger in the eighteenth century and their weapons were deadlier, but they were more separated from the civilian population, so that their impact in terms of the spread of disease and the intentional or accidental killing of civilians was smaller. Mass migrations because of warfare were fewer in the eighteenth century than earlier – and non-existent in Britain, which fought no major wars on its own territory – which meant fewer abandoned fields and years in which nothing was planted.

Historians debate exactly which of these factors – more and different food, better transport, more land under cultivation, fewer epidemics, improving public health measures, different patterns of warfare – was the most important, but there is no debate about the actual trends. Mortality crises, in which death rates shot up for weeks, months, or years because of famine, disease, or war, decreased in their intensity, so that the difference between maximum and

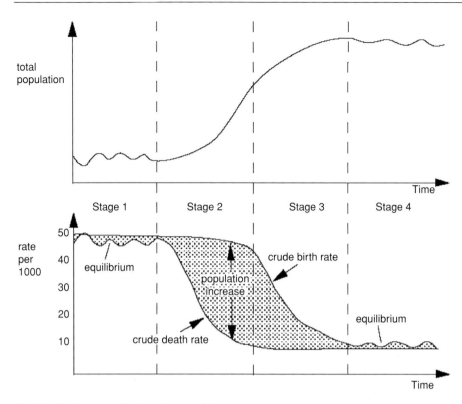

Fig. 31. The demographic transition model.

minimum death rates decreased. Life expectancy increased slowly and steadily, from twenty-eight to thirty-four in France during the period 1750 to 1850, thirty-seven to forty in England, and thirty-seven to forty-three in Sweden. This declining mortality was the beginning of what population historians have called the "demographic transition," in which death rates go down steeply, followed after some decades or even a century by a decline in birth rates (see figure 31). The first phase of the demographic transition is marked by a rapid rise in population; when birth rates begin to go down, the population increase slows, and finally both birth and death rates level off at a much lower level than they were before the transition. The demographic transition occurred first in western Europe and then in eastern and southern Europe; it began in much of the developing world only in the twentieth century with the spread of vaccines, antibiotics, and DDT spraying.

Declining death rates had other effects besides increasing the total population. They gradually regularized the process of life, so that death became associated with aging, rather than something that occurred randomly. Infant and child mortality slowly declined, so that the most perilous years of life – the period in which the greatest percentage of the population died – were no longer the first five. Even more dramatic was a decrease in mortality among older children and adolescents. In 1750, a ten-year-old child in France had a one in four chance of dying before his or her mother; by 1850 this had declined significantly (and today it is about one in sixty).

Most people aware of the growing population in the eighteenth century saw this as a cause for celebration. Mercantilists regarded it as an economic plus because more people meant both more workers and more consumers. The Physiocrats, a group of French economists in the middle of the eighteenth century, opposed the mercantalists' stress on trade, and emphasized agriculture as the source of all wealth. They thought that all restrictions on agriculture, including price controls and tariffs, diminished national wealth and sickened the body politic just as blockages and clots sickened a human body; they popularized the phrase *laissez-faire* ("leave alone"). But the Physiocrats too saw an increase in the rural population as largely beneficial, because it offered the possibility of increasing agricultural surplus, the true source of any nation's prosperity. They did worry that the growth in population might outstrip any surplus, however, an idea that was stated even more strongly by the English economist Thomas Malthus (1766–1834). In *Essay on the Principle of Population* (1798), Malthus argued that population increases geometrically while food supply increases arithmetically, so that population will always outstrip food supply. He looked to history as well as mathematical models for his proof, noting the many times that famine, disease, and war had served as a check on population growth. He was not sure when European society would reach what later economists called the "Malthusian limit" and suffer a catastrophic collapse, but he was sure it would happen, unless moral restraint or "vice" (by which Malthus meant contraception) prevented it.

Proto-industry and manufactories

Many of the growing population found work in rural areas doing tasks directly related to agricultural production. More fields meant more harvesting, and greater specialization meant more transporting of goods to market. Commercial crops such as olives, wine, and flax (for linen) were very labor-intensive, as was caring for animals year-round. Silk was even more labor-intensive, providing work in the Italian and Ottoman countryside for women and girls who gathered leaves from mulberry trees, raised the silk cocoons, and processed cocoons into raw silk by reeling and spinning. Silk-making was regarded as an appropriate occupation for women, because women, or more accurately girls, were viewed as having greater dexterity and ability to concentrate than men, both necessary for the tedious task of unwinding silk cocoons. Girls were also probably the only ones willing to accept the extremely low wages paid for this task, though the life-long damage to their eyes that could result from unwinding fine thread in low light made even poor girls think twice about steady work in silk-winding. Silk producers were often forced to hire whole orphanages (without the assent of the residents, of course) in order to have enough labor.

Landlords and more prosperous tenant farmers hired many workers for specific tasks, and they also hired permanent household servants. Servants were hired annually, often at local hiring fairs, and were supposed to stay with their employer for at least one year. Their period of service was rarely determined by a written contract, but instead by a verbal one sealed by a small sum of money. They received room, board, and some clothing from their employers, and, except for very young children, also an annual salary. This salary was paid only at the end of the year, or even held until the servant left the household, so that servants actually lent their employers the use of their salary during their term of service. Young people generally regarded service as a time to save for later marriage, though they were also occasionally forced into service to pay off their parents' feudal dues, a practice that continued in Germany, Sweden, and Finland into the eighteenth century.

Rural residents also increasingly engaged in handicraft production, using raw materials provided by merchants from nearby towns and cities, especially in the production of textiles. Such rural cottage industry developed first in the Netherlands and Flanders, where merchants sought to escape the restrictions on quantity, quality, wages, and the nature of the workforce that guilds imposed on production in cities. Rural workers would work for less, as they generally produced much of their own food. Merchants purchased raw wool or flax, and then distributed it to peasant households to be spun into yarn. From there the merchant would arrange for it to be taken to a different household for bleaching, another for dying, another for weaving, and another for final finishing, "putting it out" to each household, as the expression went at the time. Each household in this "putting-out system" would be paid for the tasks it did, but the merchant retained ownership of the product at every stage and took the largest share of the profits.

Initially cottage industry was a by-employment, done during the winter or more regularly only by certain family members, but gradually families in some parts of Europe, especially areas with large groups of landless people, engaged in production full-time. "Not only women and maids, but also men and boys, spin," commented the German religious reformer Sebastian Franck, after visiting some villages around Augsburg and Ulm, going on to say, "One sees contradictions; they work and gossip like women, yet are still vigorous, active, strong and quarrelsome people, the kind any area would want to have."[2] By the eighteenth century, increased demand for textiles, combined with a growing rural population, meant that certain rural areas of the Netherlands, Belgium, England, the Rhineland, and northern France specialized in textile production. For residents of those areas, wages were no longer simply a supplement to their food production, but a replacement for it, and they became completely dependent on market conditions that might be international in scope. Economic historians refer to this process of expanding wage labor as "proletarianization," and note that wages were often so low that families remained impoverished even if all family members worked most daylight hours. The merchants and investors who hired households to spin and weave were similarly dependent on changing styles, political circumstances, and even the weather, but those entrepreneurs who were shrewd and fortunate could make tremendous profits.

Economic historians have termed this more intensive putting-out system "proto-industrialization," and note that it had important social, as well as economic, ramifications. In parts of Europe where the land was poorest and the agriculture was more or less subsistence, entrepreneurs hired whole households, and proto-industry often broke down gender divisions. Men, women, and children who were old enough all worked at the same tasks, as the quotation from Franck notes. Domestic industry might also lead to role reversal, with women producing thread while, in the words of an eighteenth-century German observer, "men ... cook, sweep and milk the cows, in order never to disturb the good, diligent wife in her work."[3] In such areas, labor became a more important economic commodity than property, which led to earlier marriage, weaker parental control over children, and a faster rise in fertility rates. Some historians have suggested that this may have given young women more power within the family and a greater sense of independence, though these were balanced by the fact that young men were also freer, which increased the risk of young women being seduced and abandoned.

In other parts of Europe, proto-industrialization began in areas where there was a high level of seasonal unemployment, especially among women. In these areas, including parts of France, individual women, rather than whole households, were hired, with men continuing to work at wage-paying agricultural tasks. In these areas there was no sharing of domestic duties or reversal of roles, for the men's tasks were more highly paid and generally away from the household, so the women continued to do most domestic labor. Proto-industrialization in these areas did not lead to great improvements in women's status, for, though the wages women earned gave the family some disposable income, it was the men of the family who decided when and how that income could be spent, and often gathered in taverns, and by the eighteenth century in cafés to spend it. This may have been one reason why female spinners in Augsburg chose to pool their wages and live together rather than with their families or in the house of a master weaver, though the city tried to prevent this from happening.

In rural areas where the population was dense enough, entrepreneurs sometimes brought together workers under one roof rather than putting work out to individual households. They opened what are often termed "manufactories" in which workers used hand tools or hand-powered machines – often owned by the entrepreneur, not the worker – and were paid by the piece with frequent quality checks. Women were favored as workers because they would work for lower wages and were thought to have more delicate and nimble hands; the investors did not realize that these women also did rough housework and seasonal agricultural labor, so that their hands were swollen and scarred, which made their work uneven and led them to be fined for poor-quality work.

In the eighteenth century, manufactories were also opened in towns and cities, often in newer industries where craft guilds had not developed or in cities where the guilds were relatively weak. As we saw at the beginning of this chapter, Glickl bas Judah Leib owned just such a manufactory for stockings in Hamburg. Conditions in these manufactories were often unpleasant and unhealthy, with cloth fibres filling the air and boiling vats causing workers' clothes to be continually damp. Wages were low, but young people sometimes preferred work in a manufactory over domestic service because it did allow a small amount of free time and a greater sense of independence. City manufactories rarely outweighed rural production in the eighteenth century, however. In the 1740s in Silesia (part of Austria), more than 80 percent of the linen was made in rural areas, and in the 1780s nearly 75 percent of the looms in Picardy, the area north of Paris in which there was intense proto-industrialization, were in the countryside.

The economic historians who first coined the term "proto-industrialization" saw this as a middle stage in a historical process that began with independent artisanal production in craft guilds and ended with the mechanized factories of the Industrial Revolution. England led the way in this process, in this line of argument, and each stage made the previous stage obsolete, or turned areas that did not change into economic backwaters. More recently, economic historians have emphasized the fluidity and simultaneity of various forms of production rather than one single line of development. The weaving of cloth had moved into manufactories in some places by the eighteenth century, but this cloth was then sent to individual homes to be sewn into clothing, so that in this case manufactories increased rather than decreased the opportunities for domestic production. Some industries, such as metal smelting, mechanized outside factories; the machines that powered the early Industrial Revolution were made in individual shops, often by members of craft guilds, not in factories. Toward the end of the eighteenth century, steam-driven sawmills produced wooden planks that carpenters used in their own shops to make furniture. In these cases, artisans were integrated into new systems of production rather than being displaced by them, though they were more dependent on capitalist entrepreneurs for raw materials and sales of finished products than their predecessors had been.

Craft guilds remained strong in many parts of Europe throughout the seventeenth century, and in some places, such as Sweden and Austria, they were actually at their most powerful in the eighteenth century. City, regional, and royal governments worked through the guilds to regulate the economy. In France, the finance minister Jean-Baptiste Colbert issued hundreds of regulations about quality, price, production processes, competition, membership, and other guild issues, a policy imitated by other states. He also set up new guilds, particularly aimed at groups that might otherwise need public welfare.

47 Apprenticeship contract for an eleven-year-old boy, Paris 1610

Parents and guardians placing their children into service or apprenticeships often did so by means of a written contract drawn up by a notary. Here a woman apprentices her son to a ribbon and trim maker, the same occupation as her husband's, though he had long deserted her.

Marie Frevel, wife but deserted for the last nine years, she says, by Mahis Deslandres, master ribbon and trim maker in Paris ... affirms that, for the benefit of Adam Deslandres, son of the said Mahis Deslandres and of the said Frevel, aged 11 years or so, whom the said Frevel has pledged to complete faithfulness and loyalty, she has given and placed him in service and employment for the next three years. [She has placed him] with the respectable Henry Camue, master of the said ribbon and trim trade in Paris ...

[Camue] has taken and retained [Adam Deslandres] in his service for the said time, during which he will be obliged and promises to show and teach him [Camue's] trade and all in which he is involved because of it; supply and deliver what he needs in terms of fire, bed, lodging, and light, and treat him gently, as is appropriate.

And [Frevel] placing him will maintain him during the said time with all clothing, linen, footwear, and other respectable clothing, according to his status.

In consideration of this service, the said parties remain in agreement on the sum of 18 livres tournois that the said Camue promises and guarantees to pay to the said [Frevel] or someone on her behalf, to assist in the said support of the employee her son ... To make this [agreement], present [was] the said employee, who has promised to serve his said master faithfully, work to his benefit, and warn him of losses as soon as they should come to [the boy's] attention; and not to run away nor go to serve elsewhere during the said time.

And in case of flight or absence, the said Frevel promises to search in the city and outskirts of Paris and bring him back if she can find him, to complete the time of his said service ...

Done and passed in Paris at the offices of the notaries signed below, the year 1610, Wednesday, the twenty-second day of December in the afternoon. The said [Frevel] has said that she does not know how to write or sign.

(Paris, Archives Nationales, Minutier central, Etude X/15, December 22, 1610, trans. Carol Loats, in Monica Chojnacka and Merry Wiesner-Hanks, *Ages of Woman, Ages of Man: Sources in European Social History, 1400–1750* [London: Longman, 2002], p. 24.)

In 1675, for example, he set up an all-female guild of dressmakers in Paris, noting that since women were excluded from most guilds "this work was the only means that they had to earn their livelihood decently."[4] Such regulations were often difficult to enforce, especially in growing towns where the demand for products outstripped the ability of guilds to provide them. Rural putting-out enterprises provided some of the products needed to fill this gap, especially in textiles, and so did nonguild artisans, who simply made clothes, shoes, bread, or other products without guild membership and approval, selling these clandestinely or smuggling them from town to town. The economy was thus more flexible than the regulations envisioned, and even within the regulatory structure there was some opportunity for individual initiative and competition.

This flexibility was often vigorously opposed by journeymen, who thought that nonguild work lessened the available workplaces or somehow tarnished the honor of their crafts. With the support of their associations, journeymen organized strikes, refused to work next to nonguild workers, and destroyed shops and merchandise. In Germany, they termed nonguild workers *Bönhasen* (literally "bin-rabbits," because they were regarded as stealing journeymen's food in the same way that a rabbit might steal from a storage bin) and beat them up. An imperial edict ordering journeymen in Germany to relax their code of honor and halt boycotts or punishments precipitated a wave of strikes and riots in the 1720s, and again in the 1730s and 1790s. The same thing happened in Austria in 1770, after Maria Theresa issued a proclamation requiring journeymen to accept nonguild colleagues. Journeymen also opposed the new manufactories; in 1794, journeyman ribbon-makers in Berlin entered a new ribbon factory, grabbed the young women who were employed there, and beat them.

Journeymen's opposition to flexibility and change was symbolic, in the minds of many observers of the economy, of a more general problem. By the late eighteenth century, some economic planners came to regard all corporate bodies – journeymen's associations, craft guilds, merchants' associations – as impediments to growth, and called for a policy of economic liberalism with free trade and unregulated markets. In *The Wealth of Nations* (1776), Adam Smith criticized sectors of the economy where corporate bodies exerted control, and advocated the expansion of the free market to all economic endeavors. This would best serve the "common good," Smith asserted, for any attempt to "hinder the poor man from employing his strength and dexterity in what manner he thinks proper is a plain violation of this most sacred trust . . . [and] a manifest encroachment upon the just liberty both of the workman, and of those who might be disposed to employ him."[5]

In the same year, the French controller general of finance, Anne-Robert-Jacques Turgot (1727–81) abolished the guilds and called for an end to tariffs and other government regulation of the economy. Such a move was too radical for many in the French government, however, who feared social and economic anarchy if the established hierarchical relationships of master–journeyman–apprentice were simply done away with. Several months later they convinced the king to fire Turgot. In 1791, in the middle of the French Revolution, the guilds were abolished again, which happened slightly later in other parts of Europe as well. Because they were often illegal and operated somewhat clandestinely, journeymen's associations survived long afterward, but by the middle of the nineteenth century the principles of economic liberalism had more or less triumphed and government regulation of trade and other aspects of the economy had diminished significantly.

Industry and the Industrial Revolution

Industrial production involves a large concentrated workforce dependent on an owner for raw materials and tools, mass-producing one item or a small range of items. Stories of the development of industry, often described as the Industrial Revolution, usually see its beginnings in textile manufacturing in eighteenth-century Britain. This overlooks a number of earlier examples of production that have all the qualities of industry. As we saw in chapter 7, New World plantations mass-produced one thing, such as sugar, using huge slave labor forces that had no ownership of the means of production; this was also true of New World mines, where thousands and perhaps ultimately millions of people mined and processed silver and gold. In eastern Europe, noble landholders controlled hundreds or even thousands of serfs, using them to produce grain for sale in the global market. Members of the traditional ruling class, the aristocracy, controlled most of these large-scale enterprises, using the profits to purchase consumer goods for an increasingly luxurious lifestyle.

European governments also ran industrial ventures long before the eighteenth century. The city of Venice operated the Arsenal producing ships and weapons, which employed more than five thousand workers and built more than one hundred of the ships used by Venice and its allies in their defeat of the Turks at the Battle of Lepanto in 1571. Administrators and technical experts oversaw every stage of production, which was so efficient that, if pressed, the workforce could build a war galley in a few weeks, or outfit one for combat in a few hours. The armies of the Ottoman Empire and later those of western European states were also industrial in their size and provisioning structures when compared with medieval feudal levies; with contracts from Louis XIV's finance minister Colbert, French armaments manufacturers came to employ hundreds of workers.

In terms of workforce and output, agricultural, mining, and military operations were on a much larger scale than production organized by capitalist entrepreneurs until late in the nineteenth century. By the late seventeenth century, however, the proliferation of small putting-out enterprises and manufactories with just a few dozen workers had created what economic historians have recognized was the most important precondition for industrial take-off: a broad-based market for cheap manufactured goods. Families and individuals worked more hours, especially during the slow periods of the agricultural cycle, which provided both goods for the market and cash for them to purchase products made by others. Thus the consumption of goods in Europe itself was the most important stimulant to new forms of production.

The most important of these products was cloth. The majority of cloth produced and worn in Europe was made of wool, and the most profitable type of cloth for several centuries had been luxury broadcloth woven on a large loom that required several weavers to operate. In the late sixteenth century, entrepreneurs realized there was a market for lighter, cheaper woolen cloth, or cloth made of a mixture of wool and cotton, wool and linen, or cotton and linen (called fustian), that could be dyed easily. This lighter cloth, called the "new draperies" in England, was not as sturdy as the heavier, higher-quality cloth that urban guilds had long produced, but it could be easily and quickly made by rural families who lacked the long guild training. Its lower quality might actually be a benefit, for it meant that people would have to buy clothing more often; this both stimulated demand and allowed people to keep up with changes in style, which became increasingly important in fashion-conscious cities such as London or Paris.

New machinery also speeded up the production of several products that became important fashion items in the early seventeenth century. Stocking frames with needles fixed permanently on a stand made knitting stockings and gloves much faster; knitted stockings quickly replaced woven ones, especially as they draped the leg in a much more flattering way. Silk-throwing machines, which unwound cocoons and twisted silk thread, made silk slightly cheaper, so that middle-class urban people might be able to afford at least one pair of silk stockings, along with their everyday woolen ones. In an era before artificial fibers or much use of cotton, silk stockings and undergarments offered a bit of true luxury next to the skin. For fashion that could be seen by all, ribbon looms produced twelve or more ribbons at one time, making them affordable decorations for hats or collars. Lace cuffs and collars also grew in popularity (and in size); lace-making became an important cottage industry in the Netherlands, Belgium, and parts of France in the late sixteenth century, which spurred the invention of special lace-making looms that used punched-card templates to guide the pattern.

In the later seventeenth century, cotton cloth from India, including calicoes printed in bright patterns and thin muslins that were especially light and sheer, entered the European market, imported by the Dutch and English East India Companies. Consumers snapped them up, and mercantalist governments responded by putting tariffs on Indian imports or completely prohibiting them in the hopes of convincing people to buy locally produced cloth. European manufacturers also tried to imitate Indian cloth, which was initially possible only with imported Indian thread, as Europeans were not successful at producing cotton thread that was strong enough to withstand the weaving process without breaking. At first European cloth was distinctly inferior to that from India, but it gradually improved and steadily decreased in cost, largely because of technological innovations.

Transforming raw materials into finished cloth is a multi-stage process, and any stage could be a bottleneck. Initially the problem was spinning. One hand-loom weaver could use yarn or thread produced by up to twenty carders and spinners in wool and linen, and up to ten in cotton, so entrepreneurs and mercantalist government officials suggested and implemented many schemes to encourage more spinning. Most of these were directed towards women and children, whom officials regarded as a vast labor pool waiting to be tapped; although, as we have seen, in some rural areas both men and women spun, in most places spinning was seen as the quintessential woman's task. Officials attached spinning rooms to orphanages, awarded prizes to women who spun the most, made loans easier for those who agreed to spin, and set up spinning schools for poor children. Poor law authorities in England opened spinneries for poor women, providing women too poor to own their own wheels with the needed equipment. Women who were in hospital or jail were expected to spin to defray part of the cost of their upkeep, and prostitutes in some cities were expected to produce a certain number of bobbins of yarn per day, spinning when the brothel was closed to customers.

Wages for spinning were low, but more and more women spun, either as a by-employment during slow seasons or as a full-time job; in England so many women were spinning by the seventeenth century that "spinster" became the standard term for an unmarried woman. Most women spun in their own homes or the room they rented to live in, but, especially in Germany and France, they sometimes gathered together in evening spinning bees with their wheels

Fig. 32. Isaac Claesz van Swanenburgh's (1537–1614) painting of workers spinning and weaving wool in the Netherlands, c. 1600. The women in the foreground use very large wheels to spin thread onto two different types of racks, while the man in the upper left weaves, and people in the background stretch cloth and wind yarn. This domestic workshop is both a symbol of Dutch industriousness and a fairly accurate rendition of the most efficient methods of cloth production before the advent of water-driven machines.

or distaffs and spindles. Young men gravitated to these gatherings of largely unmarried women, so that the spinning was accompanied by songs, jokes, and drinking. Religious and civic authorities often worried about what went on at spinning bees and tried to prohibit them. Mercantalist reformers countered that such gatherings actually promoted good marriages by allowing young men to compare the skill and industriousness of various marriage partners, and also promoted higher production levels because the young spinners competed with one another.

Authorities were more at ease when spinning bees were gradually replaced in urban areas by manufactories where women spun under the direction of a male overseer. In Britain, this change in work organization was hastened by the development of new machines. The earliest spinning machines often broke the threads or produced thread of uneven thickness, but in the 1760s and 1770s several machines – James Hargreaves' spinning jenny, Richard Arkwright's spinning frame, and Samuel Crompton's spinning mule – allowed the production of stronger and thinner thread, and also allowed one worker to produce multiple threads at the same time. These machines were developed for cotton, but could be adapted for wool, which remained the cloth produced in the greatest quantities in Europe throughout the eighteenth century. By the 1790s in Britain spinning mules had several hundred spindles, which ended home spinning.

Inventors immediately turned their attention to mechanical looms, though these would not become practical until the nineteenth century, and most weaving continued to be done by hand-loom weavers for many decades after the introduction of spinning machines. The finishing stages of cloth production also began to be mechanized. Artificial chemicals replaced ashes, urine, and fuller's earth in the fulling process, and replaced the sun in bleaching. Patterns were increasingly printed by running the cloth through an inked cylinder rather than by stamping each section in a block press.

While wool production increased steadily throughout the eighteenth century, cotton production grew at an even faster pace; between 1770 and 1800, imports of raw cotton into Britain grew twelvefold. This growth was directly related to Britain's overseas empire, which provided both the supply of raw cotton and much of the demand for finished cloth. Lighter, brighter cottons were popular in Europe, but they were even more desirable in tropical climates or in places with hot summers, the very places in which cotton grew best.

The spinning jenny could be operated by hand and was suited to cottage industry, but the spinning frame and mule needed an external power source. Initially this was provided by falling water, and spinning mills grew up along streams and rivers in the British countryside and then in other parts of Europe and North America. Cities located in areas with favorable river-systems became centers of cotton production and trade, and their populations soared; the population of Manchester in northwestern England, for example, one of the main centers of British cotton production, grew from 17,000 in 1760 to 180,000 in 1830.

Water-powered machinery was geographically limited and could be interrupted by drought or freezing weather, however, so that there was a strong impetus to search for other sources of power. This was provided by the steam engine, which was initially developed to pump water out of mines. The earliest steam engines, such as that developed by the English tool-seller Thomas Newcomen (1663–1729) in 1712, worked by creating a vacuum inside pistons and using the suction to lift water; by the 1730s Newcomen engines were pumping out coal, copper, and iron mines in several European countries. In the 1760s, James Watt (1736–1819), a Scottish engineer and tool-maker, dramatically improved the Newcomen engine by adding a separate condensing chamber, which increased the efficiency, that is, the amount of power per unit of coal burned. Watt's engines were put to still more uses, powering cotton-spinning machines, steam hammers, blowers, and, in 1783 in France, a steamboat. The English potter Josiah Wedgwood (1730–95) adapted coal-powered steam engines to the production of pottery, mass-producing porcelain at prices that brought it within the range of many consumers.

Watt worked with other tool-makers to improve the precision of machine tools such as drills, lathes, and planers that shaped metal, so that the parts of his engines fitted together without leakage, making them even more efficient. He also developed various devices to increase and regulate the speed of pistons, and to change the back and forth motion of pistons into circular motion, which worked better for some machines. By the early 1800s, many machines and machine parts, such as frames and pipes, that had earlier been made out of wood, were made of the much more durable iron.

Steam engines require cheap fuel, which was available in the form of coal in certain parts of Europe, most plentifully in England. (One of the richest coalfields was near Newcastle in northern England, the origin of the phrase "like taking coals to Newcastle" to describe needless effort.) Coal was smoky and smelly when it burned, but shortages of wood by the middle of the seventeenth century meant that large cities such as London had little choice but to use coal for heating. Steam-driven pumps allowed ever deeper mining for coal, which was also facilitated by laying tracks or rails for carts that brought the coal from underground. These carts were first pushed or pulled by human and animal power, and then by coal-powered steam engines. In the early nineteenth century, this technology spread out from the coalfields with the construction of railroads, where steam locomotives ran along tracks. Coal increased the amount of power available exponentially when compared with traditional sources – humans, animals, wind, and water. Many economic historians see this surge in available power as the key reason the European economy came to dominate that of the rest of the world in the nineteenth and twentieth centuries.

Along with the steam engine and coal mining, iron production was an essential part of industrial development. Coal-powered steam blowers and other equipment allowed new iron-making processes that could transform lower-grade ore into higher-quality iron and steel. Steel is a very hard alloy of iron and carbon that, using traditional methods, could only be made from very high-quality ore; in Europe, most of such ore was in Sweden, which also had huge forests that produced the charcoal required to heat ore to the temperature needed to produce steel. Many of the best weapons before the eighteenth century were thus made with Swedish steel. English ironworkers, including a father and son both named Abraham Darby, experimented with using coke, a by-product of burning coal, to produce steel. Initially coke-smelted steel was difficult to work, but by the middle of the eighteenth century the process had been perfected and coke smelting spread throughout Britain.

It was cheaper to transport iron than coal, so that the iron industry grew up in coal-mining regions, including Staffordshire, Yorkshire, South Wales, and western Scotland. These had to be huge operations in order to be profitable; those of the industrialist John Wilkinson (1728–1808 – now memorialized in the "Wilkinson sword" razor blade), for example, employed thousands of people. Industrial zones developed around certain cities, rather than being more dispersed in the countryside. These cities grew at an amazing rate, but they lacked enough housing, clean water, or sanitation services, so that diseases such as typhus and tuberculosis spread easily. Their intensive use of coal made them even more filthy, and many visitors were appalled; the English poet William Blake, for example, wrote in 1805 of "dark Satanic mills" that had replaced "England's green and pleasant land." Work was structured by the need to use machines efficiently, so tasks became more routinized and the work day more structured. Machines could be tended by people with lower skill levels, including children, so that wages were low, child labor was common, and the status of adult workers declined. Wages offered to unskilled workers by the Satanic mills were often higher than those in the "green and pleasant land," however, and the opportunities to escape parental and family control were greater, so the new industrial cities never lacked workers.

Along with coal and iron, concentrated industrial production also required transportation and money. Britain was fortunate in having mines and coalfields near rivers and harbors, which engineers widened and deepened. In the late eighteenth century engineers also began building canals to link coalfields with rivers and connect ports and other cities. Money was provided primarily by individual investors who had made great profits in trade and commerce. Banks handled money – and became much more numerous in the eighteenth century – but they rarely invested directly in machinery or factories. Private investors included people from humble beginnings who occasionally became fabulously wealthy, such as Richard Arkwright (1732–92), who began life as a barber and the youngest of thirteen children. He moved into the wholesale hair business, which was booming because of the demand for wigs, and developed a hair dye that he patented and sold to wig makers. He used the money from this to work on spinning machines, gaining patents for the horse-powered and then water-powered spinning frame, and opening mills that used them. His patents were

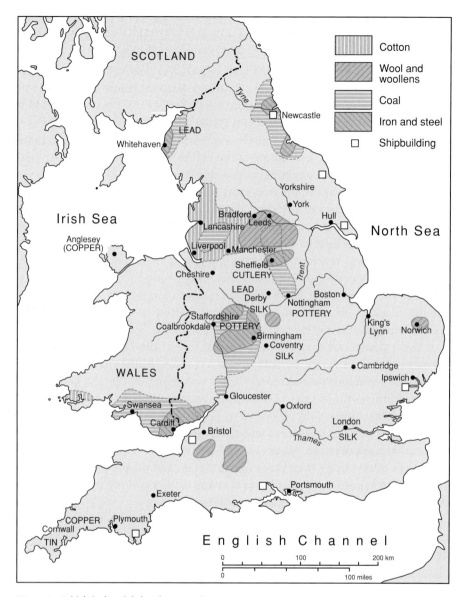

Map 12. British industrial development in 1800.

later challenged when other inventors argued that he had not changed existing technology very much, but he was knighted, and died one of the richest men in England.

Rags-to-riches stories like that of Arkwright captured people's imaginations, but much of the money in early British industrial development came from the traditional elites, that is, from titled aristocrats and landed gentry. Coal and iron mines were often on land that they owned, and they profited from the development of mining and metallurgy. Some of them had already made substantial profits in commercial farming operations, and they reinvested money from mining and agriculture in industrial ventures. Aristocrats controlled the House of Lords and gentry dominated the House of Commons, so that economic policy favored their interests, which meant protection for domestic production and commerce against foreign competition.

One aspect of Arkwright's story was very typical, however – the role of patents in creating wealth. The city of Venice was the first place in Europe to allow new devices to be registered as legal protection for their inventors, and in 1623 James I issued the Statute of Monopolies for "projects of new invention," which served as the basis for British patent law until the late twentieth century. (Before this time, royal monopolies called "letters patent" – meaning "open letter" as opposed to a sealed private letter – had been granted for the sale of all types of goods, but Parliament forced James to revoke these and limit patents to new inventions, and only for a fixed number of years.) Other countries in Europe did not start issuing patents until the 1790s, the same time as the newly independent United States also issued its first patent laws. As Arkwright's case indicates, patents could be contested, and in some cases they were evaded, but they did encourage innovation.

The technological, organizational, and legal innovations that allowed for industrialization developed first in Britain, a situation that has provoked great debate practically since the first factory opened. Was the British lead the result of cultural differences, such as a more fluid social structure than elsewhere in Europe, greater individualism, and a greater willingness to take risks and try new products and processes? Or was it the result of political differences, including the power of Parliament and the size of the British Empire? Or was it largely accidental, the result of navigable rivers and abundant natural resources located in easy-to-reach places, combined with revolution and war in France after 1789, which gave British manufacturers room to establish themselves? Explanations have pointed to all these factors, what one historian has characterized as the "pluck vs. luck" debate. Most scholars now

48 Application for a patent, Venice 1568

In this petition to the Venetian high court, six individuals, one brother and his four sisters and another man, claim to have invented two devices that would allow a person to remain underwater for several hours, which they wished to patent. This is the only record of these devices, so we have no idea of exactly what they were, though around 1500 Leonardo da Vinci had designed an underwater breathing apparatus of cane tubes and leather attached to a face mask. Early patent applications did not require exact drawings or a working model.

It has always been the custom of Your Sereneness to welcome those who with their ingenuity discover new and important inventions that can contribute to the public and the private good. In this spirit come we Salvador di Gradi g. Marc'antonio, citizen of this your Illustrious city, Laura, Isabetta, Simona, Chrestina, sisters of the above named Salvador, and Francesco Cavanei, your most faithful servants. Considering how great the damage is to ships, both armed and unarmed, when they sink under water, and how useful it would be to recover the goods and weapons and all the other things [in the ships] . . . after great effort and expense we have discovered two important secrets and inventions, the first something that allows a man or men . . . to go underwater . . . and remain able to breathe, without these men needing to enclose themselves in anything, the other to give them light so that they can see, and remain under said water for the space of approximately three hours, and they will be able to recover all of the things that they wish to [from the ship]. [This is] something truly of great service and utility because, having both air and light, the men will be able to enter the submerged ship, and with the time allowed can easily recover as we have described all of the goods that they wish . . . We Salvador, Laura, Isabetta, Simona, Chrestina and Francesco the above-named ask Your Sereneness to graciously grant us . . . the rights [to this invention] for fifty years.

(Archivio di Stato di Venezia, Pien Collegio, filza 3, no. 100, November 1568, trans. Monica Chojnacka, in Monica Chojnacka and Merry Wiesner-Hanks, *Ages of Woman, Ages of Man: Sources in European Social History, 1400–1750* [London: Longman, 2002], pp. 219–20.)

highlight the complexity of the process, and the interweaving of both techno-logical and broader changes. In terms of technology, deeper mining was only possible with steam pumps, which could only reach the temperatures they needed to run by burning coal; that coal came out of those deeper mines, and also provided coke to make the high-quality iron needed for pumps, and so on. In terms of broader changes, industry required a concentrated market for prod-ucts, which could only be provided by cities; this also concentrated workers for that industry, pulling them out of villages with more settled hierarchies and relationships and making them both easier to exploit and freer to purchase consumer goods if they could afford them.

The consequences of industrialization have been as hotly debated as the causes, though most of that debate has centered on the nineteenth and twen-tieth centuries, when industrialism became an international development. Historians of the eighteenth century have cautioned against overemphasizing the differences between early industry and what came before. Like industrial workers, guild masters and journeymen often worked twelve- or fourteen-hour days, with bells determining when they started and stopped. Cottage industry and proto-industrialization also involved jobs that required little skill, long hours, and the labor of all family members, including children. Steam engines were sometimes used by individual artisans, who rented space in a building through which steam was piped. Family connections remained the most com-mon way of gaining employment, even in industrial areas. Historians have also highlighted the very limited geographic spread of industry before 1800; cer-tain parts of England may have had cities with "dark Satanic mills," but the vast majority of people in Europe continued to live in villages. London grew from 200,000 inhabitants in 1600 to one million by 1800, but across Europe as a whole the percentage of people who lived in towns of more than 10,000 only grew from 8 percent in 1600 to 10 percent in 1800; in eastern Europe in 1800 this number was probably around 3 percent. Even in heavily urbanized areas, such as the Netherlands, only a third of the people lived in towns, and many more people worked in small family enterprises than in proto-industrial or industrial firms.

Commerce, banking, and money

The pattern of continuities amid change that characterized agriculture and pro-duction in Europe in the seventeenth and eighteenth centuries also extended to commerce and banking. Many merchants continued to operate through family firms and hired associates, while others developed new forms of busi-ness organization, including commissioned agents who took a percentage of whatever deal they negotiated but were not permanent employees. There were few international laws that applied to business matters, so merchants had to rely on their agents to be both effective and trustworthy. Commercial agents guarded their reputations carefully; deceit or open theft might provide a profit in the short run, but could ruin an agent's chances of gaining future contracts. Advice manuals for merchants and would-be merchants include long discussions of honor, honesty, and reliability along with practical concerns, for access to credit or to partners depended as much on reputation as on skill.

Local and national laws regarding personal or business bankruptcy, which were first issued in the sixteenth century, also viewed commerce as a moral issue of honor and trust. They couched bankruptcy in terms of fraud, rather than simply bad decisions or mismanagement. An English bankruptcy law of 1571, for example, spoke about merchants who "craftily obtaining into their hands great substance of other men's goods, do suddenly flee to parts unknown," or use the money obtained on credit "for their own pleasure and delicate living, against all reason, equity, and good conscience." Such laws did not prevent waves of bankruptcies, however, often precipitated by government defaults on loans, especially in Spain and France; lenders to these governments generally had little recourse when this happened, although the 1575 Spanish bankruptcy led Genoese bankers – the major creditors of the Spanish throne – to suspend all commercial credit to Spain. This suspension meant Spain could not pay its army, and in frustration soldiers sacked the city of Antwerp, sharpening the revolt of the Netherlands against Spain. The Spanish crown did get its Genoese bankers to agree to terms several years later, but they in turn called in other loans, and a series of business and personal bankruptcies resulted.

Private and public finance were interwoven in banks as well as bankruptcies. In the fifteenth and sixteenth centuries the most important banks were private international merchant banks such as those run by various families in Florence and by the Fuggers of Augsburg. Their practice of extending large loans and keeping only some of their money on reserve led to frequent bank failures, and some cities, including Barcelona, Genoa, and Naples, responded by opening public banks. In 1609, Amsterdam opened the Wisselbank, a public bank that gained a monopoly of major transactions in gold and silver, took in deposits, and loaned money to the government and to the large Dutch trading companies. During the seventeenth century in London, goldsmiths began operating as deposit banks, keeping coinage and valuables for the government and private firms and issuing deposit receipts; in 1694 they were joined in this function by the Bank of England, a public institution. Northern merchants in Antwerp, Amsterdam, Hamburg, and London gradually transformed receipts of deposit into more flexible fiscal devices; depositors could assign them to others instead of having to redeem them themselves, so that they grew into modern banknotes. Such notes were not always backed up by adequate deposits, however; in 1664, the Bank of Stockholm failed when too many depositors demanded coinage, and in 1720 a similar scenario led to a bank collapse in France. This left many people in France distrustful of banks, and a central public bank was not founded in France until 1800.

Along with banks, stock exchanges slowly evolved out of less formal arrangements. Like any other commodity, stock – shares in a private or public

49 Stock bubbles and government debt

Trade in stock and government debt was often intertwined by brokers in complicated schemes that led to speculation and rapid price spikes, usually called "bubbles." There were two dramatic bubbles in 1720, the Mississippi Bubble in France and the South Sea Bubble in England. In France, Scottish businessman John Law (1671–1729) set up a national bank with much of its capital in government debt, along with several companies that gained monopolies of trade with French territories in North America and the West Indies. Law then merged the companies with the national bank, and traded company shares for the entire national debt, making France theoretically debt-free. Speculation by investors eager to cash in on possible New World profits drove the price of a share from 500 livres to 15,000 livres in a few months. People of all social classes bought shares, and some became "millionaires" – at least on paper – a word first invented during this speculative mania; the national bank issued more banknotes to keep up with the demand for money. When it became clear that the possibility of returns was much lower than predicted, the price tumbled back down to 500 livres. Many investors had bought their shares with borrowed money and now deflated banknotes, so there was a wave of bankruptcies and the French national bank collapsed. Law fled from France.

In Britain, the founders of the South Sea Company similarly purchased government debt in return for exclusive trading rights to the Spanish colonies in the Americas. The company bribed government officials and other influential people, lied about the rights it had been granted to land in Spanish ports, opened lavish offices, and spread stories in newspapers and coffeehouses about how much profit trade would bring. Owning stock became fashionable, and the price of a share rose from £100 in January of 1720 to nearly £1000 in June. Other companies suddenly appeared, offering shares in various overseas enterprises, some as vague as "a company for carrying on an undertaking of great advantage, but nobody to know what it is." The directors of the South Sea Company realized the stock was dramatically overvalued and began selling; when word of this leaked out, other investors started selling, and the price dropped to £135 per share by September. Panicked investors sold their stock in other companies as well, which led to a general stock market crash and numerous bankruptcies. Sir Isaac Newton lost over £20,000, and later commented, "I can calculate the motions of heavenly bodies, but not the madness of people." Crowds in London demanded government action, but the directors fled the country, carrying their fortunes and the records of their bribes. Robert Walpole was brought back in as First Lord of the Treasury to deal with the mess, and he succeeded in slowly restoring public confidence in Britain's financial institutions. This cemented his political power, and he served as prime minister in all but name for twenty years.

enterprise that can be bought and sold easily – requires sellers and buyers. The earliest sellers were Italian city-states, who sold shares in the public debt to wealthy merchants and nobles. (These shares were similar to the bonds sold by municipal and national governments today; the buyers did not become owners the way they would if they had purchased stock, but creditors whose investment the cities promised to pay back with interest at a later date.) In 1602, merchants in various cities in the Netherlands joined together to form the Dutch East India Company, and offered shares to individuals who wished to invest in its overseas ventures. Specialists who bought and sold these shares began to meet at the Bourse in Amsterdam, the general wholesale market for all types of commodities, and also began to trade shares in other public and private ventures, listing prices regularly in the new Dutch newspapers. After 1688, traders in London also bought and sold public debt and shares in companies such as the British East India Company and the Bank of England; in 1773, they formed an organization to increase public confidence in their services and guarantee to investors that they would follow certain rules, and in 1801 they established themselves formally as the London Stock Exchange.

Though banknotes became increasingly important for major transactions in Europe, most buying and selling still involved coins. The expansion in the amount of gold and silver available for coins – and the inflation caused by that expansion – led to steep increases in the number of coins produced in the sixteenth century, and mint masters tried to make their coins more uniform in thickness, size, and markings. Water-powered rolling mills, cutting presses, and coin stamps slowly replaced hand-held hammers and dies, and in 1797 the first steam-driven coin press was introduced for making copper pennies. Machines also made marks around the edges of coins – called mill-marks – to prevent people from clipping or trimming off these edges, through which they slowly acquired gold or silver shavings that could be melted together and sold. Governments continued to debase coinage when they needed money for war – requiring people to turn in their old coins and accept new coins with less silver, and then keeping the difference – but currencies slowly grew more stable.

Changes in banking and business organization occurred throughout Europe in the seventeenth and eighteenth centuries, but in general the lead shifted from cities in Italy to those of northwestern Europe. In 1500 the center of European banking was Genoa, while in 1700 it was Amsterdam and in 1800 London.

The shift in the economic center of Europe from Italy to northwestern Europe was the result not only of innovations in banking, but also the changes in agriculture, production, and transportation traced earlier in this chapter. Urbanization, dense networks of exchange, technological advances, demand for consumer goods, institutions that promoted capital accumulation, and relatively high levels of literacy all promoted economic expansion in northwestern Europe, while the lack of all these made eastern Europe the least prosperous area. The shift to the Atlantic was also the outcome of processes that extended far beyond Europe. In the fifteenth and sixteenth centuries, Portuguese and Spanish voyages and colonization brought products into the harbors of western Europe, especially Lisbon, Seville, and Antwerp. Trade routes centered on the Mediterranean gradually lost volume and value when compared with those centered on the Atlantic. In the seventeenth and eighteenth centuries, Dutch, French, and British trading voyages and colonial ventures made Amsterdam and London the centers of this new Atlantic economy. These global processes enhanced the connections between Europe and the rest of the world in ways that went far beyond the economic.

Further reading

General surveys of economic developments in this era include Jan de Vries, *The Economy of Europe in an Age of Crisis, 1600–1750* (Cambridge: Cambridge University Press, 1976), and "The Industrious Revolution and the Industrial Revolution," *Journal of Economic History* 54 (1994): 249–70; Fernand Braudel, *Civilization and Capitalism, 15th–18th Century*, trans.

Sian Reynolds, 3 vols. (New York: Harper and Row, 1982); Robert Duplessis, *Transitions to Capitalism in Early Modern Europe* (Cambridge: Cambridge University Press, 1997); Keith Wrightson, *Earthly Necessities: Economic Lives in Early Modern Britain* (New Haven: Yale University Press, 2000).

For consumer goods, see Carole Shammas, *The Pre-Industrial Consumer in England and America* (Oxford: Clarendon Press, 1990); John Brewer and Roy Porter, eds., *Consumption and the World of Goods* (London: Routledge, 1993); Lisa Jardine, *Worldly Goods: A New History of the Renaissance* (New York: Norton, 1998); Wolfgang Schivelbusch, *Tastes of Paradise: A Social History of Spices, Stimulants, and Intoxicants* (New York: Vintage, 1992).

For changes in agriculture and the social dislocations these caused, see Robert C. Allen, *Enclosure and the Yeoman: The Agricultural Development of the South Midlands, 1450–1850* (Oxford: Clarendon Press, 1992); Cynthia A. Bouton, *The Flour War: Gender, Class, and Community in Late Ancien Régime French Society* (University Park, PA: Penn State University Press, 1993); Liana Vardi, *The Land and the Loom: Peasants and Profit in Northern France 1680–1800* (Durham, NC: Duke University Press, 1993); Mark Overton, *Agricultural Revolution in England: The Transformation of the Agrarian Economy 1500–1850* (Cambridge: Cambridge University Press, 1996); Steven Laurence Kaplan, *The Bakers of Paris and the Bread Question, 1700–1775* (Durham, NC: Duke University Press, 1996); Govind P. Sreenivasan, *The Peasants of Ottobeuren, 1487–1726: A Rural Society in Early Modern Europe* (Cambridge: Cambridge University Press, 2004).

For changes in the pre-industrial workplace, see Thomas Safley and Leonard Rosenband, eds., *The Workplace before the Factory: Artisans and Proletarians, 1500–1800* (Ithaca, NY: Cornell University Press, 1993); Daryl Hafter, ed., *European Women and Pre-industrial Craft* (Bloomington: Indiana University Press, 1995); James R. Farr, *Artisans in Europe, 1300–1914* (Cambridge: Cambridge University Press, 2000).

For early manufacturing, see John Rule, *The Experience of Labour in Eighteenth-Century Industry* (London: Croom Helm, 1981); Myron Gutmann, *Toward the Modern Economy: Early Industry in Europe, 1500–1800* (Philadelphia: Knopf, 1988); Maxine Berg, *The Age of Manufactures, 1700–1820*, 2nd edn (Oxford: Oxford University Press, 1994); Sheilagh Ogilvie and Markus Cerman, *European Proto-Industrialization* (Cambridge: Cambridge University Press, 1996). Arlette Farge, *Fragile Lives: Violence, Power, and Solidarity in Eighteenth-Century Paris* (Cambridge, MA: Harvard University Press, 1993), explores the impact of economic and social changes on the residents of one of Europe's largest cities.

For banking and money, see Carlo Cipolla, *Money, Prices, and Civilization in the Mediterranean* (Princeton: Princeton University Press, 1956); Eric Kerridge, *Trade and Banking in Early Modern England* (Manchester, UK: Manchester University Press, 1988); Larry Neal, *The Rise of Financial Capitalism: International Capital Markets in the Age of Reason* (Cambridge: Cambridge University Press, 1990).

 For more suggestions and links see the companion website www.cambridge.org/wiesnerhanks.

Notes

1 Glickl bas Judah Leib, *Memoirs*, trans. Marvin Lowenthal (New York: Schocken, 1987), pp. 166, 179.
2 Gustav Schmoller, *Die Strassburger Tucher- und Weberzunft: Urkunden und Darstellung*, 2 vols. (Strasbourg: Karl J. Trübner, 1879), p. 519. My translation.
3 Hans Medick, "The Proto-Industrial Family Economy: The Structural Function of Household and Family during the Transition from Peasant Society to Industrial Capitalism," *Social History* 1 (1976): 312.

4 French royal statutes, 1675, quoted in Cynthia M. Truant, "The Guildswomen of Paris: Gender, Power, and Sociability in the Old Regime," *Proceedings of the Annual Meeting of the Western Society for French History* 15 (1988): 131.

5 Adam Smith, *Inquiry into the Nature and Causes of the Wealth of Nations,* book I, ch. 10, "Of Wages and Profit in the Different Employments of Labour and Stock," paragraph I.10.67.

13 Europe in the world, 1600–1789

Europe supported by Africa & America

The English artist and poet William Blake's engraving of *Europe Supported by Africa and America*, designed to accompany John Gabriel Stedman's account of slavery in Surinam, *Narrative of a Five Years' Expedition Against the Revolted Negroes of Surinam, in Guiana, on the Wild Coast of South America; from the Year 1772 to 1777* ...(London, 1796). Blake symbolizes the wealth of Europe with the necklace of imported pearls, and the slavery of Africa and America with gold armbands, thus using their own resources to shackle them. Stedman was an officer in the Scots Brigade, a special unit of the Dutch Army, who served in Dutch Surinam fighting escaped slaves. Stedman's book, for which Blake and other artists did eighty engravings based on Stedman's drawings, detailed brutality against enslaved people and became part of the growing body of anti-slavery literature.

Timeline

1602	Dutch East India Company founded
1607	First successful British colony founded in North America
1619	First African slaves brought to North America
1620s and 1630s	French, Dutch and British colonies founded in the Caribbean
1662	Virginia assembly outlaws marriage between Europeans and Africans
1670s	Marquette and Joliet explore central North America
1682	William Penn granted charter for Pennsylvania
1699	French found Louisiana
1720s and 1730s	Vitus Bering's expeditions in Siberia
1735	Linnaeus publishes *The System of Nature*
1763	Colonial holdings shift in the treaty ending the Seven Years War
1764	British East India Company granted direct rule in Bengal
1768–79	James Cook's three voyages in the Pacific
1775–83	War of American Independence
1795	Blumenbach publishes third edition of *On the Natural Variety of Mankind*
1799	Dutch East India Company disbanded

BY A CENTURY after Columbus's first expedition, his voyages were already history. Authors and editors in many parts of Europe had used his journals and letters, along with those of other captains, mariners, soldiers, and missionaries, to weave a story of travel, exploration, and conquest, and then commented on that story, literally transforming it into history. Two English clergymen, Thomas Hakluyt (1552–1616) and Samuel Purchas (1575?–1626), were important creators of that history. As a student at Oxford, Hakluyt read everything he could about European explorations, began giving lectures on geography, and published a history of voyages, highlighting those made under the English flag. This brought him to the attention of members of court, and he was sent as the chaplain with an English delegation to Paris, where he was to listen for information about French and Spanish actions in the New World and anything else that might prove helpful to English interests. He continued to gather stories, translated and published a French history of voyages to Florida, wrote several works in Latin, and on returning to England published the first edition of his chief work, *The Principal Navigations, Voyages and Discoveries of the English Nation* (1589), which he later expanded to three volumes.

The Principal Navigations includes texts written by many voyagers, famous and largely unknown, which Hakluyt reports that he included "word for word," rescuing them from "musty darkness…misty corners…and perpetual oblivion." His prefaces make clear that he hoped these works would encourage more English voyages to the west, which would help spread Christianity, allow England to obtain tropical products such as silk and spices on its own, widen the market for English cloth, and transform England into a powerful nation.

Hakluyt's promotion of exploration was not limited to writing. He became an adviser to the British East India Company and an important voice in the group urging King James to found colonies in North America. He gained the position as vicar in the Anglican Church of the next English settlement in North America whenever it was founded, which, like most clerical posts (of which Hakluyt already had several), brought an income. When that settlement – named, unsurprisingly, Jamestown – was actually established in 1607, Hakluyt sent a curate to carry out the actual clerical duties, a standard pattern in the Anglican Church. His various church positions made him a wealthy man, and he invested in overseas voyages, becoming, in the word used at the time, an "adventurer." He also continued to translate and publish reports of voyages, and encouraged the translation of all types of works on the world beyond Europe. He was buried in Westminster Abbey, a high honor.

Samuel Purchas was not as fortunate as Hakluyt, though their careers followed similar paths. Like Hakluyt, he also became interested in the voyages of exploration while a student and held a series of church positions, writing two works of what we might term comparative religious history based on reading Hakluyt and other works: *Purchas, his Pilgrimage; or, Relations of the World and the Religions observed in all Ages* (1613) and *Purchas, his Pilgrim. Microcosmus, or the histories of Man. Relating the wonders of his Generation, vanities in his Degeneration, Necessity of his Regeneration* (1619). The two men met in 1613, but personal disagreements apparently kept Purchas from acquiring Hakluyt's voluminous papers until after his death. Those papers – both Hakluyt's own unpublished notes and the many journals, log-books, and other sources he had collected – formed the basis for Purchas's huge multiple-volume work: *Hakluytus Posthumus or Purchas His Pilgrimes, contaynyng a History of the World in Sea Voyages and Lande Travells, by Englishmen and others* (1625–6). Purchas was not as careful an editor as Hakluyt, but most of the original manuscripts on which he based his work have been lost, so the book contains information available nowhere else.

Hakluytus Posthumus also includes Purchas's reflections on the history he was telling and that Hakluyt helped to make. Purchas commented that Europe was the smallest continent, but that "the Qualitie of Europe exceeds her Quantitie" in many things:

> If I speake of Arts and Inventions (which are Men's properest goods, immortall Inheritance to our mortalitie) what have the rest of the world comparable? First the Liberall Arts are most liberall to us, having long since forsaken their Seminaries in Asia and Afrike, and here erected Colleges and Universities. And if one Athens in the east (the antient Europaean glory) now by Turkish Barbarisme be infected, how many Christian Athenses have wee in the west for it. As for Mechanicall Sciences, I could reckon…the many artifical Mazes and Labyrinths in our watches, the great heavenly Orbes and motions installed in so small a model…Who ever tooke possession of the huge Ocean, and made procession round about the vast Earth? Who ever discovered new Constellations, saluted the Frozen Poles, subjected the Burning Zones?…And is this all? Is Europe onely a fruitfull Field, a well watered garden, a pleasant Paradise in Nature? A continued Citie for habitation? Queene of the World for power? A School of Arts Liberall, Shop of Mechnicall, tents of Military, Arsenall of Weapons and shipping? Nay, these are the least of Her praises, or His rather, who hath given Europe more than Eagle's wings, and lifted her up above the Starres…Europe is taught the way to scale Heaven, not by Mathematicall principles, but by Divine veritie. Jesus Christ is their way, their truth, their life; who hath long since given a Bill of Divorce to ungratefull Asia where hee was borne, and Africa the place of his flight and refuge, and is become almost wholly and onely European.[1]

Purchas's comments about Europe's taking "possession of the whole Ocean" were a bit premature in 1625. At that point, the Spanish controlled most of Central America, Peru, the Philippines, and some islands in the Caribbean, and loosely held the north and west coast of South America. The Dutch and the Portuguese shared the coast of Brazil and some fortified trading posts on islands and coasts in the Indian Ocean and western Africa. However, the French colony in Quebec had a total population of eighty-five, and the two English colonies in North America, Jamestown and Plymouth, and the one Dutch colony, New Netherland, were also tiny and brand new. English sailors had just landed on Barbados, but there were no settlers there yet.

By 1789 the picture was very different. Spain and Portugal had effective control of much of South America, and Spanish holdings in Central America stretched into North America; Portugal had several trading colonies on the African coasts, and Goa in India. The French Empire around the world had been significantly reduced by its losses in the Seven Years War (1756–63), but still included well-populated islands in the Caribbean, French Guiana in South America, and smaller colonies around the Indian Ocean and the Pacific and along the coast of Africa. Dutch power had declined since its seventeenth century heights, and Dutch trade had been severely disrupted during the Fourth Anglo-Dutch War (1780–4) but the Dutch still held most of the East Indies, Ceylon, several islands in the Caribbean, and Suriname in South America. Purchas's own Britain was doing the best. Though it had recently lost some of its North American holdings in the War of American Independence (1775–83), it still held much of North America, many of the islands in the Caribbean, and a small colony in central America. A British company had direct rule of part of India, and indirect rule of more. Britain claimed islands in the Pacific, had a fort on Vancouver Island on the west coast of North America, and had just established the first colony in Australia.

In the years between 1789 and the beginning of World War I in 1914, European empires around the world would grow even more, of course, to include most of Africa and much of Asia. Statesmen, authors, scholars, and others in Europe would seek, as Purchas did, to explain this "rise of the West." Like Purchas, they often attributed it to European (and European-background) superiority in culture, science, economic development, military technology, and religion. Such reasoning has continued in the century or so since World War I, but the conclusions have become more varied, and less celebratory. They have generally agreed, however, that Europe's colonial possessions were not simply a consequence of European power, but also a source of that power. Not until the nineteenth century would industrialization make the gap between the West and the rest of the world – what the contemporary historian Kenneth Pomeranz has labeled the "great divergence" – truly marked. Europe's "possession of the huge Ocean" and "procession round about the vast Earth" would be central to that takeoff.

European ventures throughout the world in the seventeenth and eighteenth centuries were similar in many ways to those in the sixteenth century that we traced in chapter 7, but they also involved new themes and players. Explorers continued to search for routes from Europe to Asia, but also gathered scientific information and pushed further into the interiors of North and South America. Rulers continued to support exploration and colonization, but private companies became more important, providing financial backing, ships, and personnel. In some places these private companies became the actual territorial rulers, working with or displacing indigenous authorities. Colonies continued to provide wealth to monarchs and private investors through the extraction of natural resources such as precious metals and furs, but plantations of tropical crops using slave labor or other types of forced labor systems became the most significant engines of wealth. The European presence in some parts of the world remained limited to small isolated trading posts, but in other areas large numbers of Europeans and their descendants, along with people from other continents brought in by Europeans, came to vastly outnumber indigenous peoples. In every colonial area, Europeans developed systems of defining and regulating the various peoples under their control based on conceptualizations of difference that changed during this period.

Explorations

By the middle of the sixteenth century, Spanish expeditions had traveled north from New Spain (present-day Mexico) into the interior of North America, north from the Caribbean, around and across Florida, up the Rio de la Plata in South America to present-day Paraguay, and directly across the Pacific to the Moluccas and the Philippines and back. In the later sixteenth century Spanish and Portuguese explorers pushed up the Orinoco and Amazon river systems, with the discovery of gold and precious stones in Brazil attracting more adventurers into the South American interior. Meanwhile, the French, Dutch, and English tried to find a northern route to Asia that could allow them to compete with the Portuguese and the Spanish. Some expeditions searched for a Northwest Passage through North America. In the 1520s, Francis I of France sponsored the Italian Giovanni de Verrazzano (c. 1485–c. 1528) on a voyage up the east coast of North America; Verrazzano found rivers and bays, but nothing that led very far inland. Jacques Cartier's exploration of what he named the St. Lawrence River in the 1530s was a bit more promising, but it would be seventy years before other explorers would venture further up the St. Lawrence and into the Great Lakes area.

Meanwhile, English and Dutch expeditions sought a Northeast Passage up the coast of Norway. An English expedition made it to the Russian city of Archangel in 1553, and in the 1590s a Dutch expedition under Willem Barents (1550–97) discovered the island of Spitsbergen and wintered far to the east, though ice made it impossible for his ships to continue. Russian fur-traders and whalers were also exploring the far north, traveling into the vast areas of Siberia all the way to what is now Alaska in search of fox and sable. Peter the Great sponsored the Danish captain Vitus Bering (1681–1741) on several expeditions in the 1720s and 1730s along the north and east coast of Siberia; he was the first to map this area, and on one of the voyages he discovered the strait between Asia and America that was later named for him, along with the Aleutian Islands and the northwest coast of North America. (In the late nineteenth century, a Finnish and a Russian explorer each successfully sailed the whole length of northern Russia, and during the 1930s to the 1990s the passage saw some commercial navigation, using heavy icebreakers.) The first Russian trading post in Alaska was founded in 1741, and the first permanent colony in 1784.

In the seventeenth century, the English, Dutch, and French pushed further into North America. A series of French explorers, including Samuel de Champlain (c. 1570–1635) and Jean Nicolet (1598–1642), traveled up the St. Lawrence to the Great Lakes, and in the 1670s Jacques Marquette (1637–75) and Louis Joliet (1645–1700), along with others, explored the area from the Great Lakes to the river systems of central North America. French expeditions discovered the mouth of the Mississippi River, and by the early eighteenth century the French had established a string of forts and small settlements from Quebec to the Gulf of Mexico. Dutch-sponsored voyages under the English captain Henry Hudson (c. 1570–c. 1611) and English-sponsored voyages explored various waterways in northern North America searching for a Northwest Passage; several looked promising, but turned out to be land-locked bays or ice-blocked straits. William Baffin (1584–1622), the navigator and pilot on several of these voyages, recorded astronomical, tidal, and magnetic observations that would ultimately prove more useful than many of the voyages themselves, although it would be

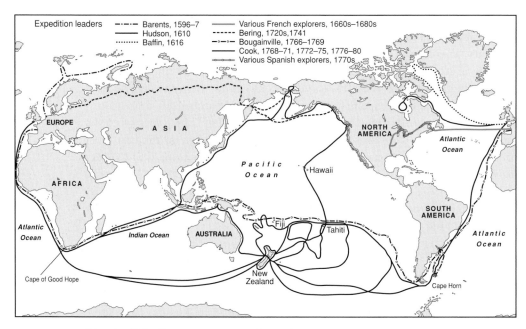

Map 13. Major European voyages, 1600–1789.

several centuries before his findings would be confirmed and a European voyage come this far north again.

Along with the search for the elusive northern passage to Asia, much exploration was driven by the search for the huge continent that Europeans expected would be in the southern hemisphere to balance all the continents in the northern hemisphere. This "Terra Australis" (a phrase simply meaning "southern land") showed up on maps throughout the sixteenth century, and in 1606 Europeans got their first glimpse of what was soon named Australia. Dutch expeditions explored and mapped the coasts of Australia, Tasmania, New Zealand, and other islands in the Pacific, at the same time as Dutch merchants and captains were challenging Portuguese trading dominance in the East Indies.

Australia was huge, but still not large enough to be the famed southern lands, and eighteenth-century expeditions continued the search, discovering and mapping much of the Pacific in the process. French and British ships reached Samoa, Tahiti, and other island groups, bringing back plants, animals, and often a few residents, along with reports and drawings of what they had seen. Such information fueled the European desire to classify, systematize, and understand the natural world.

The most important of these Pacific voyages were those under Captain James Cook (1728–79). Cook had been apprenticed as a young man in the merchant navy, volunteered in the British royal navy and served in the Seven Years War in North America, primarily as a surveyor. His land and coastal surveying brought him to the attention of the Royal Society, which hired him to go to the Pacific to record a transit of Venus across the face of the sun. On this first voyage in 1768–71, Cook sailed south around South America, made the planetary observation, and then explored and mapped both islands of New Zealand. He sailed to Australia, landing at several points to collect botanical specimens and looking for suitable places for a settlement; one bay he found was later named Botany Bay, and the first British penal colony in Australia was established there in 1788. Cook made contact with several groups of indigenous people, and communicated well enough to adopt an aboriginal word for the most distinctive animal he had seen, a kangaroo. He confirmed the existence of the Torres Strait separating Australia from New Guinea before continuing around the world back to Britain.

On his second voyage in 1772–5, again sponsored by the Royal Society, Cook sailed in the other direction around Africa and explored far south in the Pacific, crossing the Antarctic Circle at several points, though he did not land in Antarctica. His records about the weather and the seas demonstrated to all but the most adamant that there was no habitable continent south of Australia. On his third voyage in 1776–9 he dashed more hopes, sailing through the Bering Strait to the edge of the pack ice, and proving it was impossible to sail from Europe to Asia going north along either a Northeast or a Northwest Passage. (The first ship to make it through the Northwest Passage in a single season was a Canadian schooner in 1944, and a few more have done it since, though the route has been judged commercially unviable; global warming has recently thinned the ice and made getting through easier, however, and several nations are engaged in discussions about future shipping in this area, as it is thousands of miles shorter for ships traveling from New York or London to China than

50 The legacy of Captain Cook

The motivations and impact of Cook's voyages, like those of Columbus, have been hotly debated. Cook contributed enormously to European knowledge about the Pacific, both directly through the publication of his journals and through the reports, specimens, and sketches of the botanists and artists who accompanied him. He was the first to use new types of timekeeping devices to help figure longitude at sea, and was one of the best navigators and mapmakers in history. He kept his men from getting scurvy – a disease caused by vitamin C deficiency, and very common on long voyages – by forcing them to eat citrus fruits and sauerkraut, even though he did not know exactly why this worked. This view of him as an Enlightenment figure, interested in all aspects of the world around him and open to new, empirically demonstrated tools and techniques, stands in contrast to views of him as a destroyer of local cultures he viewed as inferior, bringing European diseases, introducing unhealthy products, and opening the Pacific to exploitation.

Cook's death also figures in this debate. The traditional view, based on copies of several paintings made at the time and widely reproduced as engravings, sees him as a peacemaker who got caught in a fight between native Hawaiians and his men. The original of one of these paintings was rediscovered in 2004, however, and it shows him aggressively attacking indigenous people. Hawaiian accounts also report that he was a violent man, though his own crew attributed this to irrationality brought on by an illness on his third voyage.

The actions of the islanders are even more hotly disputed. The anthropologist Marshall Sahlins and others have argued that the Hawaiians thought Cook was the human manifestation of the harvest god Lono because he appeared at the expected time in the ritual cycle; when Cook returned at a different point in the religious calendar, they killed him because he was now a sacrilegious taboo (a word that derives from the Hawaiian word *kapu*). More recently different scholars have asserted that Cook was killed because he demanded too much food from the island's residents and treated them harshly. They charge that Sahlins' view is imperialistic and ethnocentric, portraying Hawaiians as illogical savages who could not tell the difference between people and gods. Sahlins has countered that his critics' refusal to acknowledge that a very different view of reality could exist elsewhere is true ethnocentrism, because it judges Western ways of thinking as automatically superior. All sides in these debates can point to various pieces of evidence, so the discussion revolves primarily around methods of interpretation and the limits of applying anthropological and historical theory.

 For additional chapter resources see the companion website www.cambridge.org/wiesnerhanks.

the route through the Panama Canal.) Cook mapped the west coast of North America from California north, an area claimed by Spain but with very little permanent Spanish presence. This trip was also the first documented European contact with the inhabitants of the Hawaiian Islands (which Cook named the Sandwich Islands), who had themselves come from Polynesia by way of the Marquesas sometime around 500 CE. Cook was killed in Hawaii on a return visit later in the trip.

Cook's first two voyages, sponsored by the Royal Society for scientific purposes, like most explorations also had political and economic motivations and impacts. In the 1770s, Spanish expeditions traveled up the west coast of North America to what later came to be called Vancouver Island, and Spain began establishing a few garrisons and missions in the huge area north of Baja California. These included coastal settlements north of Point Loma (modern-day San Diego), Spain's northern-most firm claim, and so brought Spanish priests and soldiers into areas claimed by Francis Drake for England two hundred years earlier. (Exactly where Drake landed is not clear, though it was somewhere near Point Reyes, just north of San Francisco Bay.) After Cook's third voyage, the British East India Company established a one-building trading post at Nootka Sound on the west coast of what later came to be called Vancouver Island, which the Spanish captured in 1789. In the same year, Spain sent an expedition to the area under the leadership of Alessandro Malaspina (1754–1810), which, like Cook's, included scientists, artists, and scholars interested in local peoples, along with troops to support the tiny Spanish garrison. Malaspina explored and mapped much of the west coast, including Puget Sound, and then sailed to the western Pacific, where he also explored and mapped many of the same places as Cook. The British and the Spanish nearly went to war over rival claims to Nootka Sound, but these were resolved by treaties in favor of the British arranged by George Vancouver (1757–98), one of Cook's protégés who also carried out explorations in the area. The Pacific northwest continued to be the focus of international dispute, however, for Russian fur-traders had actually traveled in this area long before either Cook or Malaspina, and after 1783 the newly independent United States became involved as well.

France was not involved in this quarrel, but French conflicts with the British on the other side of North America – discussed in more detail below – led to French expeditions similar to those of Cook. In 1766, shortly after losing France's North American possessions to the British in the Seven Years War, Louis XV commissioned Louis Antoine de Bougainville (1729–1811), who had been a military officer in Quebec, to circumnavigate the globe. Bougainville visited the island of Tahiti and later described the islanders in a widely read book as true "noble savages." His visit also served as the basis for later French claims in Polynesia. Bougainville's book, along with a fictionalized version of his encounter with the Tahitians titled *Supplement to Bougainville's Voyage* (1771) written by the *philosophe* Denis Diderot, became key texts in Enlightenment debates about the merits of civilization. They, and Cook's journals, also inspired another French explorer and veteran of the Seven Years War, Jean François Galaup, count of

La Pérouse (1741–88) to lead a scientific expedition to the Pacific in 1785. La Pérouse explored coasts and islands all over the Pacific Rim, including the new British settlement in Australia and Russian settlements in the Kamchatka peninsula founded by Bering, before his expedition was shipwrecked and everyone died. Fortunately for future explorers, he had sent letters and documents about his expedition back to Paris, where they were subsequently published.

By the end of the eighteenth century, then, the coastlines and islands of the Atlantic and much of the Pacific had been explored and mapped, as had those of the Indian and Arctic Oceans. European interests in the nineteenth century would turn to continental interiors, especially Africa and Asia, which would also become the main focus for European conflicts over empire-building. In the seventeenth and eighteenth centuries, those conflicts were fought primarily on or near the sea, for domination of sea routes was the key to power. The world's seas, especially the Indian Ocean, the Caribbean, and the Atlantic, were crossed by faster and faster sailing ships, carrying goods, people, and ideas.

Trade and colonies in the Indian Ocean

By 1600, the Portuguese had become one of the many players in Indian Ocean trading ventures, shipping spices, precious metals, horses, and other goods, often in partnership with Asian merchants. They had a string of fortified trading posts and a few churches, but had not significantly altered centuries-old patterns of commerce involving merchants from different regions. That changed with the entry of the Dutch and then the British into Asian waters.

In the last decade of the sixteenth century, large well-built Dutch ships, often captained by mariners who had worked for the Portuguese, sailed to South and Southeast Asia, returning with huge quantities of spices. So many ships went, in fact, that Dutch markets were flooded with spices, which depressed the price and reduced profits. This situation led Dutch merchants in 1602 to agree to pool their resources in a new form of commercial enterprise, the United East India Company (Vereenigde Oost-Indische Compagnie, abbreviated VOC), which was given a national monopoly on trade with the East by the Dutch States General. The VOC separated managers from investors, who now bought permanent shares in the company rather than simply backing a single expedition; profit was given annually to investors, based on all the company's operations together, so that risk was minimized. This form of business organization became known as a "joint-stock company," and was later adopted by other companies in the Netherlands and elsewhere. Investment in joint-stock companies became generally profitable – though there were spectacular collapses – and increasingly fashionable; the circle of investors grew to include men and women with only a small amount of disposable income, as well as major merchants and bankers.

The States General provided financial support to the VOC in its early years and granted it political sovereignty over the territories under its control,

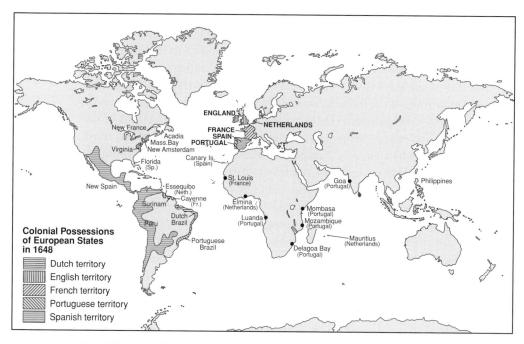

Map 14. Colonial possessions of European states in 1648.

allowing it to build forts, appoint governors, maintain armies and navies, and wage war against indigenous states. The VOC initially worked from fortified trading posts, many of which were captured from the Portuguese. Its managers, under the leadership of a governor-general, decided that the force of the Dutch navy could allow the company to reorganize the trading network to favor its interests. Dutch forces captured the Javanese port of Jakarta in 1619, renaming it Batavia, and the VOC established a naval base and ship-building yard there. The managers made alliances with Chinese merchants already living in the area, who set up sugar plantations and organized the recruitment of laborers from China for the sugar crop and for harvesting timber for ships and export. Dutch forces also defeated those of many small states in the East Indies, Ceylon (modern Sri Lanka), and the coast of India where spices were produced or traded, often in bloody battles; they sometimes enslaved the remaining population and forcibly transported them to a different location to work.

By the 1680s, the islands surrounding Batavia had become Dutch colonies and the VOC had a worldwide monopoly on spices. The Indian Ocean network was being radically transformed from one of partnerships to one in which Asian merchants were more dependent, though local and Chinese traders continued to make healthy profits. Dutch colonies also included several strongholds captured from the Portuguese in India, and Cape Town on the south coast of Africa, which became an important resupply point for ships. The Dutch were active in carrying goods of all types around Asia as well – what was termed in this era the "country trade" – making large profits from transporting Japanese silver to China, Chinese porcelain to India and Japan, and Indian opium to China.

The Dutch colonies in and around the Indian Ocean had mixed populations, of which European employees of the VOC were a tiny number; even in Batavia, the largest colony, Europeans were less than 10 percent of the population. Most Europeans were soldiers and sailors, and the vast majority of them were men. The VOC allowed employees who had served their time to stay on as "free burghers," but their numbers were very small, other than in Cape Town, where free burghers and other settlers – called "Boers," the Dutch word for farmer – began to move out into the countryside in the eighteenth century to raise crops and livestock.

Along with European, indigenous, and mixed-race people, many Dutch colonies included significant numbers of free Asians who came from elsewhere, and all included large numbers of slaves; one recent estimate finds that enslaved people were between one-third and two-thirds of the population in Dutch East Indian cities. Until the 1660s, most enslaved people were from South Asia, and after this from Southeast Asia and Africa; some were directly owned by the VOC, but most by private individuals. They were used primarily as domestic laborers with a range of tasks, though some worked in mining, shipping, and agriculture, especially on spice and sugar plantations.

Outright slavery was only one type of forced labor system in the East Indies. Chinese merchants brought in unskilled laborers – later called "coolies," a word that is now seen as derogatory in many areas – from China with terms of employment that were close to slavery. Immigration by Chinese laborers into Batavia was technically illegal, but Dutch authorities looked the other way as the Chinese were needed for sugar production; this situation kept labor cheap and the price of sugar relatively low. It was not low enough to compete with sugar produced by slave labor in Brazil, however, and, when the bottom fell out of the sugar market in 1740, unemployed Chinese laborers were ordered to be shipped to VOC tea plantations on Ceylon. Rumors spread that they would actually be thrown overboard on the way, laborers rioted, and VOC authorities responded by searching and looting all Chinese houses in Batavia. In a three-day wave of violence, every Chinese resident of the city, probably around 10,000 people, was killed. There were calls for an investigation, but these went nowhere. The toleration for diversity in their homeland that contributed to Dutch financial successes in Europe was much more limited in the colonies.

While the massacre in Batavia had no immediate ramifications, it was symptomatic of the VOC's growing inability to deal with the consequences of exploitation and to respond effectively to economic and political developments. The VOC was also slow at recognizing changing consumer demands in Europe, sticking with spices, which had always provided a solid profit, rather than investing in new commodities that had a much larger potential market. There was some change. Tea and coffee, for example, represented about 25 percent of the value of all goods imported into Amsterdam from the East Indies in 1780, whereas a hundred years earlier they had not been imported at all; during the same period, the share represented by spices dropped from 60 percent to 35 percent. Figures for other ports in other countries showed an even more dramatic shift, however, and the Dutch share of international trade declined steadily. Expenditures regularly outweighed revenues in the last half of the eighteenth century, and the company was disbanded in 1799.

Dutch preeminence in the Indian Ocean ended not only because of problems within the VOC, but also because of the rising power of the VOC's English competitor, the English East India Company. The EEIC actually received its charter two years earlier than the VOC, in 1600, but strong Dutch pressure in the East Indies led English merchants to concentrate on India. Company envoys spent much of the seventeenth century requesting an imperial decree, or *farman*, granting them regular trading privileges throughout the Mughal Empire from the powerful Mughal rulers of India. They were given privileges in a few areas, including Bombay on the west coast, but even these were revoked when the company declared war on the Mughals in 1686 to speed up the process and lost disastrously. Only abject apologies – including full prostration in front of the Mughal emperor – and a large fine persuaded the emperor to allow them back in. The EEIC then concentrated on trade through Madras and Calcutta on the east coast of India, dealing less in spices and more in new types of consumer goods, especially cotton and silk textiles, saltpeter (for gunpowder), and, by the eighteenth century, tea and opium.

British trade in and around India increased dramatically in the first half of the eighteenth century. In contrast to the VOC, which at least in theory forbade its agents to do business privately, the EEIC encouraged this. Individual British merchants along with small companies called syndicates began to specialize in the "country trade" around Asia, making alliances with Indian partners. High demand in Europe for Indian goods, and in China for Indian opium, allowed for profits at all stages of trade.

The EEIC also continued to push for an empire-wide *farman*, and in 1716, after the company threatened to pull all its business out of western India, the Mughal emperor Farrukhisiyar finally agreed. This action opened the way for the EEIC to intervene in the political affairs of India as the company defended its growing economic power. During the next several decades, company agents and private English traders, often allied with wealthy Indian merchants, took advantage of the declining power of the Mughal state and commercial opportunities of all types to expand their spheres of operation. They made treaties with Indian princes and conducted military operations, acting more like a sovereign state than a private company.

In the 1740s, the British and the French backed opposing contestants for the rule of several states in southern India, thus mixing European and local rivalries. Warfare spread back and forth for several decades, becoming part of the Seven Years War, with the British ultimately victorious, in part because they were better able to pay for Indian troops (called sepoys) who did much of the actual fighting and provided key information about the plans of rival forces. Several key battles were won through the military abilities of Robert Clive

(1725–74), who began his career in India as a teenaged clerk and book-keeper in the EEIC. When hostilities broke out between the British and the French, Clive joined the private army of the EEIC, and proved to be a very able commander. After a brief stay in England, he went back to India as a governor and military leader, and defeated a large French-backed force to secure Bengal for British interests. Clive was well rewarded financially by the EEIC and its Indian allies, and when he returned to England he became a Member of Parliament. Unrest in India drew him back again, and he helped to broker an agreement in 1764 granting the EEIC direct rule of the province of Bengal in northeastern India and several other parts of the subcontinent; Clive became the first governor-general of Bengal. Other territories had indigenous rulers, but they too were allied with the EEIC. Inquiries began in Parliament about the wealth Clive had accumulated, however. He had also long suffered from what was probably manic depression and various physical ailments, which he eased by the use of opium. All of these factors converged, and Clive committed suicide at the age of forty-nine.

In the heroic view of British imperialism – the 1911 *Encyclopedia Britannica* provides a good example of this – Clive was regarded as the founder of the British Empire in India, though more recent scholarship has seen the process as slower and more complex. As the EEIC acquired more political power, the relationship between its representatives and local merchants changed from partnership to clientage, and the company was able to dictate terms and cut into the profits of local suppliers. In 1773, for example, the governor-general of Bengal established a monopoly on the opium trade in India; the Chinese emperor had banned the smoking of opium in 1729, so the EEIC auctioned its opium to private British merchants, who then smuggled it into China, with all parties gaining solid profits. (In the nineteenth century, Britain fought two wars to force China to allow unrestricted opium imports.) Despite significant Indian resistance to British political and economic measures and a series of wars throughout the rest of the eighteenth century, British power in India continued to expand.

Historians hotly debate the extent to which imperial ambitions shaped the British takeover of India. Some view the whole process as somewhat accidental, with the EEIC and the British government simply responding to economic and political developments with no clear plan. Others see empire building as a defined aim throughout the eighteenth century or even earlier. Still others note a change in the 1740s and 1750s, and use the transformation of Robert Clive from book-keeper to general and governor as a symbol of this change.

The VOC and the EEIC were not the only European trading companies in the Indian Ocean basin. France, Denmark, Portugal, and Sweden all chartered East India Companies modeled on and designed to compete with those of the Dutch and the English. They were far less successful, however, because they depended more on government support than private investment, lacked long-range planning, and simply could not compete with the far larger and more established Dutch and British companies.

Fig. 33. An Indian miniature from about 1785 shows the wife of an East India Company officer surrounded by many servants, in a household that blends European furnishings with an Indian carpet. She appears to be receiving a line of Indian and English merchants who want her favors. Colonial settings juxtaposed gender and ethnic hierarchies in complex ways; not only are men seeking her good will, but all her servants, or at least all those shown in this painting of a public room of the house, appear to be male.

Trade and colonies in the Caribbean

While the Indian Ocean was primarily dominated by two powers, the Caribbean – the first site of extensive European colonialism outside of Europe – was contested by many. Columbus claimed the entire area for Spain, but many islands had only small, weakly defended settlements. By the middle of the sixteenth century English and French ships began to smuggle all types of goods to Spanish settlements, and English and French privateers attacked

Spanish ships. The religious wars in the sixteenth century gave Protestant captains an excuse to engage in more formal attacks on Catholic Spanish settlements, though often these were ruses; captains threatened, Spanish governors acquiesced, and then both sides engaged in trade. After 1610 or so such "attacks" grew less frequent, and smugglers went back to work, their jobs made easier by the establishment of Caribbean colonies by many nations, which shortened smuggling routes and enhanced opportunities to make a profit from contraband goods or differential tariff policies.

During the seventeenth century, England, France, the Netherlands, Denmark and even the tiny Baltic duchy of Courland (in present-day Latvia) all established their own colonies or took over Spanish colonies on the Caribbean islands and the north coast of South America. Often two countries set up tiny rival colonies on the same island, which were easily – and often – destroyed by hostile forces. The sovereignty of many colonies changed frequently; the tiny island of Sint Maarten/St. Martin, for example, changed hands at least sixteen times before it was finally divided between the Dutch and the French.

The earliest challenges to Spanish control came on the north coast of South America, where England, France, and the Netherlands all established settlements where they hoped to grow tropical crops for export and provide safe havens for ships from their own country. From these bases, military expeditions to take over the highly profitable Portuguese settlements in Brazil were launched. Several French invasions failed, but in 1630 Dutch troops conquered the northeastern part of Brazil, and continued to expand their holdings southward. At the time Portugal and its empire were ruled by the Habsburg kings of Spain, and the Netherlands was engaged in its long fight against Habsburg domination which ended with the Thirty Years War. Thus military actions in Brazil were motivated in part by Dutch aims in Europe, as well as the financial opportunities offered by Brazilian sugar plantations. Spanish troops were busy fighting in Europe, so few could be sent, and the Dutch conquered much of Brazil. After the successful Portuguese revolt against Spain in 1640, local Portuguese settlers rebelled against the Dutch, and Brazil reverted to Portugal in 1654. The Dutch then established larger settlements further north, and also captured the English colony of Suriname, later known as Dutch Guiana, which became the largest Dutch colony in the Americas by 1800.

As in Brazil and many Caribbean islands, Suriname's prosperity rested on sugar planted and harvested by slaves; by 1800, more than 90 percent of the population of the colony consisted of enslaved Africans. Much of the area was low-lying coastal plains, like the Netherlands itself. Using skills they had perfected in Europe, Dutch engineers directed slave labor in massive drainage projects that increased the total amount of cultivable land significantly. Landowners then oversaw the planting of cotton, coffee, and cacao along with sugar. Many of these goods passed through the port established by the Dutch on the small island of Curaçao, on their way to the Netherlands and then the rest of Europe. As Batavia was in the East Indies, Curaçao became a center for ship-building and ship repair in the West Indies, and a place where sailors could find captains who needed crew.

Dutch activities in the Americas began as a series of independent ventures, but in 1621 a West Indian Company (WIC) modeled on the already very successful VOC was chartered by the States General, and given monopoly trading privileges and the right to act as a government. Because the Netherlands was at war with Spain at the time, the WIC also had a clear military mission, which made investors hesitant to risk their money. WIC ships did capture the Spanish silver fleet once, and shareholders got a 50 percent dividend that year, but in general the WIC was a financial disaster. It was never able to gain a monopoly on sugar the way the VOC did on spices, and it was unable to control the activities of private merchants, not even those who were Dutch. Despite a huge payment from the VOC enforced by the Dutch government, the WIC went bankrupt in 1674. It was reorganized with new directors, but no longer had military forces or an official monopoly on anything, becoming instead simply the administrator of Dutch colonies in the Americas.

VOC-run colonies in the East Indies operated very efficiently with only a small Dutch population, but the WIC's financial difficulties led many in the Netherlands to suggest that increasing the number of Dutch settlers might be a way to make American colonies more profitable, or at least allow them to survive. The WIC granted what were termed patroonships to individuals; patroons got economic and juridical rights over a piece of land, and in return they were expected to bring in settlers. Thus many Dutch colonies were largely in private hands, though this system never accomplished its original aim of attracting more settlers.

The first French colony in this area, Cayenne (later called French Guiana), was established in 1604 on the mainland, but it never became very important economically. The core of French holdings, and France's most important overseas settlements, were islands in the Caribbean, some taken from indigenous Caribs, some from the Spanish, and some that had been largely unpopulated. Among these was the western coast of the large Spanish-held island of Santo Domingo. Spanish colonists had brought in cattle, some of which escaped, and, as in Argentina, multiplied into large herds. Like any abundant natural resource, these cattle attracted people seeking to exploit an opportunity, in this case men who lived by selling leather and meat smoked on wooden frames called *boucans* to the many ships that passed by. These settlements of *boucaniers*, or buccaneers as they came to be known in English, were lawless and violent places where men – and a very few women – of varying ethnic backgrounds mixed. In the later seventeenth century, the French began to exert some control over this western part of Santo Domingo, giving it the equivalent French name of Saint-Domingue. They slowly transformed Saint-Domingue – which later became Haiti – into the most profitable slave plantation colony in the Caribbean. Wealthy planters established huge plantations with several hundred slaves, irrigation systems, and new types of processing machinery.

Other French holdings in the Caribbean experienced a similar transformation. In the middle of the seventeenth century farms worked primarily by white indentured servants grew tobacco, with the colonies themselves poorly run by a series of short-lived chartered companies. Indentured servants were young men, often quite poor, who worked a set period of years for a landowner in exchange for their passage; their terms of service were often set by a contract. (The word "indentured," meaning "toothed," comes from the fact that the edges of a contract written in duplicate on one sheet, were then torn or cut in an uneven jagged pattern; each party was given half the sheet, so that only authentic contracts could be fitted back together properly.) They were, at least in theory, protected from over-exploitation by the local legal authorities.

By the end of the century, however, large plantations worked by enslaved Africans had been established on many islands. Former indentured servants remained as overseers, went back to France, drifted into other sorts of employment, or a lucky few became large landowners themselves. Within a century these colonies produced half of Europe's sugar and coffee, allowing France to maintain a favorable balance of trade, and spurring production in France of certain types of goods for the colonies, especially cloth. That cloth supplied clothing for the Africans who were brought into Saint-Domingue in such numbers that France became the second-largest slave-trading nation after Britain. The French military took over direct control of the colonies from the chartered companies. Colonists were expected to serve in militias, a task they resented and often avoided, and were expected to send all their products to France, a task they also often avoided by smuggling goods directly to other colonies or to Britain or the Netherlands.

Louis XIV's desire for centralized control extended to the Caribbean, and in 1685 he issued the Code Noir ("Black Code"), which among its many provisions prohibited Jews from living in French colonies, forbade the practice of any religion other than Roman Catholicism, regulated relations between masters and slaves, and declared that the legal status of children would follow that of their mother, not their father. (Later in the same year Louis extended the religious clauses to France itself, revoking the Edict of Nantes and outlawing Protestantism.) Many of its provisions were regularly ignored, however, as slaves were undernourished and tortured, and masters refused to baptize their slaves or teach them Christianity.

The Code Noir set harsh punishments for slaves who ran away, but allowed people over the age of twenty to free slaves that they owned. Some slaves were manumitted, especially women who were the sexual partners of white men, along with their children, and slowly the population of free black and mixed-race people grew. Estimates of the population of the French Caribbean in 1789 include about 56,000 whites, perhaps as many as 700,000 slaves, and 23,000 free blacks and persons of mixed ancestry. Some of these "free people of color," as they came to be known, became increasingly wealthy, owning property and slaves. They also wore French clothing, purchased French furniture, and adopted other aspects of French culture, a process white colonists

51 The Code Noir

Louis XIV issued the extensive Code Noir in March of 1685, and two years later it was officially registered in Saint-Domingue. The prologue captures Louis's understanding of his role as monarch (English translation by John D. Garrigus, Jacksonville University. Printed by permission).

Louis, by the grace of God, King of France and Navarre, to all present and to come, greetings. Since we [Louis is speaking in the royal "we" here] owe equally our attention to all the peoples that Divine Providence has put under our obedience, we have had examined in our presence the memoranda that have been sent to us by our officers in our American islands, by whom having been informed that they need our authority and our justice to maintain the discipline of the Catholic, Apostolic, and Roman church there and to regulate the status and condition of the slaves in our said islands, and desiring to provide for this and to have them know that although they live in regions infinitely removed from our normal residence, we are always present to them...we say, rule, order, and wish that which follows.

I. We wish and intend that the edict by the late King of glorious memory our very honored lord and father of 23 April 1615 be enforced in our islands, by this we charge all our officers to evict from our Islands all the Jews who have established their residence there, to whom, as to the declared enemies of the Christian name, we order to have left within three months from the day of the publication of these present [edicts], or face confiscation of body and property.

II. All the slaves who will be in our Islands will be baptized and instructed in the Catholic, Apostolic, and Roman religion...

III. We forbid any public exercise of any religion other than the Catholic, Apostolic, and Roman; we wish that the offenders be punished as rebels and disobedient to our orders...

VI. We charge all our subjects, whatever their status and condition, to observe Sundays and holidays that are kept by our subjects of the Catholic, Apostolic, and Roman religion. We forbid them to work or to make their slaves work on these days from the hour of midnight until the other midnight, either in agriculture, the manufacture of sugar or all other works...

VIII. We declare our subjects who are not of the Catholic, Apostolic, and Roman religion incapable in the future of contracting a valid marriage. We declare bastards the children born of such unions...

XII. The children who will be born of marriage between slaves will be slaves and will belong to the master of the women slaves...

XIII. We wish that if a slave husband has married a free woman, the children, both male and girls, will follow the condition of their mother and be free like her, in spite of the servitude of their father; and that if the father is free and the mother enslaved, the children will be slaves the same...

XV. We forbid slaves to carry any weapon, or large sticks, on pain of whipping and of confiscation of the weapon to the profit of those who seize them...

XVI. In the same way we forbid slaves belonging to different masters to gather in the day or night whether claiming for wedding or otherwise, whether on their master's property or elsewhere, and still less in the main roads or faraway places, on pain of corporal punishment...

XXII. Each week masters will have to furnish to their slaves ten years old and older for their nourishment two and a half jars...of cassava flour or three cassavas weighing at least two-and-a-half pounds each or equivalent things, with two pounds of salted beef or three pounds of fish or other things in proportion, and to children after they are weaned to the age of 10 years half of the above supplies...

XXV. Each year masters will have to furnish each slave with two outfits of canvas...

XXXIII. The slave who will have struck his master or the wife of his master, his mistress or their children to bring blood, or in the face, will be punished with death.

XLII. The masters may also, when they believe that their slaves so deserve, chain them and have them beaten with rods or straps. They shall be forbidden however from torturing them or mutilating any limb, at the risk of having the slaves confiscated...

XLIII. We enjoin our officers to criminally prosecute the masters, or their foremen, who have killed a slave under their auspices or control, and to punish the master according to the circumstances of the atrocity...

LIX. We grant to manumitted slaves the same rights, privileges and liberties enjoyed by persons born free; desiring that they merit this acquired liberty and that it produce in them, both for their persons and for their property, the same effects that the good fortune of natural liberty causes in our other subjects.

disparagingly called *francisation*, sometimes translated as "Frenchification." Officials increasingly regarded free people of color with suspicion, and in the later eighteenth century passed restrictive laws regarding their economic and legal position.

Like Dutch colonies, many British Caribbean colonies were established during the Thirty Years War when Spanish troops were busy fighting in Europe, and like French colonies, many first used white indentured servants to raise tobacco or cotton. Changes in agriculture, the disruptions of the Civil War era, and religious differences led some people to immigrate voluntarily through indenture contracts, while others were forced into service. Opponents of Cromwell's actions in Ireland and Scotland were sometimes transported to the Caribbean, as were vagrants, debtors, and those found guilty of minor crimes; servants and other poor people were also occasionally "Barbadosed," a slang term for being kidnapped and taken to the colonies.

As in the French Caribbean, the introduction of sugar created a much larger demand for labor than indenture contracts or even kidnapping could supply, however, and African slaves, supplied by merchants from many countries, met this need. Sugar could only be produced profitably on a large scale, so wealthy planters often bought out their neighbors, then turned the actual running of the plantation over to those same individuals or men in their families, now hired as overseers. Many poorer whites eked out a living through hunting, raising a few crops and animals, fishing, and doing the few odd jobs available. The wealthy planters called them "redlegs" because of their sunburned skin. (The American term "redneck" may also come from the sunburned skin of poorer whites who worked outdoors in the southern colonies, though an alternative derivation is the red scarves worn by Scottish opponents of the Church of England, some of whom emigrated to those same colonies.) Groups of colonists also moved from one island to another, establishing new colonies or taking over those of other countries. British troops took part of Spanish Jamaica in 1655, for example, and a few years later held the whole island; later British Jamaicans established a colony for timber in the area of Spanish Central America called the Mosquito Coast (now Belize). Such actions spurred return raids, with settlements and plantations burned and slaves captured. Beginning in the 1670s, hundreds of British colonists from Barbados settled in Carolina, where they built plantations growing rice and indigo, also using African slave labor.

In the eighteenth century, local conflicts and international disputes continued. The Seven Years War brought a reshuffling of territories between France and Britain, and the War of American Independence brought further changes. British colonists were forbidden to trade with the newly independent Americans; though much smuggling continued, it proved difficult to find substitutes for the large amounts of grain that the American colonies had provided to feed slaves and other Caribbean residents. There was famine on several islands, sometimes made worse by hurricanes that were common in the area, and yellow fever killed many immigrants. Wealthy planters and their families spent more and more time in England, where life was more secure, and there were far more schools, cafés, clubs, and other institutions of the newly emerging "public sphere" than were available in the colonies. Despite these problems, however, the British West Indian "sugar islands" were quite prosperous at the end of the eighteenth century, and the absentee landlords gathered in London were effective in making sure that national policies did not interfere with this.

Although the colonies of the Caribbean and northern South America were often at war with one another, their basic economic and social structures were very similar; most were based on plantation slavery, or in providing plantation economies with goods that they needed. African slaves had actually arrived in the Americas as early as 1502, though there were few in the early decades of colonization, as the Spanish and Portuguese hoped their labor needs would be met by indigenous peoples. When death due to disease and exploitation made this impossible, the importation of African slaves increased. Estimates of the slave trade suggest that about 75,000 slaves left Africa for the Americas before 1580, and during the same period, around 225,000 people left Europe, mostly from Spain and Portugal. From 1580 to 1700, the proportions were very different; estimates vary, but perhaps a million people left Europe for the Americas, while a million and a half to two million people were taken from Africa. In the eighteenth century, as the demand for tropical crops increased, the proportion grew even more skewed; somewhere between two and a half and five million people were taken from Africa, while less than a million left Europe. Taking all the years of the slave trade together, around 40 percent of the slaves went to Brazil, another 40 percent to the Caribbean, and the remaining 20 percent to the rest of the Americas. Somewhere around 4 percent went to North America, where higher reproductive rates among slaves allowed the maintenance of the system without a large constant influx from Africa.

In the sixteenth century the Portuguese dominated the slave trade, while in the seventeenth century the Dutch, French, and English joint-stock companies all carved out set routes and areas in which they were supposed to have a monopoly. As with other goods, however, slaves were regularly smuggled in and out of islands and ports. Laws regarding slavery in Spanish, Portuguese, French, and Dutch colonies were, like many other legal issues, based loosely on Roman law, which allowed slaves to be manumitted and forbade masters to kill them. Colonies further developed their own codes based on metropolitan directives and decrees such as Louis XIV's Code Noir, but also on local customs and needs. By the eighteenth century, for example, slaves in Spanish America were allowed to purchase their own freedom through the *coartación*; as long as they offered a fair price, their masters were supposed to free them. Britain had never adopted Roman law, nor was there much consideration of slavery in common law, so that each British colony devised its own laws and legal precedents.

Though the Code Noir and other laws regarding slavery set harsh punishments for slaves who ran away and for anyone who aided them, many did attempt to escape. Most were probably returned, but runaway slaves, called *maroons*, formed villages and settlements in mountains, swamps, jungles, and other frontier areas beyond the reach of colonial authorities. Some of these communities grew so large that they were the actual governing power in certain areas, and colonial officials occasionally made treaties with them just as they did with other neighboring states. Maroons were often central figures in slave revolts, which began in the sixteenth century and continued throughout the time of plantation slavery. Most revolts were brief, local, and small, though a few spread more widely. Fear of slave revolts was ever present, heightened by sensationalist stories that spread by word of mouth, letters, and printed accounts of plots uncovered, weapons gathered, and owners threatened. Fear of revolt was also intensified by simply looking around, for by the end of the eighteenth century the vast majority of the Caribbean population, no matter which European state controlled the colony, were slaves from Africa.

Trade and colonies in the Atlantic

The Caribbean is, of course, geographically part of the Atlantic, and its economy, social structure, and political situation tied it very clearly into what historians are increasingly calling the "Atlantic world." By the seventeenth and eighteenth centuries, that world also connected to the Indian Ocean, and to the lives of people far from any sea. Millions of pieces of Chinese porcelain made in the inland city of Jingdezhen were transported to Canton, carried on ships to Amsterdam and London, and then exported to Jamaica, Boston, Berlin, and Moscow. Calico cloth made by village residents in the Gujerati area of northwest India went to Europe, but also to the Senegambia in western Africa, where it was traded to African merchants for slaves and for the gum of the acacia tree. Acacia gum was used in Britain and France for papermaking and for producing calicoes that Europeans hoped might eventually compete with those of India. Calico was one of the many items promised "in perpetuity" to Native American tribes in treaties with British and later American authorities. Commerce in the Atlantic is often described as a "triangle trade" linking Europe, Africa, and the Americas, but no geometrical figure can accurately capture the many lines of interaction.

The colonies established in North America by powers other than Spain and Portugal were a key part of this new Atlantic world. The earliest colonies were tiny and underfunded, often dependent on indigenous peoples for their survival. Half failed, whether through conquest by another power, disease, abandonment, economic or environmental collapse, or indigenous opposition.

English-sponsored voyages to the Americas began with those of John Cabot in 1495, but nearly a century later Hakluyt and others were still trying to encourage a first successful settlement. In 1585, the English writer, explorer, and New World promoter Sir Walter Raleigh (1554–1618) founded a small colony at Roanoke Island off what is now North Carolina, but the colonists vanished within several years. About twenty years later another group settled at Jamestown in Virginia, organized by the joint-stock Virginia Company, though

52 The transportation of children

As in the Caribbean, not every indentured servant came to North America voluntarily. The following is a letter from Sir Edwin Sandys of the Virginia Company requesting a member of the king's Privy Council to give him the authority to coerce children to go to Virginia in 1620. These were children the government of the city of London had determined were "superfluous"; many were probably orphans, but we know from other sources that poor children were also simply rounded up on the streets, and transported despite the objections of their parents. Sandys makes no mention of labor needs in Virginia in his letter, but frames it in terms of relieving a burden on the city and improving the character of young people he views as dangerous and shiftless.

Right Honorable [Sir Robert Naughton of the King's Privy Council]:

Being unable to give my personal attendance upon the Lords [the Privy Council], I have presumed to address my suit in these few lines unto your Honor. The City of London have by act of their Common Council, appointed one hundred children out of their superfluous multitude to be transported to Virginia; there to be bound apprentices for certain years, and afterward with very beneficial conditions for the children. And have granted moreover a levy of five hundred pounds among themselves for the appareling of those children, and toward their charges of transportation. Now it falleth out that among those children, sundry being ill disposed, and fitter for any remote place than for this City, declare their unwillingness to go to Virginia, of whom the City is especially desirous to be disburdened, and in Virginia under severe masters they may be brought to goodness. But this City wanting authority to deliver, and the Virginia Company to transport, these persons against their wills, the burden is laid upon me, by humble suit unto the Lords to procure higher authority for the warranting thereof. May it please your Honor therefore, to vouchsafe unto us of the Company here, and to the whole plantation in Virginia, that noble favor, as to be a means unto their Lordships out of their accustomed goodness, and by their higher authority, to discharge both the City and our Company of this difficulty, as their Lordships and your Honors in your wisdom shall find most expedient. For whose health and prosperity our Company will always pray...

(From Susan M. Kingsbury, ed., *The Records of the Virginia Company of London: The Court Book, from the Manuscript in the Library of Congress,* vol. III [Washington: Government Printing office, 1933], p. 259.)

it was several decades before the colony's stability was assured. Colonists experimented with different cash crops as well as grain and root crops for their own use, and gradually established a system of indentured servitude to supply the needed labor. Ship captains recruited young people, mostly boys and young men, but also some young women, as indentured servants, then sold the contracts to Virginia colonists. The first Africans came to English North America in 1619, in a ship named the *Jesus*; though in the early decades some Africans were indentured servants, most of them were permanent slaves. Native Americans were also enslaved in many southern colonies, but their numbers were soon dwarfed by those of Africans.

These earliest ventures were organized by various chartered companies and motivated primarily by the hope of wealth, but in 1620 a group of religious separatists called the Pilgrims established a colony at Plymouth far to the north of Jamestown. Over the next several decades, other colonies were established by groups unhappy with the religious situation in England, primarily Puritans – who set up Massachusetts Bay, Rhode Island, Connecticut, and New Haven – but also Catholics, who established the colony of Maryland. Each of these colonies was chartered by the crown, which allowed the colony the right to make local laws, as long as these did not go against the laws of England. Many of them established some sort of assembly; in most colonies propertied males could vote for members in the assembly, though in Massachusetts only those men who were approved members of the church had the right to vote. In order to be full church members, men had to make a confession to the whole congregation describing their personal conversion experience. Women became church members independently through their own conversion experiences, though this did not give them political rights.

Early French colonies in North America were just as tiny and tenuous as British colonies. France attempted to found colonies in Florida and Canada in the middle of the sixteenth century, but these were either taken over by the Spanish or immediately failed. The first long-lasting French settlements were at Acadia and Quebec in the first decade of the seventeenth century, owned by a series of noblemen who worked sporadically with merchant companies to try to encourage colonization, though they were not very successful. Both Quebec and Acadia were occupied by the English for short periods during the seventeenth century, and French explorers, fur-traders and missionaries moved westward, founding forts, trading posts, and a few small missions along the coasts of the Great Lakes and the Mississippi River. These early French colonies were based on a single product – fur, especially beaver pelts destined to be made into hat felt, for such hats were the height of fashion in Europe.

As in the Caribbean, other countries joined Spain, England, and France in founding colonies in North America. In 1609, the English explorer Henry Hudson led an expedition in northeastern North America sponsored by the VOC, and claimed various places where he landed for the company. Dutch fur-traders set up a few forts near present-day Albany, New York, and in 1623 the new Dutch West Indian Company convinced the States General to declare the whole area a Dutch province, called New Netherland. In 1626 the WIC founded New Amsterdam on the southern tip of the island of Manhattan at the mouth of the Hudson River, primarily as a base to defend its fur trading operations; this became the largest Dutch colonial settlement in North America, and attracted settlers from other parts of Europe. In 1638 Sweden established the first of several colonies along the Delaware River, but in 1655 most of these were conquered by the Dutch, who saw them as a threat. Most of the Swedish colonists stayed, however, adding to the mixture of settlers in the Dutch colonies.

In the 1660s, a second wave of colonies were founded, especially by England. English forces conquered New Netherland, including the settlement at New Amsterdam, renaming both New York, in honor of the younger brother of the newly restored King Charles II, James, duke of York. Colonies were founded in South Carolina and Georgia in 1670, to form a buffer between Virginia and the Spanish colonies in Florida, and to attempt the introduction of profitable subtropical crops, including indigo, tobacco, and rice. Georgia also served as a penal colony for the transportation of debtors, vagrants, and criminals. In 1682, William Penn (1644–1718), a prominent member of the Society of Friends – the Quakers – received a charter for what became Pennsylvania, which included the former New Sweden. Most of the new colonies, including Penn's, were proprietary, meaning they were owned outright by a single person or group. Virginia had a governor appointed by the king, along with an elected assembly, and the New England colonies were largely controlled by their elected assemblies. Economically the mid-Atlantic and New England colonies depended on agriculture done by families, sometimes with the assistance of an indentured servant or two. Virginia was primarily settled by small farmers in the interior, though coastal merchants and larger landholders dominated the economy. Discontent among poorer farmers and indentured servants led to Bacon's Rebellion in 1676; the leaders of Virginia society saw importing more African slaves as a way of reducing the number of future rebels and lessening social tensions among white colonists by establishing a permanent, racially marked labor force.

As we have seen, attempts by French chartered companies to encourage permanent settlements in North America were not very successful, and in 1663 Louis XIV brought all of New France under direct royal control. He appointed a governor-general to handle military matters, and an *intendant* similar to those he was appointing in France to handle administrative affairs. Each regional colony had its own governor and *intendants*, also put in position by the king. Some historians have, in fact, seen New France as a sort of laboratory for absolutism, where traditional noble privileges meant little, no guilds restricted trade or production, and commoners could advance more quickly through service to the monarch and their own skills.

Louis XIV, or, more accurately, his finance minister Jean-Baptiste Colbert, recognized that increasing the population of New France was important if French holdings were to compete with the steadily growing English colonies. Most immigrants in the seventeenth century were unemployed young men from urban environments, who stayed briefly and then either died or went back to France. The English colonies also attracted young single men, but also young single women who married these men, and young families, so that they grew from both immigration and natural increase. For a brief period in the 1660s the French crown directly recruited young women, mostly poor women from charity hospitals, and paid for their passage; about eight hundred of these *filles du roi* (daughters of the king) did immigrate, more than doubling the number of European women who were not nuns. Colbert stated explicitly, however, that "it would not be wise to depopulate the kingdom in order to populate Canada," and so recommended instead that "the most useful way to achieve it would be to try to civilize the Algonquins, the Hurons, and the other Savages who have embraced Christianity; and to persuade them to come to settle in a commune with the French, to live with them, and educate their children in our mores and our customs."[2] Thus official policy in New France in the seventeenth century was one of the assimilation of Native Americans through *francisation*, through which they would be "made French."

The policy of *francisation* included intermarriage between French men and indigenous women, for the French hoped that such marriages would help the fur trade and strengthen ties between French and Native American communities and families. French fur traders – called *voyageurs* or *coureurs de bois* ("runners of the woods") – did frequently marry Native American women as they traveled further and further west, relying on their wives and their wives' families for many things. In contrast to free people of color in the French Caribbean, however, very few Native Americans in New France were interested in adopting French culture or integrating into French society on French terms, and the policy was abandoned at the end of the seventeenth century. Intermarriage between French traders and Native American women continued, especially in central and western fur-trading areas where European women were, in fact, banned until the 1820s. Officials now worried, however, about the man adopting "savage" customs from his wife rather than expecting that she would become French through him. Jesuit missionaries set up communities for Christian converts, but lived slightly separate from them; they translated Christian materials into local languages, and, as in China, tried to explain Christian beliefs and practices in terms of native customs. Becoming Christian no longer required becoming French.

British missionaries were far less active among native peoples than French or Spanish Jesuits and Franciscans, and intermarriage with native people was never English policy. There were separate settlements for Indian Christians in New England: "praying towns" in which converts were expected to follow Christian mores in terms of marriage and behavior as well as worship and other religious practices. There were never very many of these, however, and the rapidly expanding European population of New England made the primary story of native–immigrant relations one of European appropriation of Native American land for new settlements, war, and the eventual expulsion of natives from many parts of New England.

In the southern states there was little missionary activity and very few churches even for immigrants. Slaveowners often chose not to baptize their slaves, for they feared this might mean they would have to free them. In 1667, the Virginia assembly, called the House of Burgesses, passed a law stating that baptism did not change one's condition of servitude, but many owners still refused to allow their slaves to be baptized. This was also true in the British Caribbean, whereas Catholic slaveowners in both the French and Spanish colonies were more likely to baptize their slaves, as the Code Noir enjoined.

The eighteenth century brought further expansion and shuffling in French, British, and Spanish North American holdings. In 1699, the French founded Louisiana at the mouth of the Mississippi to prevent either the Spanish or the British from controlling trade from the interior, especially the furs that were being transported from the French Illinois colony. By 1750, Louisiana had a population of about four thousand Europeans, some of them unwilling transports from French prisons and cities, sent into what became known as "Louisiana slavery." Others were Germans attracted by brochures produced by financier John Law, whose investment schemes for spectacular profits involved recruiting thousands of new residents to French colonies in the Americas. About five thousand of Louisiana's residents were African slaves, growing tobacco, indigo, and rice. In the late 1750s, these groups were joined by French colonists from

Acadia (now part of the Canadian province of Nova Scotia) deported by the British after they conquered the area. Though the number of Acadians who came to Louisiana was probably only somewhat over a thousand, their story became an essential part of Louisiana culture, and many residents with no ties to this group also came to think of themselves as "Cajun."

The conquest of Acadia was only one part of British expansion into French territory. By 1750, the valley of the St. Lawrence River was filled with French farms that exported grain to the Caribbean, and the port town of Louisbourg on Ile Royale (now Cape Breton Island, part of Nova Scotia) was a thriving center for trade in fish from the Grand Banks and products from around the world. The entire population of New France, however, probably included only about 100,000 Europeans and Africans, while the British North American colonies had at least one and a half million inhabitants, and perhaps as many as two million. The northern British colonies had developed extensive craft industries in ship-building, pottery, and iron goods, and three towns with populations of more than ten thousand: Philadelphia, New York, and Boston. New Englanders helped British troops and the British navy take Louisbourg in 1745, a small American skirmish that was part of the War of the Austrian Succession (1740–48). The terms of the peace treaty returned Louisbourg to France, but tensions between French and British settlers continued, spreading into the Ohio River valley. In 1754, the young George Washington led a small contingent of troops against French forces in western Pennsylvania in the first battle of what came to be known in the United States as the French and Indian war (1754–63). British forces widened their attacks on New France, and North America became one battleground in the war known more widely as the Seven Years War (1756–63). Louisbourg fell again, as did Quebec, and at the end of the war France was required to cede Louisiana to Spain and the rest of its North American holdings, other than two tiny islands, to Britain.

The Seven Years War left Britain in control of most of eastern North America, with King George III and his ministers deciding that ties between Britain and what had become its most valuable colonial possession should be strengthened, and that the colonies should provide a fairer share (to British eyes) of the revenue needed to run an empire. The government decided to enforce demands for revenue and other acts previously left unenforced, and set new taxes on sugar, the stamps required for official documents, and other goods. These measures met increased resistance, and led to colonial challenges to British authority, first as protests, boycotts, mob violence, organizing, speeches, pamphlets, and essays, and then military action. Fighting began in 1775, and eventually involved white settlers, black slaves, and Native American groups on both sides, along with British troops and Germans hired by the British. France entered the war on the side of the Americans, first with money and supplies and then with soldiers and ships. Spain was allied with France, which made every British colony in the Caribbean vulnerable, and British supply lines were long and stretched thin. Many other European states, including Russia under Catherine

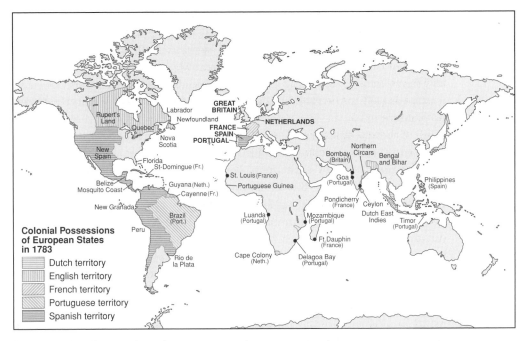

Map 15. Colonial possessions of European states in 1783.

the Great, formed a League of Armed Neutrality, which worked against British interests, blocking them from being able to substitute Baltic wood and tar for American, thus hindering ship repair and maintenance.

The colonies began the war with militia that were used to serving for a relatively short term of service, but by the end at least some of these troops had been turned into skilled, disciplined soldiers, similar to those fighting for European generals. In fact, some of the American officers *were* European generals, either veterans of the British army or continental military officers attracted to the fight. In 1781, a large British army was forced to surrender by French and American forces supported by French ships, and fighting in North America died down. Fighting continued in the Caribbean, and British and French troops were still fighting halfway around the world in India when the peace treaty confirming the independence of the thirteen colonies was signed in 1783. Loyalists streamed to other British colonies, especially several of the provinces in Canada, and British islands in the Caribbean. Britain could no longer send prisoners to North America as indentured servants, and a few years later the country established the first penal colony in Australia.

The Seven Years War, the War of American Independence, and the numerous other wars discussed in chapter 9 often involved formal naval battles on the Atlantic as well as land fighting in the Americas, especially in frontier and border areas. War disrupted connections around and across the Atlantic, but also increased those connections and made them more complex, as political exiles sought new places to live, religious refugees founded places where they could worship more freely, former indentured servants settled in lands newly appropriated from indigenous peoples, indigenous peoples moved deeper inland, and slaves were purchased in ever greater numbers to replace those killed by warfare as well as the millions who died from the normal working conditions on plantations.

All of these people carried customs, languages, stories, religious beliefs, food preferences, music, kinship structures, funerary practices, and many other aspects of their cultures with them. For some, their cultural traditions were silenced or suppressed, but in many places they existed side by side with those from elsewhere, were given new meanings as people coped with their new environment, or were transformed into entirely new hybrid forms. West Africans, for example, carried their religion, called Vodun, to the New World, where it blended with the religious traditions of people from other parts of Africa, and a few elements of popular Christianity, especially the veneration of saints, to form related, but new, religions including Vodou in Haiti and Lukumi in Cuba. Traditions officially suppressed or ignored, especially those of indigenous or enslaved peoples, were sometimes incorporated into more approved forms; Caribbean and Brazilian Christianity, for example, was shaped by African customs and beliefs, just as Mexican Christianity was shaped by indigenous practices and ideas.

Colonies, difference, and race

European colonization in all parts of the world brought peoples together who had long been separate from one another, but this was generally perceived as a problem, not an opportunity. In the earliest colonial empires, the Spanish and Portuguese crowns hoped to keep various groups – Europeans, Africans, and indigenous peoples – apart, but the shortage of European and African women made this impossible, and there were sexual relationships across many lines. The children of these relationships challenged existing categories, but the response of colonial authorities was to create an even more complex system of categories for persons of mixed ancestry, who were called *castas*. The Catholic Church and Spanish and Portuguese officials defined as many as fifteen or twenty different categories and combinations that were in theory based on place of birth, assumed geographic origin, and the status of one's mother, with a specific name for each one. In practice, whether one was a "mestizo" or "mulatto" or "caboclo" or another category was to a large extent determined by how one looked, with lighter-skinned mixed-ancestry persons accorded a higher rank than darker ones, even if they were siblings. New laws passed after 1763 in the French Caribbean colonies set out a similar system, with various categories based on the supposed origin of one's ancestors.

The social structure that developed in colonial Spanish and Portuguese America, including the Caribbean (and later in the French Caribbean) was thus a system based partly on physical appearance, but intricately linked to concepts of honor and virtue as derived from class and family status. One's social status – termed *calidad* – rested on a precarious balance of moral, physical, and class judgments that frequently shifted within the regional and social hierarchy. Since one's ability to marry or inherit, enter a convent or the priesthood, or attend university relied on official determination of ancestral purity, individuals sought to "whiten" their social status in order to obtain privileges in society. In many areas families of property and status bought licenses to pass as descendants of Europeans, regardless of their particular ethnic appearance and ancestry.

In frontier areas of Spanish America, or during times of political and social transitions, family members classified their children as "Spanish" or "Castellano" on baptismal records, often in open defiance of the presiding priest's observations about the actual appearance of the child. In addition, individuals might define themselves, or be defined, as belonging to different categories at different points in their life, so that the hierarchy became increasingly confused and arbitrary over generations.

As colonial authorities were trying to sort out and govern their increasingly diverse populations, Europeans were trying to understand differences between people both locally and globally. In many cultures, "blood" had long been a common way of marking family, clan, and eventually class differences, with those of "noble blood" prohibited from marrying commoners and taught to be concerned about their blood lines. This has been studied most extensively in Europe, but high-status people in other parts of the world were also thought to have superior blood. In several European languages the word "race" was also used to mean family line or lineage; both French and English dictionaries in the seventeenth century define race in this way, as does Samuel Johnson's enormous *Dictionary of the English Language* (1755). Both "blood" and "race" also came to be used to describe national boundaries, with those having "French blood" distinguished from those having "German blood," the "English race" distinguished from the "Spanish race." Religious beliefs were also conceptualized as blood, with people regarded as having Jewish, Muslim, or Christian blood, and after the Reformation Protestant or Catholic blood. The most dramatic expression of this was in early modern Spain, where "purity of the blood" – having no Jewish or Muslim ancestors – became an obsession, but it was also true elsewhere. Fathers choosing a wet-nurse for their children took care to make sure she was of the same denomination, lest, if he was a Catholic, her Protestant blood turn into Protestant milk and thus infect the child with heretical ideas. Children born of religiously mixed marriages were often slightly mistrusted, for one never knew whether their Protestant or Catholic blood would ultimately triumph.

As Europeans developed colonial empires, these notions of "blood" and "race" became a way of conceptualizing ethnicity as well as social status, nation, and religion. In some cases, such as Jews or Jewish converts in Spain and the Spanish empire, or Gaelic Irish in Ireland, religious and ethnic differences were linked, with religious traditions being viewed as signs of barbarity and ethnic inferiority. Religion was also initially a marker of difference in colonial areas outside Europe, where the spread of Christianity was used as a justification for conquest and enslavement. As indigenous peoples converted, however, religion became less useful as a means of differentiation, and skin color became more important. Laws in the British colony of Virginia regarding sexual relations, for example, distinguished between "christian" and "negroe" in 1662, but by 1691 between "white" men and women and those who were "negroe, mulatto, or Indian."

While Spanish and Portuguese authorities were developing hierarchies of classification, Dutch authorities were less systematic in their approach to ethnic mixing. They initially encouraged sexual relations and even marriage between European men and indigenous women as a means of making alliances, cementing colonial power, and increasing the population. The directors of the VOC gave soldiers, sailors, and minor officials bonuses if they agreed to marry local women and stay in the Dutch colonies as free burghers. This policy was opposed by some Dutch missionaries, but accepted by others, who hoped marriage with local women would not only win converts but give missionaries access to female religious rituals so that they could be overseen and suppressed. There were limits to this acceptance of intermarriage, however. Rijkloff von Goens, VOC governor-general in the 1670s, supported mixed marriages, but then wanted the daughters of those marriages married to Dutchmen so that "our race may degenerate as little as possible."[3] (By "our race" von Goens probably meant the "Dutch race," as he worried about mixed marriages with Portuguese-background women as well.) By the second and third generation, many European men preferred women of mixed race rather than fully indigenous women as marital partners. The pattern in Dutch colonies was repeated in those of other European nations in the Indian Ocean basin. The directors of the English East India Company, for example, generally approved of intermarriage in the seventeenth century; in 1687, they even decreed that any child resulting from the marriage of any soldier and native woman be paid a small grant on the day of its christening.

Most children from mixed unions in the colonial world did not get such a gift, of course, and their fate varied enormously. Some of them were legitimated by their fathers through adoption or the purchase of certificates of legitimacy, and could assume prominent positions in colonial society. For example, two of the sons of François Caron, who had worked for twenty years for the VOC and had five children with a Japanese woman, later became well-known ministers in the Dutch church. French and Spanish men in the Caribbean regularly freed and legally recognized their children with enslaved women, and often their mothers as well. Other mixed-race children did not fare as well, remaining enslaved in plantation colonies or surviving by begging or petty crime in port cities.

At the same time that the VOC and the EEIC tolerated or even encouraged intermarriage, British colonies in North America forbade it. The 1691 Virginia law mentioned above forbade marriage between an "English or other white man or woman", and a "negroe, mulatto, or Indian man or woman". Such laws were passed in all the southern colonies in North America and also in Pennsylvania and Massachusetts between 1700 and 1750. (They were struck down by the US Supreme Court in 1967, but remained on the books in some states for decades after that; the last of such "miscegenation" laws was rescinded by Alabama voters in a statewide referendum in 2000.) The relatively large number of women among white settlers and the increasingly small number of indigenous women in coastal areas where settlements were located meant that marriages or even long-term sexual relationships between white men and indigenous women were rare in the British North American colonies. As the slave population in southern colonies increased, sexual relations between white men and black women did as well, but these were never marriages. In contrast to the hierarchy of categories found in Spanish, Portuguese, and French colonies, the British North American colonies and later the United States developed a dichotomous system, in which in theory one drop of "black blood" made one black, though in practice lighter-skinned mixed-ancestry individuals may have passed over without notice into the white world.

Laws regarding intermarriage were usually framed in gender-neutral language, but what lawmakers were most worried about was, as the preamble to the Virginia law states, "negroes, mulattoes, and Indians intermarrying with English, or other white women" and the resultant "abominable mixture and spurious issue." Because initially almost all Europeans in colonial areas were men, inter-group sexual relations generally did not upset Europeans' notions of their own superiority, for the gender and ethnic hierarchies involved reinforced one another. Relations between European women and indigenous or other non-white men were another matter, however. Even in areas that encouraged intermarriage, European women's mobility and activities were restricted by custom and law. Unmarried white women who bore mixed-ancestry children were more harshly treated than those who bore white children, while white men fathering mixed-ancestry children with non-white women was accepted, whether in or out of marriage. In the British North American colonies and elsewhere, rape of a white woman by a black man could lead to castration. In places where intermarriage was allowed, European women who married indigenous men often lost their legal status as "European," while men who married indigenous women did not. (A similar disparity became part of the citizenship laws of many countries well into the twentieth century; even today in some countries a woman automatically loses her citizenship on marrying a foreign national, while a man does not.)

In most parts of the colonial world, then, migration created new types of hybrid ethnicities. In most Spanish and Portuguese American colonies, for example, about one-quarter of the population was *casta* by the end of the eighteenth century. Many persons of mixed ancestry, and poor people of all types, often simply did not bother to have an official wedding ceremony, though in many cases they did establish long-term unions regarded by their neighbors and friends as stable. For members of the white European elite, the concern with blood lines created a pattern of intermarriage within the extended family, with older women identifying the distant cousins who were favored as spouses. Thus, despite Christian norms, families in the Caribbean and Latin America were extremely diverse: elite men married, but they often had children by slaves or servants who were also part of their household; poor free people did not marry, but might live in stable nuclear households; slave unions were often temporary, and the children stayed with their mothers or became the property of their mothers' owners.

This diversity was also found elsewhere in the colonial world, though the privileges accorded to whiteness also meant that the boundary separating Europeans from all other groups was the one most firmly guarded. As more white women moved to the colonies in the eighteenth century, long-term interracial relationships became less acceptable as the European communities worried about what they termed "racial survival". Ideas about racial differences were often expressed in gendered and sexualized terms. In India Englishmen were judged "manly" while Bengali men were seen as "effeminate," while in Saint-Domingue mixed-race men were foppish and beardless while mixed-race women, according to one European visitor, "combine the explosiveness of saltpeter with an exuberance of desire, that, scorning all, drives them to pursue, acquire and devour pleasure."[4]

Ideas about differences created by social status, nation, religion, and ethnicity in the sixteenth and seventeenth centuries were often understood – sometimes by the same person – to be both culturally created and inherent in the person. Thus the same religious reformers who warned against choosing the wrong wet-nurse also worked for conversions. Rulers who supported nobles' privileges because of their distinction from commoners regularly ennobled able commoners who had served as generals and officials. French royal officials with authority over colonies spoke about the superiority of "French blood" but also advocated assimilation, in which indigenous peoples would "become French." Catholic authorities limited entrance to certain convents to "pure-blooded" white or Native women, thus excluding *castas*, but were more willing to allow a light-skinned *casta* than a "full-blooded" Native to marry a white person.

These various, complex, and sometimes conflicting understandings of "blood" and "race" – Jewish blood, white blood, the Dutch race, the noble race – continued in the eighteenth century, but educated Europeans increasingly wanted a system in which human differences could be arranged in a single schema and the reasons for them explained. In *The System of Nature*, first published in 1735 and expanded in twelve subsequent editions, the Swedish naturalist and explorer Carl Linnaeus (1707–78), set out to create a system of classification for all living things. He and his students collected botanical and zoological specimens from around the world, and Linnaeus set down the rules that are still used for naming and classifying organisms. Along with plants and other animals, Linnaeus also classified humans, dividing them into four groups, based on continent of origin: Americanus, Europaeus, Asiaticus, and Africanus. He identified each group by skin color, dominant Galenic humor (which determined temperament), posture, and general behavior: Americanus was reddish, choleric, upright, and ruled by habit; Europaeus was white, sanguine (dominated by blood), muscular, and ruled by custom; Asiaticus was sallow, melancholic, stiff, and ruled by opinion; Africanus black, phlegmatic, relaxed, and ruled by caprice. Though he clearly views Europaeus as superior, Linnaeus does not arrange these groups in a hierarchy or view them as separate species, but as varieties that resulted primarily from differences in climate and environment. The Dutch-born abbé Cornelius de Pauw (1734–99), philosopher and naturalist at the court of Frederick II of Prussia, agreed with Linnaeus about the influence of climate, and was particularly scornful of the Americas, a "vast and sterile desert" where native animals and people were "degenerate or monstrous," and European immigrants became inferior nearly as soon as they got off the boat.[5]

Linnaeus's four groups found spectacular visual expression in the ceiling fresco over the main staircase in the palace of the prince-bishop of Würzburg, painted in 1750–3 by the Venetian artist Giovanni Battista Tiepelo (1696–1770), but here the preeminence of Europe is clear. The fresco – the largest ceiling fresco in the world – presents an allegory of the planets and continents, with all the continents portrayed as women. An elaborately dressed Europe, seated on a throne and leaning against a very placid and domesticated bull representing Zeus, has musicians, artists, and courtiers holding symbols of the church and a page carrying a crown on a pillow around her. Over her head an image of the prince-bishop is held aloft by the demi-goddesses Virtue and Fame, and under her feet the allegorical figure Painting is applying color to various parts of a globe. On the other sections, the scenes with America, Asia, and Africa have no crowns, no globes, no artists, and no buildings, though they do have cannibals, slaves, pipe-smokers, and lots of wild animals.

Linnaeus, de Pauw, and many of the visiting officials and young men on the "Grand Tour" who marveled at Tiepelo's painting were part of wide-ranging discussions about why there were differences among humans and whether such differences were changeable. Christianity taught that all people descended from common ancestors – what came to be called "monogenesis" – but some writers speculated that perhaps there had been separate godly creations for different human groups – what came to be called "polygenesis." In *Of the Different Human Races* (1775), the German Enlightenment philosopher Immanuel Kant split the difference, arguing that there was only one creation, but the original pair carried the seeds for four different groups, and the division was now irreversible. Intellectual historians disagree about exactly who was the first to use the word "race" in its modern meaning, but Kant is one candidate. *Of the Different Human Races* and other works by Kant were very influential with his contemporaries, including the French naturalist Georges Louis Buffon (1707–88). Differentiation based on race had already emerged in laws, such as the 1691 Virginia law about intermarriage, and this became more common toward the end of the eighteenth century. In 1777, for example, Louis XVI of France issued a new law, the *Police des Noirs*, that banned the entry of all blacks and people of color into France. Earlier laws had distinguished between free and slave, but this law was based on a racial scheme. "Race" became the primary term for discussing human variety in the nineteenth century.

At the very end of the eighteenth century, the German anatomist and naturalist Johann Friedrich Blumenbach (1752–1840) drew on both Linnaeus and Kant, and created what became the most influential system of classification. In the third edition of his *On the Natural Variety of Mankind* (1795), Blumenbach set out five categories, not four, with the light-skinned people of Europe and western Asia as the original human form, and two lines departing from this form: one line led through Native Americans to Asians, and the second through "Malays" (a group he added to Linnaeus's system) to Africans. Blumenbach called the light-skinned group "Caucasian," because he thought that the Caucasus Mountains on the border between Russia and Georgia were most likely the original home of humans or where Noah's ark ended up after the flood, and because this area "produces the most beautiful race of men." His judgment about Caucasian attractiveness came through studying a large collection of skulls, as he measured all other skulls against one from Georgia that he judged to be "the most beautiful form of the skull." Blumenbach argued that racial differences were superficial, and that mentally and morally all groups were equal, but his hierarchical arrangement and its basis in what he called "the truth of nature" were much more influential than his more egalitarian views.

De Pauw put Americans – both Native Americans and immigrants – at the bottom of his hierarchy of human groups, and European colonists in the New World described indigenous people as clearly inferior because they died so readily from new diseases, thus opening the way for Europeans destined to occupy these new lands. European views of the Chinese also grew more negative in the eighteenth century, from Leibniz at the beginning of the century describing Chinese law as "beautifully directed … to the achievement of public tranquility," to Montesquieu writing at mid-century that "China is a despotic state whose principle is fear."

For most eighteenth-century Europeans, however, Africans were the lowest on a hierarchy of races. Advocates of polygenesis argued that blacks were descended from a different origin than whites, while the biblical story of the "curse of Ham" – in which Noah cursed the descendants of his son Ham to a life of hard labor after Ham had seen him drunk – was interpreted racially, with blacks seen as descendants of Ham. This story both explained and justified slavery, just as travelers' reports about Africans living and working in the extremely degrading conditions of plantation slavery both enhanced and confirmed racist views.

There were a few voices that opposed slavery, or at least the brutality of the slave trade, on religious grounds throughout the early modern period, and in the last quarter of the eighteenth century, these were joined by secular arguments opposing slavery on humanitarian and moral grounds. Quakers and Methodists were prominent in both these lines of argument, though some Quakers and Methodists in Pennsylvania were slave-holders. Courts in France made rulings against slavery within France itself in the eighteenth century, and several hundred slaves won their freedom by suing for it in French courts. (Louis XVI's *Police des Noirs* was in some ways a response to this, forbidding the entry of all non-white persons in an attempt to stop such lawsuits.) England and Scotland made rulings against slavery within their borders beginning in the 1770s and some northern American states outlawed slavery during the course of the American War of Independence. Antislavery activists in England formed the Society for Effecting the Abolition of the Slave Trade in 1787, and former slaves told their stories orally and a few in memoirs, slowly building support for abolition. In 1791, a slave revolt in Saint-Domingue escalated into a full-scale revolution against French colonial power which created the free black republic of Haiti, the second independent nation in the western hemisphere. Pro-slavery forces rallied in opposition to all these moves, however, extending the new theories about race into ever more vicious statements about the inferiority of Africans. It would be another century before slavery was abolished in all of the Americas.

The effects of colonialism

The ideology of race was created in part by men who never left Europe – Kant, Hume, Buffon, de Pauw, Blumenbach – but it was also created through the actual experiences of Europeans in their colonial empires. In New France, the policy of assimilation was abandoned, in part because of growing ideas about unchangeable racial differences, but in larger part because it had not worked; some Native Americans adopted Christianity, but very few wanted to "become French." Spanish, Portuguese, and French systems of socio-racial classification came from observations about what kinds of people actually lived in Caribbean and Latin American communities, which may explain why they had many more categories than the four or five proposed by the naturalists. White colonists born in the Americas – called Creoles – answered Europeans disparaging the effects of the American climate by stressing their fitness and immunity to environmental influences; they argued that their superiority to other groups was innate, not created by their surroundings. Hierarchical theories of race were thus one product of colonialism.

The expansion of Christianity was another. Catholic missionaries, especially members of religious orders such as the Jesuits, the Recollects, and the

Dominicans, accompanied Spanish, Portuguese, and French traders and officials. They also established missions in places where there was otherwise little European presence, including mountainous regions of South America and
desert regions of North America. Convents for women soon followed. In 1637,
the same year as Jesuit missionaries in Canada established the first community
for Indian converts, an Ursuline house was established in Quebec; by 1725, one
out of every hundred residents in New France was a nun. Lay confraternities
for local converts were established by Portuguese missionaries in the Indian
Ocean region, and later by French missionaries in Vietnam.

This process used to be described as a "spiritual conquest," in which indigenous beliefs and practices were largely wiped out through a combination of
force and persuasion. The spread of Catholic Christianity is now viewed very
differently, not simply as conquest and resistance – though it was that – but as
a process of cultural negotiation, during which Christian ideas and practices
were accepted but also transformed. This transformation involved indigenous
people and missionaries, and also slaves, migrants, and people of mixed background. Christianity became part of a new shared culture in many colonial
areas, though one with many local variations, often within the same colony.

Protestants were not as active as missionaries in the seventeenth and eighteenth centuries as they would be in the nineteenth century, though men and
women from radical and pietist groups such as the Quakers, Moravians, and
Methodists did teach and preach to indigenous people, often far from European
settlements. The VOC provided, paid, and controlled pastors for its own personnel, a few of whom attempted to convert indigenous people to Dutch Reformed
Christianity, especially those who had already been converted to Catholicism
by the Portuguese. In many Asian VOC trading posts, conversion to Reformed
Christianity was almost entirely the result of intermarriage, though in a few
places, including Ceylon and Ambiona, more widespread conversion occurred,
generally among those who stood to gain financially or politically from conversion. The first translation of the New Testament into a Southeast Asian
language was into High Malay by a Dutch missionary in 1688, but as literacy
levels were low, conversion remained largely an oral process. The English East
India Company was hostile to missionaries because it thought their activities
disrupted trade, though it did provide chaplains for its own employees.

Some of the British colonies in North America were founded explicitly as religious communities, with evidence of personal conversion required for men to
be allowed political rights. Religious dissenters in many colonies were whipped,
expelled or even executed, though some colonies included religious toleration
as one of their founding principles. Early settlers in Virginia and the Carolinas
were theoretically part of the Anglican Church, but there were few clergy or
churches. The mid-Atlantic colonies were a religious as well as ethnic mixture.
By the later seventeenth century, religious diversity was joined by lack of interest in many parts of North America. People chose to be part of Baptist, Quaker,
Presbyterian, Anglican, Catholic, Congregationalist, or other communities, or –
more likely – chose to join no denomination at all. In contrast to the

popular view of church-going Americans, most historians estimate that by 1700 the majority of colonial residents were not church members and rarely attended a service. Lack of interest in religion changed somewhat in the 1730s and 1740s with the spread of a religious revival movement later known as the "Great Awakening." This was a pietist movement of personal religious conversion that spread throughout the colonies, especially in frontier areas away from the coast where official state churches were the weakest. Like pietism in Europe, it emphasized emotion, the spoken word, personal experience, and leadership based on a sense of calling; it attracted Native Americans and Africans as well as Europeans. By the end of the eighteenth century religious devotion had died down again, only to be rekindled with a Second Great Awakening in the 1820s and 1830s.

Along with shaping ideologies of difference, and creating ever more diversity in Christianity, the development of colonies clearly had an economic impact on Europe, and on the world. The contours of this have been hotly debated, however. In *The Modern World System*, the sociologist Immanuel Wallerstein developed one very influential line of argument, building on the ideas of Latin American social scientists. Wallerstein asserted that economic growth in western Europe, which he terms the "core" of the modern global economy, was only achieved by using – and exploiting – the raw materials and the people of the rest of the world. Core nations enhanced their economic dominance by mercantilist trade policies that encouraged the export of manufactured goods and the import of raw materials. The opposite end of this trade was what Wallerstein calls the "periphery," areas that produced cash crops such as sugar and tobacco, raw materials such as timber and metals, and human labor in the form of slaves and serfs. The periphery initially included eastern Europe and Hispanic America, and eventually Asia and Africa as well. Southern Europe gradually became a "semi-periphery," with little industrial development and only a small share of international commerce. In world-systems theory, the periphery and semi-periphery generate wealth for the core in the same way as the proletariat generates wealth for the bourgeoisie in Marxist theory. World-systems theory fits with certain types of Marxist analysis, and also with the post-colonial theory discussed in chapter 7, with its emphasis on the subordination and exploitation of subaltern groups. Post-colonial theorists tend to put greater emphasis on the cultural aspects of domination than world-systems theorists, though Wallerstein does briefly mention the role of religion in his analysis.

Criticism of world-systems theory has come from several perspectives. Basing their argument on statistics about actual trade, some economic historians have suggested that growing demand for consumer goods within Europe itself was a more important engine for economic growth than any change in production patterns. Demand for Indian cottons meant that 80 percent of the Asian products imported by the East India Company in 1740 were finished textiles, not raw materials or cash crops. Thus the story, at least as far as Asia is concerned, is more properly one of interconnections and parallel development rather than a dominant core and dependent periphery. Some historians have posited multiple systems of cores and peripheries in different parts of the world, rather than a single system dominated by Europe. Viewing modern history as the story of the "rise of the West," they argue, comes from taking too short a view; in another five hundred years, or perhaps even another fifty, economic growth in Asia will have made "the rise of the East" the development that needs explanation.

Other economic historians, especially those with expertise in China, have pointed out that Europe's access to resources from overseas was important, but so was an access to coal and the development of technologies to use that coal; Britain's early use of coal power was a central factor in classic explanations of the Industrial Revolution, and many comparative world historians have returned to stressing its importance. Only in the nineteenth century, when coal was combined with traditional sources of power such as animals – which Britain also had in greater numbers per capita than China – did Britain begin to out-produce China.

Scholars thus debate the relative role of colonies in European economic expansion and the "rise of the West," and when they discuss other factors in that rise the debate moves from heated to blistering. Some, such as David Landes, argue in terms not much different than those of Samuel Purchas: western European dominance came not just from colonies and coal, but from superior values and culture, especially an openness to innovation. Like Purchas, and like Max Weber, Landes argues that Christianity (in its Protestant form) was part of this, generating "a new kind of man – rational, ordered, diligent, and productive."[6] According to Landes, the rest of the world was mired in unchanging despotism, for which the only solution is adopting western values.

Landes and others who write in a similar sweeping way about "culture" are dismissed by historians specializing in different geographic areas as simply repeating old ideas that have since been disproved, but new analysis has confirmed one part of this line of argument: the importance of technological innovation. This newer research, including work by Margaret Jacob and Joel Mokyr, does not see technological advance as a general cultural phenomenon separating Europe from the rest of the world over a long period of time, but points to a quite specific culture of innovation that developed in England from the middle of the seventeenth century. English scientific works, especially those of Newton on gravity and mechanics, which had even won the approval of the Anglican Church, were available to and read by artisans and entrepreneurial inventors looking for solutions to practical problems in designing and improving engines and other machines. Laws regarding property rights allowed innovators (sometimes) to make profits from their inventions, and banks – often financed by the profit from international trade – made borrowing to build machines easier than it had been earlier. As we traced in chapter 12, these machines allowed for the exploitation of coal; this meant that by the early nineteenth century, people in England had vastly more energy available to do all sorts of tasks than people elsewhere in the world.

Eventually those machines, often powered by steam-engines, would be used to produce cloth that would substitute for Indian calicoes, and pottery that would imitate Chinese porcelain. This allowed Britain to bypass Asian imports, particularly when high tariffs and trade prohibitions imposed by the government made those imports very expensive or difficult to obtain. British cloth and pottery used raw materials produced in British colonies, where the unpaid nature of slave labor also reduced costs, and helped keep British manufactured products affordable to consumers. In 1750, Britain accounted for less than 2 percent of production around the world, while in 1880 its share was more than 20 percent.

Technological and financial innovations were crucial to the industrial development that gave first Britain and then other countries in Europe distinct advantages, and they were also crucial to another reason for European preeminence: the ability to wage large-scale war on both land and sea. Systems of taxation developed to finance the nearly continuous cycle of wars in Europe in the seventeenth and eighteenth centuries were not as efficient as bureaucrats hoped, but they provided enough money to finance standing armies and ever larger and more deadly navies. Those armies and navies were deployed for reasons increasingly defined as the "national" interest, rather than the defense of a religion or dynasty. By the eighteenth century that national interest included the protection of trade, as European ships came to carry most of the world's cargo across all the seas we have discussed in this chapter. National interest also included colonies on the islands and coasts of those seas, where European soldiers and sailors fought indigenous people and each other with well-practiced tactics and new and improved weapons.

What makes this story of innovation different from that told by Purchas – or by more recent scholars who highlight cultural differences between "the West and the rest" – is its emphasis on the contingent nature of these developments. Industrialization, which Joel Mokyr has called a "peculiar path," was the result of the coincidental interdependence of many things. Its ultimate implications were only recognized later, not foreseen by a few people with a telescopic vision of the future. One of the problems in doing any historical analysis is that we know what happens later, or at least what happens later up to right now. Thus developments that are accidental or fortuitous look like destiny. Western dominance in the nineteenth and twentieth centuries had its roots in the early modern world, but unique talent or unique rapaciousness are far less satisfactory as explanations than those that consider a range of factors.

A nod to "what came next" is a common way to end histories, but the centuries covered in this book were not just a prelude to modernity, but a distinctive era of their own. If Albrecht Dürer, whose sketch of the myth of Europa from the early sixteenth century is the frontispiece to the introduction of this book, were to travel through time to the late eighteenth century of William Blake, whose engraving of Europe supported by Africa and America is the frontispiece to this chapter, what would he have thought? What changes would he have noticed, and what would have seemed familiar?

Dürer was a well-traveled individual, and accustomed to many things from far beyond Europe, as his drawings and engravings of lions and rhinoceroses, and his portraits of women with pearl necklaces and men in turbans make clear. The range of products available by 1789 even in his home town of Nuremberg, far from the Atlantic world or any bustling seaport, would still have astounded him. The "Columbian Exchange" that had only just begun in Dürer's lifetime was now what we might call the "Captain Cook Exchange," with hundreds of plants and animals intentionally taken from one part of the world to another for study or use. Naturalists collected specimens for "cabinets of curiosity," while colonists experimented with crops native elsewhere. In the 1780s, French and British ships carried breadfruit from the Pacific to the Caribbean, hoping to grow it to feed slaves. One of these ships, the *Bounty*, captained by one of Cook's former officers William Bligh, experienced a mutiny that made it far more famous than its mission. Dürer would not have found breadfruit in Nuremberg, but plenty that was new: rice, potatoes, peppers, coffee, tea, chocolate, perhaps a pineapple or two, and mounds of sugar.

Human-made products traveled even more widely. Dürer could have bought Chinese lacquerware and Indian calicoes, and have had his choice between English Wedgwood, French Sèvres, and German Meissen for porcelain teapots, candelabra, figurines, and vases. He might have paid for these with Mexican silver pesos, which circulated globally, and were especially popular in China, where people thought the hefty rulers portrayed on their faces looked like the Buddha. Merchandise in large quantities still came primarily by ship as it had in the sixteenth century, but small amounts of goods, and private letters, could now be sent through postal services. Those deliveries also brought journals and newspapers, read and discussed in cafés and learned societies even in a relative backwater like Nuremberg. Dürer was a sociable type, and would no doubt have quickly adapted to the range of other pleasures such places also offered: distilled liquor, sweet wines, coffee, tea, tobacco, and perhaps even opium, mixed with tobacco and smoked in a pipe.

Dürer's Nuremberg had been an important intellectual, artistic, and economic center, where Luther's ideas were discussed and printed, Italian products and ways of doing business introduced north of the Alps, painters, sculptors, and poets created works that were widely copied, and the first clocks small enough to be carried, nicknamed "Nuremberg eggs," were invented by a locksmith. By the end of the eighteenth century, like most other medium-sized cities in the center of Europe, Nuremberg was not very important. It was still independent and governed by a city council, though in 1806 it would be swallowed by Bavaria, one of the regional states growing ever more powerful within the Holy Roman Empire. Nuremberg's decline would have been even more noticeable had Dürer traveled to London or Paris; at its height, Dürer's hometown had perhaps 30,000 residents, but by 1789 the population of Paris was more than 500,000 and London more than 800,000. The houses of the wealthy were lavish and immense, with separate rooms where family members could find privacy from servants and each other. The homes of artisans were much plainer, and the poor were crammed into attics and cellars, but even artisans or servants might now own pocket-watches. These had a minute hand as well as the hour hand found on Nuremberg eggs, for the rhythm of the work day was guided increasingly by the clock, a regulation of labor that was spreading from slave plantations to cities.

The countryside outside of cities, by contrast, had changed far less. There traditions, customs, and religious ideas were still taught through the spoken word, stories and songs shared, and natural, supernatural, and human-produced miseries feared. Dürer had made a woodcut of the Four Horsemen of the Apocalypse – pestilence, famine, war, and death – and these had not stopped being regular visitors in the eighteenth century, though certain diseases had decreased in virulence. Had our mythical time-traveler been an eastern European serf instead of a western European urban resident like Dürer, he or she would have found family structures, housing styles, and agricultural techniques that were very familiar.

As far as the larger political scene is concerned, Dürer would no doubt have been astounded that states he regarded as barely European and barely civilized, such as Prussia and Russia, were now powerhouses with French-speaking rulers and elegant palaces. On the other hand, the continuing importance of the Habsburgs would have surprised him not at all; nor would the regularity of war, though the size of armies might have.

Dürer was an artist, and he would not have had to travel far to see spectacular baroque and rococo paintings and architecture; Tiepelo's ceiling in the bishop's palace in Würzburg was only two days' ride away by coach. Dürer would no doubt have appreciated its craftsmanship, though he would have been less impressed by its drama and spectacle, which did not follow his own Renaissance artistic ideals of harmony and balance. The gardens behind the palace, laid out according to classical principles, would have been more acceptable, though he might have been puzzled by the Chinese pagoda set as an ornament among the statues of gods and nymphs.

As the resident of a free imperial city, Dürer was familiar with the notion that citizenship brought rights and privileges, so may not have seen the ideas of Locke or the *philosophes* as dramatically new. The fact that they based these rights on nature rather than custom, and emphasized the power of human reason, might have struck him as novel, however, and perhaps as misguided. The ideas of Galileo or Newton might have been more startling, particularly their assertion that knowledge was to be discovered primarily by measuring and analyzing the natural world, not by reading the words of ancient authorities.

The residents of Nuremberg, like those of much of Europe, fought over religion in Dürer's lifetime. By the end of the eighteenth century Lutheran

Protestantism was still the official religion in the city, though its practitioners, like Christians all over Europe, varied from those who attended church
rarely to those for whom religious devotion was paramount. There were other
types of Christian churches as well, however, and a synagogue; Jews, expelled
from the city in 1499, had been allowed to return in the early eighteenth
century.

What might Dürer have thought of William Blake's depiction of Europe, so
different from his own? Her dependence on – or alliance with – Africa and
America was certainly not part of the classical tradition, which emphasized
Europe's separation from other continents. But Dürer had drawn a sympathetic
portrait of a Portuguese-African mixed race woman, and on seeing an exhibit
of Aztec art shipped back to Europe in 1520, commented in his diary, "All the
days of my life I have seen nothing that rejoiced my heart so much as these
things, for I have seen among them wonderful works of art, and I marveled
at the subtle intellect of men in foreign parts."[7] Dürer's sentiments were not
those of the majority of Europeans in their encounters with the rest of the
world in the centuries that separated Dürer and Blake, but they might have
helped him understand Blake's message of interdependence and links between
various parts of the world.

Further reading

For general overviews of issues surrounding colonialism, see Peter Kriedte, *Peasants,
Landlords and Capitalists: Europe and the World Economy, 1500–1800*, trans. Volker Berghahn
(Cambridge: Cambridge University Press, 1983); Karen Kupperman, ed., *America in
European Consciousness, 1493–1750* (Chapel Hill: University of North Carolina Press, 1995);
Anthony Pagden, *The Lords of All the World: Ideologies of Empire in Spain, Britain and France
c. 1500–c. 1800* (New Haven: Yale University Press, 1995); *Oxford History of the British Empire*,
vols. I and II (Oxford: Oxford University Press, 1998); Kenneth Pomeranz and Steven
Topik, eds., *The World that Trade Created: Society, Culture, and the World Economy, 1400 to the
Present* (Armonk, NY: M. E. Sharpe, 1999); David Armitage, *The Ideological Origins of the
British Empire* (Cambridge: Cambridge University Press, 2000); Tony Chafur and
Amanda Sackur, eds., *Promoting the Colonial Idea: Propaganda and Visions of Empire in
France* (Basingstoke, UK: Palgrave-Macmillan, 2002); Lauren Benton, *Law and Colonial
Cultures: Legal Regimes in World History, 1400–1900* (Cambridge: Cambridge University
Press, 2002).

For explorations, see Nicholas Thomas, *Entangled Objects: Exchange, Material Culture,
and Colonialism in the Pacific* (Cambridge, MA: Harvard University Press, 1991); Glyn
Williams, *Voyages of Delusion: The Quest for the Northwest Passage* (New Haven: Yale
University Press, 2002). The debate over the death of Cook began with Marshall
Sahlins, *Historical Metaphors and Mythical Realities: Structure in the Early History of the
Sandwich Islands* (Ann Arbor: University of Michigan Press, 1981), countered by
Obeyesekere Gananath, *The Apotheosis of Captain Cook, European Mythmaking in the Pacific*
(Princeton: Princeton University Press, 1992), which was answered by Marshall Sahlins,
How "Natives" Think: About Captain Cook, For Example (Chicago: University of Chicago
Press, 1996). For a fascinating – and funny – view of Cook's voyages, and attitudes
toward Cook held by modern Pacific islanders, see Tony Horwitz, *Blue Latitudes: Boldly
Going Where Captain Cook Has Gone Before* (New York: Picador, 2003).

For the Indian Ocean, start with the classic overview by Charles R. Boxer, *The Dutch Seaborne Empire, 1600–1800* (Harmondsworth: Penguin, 1965). More specialized works include Jonathan Israel, *Dutch Primacy in World Trade, 1585–1740* (Oxford: Oxford University Press, 1989); Prasannan Parthasarathi, *The Transition to a Colonial Economy: Weavers, Merchants and Kings in South India* (Cambridge: Cambridge University Press, 2000); H. V. Bowen, Margarette Lincoln, and Nigel Rigby, eds., *The Worlds of the East India Company* (Rochester, NY: Boydell, 2002).

For the Caribbean, see Robert Louis Stein, *The French Sugar Business in the Eighteenth Century* (Baton Rouge: University of Louisiana Press, 1988); Hilary McD. Beckles, *A History of Barbados: From Amerindian Settlement to Nation-State* (Cambridge: Cambridge University Press, 1990); Richard S. Dunn, *Sugar and Slaves: The Rise of the Planter Class in the English West Indies, 1624–1713* (Chapel Hill: University of North Carolina Press, 2000).

For the Atlantic world, see Nicholas Canny and Anthony Pagden, eds., *Colonial Identity in the Atlantic World* (Princeton: Princeton University Press, 1987); Alan L. Karras and J. R. McNeill, eds., *Atlantic American Societies: From Columbus through Abolition 1492–1888* (London: Routledge, 1992); Colin Kidd, *British Identities before Nationalism: Ethnicity and Nationhood in the Atlantic World, 1600–1800* (Cambridge: Cambridge University Press, 1999); Jorge Cañizares-Esguerra, *How to Write the History of the New World: Histories, Epistemologies, and Identities in the Eighteenth-Century Atlantic World* (Stanford: Stanford University Press, 2001); David Armitage and Michael J. Bradick, eds., *The British Atlantic World, 1590–1800* (Basingstoke, UK: Palgrave-Macmillan, 2002); Christine Daniels, ed., *Negotiated Empires: Centers and Peripheries in the New World, 1500–1820* (London: Routledge, 2002).

For the interior of North America, see James Axtell, *The Invasion Within: The Contest of Cultures in Colonial North America* (New York: Oxford University Press, 1985); Richard White, *The Middle Ground: Indians, Empires, and Republics in the Great Lakes Region* (Cambridge: Cambridge University Press, 1991); Daniel Usner, *Indians, Settlers, and Slaves in a Frontier Exchange Economy: The Lower Mississippi Valley before 1783* (Chapel Hill: University of North Carolina Press, 1992); Allan Greer, *The People of New France* (Toronto: University of Toronto Press, 1997).

New studies of Atlantic slavery and the slave trade include Robin Blackburn, *The Making of New World Slavery: From the Baroque to the Modern 1492–1800* (London: Verso, 1998); David Eltis, *The Rise of African Slavery in the Americas* (Cambridge: Cambridge University Press, 1999); Herbert S. Klein, *The Atlantic Slave Trade* (Cambridge: Cambridge University Press, 1999).

Studies of colonial hybrid cultures include Serge Gruzinski, *The Mestizo Mind: The Intellectual Dynamics of Colonization and Globalization* (London: Routledge, 2002); James H. Sweet, *Recreating Africa: Culture, Kinship, and Religion in the Portuguese World, 1441–1770* (Durham, NC: University of North Carolina Press, 2003).

For the development of ideas about race, Ivan Hannaford, *Race: The History of an Idea in the West* (Baltimore: Johns Hopkins University Press, 1996), is a good place to start. More specialized analyses include Sue Peabody, *"There Are No Slaves in France": The Political Culture of Race and Slavery in the Ancien Régime* (New York: Oxford University Press, 1996); Joyce E. Chaplin, *Subject Matter: Technology, the Body, and Science on the Anglo-American Frontier, 1500–1676* (Cambridge, MA: Harvard University Press, 2001); Sue Peabody and Tyler Stovall, eds., *The Color of Liberty: Histories of Race in France* (Durham, NC: Duke University Press, 2003). A new study of ideas about Asia is Franklin Perkins, *Leibniz and China: A Commerce of Light* (Cambridge: Cambridge University Press, 2004). For an analysis of the Tiepelo ceiling, with excellent color plates of the various parts, see Svetlana Alpers and Michael Baxandall, *Tiepolo and the Pictorial Intelligence* (New Haven: Yale University Press, 1994).

The role of early modern scientists in creating racial and gender ideologies is discussed in Londa Schiebinger, *Nature's Body: Gender in the Making of Modern Science* (Boston: Beacon Press, 1995). For intersections of gender and race in the colonial world, see Kathleen M. Brown, *Good Wives, Nasty Wenches, and Anxious Patriarchs: Gender, Race and Power in Colonial Virginia* (Durham, NC: University of North Carolina Press, 1996); Ann Laura Stoler, *Carnal Knowledge and Imperial Power: Race and the Intimate in Colonial Rule* (Berkeley: University of California Press, 2002); Kathleen Wilson, *The Island Race: Englishness, Empire and Gender in the Eighteenth Century* (London: Routledge, 2002).

Immanuel Wallerstein's classic work is *The Modern World System* (New York: Academic Press, 1974, 1980, 1989). The role of European consumers in promoting economic development has been discussed in many works, including Maxine Berg and Helen Clifford, eds., *Consumers and Luxury: Consumer Culture in Europe, 1650–1850* (Manchester: Manchester University Press, 1999). The book by David Landes cited in the chapter notes is written for a general audience, and presents conclusions very similar to his earlier, more scholarly study, *The Unbound Prometheus: Technological Change and Industrial Development in Western Europe from 1750 to the Present* (New York: Columbia University Press, 1969). This point of view has been countered especially by historians of China, including R. Bin Wong, *China Transformed: Historical Change and the Limits of the European Experience* (Ithaca, NY: Cornell University Press, 1997), and Kenneth Pomeranz, *The Great Divergence: China, Europe, and the Making of the Modern World Economy* (Princeton: Princeton University Press, 2000). For newer works about the role of technology, see Joel Mokyr, *The Lever of Riches: Technological Creativity and Economic Progress* (Oxford: Oxford University Press, 1990), and *The British Industrial Revolution*, 2nd edn (Boulder, CO: Westview Press, 1999); Margaret C. Jacob, *Scientific Culture and the Making of the Industrial West* (New York: Oxford University Press, 1997). A wide-ranging survey of these issues, with a huge bibliography, is Jack A. Goldstone, "Efflorescences and Economic Growth in World History: Rethinking the 'Rise of the West' and the Industrial Revolution," *Journal of World History* 13:2 (2002): 323–90. For an extensive and thoughtful discussion about the role of the state in these changes, also with an extensive bibliography, see J. H. H. Vries, "Governing Growth: A Comparative Analysis of the Role of the State in the Rise of the West," *Journal of World History* 13:1 (2002): 67–138.

Studies of the cultural impact of colonialism, and of other changes discussed at the end of the chapter include Kathleen Wilson, *The Sense of the People: Politics, Culture and Imperialism in England, 1715–1785* (Cambridge: Cambridge University Press, 1995); Victor Lieberman, ed., *Beyond Binary Histories: Re-imagining Eurasia to c. 1830* (Ann Arbor: University of Michigan Press, 1999); and Hans Joachim Voth, *Time and Work in England 1750–1830* (Oxford: Oxford University Press, 2000).

 For more suggestions and links see the companion website www.cambridge.org/wiesnerhanks.

Notes

1 Samuel Purchas, *Hakluytus Posthumus or Purchas His Pilgrimes, contayning a History of the World in Sea Voyages and Lande Travells, by Englishmen and others* (London: Hakluyt Society, 1905), vol. XX, pp. 248, 249, 250, 251.

2 Letter from Colbert to Intendant Jean Talon, January 5, 1666, quoted and translated in Saliha Belmessous, "Assimilation and Racialism in Seventeenth and Eighteenth-Century French Colonial Policy," in *American Historical Review* 110:2 (April 2005): 326, 326.

3 Quoted in Charles Boxer, *The Dutch Seaborne Empire, 1600–1800* (New York: Knopf, 1965), p. 221.

4 Baron de Wimpffen, quoted and translated in John D. Garrigus, "Tropical Temptress to Republican Wife: Gender, Virtue, and Haitian Independence, 1763–1803," unpublished paper.
5 Cornelius de Pauw, *Recherches philosophiques sur les Américains* (Berlin, 1771).
6 David Landes, *The Wealth and Poverty of Nations: Why Some Are So Rich and Some So Poor* (New York: Norton, 1998), p. 177.
7 Albrecht Dürer, quoted in Benjamin Keen, *The Aztec Image in Western Thought* (New Brunswick, NJ: Rutgers University Press, 1971), p. 69.

Index

abortion 59, 275
absolutism 284–301
Académie Française 330, 332
Acosta, José de 247
adolescence 53
adultery 58, 63, 163, 170, 211, 277
Afonso I (Nzinga Mbemba), King of Kongo 236, 239
ages of man 44–7, 254
Agricola, Georgius 201
agriculture 40, 189–99, 405–16
Ailly, Pierre d' 224
Albert II of Habsburg 24, 108
Albert of Brandenburg, Duke of Prussia 105
Albert of Mainz 154
Alberti, Leon Battista 139–40
Albuquerque, Afonso de 232
Alchemy 334–5
Alciati, Andrea 123–4
alcoholic beverages 404–5
Aleksei, tsar of Russia 304–5
d'Alembert, Jean 12, 345
Alexander VI, pope 102–125, 172, 229
Ambrose, St. 45, 130
American Revolution, see War for American Independence
Amsterdam 277, 279, 310, 331
  economy in 180, 203–4, 207, 404, 433–5, 449, 459
Anabaptists, see radical Reformation
anatomy 62, 123, 268–74
Anderson, Benedict 81, 113, 153
Angoulême, Marguerite d' 129, 133, 134
Anne, St. 35, 136, 177
Anne I, Queen of England 281, 308–9
Anne of Austria, Queen of France 126, 298, 299
Anne of Brittany 96, 126
Antwerp 180, 206–7, 433, 438
Aragon, see Spain
Archimedes 334
Argyropoulos, Johannes 127
Ariès, Philippe 52
Ariosto, Ludovico 83, 133
Aristotle 42, 48, 56, 129, 132, 333–4, 337–8

Arkwright, Richard 429–31
Armada, Spanish 181, 245
armies, standing 85–9, 99, 113, 308, 314, 447, see also warfare, military technology
Arnauld, Angélique 372
art and artists 32, 81, 113, 116–19, 139–146, 241, 329, 352–7, 471, 478–9
astronomy 336–7
asylums 75, 265, 277
Augsburg Confession 166
Augsburg, Peace of 167–70, 250–1
Augustine, St. 130, 169
Augustinians 34, 153, 173
Australia 7, 442, 444–5, 447, 465
Austria 24, 62, 89–90, 109, 287, 294–6, 313–15, 322–3, 373, 395–6, 421–2
autos-da-fé 60, 101, 233
Azores Islands 17, 223
Aztec Empire 240–1, 244, 480

Bach, Johann Sebastian 358–9
Bacon, Francis 125, 335, 348
Bacon's Rebellion 462
Baffin, William 443–4
Bainton, Roland 149
Bakewell, Robert 408
ballet 361
banks 37, 204, 429, 433
baptism 35, 52, 70, 74, 151, 154, 160–1, 176, 299, 376, 383, 463
barber-surgeons 49, 274
Barcelona 17, 204, 433
Barents, Willem 443
Barnabites 173
baroque art 352–7, 479
Basil I, grand duke of Muscovy 106
Basil II, grand duke of Muscovy 106
Batavia 407, 448–9
Bayle, Pierre 331
Beauchamp, Pierre 361
Beaumarchais, Pierre Augustin de 351
begging 169, 211–12
Beguines 34–5
Behn, Aphra 349
Bembo, Pietro 133

Benedictines 173
Bering, Vitus 443, 447
Bernard of Siena 8
Bernini, Gian Lorenzo 353
"Black Legend" 245
Blake, William 376, 429, 438, 477, 480
bloodletting 49
Blumenbach, Johann 472–3
Boccaccio, Giovanni 133, 135
Bodin, Jean 126–7
body 47–52, 68, 72, 253–5, 265–273, 281,
     339, 387, 418
body politic 253, 255–65, 281, 418
Boehme, Jakob 375–6
Bohemia 20, 38, 150, 153, 291, 313–14
Boleyn, Anne 158
Bologna 30, 123, 178
Bora, Katherina von 164
Borgia, Cesare 125–6, 172
Borgia, Lucrezia 126, 172
Borgia, Rodrigo, see Alexander VI, pope
Bosch, Hieronymus 144
Bossuet, Jacques 285–8, 322, 373
Botticelli, Sandro 140, 144, 145
Bougainville, Louis Antoine de 446
Bourignon, Antoinette 376
Boyle, Robert 256, 334
Brahe, Tycho 334, 336
Bramante, Donato 141
Brandenburg-Prussia 256, 367, 377, 416,
     479
   politics in 287, 293, 314–17
Brazil 174, 229–30, 236–8, 294, 441, 443,
     449, 453, 458
Brendan of Clonfert, St. 21
Britain, see England
British colonies
   in Asia, 441, 450–2
   in the Caribbean 441, 453–9, 463, 464
   in North America 227, 294–5, 342,
     439–443, 459–64, 469, 474
brothels 26, 60, 112, 211, 276; see also
     prostitutes
Brueghel, Peter 144
Bruges 17, 38, 180
Brunelleschi, Filippo 141
Bry, Theodor de 246
Buffon, Georges 472
Burckhardt, Jacob 46, 73, 80–1, 113, 145
Burgundy, duchy of 23, 96, 249
Burton, Robert 265, 266, 281
Butler, Samuel 364

cabala 128, 129, 367, 394–6
Cabot, John 227, 459
Cabral, Pedro 229
Cairo 17, 105, 221, 397
calculus 339, 341

Calderón de la Barca, Pedro 350
Calvin, John 122, 157, 169–71, 178
Calvinism 165, 169–72, 178–181, 187, 256,
     291–2, 303–4, 311, 366–70, 380, 382
Cambridge Group 72
cameralism 288
Campion, Edmund 174
Canary Islands 17
Canisius, Peter 174
capitalism 186–9, 213–15
Capuchins, 290
Caravaggio, Michelangelo da 354
Caribbean 232, 236–42, 248, 294–5, 441–2,
     452–9, 463–7, 470, 473
Carmelites 176
Cartwright, Edmund 6
Carvajal, Luise de 175
Castiglione, Baldassar 132, 259
Castile 25, 27, 97–100, 102, 249
castrati 137, 360
Cateau-Cambrésis, Treaty of 111, 178
Catherine (II) the Great, empress of
     Russia, 281, 321–2, 374, 386
Catherine of Aragon 92, 98, 158
Catherine de' Medici, queen of France,
     126, 361
celibacy 57, 63, 155, 164, 380
Celtis, Conrad 129
Cervantes, Miguel de 83, 134, 186
Champlain, Samuel de 443
charity, see poor relief
Charles I, king of England 304–7
Charles II, king of England 307–8
Charles III, King of Spain 302
Charles V, Holy Roman Emperor and king
     of Spain 90, 102–3, 108, 111, 205, 244,
     291
   and religious reform 149, 158, 166–7,
     169, 180
   and Spanish empire 229–30, 242
Charles VI, Holy Roman Emperor 314
Charles VII, King of France 95
Charles XII, King of Sweden 317–18, 321
Charles "the Bold," Duke of Burgundy 96
Châtelet, Emilie du 346
Chaucer, Geoffrey 135
chemistry 335–6
childbirth 35, 67, 273–5
childhood 52–5
China 213, 236, 244, 272, 472, 476, 478
   merchants in 16, 17, 232–5, 243, 318
   missionaries in 21–2, 174, 234–5, 247,
     374, 448–51
Christian III, King of Demark/Norway 170
Christian humanism 130–1
Chrysoloras, Manuel 127
church courts 11, 33, 112, 150, 151, 169,
     370

churching of women 35
Cicero 32, 122, 124, 132
circumcision 52, 99
Cisneros, Francisco Jiménez de 129
cities and towns 16–18, 26–7, 31–2, 39–41,
    59–61, 85, 109–13, 156, 204–12, 220–1,
    264, 429
citizenship 112–13, 264, 469
class, see social hierarchy
Clement VII, pope 158, 172
Clement XI, pope 373
Clement XIV, pope 374
climate, ideas about 344–6
Clive, Robert 450–1
cloistering of women 122, 176
cloth production 38–9, 92, 186, 201–3,
    214, 299, 418–27
clothing 39, 51–2, 203, 205, 210, 211, 243,
    264, 280, 346, 404, 421, 455
coal 199, 201, 428–30, 432, 476
Code Noir 455–6, 458, 463
coffee and tea 238, 244–5, 329, 402, 404,
    455, 478
coins 188–9, 204–5, 242, 243, 433–5
Colbert, Jean-Baptiste 299, 421, 424, 462
"Columbian Exchange" 244, 478
Columbus, Christopher 1, 6, 9, 18, 217–27,
    236–8, 248–9, 258
Columbus Day 248
Commedia dell'Arte 134–5
Complutensian Polyglot 129, 130
conciliar movement 33
Condorcet, Marquis de 343, 346–7
confessionalization 151–2, 181, 366
confraternities 74–5, 144, 177, 381, 474
Constance, Council of 20, 153
Constantinople (Istanbul) 19, 33, 202, 206,
    221, 394
    conquest of 6, 104, 382, 384
consumer goods 404–6, 418, 423, 428,
    432, 435, 450, 475, 477
contraception 58, 275
convents 27, 32, 34, 63, 64, 137, 156, 158,
    176, 383, 386, 470, 474
converses 99–100, 104, 393
Cook, James 444–6
Copernicus, Nicolaus 336–7
Corneille, Pierre 350
Cortes 98
Cortés, Hernan 241–2, 244
Corvinus, Matthias 81–2, 143
cosmology 336–40
Cossacks 318, 320, 322, 394
cottage industry 419–20, 425 427, 432
craft guilds, see guilds
Cranach, Lucas 8, 144
Cranmer, Thomas 157–8
Cromwell, Oliver 306–7, 370

Cromwell, Thomas 158
Crusades 19, 91

Dante Alighieri 133, 348
death 35, 67–70, 76, 414–17
Defoe, Daniel 350
deism 344
Del Cano, Sebastian 230
demography, see population
Denmark 451, 453
    economy in 17
    laws in 74, 156
    politics in 25, 80, 106–7, 167, 291, 317
    witchcraft in 392
deportation 277–8, 322
Descartes, René 266, 309, 329, 338–9, 341,
    342, 344, 350
Desmond Rebellion 93–4
diaries, see memoirs and diaries
Dias, Bartolomeu 223, 229
Diderot, Denis 12, 343, 345, 362, 446
diplomacy 25, 110–11, 125, 374
disease 47–50, 72, 86, 111, 235, 240–4,
    254, 270–3, 414–18, 458–9, 472,
    479
divine right of kings 286–8, 323, 342
divorce 63–4, 161, 165, 177, 382
Dominicans 75, 474
Donatello 139
Don Quixote 83, 134, 185–6
Dort, Synod of 368, 370
dowries 64–5, 75, 262, 414
Dózsa, György 197
Drake, Francis 245, 446
drama 132–6, 265, 280, 348–51
Dryden, John 349
Dudley, Robert 86
Duplessis de Mornay, Philippe 127
Dürer, Albrecht 144, 241, 477–80
Dutch colonies 449–51, 453–4, 458, 461,
    468
Dutch East India Company (VOC) 447–51,
    454, 461, 468, 474

early modern, concept of 1–2, 6–7, 118
Eck, Johann 154
Edinburgh 331
education 290, 316, 342, 374
    see also schools, universities
Edward IV, king of England 91–2
Eleonore of Portugal 14, 15, 89
Elias, Norbert 258–9
Elizabeth I, queen of England 51, 92,
    94–5, 124, 126, 158–9, 174, 180, 207,
    254, 303–4
enclosure 194–5, 407–10
encomienda system 237, 242
Encyclopédie 12, 343, 345

England
  agriculture in 189–91, 194–6, 406–10
  arts in 144, 331, 357, 358
  economics in 38, 238, 421–34
  education in 119–20, 122, 130
  families in 66, 71, 165
  law in 25, 212–13
  literature in 135–6, 349–50
  medicine in 272, 274
  politics in 22–4, 86, 90–5, 260–4, 286,
    303–9
  religion in 75, 153, 157–60, 170, 174–5,
    180–1, 369–71, 375–6, 378–80
English Civil War 289, 305–9, 369–71
English (later British) East India Company
    (EEIC) 434, 440, 446, 450–2, 468–9
"enlightened" absolutists 322–4
Enlightenment 328–9, 332, 343–51, 361,
    446, 471
Erasmus, Desiderius 130–1, 153
Estates General 95, 299, 310
Ethiopia 223
Eucharist 150, 153, 157, 350, 382
Europa 2, 477
Europe, concept of, 2, 480
executions 212–13

families and family structure 29, 54,
    61–75, 191–2, 208–11, 262–7, 420, 432,
    467
Febronianism 373
Fénelon, François 373
Ferdinand I, Holy Roman Emperor 169,
    291
Ferdinand II, Holy Roman Emperor 291–2
Ferrara 31, 133, 137, 206
Ficino, Marsilio 127–30, 173
Fielding, Henry 351
Filmer, Robert 126, 342
Finland 107, 317, 318, 388, 419
fishing 163, 190–1, 196, 203, 227, 229, 415,
    457
Flodden, Battle of 94
Florence 17, 24, 37, 60, 64, 110–11, 125,
    127, 194, 204, 337
  art in 141, 144
Flour War 412
Fontana, Lavinia 54, 146
Formula of Concord 157, 166–7
food 39–40, 50, 72, 188–9, 195–6, 211, 237,
    244, 408, 412, 415–19
Foucault, Michel 259–60
Fox, George 306, 375–6
Fox, Margaret Fell 306
Foxe, John 8
France
  agriculture in 40, 194, 412, 416
  economy in 203, 213, 274, 419–21, 433–4

education in 119, 122, 129
families in 67, 74
literature in 133, 350–1
military in 111, 127, 290–7
politics in 80, 94–7, 260, 294, 287–90,
    297–301
religion in 20, 22–4, 151–2, 165–72,
    177–80, 366, 371–4, 381, 396
Francesca, Piero della 139
Francis I, king of France 88, 96, 111, 129,
    178, 443
Franciscans 34, 75, 173, 212, 383, 463
Francke, August 377
Franco, Veronica 280
Frederick II (the Great), king of Prussia
    295, 317, 319, 323, 416, 471
Frederick III, Holy Roman Emperor 14–15,
    89
Frederick Barbarossa, Holy Roman
    Emperor 107
Frederick William, elector of
    Brandenburg-Prussia 316
Frederick William, king of Prussia 316–17
Freemasons 331
French colonies 295, 450–1, 453–7, 461–5,
    469, 470
French Revolution 6, 399–400, 412
Fronde 288, 298–99
Fugger family 154, 205–7, 433
funerals 34, 37, 68–9, 70, 75, 373, 394

Gainsborough, Thomas 357
Galen 42, 48–9, 268, 270, 334, 471
Galilei, Galileo 268, 331, 337–9, 348, 479
Galilei, Vincenzo 139
Galizia, Fede 146
galley service 213
Da Gama, Vasco 223
Garcia II, king of Kongo 239
Gassendi, Pierre 268
gender, ideas about 29, 49, 56–7, 113,
    126–7, 263, 268–70, 279–81
  in the Enlightenment 322, 342, 345–8
  in the Reformation 159, 164–5, 175–7
  in the Renaissance 126, 136
gender differences
  in the arts 145–6, 349, 360
  in education 32, 53, 120–2
  in families 65–7, 73–4, 385
  in law 58, 113, 262, 278, 314, 469
  in religion 366, 379–81
  in work 40, 190–1, 195–6, 215, 420, 425
Geneva 122, 169–71
Genoa 17, 202, 204, 221, 224, 271, 433, 435
Gentileschi, Artemisia 354, 355
George I, king of Britain, 309
George II, king of Britain 73, 309
George III, king of Britain 464

Germany
  art in 144, 287
  economy in 16, 38, 201, 208, 265, 422,
    425
  education in 119, 346
  families in 62, 73–4, 419
  music in 137, 358–9
  politics in 24, 107–11, 292, 295
  religion in 34, 153–6, 161, 163–70,
    366–9, 377
Giotto di Bondone 139
Glickl bas Judah Leib 256, 403–5, 421
Glorious Revolution 308
Goa 232–5, 441
godparentage 74
Golden Bull of 1356 109
Gordon riots 370–1
Graffigny, Françoise de 351
Gramsci, Antonio 219, 235
Granada 20, 25, 98–100, 102, 103, 225, 249
Grebel, Conrad 160
Greece 20, 27, 40, 85, 381–2
Greenland 22, 377
green-sickness 266
Gregory VII, pope 19
Gresham, Thomas 207
Grimmelshausen, Hans Jakob von 349
Grünewald, Matthias 9, 144
Guanches 17
guilds 38–9, 61, 75, 134, 188, 201–2,
    207–9, 213, 299, 419, 421–3
Gustavus Adolphus 291–2, 317, 407
Gutenberg, Johann 6
Guyon, Jeanne-Marie 373, 376

Habermas, Jürgen 329
Habsburg–Valois wars 84, 111, 167, 177
Habsburgs 24, 89–90, 98, 108, 180, 206,
    291–5, 300, 309, 313–14, 383, 453
Hajnal, John 63
Hakluyt, Thomas 39–40, 459
Haller, Albrecht von 268
Hals, Franz 354
Hamburg 17, 44,421, 433
Handel, George Frideric 358–9, 360
Hanseatic League (Hansa), 24, 176,
Harvey, William 268
Hasidism 367, 396, 399
Haskalah 344, 396
Hawaiian Islands 445–6
Haydn, Franz Joseph 359
Hemessen, Caterina van 145
Henry II, king of France 96
Henry III, king of France 280
Henry IV, king of France 178–80, 290, 297,
    374
Henry VII, king of England 79, 91–2, 227
Henry VIII, king of England 92, 98, 158–9

Henry the Navigator, prince of Portugal
    222–4
Herder, Johann Gottfried von 351
Hermetic texts 128, 334
Herodotus 2
Heywood, Eliza 351
Hildegard of Bingen 130
Hippocrates 48, 123
historiographical debates 5
  about the arts 118
  about the body and sexuality 47, 55–6,
    258–9
  about colonialism 219–20, 451, 476
  about the economy 187, 405, 431, 475
  about politics 81, 289, 302, 305
  about religion 150
  about science and philosophy 328, 348
Hobbes, Thomas 252–3, 266, 281, 342, 347
Holbein, Hans 144
Holy Roman Empire, see Germany
Hogarth, William 364
homosexuality, see same-sex relationships
honor 29, 53, 58, 75, 83, 209, 213, 277,
    350, 385, 422, 467
Hooke, Robert 327, 330
hospitals 212, 265, 271–2, 462
Hoyer, Anna Owen 366
Hudson, Henry 443, 461
Huguenots 127, 178–80, 297–300, 316, 371
humanism 32, 125, 128, 130–1
Hume, David 343–4, 346, 473
humors 42, 48–9, 265, 268, 270, 334, 471
Hundred Years War 6, 22, 82, 91, 95, 96
Hungary 63, 81–2, 143, 167, 197, 289,
    313–14
  religion in 161, 383, 393
Hunyadi, John 81
Hurll, Mary 255
Hus, Jan 20, 153
Hutten, Ulrich von 130
Hutter, Jacob 160–1
Hutterites 161, 163, 374
hymns 139, 162 307, 359, 377–9

Iceland 3, 21, 22, 74, 388
iconoclasm 144, 178, 180, 189
illness, see disease, mental illness
Inca Empire 240–2
Index of Prohibited Books 173, 177
India 21–2, 229, 235, 295, 425, 441,
    447–52, 459
Indian Ocean 19, 213, 220–3, 232
individualism 46, 413
indulgences 69, 153, 154, 155, 176
industry 302, 316, 418–20, 423–32
infanticide 59, 275–6, 385
inheritance 71, 262
Innocent III, pope 20

Innocent VIII, pope 387
Innocent XI, pope 360
Inquisitions 60, 89, 99–103, 152, 173, 233, 371, 389–93
intendants 298–9, 462
intermarriage 100, 208, 462–3, 468–70, 472, 474
Ireland 24, 63, 93–5, 170, 307–8, 370, 375, 416, 468
iron production 201, 428–30
Isabella and Ferdinand, rulers of Spain 98–102, 158, 393
    and Columbus 217–18, 225–6, 227
Islam
    ideas and practices in 19, 57, 123, 198, 367, 396–99
    spread of 21, 37, 220, 223, 383
    See also Muslims
Istanbul, *see* Constantinople
Italy
    agriculture in 410, 412, 415
    arts in 133, 141–3, 286–7, 354
    economy in 16, 40, 194, 202, 435
    education in 31, 128–30, 330
    families in 62–3, 73
    music in 358–60
    politics in 24, 90, 109–12, 172–3, 180, 208, 371
Ivan III, grand-duke of Muscovy 106
Ivan IV, "the Terrible," tsar of Russia 106, 320

Jacob, Margaret 476
Jacobite rebellions 73, 309
James IV, king of Scotland 92, 94
James V, king of Scotland, 94
James VI and I, king of Scotland and England 94–5, 127, 254, 261, 286, 288, 303–304, 431, 369
James VII and II, king of Scotland and England 308–9
Janissary Corps 85, 104, 312–13
Jansen, Cornelius, and Jansenism 367, 372–4, 399
Japan 232–3, 235, 448–9
Jefferson, Thomas 343–4
Jenner, Edward 272
Jesuits 122, 173–5, 177, 233–6, 247, 291, 338, 383, 463, 473–4
    suppression of 302, 323, 372, 374
Jews and Judaism 27, 120, 122, 152, 307, 309, 344, 393–6, 403, 455, 480
    ideas and practices of 37, 51–2, 55, 57, 62, 64, 70
    in eastern Europe 318, 323
    in Ottoman Empire 104
    in Spain and Portugal 99–102, 206–7, 393

Joan of Arc 95
Joao I (Nzinga Nkuwu), King of Kongo 236
John of Monte Corvino 22
John III, king of Portugal 137, 239
John III Sobieski, king of Poland 318
John IV, king of Portugal 302
John V, king of Portugal 302
Joliet, Louis 443
Joseph I, king of Portugal 302
Joseph II, ruler of Austria 314–15, 323, 373–4, 396
journals 255–8, 331–2, 376, 478
journeymen 29, 38–9, 75, 136, 208–10, 422–3, 432
Julius II, pope 235, 290

Kant, Immanuel 328, 471–2
Karlstadt, Andreas 160
Kepler, Johannes 334, 336–7, 339
Kett's Rebellion 189
kin groups and clans 70–5
Knights' Revolt 163
knitting 202, 424
Knox, John 126, 170
Kongo 223, 235–9
Kuhn, Thomas 328

La Pérouse, Jean François Galaup, count of 446
La Salle, Robert 299
Labadie, Jean de 376
lace-making 202–3
Laclos, Pierre Choderlos de 266
Landes, David 476
Las Casas, Bartolome de, 245–8
Lasso, Orlando di 137
Laud, William 304–5
Lavoisier, Antoine-Laurent 268, 335–6
Law, John, 734, 784
law
    canon 33, 55, 71, 165
    common 91, 92, 93, 174, 458
    Roman 30, 113, 389, 395, 458
law codes 10, 11, 25, 81, 124, 320, 384
Le Brun, Charles 284
Lead, Jane 376
learned societies 330–2, 478
Lee, Ann 380
Leeuwenhoeck, Anton von 268
Lefèvre d'Etaples, Jacques 129, 130, 178
Leibniz, Gottfried Wilhelm 330, 341–2, 472
Lenclos, Ninon de 280
Leo X, Pope 154
Leonardo da Vinci 20, 126, 129, 140, 431
Lepanto, Battle of 87, 105, 134, 206, 313, 424
Lessing, Gotthold 351

letters and letter-writing 9, 119, 255–8, 265–6, 478
Levellers 306, 367
life expectancy 66–7, 412–18
Linacre, Thomas 129
Linnaeus, Carl 471–2
Lisbon 181, 224–5, 302, 341, 435
literacy 30–2, 120–2
literature 30–1, 118, 132–6, 265, 348–51, 369
Lithuania 105–7, 174, 262, 383, 394
Livonia 104, 105, 106, 380
Locke, John 309, 329, 342–3, 347, 348, 350, 479
Lollards 153
London 135, 211, 254, 261, 279, 305, 333, 460
    economy in 17, 206–8, 213, 405, 428, 434–5
    Great Fire of 414
Lope de Vega, Félix 134, 135, 350
Louis XI, king of France 96
Louis XIII, king of France, 330
Louis XIV, king of France 180, 261, 277, 284–9, 297–300, 307–9, 312, 323, 350, 361, 371–2, 455–6, 462
Louis XV, king of France 280, 300–1, 446
Louis XVI, king of France 280, 300–1, 472
love 61–2, 128, 133–4, 265–7, 341, 378
Loyola, Ignatius 173–5
Lucca 21, 60
Lukaris, Cyril 382
Luo Wanzao 247
Luria, Isaac 396
Luther, Martin 1, 8, 57, 131, 132, 139, 144, 148–57, 164–5, 187

Machiavelli, Niccolò 79–80, 125–6, 134
Magellan, Ferdinand 229–30
Magna Carta 91
Maintenon, Madame de 280
Malaspina, Alessandro 446
Malherbe, François de 350
Mali Empire 6, 17, 22, 223
Malleus Maleficarum 387–8, 390, 391
Malthus, Thomas 418
Mameluke Empire 17, 105
manners 258–9, 264, 279, 280
Mantegna, Andrea 139–40
Manuel I, king of Portugal 98, 223
Manutius, Aldus 130
Margaret of Parma 180
Margrete I, queen of Denmark 25, 106
Maria Theresa, queen of Austria 289, 314, 422
Marie Antoinette, queen of France 280–1, 416
Marie de Medici, queen of France 297

marital strategies 80, 89–90, 96, 98–9 102, 105, 107, 113
Marlowe, Christopher 135
Marquette, Jacques 443
marriage 18, 53, 57–64, 70–4, 100, 266–7, 380–5, 394, 462, 468–9
    in the Reformation 151, 155–6, 160, 164–5, 177
marriage contracts 11, 62, 121
Marx, Karl 187
Mary I, queen of England 126, 158–9
Mary of Burgundy 78–9, 89, 96, 98, 180
Mary (Stuart), queen of Scotland 94–5, 125, 126, 180–1, 303
Mary, Virgin 16, 35, 57, 142, 155, 176–7, 382
masturbation, see onanism
mathematics 334, 336, 338–40
Mather, Cotton 272
Maximilian I, Holy Roman Emperor 78–9, 89–90, 96, 109, 138
Mazarin, 298–9
Medici, Cosimo de' 127
Medici, Lorenzo de' 128, 132, 141
Medici family 116, 125, 144–5, 227, 337
Medicine 49–50, 123, 270–5
Mehmed II 6, 123
melancholy 48, 265–6, 281
Melanchthon, Philipp 155, 157, 166, 382
Memling, Hans 144
memoirs and diaries 11, 255–8, 319, 403–4
Mendelssohn, Moses 344, 351
Mennonites 161, 374
menopause 66
menstruation 49, 55, 266, 275
mental illness 265–6
mercantalism 188, 271, 340, 418, 425, 427, 475
Mercator, Gerardus 229
Merchant Adventurers 206
merchants 16–21, 29, 186–91, 202–9, 419, 432–5
    in northern Europe 262, 304, 310–12
    and overseas trade 41, 87, 220–4, 232–236, 243–4, 447–55, 459
    in southern Europe 37–40, 110, 112
Merici, Angela 175
mestizo culture 243, 248, 466
metals, precious 38, 188–9, 204–5, 245, 442, 447
Methodists and Methodism 367, 373, 377–81, 473, 474
Mevlevi orders 397, 399
Mexico 240–3, 247, 415
Michelangelo (Buonarotti) 116, 132, 141, 143, 144, 145, 146, 154
microscope 268
midwives 113, 273–5, 390

military technology 41, 82–9, 107, 249, 294, 296, 313, 429, 477
Miller, Mattheus 255
Milton, John 254, 349
mining and miners 38, 199–206, 242–3, 428–30, 432
Mirandola, Pico della 128, 145
missionaries 21, 174–7, 231–6, 243, 246, 374–5, 377–8, 383, 463, 468– 473–4
Moctezuma 241
Mohacs, Battle of 82, 85, 314
Mokyr, Joel 476–7
Molière 350
Molinos, Miguel de 373
monasteries 27, 34, 63, 156, 158–9, 199, 212, 323, 373, 383, 386
Mongol Empire 21, 22, 104, 105, 222
Montagu, Mary Wortley 272
Montaigne, Michel de 338
Montesquieu, Baron de 343–6, 348, 472
Monteverdi, Claudio 358
Moravia 153, 161, 375
Moravians 367, 377–8, 380, 474
More, Thomas 130–1, 159, 194
Moriscos 101–4
Moscow 152, 198, 320, 382, 384–5
mothers and motherhood 68, 267, 390
Mozart, Wolfgang Amadeus 351, 359, 360
Münster 161
Müntzer, Thomas 161
Murad II, Ottoman Sultan 245
Muscovy, see Russia
music 118, 136, 137–9, 155, 256–7, 265, 333, 349, 352, 357–61, 399
Muslims
    practices of 19, 27, 37, 51, 58, 64, 70, 220, 397–9
    treatment of 20, 25, 97–103, 222, 301

names 73–4
Nantes, Edict of 180, 297, 300, 309, 371, 455
Naples 98, 111, 188, 204, 209, 411, 433
Nasi family 206
nation-states 80–2, 113, 249, 316, 371
Native Americans
    in Caribbean 226, 246–8
    in North America 378, 459–64, 469, 472
    in South America 242–3, 468
natural rights 342–3, 348
naval technology and warfare 41, 87, 107, 213, 294–5, 465
navigational instruments 40, 220, 223
Nebrija, Antonio de 129
Nestorians 21
Netherlands
    agriculture in 406, 410, 416
    art in 144–5, 354

economy in 189, 194, 203, 207, 238, 425, 434
religion in 151, 170, 172, 180–1, 367, 370–6
politics in 290, 292, 301, 309–12
and war 314, 441
Newcomen, Thomas 428
newspapers 332, 478
Newton, Isaac 326–8, 334, 339–40, 346, 434
Nicolet, Jean 443
Nicot, Jean 244
Nikon, Patriarch 385
nobles 26–7, 50, 71, 83–4, 86–7, 137, 208, 249, 259–64, 358, 470
    in eastern Europe 25, 82, 105–113, 161, 174, 197–202, 312–14, 316–21, 423
    in England 91–5, 135, 159, 308, 410
    in France 20, 95–7, 172, 178, 286, 297–9
    in Spain 97–100, 193–4, 301–2
    in western Europe 24
Nobunaga, Oda 233
Northeast and Northwest Passage 443, 445
Norway 17, 25, 106, 191, 416
novels 8, 265–6, 350–1
Nuremberg 27, 110, 144, 206, 264, 478–9

offices, sale of 96–7, 103, 178, 297
O'Gorman, Edmundo 218, 262
old age 66–7
Old Believers 367, 385–6
onanism 278
opera 351, 357–62
opium 449–51
Oppenheimer, Samuel and Joseph 394
oral traditions 12, 32, 132, 136–7, 349
orphanages 26, 112, 173, 177, 210, 276, 311, 360, 419, 425
orphans 17, 75, 170, 212, 271, 460
Orthodoxy, Eastern 33, 55, 57, 63, 152, 367, 381–6, 399
Ottoman Empire 272, 414
    art in 143
    economy in 198–9, 245
    education in 119, 123
    military in 81–2, 85, 104–5, 293, 314, 318, 424
    politics in 25, 27, 37, 312–13
    religion in 101, 382, 394–9
Oxenstierna, Axel 73, 317

Pacific, exploration of 444–447
Palestrina, Giovanni 137
Palladio, Andrea 357
papacy and Papal States, 20, 24, 33–4, 109, 150, 172–3, 178, 371–4
Paracelsus 334–5
Paré, Ambrose 56, 83

Paris 30, 96–7, 123, 127, 178–9, 277, 279, 299, 357, 361, 412
   salons and clubs in 330, 331, 332, 404
   work in 59, 196, 213, 422
Paris, Treaty of 296
parlement of Paris 96–7, 299–300, 392, 393
Parliament, English 91–2, 257, 305–9, 320, 367, 370, 396, 408, 431, 451
Parliament, Polish (*Sejm*) 105, 197, 318, 319–20, 395
Parmentier, Antoine-Auguste 416
Parsons, Robert 174
Pascal, Blaise 372
Pasek, Jan Chryzostom 319
patents 429, 431
patronage, artistic 129, 144, 329, 330, 359
Paul III, pope 141, 172–6
Paul IV, pope 173
Pauw, Cornelius de 471
pawnbrokers 205–6
peasants 26–7, 74, 121, 190–9, 260, 288, 298–301, 316–23, 410
peasants' revolts 39, 82, 91, 179, 189, 412
Peasants' War, German 161, 163–4, 205
penance 35, 69, 372
Penn, William 461
Pepys, Samuel 256–7, 360
Perrault, Charles 136
Peru 241–2, 441
Peter the Great, tsar of Russia, 286, 288, 289, 320–2, 330, 385–6, 443
Peter II, king of Portugal 302
Petersen, Johanna Eleonora 379
Petrarch 83, 117, 132, 135
Philadelphian Society 376
Philip II, king of Spain 100, 102–3, 169, 172, 180–1, 291
Philip III, king of Spain 301, 302
Philip V, king of Spain 300, 302, 360
Philip Augustus, king of France 95
Philip "the Good," duke of Burgundy 96
Philippe d'Orléans 280
Philippine Islands 229–30, 233, 295, 441, 443
philosophy 30, 122, 127–8, 131, 141, 333, 337–40, 347
physiocrats 418
pietism 376–81, 399, 474, 475
Pigafetta, Antonio 230, 255
Pilgrimage of Grace 159
pilgrimages 16, 19, 36, 53, 131, 153, 383, 399
pirates 87, 181, 204–5, 238, 245
Pitt, William 309
Pius II, Pope (Aeneas Silvius Piccolomini) 14–16, 20, 129
Pius IV, Pope 124, 173
Pizan, Christine de 67

Pizarro, Francisco 241
plague, bubonic 17, 27, 188, 206, 240–1, 270–1, 273, 292, 414–15
Plato 124, 127–8, 133, 139, 334, 336
Poland
   education in, 122
   mining in 38, 407
   partitions of 7, 319
   politics in 73, 105–7, 197, 262, 317–18
   religion in 19, 161, 170, 174, 374, 383, 394–6
police forces 106, 211, 277, 279
political theory 124–7, 253–5, 285–8, 342–8
Poliziano, Angelo 127, 132, 145
Polo, Marco 16, 224–5
Pombal, Marquise de 302
Pomeranz, Kenneth 442
Pompadour, Madame de 280
poor relief 65, 169, 177, 211–12, 288, 462
Pope, Alexander 327–8, 333, 340
popular beliefs 55, 152, 154
population 187–9, 412–18
Portugal
   economy in 206, 210
   education in 30, 123
   politics in 98–103, 301–3
   religion in 75, 177, 374, 390–1, 393
Portuguese colonies and voyages 6, 17, 222–4, 236–9, 441, 466–9, 473–4
   in Americas 229–30, 240, 243, 294, 453, 458
   in Indian Ocean 232–5, 447–8
"post-colonial" theory 219, 224, 475
postal service 255, 265, 332, 478
potatoes 244, 288, 321, 406, 415–6
Poussin, Nicolas 357
Pragmatic Sanction of Bourges 95–6
pregnancy 48, 57–60, 63, 210, 273–6
Prester John 223–4, 236
Prez, Josquin des 137
prices 188–95, 205, 211, 412–13
Priestley, Joseph 268, 335–6
printing 6–10, 42, 154, 225, 230, 248, 394
prisons 211, 277–8, 379
Procopius 21
prostitutes and prostitution 51, 60, 75, 211, 275–9, 425, *see also* brothels
proto-industrialization 71, 418–21, 432
Prussia, *see* Brandenburg-Prussia
Ptolemy 224–5, 333–4, 336
public health 271–3
public welfare, *see* poor relief
Pugachev Rebellion 322
Purchas, Samuel 439–442, 476–7
purgatory 69, 75, 154
Puritans and Puritanism 124, 146, 170, 300, 304–5, 307, 364, 366, 369–70, 460

"purity of the blood" laws 100, 301, 467
putting-out system, *see* cottage industry
Pythagoras 128, 334

Quakers 256, 300, 306, 367, 370, 375, 380,
    461, 473, 474
Quietism 373

Rabban Sauma 21–2
Rabelais, François 133
race, ideas about 219, 248, 259, 344–6,
    466–473
Racine, Jean 350–1
radical Reformation 151, 157, 160–4
Rákóczy, Francis II 314
Raleigh, Walter 459
rape 2, 58, 351, 469
Raphael (Sanzio) 141–5
reading, *see* literacy
Reconquista 25, 225
Reformation, Catholic 172–7
    effects of 57, 122, 124, 131, 177–81, 233,
    374
Reformation, Protestant 1, 8, 109, 111,
    149–63, 169–72
    effects of 63, 69, 124, 139, 146, 163–9,
    230, 249, 287, 290
Reinhart, Anna 164
religious wars 124, 165–9, 180–1, 202, 249,
    290, 453
    in France 111, 127, 177–80, 194
Rembrandt van Rijn 354, 356
Renaissance 1, 32, 46, 116–19, 139–146,
    219, 249, 328, 330, 352, 361, 479
representative assemblies 89, 91, 95, 98,
    107–8, 113, 127, 260, 289, 310, 314,
    318, *See also* Parliament, Estates
    General, *Cortes*
"Republic of Letters," 331–2, 246, 361–2
resistance theory 127
Reuchlin, Johann 129
Reynolds, Joshua 357
Ricci, Matteo 234
Richardson, Samuel 266, 351
Richelieu, Armand-Jean du Plessis,
    Cardinal 297–9, 330
riots 99, 144, 151, 179–80, 188–9, 370, 378,
    408–9, 412, 422, 449
rituals 35, 37, 50, 53, 68–9, 101, 136, 197,
    209, 367, 383–5, 397, 399
Roches, Madeleine and Catherine des 133
rococo art 352, 357
Roma 199
Romania 63, 81, 105, 313
Romanov, Michael, tsar of Russia 320–1
Rome 109, 111, 141, 154, 158, 330, 352, 360
Ronsard, Pierre de 133
Roser, Isabel 175

Rossi, Properzia de' 145
Rossini, Gioacchino 351
Rousseau, Jean-Jacques 332, 347–8, 351
Royal Society 256, 272, 330, 332, 335,
    339–40, 445, 446
Rubens, Peter Paul 354–5, 357
rulers, female 113, 126–7, 322
rulership, theories of 80
Russia 3, 7
    agriculture in 197–9, 410
    economic life in 71
    explorations by 443, 446
    politics in 287–8, 294–5, 317–23
    religion in 33, 89, 152, 161, 384–6

Safavids 105, 313, 399
Sahlins, Marshall 445
St. Bartholomew's Day Massacre 127,
    178–9
St. Thomas Christians 21, 234
saints 16, 21, 35, 57, 131, 136, 155, 176,
    354, 382, 397
Salamanca 30, 123
Salic Law 314
salons 332–3, 343, 361
same-sex relationships 18, 55–6, 60,
    278–81, 385
São Tomé 17–18
Scheele, Carl Wilhelm, 335
Schiller, Friedrich 351
Schmalkaldic League 166–7
schools 30–2, 101, 119–22, 129, 131, 174,
    289, 317, 323, 377
    Jewish 37, 122
    Muslim 37, 123, 143
    see also education, literacy
Schrader, Catharina van 256
Schwenkfeld, Kaspar von 160
Schwenkfelders 161–2
Scientific Revolution 328–9, 334
Scot, Reginald 392
Scotland
    economy in 191, 429
    law in 165, 276, 473
    politics in 24, 94–5, 303–4, 308–9
    religion in 170
Selim "the Grim," Ottoman sultan 105
Selim II, Ottoman sultan 206
Serbia 26, 33, 136, 152, 366, 382, 383
serfs 40, 64, 197–9, 201, 318, 320, 323–5,
    394, 410
servants 39, 58–63, 73, 208–10, 264, 267,
    404, 419, 452, 479
    indentured 198, 455, 457, 460, 462, 466
Seven Years' War 290, 294–5, 309, 317, 441,
    450, 457, 464
Sévigné, marquise de (Marie de
    Rabutin-Chantal) 258

sexuality 46, 55–61, 278–81, 346, 380
Shakers 380
Shakespeare, William 45, 73, 35–6, 253–4
ships and ship-building 22, 203, 299, 448,
      464
Sidney, Philip 135
Sigismund II Vasa, king of Poland 174
silk and silk-making 21–2, 51, 96, 196,
      202–3, 232, 243, 418, 424, 450
silver, see metals, precious
Simons, Menno 160
Sinan, Mimar 143–4, 145
Sixtus IV, pope 99
slave revolts 198, 246, 349, 459, 473
slave trade 221–3, 232, 235–9, 248, 343,
      346, 349, 458, 473
slavery 468–79
    in Americas 242–7, 438, 442, 453–64
    in India Ocean area 448–9
    in Muscovy 64, 197–8
    in Ottoman Empire 85, 198–9
    in western Europe 17–18, 102, 210
smallpox 240, 272, 415
Smith, Adam 186–7, 266, 346, 423
smuggling 331, 414, 422, 451, 452–3, 455,
      457, 458
social discipline 151, 169, 259
social hierarchy
    ideas about 164, 253–4, 260–5, 375,
      468–72
    differences within 29, 84, 113, 191, 249,
      467
Society for the Reformation of Manners
      279
Socinians 161, 174
sodomy, see same-sex relationships
sources 7–11
Sozzini, Fausto 160, 161, 376
Spain
    arts in 134, 143, 146, 354, 360
    economy in 38, 193–4, 202, 205, 433
    education in 119–20, 122
    military in 85, 111, 180–1, 290–4
    politics in 80, 97–103, 261–2, 299–304
    religion in 20–1, 152, 371, 393
Spanish colonies 225–7, 229–31, 242–5,
      295, 441, 446, 452–4, 464
Spee, Frederick 393
Spener, Philipp 376
Spenser, Edmund 93, 135
spices 17, 206, 220–3, 232, 243, 404, 440,
      447–50
spinning 53, 211, 418, 425–9
Spinoza, Baruch 341
spiritualism 375–80
Stahl, Ernst 335
steam engine 6, 421, 428, 432, 477
stock bubbles 434
stock exchanges 207, 433

Stone, Lawrence 70, 72, 73
Stradivari, Antonio 359
Strasbourg 61, 155, 300
Stuart, Charles Edward 73, 309
Stubbes, Phillip 68
Sturm und Drang 351
Sufism 21, 367, 397, 399
sugar 17, 203, 223, 235–8, 243–5, 404,
      448–9, 453–8, 464, 475
suicide 69, 267
Süleyman "the Magnificent," Ottoman
      sultan 85, 105, 123, 143, 145, 167,
      206, 399
Sully, Maximilian de Béthune, Duke of
      297
sumptuary laws 51–2, 210, 254, 264
Sweden
    economy in 407, 416, 419, 421
    mining in 38, 201, 429
    politics in 25, 107, 167, 260, 292,
      317–19, 322
    religion in 156, 392
Swedenborg, Emanuel and
      Swedenborgians, 376
Swedish colonies 451, 461
Swift, Jonathan 340, 350
Switzerland 71, 122, 150, 156, 165–6, 292,
      331, 392, 416
syphilis 111, 211, 271, 272, 292

Taino people 226
tax policies 26–7, 80–1, 89, 98, 112–13,
      163, 188, 190, 208, 210, 242, 260–1,
      410
    in British Isles 91–3, 304, 307
    in eastern Europe 104, 107, 109, 197–9,
      315–17, 323
    in France 95–7, 194, 288, 297–301
    in Ottoman Empire 105, 312–13, 382
Taxis family 255, 265
Tenochtitlán 240–1
Teresa of Avila 176, 256
Tetzel, Johann 154
Teutonic Knights 104, 105
textiles, see cloth production
Theotokópoulos, Doménikos (El Greco) 141
Thirty Years' War 181, 291–5, 299, 302,
      313–14, 316, 317, 349, 366, 416
Tiepelo, Giovanni Battista 471, 479
"Time of Troubles" 320, 384
Tintoretto, Jacopo 141
Tissot, Samuel-August 278
Titian 141, 144, 145
tobacco 204, 244–5, 386, 402, 455, 457,
      463, 475
toleration, religious, 100, 174, 180, 297,
      308, 311–12, 316, 323, 351, 366–8,
      370–1, 373, 375, 396, 399, 474
Tordesillas Line 229–30

Toscanelli, Paolo 225
towns, *see* cities
Townshend, Charles 407
Trent, Council of 122, 157, 172, 176, 235, 371
"triangle trade" 238, 459
Tudor, Margaret 92, 94
Tull, Jethro 401
Turgot, Anne-Robert-Jacques 423
Tyrone's rebellion 93–4
Tzevi, Shabbetai 395

Ukraine 105, 318, 39, 396
Uniates (Eastern Rites Catholics), 650
Union of Kalmar, 39, 176
universities 30–1, 53, 123–4, 169, 321, 329, 333, 370–1
unmarried people 39–40, 60, 63, 71, 192, 266, 275–6, 425, 427
Urban II, pope 19
Ursulines 122, 176, 474

Valdés, Juan de 130
Valla, Lorenzo 117
Van der Weyden, Rogier 144
Van Dyck, Anthony 357
Van Eyck, Jan 144
Vancouver, George 446
Vasa, Gustav, king of Sweden 107, 156
Vasari, Giorgio 117–18, 139, 144, 145, 327, 354
Velázquez, Diego 354
Venice 60, 110, 141, 152, 177, 358, 360
    economy in 17, 194, 202, 204, 221, 424, 431
Vergil, Polydore 79–80, 92, 129
Vermeer, Jan 311, 354
Vermigli, Peter Martyr 129
vernacular languages and literature, *see* literature
Verrazzano, Giovanni da 443
Versailles 261, 284, 286–7, 312, 352
Vesalius, Andreas 78, 89, 454
Vespucci, Amerigo 227, 229, 230, 247, 255, 258
Vienna 15–16, 129, 167, 174, 261, 313, 359, 360, 394
Vikings 22, 40, 227
village governments 25–6, 61, 104, 112–13, 190–2, 197, 383
virginity 57
Visconti, Giangaleazzo 110
Vivaldi, Antonio 359–60
Vives, Juan Luis 130
Vodun 466
Voltaire 341, 346
voyages
    in Atlantic 225–9

in Indian Ocean 222–4, 232
in Pacific 230, 444–7

Waldseemüller, Martin 227
Wallenstein, Albrecht von 291–2
Wallerstein, Immanuel 475
Walpole, Robert 309, 434
War of American Independence 290, 309, 441, 457, 465
War of the Austrian Succession 294, 314–5, 464
War of the Bavarian Succession 416
War of Jenkins' Ear 294
War of the League of Augsburg 294
War of the Roses 91
War of the Spanish Succession 294, 300, 302, 310, 314
warfare 6, 41, 81, 86–7, 290–7, 416 *see also* military technology; armies, standing
Washington, George 464
Watt, James 428
Watteau, Antoine 357
weaponry, *see* military technology
Weber, Max 187
weddings 35, 37, 52, 137, 164, 470
Wedgwood, Josiah 428
Wesley, John 378–9, 380
Westphalia, Peace of 292–3, 295, 302
Weyer, Johann 392
Whitefield, George 378
widowers 61, 65–6
widows 29, 61, 65–6, 75, 170, 190, 254, 271, 342, 386
    work by 39, 113, 209
Wilkinson, John 429
William, duke of Normandy 91
William and Mary, rulers of England 308, 310, 375
William the Silent, Prince of Orange 180, 310
wills 10, 11, 35, 69, 120–1, 222
Winstanley, Gerrard 306
witchcraft 151, 276, 367, 386–93
Wittenberg 149, 153–4, 160, 377
Wollstonecraft, Mary 7
Wolsey, Thomas 158
world-systems theory 475–6
Wyclif, John 153

Xavier, Francis 173

Zarlino, Gioseffo 139
Zheng He 22, 222, 224, 232
Zinzendorf, Erdmuthe von 380, 381
Zinzendorf, Nicholas von 377–8
Zurbarán, Francisco de 354
Zwingli, Ulrich 150, 155, 156–7, 160, 164, 166